Explorations
in
Planning
Theory

Explorations in Planning Theory

EDITED BY

Seymour J. Mandelbaum
Luigi Mazza
Robert W. Burchell

CENTER FOR URBAN POLICY RESEARCH

CENTER FOR URBAN POLICY RESEARCH
Rutgers, The State University of New Jersey
New Brunswick, New Jersey

Published by the Center for Urban Policy Research
Civic Square • 33 Livingston Avenue • Suite 400
New Brunswick, New Jersey 08901–1982

Printed in the United States of America

Library of Congress Cataloging-in-Publication Data

Explorations in planning theory / edited by Seymour J. Mandelbaum,
    Luigi Mazza, Robert W. Burchell.
        p.   cm.
    Includes bibliographical references and index.

    ISBN 0-88285-153-5 (cloth) — ISBN 0-88285-154-3 (paper)

        1. City planning—United States.   2. Regional planning—United
States.   3. Urban policy—United States.   I. Mandelbaum, Seymour J.
II. Mazza, Luigi.   III. Burchell, Robert W.
HT167.E97   1996
320'.6'0973—dc20   95–20379
                                                            CIP

Cover design: Helene Berinsky   *Interior design:* Arlene Pashman

Contents

[handwritten annotation next to "4": top 67 m vol 73]

PART II

The Latitude of Planners

PART III

The Planning Encounter and the Plan

need for
9/15/00

Preface

This volume began in Washington, D.C., in 1987 with a conference on planning theory organized by Robert W. Burchell for the Center for Urban Policy Research. The conference intended to generate a book, *Planning Theory in the 1990s*, to complement the very successful *Planning Theory in the 1980s: A Search for Future Directions*, which CUPR had published in 1978. Along the way to hard covers, Burchell presented several of the essays in a symposium on "Planning, Power, and Politics" published in *Society* 26, 1 (1988). Those papers caught the eye of Peter Hall, who included them in his severe critique of the state of academic planning theory published in the *Journal of the American Planning Association* in 1989. Several of the gored authors replied in kind, and Burchell and Seymour J. Mandelbaum (who had by then hired on as co-editor of the intended volume) would have been delighted if the expected book had been able to take advantage of its serendipitous notoriety.

Alas, it was not to be! The project, instead, was overcome by a second conference when, in 1991, Mandelbaum and Luigi Mazza cooperated in organizing the "theory track" at the first joint conference, held in Oxford, England, of the Association of Collegiate Schools of Planning and the Association of European Schools of Planning. Before we left Oxford, a scheme was afoot to publish the papers from that track. Negotiations between the two associations and potential publishers proceeded very slowly until Mandelbaum suggested that the CUPR and Oxford papers be merged into a set from which a single volume would be crafted. This book—finally— is the result of that merger.

The division of labor among the three editors was relatively simple. Burchell had, in effect, done his part in the organization of the 1987 conference and the *Society* symposium. Mandelbaum and Mazza, continuing the active collaboration begun in the preparation of the Oxford conference, worked together in the selection and grouping of the essays, the solicitation of commentators, and the preparation of introductions to each section. They also joined in the often difficult task of mitigating the North American dominance of the planning theory game as it is played in English. Mandelbaum did most of the detailed editorial work on the essays selected for inclusion and wrote the general introduction.

In all of these tasks, we were helped enormously by Robert W. Lake, the editor in chief (and principal midwife) of CUPR Press. He kept the project moving when authors and editors were ready to despair. We are deeply grateful to him and only hope that other CUPR books are born more easily than our stubborn baby. We are also grateful to the authors and commentators who stayed with us through a long gestation and who tolerated with remarkable grace what was often an aggressive editorial hand.

All of the essays in this volume were written to address arguments that are salient in the community of planning theoreticians, and they are crafted in the language of that community. The community is not, however, a free-floating or self-absorbed band whose members talk only to each other. While authors differ in their styles and in their images of their audience, we are confident that students, experienced practitioners, and friends of city and regional planning, wherever they are, will find that these essays illuminate their various enterprises and help them (in John Forester's phrase) "when they are stuck."

Seymour J. Mandelbaum
Luigi Mazza
Robert W. Burchell

Seymour J. Mandelbaum

Introduction

THE TALK OF THE COMMUNITY

The growth of university-based instruction in what is variously described as "city and regional," "town," or "urban" planning has encouraged the development of a community of academic planning theoreticians. The members of this community read each other's work, speak to one another across the printed page and, often, know each other personally. The small size of the community and its ties to schools of a "minor profession" limit its audience and external prestige but not its intellectual ambitions. "Planning"—as idea and activity—carries the theoreticians into the center of debates over the nature of social and ethical inquiry and the great choices that confront us when the future seems open to our efforts. Large areas of the social sciences and humanities—read as reflections on the links between planning processes and their outcomes— are incorporated into the domain of the community even if it sometimes seems that a minnow has swallowed a whale.

The essays in this collection are the substantially revised descendants of papers presented at two gatherings of this community. The first, in Washington, D.C., in 1987, was organized by the Center for Urban Policy Research at Rutgers University; the second, in Oxford, England, in 1991, was the "theory track" in a joint conference of the Association of Collegiate Schools of Planning and the Association of European Schools of Planning. Even were we to publish every paper read at those two celebrations of the joys of theorizing, some established and many new voices would be excluded from this volume. Taken together, however, these essays—roughly half the candidates we considered—capture the concerns and the tone of the talk of the community writing in English about planning theory.

"Current talk" does not, of course, capture everything that the members of the community know or care about. Individually and collectively, we do, indeed, remember texts (such as the "classics" of general systems theory) that are no longer central to our conversations because we have integrated them into our terms of reference; we remember but do not talk much about issues that we have decided are either settled or intractable. Symmetrically, we are prone to exaggerate the influence of authors whose work is only partially integrated into our thought and who still appear as a "cause" calling for a champion or demanding rebuttal.

Current talk is also not a measure of a communal destiny. Most of the scholars represented in this collection announced a broad and ambiguous problem early in their careers and have pursued it in various guises over time: they are not likely, therefore, suddenly to change direction in response to external "imperatives," immediate "problems," or even a particularly insightful essay. The subtle dynamics of the community encourage, however, a constant process of realignment and redirection. As beginning theorists craft their identities, they must establish that theirs is a new though recognizable path. Senior figures must assimilate phenomena into the problem within which they have grounded their identities if they are to remain both cogent and vital. In the course of this assimilation, they shift their grounds, retaining the intellectual benefits of persistence while avoiding mere repetition.

Conferences of the sort that gave birth to this volume also provide opportunities for collective reflection and repair. The Oxford conference, for example, has already encouraged conversations about ways of bridging the gap between the interpreters of planning practice who dominated the theory track (and now this volume) and the formalists designing new planning techniques who were largely missing from the track and who are poorly represented here.

Each section in this collection is organized in an identical way. A set of essays is sandwiched between an editorial introduction that justifies the clustering and a critical commentary. In effect, the volume as a whole constitutes a third conference, awaiting only the response of readers to make it complete.

The outline into which we have poured the papers should not confuse any of those readers—may they be many! This is not a book designed by a single intelligence and moving systematically from one idea to another. The essays are fragments from what we believe is a shared but not very tidy conversation. The weak order we have imposed upon the texts was never intended to discipline them tightly into a coherent exposition of a single theoretical position or even a single conception of the generative issues of the field. They remain fragments.

Publication of this collection by CUPR Press deliberately identifies us with *Planning Theory in the 1980s: A Search for Future Directions* (New Brunswick, NJ: Center for Urban Policy Research, 1978), the product of an earlier CUPR conference. I was tempted to locate this volume in time and intellectual space by explicitly contrasting it with its predecessor. The contrasts are, however, so intriguing that I leave them to the reader who may go back and forth between the two collections without my guidance wondering whether they indicate a sea change in academic discussion over nearly two decades or minor variations in two samples from an essentially stable universe of reflection and argument.

As in any epistemic community, the talk of the planning theoreticians (in the 1990s) is structured around arguments, uncertainties, and disagreements. There is barely an essay in this collection that does not insist (sometimes more emphatically and sometimes less) that there are several ways of looking at an issue, and *this* way is better than *that*; that the evidence should *really* be interpreted in this particular manner; that the sensible and cogent conception of *planning* or *rationality* or *democracy* should lead us to abandon (or adopt) this or that research strategy; that more or better research might allow us to act confidently where now we hesitate and stumble.

I leave these disputes to the essayists and commentators, choosing, instead, an unusual and risky introductory tactic. Despite the stylized emphasis on disagreements and despite its expansive reach, the community seems to me to be remarkably consensual. There is no reason, however, to accept my interpretation as authoritative. As they explore what I believe is a rich treasure of essays, readers will be able to judge for themselves whether I have this agreement right or whether my emphasis on consensus has robbed the field of its distinctive flavors.

It seems to me that we agree on four major issues: a capacious conception of theory and theorizing, a commitment to writing in public, a reconciliation of agency and structure, and a pervasive interest in practices and practitioners. These agreements shape our conversation, diffusing rather than sharply articulating our differences. Our consensus does not provide a fixed point in the heavens to guide planning choices but, paradoxically, it makes it possible to respond with depth and insight to the repair and replacement of particular practices.

THEORY AS A CAPACIOUS RHETORICAL FORM

Once upon a time—I am not sure when—"theory" was a prestigious and restrictive term. Its rhetorical standards could not be satisfied by even a carefully crafted narrative of particular events, and certainly not by an

everyday story. Theory was not to be confused with empirical generalizations or statistical patterns nor with a normative catechism or a policy proposal. In its full rhetorical splendor, theory was composed of a set of propositions brought together in a symbolic world that generated accurate forecasts and postdictions, that disciplined the chaos of our sensory observations so that the rhetorical form revealed and mirrored what we assumed
was the hidden order of Nature, Man, and Society. Theory forced our
jumbled expressions of value, virtue, and preference into a coherent hierarchy so that immediate choices followed ineluctably from a small set of
principles and decision rules.

Because the form was so demanding it was, of course, rarely observed
outside the diagrams and fictive illustrations of textbooks and treatises.
Everyone understood, however, that the varied practices of aspiring theorists were part of a development process that was common across all the
sciences: today an imaginative observation, a statistical correlation, a history,
a value clarification; tomorrow or the day after, a theory. The prestige
attached to theorizing in the present derived from the confident sense that
the voice of theory was the voice of tomorrow's progressive scientific
culture.

That ambitious image of theory and theorizing was never uncontested
and, perhaps, dominated only small (though prestigious) intellectual stages;
nor is it now completely vanquished or quiet. The image does not, however, provide a compelling or even salient discipline for the community of
planning theoreticians. Within that community, it would seem both personally gauche and intellectually old-fashioned to read the essays in this
volume only to dismiss most of them as not "really" theoretical. The community of planning theoreticians, without an explicit decision (of a sort it
is, of course, incapable of making) has tacitly dismissed the idea that there
is a cogent form of knowledge that is justified by a human desire for understanding that is so universal and so powerful that it cannot be ascribed
to any particular purpose nor tested against any localized pragmatic standard of value. The severe forms of both positive and normative theory that
used to command the intellectual heights and draw us to them now appear as a mirage that retreats or disappears as we approach it. Planning
theoreticians characteristically represent themselves as engaged in worlds
in which knowledge is always directed to improving or maintaining "good"
practices or crafts. Our rhetorical variety is appropriate to *praxis* and to
techne—the only forms of knowledge within our grasp. Aristotle's *theoria* is
an empty category.

The catholicity of the community and its rhetoric restructures the ordinary way of imagining the relations between theorists and practitioners.

The willingness of theoreticians to accept a capacious conception of theory for themselves simultaneously grants a comparable standing to the clamorous buzz of "talk-about-planning" that accompanies everyday practices in agencies, consulting firms, courts, legislatures, and on the street. The talk of theorizing priests and laity alike is marked (among other forms) by archetypes, abstract symbolic and iconic models, tacit protocols, stories, conventionalized dilemmas, dichotomous semantic structures, and all of the tropes beloved of rhetoricians. When those of us who make our living theorizing enter a conversation with practitioners, we never meet the silence of "planners without theory." Instead, we are engaged by a crowded field of theories (and lay theoreticians) entangled in one another and embedded in social relations. Without the glow of the mirage or the support of short-lived professorial authority over novices, our messages do not soar above the field but struggle for attention on the ground as a part of the ordinary sounds of the madding crowd.

WRITING IN PUBLIC

Some of the planning theoreticians represented in this volume would probably insist that their talk is distinguished from ordinary sounds by its commitment to the norms of science; others would demur or would attach complex caveats to the term. I am content to leave science and its close cousins to the contested or at least ambiguous ground of the community. There is, however, a simpler and less contentious version of that notion: planning theoreticians are committed to writing in public.

The "in public" provision distinguishes our talk from all of the communication that surrounds planning within organizations and communities in which members learn to maintain their private domain by public discretion; learn to encode their emotions in forms that maintain and protect established social relations. The community of theoreticians is subject to the same disciplines within its own borders. As they face the world, however, theoreticians are purposefully indiscreet: they reveal secrets and explicate the conservative power of discursive forms even as—as in so many essays in this collection—they write appreciatively of private domains, the richness of planners' stories, and the wisdom of citizens.

The indiscretion and essential irresponsibility of theoreticians are sustained by their commitment to the written word. The origin of this volume in two conferences and the delights of face-to-face meetings should not obscure the essential dependence of the community upon (public) reading and writing. Theoreticians—in their communal role—do not manage agencies, organize neighborhoods, whisper in the mayor's ear, solve difficult design problems, teach students, or negotiate with developers. In character, they write in a community of active readers that is sustained by the creation of new texts and the maintenance of old ones. Those who do not read cannot be persuaded. Those who do read must persuade themselves. We may scorn theorists who have given us bad advice but—reading at arm's length outside the bonds of organization—we cannot blame them or hold them to account. Theorists require no malpractice insurance.

I am not able here to probe very deeply the implications of this reliance upon writing. Even superficially, however, it is obvious that theoreticians who do not write are suspect or, more precisely, they are invisible. The written conversations that are recorded in the annotations that mark every essay in this volume are asymmetrical. Theoreticians can "speak" with dead authors and with living ones who do not attend to them, introducing strange gods into the oral culture of planning. (Derrida talks to the planning theoreticians but, I suspect, they do not talk to him.) Writing allows for enormous argumentative complexity, multiple voices, and an extended memory, but the absence of sustained interaction decisively shifts the control of texts from writer to reader. Once it is out of my hands, this introduction is no longer mine to interpret; it belongs to the reader. In ordinary face-to-face conversations, in contrast, speakers often correct and readjust their words in repeated attempts to be understood by their listeners. They remain in control of their own words until the encounter is concluded.

AGENCY AND STRUCTURE

I have deliberately tiptoed around the word "planning," since that term is part of the contested ground and, as will be apparent in the first section of the volume, I am one of the contestants. I suspect, however, that virtually all members of the community of theoreticians represent planning as some sort of process in which individual or collective agents exercise discretion: they choose to do *A* (whether it is a simple momentary act or a complex behavioral chain over extended time) in a field in which it always is possible to select at least one other alternative.

The modes of choice are planning processes and are the central concern of the theorizing community. I am disposed to treat all modes—flipping a coin, reading entrails, and conferring with stakeholders—as planning processes. Though most theoreticians would be more restrictive in their definition of the central term, the differences among us do not disrupt a broadly shared consensus on what has been an extremely difficult issue in the representation of agency and structure.

Most of us have struggled at one point or another in our lives with the classic conflict between free will and determinism. Even when the deep metaphysical issue is resolved in favor of human discretion, we characteristically face a conflict between two sensibilities. On the one side, we are eager to treat individuals and collectivities as agents and to empower them by illuminating the dynamics of planning. On the other side, the search for that illumination leads us (Prometheus-like) to steal the insight of the gods so that we can understand the "structures" that shape our lives, making events predictable and knowledge possible. In the search for structure and predictability, agency appears as a troubling indicator of a still-incomplete explanation—an intellectual problem to be overcome.

For many years, the community of planning theoreticians was dominated by the conflict between these two sensibilities, particularly as it appeared as a struggle between Marxist analyses of capitalist societies and the attempts to enhance the intelligence of professional planning within those societies. If the Marxists were right in their structural analysis, did the professionals have any choices? Should planning theorists even attend to the professionals if they wanted to understand how and why cities and regions were *really* planned?

The echoes of that struggle have not faded completely and are not likely to disappear. Indeed, they are recreated over and over again as one structure or another—the global economy, culture, urban regimes, networks of innovators—appears to offer fresh insight into the worlds we construct. The sensibilities that command our attention to both agency and structure are elements in a dilemma that we should not dismiss even if we could. As I read the essays in this volume, however, I am struck by how little of the venom remains from the old battles. Without much ado, virtually everyone has adopted an image of a world in which agency is rampant and virtually anything is possible: nations, cultures, empires, regions, and complex institutions may all be designed by human agents.

Some things are, of course, harder than others to accomplish. Our representations of the social world are shaped by our attitudes toward those difficulties. When we adopt the image of "structure" and seek knowledge within it, we are, in effect, announcing that (at least temporarily) some risks are too great to bear; some pleasures too great to put at risk; some gains not worth the struggle; some adversaries too formidable. When we are ready for the fray, then structures dissolve into systems of agents vulnerable to incentives, to persuasion, and to power. In large matters and in small, we understand those systems in relation to our own capabilities to address them.

PRACTICES AND PRACTITIONERS

In the simplest but not fully adequate terms, this final element in the shared framework of these essays captures a pervasive interest in the behavior, values, character, and experiences of professional planners at work. If anyone still thinks that theoreticians don't care about "the profession," they haven't been reading "theory" for a very long time.

There is, however, a deeper meaning to this interest in practices and practitioners. The theorists writing in this volume characteristically represent the behavior of men and women as organized in "practices"—ways of talking, rituals, implicit protocols, routines, relational strategies, character traits, and virtues. The complex web of these practices—rarely reducible to a few generative principles or hierarchical ethics—is the primary source of social stability. Simultaneously, however, the conception of a "practice" is an attempt to locate important behavioral clusters that are small enough to be amenable to externally encouraged change but large enough to sustain themselves within the environmental web.

In some formulations, practices—notably discursive forms—appear almost disembodied, shaping and driving individuals and groups in ways they barely understand and cannot control. For planning theoreticians, however, practices are characteristically linked to actors (practitioners) who have an ambivalent or dilemmatic relationship to their own behavioral patterns rather than being trapped within them. New intentions and new possibilities repeatedly lead us to devalue and to dismiss old practices. We are bound, however, to fill the containers formed by new artifacts, communities, institutions, or policies with new practices: they cannot stay empty because without practices, social forms have no character or predictability. They can sustain neither trust nor respect. Filling forms with entirely new practices is so difficult, however, that inevitably, old wine is required to fill the innovative bottles. In effect, we spring the trap and reconstruct it over and over again.

AGREEMENT AND DISAGREEMENT

The elements of this consensus—if I have correctly characterized them—have important implications for the ways in which disagreements (and hence contributions) are articulated. Imagine, if you can, an intellectual domain in which the participants think that there should be a single compelling way of representing the world; that positive theorizing will provide a coherent, abstract order for that world; and that normative theorizing provides a hierarchical set of ethical mandates. In such a domain, a great deal rests on differences in the architecture of positive theory, on the implications for theory of particular empirical observations (and vice versa), and on the placement of ethical propositions within a hierarchical form. The structure of the domain locates issues of conflict and uncertainty with great clarity. *comprehensive, wide view*

Capacious theorizing has the opposite effect. The abandonment of *theoria* and its severe domain diffuses disagreements. The community of planning theoreticians speaks of a plurality of worlds in terms that are expressive of variable intentions and expectations. Rampant agency makes all knowledge seem historical and contingent. Misfits and conflicts are difficult to distinguish in a *bricollage* in which the mortar holding collections of abstractions together consists of practices that are dilemmatic and protean.

There is a paradoxical quality to the talk of the community. Its pluralism and its abandonment of the images of a grand theoretical synthesis may leave some readers, including professional planners, unsatisfied, still "searching for new directions." At the same time, the emphasis on agency and the forms of representation should free the design and repair of practices from the overwhelming burden of locating a singular hierarchical form in which to organize both our knowledge of the world and our conception of its virtues. I hope you will find that a precious gift available to the active reader who is attentive to the talk of the community.

theoria — Greek — a looking at contemplation, speculation, theory

protean — things that are extremely variable & can swiftly change. Proteus — Shape changing God

Explorations
in
Planning
Theory

PART I

Designing a Domain
for
Planning Theory

Luigi Mazza

Designing a Domain for Planning Theory

INTRODUCTION

FOR a long time, planners have been searching through their history to find the roots and meanings of their activity. Planning accounts tend to be biased toward certain types of practice or theoretical hopes in an attempt to assign a domain to planning that can boast homogeneity and consistency, characteristics considered typical of a well-defined technique if not of a science. In this way, even the best planning accounts become willing reductions of the multiplicity of planning practices to the coherence of general theoretical systems. The results are sometimes exciting, but because they are either too partial or too removed from reality, they are necessarily fictitious.

Friedmann's chapter, which opens this section, is the first account of a wide perspective that restores the roots of contemporary planning without forcing coherence and without fearing to show how much these roots are contradictory and ambivalent—and how many important questions remain without definitive answers from the four planning traditions that he identifies in the political and social thinking of the last two centuries. In this chapter, the concerns and aims of historians are subordinated to a dual task: to design a conceptual framework in which to locate the extraordinary multiplicity of contributions that so widely influenced planning activities and, secondly, to graft onto this framework a program for planning that asserts the priority of democracy over planning. Even though Friedmann's second aim is not explicit here, it seems helpful to recall it in

3

order to grasp fully the meaning of two possible levels on which his chapter may be read. What is immediately essential is the design of the conceptual framework and the acknowledgment of the four main planning traditions. Within that framework, the traditions overlap, conflict, and are inseparably related. What was seen as a great synoptic scheme exposes an interpretative capability that breaks out of the original framework and develops the connections among different contributions, however distant in space and time.

Throughout these articulations and patterns, the chapter may also be read as a definitive confirmation that the "age of innocence" for planning is over, in the sense that planners have to abandon their technocratic illusions and their illusions of renouncing the power (however meager) bestowed on them by their professional activity. Neither the reflective planner nor the radical planner is innocent. The ambiguous relationship between action and knowledge is a daily reality, and everyone may respond to it with different intentions and commitments, whether to raise awareness and change power relationships or to unveil power and take one's distance from it.

To simplify Friedmann's scheme, we might paraphrase Sen (1987, 3) and say that planning has two origins, "both related to politics, but related in rather different ways, concerned respectively with 'ethics' on the one hand, and with what may be called 'engineering,' on the other." Friedmann's planning traditions and other contributions to this section show how planners' different aims and ways of considering the relationship between action and knowledge, knowledge and power, reflect a dual and rather conflictual nature of planning. The two origins become two planning approaches that mingle variously with theoretical contributions. A balance is not always reached between the two approaches: at times the concerns of one prevail over the other. For example, among the authors of this section, although in different ways, ethical concerns are predominant in Hoch and Mandelbaum, and methodical concerns in Alexander and Faludi. Faludi, though claiming the need for planning methodology and the positive implications of rationality in practice, advances a "weak" version of the rational model and develops the concept of "planning doctrine" as defined some years ago together with Alexander. This, in my opinion, may offer a bridge between the two approaches, for it contributes to the definition of decisional situations and consensus building. Faludi notes the independence of such a strong concept and suggests that the efficacy, comprehensiveness, and consistency of a doctrine have to be subject to the control of rational debate, but he acknowledges that a doctrine is an amalgam of heterogeneous elements and "relies on sometimes deceptively simple but ambiguous concepts." Ethical dimensions are also present in Alexander's research, which suggests a contingent framework for planning that includes critical rationality and communicative action. Hoch's aim is to untie the knot of the relationship between power and knowledge and resolve it into political pragmatism. His interest in technical knowledge is a defensive interest, aimed at preventing knowledge from becoming a tool of professional coercion and power. Mandelbaum, on the other hand—for the very reason that he acknowledges that his replies to the limits of social sciences fluctuate conflictually between regret for "political" influences, which limit the application of "knowledge," and enthusiasm for the wisdom of experience—is looking for a space for freedom and research within the claims of moral communities that give sense and value to our actions. Formal theorizing is defined by Mandelbaum as the production of a medium of escape from the vindications of moral communities—that is, the production of alternatives to what communities argue as being just. His program involves social sciences, while planning knowledge is in the background.

The importance of the two origins seems to be confirmed and expressed by the long and intractable debate about the rational model, a debate that has concerned planners for decades and turns up again in the chapters of this section. Whatever one's judgment of this debate, it is natural to wonder why it has taken us so long to understand it—and understand ourselves. It has been observed that this debate is prompted by planners' difficulty in finding their way through the complex Weberian discussion on the limits to rationality, without reducing it to a mere contrast between formal and substantive rationality. I do not want to ignore the question of planners' limits in action and understanding. I would merely like to suggest the possibility that such a schematic contrast has been, and perhaps still is, a more or less unconscious screen concealing a reluctance to develop a more open debate on the nature of planning.

One of the more generally agreed-upon accounts of planning activities depicts them as activities aimed at designing the future. The expression "designing the future" is usually meant as the design of something new. This has strong appeal because it hints at the generosity of those who are in favor of challenging power, uncertainty, and risk to foster change and help the community thrive. Designing the future may, however, also mean opposing change in favor of environmental or social conservation, or acting aggressively to promote the survival of what seems worth conserving and defencing. In both modes, designing the future implies questioning and discussing moral values. But this account of planning activities is a partial one.

In the last few years, numerous studies of planners' daily activities (some of which are published in this book) have shown that most involve forms of routine administrative activities and control. A substantial quota of planning activity is not carried out either for or against change, for or against expansion or exclusion. In short, it is not aimed at "designing the future" but at managing the present on the basis of a known past.

If this development of the account of planning activities has a base, planning nature reveals not only two origins but also a blend of two basic types of action that are different from each other, and to which different forms of rationality and justification correspond. These are anticipatory actions based especially on the logic of consequence and obligatory actions based especially on the logic of appropriateness. This distinction has more than an analytical value. It is present in practice and at times is formally authorized, even though it is evident that designing the future and managing the present are interdependent and in many instances affect each other reciprocally. The use of the two logics is not divided—even the more consolidated routines can give rise to dilemmas. The planner's daily activity nearly always implies discretion and negotiation. It is often not easy to define the proper choice in a given situation. The rule must be interpreted and, within different interpretations, choice may be defined following a consequential logic. The interlacing of the two logics is strengthened by the fact that planning activities have both a technological and an institutional nature. Sometimes technological fragments are embodied in the laws that define the planning system, and the outcome is a further meshing of technical knowledge and procedural rules. In turn, technological components embody consequential logics and calculability. Procedural rules embody obligation and appropriateness.

Since planning activities are almost everywhere a formal government tool, another generally agreed-upon account is that planning activities have become institutionalized. While this is formally true for obligatory actions, it is less true for action aimed at designing the future. In general, due to its characteristic blend of actions and logics, planning appears as a rather incomplete institution, a "non-defined" one, which is continuously urged to define its task, its position. Formally, planning's role is a given—subservient to the needs of the community. But in practice planners are continuously redefining it within and outside the institutional form. Conflictual values, present within any democratic process, constantly widen the field and the contingency of choices, questioning anew any attempt to reduce all planning practices to predetermined and conclusive formal logics, to contain them in a general system of predefined procedures. Planning activities and practice seem to resist general rationalization and bureaucratization processes because they are anthropologically—and not technically—committed to the future, and within them the temporal order of decision processes, within and outside institutions, overcomes the sequential order of technological processes. The result is an institutional incompleteness that shows itself not only at a technical level but as a continuous tension between an accomplished form and rationality and the need to break out of the form in order to foresee and provide. It is, therefore, not surprising that in the attempt to resolve this tension, the search for a general theory is not abandoned. But the nonexistence of a general theory is consistent with planning's inherent characteristics as described so far, and Mandelbaum's arguments are quite difficult to refute. Those arguments, furthermore, lead us to conclude that "we don't need a complete general theory of planning and we don't even need to agree on the definition of the field." Besides, how many sciences have a complete general theory?

If planning activities were committed only to designing the future, to breaking established balances in order to build new and different ones, then the tension that runs through them could be considered the result and expression of conflicts between conservation and change. The search for a planning rationality could be dismissed either as an attempt at rationalizing the balances established in the form and rationality of power or as the scientifically and historically failed attempt to develop a form of total planning. But a significant portion of planning activity is not aimed at the future. It is, on the contrary, committed to removing uncertainty and risk and to excluding these from life-plans by implementing established models and routines that are formally expressed in the form of plans and bylaws and informally by the actions of the planner. The basis of these regulative policies is formed by the methodical rationality of a disregarded planning knowledge—we could say a planning "science"—that is the result of "unforced agreements," slowly sedimented in time and spread out in the knowledge of our communities. A sense of voluntary obligation springs from these agreements and allows for "acknowledging" and hence "expecting"—that is, of describing in a rational manner, in accordance with the established and accepted way—and, as long as solidarity and obligation are respected, of projecting into the future the if–then relationship, beyond uncertainties and risks.

If by rational we mean "methodical," most planning activity has been rational for a long time, in terms of both obligatory and anticipatory actions. If by rational we mean "reasonable" rather than methodical, then anticipatory actions, directed toward designing the future—hazardous activities, characterized by a measurable probability of failure, punctuated by successes but also by disasters of varying dimensions—are reasonable, and their reasonableness is constructed through the justified composition of fragments of methodical rationality, of technical knowledge. Methodical rationality and reasonableness are no strangers to planning. On the contrary, they are both intrinsic to its processes and follow interlocking paths that are not always easy to distinguish at first glance. Planners' difficulty in understanding (and in understanding each other) could perhaps be traced back to the complexity of this mesh, particularly as planners sometimes try to be rational in cases where it is possible to be only reasonable, while they fail to consider the rationality applied in daily practices, governed by a technical knowledge. That knowledge is not technical merely because it is shared but is so shared that it is sometimes applied in an unconscious way.

Surprisingly, the premises of methodical rationality are little known and rarely analyzed or developed. Planners know very little about technical knowledge and its application in discretionary action, in mediation and negotiation, or in explicit anticipatory action. We can acknowledge, and to some extent also regret, that planning's methodical rationality—as shown by the analysis of the rational model developed in Faludi's chapter—has always been weak. The technical knowledge that substantiated it is even weaker. Its weakness and inability to fulfill promises and expectation and, therefore, to support the meager solidarity of the planning community, are perhaps the best explanation for the lengthy debate among supporters and detractors of the rational model. If the "engineering" approach to planning had been more developed, the rationality debate would have been over long ago—and probably confined to discussions of professional ethics.

I think that we must take the rationality debate seriously because the real and supposed departure of planning activities from methodical rationality is proportional to the poverty of our technical knowledge—both the technical knowledge proper to planning and that of natural and mechanical sciences used in planning actions. Albeit slowly, growth of technical knowledge is doomed to continue and to constitute a regulation form, of which it is vital to be very conscious to avoid authoritarian regulation forms of planning and to keep open "a medium of escape." It is possible that a fair amount of the current hostility of planners to methodical rationality has arisen because the negative effects produced by certain regulation forms have been attributed to rationality when, instead, it is the growth of knowledge that brings rationality with it; the planner's ideological use of knowledge is responsible for the negative effect of regulation. The planner's vulnerability is not simply the human vulnerability of the weak; it is also the vulnerability of weak technical knowledge. In a democratic context, the capacity to resist is also a function of available technical knowledge and of how it is put to use politically. The stories of planning and power through which Hoch would like to construct a community "in which we can work to improve the democratic quality of practice" are also the stories of the transformation and uses of technical knowledge. The quality of the identification and description of an action's consequences, and the democratic quality of planning processes—both key factors for Hoch's pragmatic approach—are not indifferent to the quality and use of the planner's technical knowledge.

There is, of course, the further possibility that there are more than two origins of planning. If we glance at planning history beyond the Enlightenment, we might perceive a third origin—that of the rite. The ritual foundation of towns and cities reflects a form of rationality—certainly not only superstition. To distinguish town from country, citizen from alien, is functional to the symbolic construction of power and offers a means of defense against uncertainty and the self-destructive violence that always runs in a community's veins. This form of rationality is functional to the construction of an institutional violence designed to overcome instinctive violence.

What is left of this ritual origin in contemporary planning? Perhaps nothing, or perhaps more than we suspect, as the original ritual function may have taken on new forms. How many (disregarded) ritual undercurrents lurk beneath market practices and theories? And is this disregarding of the ritual aspects of competition preventing us from acknowledging that some of these policies are unreasonable? Actually, in some planning concepts aimed at safeguarding the environment against uncontrolled and destructive market expansion, one can detect a defensive function typical of ritual proceedings—a function that is, at least in part, still ritually developed. Similarly, the application of planning ideas such as "green belt" and "green heart" betrays a stronger ritual connotation, in the positive and rational meaning of the term, than an engineering or scientific content. Even if there is no intrinsic and compulsory ritual dimension in the concepts expounded here, this quality, if it exists, is rooted in the link between concepts and powers—and this link is developed in the ways of constructing our specific technical knowledge. Once again, our poor understanding of the nature and multiple dimensions of our technical knowledge leaves us with not a few embarrassing theoretical shortcomings.

John Friedmann

1 Two Centuries of Planning Theory: An Overview

INTRODUCTION

The idea that scientifically based knowledge about society could be applied to society's improvement first arose during the eighteenth century. Figure 1.1 describes the forms of that idea over the last two hundred years, mapping the intellectual influences that have shaped contemporary planning theory in the United States. Schools of thought and individual authors are placed along a continuum of social values, from conservative ideology on the left-hand side of the figure to utopianism and anarchism on the right. To simplify exposition, we may divide this continuum into three parts. On the extreme left of the diagram are shown those authors who look to the confirmation and reproduction of existing relationships of power in society. Expressing predominantly technical concerns, they proclaim a carefully nurtured stance of political neutrality. In reality, they address their work to those who are in power and see their primary mission as serving the state.

Systems Analysis derives from a cluster of theories that may be loosely grouped under the heading of *Systems Engineering* (cybernetics, game theory, information theory, computer science, robotics, and so on). Scientists in this tradition work chiefly with large-scale quantitative models. In specific planning applications, they may use optimizing techniques such as

This chapter is adapted from John Friedmann, *Planning in the Public Domain: From Knowledge to Action* (Princeton, NJ: Princeton University Press, 1987), chapter 3, with permission of the publisher.

An earlier version of this chapter appeared in *Society* 26, 1 (November/December 1988), Transaction Publishers, New Brunswick, New Jersey.

Operations Research; alternatively, they may construct long-range forecasting models. Most futures research leans heavily on systems-analytic languages.

More closely allied to public administration than to systems analysis, *Policy Science* subjects specific issues in public policy to socioeconomic analysis. Stock-in-trade concepts include the analysis of costs and benefits, zero-base budgeting, cost effectiveness, and program evaluation. Theorists of this school generally prefer problems that are well-bounded and goal statements that are unambiguous. Note, too, that policy science is heir to a long intellectual tradition. Such logic as it has derives largely from neoclassical economics with its several offshoots of welfare economics and social choice theory. An amalgam with the institutional approach of public administration, however, is its very own.

Public Administration, finally, has been more generally concerned with the functions of central planning, the conditions for its success, and the relationship of planning to politics. In recent decades, a special area of concern has been the implementation of public policies and programs. A central contribution to planning theory from the traditions of public administration was made by Herbert Simon, whose early work, *Administrative Behavior* (Simon 1976 [1945]), approached the bureaucratic process from a behavioral perspective that stressed conditions limiting rationality in large organizations.

On the opposite side of the spectrum (extreme right of Figure 1.1) are authors who look to the transformation and transcendence of existing relationships of power within civil society. Here it is no longer the state that is addressed but the people as a whole, particularly those of working class origins who, it is believed, are fundamentally opposed to the bureaucratic state and, more generally, to every form of alienated power. The mode of discourse adopted by these authors is frankly political.

Most extreme in their rejection of power are the *utopians* and *social anarchists*, who deny all claims of higher authority in their search for a world of non-hierarchical relations. Parallel to this tradition is *Historical Materialism* and, more recently, *Neo-Marxism*. Writers in this vein tend to espouse the revolutionary transformation of the prevailing "mode of production." In contrast to utopians, they accept the state as a necessity. Class relations constitute a central analytical preoccupation of historical materialists. It is through relentless class conflict, they argue, that existing relations of power will eventually be "smashed" and replaced with a socialist state that will reflect the organized power and material interests of the working class as a whole.

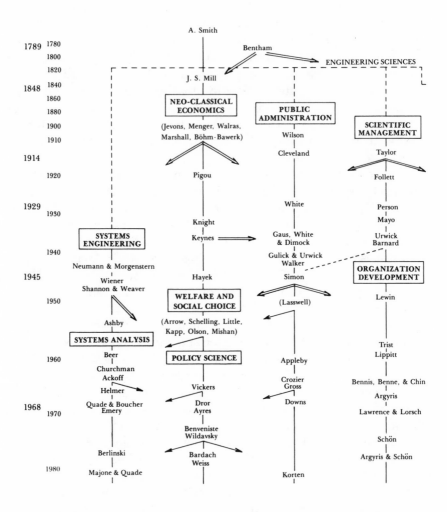

FIGURE 1.1
Intellectual influences on American planning theory

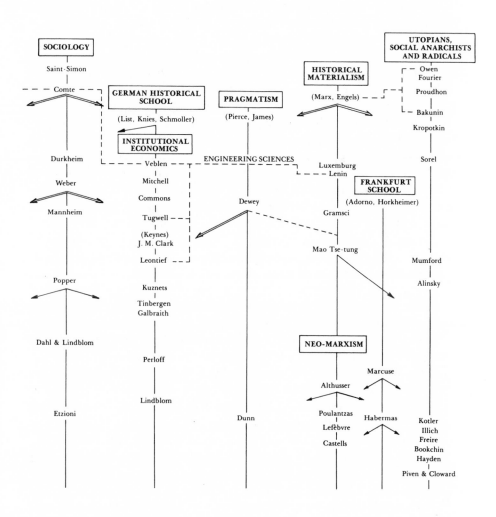

FIGURE 1.1 (continued)

Midway between utopian anarchism and historical materialism, I have located a secondary tradition, particularly important to planning theorists, in the "Frankfurt School of Critical Sociology" (Jay 1973). This school's radical critique of the cultural manifestations of capitalism (including the deification of technical reason itself) is grounded in Hegelian and Marxist thought.

Moving toward the central portions of Figure 1.1, we enter the gray area of overlap between the conservative pole of "ideology" where present relations of power remain largely unquestioned and the radical pole of "utopia," with its transcendent moral vision. Here we encounter the reformist traditions of planning and the related fields of *Public Administration* and *Scientific Management* and the seminal work of Frederick Winslow Taylor (1919 [1911]). Taylor's notion that management could be rationalized through the application of science enjoyed remarkable success in its time. Though he directed his attention to capitalist firms, his doctrines were attractive to radical thinkers such as Veblen and Lenin, who conceived of society as a large workshop or factory and of planning as a form of social engineering. For all of them, conservatives and radicals alike, the watchword was efficiency. In an age of industrialism, they thought, its invocation would magically unlock the gateway to the future.

After 1945, work on scientific management spawned the new field of *Organization Development*. Its principal client was the large, private corporation, to which it tendered a message steeped in humanistic rhetoric. With works by Eric Trist, Chris Argyris, Donald Schön, Charles Hampden-Turner and others, the field produced a literature that gradually moved away from profit as the sole criterion of management, bringing psychological values of self-development to the foreground.

Along more conventional liberal lines is *Institutional Economics*. An American branch of the nineteenth century "German Historical School," but by no means rigorously defined, it emphasizes the study of existing economic and social institutions over abstract theorizing in the style of neoclassical economics. Institutionalists prefer to examine the failings of specific institutional arrangements in relation to social purpose, and to identify reforms. They have contributed major ideas for planning full employment, economic growth, regional resources development, New Towns policies, public housing schemes, and social welfare. In the 1930s, the institutionalization of a central planning function was one of their major concerns.

Institutionalists tend to regard the state as a benign and rational actor, responsive to political pressure. In this sense, they stand very much in the tradition of Auguste Comte, who thought that social scientists should offer their knowledge to the rulers of nations. Like the father of positive philosophy himself, they believe in the powers of technical reason to determine what is correct, to persuade the ignorant and doubtful, and to forge the consensus needed for public action. Suspicious of free-wheeling democratic politics, they place their faith in a technocracy of the meritorious. Located between the traditions of institutionalism and historical materialism, we find the philosophical school of *Pragmatism*. For present purposes, this is an important tradition primarily because of John Dewey's exceptional influence on the intellectual history of planning. His influence is especially notable among institutional economists, many of whom came to accept Dewey's championship of a "scientific politics" in which learning from social experiments was regarded as fundamental to the development of a healthy democracy. A more recent exponent of a Dewey-like pragmatic philosophy is Edgar Dunn.

The center line of Figure 1.1 is labeled *Sociology*, for want of a better term. Here we meet the great synthesizers of social knowledge. Without exception, the great sociologists of the past stressed the importance of technical reason in human affairs. The classic European masters of this tradition include Emile Durkheim, Max Weber, Karl Mannheim, and Karl Popper. Durkheim stressed the importance of consensual values in social organization and the "organic solidarity" of the division of labor, while Weber emphasized the dominant role of bureaucratic structures in an industrial society devoted to the worship of functional order. Mannheim, the most distinguished continental sociologist of his time, was a critic of mass society and an advocate of "rational planning" as a way of overcoming the evils of unreason that had overtaken inter-war Europe. In contrast, Popper, an Austrian emigré scholar living in England, inveighed against the image of a totally planned society and defended the intellectual and moral credibility of piecemeal social engineering.

This classic tradition has been carried forward in the United States by Robert Dahl and Charles Lindblom whose *Politics, Economics and Welfare* (1957) was the first major American theoretical statement on planning, and by Amitai Etzioni, whose *The Active Society* (1968) may be read as a worthy successor to Mannheim's *Man and Society in an Age of Reconstruction*, written during a period of general crisis a generation earlier (1949b [1940]).

A dashed line, labeled *Engineering Sciences*, runs across the top of Figure 1.1, connecting Saint-Simon and Auguste Comte in the center with *Scientific Management, Public Administration, Systems Engineering,* and *Institutional Economics*. (An influence on Lenin is also shown.) A case can be made that the methods of engineering inform major sectors of the planning theory tradition down to this day. At his celebrated Paris dinners during which his basic ideas took shape, Saint-Simon played host to some of the leading professors of the new "École Polytechnique" (established in 1794); later, he surrounded himself, by preference, with young polytechnicians who were both his audience and inspiration. Among them was Auguste Comte, who was expelled from the École for disciplinary reasons only months before he was to graduate.

The École Polytechnique may be seen as the prototypical institution of the new Industrial Age and the source of its managerial ideology. Engineering applied the knowledge of natural sciences to the construction of bridges, tunnels, and canals. By the same logic, why should not a new breed of "social engineers" apply their knowledge to the task of reconstructing society? In a brilliant essay on the École tradition, Friedrich von Hayek tells us how the new institution, born in revolutionary times, shaped the character and outlook of its pupils.

> The very type of the engineer with his characteristic outlook, ambitions, and limitation was here created. That synthetic spirit which would not recognize sense in anything that had not been deliberately constructed, that love of organization that springs from the twin sources of military and engineering practices, the aesthetic predilection for everything that had been consciously constructed over anything that had "just grown," was a strong element which was added to—and in the course of time even began to replace—the revolutionary ardor of the young polytechnicians. . . . It was in this atmosphere that Saint-Simon conceived some of the earliest and most fantastic plans for the reorganization of society, and . . . it was at the École Polytechnique where, during the first twenty years of its existence, Auguste Comte, Prosper Enfantin, Victor Considerant, and some hundreds of later Saint-Simonians and Fourierists received their training, followed by a succession of social reformers throughout the century down to Georges Sorel. (Hayek 1955, 113 [1941–44])

The engineer's sense of certainty (and his ignorance of history) informed some of the most prominent of later planning theorists, among them Thorstein Veblen, Rexford Tugwell, and Herbert Simon, all of whom were enthralled by the idea of "designing society."

Even Simon, who was certainly aware of the difficulties inherent in the project, could not resist discussing social planning as the task of "designing the evolving artifact," as though society were merely a complex piece of machinery (Simon 1982 [1969]). It is precisely when we turn from designing genuine artifacts to society, however, that the design model breaks down. Simon seems to be conscious of the contradiction:

> Making complex designs that are implemented over a long period of time and continually modified in the course of implementation has much in common with painting in oil. In oil painting, every new spot of pigment laid on the canvas creates some kind of pattern that provides a continuing source of ideas to the painter. The painting process is a process of cyclical interaction between painter and canvas in which current goals lead to new applications of paint, while the gradually changing patterns suggest new goals. (Simon 1982 [1969], 187)

An oil painting is not a machine, and urban designers do not paint in oils. What is more, and to confuse the metaphor, society is not a canvas to be painted by an inspired artist. Engineers can build bridges and automata; it is an illusion to think that they can "build" society. There was a moment in time when aeronautic and space engineers thought that, having reached the moon, they could now turn their energies to solving the problem of growing violence in cities along with other urban "crises." But the two types of problems—how to conquer space and how to eliminate urban violence—were of an essentially different nature, and their discovery that urban violence would not yield to engineering solutions was not long in coming (Rittel and Webber 1973).

This "quick read" across the horizontal axis of Figure 1.1 needs to be complemented now with a more detailed discussion of the time dimension in the evolution of planning thought. Certain key dates are marked in bold type on the left-hand margin.

FOUR TRADITIONS OF PLANNING THOUGHT

A slightly different approach to essentially the same intellectual history appears in Figure 1.2. I have placed key figures in the history of planning thought within four major traditions, each addressing the links between knowledge and action. To be grouped into a common "tradition," authors had to meet three requirements:

1. They had to speak in the "languages" (such as economics or mathematics) of the tradition;

2. They had to share a certain philosophical outlook; and

3. They needed to address a small number of central questions that defined the particular intellectual tradition.

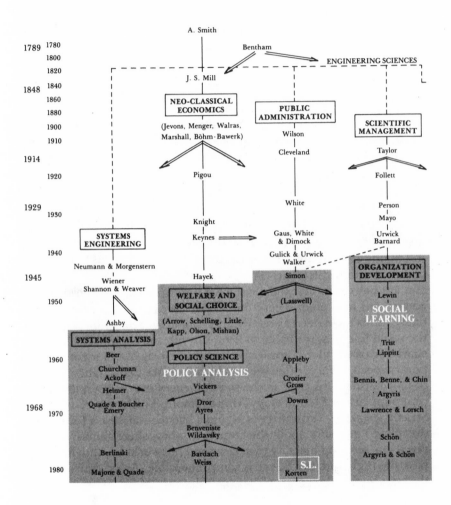

FIGURE 1.2
Major traditions of planning theory

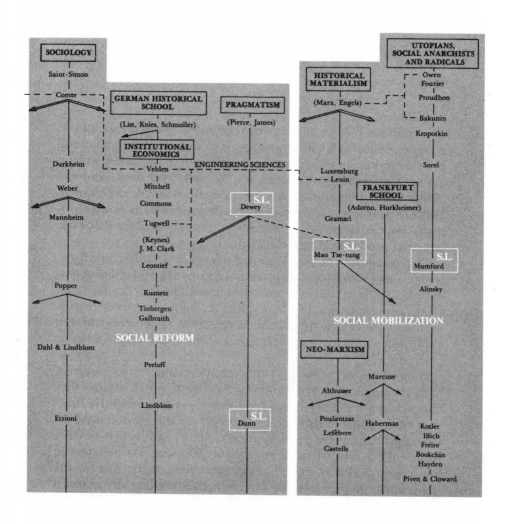

FIGURE 1.2 (continued)

The traditions extend across the entire ideological spectrum, from support for the state and affirmation of its authority to the abolition of every form of authority, including that of the state. The two older traditions, *Social Reform* and *Social Mobilization*, reach back to the first half of the nineteenth century. The other two, *Policy Analysis* and *Social Learning*, have their origins in the period between the Great Depression and World War II.

Social Reform

This tradition focuses on the role of the state in societal guidance. It is chiefly concerned with finding ways to institutionalize planning practice and make action by the state more effective. Those writing in this tradition regard planning as a "scientific endeavor"; one of their main preoccupations is with using the scientific paradigm to inform and to limit politics to what are deemed to be its proper concerns. *Policy Science*—Karl Mannheim's *wissenschaftliche Politik*—is one of its products (Mannheim 1949a [1929]).

The vocabulary of social reform derives primarily from three sources: macrosociology, institutional economics, and political philosophy. In their political convictions, the authors in this tradition affirm liberal democracy, human rights, and social justice. Within limits, they are tolerant of positive social change. They believe that through progressive reforms, both capitalism and the bourgeois state can be perfected.

Philosophically, authors in this tradition understand planning to be the application of scientific knowledge to public affairs; they also consider it a professional responsibility and an executive function. Many fields in the planning terrain are, therefore, fenced off from the intrusions of politicians and ordinary citizens who, it is argued, are not sufficiently informed to be seriously engaged in planning. As planners in the reform tradition, these authors advocate a strong role for the state, which they understand to have both mediating and authoritative roles. Since the publication of Keynes's *General Theory* in 1936 (Keynes 1964), they have argued for three areas of scientifically based and legitimate state intervention: the promotion of economic growth, the maintenance of full employment, and the redistribution of income.

The central questions addressed by planners in this tradition tend to be of a broad philosophical nature:

1. What is the proper relation of planning to politics?

2. What is the nature of the public interest, and should planners have the power (and the obligation) to articulate and promote their version of it?

3. In the context of planning, what should be the role of the state in a market economy? To what extent would "social rationality" be served through market interventions by the state? Under what conditions would such interventions be considered legitimate?

4. If planning is a "scientific endeavor," what is meant by science? Is it Karl Popper's (1974 [1945]) view that scientific knowledge is the residue of hypotheses that have successfully resisted all efforts at "falsification" through contradictory evidence? Is it Thomas S. Kuhn's celebrated theory of science as the dynamic interplay of "normal paradigms" and "scientific revolutions" (Kuhn 1970 [1962])? Or is it John Dewey's (1927) pragmatic epistemology, in which knowledge exists only in the act of knowing, and the validity of any statement is derived from its usefulness in application? Which of these views is most appropriate for planning, and what implications follow from adopting it?

5. There is great debate within the social reform tradition over the institutionalization of planning. Should planning be used comprehensively as an instrument of central guidance, coordination, and control by the state? Should it be divided among a large number of relatively autonomous actors working on more narrowly defined problems, who can, therefore, adapt their calculations more precisely to a constantly changing environment for decision making? Or does the "correct" organization for planning lie somewhere in between synoptic central planning and a decentralized planning that involves "mutual partisan adjustments" among actors?

In addition to debating these philosophical questions, social reform theorists, and particularly the economists among them, have fashioned the tools needed by a state that is increasingly determined to manage the economy "in the general interest." These instruments, so important to mainstream planning, include business cycle analysis (Mitchell), social accounting (Kuznets), input–output analysis (Leontief), economic policy models (Tinbergen), urban and regional economics (Perloff), and development economics (Hirschman). Major specialized fields of study have evolved out of these pioneering efforts, and several of the inventors of planning tools have been honored with the Nobel Prize in economics.

Policy Analysis

This tradition was strongly influenced by the early work of Herbert Simon, whose revolutionary study of 1945, *Administrative Behavior*, focused on the behavior of large organizations and particularly on how they might improve their ability to make decisions. Simon had absorbed several intellectual traditions into his own thinking, among them Weberian sociology and neoclassical economics, and his approach stressed synoptic analysis and decision making as the means of identifying the best possible courses of action. What was "best," of course, would inevitably be limited by the normal constraints on rationality, which include the resources, information, and time that are available for making decisions. Simon's was a model of "bounded" rationality.

The ideal-typical decision model applied by authors in the policy analysis tradition has the following identifiable "stages":

1. Formulation of *goals and objectives*.

2. Identification and design of *major alternatives* for reaching the goals identified within the given decision-making situation.

3. Prediction of major sets of *consequences* that would be expected to follow upon adoption of each alternative.

4. *Evaluation* of consequences in relation to desired objectives and other important values.

5. *Decision* based on information provided in the preceding steps.

6. *Implementation* of this decision through appropriate institutions.

7. *Feedback* of actual program results and their *assessment* in light of the new decision-situation.

For the most part, policy analysis has concentrated on stages 2, 3, and 4. In recent years, some excitement has also been generated about the implementation problems of policies and programs (stage 6). This has led to a modification of the original decision model, in which implementation concerns are now incorporated as early as stage 2—the design of alternative courses of action. The vocabulary of policy analysis tends to be specialized. Most analysts are versed in neoclassical economics, statistics, and mathematics. Beyond this, they tend to cluster into specialized subdisciplines such as systems analysis (with its emphasis on mathematical modeling), policy science (with its combined emphasis on neoclassical economics and political science), operations research (that tends to focus on problems having determinate outcomes), and "futures research," which is still a rather eclectic field. In addition, much of the language of policy analysis derives from work with specific analytical techniques such as gaming, simulation, evaluation research, linear and nonlinear programming, and the like.

Policy analysis has, strictly speaking, no distinctive philosophical position. On larger issues of society and justice, its practitioners are typically conventional in their thinking. They tend to think of themselves as technicians or, more flatteringly, as "technocrats" serving the existing centers of power—large private corporations and the state. On closer inspection, some of their views are remarkably similar to those of Saint-Simon and Auguste Comte. They believe that by using appropriate scientific theories and mathematical techniques, they can, at least in principle, identify and precisely calculate "best solutions." They are social engineers. If challenged on epistemological grounds, policy analysts are likely to reply that it is better to arrive at decisions through an imperfect (but perfectible) science than through a process of unmediated politics that is subject to personal whim, fickle passion, and special interest. The reliance of policy analysts on the tools of neoclassical economics implies that the value premises of that discipline are built into their work; chief among these values are individualism, the supremacy of the market in the allocation of resources, and the inherent conservatism of the equilibrium paradigm. Because market outcomes are regarded as "rational" for the actors involved, deviations from them are normally thought to require special justification and are admitted only reluctantly.

The central questions informing this tradition, in keeping with its basic ethos, are of an essentially technical nature:

1. What are the relative advantages of comprehensive and incremental policy analysis? Comprehensive models provide an extensive overview of a given terrain but they are subject to huge, if indeterminate, error. Incremental analysis is parsimonious in its demands for information, concentrates on the consequences of limited change, and can be modeled to yield determinate solutions. Which model is to be preferred, and under what conditions?

2. Different models yield different types of solutions. Some are structured to allow for the maximization of "payoff" variables such as profits, employment, or savings in travel time. Others are essentially "optimizing" models that yield "best combinations" of results over a variety of objective variables. Still others yield only second-best solutions (in Herbert Simon's neologism, they are merely "satisficed"). The choice of a model for evaluating consequences and recommending technically correct solutions to political decision makers matters a great deal in policy analysis. And how should decision makers be informed? Should

they be given, for example, the one "best" solution? Should they be given the results of various "simulations" together with the assumptions that were used to obtain them? Or should they be asked to take part in "gaming situations" where they simulate the group dynamics of strategic choices, much as the Army General Staff might simulate war games or conduct field maneuvers?

3. How might market prices be modified to express social criteria of valuation? Should cost–benefit studies, for example, use current market rates of interest or some "shadow" price of money that reflects social preference? If so, and in the absence of political guidance, how might shadow prices be calculated? Or, in the case of goods for which there is no ready form of market valuation, what conventions of "social accounting" might permit them to be included in the overall policy calculus? Should women's household work, for instance, be assigned a shadow price and, if so, what should it be?

4. Policy analysts make forecasts about economic variables, expected changes in reproductive behavior, environmental impacts, technological innovations, changes in settlement patterns and land use, and many other things. What are the most reliable methods for mid- and long-range forecasting?

5. Most policy analyses contain huge areas of uncertainty about the future and even greater areas of ignorance. ("What is the probability of global warming within the next fifty years?") How should these great unknowns be treated, and what advice should be given to those responsible for decisions? Are there ways of controlling for uncertainty, and what mathematical values should be assigned to express different degrees of subjective uncertainty? Should alternative courses of action be designed to be compatible with the known areas of ignorance ("planning without facts"), especially when the consequences of a "wrong" decision might be politically, environmentally, or in some other way disastrous?

Social Learning

This tradition focuses on overcoming the contradictions between theory and practice, or knowing and acting. Its theory derives from two streams.

The first is the pragmatism of John Dewey and, more specifically, his epistemology that put so much stress on "learning by doing." A second stream, evolved within Marxism, has its origins in Marx's "Theses on Feuerbach" (1978 [1844]) that ends with the famous declaration, "The philosophers have only *interpreted* the world, in various ways; the point, however, is to *change* it." From this immortal sentence derives the basic Marxist proposition concerning the essential unity of revolutionary theory and practice, that found its fullest expression in Mao Tse-Tung's 1937 essay "On Practice" (1968).

Social learning may be regarded as a major departure from the planning paradigms of Saint-Simon and Comte. Whereas these early founders of the planning tradition had treated scientifically based knowledge as a set of "building blocks" for the reconstruction of society, theorists in the social learning tradition have claimed that knowledge is derived from experience and validated in practice, and is therefore integrally a part of action. Knowledge, in this view, emerges from an ongoing dialectical process in which the main emphasis is on practical undertakings: Existing understanding (theory) is enriched with lessons drawn from experience, and this "new" understanding is then applied in the continuing process of action and change. Whereas Comte and his fellow positivists believed that the social world behaved according to immutable "social laws," social learning theorists assert that social behavior can be changed and that the scientifically correct way to do this is through social experimentation, the careful observation of the results, and a willingness to admit to error and to learn from it.

Not surprisingly, then, the central questions of the social learning tradition are primarily instrumental:

1. How can the normal processes of social learning, which are found in all cases of successful and extended action, be used to spread social learning techniques to all forms of social undertaking?

2. Since human beings are reluctant to alter their habitual ways and are prone to believe that their own opinion or ideology is the only correct one, and since there is an evident connection between ideology and power, how can change be accomplished? How might people be motivated to participate in a form of social learning that depends on openness, dialogue, a willingness to risk social experiments, and a preparedness to let these experiments affect their personal development as human beings?

3. How might formal and informal ways of knowing be linked to each other in a process of change-oriented action that involves mutual learning between those who possess theoretical knowledge and those whose knowledge is primarily practical, concrete, and unarticulated?

4. The social learning paradigm involves, among other things, frequent face-to-face transactions that require a relation of dialogue between the participating parties (Friedmann 1979, 1981). But under conditions where specific tasks must be performed, dialogic relations are difficult to bring about and maintain. What techniques might facilitate relations of trust and dialogue, especially between "planners" and "client-actors?"

5. What is the relationship of the social learning paradigm—with its emphasis on dialogic, non-hierarchical relations and its commitments to experimentation, tolerance for difference, and openness in communication—to democratic political theory? And what is its relationship to the growth and development of the autonomous, self-actualizing personality?

Social Mobilization

This departs from all other planning traditions by asserting the primacy of direct collective action "from below." It stands in stark contrast to the traditions of social reform and policy analysis, which address the role of the state and look toward a "scientific politics." In the social mobilization tradition, planning appears as a form of politics, conducted without the mediations of "science." Nevertheless, scientific analysis, particularly in the form of social learning, plays an important role in the transformative processes sought by social mobilization.

The vocabulary of social mobilization comes in part from the long tradition of mutually antagonistic social movements on the left: Marxists on the one hand, and utopians and social anarchists on the other. Only Marxism developed a full-fledged ideology, but the mutual attractions and repulsions of various factions and groupings on the left provide much of the rhetoric in which many popular struggles are expressed. A good deal of this rhetoric also stems from the collective memory of two centuries of conflict and communitarian effort. It is a history of oppression and triumphant revolutionary movements, from the Paris Commune to the Spanish Civil War, with its own pantheon of heroes and heroines, its own moments of glory in defeat. The language of social mobilization draws on this history as much as it does on the more abstract discourse of its philosophers, theoreticians, and gurus.

Philosophically, this tradition embraces utopian communitarianism, anarchist terrorism, Marxist class struggle, and the neo-Marxist advocacy of emancipatory social movements. These divisions are chiefly historical, however, and reflect disagreements over strategy and tactics more than basic differences in ideology. One might reasonably claim, for example, that the various proponents of social mobilization are of one mind in their condemnation of the pervasive oppression and alienation of human beings under the institutions of capitalism and the bourgeois state. Social mobilization is an ideology of the dispossessed whose strength derives from social solidarity, from the seriousness of their political analysis, and from their unflinching determination to change existing relations of power.

Two kinds of emancipatory politics may be involved in social mobilization. For utopians and anarchists, there is a "politics of disengagement" carried on by "alternative communities" that demonstrate to others new ways of living. For Marxists and neo-Marxists, there is a "confrontational politics" that emphasizes political struggle as necessary to transform existing relations of power and to create a new order that is not based on the exploitation of labor and the alienation of man from what is distinctly human.

Among the central questions faced by adherents to this tradition are the following:

1. What is the proper role of "vanguards," community organizers, and the leaders of movements for social mobilization? If emancipation from various forms of social oppression is the ideological goal, does it not require leadership elites to abide by thoroughly democratic procedures, including the full participation of movement members in collective decisions, a tolerance for open dissent, and non-manipulative methods of organizing group action?

2. How can the disinherited and those who have never had effective power suddenly gain confidence in their ability to "change the world"? How can the poor empower themselves to gain their freedom from oppression?

3. How can the commitment to a new life in community (utopians and anarchists) or a new life in struggle (Marxists and neo-Marxists) be maintained when only an occasional and partial

victory is gained in the seemingly interminable struggle against
oppression?

4. What should be the basic components of a strategy? What role
    should be given to violence, to the choice of arena, to the timing
    of actions and their duration ("long march" or Armageddon),
    and what kinds of specific actions should be undertaken (strikes,
    demonstrations, street theater, terrorism, noncooperation with
    the state, formation of political alliances, establishment of alter-
    native communities)?

5. What should be the characteristics of the "good society," the so-
    cial ideal to be realized in practice, now or in the future? What
    importance should be given to such goals as a non-hierarchical
    and inclusive social order, the practice of self-reliance, volun-
    tary cooperation, dialogic processes, and a radical leveling of
    social hierarchies?

New chapters in the history of planning thought are still being written. Specific modalities and styles of planning may become obsolete, but
the linkage between knowledge and action will remain a lively concern,
both ideologically and in practice. We cannot wish *not* to know, and we
cannot escape the need to act. As social conditions and human understanding change, the actual and theoretical links between knowledge and action
will surely undergo changes as well. If we wish to ensure the continued
vitality of planning in the public domain, we would do well to examine,
carefully and in a critical spirit, the traditions we now have.

REFERENCES

Dahl, R. A., and C. E. Lindblom. 1957. *Politics, economics, and welfare*. New York:
    Harper & Bros.

Dewey, J. 1927. *The public and its problems*. New York: Henry Holt.

Etzioni, A. 1968. *The active society: a theory of societal and political processes*. New
    York: Free Press.

Friedmann, J. 1979. *The good society*. Cambridge, MA: MIT Press.

_____. 1981. *Retracking America*. Emmaus, PA: Rodale Press. (Original edition
    1973. Garden City, NY: Anchor Books.)

Hayek, F. A. 1955 [original editions 1941–44]. *The counterrevolution of science: studies on the abuse of reason.* New York: Free Press.

Jay, M. 1973. *The dialectical imagination: a history of the Frankfurt School and the Institute of Social Research, 1923–1950.* Boston: Little, Brown & Co.

Keynes, J. M. 1964 [1936]. *The general theory of employment, interest, and money.* New York: Harcourt, Brace, Jovanovich.

Kuhn, T. S. 1970 [1962]. *The structure of scientific revolutions.* 2d ed., enlarged. Chicago: University of Chicago Press.

Mannheim, K. 1949a [1929]. *Ideology and utopia.* New York: Harcourt-Brace.

———. 1949b [original edition 1940. London: Kegan Paul]. *Man and society in an age of reconstruction.* New York: Harcourt-Brace.

Mao Tse-Tung. 1968 [1937]. "On practice," in *Four essays on philosophy.* Peking: Foreign Language Press.

Marx, K. 1978 [1844]. Theses on Feuerbach, in R. C. Tucker, ed., *The Marx-Engels reader.* 2d ed. New York: W.W. Norton.

Padilla, S. M. 1975. *Tugwell's thoughts on planning.* San Juan: University of Puerto Rico Press.

Popper, K. R. 1974 [1945]. *The open society and its enemies.* 2 vols. London: Routledge & Kegan Paul.

Rittel, H. W. J., and M. M. Webber. 1973. Dilemmas in a general theory of planning. *Policy Sciences* 4, 2 (March): 155–69.

Simon, H. A. 1976 [1945]. *Administrative behavior.* 3rd ed. New York: Free Press.

———. 1982 [1969]. *The sciences of the artificial.* 2d ed. Cambridge, MA: MIT Press.

Taylor, F. W. 1919 [1911]. *The principles of scientific management.* New York: Harper & Bros.

CHARLES HOCH

2 A Pragmatic Inquiry about Planning and Power

INTRODUCTION

For several centuries, as John Friedmann (1987) recounts in chapter one of this volume, philosophers and social scientists have adapted the principles and methods of science to the analysis of human social activity and individual behavior in an effort to explain, predict, and thereby control the uncertainties of social life. While still a viable and robust enterprise in our own day, the presuppositions and claims of the social sciences about the generalizability and objectivity of knowledge have been subjected to vigorous criticism. Planning practitioners may long for new theoretical breakthroughs that will offer a reassuring version of the rational model as a proper guide for practice, but pragmatists, like Richard Rorty and Richard Bernstein, dismiss the quest and with it the separation between theory and practice.

Rorty criticizes the transcendental aspirations of analytic philosophy, a pillar of intellectual support for the rational paradigm (Rorty 1979). He uses the pragmatism of Dewey to argue that philosophers enjoy no privileged standpoint outside history. Philosophers, he contends, should take the world of practice as the focus of study rather than a condition one seeks to transcend. Instead of searching for a vision of the really real, and insisting on a "transcendental privilege," pragmatic inquiry critically compares the relative efficacy of different varieties of speech and action people use to identify, meet, and interpret their goals (Rorty 1985, 109).

An earlier version of this chapter appeared in *Society* 26, 1 (November/December 1988), Transaction Publishers, New Brunswick, New Jersey.

Epistemological worries disappear for the pragmatic and interpretive analyst, replaced by political concerns over the purposes expressed within and among different moral communities. The paradox between general theory and specific practice gets replaced with the complex relationships among different communities.

Bernstein reaches beyond "totalizing schemes or totalizing critiques" to embrace "a robust pluralism that does justice to the tangled quality of our experience" (Bernstein 1986, 18). But plurality has its difficulties and dangers. The diverse social communities of the modern world may be neither completely isolated nor held together solely by manipulative power relations, but Bernstein insists this does nothing to assure unity. We face the danger of a "wild pluralism in which we no longer even know how to communicate with each other." He takes such danger as stimulus to the critique and reconstruction of our social practices, especially those contributing to the formation of democratic community (Bernstein 1986).

Elsewhere, I have argued that a significant body of planning theory bears a close family resemblance to the theory of pragmatic action best elaborated by John Dewey. Dewey imagined modern liberal societies becoming clusters of communities held together by a diverse assortment of agreements, traditions and conventions, arrived at through democratic deliberation. His was a hopeful, even optimistic, view of the prospects for solidarity through practical democracy. My purpose has been to point out the close conceptual ties between different theories of planning and pragmatic theory (Hoch 1984a) and to argue that a pragmatic orientation provides important insights for the reconstruction of a type of planning that can resist the encroachment of coercive power relations while contributing to the practical formation of powerful democratic communities (Hoch 1984b; Kaufman-Osborn 1985).

Pragmatists assess ideas based on their usefulness for guiding purposeful conduct in diverse contexts. Many planning theorists and practitioners, harboring rational expectations, criticize this practical approach as relativistic. Good rational arguments, they believe, transcend the contingent circumstances of history. But this criticism misses the mark. Pragmatists do not find the correspondence between truth and practice but identify and describe the consequences of action.

> For the pragmatists the pattern of all inquiry—scientific as well as moral—is deliberation concerning the relative attractions of various concrete alternatives. The idea that in science or philosophy we can substitute "method" for deliberation between alternative results of speculation is just wishful thinking. . . . The great fallacy of the tradition, the pragmatists

tell us, is to think that the metaphors of vision, correspondence, mapping, picturing, and representation which apply to small, routine assertions will apply to large and debatable ones. This basic error begets the notion that where there are no objects to correspond to we have no hope of rationality, but only taste, passion and will. (Rorty 1987, 164)

Pragmatic planning theory does not require necessary and certain knowledge but reasons, descriptions, and beliefs that others can recognize, understand, and use to guide their actions. Planning in this sense need not include knowledge of everybody and everything but just the relevant and important things other people involved with the subject or problem at hand want included. A pragmatic approach trades in epistemological problems for social and political ones.

The pragmatists imagine individuals taking actions within competing versions of liberal community. Bernstein's worry about wild pluralism testifies to his desire to protect the boundaries of liberal tolerance, freedom, and justice. Skeptics argue that pragmatists rely upon an ethnocentric version of Enlightenment humanism that disguises repression in the language of liberal hope. Power relationships, they contend, not only undermine the promise of pragmatic planning but infect the entire planning enterprise.

How does this criticism work, and how do planning analysts with a pragmatic bent respond? What implications does the outcome of such a debate have for planning practitioners? In answering these questions, I will first examine the relations between power and knowledge and then argue for a revised pragmatic approach to planning that addresses the power issue. I will conclude—in a style appropriate to the community of theoreticians—with questions for planning research.

FROM PATH TO PLANE

The quest for transcendental certainty has been a philosophical journey toward enlightenment shaped by a Promethean desire to overcome the practical limits of necessity. The peculiar alliance of the search for scientific knowledge and for technical mastery has generated a series of contradictions in understanding and in the application and organization of power. The pathway to discovery has become, in the course of time, a massive limited-access toll road built on the foundations of technical knowledge, bureaucratic organization, and capitalist accumulation. What was once a path of progress has become a limitless and forbidding plane in which many travelers lose their bearings searching for a pathway. The mode of rational inquiry that transports them so swiftly about proves distressingly inadequate. Worse yet, the foundations of this roadway cast an ever-expanding shadow on the surrounding landscape and passersby, not only hiding these communities from the view of those on the plane but subjecting both travelers and communities alike to a twilight existence on the periphery of power.

This apocalyptic tale of modernity captures the critical spirit of the work of Michel Foucault. Foucault peers deeply into the dark side of the Enlightenment, developing a form of critique that challenges the possibility of a socially benign and democratic planning. Foucault argues, using his unique and provocative method to reconstruct historical evidence, that the quest for predictability in the pursuit of progress has introduced and legitimized the creation of liberal care-taking institutions (run by middle-class professionals) which, paradoxically, liberate individuals by subjecting them to new relations of power (Foucault 1977).

I use Foucault's concept of power relations in this chapter because it provides an important critique of professions (such as planning and policy analysis) that claim to serve the common good. Foucault's work focuses precisely on how the human sciences, when used by professionals as a guide for social reform, produce new techniques of subjection. I believe we can read his critique not only as a probing and insightful empirical analysis but as a useful warning about the insidious power of those who seek to "do good."

Learning from our strongest critics secures our footing in the search for a coherent intellectual justification for planning. If we do not respond to the challenge, the opponents of any sort of planning can too easily use the ideas of critics like Foucault to dismiss efforts to reconstruct a pragmatic justification for planning as simply another misguided utopian power trip.

THE SCAFFOLDING OF POWER

Foucault offers a trenchant analysis of how professionals unwittingly build repression into the institutional order of care-giving institutions using a unique scaffolding of power relations. Foucault rejects the search for an ultimate foundation to justify modern social development. Instead, he focuses on the power relations that inform this quest and which, he argues, provide not a foundation but a disciplinary network. Foucault dismisses the idea of the subject precisely in order to illustrate how the power relations of modernity invest subjectivity with an almost cybernetic system of self-repression (Foucault 1980). He conducts his analysis of the magnitude and intensity of the power relations of modernity by uncovering in detail how efforts to categorize individuals based on the standards of a professional discipline (the practices of "micro-power") seek to control subjects through procedures of moral indoctrination designed to make the subjects their own keepers. Yet, subjection is not total for Foucault, else he would succumb to the foundational desire. He documents how the application of disciplinary techniques evokes new forms of resistance by the subjects.

Foucault explores the shadows of the scaffolding of power uncovering the struggles that lie beneath the plane of progress. His method discourages any effort to recover the past as a story of development or progress. Foucault does not reconstruct a narrative account because to do so would be to cast the sort of shadow he hopes to penetrate. His skeptical method can trace the record of power relations in the shadows only because it both incorporates and resists the seduction of the quest for moral certainty so central to the Enlightenment project. Foucault cares so much about liberation that he starts his analysis of modern care-taking institutions with the immediate and local struggles of individuals trying to control their own bodies (Gandal 1986). Foucault's work demonstrates in detail how the disciplinary knowledge of the human sciences has been etched into the conscience of modern individuals by subjecting human action to a "political 'double bind,' that is, the simultaneous individualization and totalization of modern power structures" (Foucault 1983, 216). Foucault's distinctions provide an unsettling critique of the roles played by professionals in the corporate institutions of the welfare state.

Let me illustrate. Homelessness emerged as a serious social problem in the United States during the early 1980s. Why did the problem gain such notoriety at that time? Analysts offered two arguments to account for the origins of the new homeless: first, the number of homeless people had grown dramatically; and second, these people included a wider diversity of social types than previous cohorts of homeless people. These debates, conducted mainly by professionals, caretakers, and public officials, center around the two themes that Foucault argues are central to the use of the human sciences in the organization of the welfare state: totalization—the quantitative assessment of the scope of a problem population, and individualization—the qualitative definition of that population as subjects.

Each argument about the number or type of the homeless draws on the professional discipline of the analyst who applies these categories to define this population. In addition, analysts also draw on their political authority to determine the practices that are followed in conducting treatment of the homeless. The disciplinary authority of their assessments is expressed in state policies, programs, and practices to govern this population.

Public debates among professionals produced competing estimates of both the size of the homeless population and the number of different types of homeless individuals whose "needs" match the professional disciplines and institutions ready to provide care. Professionals and state agencies collaborate to allow each discipline (e.g., psychiatrists, social workers, police, planners, administrators) to retain authority over "their" homeless (e.g., mentally ill, women with children, families, runaways, deviants, addicts, the unemployed). The liberal caretakers and planners produce a framework for cooperative benevolence that ends up organizing and legitimizing subjugation.

Under Foucault's scrutiny, the practice of professionals serves a perverse modernity that promises security as it ensnares individuals in the categories of need. Foucault's critique cuts to the very heart of any theoretical effort to justify planning as a privileged moral and scientific practice in the service of a public interest.

Foucault uses his work to illustrate the terrifying danger that the rationality of modernity has unleashed—terrifying because the relations of power he uncovers seem otherwise so benign. What is more natural than that psychiatrists should treat the mentally ill and relief agencies feed the hungry? One might argue that Foucault leads us to an inevitable nihilism. But I think otherwise. As he said himself: "We have to promote new forms of subjectivity through the refusal of this kind of individuality which has been imposed on us for several centuries" (Foucault 1983, 216).

Nevertheless, for planners, who aspire to improve the public good, such analysis as Foucault offers provides little grounds for hope—much less moral justification. Seeing the world through his eyes, what can we say that is positive about practices that subject us all to the power of organized discipline and technique? Are we doomed myopically to skitter about the plane? Foucault's prose is intimidating and requires a competing image to preserve the germ of insight without giving way to numbing nihilism. I find that image in the pragmatic philosophy of Charles Pierce, William James, and, particularly, John Dewey.

PRAGMATIC REVIVAL

Pragmatism, Richard Rorty argues, was postmodern ahead of its time. John Dewey long ago abandoned the search for meta-narratives or ultimate foundations that had shaped the Enlightenment tradition. In this respect, Dewey and Foucault are alike, although they differ dramatically in their outlook on knowledge (Rorty 1987, 204–5). Dewey writes with hope, Foucault with despair. Dewey's instrumentalism taps into a network of power relationships searching for ways to put human desires and creativity to practical use. Foucault's skeptical assessment makes all such efforts at amelioration appear self-deluding—acts of imprisonment and subordination. Foucault does not believe that existing conditions offer much practical opportunity for innovations that will not prove self-limiting (Rorty 1987, 205–8).

Communities are shaped not solely by mutual interdependence among members but also by the imposition of power relations that undermine or sustain this solidarity. In Foucault's framework, the diverse communities Dewey imagines are not the product of intersubjective agreement or consensus but the product of power relations. Foucault claims that public good and public discipline together have shaped the norms of modern life. "The powers of modern society are exercised through, on the basis of, and by virtue of, the very heterogeneity between a public right of sovereignty and a polymorphous disciplinary mechanism" (Foucault 1980, 106). Hence, he does not believe we can return to the right of community sovereignty to limit the coercive effects of modern disciplinary power because the two define each other. Liberation, he argues, requires a new form of right, one that must be anti-disciplinarian, liberated from the principle of sovereignty (Foucault 1980, 108). In other words, encouraging each community to form its own domain of democratic sovereignty in order to escape or overcome the techniques of coercive power will not work. Unless the desire for sovereignty is left behind, decentralization will simply disperse disciplinary power without mitigating it.

Rorty argues that Foucault reaches a skeptical impasse because he wants to obtain individual fulfillment through public means, a wish for self-definition that Rorty believes cannot or should not take place in institutions. Foucault sees only the limits within our liberal self-definition because he expects the public domain to give way before critical and ironic resistance. Transgression and the pursuit of autonomy leave Foucault reaching for a deep rupture in the network of power relations sufficient to allow for a community of other critical souls. But how can they come together without collapsing their individual freedom into some disciplinary order? Rorty suggests that we can read Foucault with less frustration or disbelief if we use Foucault's ideas to inspire and guide efforts at poetic self-expression rather than public policy. Planners, as public servants, would do well to leave Foucault at home (Rorty 1989, 64–6) and to carry Dewey with them.

PRAGMATIC PLANNING AND COMMUNITY

Instead of emphasizing autonomy and instrumental control, a critical pragmatism emphasizes solidarity based on shared inquiry and common purpose—solidarity based on the kind of community that makes up what Jürgen Habermas, the German social theorist, calls the "lifeworld." The roots of individual emancipation are attached to communal traditions we already share and from which we can recollect our experience of what it means to choose responsibly as an individual, to communicate without distortion, and to govern ourselves democratically (Hoch 1984b).

How would this pragmatism help planners bridge the social differences within and between communities, especially when these are generated or exacerbated by different forms of power, without simply enforcing one will as the right one? John Dewey believed that local communities had once been the center of public life in the United States and that this made it possible to rebuild the ties between distinct communities and the broader concerns of public life. He wrote,

> Unless local communal life can be restored, the public cannot adequately solve its most urgent problem, to find and identify itself. But if it be re-established, it will manifest a fullness, variety and freedom of possession and enjoyment of meanings and goods unknown in the contiguous associations of the past. For it will be alive and flexible as well as stable, responsive to the complex and world-wide scene in which it is enmeshed. While local, it will not be isolated. (Dewey 1927, 127)

The close attachments necessary to create bonds of trust and mutuality strong enough to sustain social ties in the midst of serious disputes, and flexible enough to accommodate the differences among individual members, end up limiting the size of the unitary community Dewey envisioned. Furthermore, these communities are crosscut by different functional and organizational domains. If we rely solely on the unified community as the context for practicing a democratic rationality, the fragmentation of modern life quickly imposes itself as an obstacle to meaningful participation. To which community do we turn to enact democracy? How do we avoid provincial selfishness?

Communities, in the strong sense, exist in abundance in the United States but most usually do not play an active role in the conduct of public life. There are, however, important exceptions. Such exceptions include the social communities of the capitalist class in which members are prepared to fill positions of authority in corporation and state (Domhoff 1970,

1974, 1979). The bonds of this community strengthen the political power of a class. This is hardly cause for democratic celebration even if that class is open to new recruits remarkable for their wisdom and virtue.

Less well-positioned or poorer communities usually "go public" only when subjected to threats of economic ruin, physical displacement, social invasion, or political domination. Even then, these stories of resistance are not necessarily tales of democratic and cooperative action. J. Anthony Lukas, in his excellent book, *Common Ground* (1985), illustrates this dilemma in a lucid reconstruction of the segregation and desegregation of Boston schools. Lukas assesses the impacts of forced busing on three communities in Boston by tracing how the social identity of three households was challenged by the implementation of a liberal policy, how each responded to the threats, and how their responses were separated from each other in ways that intensified isolation and the resort to violent resistance.

The social distance between diverse communities poses a serious obstacle to any effort to build uncoerced solidarity in a single "Great Community." Such efforts cannot be undertaken, as Dewey proposed, exclusively through problem-focused participation and education. Such an approach ignores the shadow cast by undemocratic power relations that shape the identities of the community and its members. Minority planners who encounter racial discrimination on the job will likely resist and struggle for fair treatment and respect. Planners may openly oppose neighborhood resistance to the siting of a group home after educational efforts fail to obtain consensus. In such cases, planners participate in the sorts of power relationships Foucault describes. They classify, subordinate, and order the desires of others to fit within a framework of liberal justice.

Planners who take up the struggle for social justice in such adversarial settings imagine themselves as advocates. They justify their use of coercion as necessary intervention to protect the boundaries of the liberal arena within which the formation of diverse communities of consensus is made possible. But how can advocates retain their legitimacy as professional experts and liberal democrats? I may have left Foucault at home, but he awaits me there at the end of the day to cast a dark shadow on my benevolence.

PLANNING IN THE FACE OF POWER

Recent work by John Forester has addressed the issue of power for planners and policy analysts without succumbing to the modernist seduction of an ultimate truth or to Foucault's skepticism (Forester 1982, 1985, 1989). Forester writes in the pragmatic tradition, although the links to Pierce,

James, and Dewey run through Jürgen Habermas, especially Habermas's theory of communication. Habermas agrees with American pragmatists (drawing especially on the work of Charles Pierce) that meaningful social practice depends on the quality and efficacy of democratic participation among community members. Forester shows how planners tacitly draw upon relations of trust, sincerity, comprehension, and legitimacy in their conduct but then get tripped up or seduced by power relationships. The efficacy of practical social communion for Forester flows from the mediation between two distinct domains: the domain of solidarity and the domain of control. Both are necessary, but knowledge based on solidarity should call the shots.

In *Theory of Communicative Action*, Habermas (1984) develops a social theory to demonstrate how the systems rationality of the modern industrial society, with its instrumental orientation, depends on and yet threatens what he calls the "lifeworld" of communicative rationality. Habermas explores this paradox with vigorous and exhaustive argument, contending that the "colonization of the lifeworld" by systems rationality is neither necessary nor inevitable. He believes that the spread of instrumental rationality has been selective and strategic but not total. Resistance to the imposition of such rationality, whether in the form of market relations, state bureaucracies, or even professional planning, stakes out not only a boundary marker for the lifeworld but also a political indicator of the social pathology of an untamed instrumentalism and, hence, an opportunity for both resistance and democratic practice.

Foucault and Habermas meet at this point, although from very different directions. Both recognize and support meaningful efforts to resist and struggle against the imposition of instrumental rationality or subjugation. Neither would characterize these struggles in categorical terms. In other words, neither believes that instrumental rationality can be totally overthrown or subdued by those who resist. The interdependencies of modern life rely on a systemic infrastructure that ties the partners in struggle to each other. Political conflict and the struggle to reproduce freedom through democratic practice remain intertwined. Habermas, like Dewey, offers the more hopeful conception of the social conditions necessary to make such resistance both liberating and socially binding without requiring the exclusive imposition of power relations. Foucault is less sanguine and more skeptical about a communication that can escape the tendrils of power.

Habermas proves a useful guide to action, although he stops short of Dewey's and Foucault's critical rejection of the Enlightenment. Habermas still hopes to salvage rational universality by replacing subject-centered varieties of reason (from the Frankfurt School versions of his colleagues

Herbert Marcuse, Theodor Adorno, and Max Horkheimer all the way back to Hegel and Kant) with the intersubjective and universal pragmatics of social communication. If we follow Rorty's and Dewey's advice, we need not concern ourselves too much with reassuring arguments about the universality of rationality, whether subjective or intersubjective. Reason does not harbor the solidarity we may long for or believe in. The liberties we enjoy, the limits we suffer, and the possibilities we imagine come from the contingent history of modernity.

THE POWERS OF THE WEAK

Planning practitioners work, for the most part, as employees in state or corporate bureaucracies that require professional employees to collaborate in the uneven distribution of uncertainty among subordinates or clients. This bureaucratic setting, however, also means that planning practitioners will be subject to authority as well. Like other subordinates, planners frequently conspire with their peers when threatened by the actions of their superiors. Building on informal ties of mutual care and solidarity, they develop ways to resist and frustrate the imposition of additional burdens of uncertainty. When those ties are weak, practitioners identify with authority and its promise of autonomy through the exercise of power.

In order to avoid the seduction of power as the crucial ingredient for establishing a successful career and a strong professional identity, individual planners should recognize that they are members of a weak professional community working as employees in vulnerable occupational positions. The popularity of instrumental rationality, with its accompanying fear of dependence and desire for professional prowess, does not stop planners from recognizing their weakness. In fact, it is this recognition that leads to ambivalence and doubt as planners are unwilling to use power yet want the personal prestige that accompanies individual success. The pragmatist tradition points out to these practitioners that they are hanging onto false expectations that prevent them from recognizing that the uncertainty they face is shared and not unique.

Embracing weakness appears to Foucault little more than an act of self-immolation. Freedom, for him, flows from transgression based on individual resistance. That Foucault can, however, be left at home. The skeptical and ironic artist or designer cannot make way for others without diminishing himself or herself. Extending such possessive individualism to matters of public justice cuts planners off from the social resources for resistance and innovation. In *Habits of the Heart*, Robert Bellah and his associates (1985) make a similar point when they discuss why middle-class individuals fear making social commitments:

> What we fear above all, and what keeps the new world powerless to be born, is that if we give up our dream of private success for a more genuinely integrated societal community, we will be abandoning our separation and individuation, collapsing into dependence and tyranny. What we find hard to see is that it is the extreme fragmentation of the modern world that threatens our individuation; that what is best in our separation, individuation, our sense of dignity and autonomy as persons, requires a new integration if it is to be sustained. (Bellah et al. 1985, 286)

This integration, I think, hinges on the social recovery of the experience of vulnerability that we share as human beings. We can experience solidarity with members of alien and distant communities when we recognize our vulnerability and susceptibility to shared dangers of exploitation, domination, and subjection (and death). Unilateral vulnerability promotes exploitation because the vulnerable remain tied to the social norms of the more powerful. When vulnerability is recognized across communities, however, it may become a source of resistance and strength. Craft in negotiation may cultivate this recognition, but it is principally nourished by empathy, compassion, and a shared sense of injustice. Even unsuccessful resistance becomes a source of strength for those who are able to identify with the victims as members of their own community. They experience the loss as their own, conquer the fear that what happened to the victims will happen to them if they resist, and react with outrage against the authorities who have attacked them.

The moral rejuvenation of a republican and biblical tradition of community responsibility builds on the practical awareness of shared vulnerabilities. This is the very sort of belief Nietzsche held in contempt and Foucault identified with new powers of subjugation. Its foundation is the social interdependence among citizens, but its cultivation is a conscious process by which individual citizens develop their own characters through a "shared enthusiasm for the ideals of dignity and justice that the political community represents" (Sullivan 1983, 313-14). The catalyst for translating these shared vulnerabilities into springboards for collective resistance hinges on voluntary participation by members from different communities, participation that, Sara Evans and Harry Boyte argue, requires free spaces in which people can "build direct, face-to-face and egalitarian relationships beyond their immediate circle of friends and smaller communities" (Evans and Boyte 1986, 191).

Instead of relying on rational methods that require practitioners to seek greater political authority and more professional power in order to do good, planners might benefit more from a critical review of the limits to bureaucratic command and adversarial democracy. Planners might consider identifying with the powers of the weak, identifying with colleagues, neighbors, and citizens rather than with the protocols of professional expertise. Recognizing weakness need not be cause for shame but may be the first step in putting human vulnerability in the service of a democratic planning that resists and even tames instrumental and hierarchical authority—the first step in helping to construct a free space where technique can serve democratic community. These spaces cannot be produced by a welfare state or by philanthropic employees. They require the active democratic participation of the subordinates whose success in mutual resistance inspires hopes for making practical improvements. "Once the weak lay hands on their powers and weave individual doubts into joint resistance, the political process moves them toward positive action and starts teaching courage to improvise and undertake the action necessary, practical or impractical. Probably both." (Janeway 1981, 284)

No longer need planners claim that their methods have been certified scientific, certain, and true. As the critics of the rational paradigm make clear, when practitioners appeal to universal truth, they are more likely to be on a power trip than a theoretical journey. The irony is that most planners do not enjoy the power necessary to make good on their instrumental designs, yet they cannot seem to let go of the professional protocol. How does one persuade them even to try?

CONCLUSION

The big question for the pragmatic analysts is how practitioners construct the free spaces in which democratic planning can be institutionalized. Recent efforts by theorists to study practitioners, I think, have been undertaken to answer this question. The idea, in part, is to uncover examples of planning that are both competent and democratic, and then to explore who the practitioners were who did it, what actions they took to make it happen, and what sorts of institutional conditions helped or hindered their efforts. The results of this sort of research can provide us with knowledge about the architecture of free spaces in the midst of existing power relations. We need these cases and stories if we are to persuade others not only of the hidden dangers and costs of the rational paradigm but also of the viability of alternatives that offer evidence of effective democratic planning in the face of power. While the more cynical among us may protest that this is like looking for a needle in a haystack, other researchers are more confident. As Foucault argues, few of us consent completely to the imposition of power. We resist in a variety of ways, many of which are neither obvious nor dramatic.

Unlike Foucault, however, for the pragmatists the roots of this resistance can be traced to our growth and development in communities where we learned what it means to become an individual in a context of social interdependence (e.g., family, neighborhood, church, clubs, and the like). Thus, stories of resistance are likely to be quite common, given that power relations are virtually inescapable in most planning activities. Research on contemporary practice aims at uncovering these stories so that practitioners will not only recognize the opportunities for creating free spaces but also experience the sense of solidarity necessary to take the risk of trying.

In order to grasp the practical prerequisites for pragmatic action that are both sensitive to the dangers of power and informed by the promise of democracy, we need to reconstruct the personal and institutional narratives of struggle produced by practitioners. Instead of vying with one another to establish the definitive rational model, we may do well to settle for the more modest expectations of a critical pragmatism. Instead of striving to be experts on truth, we may be better off becoming storytellers of practice. Telling stories of planning and power from the present and the past in a context of ongoing inquiry and debate—sharing our interpretations as researchers and theorists not only with each other but with practitioners as well—offers, if not a new paradigm, at least a new sort of community in which we can work to improve the democratic quality of practice.

REFERENCES

Bellah, R., R. Madsen, W. W. Sullivan, A. Swindler, and S. Tipton. 1985. *Habits of the heart.* Berkeley: University of California Press.

Bernstein, R. 1986. *Philosophical profiles: essays in a pragmatic mode.* Cambridge: Polity Press.

Dewey, J. 1927. *The public and its problems.* New York: Henry Holt.

Domhoff, G. W. 1970. *The higher circles.* New York: Random House.

_____. 1974. *The Bohemian grove and other retreats.* New York: Harper & Row.

_____. 1979. *The powers that be.* New York: Random.

Evans, S., and H. Boyte. 1986. *Free spaces: the sources of democratic change in America.* New York: Harper & Row.

Forester, J. 1982. Towards a critical empirical framework for the analysis of public policy. *New Political Science* 9, 10: 33–61.

———. 1989. *Planning in the face of power.* Berkeley: University of California Press.

Foucault, M. 1977. *Discipline and punish.* New York: Random House.

———. 1980. *Power/knowledge: selected interviews and other writings.* Edited by C. Gordon. New York: Pantheon.

———. 1983. The subject and power. In H. Dreyfus and P. Rabinow, eds., *Beyond structuralism and hermeneutics.* Chicago: University of Chicago Press, 208-26.

Friedmann, J. 1987. *Planning in the public domain.* Princeton: Princeton University Press.

Gandal, K. 1986. Michel Foucault: intellectual work and politics. *Telos* 67: 121–34.

Habermas, J. 1984. *Theory of communicative action.* Boston: Beacon Press.

Hoch, C. 1984a. Doing good and being right: the pragmatic connection in planning theory. *Journal of the American Planning Association* 50, 3: 335–45.

———. 1984b. Pragmatism, planning and power. *Journal of Planning Education and Research* 4, 2: 86-95.

Janeway, E. 1981. *Powers of the weak.* New York: McGraw Hill.

Kaufman-Osborn, T. 1985. Pragmatism, policy science, and the state. *American Political Science Review* 29: 827–49.

Lukas, J. A. 1985. *Common ground.* New York: Knopf.

Rorty, R. 1979. *Philosophy and the mirror of nature.* Princeton, NJ: Princeton University Press.

———. 1985. Epistemological behaviorism and the detranscendentalization of analytic philosophy. In R. Hollinger, ed., *Hermeneutics and praxis.* Notre Dame: University of Notre Dame Press.

———. 1987. *Consequences of pragmatism.* Minneapolis: University of Minnesota Press.

———. 1989. *Contingency, irony, and solidarity.* New York: Cambridge University Press.

Sullivan, W. 1983. Beyond policy science: the social science as moral sciences. In N. Haan, R. Bellah, P. Rabinow, and W. Sullivan, eds., *Social science as moral inquiry.* New York: Columbia University Press.

Ernest Alexander

3 After Rationality: Towards a Contingency Theory for Planning

INTRODUCTION

P lanning theoreticians are in a state of turmoil. Nothing is accepted; everything is questioned. The requirements that theory must meet have been well stated (McConnell 1981, 20–2; Healey and Thomas 1982, 19–22), but no coherent body of thought has been accepted as meeting these criteria. Indeed, Mandelbaum (1979) and others (Rittel and Webber 1973; Tenbruck 1972) have questioned whether a "general theory of planning" is even possible. Given these cogent reservations about the feasibility of a general theory of planning, it is clear that a more modest approach is indicated. Consequently, a contingency framework is suggested here as a way of addressing the problems planning theoreticians face today.

Two theories are juxtaposed within the contingency model. One is the "classic" theory of rational decision making and planning that is grounded in a utilitarian assessment of consequences. The other is the critical theory of "communicative action." Both rationality and critical theory offer idealized prescriptions for choice. But rationality is limited to individual deliberation, while critical theory deals only with communicative interaction. Each of these models is almost a mirror image of the other, focusing exactly on what its counterpart neglects. The complementary character of the two theories is the core of my claim that a contingency framework that combines them offers a promising way to provide an adequate account of

An earlier version of this chapter appeared in *Society* 26, 1 (November/December 1988), Transaction Publishers, New Brunswick, New Jersey.

planning. The contingency framework defines the domain in which each theory is valid, taking into account the necessary distinction between the normative and descriptive aspects of planning theories.

To show the broader application of this approach, I can tentatively elaborate the contingency structure by adding some dimensions that reflect the focus and orientation of this chapter. I illustrate the use of a contingency model as an organizing framework for an array of planning and decision-making theories, without necessarily claiming that this particular scheme of organization is exhaustive or definitive. Although the contingency model has limits (that will be discussed later), it offers what may be the only feasible way to frame research and practice in a fashion that can generate some useful prescriptions and insights. A contingency model comprised of a set of well-chosen dimensions can be at once sufficiently abstract to be relatively general and concrete enough to prescribe and describe specific behavior in the richness and diversity of the situations we experience every day.

RATIONALITY AND PARADIGM BREAKDOWN

As a prescription for, and description of, actual decision making, rationality has been the object of numerous critiques since the 1950s. In spite of these challenges, rational planning filled the role of a "general theory of planning" over a considerable period of time and has generated a body of significant concepts and many useful applications. Rationality has yet to be superseded as the prevailing paradigm for both theorists and practitioners, although attempts to replace it continue apace. We need a synthetic idea that will span related and interdependent areas (Alexander 1984).

Rationality serves two distinct roles. In describing and evaluating some of the substitutes that have been offered, it is important to be clear about the differences between these roles:

1. *Rationality as a descriptive model, enabling empirically realistic description, hypothesis testing, and explanation of individual and collective decisions and actions.* In effect, we ask ourselves, suppose we imagine that individuals and collectivities act *as if* they were rational. Does that representation make sense of their observed behavior?

2. *Rationality as a normative paradigm.* The normative paradigm acts in two ways. One is analytic, where the rational model is the abstract standard used to describe and analyze decision behavior (e.g., in economics and psychology). The other is prescriptive,

though critics (e.g., Dworkin 1977; Lyons 1984) have pointed out its utilitarian-consequentialist bias. In spite of its short-comings, rationality continues to be the normative basis for the methods used in planning, policy analysis, and administration, and for planners' and related practitioners' claims to professional expertise (Teitz 1985, 139–40).

In evaluating would-be successors to rationality, we must bear these two aspects in mind. This is not to say that any one alternative must necessarily fill both of these roles. But it does suggest that a future paradigm must consist of a theory or model—or a set of related theories—that can fulfill the same range of functions served by the rational paradigm. Below, I review some of the candidates to become the next dominant paradigm for planning and ask how they meet this test. Finally, I develop one direction that, as I have already suggested (Alexander 1984, 67), may offer the most promising prospects: a contingency framework for the development of a new planning theory and practice.

AFTER RATIONALITY:
PREPARADIGMATIC ALTERNATIVES

What have been the responses to the breakdown of rationality as a dominant paradigm? I have described these as "the ritual response," the "avoidance response," the "abandonment response," and the "search response" (Alexander 1984). In the "ritual" response, widespread in planning education and practice, adherence to the rational model continues with only token acknowledgment of its anomalies. The "avoidance" response is common among social scientists. It involves substitution of essentially descriptive decision-making models for the rational paradigm, or modifications of the rational model that generally fail to develop their practical implications to any logical conclusion.

The "abandonment" response suggests that the rational model, or indeed any "process" model at a similar level of generality and abstraction, is unnecessary and should be abandoned. In one version, substitutes are proposed at a lower level of abstraction, either summoning up the practitioner's intuition and experience as a basis for action, or suggesting a pragmatic limitation of planners' roles. In another version, a concrete, substantive, political or social ideology is substituted for the "value-neutral" rational model. Finally, in the "search" response, radically different models are offered as alternatives to the prevailing paradigm, which is crumbling under its acknowledged anomalies.

Here, I want to focus on those responses that constitute the pre-paradigmatic alternatives to the rational model. To win acceptance as a new dominant paradigm for planning and the related decision sciences and professions, each, some, or all of them together must encompass the different roles that rationality filled, as described above. Ideally, a new paradigm should also meet the criteria for adequate theory enumerated before, but apparently this is not a necessary condition. After all, the rational model itself does not meet these criteria, yet it fills the paradigm role—although how well it does so is, of course, a matter of perception and argument.

One type of response is to substitute for the rational model an alternative model of decision making. Many critiques of classic rationality have been prefaces to this type of response. Simon's "satisficing" (1955) and Lindblom's "disjointed incrementalism" (1959, 1965) are examples. However, these models themselves have been subject to many of the same critiques that they advanced against the rational model: they too are based on limiting assumptions that are not always supported in reality (Alexander 1972, 326–7). These come under the "avoidance" response referred to above.

Another set of responses falls into the "abandonment" category but still offers a "substantive" model as an alternative paradigm. Neo-Marxist planning theorists are the most prominent example of this approach (for example, Cooke 1983 or Castells 1977). The problems with this or, indeed, any substantive approach, are well set out by Camhis (1979). Proposals of a substantive paradigm are not limited to neo-Marxism, however. Systems-based and ecology-oriented approaches have been presented making similar claims (Travis 1977, Portugalli 1981). As a counterblast to the neo-Marxists, Poulton (1991) proposes public choice theory as the uniquely compelling positive theory for planning.

And there are more. Friedmann has proposed his model of "trans-active" or "radical" planning that modifies some of the procedural characteristics of the rational model and introduces some significant substantive assumptions about ethics and society (1973, 1979, 1987). Sillince (1986) developed a syncretic blend of bounded rationality and interactive approaches, presenting a new "Theory of Planning." But its substantive analysis stops short of even contingent generalizations, and its prescriptions remain well within the conventional procedural domain. Without entering into a detailed critique, it is clear that none of these can replace the rational paradigm. All of them are either limited to specific contexts or, if universalized, require an improbable act of faith in their underlying ideological assumptions.

These various alternatives have often been shaped within a long-running, but essentially sterile, debate between proponents of "procedural" and of "substantive" planning theories (Taylor 1984). Many of the assertions underlying this debate are rooted in what I believe is a fundamental misunderstanding of the role of abstraction in theory building. Thus, the contention that "procedural" theory is abstract and devoid of substance and that "substantive" or "positive" theory alone can offer models based on reality (Cooke 1983, Poulton 1991) is misplaced. It should be obvious that at some level of abstraction, process and procedure are bound to become divorced from each case-specific context and substance: without such abstraction, any generalization across cases is impossible. But this is equally true for substantive or structural variables (e.g., Castells 1983; Healey and Underwood 1977).

In fact, there are two orthogonally distinct dimensions on which we can map any discourse on planning (Figure 3.1):

1. The focus of conceptualization, ranging from totally procedural at one pole to totally structural at the other, with various procedural–structural mixes between; and

2. The level of abstraction, from the totally concrete case-specific or phenomenologic approach at one extreme to the completely abstract, contextless, and general, perhaps even universal, model at the other.

The debate between "process" and "substance" has been mostly about something else: the appropriate level of abstraction for fruitful discussion and learning about planning. That is a question of some importance, but it cannot be constructively addressed through a contrived conflict between essentially complementary concepts.

This realization can help us evaluate some of the philosophical borrowings that have been proposed as alternative paradigms for planning. Models such as Schön's "reflective practitioner" (1983) that rest on an essentially phenomenological approach to action (Krieger 1974) cannot serve as a general normative base for decision and action. Pragmatism, as described by Hoch in chapter two in this volume, may have some value, although it is difficult to see how the pragmatic calculus can be operationalized (except as a guide to sound intuition) for actual decisions.

Another alternative paradigm has been transferred from critical theory (Albrecht 1985; Forester 1985). Based on the thinking of the Frankfurt School of German philosophers and elaborated by Jürgen Habermas, this model

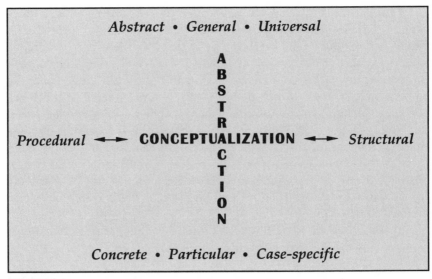

Abstract • General • Universal

Procedural ←→ **CONCEPTUALIZATION** ←→ *Structural*

Concrete • Particular • Case-specific

FIGURE 3.1

has been the subject of widespread discussion among philosophers and planning theorists (Thompson and Held 1982; Albrecht and Lim 1986; Forester 1989a). Critical theory has, I believe, many—though not all—of the attributes needed for a paradigm, and it can offer a very significant contribution. Accordingly, I will postpone discussing it until it is incorporated into the contingency framework.

Finally, representatives of the "search" response have proposed a variety of contingency theories as a way to sidestep the recognized problems of a general model. Examples of such contingency models in planning theory are Hudson's (1979) SITAR model and Lim's (1986) synthetic framework, Banai's (1988) "dialectic" of planning paradigms, and Yiftachel's (1989) taxonomy of planning theories. In decision and organization theory, such frameworks have also been proposed as a way to integrate different and competing models (Thompson and Tuden 1959; Grandori 1984).

The very proliferation of alternative contingency models illustrates their intrinsic problem. A contingency theory is in essence a meta-theoretical framework for identifying and relating a set of relevant contingencies into which the universe must be partitioned. Such frameworks suffer from the same shortcomings as the ideologically based substantive models described above. The selection of the relevant contingencies, or the identification of the specific partitioning factors, is absolutely critical. Yet in any contingency model, this selection is essentially arbitrary, and any attempt to justify it is the beginning of an infinite regress.

In spite of this reservation, I believe that a contingency framework offers the most promising direction out of our preparadigmatic impasse. The contingency models offered to date do not fit the bill because they essentially limit themselves to integrating classic rationality with a few of the "modified rationality" models. They fail to respond to critical theory's valid critiques of formal utilitarian rationality: in particular, the fact that neither classic nor modified rational models address the social and interactive aspects of decision and action.[1]

If I am optimistic about the potential contribution that a contingency theory can make, it is because I see no better alternative. I will be rash enough to join the long line of proponents of contingency models on the assumption that an inductive approach, based on a valid intersubjective experience of a common "lifeworld" in practice, can generate a set of useful contingencies.

The test of such a model will be both theoretical and pragmatic. Are its dimensions a valid reflection of some critical factors in the real world that facilitate description, analysis, and explanation of phenomena? Does the framework offer answers to practical questions and dilemmas, answers that offer the foundation for the development or application of skills and tools that offer processes superior to intuition alone? No model or paradigm can be perfect on these criteria, but another virtue of a contingency model is that it offers the best framework for discourse in the ongoing process of theory generation and generalization.

RATIONALITY AND CRITICAL THEORY: COMPETITIVE OR COMPLEMENTARY?

The point of departure for the contingency framework proposed here is the juxtaposition of the rational model with a proposed new paradigm: critical theory. Critical theory has expanded the base of reference of our thinking on decision making and action with two important contributions:

1. *The idea of reflexive consciousness.* What is good in a particular setting is not merely (for Habermas) what is traditional or customary but how participants in that world would choose to act if they communicated openly and without coercion—if they spoke with full "reflexive consciousness."

2. *A shift from decision to interaction as the focus of theorizing.* Interaction implies communication between persons or, by implication, between homogenous social units acting like individuals. Thus,

the classic theory of decision is transformed into a "Theory of Communicative Action" (TCA) offered as the new paradigm for thinking about individual and societal action.

TCA is also inadequate as a general paradigmatic model for planning and decision making. It is subject to some of the same flaws that have been identified in critiques of classic rationality. It is normative, not descriptive; procedural, not substantive. Like rationality, it omits a significant portion of the relevant universe from its intellectual domain:

1. *TCA is a normative theory.* It is abstracted from the real world and does not purport to describe real behavior. "It is not my aim," Habermas notes, "to characterize behavioral dispositions empirically, but to grasp structural properties of reaching understanding, from which we can derive general pragmatic presuppositions of communicative action" (Habermas 1984, 286).[2] Communicative action is characterized by an *a priori* orientation toward consensus among the participants in the interaction or, more accurately, the discourse. In this respect, it is clearly distinguished from strategic action, directed toward success on each actor's own terms (Habermas 1981, 385–7).

   Unlike communicative action that aims at persuading participants to coordinate their actions based on commonly arrived at convictions, strategic action (that Habermas refers to only in passing and includes in his schema for completeness rather than giving it much attention) does not use the force of rational argument to accomplish its ends. Both open and covert strategic action uses power, influence and manipulation, or systemically distorted communication in unconscious deception, to coordinate the participants' behavior in pursuit of the actor's objectives (Habermas 1981; 1983, 68–9).

   Habermas's complete schema is a powerful analysis of the potential universe of interactive behavior. But communicative action, which commands most of Habermas's energy and has riveted his readers' attention, is only part of that schema. It does not take an extreme degree of cynicism to recognize that it is strategic action that describes interactive behavior most accurately, and that most observed interpersonal, interorganizational, and social interactions are strategic—not communicative.

2. *TCA is entirely procedural.* It is as divorced from substance as is classical rationality, in the sense of the many critiques that have

been aimed at rationality over the last twenty years. Communicative action is a process that is regulated by a highly abstract set of rules that can be applied in any substantive context and that are designedly independent of social structure. Indeed, they can be criteria to evaluate and assess social structures as contexts for interaction. Communicative action is a general and universal theory, demonstrated by its most basic law: the "universalization principle." This is the principle that a norm can be valid only if it is unconditionally and freely accepted by all affected parties (Habermas 1983, 71–8, 96–9, 131).

A revealing illustration of the deliberately procedural orientation of TCA is Habermas's comparison of communicative action with Rawls's criterion of distributive justice. Habermas is quite explicit in describing Rawls's approach as nothing more than a special case of a possible substantive consensus that could be reached through communicative action, a particular working out of the "universalization principle" that he and Rawls share (Habermas 1983, 103–4).

3. *TCA cannot become a paradigm for planning and decision making because it covers only a limited part of the universe of action and interaction.* Habermas implicitly acknowledges this limitation when he complements his essentially normative model of communicative action with a much more realistic model of strategic action.

There is another sense, however, in which Habermas's entire construct of communicative and strategic action is incomplete. TCA is limited to the "public" or social-interactive dimension of action. It does not prescribe and cannot account for preinteractive decision making or deliberation. How does an individual or a social unit arrive at the choice of the course of action desired, before entering the arena of interaction and discourse? How should individuals or social units, acting as units, decide on the strategy that they enter this arena to promote? In this sense, TCA is the mirror image of classic rationality, which ignores the interactive and collective aspects of action.[3] This dichotomy is reflected in the "dual role" of planning theories and approaches described by Albrecht (1985, 16–22), split between "thinking and being, cognition and reality . . . knowledge and action" (p.17).

Clearly, the lifeworld is not limited to either of these dimensions: the domain of internal reasoning or the arena of social interaction. The universe of decision and action must comprise both. Therefore, the conclusion suggested by the above diagnosis of the reciprocal gaps in the rationality model and TCA is compelling. One paradigm cannot supplant another. Rather, these two models are complementary, each covering an aspect of the process that transforms ideas into reality that the other does not. Any model that claims the status of a new paradigm must include both.

TOWARD A CONTINGENCY FRAMEWORK
FOR PLANNING THEORIES

The framework I have designed, incorporating both classical rationality and TCA, makes sense of the array of theories and models intended to address the flaws of formal rationality. The strongest claim I can make for my framework is that it is a better way of approaching planning and decision making *at the highest level of abstraction* than any of its partial competitors. The juxtaposition of TCA and classical rationality in one contingency matrix is based on the understanding that both are complementary, each addressing a different aspect of the idea of translating ideals into realities.[4]

This contingency framework spans several levels of abstraction. At the highest level, as shown in Figure 3.2, it aspires to be comprehensive and universal. At the lower levels, it cannot hope to be complete, so that my examples are partial illustrations intended only to bolster the cogency of the approach.

Figure 3.2 distinguishes three dimensions: 1. the type of theory; 2. the purpose of the actors; and 3. the domain of action.

1. *Type of Theory.* Theories are of two types. They are either logical-deductive—*ideal*—or positive-descriptive—*real*. Ideal theories are, by definition, normative; real theories, in contrast, describe and explain.

2. *Actor's Purpose.* This partition is proposed by Habermas, who uses it to distinguish between strategic and communicative action. An actor may seek to reach discrete goals or may focus on the interactive process and the ways in which action is grounded in mutual understanding and agreement.

3. *Action Domain.* This partition distinguishes between models that refer to decision making or action by individuals, or units

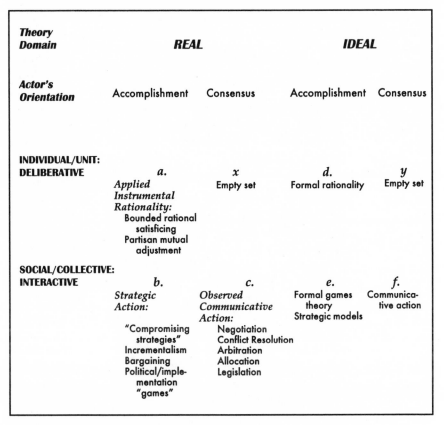

FIGURE 3.2
Contingency Framework

conceived as individuals, and those referring to the necessarily interactive decisions and actions of collectivities.

As shown in Figure 3.2, these three dimensions divide the universe of decision and action models into eight possible cells, but two of them are empty. One of these is labeled x; the other y. Cell x is empty by definition since consensus and understanding are properties of interactive, not individual-deliberative, behavior. Cell y is empty because ideal theories cannot deal with the sort of logical inconsistencies that characterize social interaction.

The remaining six cells order the array of known decision models.[5] This order can be understood as a series of "If . . . Then" statements, where the contingency (If) applies to the cell dimensions and the resultant (Then) identifies the applicable theories of choice.

a. *Real, Individual, Accomplishment-oriented:* This cell contains the descriptive models developed in response to critiques of "classic" rationality: models of instrumental rationality applied to practical situations. These include various versions of "bounded" rationality, satisficing, and disjointed incrementalism, and contingent "blends" of these, such as mixed scanning.

b. *Real, Collective, Accomplishment-oriented:* Here is Habermas's strategic action. This cell may include instrumental or substantive rationality (in the sense defined by Mannheim 1940) and interactive pluralist incrementalism (Forester 1984: 26–7). These may be manifested in "compromising strategies" (Thompson and Tuden 1959) such as bargaining, negotiation, and political "games."[6] Strategic planning as a process through which organizations determine their aims and priorities (Bryson 1988) also fits into this cell as an interactive exercise in substantive rationality. Here also belong coordinative planning and institutional design (Alexander 1992a; Bolan 1991) that involve interaction among participants in a project or among an "implementation set" of organizations (Hjern and Porter 1981).

c. *Real, Collective, Consensus-oriented:* This cell contains models of communicative action that can be observed and described. Such models could include mediation, conflict resolution, arbitration, allocation, regulation, and legislation. This set may also include strategic planning, an institutionalized interaction that produces policies or plans that constrain future implementation decisions and actions (Faludi 1987) and frame-setting (Alexander 1992b, 51). However, to fall into this set, such actions must be by a neutral participant or by a consensus-oriented collectivity—obviously rare cases. Models in cell *c* involve actions and interactions that are unself-interested by definition. To the extent that they do not conform to this requirement and involve actors that seek their own goals and success, they would be strategic action and fall into cell *b*. Alternatively, if the models are only analytic or normative idealizations of behavior, they would be assigned to *f*.

d. *Ideal, Individual, Accomplishment-oriented:* This is where the formal models of both instrumental and substantive utilitarian rationality belong. Rationality has its place, including both instrumental and substantive rationality. Rationality-related normative analytic models such as optimization, linear programming, and multi-objective decision making also fall into this cell.

e. *Ideal, Social-Interactive, Accomplishment-oriented:* Game theory, formal models of teams and coalitions, and both formal strategic models and simulations appear in this cell.

f. *Ideal, Social-Interactive, Consensus/Understanding-oriented:* Here is the place of "communicative action" as defined and described by Habermas.

DISCUSSION AND CONCLUSIONS

A framework for a contingency model of theories of planning, decision, and action has been presented. This framework is developed at only the highest and most general level of abstraction. It is intended to serve as a point of departure for thinking and discourse about deliberation, action, and interaction, and for the development of more specific, detailed, and concrete contingency dimensions to further partition some of the cells in Figure 3.2.

There is already a significant body of work along these lines that could be integrated into this framework. For example, Grandori (1984) has focused on models of modified rationality that are all included here in set *a*. She suggests how the choice of an appropriate model among maximizing models (such as linear optimization), heuristic models (including satisficing), incrementalism, cybernetic or random strategies may be affected by types of uncertainty and knowledge about expected conflicts of interest. Duncan (1972) and Alexander (1973) also distinguish among decision models according to the degree and types of uncertainty that prevail. Thompson and Tuden (1957) and Walton (1972) array approaches to decision and action (spanning cells *a* and *b*) according to agreement on goals, knowledge of cause–effect relationships, and whether the values at stake are instrumental or expressive.

This framework may also serve to integrate procedural and structural orientations to theory. Structural dimensions can be introduced at any relevant level of abstraction. Decision, action, and interactive models in *a* and *b*, for instance, could be analyzed, and new or elaborated models could be generated using as structural dimensions (following Healey 1986, 115) the internal organization of the state, spatial relations, land use, development interests, and the demand and need for land by distinct sectors.[7]

Is a contingency framework such as the one developed here (and, eventually, its elaboration at more specific and concrete levels) a viable candidate to replace the rational model as a conceptual paradigm for the planning, policy, and decision disciplines and professions? I believe that it is and, indeed, that such a framework is the only approach that can span the expanding universe of decision and action and at the same time bridge the widening gap between theory and practice.

In a knowledge world in which we have come to appreciate complexity, the replacement of one simple paradigm by another is unlikely, however desirable that may be. A contingency framework offers the only hope (perhaps no more than a hope) of a paradigm that can incorporate complexity and that can grow, change, and adapt in response to new insights and accretions of knowledge. Perhaps this is a step in that direction.

Notes

1. One exception to this critique is Forester's (1984) conditional table of administrative and planning actions. This incorporates a form of bounded rationality that is based on critical theory and spans the range of agents from the individual actor to the interactive social collectivity. While making a significant contribution, Forester stops short of highlighting several other important dimensions of theory and action that are incorporated into the contingent framework proposed below.

2. In the original text (Habermas 1981, 386), the normative orientation is even more strongly expressed than in McCarthy's translation: "general pragmative presuppositions" is *"formal zu charakterisierende Teilnahmebedingungen,"* which means "formally characterized conditions of participation." Habermas's normative intention is not unambiguous; it is contradicted in a previous passage, which implies a positive orientation: "In identifying strategic action and communicative action as types, I am assuming that concrete actions can be classified according to these points of view. I do not want to use [these] terms only to describe two analytic aspects under which the same action could be described . . . [but to] distinguish . . . [them] according to whether the participants adopt either a success-oriented attitude or one oriented to reaching understanding" (p. 286). But this claim is made more specifically for his general taxonomy (discussed in more detail below). I must emphasize that I am using the term "normative" here in the dual sense set out above, that is, both as a prescriptive model and as an analytical "ideal type." The normative orientation of TCA in the latter sense is well supported by a cumulative reading of Habermas's work, while the prescriptive intention is expressed in *Moralbewusstsein*

und kommunikatives Handeln (1983). Some critics (e.g., Lukes, in Thompson and Held 1984, 135–8) give Habermas's TCA an even narrower normative reading than suggested here; this is actively refuted by Habermas (Thompson and Held 1984, 235–6), but here he also concedes TCA's "ideal type" and normative character (in the sense used here) when he describes his "ideal speech situation" as one to be inferred by an outside observer in a hypothetical transition from "real life" to "discourse."

3. The formal rational model cannot encompass collective decisions (Arrow 1983), and its limitations, even when surmountable (e.g., Sen and Williams 1982), demand its practical replacement by "soft" models of political interaction (Braybrooke and Lindblom 1985; Steinbruner 1974; Wildavsky 1979).

4. A review of the planning and decision-making models and theories shown in Figure 3.2 and their distribution among the cells must be the best evidence for the comprehensiveness and inclusiveness of the framework and its effectiveness as a way of accounting for their relationships and differences.

5. For the knowledgeable reader, the brief reference given here to these decision models is hopefully enough; space does not permit elaboration. For more detail, see Alexander (1992b, 39–60) and the cited sources.

6. As a ready illustration of the value of contingency models, we can observe the integration of implementation processes and "games" (Alexander 1985; Alterman 1982; Mazmanian and Sabatier 1983). Forester's (1984) conditional table of administrative/planning actions also generates some of these strategies.

7. Healey's contrast between the contingency approach (that she dismisses) and her suggested structural "political economy" approach, which in her words "should emphasize the enormous variability of 'constrained choice' situations," is a false dichotomy (Healey 1986, 112–3). In fact, both these approaches share this characteristic, and I hope that the contingency framework suggested here demonstrates that the "political economy" framework is actually a subset (one of many that are possible) of a more general contingency approach.

REFERENCES

Albrecht, J. 1985. Planning as social process: the uses of critical theory. Frankfurt am Main: Verlag Peter Lang.

_____, and G-C. Lim. 1986. A search for alternative planning theory: use of critical theory. *Journal of Architecture and Planning Research* 3, 2 (May): 117–31.

Alexander, E. R. 1972. Choice in a changing world. *Policy Sciences* 3, 3 (September): 325–37.

_____. 1984. After rationality, what? A review of responses to paradigm breakdown. *Journal of the American Planning Association* 50, 1 (Winter): 62–9.

_____. 1985. From idea to action: notes for a contingency theory of the policy implementation process. *Administration and Society* 16, 4 (February): 403–26.

_____. 1992a. A transaction cost theory of planning. *Journal of the American Planning Association* 58, 2: 190–200.

_____. 1992b. *Approaches to planning*. 2d ed. Philadelphia: Gordon & Breach.

_____, and A. Faludi. 1992. Planning doctrine: its uses and implications. In G. McDougall, ed., *Planning theory: prospects for the 1980s*. Aldershot, Hants.: Gower.

Allison, G. T. 1971. *Essence of decision: explaining the Cuban missile crisis*. Boston: Little, Brown.

Alterman, R. 1982. Implementation analysis in urban and regional planning: toward a research agenda. In P. Healey, G. McDougall, and M. J. Thomas, eds., *Planning theory: prospects for the 1980s*. Oxford: Pergamon.

Arrow, K. 1963. *Social choice and individual values*. New York: Wiley.

Banai, R. 1988. Planning paradigms: contradictions and synthesis. *Journal of Architecture and Planning Research* 5, 1 (Spring): 14–34.

Blanco, H. 1993. *How to think about social problems: American pragmatism and the idea of planning*. Westport, CT: Greenwood Press.

Bolan, R. S. 1991. Planning and institutional design. *Planning Theory* 5/6 (Summer–Winter): 7–34.

Braybrooke, D., and C. E. Lindblom. 1985. *The strategy of decisions: political evaluation as a social process*. New York: Free Press.

Bryson, J. M. 1988. *Strategic planning for public and nonprofit organizations*. San Francisco: Jossey-Bass.

Buchanan, J. M., and G. Tullock. 1969. *The calculus of consent*. Ann Arbor, MI: University of Michigan Press.

Camhis, M. 1979. *Planning theory and philosophy*. London: Tavistock.

Castells, M. 1977. *The urban question: a Marxist approach*. London: Edward Arnold.

_____. 1978. *City, class and power*. London: Macmillan.

_____. 1983. *The city and the grassroots: a cross-cultural theory of urban social movements*. Berkeley, CA: University of California Press.

Cooke, P. 1983. *Theories of planning and spatial development*. London: Hutchinson.

Darke, R. 1985. Rationality, planning, and the state. In M. Breheny and A. Hooper, eds. *Rationality in planning: critical essays on the role of rationality in urban and regional planning*. London: Pion, 15–26.

Dror, Y. 1971. *Design for policy sciences.* New York: Elsevier.

Duncan, R. B. 1972. Characteristics of organizational environments and perceived environmental uncertainty. *Administrative Science Quarterly* 17, 3 (September): 313–21.

Dworkin, R. 1977. *Taking rights seriously.* Cambridge, MA: Duckworth.

Ehrlich, I. 1975. The deterrent effect of capital punishment: A question of life and death. *American Economic Review* 65 (June): 314–25.

Faludi, A. 1987. *A decision-centred view of environmental planning.* Oxford: Pergamon.

———. 1986. Procedural rationality and ethical theory. In *Planning theory in practice,* vol. 1. *Proceedings* of the 2nd International Conference, Turin. September.

Fischer, F., and J. Forester, eds. 1987. *Confronting values in policy sciences: the politics of criteria.* Newbury Park, CA: Sage.

Forester, J. 1982. Understanding planning practice: an empirical, practical and normative account. *Journal of Planning Education and Research* 1, 2 (Winter): 59–71.

———. 1984. Bounded rationality and the politics of muddling through. *Public Administration Review* 44, 1 (Jan.-Feb.): 23–31.

———, ed. 1985a. *Critical theory and public life.* Cambridge, MA: MIT Press.

———. 1985b. Practical rationality in planmaking. In M. Breheny and A. Hooper, eds. *Rationality in planning: critical essays on the role of rationality in urban and regional planning.* London: Pion, 48–59.

———. 1989. *Planning in the face of power.* Berkeley, CA: University of California Press.

Friedmann, J. 1973. *Retracking America: a theory of transactive planning.* Garden City, NY: Anchor Books.

———. 1979. *The good society.* Cambridge, MA: MIT Press.

———. 1987. *Planning in the public domain.* Princeton, NJ: Princeton University Press.

Grandori, A. 1984. A prescriptive contingency view of organizational decision making. *Administrative Science Quarterly* 29: 192–209.

Habermas, J., 1981. *Theorie des kommuikativen Handelns.* Band I. *Handlungsrationalität und gesellschaftliche Rationalisierung.* Frankfurt am Main: Suhrkamp Verlag.

———. 1983. *Moralbewusstsein und kommunikatives Handel.* Frankfurt am Main: Suhrkamp Verlag.

————. 1984. *The theory of communicative action: Vol. 1. Reason and the rational-ization of society.* Translated by T. McCarthy. Boston: Beacon Press.

Harsyani, J. 1972. Rational choice models of political behavior vs. functionalist and conformist theories. In D. E. Apter and C. F. Andrain, eds., *Contemporary analytical theory.* Englewood Cliffs, NJ: Prentice-Hall.

Healey, P. 1986. Policy processes in land use planning. In *Planning theory in practice,* vol. 3. *Proceedings* of the 2d International Conference, Turin. September.

Healey, P., and M. J. Thomas. 1982. Theoretical debates in planning: towards a coherent dialogue. Conference Position Paper. In P. Healey, G. McDougall, and M. J. Thomas, eds., *Planning theory: prospects for the 1980s.* Oxford: Pergamon, 5–22.

Healey, P., and J. Underwood. 1978. Professional ideals and planning practice. In D. Diamond and J. B. McLoughlin, eds., *Progress in planning.* vol. 9, pt. 2. Oxford: Pergamon, 75–127

Hjern, B., and D. O. Porter. 1981. Implementation structures: a new unit of administrative analysis. *Organization Studies* 2, 3: 211–27.

Hoch, C. J. 1984a. Doing good and being right: the pragmatic connection in planning theory. *Journal of the American Planning Association* 50, 3: 335–45.

————. 1984b. Pragmatism, planning and power. *Journal of Planning Education and Research* 4, 2: 86–95.

Hudson, B. 1979. Comparison of current planning theories: counterparts and contradictions. *Journal of the American Planning Association* 45: 387–405.

Krieger, M. 1974. Some new directions for planning theory. *Journal of the American Institute of Planners* 40, 3: 150–63.

Lang, R. 1984. Contingent theory and planning practice. Paper presented at the Conference of Association of Collegiate Schools of Planning, New York, October 19–21.

Lim, G-C. 1986. Toward a synthesis of contemporary planning theories. *Journal of Planning Education and Research* 5, 2: 75–85.

Lindblom, C. E. 1959. The science of muddling through. *Public Administration Review* 19: 79–99.

————. 1965. *The intelligence of democracy.* New York: Free Press.

Lyons, D. 1984. Ethics and the rule of law. Cambridge: Cambridge University Press.

Mandelbaum, S. J. 1979. A complete general theory of planning is impossible. *Policy Sciences* 11, 1 (August): 59–71.

Mannheim, K. 1940. *Man and society in an age of reconstruction.* London: Kegan Paul.

Mazmanian, D.A., and P. A. Sabatier. 1983. *Implementation and public policy.* Glenview, IL: Scott Foresman.

McConnell, S. 1981. *Theories for planning: an introduction.* London: Heinemann.

Portugalli, J. 1981. Distribution, allocation, social structure and spatial form: elements of planning theory. In D. Diamond and J. B. McLoughlin, eds., *Progress in planning,* vol. 14. Oxford: Pergamon, 227–310.

Poulton, M. C. 1991. The case for a positive theory of planning. *Environment and Planning B: Planning and Design* 18: 225–32, 263–75.

Reade, E. 1985. An analysis of the use of the concept of rationality in the literature of planning. In M. Breheny and A. Hooper, eds. *Rationality in planning: critical essays on the role of rationality in urban and regional planning.* London: Pion, 77–97

Rittel, H., and M. M. Webber. 1973. Dilemmas in a general theory of planning. *Policy Sciences* 4, 2 (March): 155–69.

Schön, D. A. 1983. *The reflective practitioner: how professionals think in action.* New York: Basic Books.

Sen, A., and B. Williams, eds. 1982. *Utilitarianism and beyond.* Cambridge: Cambridge University Press.

Sillince, J. A. 1986. *Theory of planning.* London: Gower.

Simon, H. A. 1955. A behavioral model of rational choice. *Quarterly Journal of Economics* 69: 99–118.

Steinbruner, J. 1974. *The cybernetic theory of decision.* Princeton, NJ: Princeton University Press.

Taylor, N. 1984. A critique of materialist critiques of procedural planning theory. *Environment and Planning B: Planning and Design* 11: 103–26.

Teitz, M. 1985. Rationality in planning and the search for community. In M. Breheny and A. Hooper, eds., *Rationality in planning: critical essays on the role of rationality in urban and regional planning.* London: Pion, 137–44.

Tenbruck, F. H. 1972. *Zur Kritik der planenden Vernunft.* Freiburg: Verlag Karl Alber.

Thompson, J. D. 1967. *Organizations in action.* New York: McGraw-Hill.

Thompson, J. D., and D. Held, eds. 1984. *Habermas: critical debates.* London: Macmillan.

Thompson, J. D., and A. Tuden. 1959. Strategies, structures and processes of organizational decision. In J. D. Thompson, ed., *Comparative studies in administration*. Pittsburgh, PA: University of Pittsburgh Press, 195–216.

Tips, W. E. J. 1986. On the relationship between the uncertain role concepts of third world planners and the substantive vs the procedural argument in planning theory. *Environment and Planning B: Planning and Design* 13: 279–92.

Travis, A. S. 1977. Planning as applied ecology: the management of alternative futures. *Town Planning Review* 48, 1: 5–16.

Walton, R. E. 1972. Interorganizational decision making and identity conflict. In M. Tuite, R. Chisholm, and M. Radnor, eds., *Interorganizational decision making*. Chicago: Aldine, 94–111.

Wildavsky, A. 1979. *Speaking truth to power: the art and craft of policy analysis*. Boston, MA: Little, Brown.

Willard, C. A. 1979. The epistemic functions of argument: reasoning and decision making from a constructivist/interactionist point of view. *Journal of the American Forensic Association* 15, 3 (Winter): 169–91.

Yiftachel, O. 1989. Towards a new typology of planning theories. *Environment and Planning B: Planning and Design* 16, 1 (January): 23–39.

ANDREAS FALUDI

4 Rationality, Critical Rationalism, and Planning Doctrine

INTRODUCTION

These days, nobody dares to be positive about planning thought. It is said to be "in the doldrums" (de Neufville 1983, 35). The "old paradigm" appears obsolete (Galloway and Mahayni 1977; Alexander 1984). Planning theory is said to be based on the assumption of certainty (Christensen 1985, 66), a consensus view of society (Thomas 1979), and/or on technocracy (Friedmann 1973, 68).

I disagree. The arguments presented in this chapter maintain that the rational planning model as originally conceived preempts many of its critics, that later developments are but extensions of the original model, and that the decision-centered view gives an adequate formulation to insights gained during three decades of planning thought.

THE RATIONAL PLANNING MODEL AS ORIGINALLY CONCEIVED

I start this reconstruction with the "Note on the Conceptual Scheme" by Banfield at the end of *Politics, Planning, and the Public Interest* (Meyerson and Banfield 1955). This seems to be the first discussion of the rational

65

model in the planning literature. Of course, rationality has been discussed before in the social science literature. Banfield refers to Parsons (1949), and through him there is a link to Max Weber. Simon, too, has been influential, and he, in turn, professes to be drawing on logical positivism (Simon 1976, [1945], 45–50). It appears that his main inspiration was Rudolf Carnap, then of the University of Chicago, who had been a member of the Vienna Circle. Banfield's merit is to have made this diverse body of thought accessible to planners. His contribution is not found wanting as regards awareness of the problems of rationality. He relates planning to politics, which concerns the element of conflict that critics of the rational planning model say it cannot handle:

> When there is conflict . . . between the ends of different actors (or within the end system of a single actor) and not all conflicting ends can be realized, an *issue* exists and the actors whose ends conflict are parties to the issue. . . . The ends which are made the basis of action ending a conflict form the *settlement* of an issue. (Myerson and Banfield 1955, 304)

Banfield then discusses planning, starting with the concept of a plan. A plan is, he explains:

> a course of action which can be carried into effect, which can be expected to lead to the attainment of the ends sought, and which someone . . . intends to carry into effect. . . . As distinct from planned ones, opportunistic decisions are made as the event unfolds and they are, therefore, not mutually related as a unit having a single design. The execution of any planned course of action involves the making of opportunistic decisions as well as planned ones. (Myerson and Banfield 1955, 312–13)

This is very much like the IOR (so named after the Institute for Operational Research in London) school's view of strategic choice. Banfield then introduces the rational planning model:

> Since planning is designing a course of action to achieve ends, "efficient" planning is that which under given conditions leads to the maximization of the attainment of the relevant ends. We will assume that a planned course of action which is selected rationally is most likely to maximize the attainment of the relevant ends and that therefore "rational" planning and "efficient"planning are the same. As a practical matter, of course, this assumption may in many cases be unwarranted: sometimes the most careful deliberation will result in a worse selection than might be made by flipping a coin. (Myerson and Banfield 1955, 314)

start

It is in Banfield's elaboration of the model that awareness of its limitations becomes evident:

> Obviously no decision can be perfectly rational since no one can ever know all of the alternatives open to him at any moment or all the consequences which would follow from any action. Nevertheless, decisions may be made with more or less knowledge of alternatives, consequences, and relevant ends, and so we may describe some decisions and some decision-making processes as more nearly rational than others. (Myerson and Banfield 1955, 314–15)

However, rationality can be approximated. Nowadays, a range of methods is available for each of the steps involved. Banfield details these steps:

1. *Analysis of the Situation:* Various aspects of the situation in which an actor finds himself must be investigated: the limiting conditions restricting the range of actions open to him, and opportunity areas as comprising "all those acts or courses of action which the effectuating organization is not precluded from taking." (Myerson and Banfield 1955, 316).

2. *End Reduction and Elaboration:* This refers to the selection of the relevant ends and the weights attached to them. Banfield distinguishes between active and contextual elements of ends:

   > In designing a course of action the planner must find a way to attain the active elements of the end. But although this is a necessary condition . . . it is not a sufficient one. For if the end is fully stated, the desired situation is seen to consist . . . of several . . . elements, and it is, of course, all elements—the desired situation as a whole—which the course of action should attain.

   > When the content of an end is fully elaborated, it may appear that its active elements cannot be attained without sacrifice of certain contextual elements. In such a case, if the contextual elements are valued more highly, the end may be rejected altogether (Myerson and Banfield 1955, 317).

So Friedmann's contention that Banfield treats ends as given (Friedmann 1973, 3) is ill-founded.

3. *The Design of Courses of Action:* Banfield defines a decision as "an action which obliges the effectuating organization to take certain other acts or which limits its choice of acts in the future by foreclosing certain action possibilities which would otherwise exist" (Myerson and Banfield 1955, 318). He distinguishes between developmental, program, and operational levels of choice and relates this to functional and substantive rationality. His inspiration is Mannheim (1940).

4. *The Comparative Evaluation of Consequences:* Banfield defines a consequence as "a change in the situation which is caused by an act . . . i.e., which follows the act and would not occur without it. Consequences may be anticipated or unanticipated, and anticipated consequences may be either sought or unsought. . . . " (Myerson and Banfield 1955, 319). He adds in a statement, the importance of which will become clear when discussing the decision-centered view below: "The situation consists only of those objects which have relevance in terms of the end-system of the organization: therefore, consequences . . . exist only in relation to ends" (Myerson and Banfield 1955, 319).

Banfield also appreciates uncertainty, another of those aspects to which the rational model is said to be averse. So he realizes that planning cannot be rational. He has not been able to square this circle other than by affirming that rationality is an ideal worth striving for (see also Banfield 1959, in Faludi 1984 [1973], 149).

Extensions of the Model

Under this heading I discuss advocacy planning together with other notions of the planning process said to be in opposition to optimization. Optimization is, of course, at the core of the rational planning model.

The key statement as regards advocacy planning is that of Davidoff (1965). The aim of that seminal article was to build a bridge between the rational planning model and the quest for relevance—which was the reaction to poverty and discrimination in the 1960s. Davidoff has, nevertheless, been described as being opposed to rational-comprehensive planning (Healey et al. 1982; Hoch 1984). However, Davidoff's contribution to planning as a generic process is no less significant than his later and more widely known writings on advocacy and pluralism (Stegman 1985, 375); the latter writings are also organically related to the former. Davidoff's article does not signify the demise of the rational model; rather, it represents a plea for its radical interpretation.

The article opens flamboyantly: "The present can become an époque in which the dreams of the past for an enlightened and just democracy are turned into reality" (Davidoff 1965, in Faludi 1984 [1973], 277). The distinct contribution of planners is their command of the planning process (sic!) and their substantive skills. "The prospect . . . is that of a practice which openly invites political and social values to be examined and debated. Acceptance of this position means rejection of prescriptions . . . which would have the planner act solely as a technician" (Davidoff 1965, in Faludi 1984 [1973], 277). Consequently, "the planner should do more than explicate the values underlying his prescriptions for courses of action: he should affirm them; he should be an advocate for what he deems proper" (Davidoff 1965, in Faludi 1984 [1973], 279). This is because determination of what is in the public interest is an adversarial process.

In contrast to his latter-day followers, Davidoff is also impressed by cost–benefit analysis, but he says its weak spot is the determination of values. Advocacy planning helps to make this explicit: "There are no neutral grounds for evaluating a plan; there are as many evaluative systems as there are value systems" (Davidoff 1965, in Faludi 1984 [1973], 283).

If advocacy planning cannot be construed as destructive of the rational planning model, what about satisficing, disjointed incrementalism, and mixed scanning? Above, I noted the influence of Simon on Banfield. In *Administrative Behavior* (1976 [1945]), we find the notion of "administrative man" making rational choices. But in the introduction to the third edition of *Administrative Behavior*, Simon asserts that administrative man satisfices, that he "looks for a course of action that is 'good enough'" (p. xxix). This comes from research in psychology and on artificial intelligence. Such research has influenced Lindblom too. His alternative is described variously as "limited comparisons" (Lindblom 1959), "disjointed incrementalism" (Braybrooke and Lindblom 1963), or "mutual adjustment" (Lindblom 1965). As Etzioni (1968, 271–72) comments, the formulations have in common their reliance on market-like structures. Etzioni's alternative, "mixed scanning," is an approach by which the decision maker quickly scans the field of action, identifies the preferred strategy on the basis of incomplete information, then explores that strategy in more detail, occasionally returning to the general level to reestablish the overall direction.

Such adaptations reflect awareness of the limitations of the human mind. Indeed, the rational model cannot be followed, and adaptions are needed. But the model can provide a yardstick for determining whether decisions are correct. This interpretation of the model is not affected by criticisms leveled against it in the literature, and so-called alternatives are no substitute for it. However, account may be taken of the problems of rational planning by defining decision situations with such limitations in mind.

The Decision-centered View of Planning

As has been pointed out, the controversy around the rational planning model has concentrated on whether making a plan can and should be a rational process. Implementation has been assumed to follow plan making without much ado. However, as Barrett and Fudge (1981, 25–6) say, depending on one's perspective, departing from a plan can be as rational as following it. In starting from ordinary decision making, the decision-centered view takes account of studies showing that plans and policies are but one input into the negotiations around proposals for action. As far as this is concerned, the decision-centered view accords well with "transactive planning" (Friedmann 1973) and with the argumentative approaches of the "second generation" that Rittel and Webber (1973) propose.

An important distinction among decisions concerns the commitments that they entail. Operational decisions result in definite commitments, like exchanging contracts or the granting of a permit. This is not necessarily the same as "implementation." Planning agencies are not always engaged in direct action. Often, they must be content with stimulating others to act in particular ways. Their operational decisions provide an input into the decision making of others. Such decisions are, nevertheless, operational by virtue of entailing definite commitments to use available planning powers.

Adopting a plan, by contrast, entails only tentative commitments. Of course, this does not make the decision to adopt a plan trivial. Plans are necessary as a backup to operational decision making. Imagine an actor involved in decision making day in, day out. The likely effects of these decisions form a source of constant concern. Paying attention to the consequences of proposals and relating them to each other, he or she must set certain guidelines. This, then, is what the decision-centered view regards plans to be: guidelines for day-to-day decisions. Their purpose is to draw attention to the broader context and implications of decisions. There may also be opportunities for joint action of which individual decision makers are unaware.

Planning, therefore, is a process of coordinating decisions by making them fall into a coherent pattern, their purpose being to make sense out of the actions that one takes. The requirement that decisions by public bodies make sense is enshrined in constitutional provisions, like due process, and parliamentary rules, like question time (Grauhan 1969; see also Davidoff 1965; Davidoff and Reiner 1962; Webber 1978, 1983). Such provisions ensure that decision makers answer for their decisions. Rationality relates to arguments advanced to justify decisions. It is in this context that decision makers (including those criticizing proposed decisions) need to refer to plans, lest they get lost in a plethora of detail. Plans predefine the definition of the situation for operational decision makers, thereby enabling them to make a well-considered choice.

Considering choices, the decision maker must know what can be done about the situation, what he or she wants to get out of it or to avoid, and which weights must be attached to consequences. The answers to these questions add up to the definition of the decision situation. The concept of the definition of the decision situation is a key to resolving many theoretical issues. This definition is a logical prerequisite of rational decisions, just as March and Simon (1958, 138) have concluded: "Choice is always exercised with respect to a limited, approximate, simplified 'model' of the real situation." Indeed, they call this the chooser's "definition of the situation." It follows that talk about decisions being objectively rational is meaningless. The idea of objective rationality is wrongly imputed to advocates of rational planning by their opponents. To come to this conclusion, one only has to consult, yet again, Banfield. Alternatives, constraints and ends refer to a specific decision maker faced with a unique situation. Davidoff, too, has been shown above to insist that plan evaluation can never be neutral. In strategic choice it is the same: decision areas, options, option bars, and sources of uncertainty (terms in which the IOR school discusses planning) are identified from the point of view of the decision maker.

It follows that rationality is always relative to the definition of the decision situation. Limitations of knowledge and time for preparing decisions cease to be theoretical issues. Such limitations simply form part of the definition of the decision situation. This is really the same as Simon, Lindblom, and Etzioni have been arguing, which is why I have treated their alternatives as modest extensions of the rational planning model.

Saying that the definition of the decision situation is subjective also takes care of conflict. Where there are irreconcilable differences, it is impossible to arrive at a joint decision, let alone to plan rationally. Banfield has understood this well. So, by claiming that rationality purports to transcend conflict, its critics have created a strawman. In reality, following the rational model may serve equally well to make evident that there can be no generally acceptable solution, because there is no common definition of the decision situation. In this way, rational planning may engender, rather than avoid, conflict.

This view has parallels in personal construct theory (Low 1982) and the view of reality as a social construct (Berger and Luckmann 1967; see also Barrett and Fudge 1981). It is also understood that the power structure preshapes definitions of the decision situation. This brings the decision-centered view close to the reconstructed pragmatism of Hoch (1984). In principle, there is no difference between the view here advanced and that of Forester (1985) speaking in terms of situated rational action.

One of the consequences of this view is to focus attention on how decision situations are defined. The process of defining decision situations can be approached on a micro scale, looking at concrete actions and who influences how they are shaped by the perceptions and interests of particular actors. The same process can also be approached on a macro scale, looking at the deep structure behind definitions of decision situations, the institutionalization of assumptions and belief systems on which such definitions rest. Below I discuss this deep structure of planning under planning doctrine. First, I take the discussion about rational planning to the level of planning methodology.

CRITICAL RATIONALISM

How should we talk about rational planning? What is the appropriate discursive form? In *Critical Rationalism and Planning Methodology* (Faludi 1986), I draw parallels between the language of rationality and the methodology of science. The difference between decisions and scientific statements is that decisions must be justified *before* they are taken. Or, as Rittel and Webber describe the difference:

> It is a principle of science that solutions to problems are only hypotheses offered for refutation. This habit is based on the insight that there are no proofs of hypotheses, only potential refutations. . . . Consequently, the scientific community does not blame its members for postulating hypotheses that are later refuted. (Rittel and Webber 1973)

In the world of planning and wicked problems, no such immunity is tolerated. Here the aim is not to find truth but to improve some characteristics of the world where people live. "Planners are liable for the consequences of the actions they generate; the effects can matter a great deal to those people that are touched by those actions" (Faludi 1986, 166–67). For another critical discussion of the frequently drawn analogy between the implementation of plans and scientific experiments, see Alexander (1981, 139).

Ultimately, the rational planning model is a means of sharing responsibility for the consequences of actions, and this is the most important reason for advocating it. Planning involves risks, so there must be a way of legitimizing decisions. The undertone of rationalization after the fact is accepted. There is nothing wrong with rationalizing decisions after they have been formulated as long as the attempt is successful—as long as decisions, formulated in whichever way, can be shown to *be* rational.

Being concerned with the justification of decisions, planning methodology is what much planning thought is really about. I prefer planning methodology to the term "conceptual analysis" used by Taylor (1984, 1985). Putting it this way draws attention to the analogy with the methodology of science. As with the methodology of science, planning methodology is a theory of methods, only in this case we are talking about the methods of planning and not of scientific analysis. Planning methodology also concerns the assumptions of planning and clarifies its procedures, methods, and the underlying logic. Lastly, planning methodology seeks to resolve issues concerning the structure, status, and validity of the products of planning: plans and, ultimately, operational decisions.

All this relates to my *Critical Rationalism and Planning Methodology* (Faludi 1986). As the title suggests, I develop the analogy with Popper's critical rationalism. Concerning empirical theory, Popper (1959) suggests that the task of methodology is "to give a logical analysis of this procedure; that is, to analyze the method of the empirical sciences" (Popper 1959, 27). He then goes on to ask: "What are these 'methods of the empirical sciences?' And what do we call 'empirical sciences?'" Planning methodologists should ask likewise: "What are the 'methods of planning' and what do we call 'planning'?"

Now, of course, the meaning of terms is ultimately a matter of agreement. It should be clear that my view of planning is that of *decision making concerning future courses of action.* It results in statements of intent, or *decisions.* Planning methodology concerns questions about the *rules to be applied to proposals for decisions,* so that one can accept or reject them in a reasoned manner. As in empirical research, these are *standards* concerning the *procedures by which proposals are to be judged.*

Popper proposes one such standard for empirical research. He insists that only such statements should be admitted as scientific as can be falsified. He calls this his demarcation criterion between scientific and nonscientific statements:

> My criterion of demarcation will accordingly have to be regarded as a *proposal for an agreement or convention.* As to the suitability of any such convention opinions may differ; a reasonable discussion of these questions is only possible between parties having some purpose in common. The choice of the purpose must, of course, be ultimately a matter of decision, going beyond rational argument. (Popper 1959, 37)

Popper also indicates how to decide between two or more hypotheses, each falling well within the demarcation criterion of falsifiability. His suggestion is to give preference to those hypotheses that have withstood the most stringent tests and/or are more specific in their formulation. The reason is that their informative content is greater. In technical terms, there are more "falsifiers," and so the hypothesis runs a greater risk of being found wrong. Now, Popper's decision rule is to give preference to the hypotheses with the greatest informative content. So we see that his methodology of the empirical sciences starts with a regulative idea (to search for truth), from which he derives a demarcation criterion (falsifiability) and a decision rule (take the proposition with the greatest informative content).

Popper discussed other problems, too—for instance, the adoption of standards. This provides a clue for formulating a convention for accepting planning decisions comparable to Popper's convention for the empirical sciences. As with empirical propositions, Popper says there is also a regulative rule for the adoption of standards. This idea "can be described in many ways . . . for example by the term 'right' or 'good'" (Popper 1966, vol. 2, 384–5). The same goes for planning, which may be said to be about taking correct decisions. This is the regulative idea on which the methodology of planning should orient itself—knowing, of course, that this aim is as distant as Popper's regulative idea for science of attaining truth.

What demarcation criterion and decision rule does this imply? One of the occasions of Popper discussing decisions is when he gives his reasons for accepting rationalism (Popper 1966, vol. 2, 232). Popper describes this as ultimately a moral decision. This is one of the bones of contention in *The Positivist Dispute in German Sociology* (see Adorno et al. 1976). But Popper also considers what the consequences would be of irrationalism. There are plenty of other indications of Popper holding that both moral and practical decisions should be taken with a view to their consequences. Based on this, my argument in *Critical Rationalism and Planning Methodology* (1986) goes as follows: To work toward the regulative idea of correct decisions, a Popperian must always pay regard to the consequences of proposed actions. Proposals for taking decisions that fail to state the expected consequences do not help us aim at correct decision making. Thus, consequentialism (the insistence that we should consider only proposals, the consequences of which have been analyzed) fulfills a role analogous to that of falsifiability in the empirical sciences. It is a demarcation criterion separating out those statements about decisions that lend themselves to being rationally assessed from others. In these terms, all the authors quoted here, including the critics of the rational planning model, are consequentialists. (For the opposite deontologist position see Faludi 1986, 127–8; see also Kaufmann 1981.)

Now, much as with falsifiable hypotheses, there can, of course, be a range of alternative proposals, each duly analyzed in terms of its consequences. To select one, we need a decision rule as before. The decision rule is that, after comparing all consequences of all alternatives, we should opt for the best as measured in the light of our goals. This not only makes sense, it also has an indirect effect in terms of the learning curve resulting from failure. Claiming that an alternative is the best maximizes the risk of proposals being rejected. After all, every time a realistic alternative is advanced, and every time somebody points out a consequence that has not been considered previously, proposals need to be reviewed. There is an analogy here with Popper's insistence that hypotheses should be exposed to as much risk as possible, leading to the survival of the fittest. Only those hypotheses that have been submitted to the most grueling tests deserve our trust, says Popper. The same goes for proposals for decisions.

This decision rule is, of course, identical with the prescriptions of the rational planning model. The advantage of this analysis lies in the insight it offers to the nature of the model as a rule for testing proposals for decisions—which, of course, does not mean to say that planning methodology has nothing to do with the practical pursuits of planners (Hart 1987; Needham 1987). On the contrary, planning methodology shows what planning is about. Accordingly, planners must formulate proposals that meet the requirements of the rational model, availing themselves of methods of analyzing alternatives and their consequences. Thereby, they formulate proposals in such a manner that others can react to them, if need be rejecting them based on reasoned argument. In this way, rationality has an obvious bearing on practice. But it does not insist on any particular manner of working nor, I might add, is it inimical to the exercise of creativity.

PLANNING DOCTRINE

Can these conceptions of rationality be applied to planning doctrines, the deep structure of values, assumptions and concepts that underlie plans? Together with Ernest Alexander (Alexander and Faludi 1990), I have previously identified preconditions of, and criteria for, the evaluation of planning doctrine. This is not the place to go into details. Broadly, however, doctrines are like paradigms. They frame puzzle-solving inquiry and make "normal" planning possible. Normal planning involves primarily professional, administrative, and bureaucratic actors. Within the context of agreed-upon values and a generally imaged principle of spatial organization, professional-bureaucratic debate and political discourse can produce a succession of planning concepts to respond to changing situations. A related benefit of having a doctrine is to reduce the burden of plan making. Planning becomes cumulative and progressive. (This may account for the effectiveness of Dutch planning; see Faludi and Van der Valk 1994.) The reverse may also be true: absence of an agreed-upon doctrine may explain ineffectiveness in planning.

There is also the issue of doctrinal change. Planning doctrines that have lasted and that have been successful have, at times, displayed significant differences. At the same time, we are saying that these are the same doctrines throughout. How do we account for this? Alexander and Faludi (1990) invoke once more the analogy between doctrines and paradigms. Lakatos (1974) makes a distinction, for paradigms, between negative and positive heuristics. The "hard core" of a research program cannot be altered by a negative heuristic. A positive heuristic, in contrast, encourages development of a "protective belt" of theories, models, and observations elaborating the core. These may change.

The same distinction exists in planning doctrine. Various concepts may be replaced throughout the life span of the doctrine. Thus, the emphasis in Dutch strategic planning has gone from concentric development around towns and cities to a policy of controlled dispersal and back to what is called the "compact-city" policy, all within the same spatial doctrine. The robust central metaphor of the doctrine has been stable, though it appears in quite different discursive settings.

Doctrinal discourse—putting deeply embedded notions at risk of dissolution—is exceptional. In planning, as in science, it is usually initiated by anomalies that cannot be ignored. Can such discourse be rational? The question is difficult because the core of a doctrine is often expressed in deceptively simple concepts and ambiguous metaphors. Such concepts can be marketed, but can they be rationally assessed? A doctrine's validity, comprehensiveness, and consistency are subject to rational debate. But is the same true for its core that permits it to generate consensus?

My optimistic answer to all of these questions is resolutely positive. The essential feature of a critical rationality applied to doctrine is openness. Complete openness in a doctrine is self-defeating, since it would prevent doctrine from framing and shaping planning conversations. We can and should, however, apply a set of critical questions to the core of doctrines: What is the scope of the doctrine's metaphoric core? Does it allow for the generation or absorption of diverse concepts? How fertile is a doctrine in eliciting elaboration in response to a range of problems? Does the doctrine include multiple strategies, or does it have only one response to every contingency?

These are important issues. They require intense political inspection and difficult choices. That is not, however, a reason for professional planners to avoid them, even if no one would sensibly seek to make doctrinal discourse a daily habit.

CONCLUSION

The last comment about the political element in doctrine relates to a wider consideration. In developing the concept of doctrine, issues have been taken on board that the critics of procedural planning theory have alleged it excluded. Thus, the study of the development of doctrine leads naturally to a consideration of the planning community and of patterns of dominance within it. It also leads to a consideration of how planning relates to wider concerns so that it can generate the necessary consensus. Being composed of substantive as well as procedural elements, doctrine also bridges the divide between procedural and substantive theory. This does not change the fact that there is a core concern that is precisely what the critics of planning theory assert it is: conceptual, concerned with what correct decision making and planning entail. Above, I have demonstrated that this approach can be extended to planning doctrine. As with decisions and plans, we can ask of doctrine what it is and which criteria to apply to its evaluation. These, too, are conceptual issues.

REFERENCES

Adorno, T. W. et al. 1976. *The positivist dispute in German sociology*. London: Heinemann, ix-xliv.

Alexander, E. R. 1981. If planning isn't everything, maybe it's something. *Town Planning Review* 52: 131–42.

_____. 1984. After rationality, what?: a review of responses to paradigm breakdown. *Journal of the American Planning Association* 50: 62–9.

_____, and A. Faludi. 1989. Planning and plan implementation: notes on evaluation criteria. *Environment and Planning B: Planning and Design* 16: 127–40.

_____. 1990. Planning doctrine: its uses and applications. Working Paper 120, Institute of Planning and Demography. Amsterdam: University of Amsterdam.

Banfield, E.C. 1959. Ends and means in planning. *International Social Science Journal* 11, 361–8; see also: A. Faludi, ed. 1973. *A reader in planning theory*. Oxford: Pergamon Press, 139–49.

Barnett, J. 1974. *Urban design as public policy: practical methods for improving cities.* New York: Architectural Record, McGraw Hill.

———. 1982. *An introduction to urban design.* New York: Harper & Row.

Barrett, S., and C. Fudge. 1981. Introductory review: Examining the policy-action relationship. In S. Barrett and C. Fudge, eds., *Policy and action: essays in the implementation of public policy.* London, New York: Methuen, 3-32.

Berger, P. L., and T. Luckmann. 1967. *The social construction of reality.* Harmondsworth, UK: Penguin.

Braybrooke, D., and C. E. Lindblom. 1963. *A strategy for decisions.* New York: Free Press.

Christensen, K. S. 1985. Coping with uncertainty in planning. *Journal of the American Planning Association* 51: 63–73.

Cooke, P. N. 1983. *Theories of planning and spatial development.* London: Hutchinson.

Davidoff, P. 1965. Advocacy and pluralism in planning. *Journal of the American Institute of Planners* 31: 331–8.

———, and T. A. Reiner. 1962. A choice theory of planning. *Journal of the American Institute of Planners* 28: 108–15.

Dror, Y. 1971. *Ventures in policy science: concepts and application.* New York: American Elsevier.

Dyckman, J. W. 1961. What makes planners plan? *Journal of the American Institute of Planners* 27: 164–67; see also: A. Faludi, ed. 1973. *A reader in planning theory.* Oxford: Pergamon Press, 11–39.

Etzioni, A. 1968. *The active society.* London: Collier-Macmillan.

———. 1984 [1973]. *Planning theory.* Oxford: Pergamon Press.

Faludi, A. 1986. *Critical rationalism and planning methodology.* London: Pion Press.

———. 1987. *A decision-centred view of environmental planning.* Oxford: Pergamon Press.

———. 1989a. Conformance vs. performance: implications for evaluations. *Impact Assessment Bulletin* 7: 135–51.

———, ed. 1989b. Keeping the Netherlands in shape (special issue). *Built Environment* 15: 5–64.

———, ed. 1991. Fifty years of Dutch national physical planning (special issue). *Built Environment* 16: 1–77.

_____. 1992. Dutch growth management: the two faces of success. *Landscape and Urban Planning* 22: 93–106.

Faludi, A., and J. M. Mastop. 1982. The I.O.R.-School: The development of a planning methodology. *Environment and Planning B: Planning and Design* 9: 241–56.

Faludi, A., and A. J. Van der Valk. 1994. *Rule and order: Dutch planning doctrine in the twentieth century*. Dordrecht, Holland: Kluwer Academic Publishers.

Fisher, F. 1980. *Politics, values, and public policy: the problem of methodology*. Boulder, CO: Westview Press.

Foley, D. L. 1963. *Controlling London's growth: planning the great wen, 1940–1960*. Berkeley, CA: University of California Press.

Forester, J. 1985. Practical rationality in planmaking. In M. Breheny and A. Hooper, eds. *Rationality in planning: critical essays on the role of rationality in urban and regional planning*. London: Pion Press, 48–59.

Friedmann, J. 1973. *Retracking America: a theory of transactive planning*. Garden City, NY: Doubleday–Anchor.

_____, and C. Weaver. 1979. *Territory and function: the evolution of regional planning*. London: Edward Arnold.

Friend, J., and A. Hickling. 1987. *Planning under pressure: the strategic choice approach*. Oxford: Pergamon Press.

Galloway, T. D., and R. G. Mahayni. 1977. Planning theory in retrospect: the process of paradigm change. *Journal of the American Institute of Planners* 43: 62–71.

Grauhan, R. R. 1969. Zur Struktur der planenden Verwaltung. *Stadtbauwelt* 60: 132–37; see also: "Notes on the structure of planning administration." In A. Faludi, ed. 1973. *A reader in planning theory*. Oxford: Pergamon Press, 297–316.

Hajer, M. A. 1989. *City politics: hegemonic projects and discourses*. Aldershot, UK: Gower Publishing.

Harris, B. 1978a. A note on planning theory. *Environment and Planning A* 10: 221–24.

_____. 1978b. Planning theory: a response to Scott and Roweis. *Environment and Planning A* 10: 349–50.

Hart, D. A. 1987. Planning no-man's land?: Review of A. Faludi, Critical rationalism and planning methodology. *Built Environment* 12: 179–81.

Healey, P., G. McDougall, and M. J. Thomas. 1982. Introduction. In P. Healey, G. McDougall, and M. J. Thomas, eds., *Planning theory: prospects for the 1980s.* Oxford: Pergamon Press, 1–22.

Hoch, C. J. 1984. Doing good and being right. *Journal of the American Planning Association* 50: 335–45.

Kaufmann, J. L. 1981. Teaching planning ethics. *Journal of Planning Education and Research* 1: 29–35.

Kuhn, T. S. 1970 [1962]. *The structure of scientific revolutions.* Chicago: University of Chicago Press.

Lakatos, I. 1974. Falsification and the methodology of scientific research programmes. In I. Lakatos and A. Musgrave, eds., *Criticism and the growth of knowledge.* London: Cambridge University Press, 91–196.

Lindblom, C. E. 1959. The science of muddling through. *Public Administration Review* 19: 79–88; see also A. Faludi, ed. 1973. *A reader in planning theory.* Oxford: Pergamon Press, 151–69.

Lindblom, C. E. 1965. *The intelligence of democracy: decision making through mutual adjustment.* New York: Free Press.

Low, N. 1982. Beyond general systems theory: a constructivist perspective. *Urban Studies* 19: 221-233.

Mannheim, K. 1940. *Man and society in an age of reconstruction.* London: Kegan Paul.

March, J. G., and H. A. Simon. 1958. *Organizations.* New York, London: John Wiley.

Meyerson, M., and E. C. Banfield. 1955. *Politics, planning and the public interest: the case of public housing in Chicago.* New York: Free Press.

Needham, B. 1987. Review of A. Faludi, Critical rationalism and planning methodology. *Stedebouw en Volkshuisvesting* 68: 78-79.

Neufville, J. I. de. 1983. The doldrums of planning theory. *Journal of Planning Education and Research* 3: 35–45.

Parsons, T. 1949. *The structure of social action.* Glencoe, IL: Free Press.

Popper, K. R. 1959. *The logic of scientific discovery.* London: Hutchinson.

————. 1966 [1945]. *The open society and its enemies.* 2 vols. London: Routledge and Kegan Paul.

Postuma, R. 1991a. The National Plan: the taming of a runaway idea. In A. Faludi, ed., Fifty years of Dutch national physical planning (special issue). *Built Environment* 17: 14–22

_____. 1991b. Strijd om het streekplan: aan de wieg van de regional ruimtelijke planning (1920-1950), Publicatie 11 van de Werkgroep PSVA ingesteld door het NIROV. The Hague: NIROV.

Rein, M., and D. Schön. 1986. Frame-reflective policy discourse. *Beleidsanalyse* 15, 4: 4–18

Rittel, H. J. W., and M. M. Webber. 1973. Dilemmas of a general theory of planning. *Policy Sciences* 4: 155–69.

Ruijter, P. de. 1987. *Voor volkshuisvesting en stedebouw: Voorgeschiedenis, oprichting en programma van het Nederlands Instituut voor Volkshuisvesting en Stedebouw 1850-1940.* Utrecht: Uitgeverij Matrijs.

Scott, A.J. 1984. A comment on Taylor's procedural theory of planning. *Environment and Planning B: Planning and Design* 11: 127–129.

_____, and S. T. Roweis. 1977. Urban planning theory and practice: a reappraisal. *Environment and Planning A* 9: 1097–119.

_____, and S. T. Roweis. 1978. A note on planning theory: a response to Britton Harris. *Environment and Planning A* 10: 229–31.

Selznik, P. 1953 [1949]. *TVA and the grass roots: a study in the sociology of formal organizations.* Berkeley and Los Angeles, CA: University of California Press.

Simon, H. A. 1976 [1945]. *Administrative behavior: a study of decision-making processes in administrative organizations.* New York: Free Press.

Stegman, M. A. 1985. Paul Davidoff: symbol and substance. *Journal of the American Planning Association* 51: 375–77.

Taylor, N. 1984. A critique of materialist critiques of procedural planning theory. *Environment and Planning B: Planning and Design* 11: 103–126.

_____. 1985. The usefulness of a conceptual theory of rational planning: a reply to Scott's comment. *Environment and Planning B: Planning and Design* 12: 235–40.

Thomas, M. J. 1979. The procedural planning theory of A. Faludi. *Planning Outlook* 22: 72–6; see also: C. Paris, ed. 1982. *Critical readings in planning theory.* Oxford: Pergamon Press, 13–25.

Valk, A. J. van der. 1989. Amsterdam in aanleg: planvorming en dagelijks handelen 1850-1900. *Planologische Studies 8.* Amsterdam: University of Amsterdam.

Webber, M. M. 1978. A difference paradigm for planning. In R. W. Burchell and G. Sternlieb, eds., *Planning theory in the 1980s: a search for future directions.* New Brunswick, NJ: Center for Urban Policy Research, 151–62.

Webber, M. M. 1983. The myth of rationality: development planning reconsidered. *Environment and Planning B: Planning and Design* 10: 89–99.

Zonneveld, W. 1989. Conceptual complexes and shifts in post-war urban planning in the Netherlands. In A. Faludi, ed., Keeping the Netherlands in shape (special issue). *Built Environment* 15: 40–48.

_____. 1991a. Conceptvorming in de ruimtelijke planning: patronen en processen. *Planologische Studies No. 9A*. Amsterdam: University of Amsterdam.

_____. 1991b. Conceptvorming in de ruimtelijke planning: encyclopedie van planconcepten. *Planologische Studies No. 9B*. Amsterdam: University of Amsterdam.

Seymour J. Mandelbaum

5   *Open Moral Communities*

ARGUMENTS, IMAGES, AND STYLIZED MYTHS

Whether we are engaged in the affairs of a firm, a nation, or a family, when we try to persuade one another about the "right" course of action, we set our arguments within images of a community whose members are capable of listening to our words and understanding our experiences, our fears, and our aspirations. Only within a community that sustains, legitimates, and disciplines practices does it make sense to "talk that way," to believe that anything is worth knowing, or to invest our energies and passions in the expectation that our symbolic gestures will inform our deeds. Consenting, albeit often tacitly, to argue within an image, we create a world that shapes our speech.

The communities that infuse our arguments with meaning are always creations of our imagination. We represent a community in our minds, act, and then monitor and interpret the external response. Even in their most obscure and anonymous modes—even when they are infused with legends and fantasies—these communities of our minds are stamped with the marks of shared events, persons, and practices: familiar dramas in which we have cast ourselves or been cast. These grainy images, however, are subtly and, it often seems, secretly shaped by stylized myths capable of sustaining abstract and formal arguments that may persuade skeptics or strangers. The stylized myths that serve this shaping role are few in number, enormously influential, and remarkably stable over time.

An earlier version of this chapter appeared in *Society* 26, 1 (November/December 1988), Transaction Publishers, New Brunswick, New Jersey.

Without claiming to be exhaustive, I distinguish a set of three such stylized myths that appear in social settings across the globe. (The particular way I have represented the myths and my illustrations may be "Western" and predominantly "American," but the stylized forms are ubiquitous.) Each form sustains arguments in a particular mode and generates rhetorical difficulties that are the vulnerable side of its intellectual and emotional strength. Each also implicates the other two so that even when they explicitly conflict, the three seem to require one another. In large social settings —nations, corporations, cities, major religious groups—one stylized myth rarely appears without the others.

I have labelled these three myths as distinguishing moral communities as "contractual," "deep," or "open." I am principally concerned with the final form—the myth of "open moral communities"—but it is impossible to describe it effectively without setting it within the triad.

CONTRACTUAL MORAL COMMUNITIES

The contractual myth is grounded in two complementary ideas. The first holds that communities are legitimate only if they are initiated by a voluntary contract between their members. In the absence of an explicit agreement, a community is justified if the members voluntarily agree to its practices and relations—if they engage in a process of uncoerced negotiations. When explicit and tacit contracts conflict, they are encouraged to seek a "new covenant" consistent with respect for the authority of mutual promises.

The second idea at the core of the contractual myth responds to the problems attached to the notions of voluntary consent and the authority of promises. Every process of bargaining proceeds in a structure that constrains the choices of all of the participants. To those processes we bring experiences and dispositions we cannot freely jettison, reshaping ourselves so that we can "voluntarily" engage with others. The very acts of promising and depending on promises require background institutions that allow us to respond to unimagined contingencies, protect ourselves from destructive interpretations, and balance the claims of tacit and explicit contracts. Those institutions cannot, however, survive and function if they are at risk in every promise we make, every contract we write (Attiyah 1981).

Without bolstering the contractual myth, the first idea would set such a stringent standard that we would be forced to deny legitimacy to most communities. If, however, we back off from that counsel of perfection, the first idea does not help us judge how much "structure" (or "coercion") is acceptable before contractual arguments about collective choices lose their meaning. The second idea, central to much of what we think of as "modern" and "liberal" thought, provides that bolster. Imagine, we are told, that the biological organisms we identify as "human beings" are also moral entities endowed with elemental rights that precede any social arrangement or bargain. These pre-social Selves engage with one another in order to protect their lives and well-being or to achieve a goal that is unobtainable without the discipline of community and the order of settled institutions. This primal contract provides a frame within which it is possible to articulate standards for particular and necessarily flawed bargains.

Alasdair MacIntyre (1984) has written an obituary for the attempt—he calls it the "Enlightenment Project"—to construct a social order and to define a moral code within the contractual myth. The death notice is premature. The myth has passionate advocates and is so deeply embedded in the language of collective choice and individual rights that we can barely speak without employing its terms. In Charles Taylor's magisterial account *Sources of the Self: The Making of the Modern Identity* (1989), it appears at the core of much of what we mean by modernity; in James S. Coleman's *Foundations of Social Theory* (1990), it continues to define the central issues of the sociological imagination.

The power of the myth lies in the interplay of its two elements. Looked at from one direction, the ubiquitous use of the contract as a model of association is sustained and disciplined by a general social bargain. That bargain commands our attention to a superordinate community that must be maintained if the entire web of associational life is not to come unraveled. (If that community is threatened, "anarchy" takes hold and no particular contract—explicit or tacit—is safe.)

Looked at from the other direction, the image of the uncoerced contract as a ubiquitous social form disciplines our representations of the general arrangement. The conditions in which the general contract was (or might be) struck cannot violate our ordinary conceptions of voluntary bargains: signatures elicited with a machine gun or with fraudulent representations are not binding (Gauthier 1990).

The discursive forms of the contractual myth are so dense, so pervasive, and so attached to experience (even children enter into contracts with their teachers) that we often forget that we are dealing with stylized images rather than ethnographic descriptions. The individuals we observe on the street, in legislative halls, and in our bedrooms are protean bundles of attributes. Even those who pride themselves on the constancy of their character appropriately match their face and speech to local circumstances. The Self can never be observed as a timeless essence outside of a particular context. When we posit such an essence within the myth in order to establish the bases of a general contract, we must imagine human beings in a way that violates our deepest sense of them as inevitably social. They are without gender or class or language. Their behavior and character warrant neither merit nor stigma (Sandel 1982). If we respond to this difficulty by imputing a generalized culture to the mythic founders, then we are bound to justify its terms in what promises to be an infinite regress leading from one layer of belief and practice to the one below (Rawls 1993, 13).

In the same way, the mythic image of contractual relations—though it has the feel of everyday experience—is a highly stylized expression of a complex social act. Within the myth, the structure of both overt and tacit bargaining processes—unequal power, the language we employ, the background institutions—are taints on voluntarism and require a normative response if contracts are to legitimate collective choices. Outside that mythic form, the taints are often represented as vital elements of the social order. They command our attention while contracts are seen as expressions of comity. In the common, but not fully adequate, spatial metaphor: Our mutual promises are grounded in community rather than vice versa.

DEEP MORAL COMMUNITIES

The myth of deep community—the second in the group of three— treats all human beings as social. Only in horrific fantasies are they wholly stripped of their communal identities. The counterpart to the image of the Contract is an insistence that arguments about both personal and collective choices fit within the discursive forms of a community that engages its members in an integrated view of their place in the cosmos, their history, their culture, and the meaning of personal experiences. Practices in overtly distinctive domains—factory, family, mosque, club—are represented as part of a single fabric so that a violation in one area endangers the entire skein. With or without a theistic claim, the ordinary events of daily life, the protocols of social relations, and the cycles of the natural order are invested with a sacred meaning. The most passionate arguments often deal with the conditions of entry, the punishment and even exclusion of violators, and the interpretation of apostasy.

The myth of deep community may seem the stuff of anthropology: tales told of little communities, primitive peoples and the insular groups who resist the blandishments of modernity. Members of complex civilizations, which confront cultural conflicts both inside and outside their borders, also speak, however, of deep and extensive mutual obligations, a shared history, and a sacred ethical code. The intellectual advocates of nations and empires as moral entities have often represented them as communities whose claims to superordinate authority—above family, religion, locality, or clan—rest on the shared identity of a "people." Neighborhood associations, large corporations, and suburban churches in American cities may in a similar way present themselves as extensive (even if not all-embracing) moral entities.

Rationality within the contractual myths means (in one of its many aspects) that collective choices accurately express personal preferences (Hardin 1988). The myth of deep moral communities, in contrast, is centered in the range and coherence of the moral order. To be "rational" means to fit within that order and to respect it (Horkheimer 1984; MacIntyre 1988; Nozick 1993). Contracts are rife but, as I have already suggested, they express rather than create communal orders.

Both on the ground and in their mythic representations, deep communities are marked by individual deviance, group differences, social conflict, and the stress of collective decision making. (They are in and of the world of human beings, not angels.) In the contractual myth, the processes of control, management, and planning that prevent variety and conflict from "getting out of hand" are often treated with suspicion, tested critically against standards of voluntarism. The demonstration that a "way of life" has been designed by one group to control another strips the supposed contract of its mantle of legitimacy.

In contrast, arguments set within a deep myth characteristically assume that true belief and correct practice must be designed and maintained; that voluntary recruits and children must be socialized so that they come to believe that "Japan," "America," or "General Motors" is a deep community that defines and nourishes them. Authority is not the danger but primitivism and antinomianism. One devalues current practices and historical experience by calling the community back to its origins; the other circumvents authority and narrows its domain.

The myths of deep and of contractual communities are related in complex and unexpected ways. At one level, they appear simply to compete. From the perspective of deep communities, the contractual myth seems idolatrous and shrill (readily enlisted in the service of ethically distorted and outrageous judgments) or, at the other extreme, banal and self-serving. If we specify the environmental constraints appropriately, even the most complex social arrangements may be represented as products of a sequence of contractual exchanges between (superficially) rational actors. Seen from the other bank, talk of deep and sacred obligations is often both obscure and deliberately obscurantist.

At a more profound level, the two myths depend upon and merge into one another. The voluntarism, the suspicion of coercion, and the notion of a radically free Self that mark the contractual myth have been repeatedly forged in the search for respite from the violent clash of deep claims as if only an uncoerced social compact could establish peace and, paradoxically, create a virtuous commonwealth that would (in various times and places) serve Muslim and Hindu, Catholic and Protestant, Jew and Greek, or Puritan and Friend. Inevitably, the definition of that commonwealth—including the uses and limits of "tolerance"—were shaped by the practices of the deep communities that gave it birth; the character of the deep communities by the ways in which the contractual alternatives were represented.

OPEN MORAL COMMUNITIES

I am tempted to describe the myth of open moral communities—the principal subject of this chapter—as lying between the other two. I have not, however, established much room in the middle ground. When the first two myths compete, they often appear to drive out any tepid alternatives. If you reject what George Parkin Grant (in a critique of John Rawls) calls "English-speaking justice," then the coherent options appear to be the deep agreements expressed by one of the great religious faiths (1985). Any other version of communitarianism seems pale by comparison. When they are not competitive but complementary—when we embed one myth in the other or shift back and forth between them—then the middle ground is similarly eroded.

The appropriate spatial metaphor locates the myth of open moral communities as suffused through the more familiar forms of deeply consensual or contractual justifications of the social order. Consider the simple question: "Where are you from?" Those of us who have moved from one city to the next know that the answer expresses a morally significant choice. We can respond with the name of the place in which we were born, in which we were raised, or in which we currently reside. In some settings, that is all that is called for or all that we are willing to offer. In its most compelling version, however, the question asks for marks of identity and affiliation: "I was born in Chicago but I am from New York," or " I'm from Calcutta though I have lived in Delhi for a long time."

What are the implications of a voluntary act of affiliation with a place? What rights are implied? What obligations?

Even the most ardent civic booster (eager to provide maximal answers) will understand that the communities implied by the terms of these questions engage us only partially. We are simultaneously members of many communities and assess the implications of affiliation with one or another by locating it within the dense pattern of the entire set.

The myth of deep moral communities represents this pattern as a jigsaw puzzle in which each association has its place within a relatively closed society. Temporary confusions or uncertainties about the placement of a particular piece will be resolved as the pieces are meshed in a uniquely appropriate order. In a jigsaw puzzle, each community—each nation, city, neighbor, family, firm, and church—would create a distinctive ethical domain. When we were undecided as to whether one set of obligations or another applied to a particular issue, we would evoke a rank order: nation over family, family over firm, firm over city. Deep communities may be pluralistic on the ground, but in the normative world of myths, their major institutions "fit together into one unified system of social cooperation from one generation to the next" (Rawls 1993, 11).

The myth of open moral communities denies the jigsaw image and the rhetorical insistence on "fit" and "fabric." In the open myth, the boundaries of the total "society" are contested and emergent so that we cannot securely set the external straight pieces in place before we begin to fill in the pattern. We are forced to link the pieces in order to represent the boundaries. That would be difficult enough with an ordinary puzzle, but in the open myth, some of the elements are overlapping, many are conflicting, and others are only loosely coupled so that the principle of "fit" and the geometry of the pattern are obscure. The puzzle, in its mysterious ways, must even accommodate the strange communion of long-term adversaries whose identities (shaped by their battles) come to depend upon one another. We move within this complex pattern, now emphasizing one group of claims and then another, leaving one identity and adopting a new one, without usually encountering a charge of apostasy. The possibility that its members will exit is immanent in every community. Images of routes of movement between communities and free spaces in which we can be anonymous or unidentified without being stigmatized sustain the openness of the entire structure.

The openness of the field to movement and the paradoxical freedom in the recognition of conflicting moral claims do not imply a completely voluntaristic order. Our movements are constrained and our characters shaped by practices that are not completely of our own making or choice. Even in a temporary community in which I am engaged, I can speak sensibly only if I acknowledge the words of my colleagues and respond to them. The dense fabric of overlapping communities as it appears in this mythic representation is subject to a flow of criticism and conflict that is so pervasive that it is sensibly understood as part of the internal structure of the stylized image rather than as an external critique. The CEO of a large corporation may, for example, want to encourage employee identification with small units while retaining a sense that every part of the firm is a cog in a single machine. The employees, for their part, may resent the folks upstairs who periodically intrude into the vital community of co-workers. Their firm is a field: out of one, an intractably messy many. In the same way, nation-builders may denigrate "tribalism" only to find that their attack generates a defensive though ambivalent reaction. "Thus egalitarian, nationalistic ideologies," Peter Marris observes, "generate tensions which they cannot handle, unless they also embody their apparent contradiction" (1986, 71).

The stylized myth of communal openness allows us to navigate within a field of communities without either minimizing the claims upon us or diminishing them as inferior to those of a "real" community. They do not, however, provide a simple standard—comparable to a contract or an inte-grated moral order—that would cogently shape and discipline our speech within this myth. How should we argue when we represent ourselves as belonging simultaneously to an array of moral communities (Galston 1991, 22–41)?

The myth of deep communities points to a shared lexicon that orga-nizes arguments and the worlds they make, a shared understanding even of speech differences. The prince and the pauper, the theologian and the peasant, may attribute significantly different shades of meaning to the same terms. (They certainly pronounce them differently!) The linguistic variety integrated into social roles enables deep communities to act collectively by providing markers of authority and allowing vulgar and elite perspectives to coexist. Both are protected by acknowledged differences.

The contractual myth does not elicit a comparable imagery of social differences and of language. The parties to the general social contract are impelled by powerful requirements, such as the incipient threat of warfare or the search for justice, that are not inflected by shades of competing mean-ings. (Or, at least, the philosophers have failed to describe these inflections.) The parties to ordinary contracts may and often do mistake each other's words, but in the event of a dispute, background institutions impose con-ventional meanings. If misunderstanding is endemic, then the entire con-tractual structure as the foundation of a moral order collapses.

The myth of open moral communities sets the problem in a quite dif-ferent light. If communities overlap and if they are located in a shifting and amorphous field, then it follows that they cannot fully control their own discursive order. The myth transforms our perception of communicative failure into a measure of the intrinsic (and often deeply valued) structure of our worlds. Even intense communities cannot fully control their own conversational forms. Parents and children living in a complex communal field find that words are polymorphic: They mean different things to different people and assume varied forms as contexts shift. In large (and perhaps less intense) communities—cities, labor unions, neighborhoods, professional associations—ambiguity of speech and indeterminacy of interpretation are ubiquitous. Asked to choose a mix of "guns" and "butter" in the classic image of policy analysts, the myth of moral openness encourages us to ask after the meaning of the terms and the social context in which the balance would be struck. Absent a lexicon and a location, we should—within the myth—refuse to choose.

Lexical variety and polymorphism structure the ways we argue about means as well as ends. Consensual instrumental knowledge depends upon stable conceptions of the forms employed to describe our actions, the settings in which we are engaged, and the valued outcomes of our behavior. If our descriptive protocols are ambiguous and our interpretations embedded in conflict, then we are likely to argue over means as well as ends. The overtly simple designation of one bundle of technologies as more "efficient" than another becomes a complex process of bargaining among the advocates of rival measures of both inputs and outputs. Again, absent a lexicon and a location, we should—within the myth—refuse to choose.

That rule of refusal and the premises upon which it rests provide a point of departure for my search for rhetorical forms appropriate to the myth of moral openness. They also articulate a threat. Suppose the rule is crudely summarized as: "All social knowledge and all choices are political." If that is the case, must we abandon all faith in the dream of a consensual social knowledge as the working clay of collective choices? How do we agree on what we "know" within the myth of open moral communities? How do we sustain a bargaining process that results in a workable public discursive order? What are the institutional and rhetorical forms of this bargaining?

KNOWING AND REPAIRING THE WORLD

The enterprise of theorizing about planning as it is represented in this volume fits within a tradition of dreaming about the possibilities of knowledge that is very old and that has appeared (from time to time and in different accents and modes) in virtually every corner of the globe. Two aspirations are coupled in the dream of knowledge. The first asserts that it is possible to develop a shared understanding of the social world; the second, that the understanding will support a consensual repair of that world.

That cryptic summary does not, of course, capture the complexity, conflicts, and subtleties of the communities that have pursued the dream—as the chapters in this section should abundantly attest. Some of the dreamers have radically distinguished between the first and the second aspirations: We may be able to know the past, but we cannot pretend to know a future that as yet lies outside the world of fact. Others have turned that proposition on its head: We cannot pretend to know the past until we can forecast the future with confidence and shape it with the tools of a robust science. (A small voice replies with incredulity: How can we forecast a future that we are capable of changing?)

The aspiration to control change is particularly contentious. (George Orwell's *1984* [1949] and Karl Popper's *The Open Society and Its Enemies* [1945] hover over the contemporary discussions.) For some, the dream has been confined to the intellectual technologies of instrumental planning and does not extend to objectives and values that are likely to remain intractably and appropriately varied. We may expect to agree on the ways of minimizing travel costs in a complex network, controlling inflation, reducing pollution, or teaching reading. There is no prospect, however, of consensually establishing an ethically compelling level or distribution of travel costs, inflation, pollution, or reading competence.

Others have been more ambitious. They have seen fact, value, and method as intertwined. If we believe that we can develop a science of planning (or "repair") then, at the very least, it follows that some social forms are ethically impossible or, more classically phrased, "irrational." "Racism," for example, may violate what we securely "know" about human differences; coercive persuasion may violate our commitment to the methods of scientific inquiry. The dreamers—as is to be expected—have argued among themselves: How large is the set of excluded forms? What is left when the excluded forms are deleted? Are there ethically compelling positive mandates that are attached to the dream of knowledge?

MYTHS AND DREAMS

The enterprise of dreaming about knowledge—including all of these arguments—sustains the mythic forms of both deep and contractual communities. Within both myths, it is essential that in principle a community should be capable of developing a common understanding of both its internally defining elements and its relations with the external environment. Even when—on the ground—the common understanding is contested and the dreamers are controversial, there is no essential conflict between the aspirations articulated in those myths and in that dream.

In contrast, the myth of open moral communities poses an essential threat to the dream. In principle and in practice, a field of communities without a settled boundary and with overlapping memberships may not be able to create a consensual body of knowledge about itself and about its multiple environments. The same idea reversed: The notion that social knowledge can be formulated in a coherent synthetic theory threatens the credibility of the myth. If we are capable of understanding each other consensually, why can we not eliminate the conflicts and the disconcerting babble that characterize the field?

My answer to that question, simply stated, is: "We are not capable." Rather than ruing that failure, I embrace it. Only when we abandon the notion of a consensual social knowledge can we fully accept that we live in worlds in which conflicting communal myths sustain and re-create one another. Our instrumental judgments are intractably ambiguous and dilemmatic, our plainest words subject to diverse interpretations.

Every association that imagines itself as a deep community must develop a shared conception of its history and an instrumental technology to control its future. It must know enough of the world outside its borders to respond effectively to threats, to elicit the external resources it may require, and to assess its obligations to strangers. Its ethical discourse must allow it to address and tame the variety of normative claims it characteristically encounters among its members and in the outer world.

Some small communities address these tasks by insulating their members from external contacts and socializing them intensely. Larger and less insular communities that wrap themselves in the mantle of a deep moral order—whether that of a "way of life," a collective mission, or a religious tradition—have characteristically endorsed and promoted the dream of knowledge. The promoters have, of course, sometimes been disappointed by their creations. As epistemic communities, in their various forms and elements, develop their own internal norms and disciplines, they characteristically become more difficult to control externally. In a play repeated many times in different costumes and accents, both secular and religious regimes, gored by the scholars whom they have appointed and trusted, come to wonder about these new guardians. Communities dedicated to writing produce a corpus of texts that outsiders often find overwhelming and impenetrable. Inside critics, in a complementary way, lament that their colleagues have become so self-absorbed that the links between knowledge and the social order are invisible or distorted.

The arguments over these issues, familiar in our own day but repeated many times in the past, only highlight the intensity of the connection between the dream of consensual social knowledge and the myth of deep communities. If the dream were an indulgence, there would be no passion for the indictment of failure.

There is an equally intense connection between the contractual myth and the dream of knowledge, but it characteristically takes a quite different form. While a concern with Contract as the basis of social order commands attention to the historical record of contractual engagements, the historicist regard for the fabric of a culture is missing. The contractual myth replaces it with an intellectual strategy that often treats the historical record as imperfect and distracting. In order to free the world from the taint of coercion, we must perfect it in our minds, peering over the obscuring wall of current conditions to explore what only might have been.

There is no conventional name for this perfectionist strategy, but it is ubiquitous. The contractual myth requires that we repeatedly assess the legitimacy of tacit agreements. How, we must ask, would we arrange our collective affairs if we were not constrained by our ignorance and fear, if we were not intimidated by power and the difficulties of replacing one set of social forms with another? Will this or that arrangement, interpreted as a series of contractual bargains, meet the standards set by those idealizations? The strong presence of Michel Foucault and Jürgen Habermas in this volume is testimony to the power of these questions.

When these questions are addressed strictly within the terms of the stylized contractual myth—as, for example, in welfare economics and the theory of public choice—they demand a high level of artistic craft, carefully adjusting assumptions about the nature of the Self and the terms of engagement. The terms of legitimate bargains are constructed on the strongly determinative foundations of a normatively compelling but unobservable Self (Frohock 1987). The forms and language of knowledge become, in effect, ways of elaborating upon the primal notion of Contract.

The same sensibility appears repeatedly in a more empirical and less formal vein that accepts some but not all of the imperfections of the world. Suppose we assume that in every setting some (imperfect) background arrangements are not amenable to change. All we can do is attempt to tease from the historical record an assessment of the differences between arrangements. Which enhance freely chosen bargains and which discourage them? What is the best we can do within a particular set of constraints? Within the world of these questions and the answers we provide, the contractual myth is sustained by its elaboration in the language of science and the dream of social knowledge.

The connection between myth and dream is particularly intense when the attempt to reduce or eliminate the taint of coercion is morally centered in the dream. We may employ the most imaginative thought experiments to remove the taint of coercion from imperfect social relations by an act of surgical analysis. It is unlikely, however, that we will have similar success in a world in which the players are real men and women interacting with one another rather than ethereal parties to an abstract game. Suppose, however, that a consensual knowledge of the world as seen from the myth requires a method (and a community of votaries) that is uniquely open to experiment and inquiry (Gouldner 1979). The practices of that community of inquirers, as John Dewey (1916) imagined them, would then approximate the ideal of the uncoerced agreement. Social practices would be tested against the standards of this community: Do they sustain experimentation and error-correcting inquiry? Do they engender and maintain imperfections in information that generate inefficient instrumental choices and unstable bargains? Do the rules that govern the relations between organizations encourage truth-telling or strategic bluffing? Subjected to these tests, over time only liberal contractual societies could sustain the experimental temper. The experimental temper given free rein would sustain only liberal contractual societies.

A FABLE

The notion that we argue within a field of overlapping and open communities speaks to a ubiquitous fact and to a common practice. The myth itself, however, lacks a grand tradition. I am reluctant, therefore, to impute to the myth—as person or as a canonical series of texts—a particular attitude to the dream of knowledge. Instead, I have constructed a fable that allows me to describe how the dream fares when it confronts overlapping communities without a fixed collective boundary, a uniquely specified environment, or the mooring provided by the notions of either moral integration or Contract.

Suppose (fictionalizing the activities of my colleagues) that a band of planning theoreticians working within a field of overlapping communities, captivated by the dream of knowledge, seeks to develop a theory of social guidance that would be both complete and general. (I could tell an identical story as a quest for a social theory intended to explain the past rather than to shape the future. By any other name or focus, the lesson of the tale would be the same.)

In principle, the core of such a theory is not particularly difficult to construct. (At least it is no harder than that in any other social field.) The core should include relatively few elements and not present massive problems of organization, data quality, or information storage and retrieval.

The difficulties appear when the theorists in my fable step outside the core in order to subject it to empirical testing and revision. (My fable is only a pleasant fiction but theories, after all, are not to be simply judged on their aesthetic appeal or internal logic. They must work.) As they step outside the core, the theorists—as I have imagined their ambitious goals—face an enormous array of partially formed generalizations and ideographic accounts of planning practice. Will they be able to bring their core to bear upon this array, first organizing it in a compelling way into statements of the potential relationships between the attributes of each planning process (or combinations of processes), the settings in which they operate, and valued outcomes, and then testing those statements empirically? If we seek justice, defined in one or another way, how should we plan in this or that circumstance? If we plan in a particular way, what sort of justice (or injustice) will result? What about the relationship between process and setting when effectiveness, stability, coherence, efficiency, or beauty is the valued outcome?

Will the theorists succeed in this enterprise? Will they be able to develop and refine a theory that will allow them to inspect any list of assertions about the relationships between processes, settings, and outcomes, and then accurately to predict those that will survive both historical and practice tests—that will make sense of the past and guide the future?

Within the terms of the characters and plot of the myth of an open field, I think there are only two credible answers to those queries, only two possible conclusions to the fable. If I assign vast resources and heroic discipline to my theorists, they will succeed in their labors although the intellectual tools they create are likely to be unusable. If I am more limited and more realistic in my assignment of resources or if I am more insistent on practicality, they will fail.

A general theory of planning must generate a set of propositions that relates all the necessary categories of processes, settings, and outcomes. Imagine these propositions arrayed in a table in which the columns are designated as types of planning processes, the rows as settings. Outcome measures appear in the cells. There may be many such tables arrayed in a hierarchical order. The first, or prime, table summarizes the most general empirical propositions that flow from the core of the theory. It includes only those descriptors that cannot be derived from some other attribute.

The canon of descriptors for the prime table cannot be settled through formal literary or linguistic analysis. We cannot closely read a set of texts, compare usage and interpretations, and know confidently that terms derive from one another. Setting the canon and adjusting it requires that we leap into the act of inquiry directly, assessing the performance of symbolic indicators and then circling back to adjust the way we describe processes, settings, and outcomes.

With enormous resources and discipline far exceeding any real-world epistemic community, my fabled theoreticians could maintain an archive of tables and propositions, a record of research and of debates over contested measures. Noting an anomalous finding, a game played against yesterday's knowledge or a lacuna in the information system, they could commission studies, lexical revisions, and (most seriously) the elaboration of alternative theoretical cores. The catalogue of the archive, far more elaborate than any conventional information system, would update the tables and core options, signal problematic findings, and lead users to alternative ways of framing issues or interpreting evidence.

This mythical archive is an information scientist's response to Jorge Luis Borges's (1964) nightmare of a library that includes all human knowledge but whose order passes human understanding. For ordinary users, however, the differences would be trivial. When the theoreticians returned to their communities for a short visit (the work of theory building would not allow a protracted absence), the home folk might well wonder what they had wrought. Would any but the builders move easily through the system? Would engagement in the archive sophisticate a reader's sense of the complexity of the world but reduce his or her capacity for decisive action? Finally (and perhaps most decisively), had the analysts forgotten the language, the experiential wisdom, and the purposes of the communities from which they had come?

Suppose—to continue the fable for just a little while longer—that the communities rejected the archive and sent the analysts back to work with new and more stringent design criteria: In order to be useful, they insist, the prime table must be brief, and it must be neutral.

The criterion of brevity is simple enough to understand. If the core of a theory cannot generate a powerful but relatively short set of general propositions, the theory is likely to be too complex to use and very expensive to maintain. A long prime table would enter again into the world of the capacious but daunting archive.

The neutral criterion may seem less obvious, but it flows directly from the conception of the open field. Suppose a particularly creative scientist proposed an imaginative core theory and a prime table brief enough to be tested and refined within the resources of the group. The brevity would be aesthetically pleasing but inadequate if the table failed to address four matters that would be critical to the communities. First, it would have to include the various terms in which each of them described processes, settings, or outcomes, or it would have to justify the appropriate location of the terms in secondary tables. To ignore the words of a community would be to devalue its identity and the rules it used to make sense of its moral universe.

Second, beyond attending to their lexicons, communities (as I have imagined them in this fable) would be concerned with the balance of the prime table. Suppose, for example, that the theoreticians, sketching with very broad strokes, assigned all planning processes to a single continuum from "market" to "hierarchy." Such a canon for the description of processes would be general but vulnerable to fair complaints that it biased the potential products of research by structuring the dimensions of relevant settings and outcomes. Alternative descriptors focusing attention in quite different ways (with different biases) would be necessary to balance the normative implications of the elegant market-hierarchy continuum.

Third, the theorists would have to assure that the table was neutral in regard to the contested boundaries of individual communities and of the field itself. (The open myth, remember, does not describe a jigsaw puzzle.) Within that polymorphic geography, a neutral table would have to address the attributes of individual communities and the field in which they were embedded since, presumably, the dynamics of planning are influenced by the pattern of overlap, the costs of movement from one communion to another, and the ways of resolving disputes between communities and within them.

Finally—to add to the complexity of that geography—the table would have to be neutral in regard to the contested world of moral objects. Imagine two communities with overlapping but not wholly identical memberships. Some members of the first community will treat everyone in the second community as "strangers" potentially, but not certainly, meriting respect as "moral objects." Others in the first community, however, will treat members of the second as fellow citizens, "moral subjects" engaged in a web of obligations, rights, and disciplines. The theorists must find a way of representing these differences if the prime table and those that flow from it are to be regarded as neutral.

A table would be complete and neutral when no additional adjustments were necessary to satisfy any community. That is, however, a demanding criterion. Presumably, every community in this fabled world would come to understand itself and the field in new ways through the process of evaluating the work of the theoreticians. Propositions that were satisfying at one stage of the process may seem either irrelevant or biased as communities changed their own images of the geography of the field. Indeed, they might even come to bargain with the theorists to get the best possible deal in the construction of theory. (Many theorists will be amused by this possibility: Would that communities cared so much for our labors! Perhaps, however, the fabled contingency is not so outrageous. In Eastern Europe and the areas of the former Soviet Union, debates over markets engage theorists and politicians in a passionate conversation that is similar to the critique sketched in my account.)

The easiest way to meet the criterion of neutrality would, of course, be to add descriptors to the prime table until the fund of complaints was exhausted. Such a procedure would quickly violate the criterion of brevity, making it impossible for the theorists to avoid the complexity of the clumsy archive. The task would be more manageable if the theorists could throw out ignorant or inappropriate objections. They would be empowered to turn away a complainant who did not understand the canon, could not demonstrate bias, or failed to appreciate the necessity for a hierarchy of descriptors.

Even bolstered by such authority, brevity would not survive. Suppose, for example, that the theorists, acting as a panel of judges, faced a community in which differences in language or dialect were laden with social and cultural meaning: One group spoke the parole of subjects, the other of colonizers; one of wealth, the other of poverty; one of tradition, the other of faraway cosmopolitan centers. A complainant insists that while terms may appear to outsiders to carry identical meanings, native speakers understand that their connotations are distinct and the moral implications of the differences profound. Could the judges legitimately dismiss this complaint as unfounded? Could they possibly meet the criteria of brevity and neutrality the moment they entered the world of linguistic variety and power? Would they not be forced to turn again into the archival labyrinth, with or without the guiding discipline of a magnificent information system?

PUBLIC ORDERS

End of fable! If we represent the world as a field of overlapping, open communities and seek a moral order within that framework, we cannot construct a consensual body of social theory—whether directed to the past or the future. The classic literary form I imposed on the theorists of the fable—a simple core amplified in a complete hierarchical set of empirical propositions—is never realized and rarely attempted. Because the theorizing enterprise within the myth of open moral communities is inevitably so partial and so episodic, it cannot soar above the world it describes and expect to shape it decisively.

That is not a terrible failing and need not be corrected. No community—at least none I know—guides collective choices by relying in any direct or simple way upon the theories of formal social science. Even overtly straightforward assertions of "fact" enter into policy arguments as value-laden expressions of competing images of the world and of the possibilities of action. Causal propositions, models and theories—the high talk of serious scholarship and of my fable—form a glow of often ambiguous enlightenment-suffusing debate and practice without dominating them (Lindblom and Cohen 1976). The enlightenment establishes or, more modestly, confirms the salience of tentative explanations and hypotheses embedded in practice. It rarely, however, penetrates deeply enough into the foundations of belief to stigmatize ideas effectively as outside the domain of justifiable speech or action.

The high talk of scholarship appears within the myth of open moral communities as part of a public symbolic order—conventions of speech that sustain the belief that we understand each other, our collective actions, and the world around us. Such orders are dominated by the structures of ordinary speech, a repertoire of common metaphors, and a fund of archetypal stories (such as biblical accounts and Greek myths) that both explain behavior and assert the comforting continuity of past and future. This dense mass of conventions is difficult to manipulate directly—indeed, it is remarkably resilient in the face of external assaults—but it is not impervious to change.

The language of formal social inquiry is *in* but not quite *of* this dense order. At one level, if you scratch the overtly severe and tightly specified talk of any of the epistemic communities that dream of knowledge, you discover a layer of metaphoric speech that elicits assent because it is attached to widely shared conceptions of the world whose stability depends, at least in part, upon their ambiguity. We could barely speak if we were forced to explicate each metaphor and address every variant of meaning in describing "mechanical" and "organic" institutions, the "diffusion" of ideas, the "development" of a labor "force," or the "structure" of an economy (McCloskey 1985). We can—and often do—manage to argue about collective decisions without ever defining terms or enumerating those which fit into the categories we have created. We explain phenomena, judge the parties, and articulate who we are in relation to them, but we do not specify our meanings, and we do not count.

At another level, however, the symbolic order of the dreamers has a distinctive quality that separates it from the conventions of ordinary speech and cultural tradition. It is both peculiarly plastic and peculiarly subject to frequent and overt, although hardly uncoerced, negotiations creating public orders that operationalize meanings and measure the world. Under most circumstances, we inherit those orders and treat them casually as if they were as natural as common speech. If we are arguing about employment in the United States, for example, we are bound by fragile chains to the terms set by the Bureau of Labor Statistics. We may choose to break from those terms (challenging, for example, the Bureau's definition of the labor force and its treatment of discouraged workers), but we do so at the risk of falling into the free form of unspecified argumentation.

Public orders appear both within and between communities. In a city, a university, a labor union, or a business firm, for example, accounting procedures provide a way of describing costs and resources, allowing participants in these communities to debate policy options without simultaneously arguing over the framing protocols. The internal accounting order is disciplined by general norms that allow external supervision and support the flow of funds between communities. When the intentions and forms of the two orders conflict, communities often adopt multiple "books"— one serving external requirements and the other capturing internal understandings of goals, costs, and resources. In open moral communities, participants must repeatedly struggle to define the relationship between conflicting modes of speech. Should a school be run like a business? Does productivity mean the same thing in every setting? If we have agreed in political discussions to designate a group as "victims" who are immune from blame, are we required to abide by that convention everywhere? Can people be trusted if they fail to observe the public orders of particular settings even at the cost of honesty? What are the limits of mature hypocrisy?

The character of these public orders is set both in explicit negotiations and in tacit agreements struck during intense periods of argument. Beyond their generative moment, orders are also constantly disciplined by the threat of exit. If a great many participants in debate reject a set of concepts and measures in order to express their values and images of the world, then the bridge of convention is weakened even if it does not fall. The number of "books" is multiplied, and sincere assent is replaced by ritualistic obeisance. People routinely speak ironically, signaling that words are not what they seem (Booth 1979). Bridgekeepers—if they are alert and caring—respond to the decay of terms and the disaffection from measures with new organizing forms: The BLS creates a new category of discouraged workers, the Census Bureau revises the definition of metropolitan areas, health officials broaden their notions of illness to include chronic as well as acute conditions.

In every open field, public orders are also disciplined and justified by tests of efficacy. We note with relief that an agreement to bound an issue in a particular way breaks a "logjam." This may not make sense to you, we explain to a skeptic, but it "works" for us. Don't scratch at that agreement, we warn critical interlopers. It may not be perfect, but it keeps us together.

Procedural theories of social guidance—the subject of my extended fable—enter directly into these public orders. In various settings, we debate whether we should think of a problem within the framework of market adjustments or of public regulation and development. We agree to designate some arrangements as "centralized" or "decentralized" and then proceed from there to argue over alternative designs. We assume that we can measure "power" and operationalize "accountability" so that we need not stumble over fundamental meanings as we rank and blame. We put aside our philosophic quarrels over the meaning of justice and insist that we all want public actions to be "equitable" as if it were impossible to imagine or to speak otherwise.

Active practitioners in the guidance professions—planners, managers, policy analysts, and the like—are often ambivalent toward this subtle penetration of the language of theory into everyday practice. On the one side, they are engaged by their obligations to particular communities and with the ways in which those communities define and deal with problems. The professionals share with their communal colleagues an understandable skepticism about anyone who asserts that "local" practices can be understood—let alone corrected—by outsiders who arrogate authority to themselves in the name of theory.

On the other side of the ambivalence, the professionals themselves assume that their claims to respect rest upon the foundations of theory. Without theory, they are bound into the local orders and cannot move from one community to another in order to plan, manage, or analyze; without theory, they are not a community. If theory fails them—if the library is too complex for ordinary use, if theorists speak incomprehensibly, or appear to be involved in themselves—then the practitioners feel neglected and threatened. They seek a reorientation of theorizing toward practice and a restoration of the faith that ultimately all differences can be reconciled through rational argument and scientific inquiry.

The myth of open moral communities suggests a quite different role for formal procedural theory and theorizing. In the face of contested words, deliberate ambiguity, and resistance to control, their limits are severe, their internal complexities, profound. The set of tables imagined in the fable defies the best ordering temperaments. Indeed, imaginative synoptic efforts always seem to suggest possibilities that lie just outside their scope. Theorizing communities must necessarily be self-concerned if they are to mobilize and discipline the effort required to construct even portions of the tables. The communities' influence on practice is mediated through necessarily imperfect public orders and principles.

Communities of theorists and the enterprise of thinking about things in general operate within the field of moral communities as temporary settings for escape from conventional practices and as a resource in times of particular confusion. If ordinary terms—"justice," "community," "efficiency"—have become so hollow that they interfere with conversation, formal theorizing provides a way of clearing the terrain and establishing a new set of meanings. If GOSPLAN collapses, theorizing provides a newly charged image of the Market as a substitute. If narrow contingency tables— *in case of this, do that*—are framed oppressively, theorizing suggests alternative frames.

The image of theorizing communities as temporary and necessarily flawed settings for escape is not as grand as the vision of the scientific method as the cornerstone of a liberal society. It cannot match the soaring conception of Marxism as a theory of deep moral integration. The ironic rhetoric of public orders that are not quite what they seem is not as heroic as the perfected contract freed of coercion. It does, however, accommodate the dream of social knowledge to an intractable and (for me) valued social pluralism.

REFERENCES

Attiyah, P. S. 1981. *Promises, morals and law.* Oxford: Oxford University Press.

Booth, W. C. 1979. *A rhetoric of irony.* Chicago: University of Chicago Press.

Borges, J. L. 1964. The library of Babel. *Labyrinths: selected stories and other writings.* New York: New Directions. pp. 51–58.

Coleman, J. S. 1990. *Foundations of social theory.* Cambridge: Harvard University Press.

Dewey, J. 1916. *Democracy and education: an introduction to the philosophy of education.* Reprint, New York: Macmillan, 1953.

Frohock, F. 1987. *Rational association.* Syracuse. NY: Syracuse University Press.

Galston, W.A., 1991. *Liberal purposes: goods, virtues, and diversity in the liberal state.* Cambridge: Cambridge University Press.

Gauthier, D. P. 1990. *Moral dealing: contract, ethics and reason.* Ithaca, NY: Cornell University Press.

Gouldner, A. W. 1979. *The future of intellectuals and the rise of the new class: a frame of reference, theses, conjectures, arguments, and an historical perspective on the role of intellectuals and the intelligentsia in the international class contest of the modern era.* New York: Seabury Press.

Grant, G. P. 1985. *English-speaking justice.* Notre Dame, IN: Notre Dame University Press.

Hardin, R. 1988. *Morality within the limits of reason.* Chicago: University of Chicago Press.

Horkheimer, M. 1984. *Eclipse of reason.* New York: Continuum.

Lindblom, C. E., and D. K. Cohen. 1976. *Usable knowledge: social science and social problem solving.* New Haven, CT: Yale University Press.

MacIntyre, A. 1984. *After virtue.* 2d. ed. Notre Dame, IN: Notre Dame University Press.

_____. 1988. *Whose justice? which rationality?* Notre Dame, IN: Notre Dame University Press.

McCloskey, D. N., 1985. *The rhetoric of economics.* Madison: University of Wisconsin Press.

Marris, P. 1986. *Loss and change.* rev. ed. London: Routledge & Kegan Paul.

Nozick, R. 1993. *The nature of explanation.* Princeton, NJ: Princeton University Press.

Orwell, G. 1949. *1984: a novel.* Reprint, New York: New American Library, 1961.

Popper, K. R. 1945. *The open society and its enemies.* 2 vols. Reprint, London: Routledge & Kegan Paul, 1974.

Rawls, J. 1993. *Political liberalism.* New York: Columbia University Press.

Sandel, M. 1982. *Liberalism and the limits of justice.* Cambridge, UK: Cambridge University Press.

Taylor, C. 1989. *Sources of the self: the making of the modern identity.* Cambridge, MA: Harvard University Press.

Commentary

ROBERT A. BEAUREGARD

Advocating Preeminence: Anthologies as Politics

Reflecting on African-American literature in the United States, Henry Louis Gates, Jr. (1992, 31) wrote that "[a] well-marked anthology functions in the academy to *create* a tradition, as well as to define and preserve it." One could make a similar statement about this collection of readings on planning theory. Seymour Mandelbaum's catholic claims to the contrary, his inclusionary and accommodating introductory essay, "The Talk of the Community," signals the emphasis on communicative practice that follows. Consequently, these initial chapters can be read as an attempt to establish the boundaries of an emerging, dominant domain of planning theory, with the remainder of the anthology exploring its internal diversity.

Nestled in the quasi discipline of planning, a debate is forming over the relative positioning of various planning theory domains. For example, John Friedmann recently has written a number of papers calling for less eclecticism and greater articulation of where theorists intersect (Friedmann 1994, 1995). Judith Innes (1995), though, has made the boldest of claims: Theorists who have toiled in the elevated realms of abstract theory (the rationalists being the culprits here) and those who have probed the structural dynamics of liberal capitalism (the Marxist and neo-Marxist political economists mainly) are passé. The theorists who have finally discovered the theory–practice nexus of most use to practitioners and of most interest to theorists are those who focus on communicative practice.

105

The domain of communicative practice is not new. As an identifiable approach to planning theory, it has been with us for the last fifteen years or so. Its ascendancy in the United States is a result not only of a general conservative swing that has weakened Left theorizing in academia and an increasing skepticism as to the efficacy of high theory but also of a discursive turn with roots not only in the work of Jürgen Habermas but also in the 1980s' enthrallment with postmodernism and, more specifically, issues of representation. In the case of communicative practice, representation appears as a driving force for communication itself and, as will be discussed later, an important link to a democratic ideal. Yet, while the project of this anthology is historically conditioned and political within the subfield of planning theory, the first set of readings is both ahistorical and apolitical.

The five chapters in this section include two theorists—Ernest Alexander and Andreas Faludi—whose reputations are anchored in a rationalist perspective that has been under siege for decades and that can be described only as in decline. They are juxtaposed against two theorists—Charles Hoch and Seymour Mandelbaum—whose work has been instrumental in constructing the ascendant domain of planning theory, communicative practice. John Friedmann's piece simultaneously reinforces the imputed political project and undermines it. Together, these chapters constitute the anthology's premise: Communicative practice is the future.

One of the enduring domains of planning theory, arguably its first, is that of the rationalists. Existing somewhat uncomfortably with a behavioralism that can be traced back to Patrick Geddes, the rationalists, from the beginning, threw themselves headfirst into the rarified realms of high theory. They posed themselves the Enlightenment goal of progress and cast rational behavior as the sine qua non of societal advancement. Rationalists thus owe their allegiance historically to Max Weber but more contemporareously to technologically inspired theorists of the post World War II period who took root in sociology, economics, and political science but formed such new "disciplines" as decision theory, policy science, systems analysis, and operations research.

For the rationalists, the dilemma faced by planners is not the bounded rationality of planners themselves (a minor problem we are assured) but the incomplete socialization of non-planners. Society's progress—that is, its increasing rationalization—is dependent upon the rationality of the individuals who comprise it. Although planning works best when people and organizations have internalized the rules of rational behavior, it is also designed to impose that rationality, if necessary.

Planning is thus a mechanism for controlling and guiding society. The function of planning theory is to discipline the understandings that precede action; the function of planning practice is to discipline with commands, regulations, and incentives the people and organizations who carry out those actions. As a result, rationalist planning theorists are constantly searching for an appropriate deductive logic, that is, for the principles of rational behavior from which we can derive appropriate reinforcement or, when rationality fails, disciplinary counteractions.

Theorizing in this domain almost always involves extensive categorization with rigid boundaries being drawn around different ways of thinking and acting (Zerubavel 1991, 33–60). The rationalist domain is populated by clearly defined concepts whose relationships are explicitly and exhaustively specified. All of this takes places quite abstractly, such that empirical examples or systematic evidence are hardly ever admitted into the discussion.

Ernest Alexander and Andreas Faludi are skillful practitioners of rationalist planning theory and are sensitive to its limitations. Over the years, their work has evolved, becoming more and more sophisticated and pushing against the constraints of high theory. Their contributions here, most notably, are quite fascinating in light of my portrayal of this anthology as a political project.

Alexander's offering can be read as a preemptive move to subsume communicative practice under a rationalist framework and thus to deflect, at least temporarily, its undermining of the rationalist project. His contingency model and quest for synthesis, however, vibrate with anxiety; a contingency plan is designed to be used when our preferred plan goes awry. On the other hand, we could be witnessing a conversion, a change of domains. My best guess is that the "after rationality" in his title is, for now, irony.

Andreas Faludi puts up more resistance to the advance of communicative practice. He rejects Alexander's defensive move for a more offensive posture that accuses rationalism's critics of misinterpretation and pulls them onto his terrain by labeling proponents and critics alike as consequentialists. Consequently, Faludi offers critical rationalism, a form of rationalism that recognizes the context in which decisions are made and thus makes rationality relative to the situations in which it is applied.

Most interesting is critical rationalism's notion of planning doctrine, a concept Faludi developed with Ernest Alexander. Doctrines frame and shape "planning conversations," they often contain "ambiguous metaphors," and they are in constant flux. Faludi at one point proclaims that these "doctrines are like paradigms" but he could just as easily have likened them to "discourses." In fact, his use of conversation and metaphor and his allusion to their negotiable quality suggest that this core concept of critical rationalism could be transplanted easily into the domain of communicative practice. Thus, what seems to be resistance could be no more than a strategic adjustment. Faludi is more defiant than Alexander but he too recognizes the ascendancy of a new core to planning theory.

Clearly, Alexander and Faludi, proponents of the dominant domain of the past, have not denounced their rationalist commitments and declared undivided allegiance to communicative practice. Nonetheless, both chapters make it clear that rationalist theory is on the wane and must change significantly, specifically by merging with communicative practice, in order to remain viable. These two chapters thereby prepare us for the arguments put forth by Charles Hoch and Seymour Mandelbaum, both of whom write squarely in the ascendant domain.

In communicative practice, rationality plays a much different role than it does in rationalism. The rationalists assume that rationality is the natural inclination of people and organizations and it resides in their thoughts and actions, which are rational or not. Individualism reigns. Deficiencies are caused by exogenous forces or internal weaknesses that have to be dispelled by planning.

People engaged in communicative practice are reasonable, but their reasonableness resides not in individual actions or thought processes but in negotiated and communicated intentions and understandings. People create understandings and design rational actions by talking and listening to each other. This works, however, only if those communicating do so in ways that allow discussion—discourse—to proceed sincerely, comprehensibly, legitimately, and accurately (Forester 1989, 36). Simply put, rationalists hope to make the actions of planners rational and the outcomes of planning functional, while theorists of communicative practice hope to improve the quality and openness of the debate. Rationality is socially and discursively constructed rather than imposed.

The notion of discursive reasonableness is central to both Hoch's and Mandelbaum's formulations of the domain of communicative practice. In order to avoid the paternalism of social reform and the epistemological problems posed by rationalism, Hoch champions a critical pragmatism anchored in the work of John Dewey. Planning under this formulation is not a search by experts for the correct knowledge, rational actions, and well-designed organizational relations that achieve collective goals but a shared inquiry in which moral individuals, recognizing their vulnerability, debate differing versions of the good society. The job for practitioners is to construct "free spaces" for democratic inquiry and debate, and the task for theorists is to tell stories about practice that convince other theorists and practitioners of the necessity of critical pragmatism.

Mandelbaum deepens critical pragmatism by articulating the possible modes of discursive organization of moral communities. His belief that democratic inquiry and debate occurs "within a field of overlapping and open communities" leads him to warn of the "intractably ambiguous and dilemmatic" nature of the instrumental judgments that are the substance of rationalist planning. Hence, he rejects the possibility of a consensual body of social theory. By implication, an unavoidable need exists for constant debate not only within the community of theorists but also between theorists and practitioners of planning, all of whom hold on to different myths. Thus, while Mandelbaum provides an argument for incommensurable domains of planning theory, he offers a solution to their irresoluable differences in the form of communicative practice.

Reminiscent of the rationalists, theorists of communicative practice write mostly, but not always, at a high level of abstraction. Less rigid than the rationalists and generally uninterested in the drawing of tightly bound concepts and fixed relationships, they share a reluctance to write a middle-ground theory that integrates theory and practice. Note, for example, the quite abstract nature of the presentations by Hoch and Mandelbaum. No attempt has been made to ground the arguments historically and spatially, one more indication of the observation that "matter muddles" (Goldstein, 1983, 117), particularly when one's aim is high theory. On the other hand, a number of important empirical studies have been done to demonstrate the utility of communicative practice theory in practice (see Forester 1992; Krumholz and Forester 1990; Schön 1982).

While the chapters by Hoch and Mandelbaum introduce the basic themes and theoretical style of the domain of communicative practice, Friedmann's chapter speaks elliptically to its ascendancy. At first glance, Friedmann is an obvious choice for this introductory section. His chapter, derived from his impressive intellectual history of planning thought, *Planning in the Public Domain* (1987), is a catholic review of the domains of planning theory. Yet, read against the political project of this anthology, and in light of two chapters revising rationalism and two chapters describing communicative practice, it seems less than an ideal choice.

One way to read Friedmann's history is as a statement about the futility of any domain becoming the dominant paradigm of planning theory. A more appropriate reading in this context, though, would highlight the emergence and displacement of theoretical communities. Domains of theory are in constant flux; thus, succession is a distinct possibility. Subsequent chapters hold up communicative practice as the ascendant domain. By appearing neutral, Friedmann's argument opens up historical and intellectual space for communicative practice to become dominant.

Read politically, then, this anthology is academic advocacy. The political project is to establish the dominance of communicative practice with the initial five chapters establishing the foundation for that ascendance: the capitulation of rationalist theory.

This is a bold move, one with great potential with regard to our ability to theorize planning and contribute to its practice. The path to any paradigmatic pinnacle, however, is littered with discarded questions and excluded domains. Recognizing the political nature of the chapters assembled in Part I of this volume will enable the reader to ask those questions and reflect on approaches to planning theory that remain absent.

REFERENCES

Forester, J. 1992. Critical ethnography: on fieldwork in a Habermasian way. In M. Alvesson and H. Wilmott, eds., *Critical management studies*. Newbury Park, CA: Sage, 46–65.

_____. 1989. *Planning in the face of power*. Berkeley: University of California Press.

Friedmann, J. 1987. *Planning in the public domain*. Princeton, NJ: Princeton University Press.

_____. 1994. Urban planning at UCLA: a prospective view. Lecture given at the Graduate School of Architecture and Urban Planning, University of California, Los Angeles, March 8.

_____. 1995. Teaching planning theory. *Journal of Planning Education and Research* 14, 3.

Gates, H. L. Jr. 1992. *Loose canons: notes on the culture wars*. New York: Oxford University Press.

Goldstein, R. 1983. *The mind–body problem*. New York: Dell.

Innes, J. E. 1995. Planning theory's emerging paradigm: communicative action and interactive practice. *Journal of Planning Education and Research* 14, 3.

Krumholz, N., and J. Forester. 1990. *Making equity planning work*. Philadelphia: Temple University Press.

Schön, D. 1982. Some of what a planner knows. *Journal of the American Planning Association* 48. pp. 351–364.

Zerubavel, E. 1991. *The fine line: making distinctions in everyday life*. New York: Free Press.

PART II

The Latitude of Planners

SEYMOUR J. MANDELBAUM

The Latitude of Planners

INTRODUCTION

I f the four chapters in this section were simply accounts of the travails of planning, they would present no special difficulties for the pragmatic reader. "Here is the way it was in a particular setting in time and space," we might say to ourselves. "We may in the future want to extract lessons from these stories of past planning wars, but that should always be done with a sense that there are no guarantees that what worked yesterday will work tomorrow, no certainty that the world will be predictable and our knowledge more than a comforting illusion."

The caution—or even the deeper skepticism—suggested by that radical separation of past and future has certainly touched the community of planning theoreticians. Even the most ambitious accounts of the promise of theorizing in Part I of this volume hold out little prospect that empirical (and, therefore, always historical) research will culminate in a set of timeless universal principles or tools for every occasion. "Contingency" and "uncertainty" are the slogans of the theorizing community.

It is, however, difficult for us to theorize without locating ourselves in a present that stretches across the past and the future, without assuming stabilities in the ways human beings relate to one another and in the continuity of meanings that allow us to talk coherently about "planning processes" and their "outcomes." Alas, the passion for this ordered world creates difficulties. Once we begin to cast the world in that seamless mold, we confront a dilemma at the core of our own imagery. Our understanding of the past depends first upon our retrospective assessment of events-that-did-not-happen—formally described as "counter-factuals." It also depends, however, upon our prospective assessment of events-that-cannot-yet-have-happened because they are merely anticipations of the future. Our understanding seems coherent and compelling when past and future are tightly woven together in our minds.

The tight weave is the source of the dilemma. The more confident we are of our knowledge, the harder it appears to shape events through our plans. The more plastic our representations and the more amenable to the craft of planning—the stronger our sense that we are competent agents—the less confident we are of our knowledge. That is not a very endearing choice: Plan in ignorance versus knowledgeably accept that we probably can no more change the future than we can alter the past.

Each of the four authors in this section struggles with this dilemma. Michael Brooks opens with a broadside against the theorists whose analyses of politics (or political economy) leave little room for professional planners to influence collective choices. He then elaborates a "Political Feedback Strategy" that, he argues, will expand the latitude of planners, the choices that they can make, and the changes they can effect without confronting the vetoes of the larger political system. Bishwapriya Sanyal, following in the same vein, describes three "vignettes" in which Indian planners skillfully created "institutional autonomy" for the formulation and implementation of policies they favored against the grain of the regimes within which they labored. Finally, illustrating a common strategy in the construction of latitude, the essays by Judith Innes and Andy Thornley use comparative and historical analysis to locate variation and change within overtly similar political or economic systems.

The approaches of the four authors are distinctive but overlapping. Each of them accepts the notion that institutions must express a discipline that constrains behavior. At the same time, they assert directly or by implication that it is impossible to imagine a stable or competent institutional order that does not adapt to variations in the world by assigning some discretion to its participants and then—often with considerable ambivalence—protecting their latitude. As a result of the constant process of balancing discipline and latitude, professional planners (as they appear in these chapters) are able to redirect public policy on the ground, campaign for favored projects and programs against the grain of established opinions, and reshape the ways in which preferences and collective bargains are articulated.

In order to engage us in this dynamic balancing of discipline and latitude, the authors call our attention repeatedly and critically to the ways in which our conceptions of the dilemma are informed by figures of speech: the overwhelming notion of a political economy that "dominates" all other institutions, social "forces" that are resolved in unique vectors, social "structures" that are as rigid as the frame of a building, and influence that flows like water from the "top" to the "bottom" of the social terrain.

The chapters of this section bring to bear upon these metaphors, and their suggestions of permanence and control, a language of process, flux, and negotiated institutional dynamics that sustains the sense of agency and planning discretion. The dilemma is not, of course, resolved by this symbolic refocusing, only put to the side. It remains (as Glen McDougall's critical commentary that closes this section reveals) a powerful expression of our simultaneous search for freedom and for knowledge.

MICHAEL P. BROOKS

6 Planning and Political Power: Toward a Strategy for Coping

PLANNING THEORY AND POLITICAL POWER

There is a widely held view, among those who think and write about such matters, that planning practitioners are suffering at present from a dearth of compelling and workable planning theories. Robert Beauregard, for example, is critical of the current state of planning theory on the grounds that it has become largely irrelevant to the physical and political realities of the city (Beauregard 1990; also see Alexander 1984). I agree with his assessment.

It is reasonable to inquire, then, as to what has gone wrong with planning theory. Why does it seem to offer so little help to those who practice planning, and why do we feel so keenly the need for new paradigms capable of integrating our knowledge of the planning process?

The answer, in my view, resides in the extent to which planning theory has been overwhelmed by our understanding of contemporary political processes. Early writings on planning characterized it as an act of visionary design or creative problem solving. Over time, however, these views have given way to theoretical formulations in which the political system (or, more broadly, the political economy) is all-pervasive, with the planner being relegated to minor walk-on roles under highly constrained conditions. This point can be illustrated by brief references to some of the staples of the planning theory literature.

116

Out of the 1950s, strongly influenced by the thinking of those connected with the short-lived but influential planning program at the University of Chicago, came the idea of planning as an exercise in applied rationality (see, e.g., Meyerson and Banfield 1955), typically involving the identification of goals, alternative means of pursuing those goals, and the criteria to be used in selecting among the alternatives. This approach, with its focus on the analysis of ends, means, and consequences, was for many years the dominant paradigm in planning theory. With their strong emphasis on the central role of the rational planner, however, rationality-based planning strategies tended to view politics as a dysfunctional external disturbance. Such strategies would have worked fine, according to their proponents, if only elected officials and policymakers had listened to planners and had been willing to set aside their customary political grounds for making decisions and allocating resources. It was this political naivete in the rational approach that led to its ultimate decline. I view the mega models of the 1960s—the Penn-Jersey project, the Chicago Area Transportation Study, and so on—as the last gasp of hope among planners that the elegance and sophistication of their analyses would carry the day. Clearly it did not work out that way. (See Black 1990, however, for a different point of view.)

A major corrective to the naivete of rationality-based approaches emerged with the writings of Charles Lindblom and his concept of incrementalism (Lindblom 1965). Lindblom accepted the political system as a given and commended planners to settle for minor changes—small victories—as all that could reasonably be expected. Lindblom's importance to the development of planning theory cannot be overemphasized, given his reminders to us that all planning occurs within a political context and that this context is a highly significant variable in any system of planning activity.

Paul Davidoff's advocacy planning (1965) also accepted the political system as a given but urged planners to join the fray and try to beat the system at its own game by providing specific interest groups—especially the relatively powerless—with access to the planner's kit bag of analytical tools and plan-making capabilities. Davidoff's approach did not abandon the concept of rationality; he simply wanted to make its purported benefits available to a wider spectrum of citizens. Advocacy eventually fell from grace as a major planning theory primarily because of its failure to recognize that having the services of a trained planner did not necessarily give a group of people the political power they needed in order to attain their objectives. In other words, advocacy did nothing to alter the basic political processes by which a community's resources are allocated. Advocacy too, then, was ultimately judged to be politically naive.

More recently, a great deal of planning theory literature has been produced by progressive or critical theorists who tend to view politics as all-
encompassing and to see planning as hostage to the nation's prevailing
political economy (see, e.g., Harvey 1978; Scott and Roweis 1977). In the
capitalist context, then, the planner is urged to function as a watchdog, as
a "guerilla in the bureaucracy," as an agent of radical social change or as
one who monitors communication flows and guards against the dissemination of false information (see, e.g., Beauregard 1990; Forester 1982;
Kraushaar 1988). These are indeed important roles, but it strikes me as
naive to expect them to be played by the vast majority of governmentally
employed planners who function in systems that do not generally reward
such activities. As I have noted elsewhere, "the progressive spirit thrives
far more readily in the halls of academe—where there is virtually no risk
attached to its espousal—than it does in the nation's city halls" (Brooks
1990).

The overwhelming power of politics is also a key element in formulations urging the planner to function as a negotiator or mediator among
competing interest groups, typically developers on the one hand and the
city government or a neighborhood organization on the other (see, e.g.,
Forester 1987; Susskind and Ozawa 1984). This too is a useful role, but it is
not clear that sizable numbers of planners are well-equipped, through training or professional orientation, to play it. It is certainly far removed, in any
event, from the creative, plan-generating roles posited for planners in earlier planning models.

The purpose of this brief overview has been to illustrate a historical
trend line, in which the *planning* content of planning theories has gradually given way to *politics* as the key process involved in shaping our communities. The early rational models featured a major role for planning and
paid scant attention to politics (to their ultimate peril); current planning
theorists acknowledge the full force of the political economy—and search
for a role for planning that is sufficiently efficacious to justify the existence
of planners as a distinct body of professionals.

Some find solace in the current popularity of strategic planning, an
approach touted widely in publications (both scholarly and popular),
conference sessions, and "how to" short courses. Unfortunately, there are
almost as many versions of strategic planning as there are people writing
about it. While all the evidence is not yet in, my own inclination is to view
strategic planning as the latest version of rationality-based planning,
belonging to the same family of ideas that produced systems analysis,
planning–programming–budgeting systems (PPBS), zero-base budgeting,

management-by-objectives, and other highly marketable versions of ends–means–consequences planning. It may well be an improvement over past models because of its inclusion of analysis of factors in the political environment that will help or hinder goal attainment; it places great emphasis on making sure that all key actors ("stakeholders") are made a part of the process; and its very popularity at present (derived in part, I suspect, from its private-sector origins) gives it a measure of political clout that may indeed help produce some successes here and there. In the final analysis, however, it retains the old notion that major problems are susceptible to resolution by means of analytic processes overseen by planners and other bureaucrats. I am not optimistic that the political system will ultimately yield to strategic planning any more than it has to other embodiments of the rational planning idea.

Where does all of this leave the planning theory enterprise? As I noted earlier, a number of authors have commented on the current absence of compelling planning paradigms and on our seeming inability to generate new ones. I read this in part as an expression of despair about the role of planning in capitalist societies. We have conceded the primacy of politics, and we don't know what to do about it. Stated rather baldly, the choice seems to be between 1) planning that "goes along with" the political system and, as a result, rarely accomplishes anything of significance; and 2) planning that attempts to operate in contravention of the prevailing political system—and, as a result, rarely accomplishes anything of significance. This is hardly an acceptable situation.

What, then, should be done? I am convinced that the emergence of more viable planning paradigms will require closer relationships between planning educators and planning practitioners. Academicians will benefit from acquiring a keener understanding of the daily activities of practicing planners and of the political realities within which planning practice takes place. Working jointly, educators and practitioners should strive to develop action theories of planning that pay heed to political constraints but that nonetheless illuminate ways of breaking through those constraints to provide opportunities for planning that is genuinely creative, visionary, and effective. I concur with Judith Innes de Neufville, for example, in her view that we need theory that is "grounded in practice," that is "based in empirical research and lessons from the field" (Innes de Neufville 1983). It is encouraging to note that many are now working in this vein—Howell Baum, Susan Fainstein, John Forester, Charles Hoch, Elizabeth Howe, and Jerome Kaufman are among those who come immediately to mind.

TOWARD A STRATEGY FOR COPING

The remainder of this chapter presents a normative planning strategy intended to address the problem and constraints that I have described thus far. The challenge is to provide a planning strategy that will assist planners in playing roles that are both efficacious and politically realistic. I will describe, in the following pages, a strategy that is intended to meet this challenge. For lack of a better name, I call it the "Political Feedback Strategy." Like many of its predecessors, it is an action theory of planning, one that prescribes a set of procedures that the planner might follow in the pursuit of planned change.

It is also grounded, however, in some assumptions regarding the realities of planning practice. It is based on a set of empirically testable assertions regarding the nature of the political pressures that are brought to bear upon the planner in a practice setting. In other words, it focuses attention on the social and political context in which the planner is operating and makes that context a part of the strategy.

The Political Feedback Strategy *builds in* politics as a component of the planning process; that is, it recognizes that each step in any planning process generates political feedback, and it calls upon the planner to analyze and act upon that feedback in the process of formulating each successive step. It therefore views planning explicitly as an exercise in *trial ballooning*, with a set of instructions for learning from, and responding to, the feedback generated by the trial balloons floated by the planner. So that the trial ballooning process may operate effectively, the strategy places great emphasis on the dissemination of information about each step to those whose responses are most significant. It also requires the planner to make some ethical choices regarding the relative weights to be given to the various sources of feedback in the political environment.

Some Underlying Assumptions

Four assumptions will be mentioned here. The first is the rather obvious point that planning always occurs in a specific social and political environment and that this environment plays a large part in structuring the opportunities and constraints of the situation. (This point is acknowledged, of course, in the "environmental scan" contained in most formulations of strategic planning.) Obvious as this point may be, however, very little attention has been devoted in the planning literature to the precise nature and impact of the planner's social and political context. Were we to ask, for example, from what sources the planner typically derives his or her ideas and what impact the social and political context of the situation has upon his or her ultimate choice among these ideas, we would find little to guide us. One might begin, however, by suggesting a *typology of idea sources:*

I. ONE'S SELF
    A. Knowledge, reason
    B. Ideology, values
    C. Intuition based on past experience

II. REFERENCE GROUPS
    A. Local (e.g., colleagues in the same organization, other governmental officials, friends and social contacts)
    B. Professional (e.g., graduate schools and professional societies, in which one is "socialized" to a set of professional standards, ethics, and modes of behavior)

III. INFLUENCE-WIELDERS
    A. Superiors in one's organizational hierarchy
    B. Elected officials (especially chief executives, council members)
    C. Social and economic "power figures"
    D. Providers of resources (e.g., state and federal governments, foundations)

IV. CLIENT GROUPS

Having generated such a typology (which could undoubtedly be expanded or refined in numerous ways), it might then be possible to ask questions about

1. the relative frequency with which these various sources are actually used;
2. the relative power of the sources under varied conditions;
3. the relationship of these sources to differing "styles" of planner behavior;
4. the difficulties inherent in attempting to rely on several sources simultaneously;
5. differential reliance, by the planner, on various idea sources depending on such factors as his or her position in the organizational hierarchy, or stage in life, or changes in social status, and so on; and
6. the extent to which differing sources are likely to generate ideas for significant social change, as opposed to ideas that are purely incremental.

Just as the planner operates in a social and political context (rather than in isolation) when deciding what ideas to consider, so does that context affect his or her ultimate choice among those ideas. Actors in the planner's environment—colleagues, superiors, concerned citizens and others—will be aware of the array of ideas ("alternatives") under consideration. On the basis of the information they have received, these actors will "feed back" a variety of responses and pressures that serve, ultimately, to influence the planner's decision. Some of the feedback will be positive, advocating the selection of a given alternative; other feedback will be negative, threatening sanctions (e.g., the withdrawal of support, dismissal, the loss of friends or status, decreased funding, public demonstrations) if a particular alternative is selected.

These pressures operate at all other stages of the process as well. Indeed, the entire planning process—from the identification of a problem to be tackled to the implementation of a course of action intended to resolve it—is strongly influenced by a number of pressures and forces external to the planner. It is unfortunate and perhaps even surprising that we know so little about the dynamics of these variables.

The second underlying assumption is essentially an ethical stance, holding that the appropriate division of labor between the planner and his or her client is one in which the latter is responsible for goal formulation, while the planner's major task is the design of courses of action aimed at helping the client to achieve those goals. This requires, of course, a clear determination of the client's identity in a given planning situation.

The third underlying assumption is that the trial balloon is an effective vehicle for obtaining information about a client group's goals. This proposition is based in part on the difficulties planners typically experience in attempting to formulate client group goal structures through traditional methods such as surveys and public hearings (see Patton 1983). It is also based, however, on the notion that people express their goals quite effectively when these goals are embodied—positively or negatively—in actions to which they can react (e.g. a program or facility that purports to serve them or a policy that affects them). If a program, policy or action is a manifestation of their goals, they will tend to support it; if it conflicts with their goals, they will bring pressure to bear against it. A key feature of the trial balloon is, of course, its openness to such pressures; indeed, the trial balloon should be designed to receive and process them efficiently.

Finally, the fourth underlying assumption is the importance of an explicitly experimental orientation to the planner's task. (Sound advice to this effect was offered by Seymour Mandelbaum in a 1975 article.) Rarely if ever, in the public policy arena, do we have perfect knowledge regarding the "best" course of action to pursue. In our usual all-or-nothing approaches to specific societal ills, however, we tend to behave as though there were no longer any doubt about the "correct" steps to be taken. Hence programs are all too often carried out for extended periods of time with little regard for their effectiveness. If, on the other hand, each planned course of action were to be conceived of and designed as an experiment aimed at acquiring information about its effectiveness as a means of achieving client-group goals, then our store of knowledge concerning appropriate problem-solving strategies would increase dramatically. Indeed, planning might best be viewed as a process of social experimentation wherein ideas are tested—and continuously evaluated—against the possibilities and constraints of reality.

Two kinds of evaluation are important to the planning process. Objective evaluation entails an assessment of the effectiveness of a course of action in solving the problems, or achieving the goals, at which it is aimed. Subjective evaluation, on the other hand, assesses the attitudes and opinions that a client group has about that course of action. In planning, neither type of evaluation is complete without the other.

The Political Feedback Strategy

The strategy contains six stages and is shown diagrammatically in Figure 6.1. Since this is a normative strategy—that is, one suggesting my conception of how planning *ought* to be carried out—the stages are presented sequentially. In reality, of course, few planning situations will be amenable to the orderliness that is implied in such a sequential listing of stages. I do not consider this to be a problem. In the final analysis, the Political Feedback Strategy is more appropriately viewed as an attitude toward the planning process than as a lock-step set of procedures.

1. The process begins with the emergence or identification of a problem requiring action of some sort, a problem that appears to fall within the range of the planner's professional concern. (I am not troubled by the lack of well-defined boundaries around that range of concern. The parameters of planning have expanded and contracted frequently through the years, depending on a variety of factors both internal and external to the discipline. In any event, if the planner indeed oversteps his or her boundaries, feedback from the social and political environment will so indicate—and the planner will have to decide whether to drop the matter or engage in a jurisdictional dispute.)

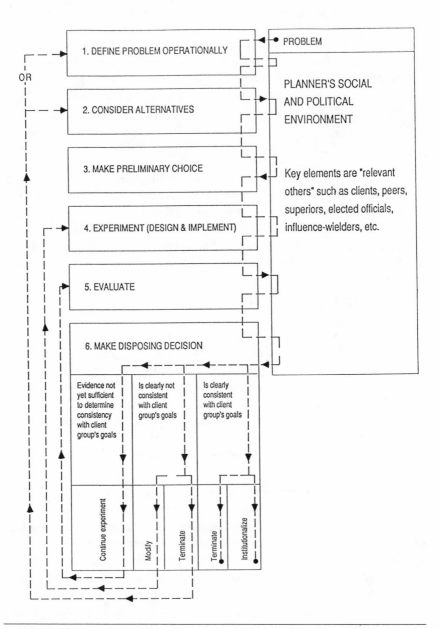

FIGURE 6.1
The Political Feedback Strategy

The planner's chief task in this, the first stage of the strategy, is to define the problem operationally. That is, he or she should break it down into its constituent parts (if any) and identify those aspects of the problem that are susceptible to treatment, alleviation, or resolution through a program of action. Having defined the problem in operational terms, the planner should communicate that definition to "relevant others" in his or her social and political environment—and it is at this point that the feedback process begins in earnest. For if the planner's own definition of the problem is inconsistent with that held by relevant others (interest groups, colleagues, superiors, and the like), this fact will soon be fed back and the planner will need to decide what adjustments in the definition, if any, to make.

I also suggest—and here I depart from the tenets of "rational planning"—that no effort be made at this point to formulate goals and objectives. The critical goals in the process are those held by the client group whose interests the planner intends to serve; these will become apparent, if at all, in feedback from the clients to the planner once they are experiencing a specific course of action. This implies, of course, that the client group has indeed been identified—an essential first step in the Political Feedback Strategy.

Frequently, of course, planning issues are characterized by the involvement of a number of groups with differing, perhaps even conflicting, interests. Identifying the client group may entail selecting one of these groups or focusing on some combination of groups among whom a measure of agreement or compromise can be anticipated. Attempting to satisfy everyone, however, is a recipe for failure. To be sure, the client may vary from project to project and may even change during the course of a single project. Indeed, identifying one's client group is not always a simple matter. But to ignore this issue (perhaps with the hope that one is somehow serving the "public interest," thus affording client status to the entire community) is to indulge in self-delusion. Planning projects or activities rarely distribute their benefits and costs in an equal manner; some people gain while others lose (or at least gain differentially). In reality, all planners serve some groups better than they serve others. The task here is to render this a matter of explicit choice rather than a mindless resultant.

2. The planner then considers several alternative actions that might be taken to deal with the problem. This step sounds suspiciously similar to one that the "rational" planner supposedly takes, but the similarity is superficial. The difference is seen in response to two questions that the planner following the Political Feedback Strategy must address at this point.

First, given the virtually unlimited number of alternatives that are potential candidates for adoption, which ones should the planner select for consideration? Earlier I suggested four major sources of alternatives in a planning situation: the planner himself or herself, reference groups, influence-wielders, and clients. Typically, then, the planner will give consideration both to those ideas—usually a limited number—that he or she thinks of and believes are worthy of further analysis and to those ideas that are suggested—with varying degrees of intensity—by any of the three external sources. The likelihood that a given externally generated alternative will be afforded full consideration by the planner is a function of 1) the extent to which the planner finds the idea an attractive one, and 2) the extent to which pressure (or influence) is brought to bear upon him or her to so consider it. How the planner weights the various sources of alternatives will be determined to a large extent by his or her personal values and style and by the degree of freedom inherent in the situation (i.e., Is the planner constrained by commitments to or potential sanctions by "relevant others"?).

Second, how extensively and by what methods is each alternative to be assessed? My answer is that each alternative should be evaluated as fully and with as sophisticated a set of methods as the situation permits. Before the planner proceeds to evaluate a set of alternatives, then, there should be a reasonably precise determination of just what the situation *does* permit.

A number of constraints serve to limit the comparative analysis of alternatives in most planning situations. The most important of these constraints are

a. the *resources* at the planner's disposal, especially funds, staff, expertise, and equipment (such as computers);

b. *time deadlines,* which in turn frequently depend on such factors as the extent to which the problem at hand constitutes a "crisis situation," the anticipated life span of the planner's organization (is it temporary or "permanent"?), whether the problem is one on which elected officials have promised rapid action, and the fiscal year of the funding body; and

c. the *political constraints* on analysis, featuring some combination of the number of persons and organizations who have generated alternatives, the relative intensity of their feelings on the matter, and how much power they possess.

The planner should assess these (and other) constraints at the outset of analysis, deciding how much time, resources, and objectivity can be applied to the evaluation of alternatives; to enter this task on an open-ended basis is to invite considerable frustration at a later time. In some cases there may be sufficient time, expertise, equipment, and freedom from political constraints for the development of simulation models and/or sophisticated benefit-cost studies; in other cases—more typical for the urban planner— there may be but a week in which to prepare a recommendation.

3. Next, the planner *makes a preliminary choice* among the various alternative courses of action that he or she has evaluated. The most important concerns at this point are those of criteria and feedback.

Several types of criteria are potentially applicable at this point. If the planning situation is one of low visibility and/or generates little public or client-group interest, then it may be possible to use economic efficiency criteria of the sort involved in benefit-cost analysis. Some alternatives may lend themselves to a much more basic form of economic analysis; it may readily be seen from the most cursory inspection, for example, that they are too costly in relation to the benefits that could be expected. Having eliminated one or more alternatives on this basis, however, the planner will generally still have to contend with several others that are roughly similar in potential cost, thereby reducing the utility of further economic comparisons.

Other criteria thus come into play, the most important being 1) political feasibility, and 2) the planner's perception, whether backed by data or merely subjective, of the "fit" between a given alternative and the needs of the clientele to be affected by the decision. Again, the relative importance of these two criteria will be determined by the values of the planner and by the number and intensity of external constraints.

All other things being equal, the best alternative is that which is adjudged to best fit the client group's needs, consistent with the constraints imposed by the political dynamics of the situation. Ideally, of course, "best fit" should be determined through sophisticated analysis; more typically, however, it will emerge from a combination of inadequate data, hurried analysis, and the planner's subjective conclusions. And we need not worry too much about this, given the critical role played by feedback.

Feedback will generally be received both before and after the preliminary choice is made. Once an array of alternatives has been identified for consideration, "relevant others"—colleagues, superiors, client groups, politicians, fund-providers, and other wielders of influence—will make their opinions known. (As in all other stages of the planning process, the planner should take pains to ensure that feedback is indeed generated, in this instance by publicizing the range of alternatives under consideration.) Some alternatives will quickly be recognized as politically infeasible, no matter how attractive their estimated excesses of benefits over costs. Here, of course, the planner can attempt to play an educative role, endeavoring to show relevant groups why they should favor one or another alternative. But one should not expect too much to result from this role; most of the reasons for which groups will favor or oppose a given alternative will have little to do with criteria typically espoused by planners.

It may be useful, in summarizing the above, to think of the preliminary choice process as the application of a set of filters. Some alternatives may be screened out by an economic filter; these are the alternatives whose costs are obviously too high, either absolutely or in relation to such benefits as they can reasonably be expected to produce. Other alternatives will be screened out by a political filter, as manifested in feedback from "relevant others." Finally, of those alternatives that are left, the planner can do little more than make a subjective judgment as to which will best serve the needs (or, stated alternatively, solve the problems) of the client group. This would be a hopelessly inadequate criterion for making a public policy decision if, as has typically been the case in the past, the decision were to be considered final and definitive. As will be seen below, however, the preliminary choice in the Political Feedback Strategy functions as a hypothesis; hence the desperate need for the choice to be the "right" one is lessened somewhat. One of the strategy's key features is, in fact, its acceptance of, and attempt to build upon, the fact that we almost never have sufficient knowledge for claiming our policy decisions to be "correct" in any absolute sense. Referring to the choice made in this stage as a preliminary one implies that the final decision is to be deferred until a later time, when more knowledge is available. And the critical piece of knowledge needed to make a valid final decision is, quite simply, how the course of action actually turns out in practice.

Once a preliminary choice has been made by the planner, feedback will again come into play—more heavily, in fact, than at any point thus far. As suggested earlier, it may be necessary to engage in a number of bargains, compromises, and trade-offs before the chosen alternative is implemented, which means, of course, that the action finally taken may differ significantly from that initially chosen and announced by the planner.

4. Having made a preliminary choice of a course of action to be pursued (as modified in response to post-choice feedback), the planner then proceeds to experiment with the idea, i.e., he or she designs and implements

a program or course of action embodying the chosen alternative. It is in this, the program development or design stage, that the planner's creative capabilities are often given widest scope. The actual management or administration of the course of action may or may not fall to the planner, depending on the nature of the organization; most typically, this role will be played by others, leaving the planner free to oversee the workings of the strategy's feedback mechanisms.

That the course of action is to be conceived as an experiment has several implications for its design. The hypotheses on which it is to be based should be clearly stated; indicators by which these hypotheses can be tested should be identified; and a methodology for evaluation should be decided upon and "built in" at the outset. Time parameters should be established. If the course of action is intended to solve a given problem in a relatively short period of time (say a year or two), then the final output or result will be the primary object of evaluation. If, on the other hand, it is believed that the problem can be alleviated only in the long run, then a series of short-run "guideposts" should be identified against which progress in eliminating the problem over the long run can be assessed.

5. The planner then evaluates the course of action being implemented. Given the experimental orientation of the Political Feedback Strategy, this is perhaps its most critical stage. In brief, the strategy impels us to learn from experience. Evaluation gives both planners and "relevant others" information on which to base final decisions about the value of a course of action (such decisions to be referred to hereafter as "disposing decisions").

Evaluation should be focused on two primary questions. First, to what extent is the course of action successfully alleviating the problem at which it is aimed? And second, what are the attitudes and opinions that "relevant others" hold with regard to the course of action? As the planner receives and analyzes these two types of feedback, the results should be disseminated broadly. Armed with this information, "relevant others" in the planner's social and political environment will thus be readied for their final act of feedback, namely, their influence on the planner as he or she carries out the next stage of the Political Feedback Strategy.

6. In the sixth and final stage, the planner makes a disposing decision with regard to the course of action that has been tested. As in all other stages of the strategy, reliance will be placed on the planner's interpretations of the relevant data as well as on his or her intuition in making this decision; here too, however, the planner will be subject to a number of pressures from "relevant others."

It is at this point, finally, that the planner will best be able to perceive the goals of the client group. If the planner performs the evaluation task correctly, the client group (or its chief representatives) will have received information concerning the objective impact of the course of action on its problems, how various relevant groups feel about it, and the nature of those issues that remain unresolved even after the evaluation has been completed. It should not be too difficult, then, to deduce group goals (at least with regard to the problem under attack) from the group's reaction to the course of action at this point.

The disposing decisions that the planner can make in response to the goals that the client group has revealed are several, as indicated in Figure 6.1. First, it may be that at the predetermined time when a disposing decision is to be made, there is insufficient evidence to enable the client group to determine whether the course of action is indeed consistent with its goals. This indicates the need for more information; the experiment continues, the planner returns to the fifth stage—evaluation—and a new time frame for a disposing decision is established.

Second, the client group may determine that the course of action as currently conducted is not consistent with its goals. In this event two options are open. If the approach appears to be on the right track but requires relatively major adjustments nonetheless, it should be modified; here the planner returns to the fourth stage—experimentation—and in effect "retools" or redesigns the course of action. If, on the other hand, it is by now clear to the client group that the course of action is totally wrong-headed and inconsistent with (perhaps even detrimental to) its goals, then it should be terminated; here the planner must either return to the second stage for consideration of a new set of alternatives or to the first stage for a redefinition of the problem.

Third, the client group may determine that the course of action is indeed fulfilling its goals. Here again there are two options. In some extremely rare cases, it may be that the problem has been completely alleviated by the course of action; hence it can be terminated. If, on the other hand, the client group determines that the course of action is clearly consistent with its goals but the problem is obviously one that will be around for many years (if not permanently), then the course of action may be institutionalized; that is, it loses its status as an "experiment," is turned over in its entirety to the realm of administration (as opposed to planning), and becomes an established function of government. Needless to say, extreme caution should be exercised in reaching this decision; in most instances it would be wise to make the "insufficient evidence" decision and recycle for several rounds of evaluation before the course of action is finally institutionalized.

In summary, then, the Political Feedback Strategy may be outlined as follows.

1. The planner begins with a problem (not a goal) that is quickly defined and operationalized to his or her own satisfaction—but subject to modification through feedback.

2. The planner considers several alternatives, derived from several sources (including his or her own insights and those of relevant others) and analyzes each within a set of predetermined resource, time, and political constraints.

3. The planner makes a preliminary choice of the alternative that seems "best" in the light of gross economic considerations, political feasibility, and "fit" between the alternative and the problem at which it is aimed (or, alternatively stated, the needs of the client group), with considerable feedback both before and after the selection having a strong impact on this choice.

4. The planner designs and implements the decision in the form of an experiment.

5. The planner evaluates the resulting course of action, devoting particular attention to the extent of problem alleviation, on the one hand, and on the attitudes of "relevant others" toward the course of action, on the other.

6. Based on feedback from the client group concerning the extent to which the course of action is consistent with its goals, the planner makes a disposing decision to continue, modify, terminate, or institutionalize the course of action, re-cycling to earlier stages of the strategy if necessary.

I conclude with three observations. First, as noted earlier, it is unreasonable to expect that any given planning situation can be managed as neatly as the above description would seem to suggest. Hence, my contention that the Political Feedback Strategy is essentially an attitude toward planning and problem solving, one that emphasizes the critical importance of feedback from those who matter in a planning situation, and the importance of using that feedback creatively in the formulation of each successive step.

Second, while I have presented this strategy in normative terms, I also suggest that it is descriptive of the way that much planning actually occurs. Many practicing planners are already using elements of the Political Feedback Strategy in their approaches to planning problems. Research would be needed, of course, to determine the actual extent of this usage.

Finally, I suggest that the Political Feedback Strategy can be an effective means of addressing critical urban and societal problems. The skillful user of the strategy will not be overwhelmed by political constraints but instead will use it to expand the parameters of the possible. A careful assessment of the political constraints in a given planning situation can provide the planner with knowledge usable in devising ways to break through those constraints. In short, I offer the Political Feedback Strategy as a means of enabling planners to play roles that are both efficacious and politically realistic, thus addressing the problem described in the first section of this chapter.

REFERENCES

Alexander, E. 1984. After rationality, what? A review of responses to paradigm breakdown. *Journal of the American Planning Association* 50: 62–9.

Beauregard, A. 1990. Bringing the city back in. *Journal of the American Planning Association* 56: 210–15.

Black, A. 1990. The Chicago Area Transportation Study: a case study of rational planning. *Journal of Planning Education and Research* 10: 27–37.

Brooks, M. 1990. The city may be back in, but where is the planner? *Journal of the American Planning Association* 56: 218–20.

Davidoff, P. 1965. Advocacy and pluralism in planning. *Journal of the American Institute of Planners* 31: 331–38.

Forester, J. 1982. Planning in the face of power. *Journal of the American Planning Association* 48: 67–80.

_____. 1987. Planning in the face of conflict: negotiation and mediation strategies in local land use regulation. *Journal of the American Planning Association* 53: 303–14.

Harvey, D. 1978. On planning the ideology of planning. In R. W. Burchell and G. Sternlieb, eds., *Planning theory in the 1980s: a search for future directions.* New Brunswick, NJ: Center for Urban Policy Research, 213–33.

Innes de Neufville, J. 1983. Planning theory and practice: bridging the gap. *Journal of Planning Education and Research* 3: 35–45.

Kraushaar, R. 1988. Outside the whale: progressive planning and the dilemmas of radical reform. *Journal of the American Planning Association* 54: 91–100.

Lindblom, C. 1965. *The intelligence of democracy: decision making through mutual adjustment.* New York: Free Press.

Mandelbaum, S. 1975. On not doing one's best: the uses and problems of experimentation in planning. *Journal of the American Institute of Planners* 41: 184–90.

Meyerson, M., and E. Banfield. 1955. *Politics, planning, and the public interest: the case of public housing in Chicago.* Glencoe, IL: Free Press.

Patton, C. 1983. Citizen input and professional responsibility. *Journal of Planning Education and Research* 3: 46–50.

Scott, A., and S. Roweis. 1977. Urban planning in theory and practice: a reappraisal. *Environment and Planning A* 9: 1097–1119.

Susskind, L., and C. Ozawa. 1984. Mediated negotiation in the public sector: the planner as mediator. *Journal of Planning Education and Research* 4: 5–15.

BISHWAPRIYA SANYAL

7 Meaning, Not Interest: Motivation for Progressive Planning

INTRODUCTION

None of the three dominant theories of bureaucratic behavior is able to explain "good bureaucratic behavior." The neo-Marxists argue that bureaucratic action is motivated by class interest. Public choice theorists claim that bureaucrats' "rent-seeking" tendencies dictate their actions. And Max Weber predicted that bureaucrats would follow rules and precedents. There are instances, however, when bureaucrats (hereafter referred to as planners) initiate distributional policies that serve the interests not of the elite but of the masses, reduce the possibilities of rent-seeking by the planners themselves, and are not guided solely by standardized rules and procedures. In other words, innovative policies in support of the poor do emerge within the so-called "capitalist," "rent-seeking," and "bureaucratic" state. So far, we have been unable to explain the emergence of such policies, which are routinely dismissed as motivated by the state's need to co-opt the poor or as the result of prolonged class struggle, or—at best—as an aberration brought about by one or two exceptional individuals who are unlike the rest of the unheeding planners.

An example is the case of informal business activities (IBAs) of the urban poor in developing countries.[1] As early as the 1970s, governments in many of these countries initiated various policies to support IBAs. These included regularization of IBAs and provision of various types of assistance such as low-interest loans, access to raw materials and markets, technical advice, and so on.[2] Yet, the literature pertaining to IBAs portrays the government (and, by implication, the planners) as hostile to these activities (De Soto 1989). Governmental efforts to assist IBAs are dismissed either as symbolic gestures intended to co-opt the urban poor at a time of deepening fiscal and legitimation crises in Third World states or as new tools for retaining old patronage politics (Tripp 1989). Public choice theorists argue that planners will never formalize these activities fully because their informal status provides planners opportunities to seek "rents" by "rationing" their right to transact in the market (Bates 1988). Even Weberian social theorists question the efficacy of these policies by pointing out the limitations of standardized policies in meeting the varying needs of the urban poor.

The empirical evidence from developing countries, however, does not fit any of the dominant theories. Planners, in increasing numbers, are implementing pro-IBA policies, and groups that have benefited from these policies continue to demand more support from the government. This evidence flies in the face of the argument that the primary motivation of pro-IBA policies is to co-opt the poor. What is more, planners in many countries have begun to work jointly with nongovernmental organizations (NGOs) to address the varying needs of the poor (Stearns and Otero 1990). This evidence, too, undermines the Weberian critique of state planners as rigid and driven by bureaucratic rules alone. And in contrast to the pronouncements of public choice theorists, IBAs are being formalized by planners in an increasing number of countries (Portes et al. 1989).

How did these progressive policies emerge within the so-called "capitalist," "rent-seeking," and "bureaucratic" state? What role did planners play in the initiation, support, and implementation of these policies? Were the planners relatively autonomous in influencing the policy process? Or, as the three dominant theories of bureaucratic behavior imply, did they lack the autonomy for independent action? Further, who are the "good and innovative planners?" What motivates them to support pro-poor policies? How do they manage to sustain pro-poor policies in the face of opposition from dominant social groups? These are the questions that motivated me in writing this chapter.

The present chapter is divided into three parts. I begin with a discussion of three dominant views of bureaucratic behavior, all of which argue that planners, in general, lack the autonomy to pursue progressive and innovative policies. One cannot accept these arguments, however, and still believe in the possibility of progressive and innovative planning. The very term "planning" assumes the autonomy of the state and, by implication, that of the planner to formulate progressive and innovative policies.

In the second part of the chapter, I provide three examples of how progressive, pro-IBA policies emerged in India, where I conducted field work for four months to collect data on the emergence of these policies.[3] The examples demonstrate how progressive planners create autonomy within institutional constraints, how the two-way movement of actors between the state and civil society may initiate progressive policies, and how progressive planners as state actors may utilize NGOs to better implement pro-poor policies.

In the third and concluding section of the chapter, I distill out of the Indian experience the motivations of progressive planners. I conclude that contrary to currently dominant views that planners are motivated solely by their self-interest, progressive planners are guided by multiple and overlapping motivations such as a sense of public interest, pride in doing a job well, simple altruism, and deep respect for leaders from civil society who drew the planners' attention to the plight of the poor. These factors, along with a concern for self-interest, jointly provide a "sense of meaning" that guides their actions in support of redistributive policies.

DOUBTS ABOUT PLANNERS' AUTONOMY

The notion that planners in capitalist countries lack the autonomy to pursue progressive policies is not new. As early as the 1850s, Marx argued that the capitalist state is the "executive committee" of the bourgeoisie, meaning that the state acts in the interest of only the bourgeoisie (Marx 1934).

Borrowing from Marx, the neo-Marxists writing in the 1960s argued that the capitalist state was neither the protector of public interest nor did it have the autonomy to restructure the relations of production and reproduction through planning. The state is considered captive to the dominant classes, both national and international, and it uses its "monopoly power over the means of coercion" to further the dominant class's interests.[4]

Planning, according to the neo-Marxists, is not intended to facilitate broad-based development. Rather, its primary purpose is to help the capitalist system survive the periodic crises it creates for itself (Harvey 1978). And the planners, the so-called guardians of public interest, are in reality handmaidens of the dominant classes. Their worldview, which they acquired partly from the educational process and partly from their middle-class upbringing, is petit-bourgeois. These "state actors" are not interested in using the state machinery to alter the relations of production so as to improve "the public's" quality of life. At best, they tinker at the margin with disjointed incremental policies to avert direct class warfare. But this "reform mongering" at the margin does not work well to fully pacify the dominated social group. What is more, state policies create new contradictions that further destabilize the capitalist system.

Public Choice Theorists and Attack from the Right[5]

The attack on the state and on planning from the right of the ideological spectrum emerged in the early 1970s as both rich and poor countries entered a period of sluggish growth, increasing internal debt, and "stagflation"—a stagnant economy with high unemployment but high inflation at the same time, a peculiar juxtaposition of trends that could not be adequately explained by the conventional "Phillips curve" and Keynesian macro-economic theory (Killick 1989).

Who was to blame for this "disjuncture" in economic growth? A group of economists, under the banner of new neoclassical economics, proposed that in both rich and poor countries the governments were solely to be blamed. The charge against these governments was that their attempts to plan, regulate, and control the economy distorted the functioning of the capital, labor, and commodities markets, created disincentives for private investment, gave rise to parallel markets, and overextended the involvement of the public sector in the economy. The critics argued that planning, which was originally intended to correct "market failures," led instead to "state failure," retarding economic growth to a much greater degree than what would have occurred even with market failures.

In condemning the state, the right-wing economists constructed a theory of the state using economic logic. The purpose was to explain why the state was pursuing policies that were clearly irrational in economic terms. Much has been written about this already, so I will only recapitulate those arguments that are central to right-wing theorizing: the rational choice model and the related notion of the rent-seeking state. According to this model, state policies that appear to be economically irrational from the point of view of the general public interest are politically and economically rational in terms of serving the private interest of the politicians and the planners who create these policies (Bates 1993).

That it is of personal interest to politicians to be elected to office is hardly a new insight; however, the economists' interpretation of planners' behavior is of some interest to us. According to this interpretation, planners act on behalf of their own interests instead of the public's. One way they further their own interests is by creating regulations that restrict market transactions and then charging "a rent" from market participants who would like to earn a "scarcity premium" as a result of the regulations. There are many variations on this central idea, but what is important for our purposes is to understand how the "rent-seeking" portrayal of the state adversely affects the legitimacy of planning. In essence, the rent-seeking analysis implies that the state is neither an autonomous nor a benign actor but has been captured by a "special-interest group," internal to the state, whose members are part of a new class that, by controlling the state apparatus, controls some of the means of production and all of the means of distribution.

Similarity between Public Choice and Neo-Marxist Theories

Although the two strands of criticism about state and planning come from opposite ends of the ideological spectrum, they are alike in two ways. First, both deny that the state has the autonomy to pursue public interest; this means both points of view dismiss the intellectual foundation on which public planning rests. The two views differ, however, about why the state lacks autonomy: The neo-Marxists blame the dominant classes for restricting the autonomy of the planners, while the neoclassical economists blame the planners themselves for undermining the autonomy of the state from within.

Another similarity between the two schools of thought is that both hold that self-interest alone is what motivates individuals to act. In this interpretation, every action is assumed to be guided by one's desire to further one's own interests; what is more, such self-serving action is valued as "rational behavior." This notion of rationality undermines the social logic of "public interest" on which the activity of planning rests. In fact, it undermines the logic and rationale not only for planning but also for many other activities that we undertake daily (Sen 1977). That aside, let us recognize for the time being that these common elements in neo-Marxist and neoclassical economics lead both views to dismiss the possibility and feasibility of planning in capitalist societies. To find such a rationale, one must look elsewhere.

Weberian Theory and the Bureaucratic State

Max Weber's theory of the state (Weber 1958) comes closest to endorsing the notion of planning—meaning that the state is autonomous in pursuing policies on behalf of the public interest. But Weber, too, was doubtful about whether planners employed by the state are autonomous agents who can pursue progressive policies on their own. The Weberian argument against planners' autonomy is well known; I will not discuss that argument here except to remind the reader that Weber was primarily concerned with bureaucratic rules and procedures that, he thought, would have a positive effect in terms of reducing the personal idiosyncrasies of individual rulers. More than a hundred years later, we are now concerned with reducing the rigidity, inflexibility, and impersonality of those bureaucratic rules and procedures. And we, as planners, would like to know how to abide by bureaucratic rules and still have sufficient institutional room to reform old policies and initiate new ones.

To sum up then: None of the three dominant theories of bureaucratic behavior adequately explains the emergence of progressive and innovative policies. The neo-Marxists and public choice theorists dismiss the notion that planners could be interested in progressive and innovative policies. The Weberians, on the other hand, do not dismiss that possibility but argue that as state actors, planners are strictly limited in their latitude by bureaucratic rules and procedures that do not leave much room for innovative policies.

EVIDENCE OF PROGRESSIVE PLANNING: THE CASE OF INDIA

The most effective way to counteract anti-planning theories of the kinds mentioned above is to leave armchair theorizing behind and talk to planners, politicians, and social activists who are involved in policy formulation, opposition, and/or implementation. In 1989, for that purpose, I visited India.[6] My objective was to find out why and how the Indian government maintained a generally progressive orientation vis-à-vis the urban IBAs and how and why a bureaucracy that is commonly attacked as both imperious and tangled in layer upon layer of obscure regulations often initiates and implements policies on behalf of large but unorganized groups of poor people. In particular, I chose to study the government-initiated programs to support women engaged in IBAs. Paradoxically, I came to think of Indian society as graced by a state that is more progressive than the fragile institutions of electoral politics warrant. What follows are some findings that illustrate my pleasant surprises about the Indian state and its planners.

Progressive Planning at All Three Levels

There is ample evidence that the Indian state at all levels—national, state, and local—had formulated a range of pro-IBA policies as early as the

1970s. For example, at the national level, the government had passed legislation in 1971 requiring all nationalized banks to lend, at a minimum, one
percent of their portfolio to IBAs, at lower than market interest rates. Later,
in 1986, the government set up a national commission, headed by a prominent grassroots leader of IBAs, to investigate the problems commonly faced
by poor women engaged in IBAs. The commission was not set up as a
public relations stance. It was endowed with all the necessary resources and
the administrative autonomy to pursue a detailed and impartial evaluation of existing government policies for women-headed IBAs.

At the state level, in Gujarat, a relatively conservative state of the Indian Union, the government passed legislation that required compulsory
procurement of handicrafts from women-headed IBAs to be sold in government-run stores. To further assist these women, not all of whom produced handicrafts, government-run hospitals and prisons regularly purchased vegetables from poor women vendors. The state government had
also created a maternity benefit scheme, and it directed India's largest life
insurance agency to start a life insurance plan for these women.[7] In
pursuing these policies, the state government planners did not restrict all
activities to the government ministries. They often sought the assistance
of NGOs to create and implement innovative programs and projects that
were targeted toward the same group of poor women who were to benefit
from the government-administered programs—a clever bureaucratic strategy that I discuss later in this chapter.

At the local level, in the city of Ahmedabad, the urban planners acknowledged their responsibility to provide physical space for street vendors. This was a direct consequence of the Indian Supreme Court's decision that all local authorities were responsible for protecting the right to a
livelihood of street vendors who, if dislocated by the authorities, were to
be provided alternative locations for conducting their businesses. True, the
legal case that led to this landmark decision by the Indian Supreme Court
was initiated by NGOs, so the credit for this progressive reform cannot
be bestowed on the planners. Still, since the Supreme Court is part of the
Indian state structure, it is an interesting example of progressive and hu-
manitarian action on the part of a state that is commonly dismissed as bureaucratic, repressive, and blatantly pro-elite in policy orientation.

The Self-Disciplining State?

In my interviews with state-level planners, it became increasingly clear
that the planners based in the state capital, Gandhinagar, were fully aware

of the inefficiencies of the government programs targeted toward IBAs. One program in particular, an "integrated scheme" to provide subsidized loans and assets to IBAs, had been evaluated by the ministry responsible for implementing the program. The evaluation indicated that the majority of the program beneficiaries were not the poor but relatively well-off groups. The evaluation had also indicated that significant portions of the program funds were not distributed and that the impact of the funds distributed, in terms of increased income and employment, was insignificant.

The planners in Gandhinagar who were responsible for administering the program were quite candid in acknowledging the evaluation findings. In discussions with me, they blamed the field-level officers—the "street level bureaucrats," according to Lipsky's nomenclature (Lipsky and Weatherley 1977)—who were to implement the program by enlisting poor families and providing them loans without the kind of paperwork commonly required by standard banks. The upper-level planners were certain that the field officers had not done their job well. They suspected that many of the field officers might have been bribed by relatively well-off and locally powerful individuals who took advantage of the well-intentioned programs. Some complained that the field officers rarely go "to the field," and that is why the loan disbursement rate is low.

In discussing these problems, the upper-level planners openly acknowledged that they lacked institutional mechanisms for disciplining the field officers and for making them accountable. They said it was very difficult, if not impossible, to gather evidence of mismanagement on the part of the field officers and that any disciplinary action initiated at the upper level was likely to be resisted at the lower levels in ways that could further reduce the already slow pace of progress. Some planners also feared that investigation of program mismanagement at the local level might anger politicians of the ruling political party who had coerced the field officers into making loans available to supporters. These politicians could harm the upper-level bureaucrats by complaining to their political bosses who could, in turn, transfer them to obscure locations within Gujarat.

The planners who still cared about improving the effectiveness of the loan program devised an innovative strategy. They persuaded the government to involve well-reputed NGOs in administering the program. The purpose was to create a mechanism by which the government field officers could be held accountable for unsatisfactory performance. How so? As the NGOs managed to disburse more loans and reach a larger percentage of poor families than the government-administered programs, the upper-level planners used that evidence to demand that the field officers match the level of performance of NGOs. The field officers who, in the past, usually provided a host of reasons for poor program performance, could do so no longer. The poor performance of the government program stood out because the NGOs demonstrated that they were much more efficient with far fewer resources than the government's field officers.

Whether this form of induced competition enhanced the performance of government programs I do not know, because I did not find any comparative evaluation of government programs after the NGOs began to participate in program implementation. I do know, however, that many upper-level planners in Gujarat are deeply concerned about how to increase the effectiveness of various government programs, including the ones directed toward the urban poor. These planners are fully aware of the institutional constraints of operating within "the state," but they are also keenly aware of how the power and resources of the state may be used strategically to enhance program effectiveness. And in devising institutional strategies for that purpose, the planners do not think of the state in monolithic terms. On the contrary, they constantly seek competing groups who provide opportunities for comparison and autonomous action.

The Power of Weak Agencies

How did the progressive planners create the autonomy to devise pro-IBA policies? The case of the national commission on poor informal-sector women, mentioned earlier, provides an interesting insight into this difficult question.

According to Ela Bhatt, chairperson of the commission, she had proposed the idea to then Prime Minister of India, Rajiv Gandhi, after he addressed a large rally of poor, informal-sector women whom Mrs. Bhatt had helped to organize. At this time, the Prime Minister was trying to shore up his political support among women voters, many of whom had been upset by his earlier support of antifeminist legislation.[8] In response to Mrs. Bhatt's request, the Prime Minister asked her to draft a proposal to set up a national commission and to contact his secretary, which Mrs. Bhatt promptly did. After a rather long wait, during which time Mrs. Bhatt had the opportunity of meeting the Prime Minister once more and reminding him about the pending decision, the Prime Ministers' secretariat formally announced the formation of the commission and nominated Mrs. Bhatt to chair it.

Institutionally, the new commission had to be located within a ministry and, as chair of the commission, Mrs. Bhatt was asked her preference. One would think that Mrs. Bhatt would choose a strong ministry, like the

Ministry of Labor or the Ministry of Industries, so that the commission's activities could be well-funded and its recommendations could have the backing of a powerful member of the Prime Minister's cabinet. Instead, Mrs. Bhatt chose to house the commission within the rather weak Ministry of Social Welfare, which administered a relatively small budget. It was headed by a woman who had never been in the cabinet before, and its highest level bureaucrat was not particularly well-known within the Indian Civil Service.

Why did Mrs. Bhatt opt for a weak ministry to house the commission? In interviews with me, Mrs. Bhatt indicated that she was concerned that if the commission were housed within a powerful ministry, she would have had very little autonomy, little ability to direct the commission's work and recommendations. Elaborating on her position, Mrs. Bhatt mentioned that if, for example, the commission were housed within the Ministry of Labor, the Minister would have pressured her to select representatives of organized formal-sector labor as commission members. Since the mandate of the commission was to investigate the problems of unorganized informal-sector women, Mrs. Bhatt feared that representatives of organized formal-sector labor, who are all male, would have deviated the commission from its original intention and used it to further the interests of labor unions to which they belonged. Mrs. Bhatt was also concerned that in a powerful and busy ministry, senior-level bureaucrats would have had little time to assist her in the day-to-day operation of the commission, yet they would have tried to influence the nature of the commission's final recommendations.

In contrast, a weak and low-key ministry lacked the type of personnel who would have curbed Mrs. Bhatt's autonomy as leader of the commission's work. The activities of a weak ministry, including the work of the commission, were less visible and, hence, subjected to less scrutiny by the powerful politicians who devoted most of their attention to the internal workings of important ministries such as the Ministry of Finance, the Ministry of Industries, and so on. This allowed Mrs. Bhatt, as the commission's chair, the institutional autonomy she needed to direct the commission's recommendation toward progressive objectives. True, Mrs. Bhatt was concerned at times that the commission's recommendations might not receive adequate institutional support for rapid implementation. However, she was aware that once the commission's report was formally published, she could use her contacts with selected politicians to draw the attention of the parliament to the report and thereby pressure the Prime Minister to act on its recommendations.

Planners' Autonomy and the Permeability of the State

It is a widely held belief among planning academicians that the more permeable a state is to the inflow of market actors, the less likely planners are to be autonomous of dominant market forces.[9] To elaborate: The easier it is for market agents to be employed by the state, particularly at the upper level, the more difficult it will be for planners to formulate policies independent of market interests. Proponents of this view often refer to the U.S. government executive branch to illustrate their point. They argue that "the revolving door," through which large numbers of corporate executives enter, exit, and reenter the American government structure, reduces the chances for state policy making that is autonomous of business interests. The consequence of this trend for progressive planning is straightforward: The permeability of the state to corporate agents reduces the possibilities for progressive planning, which usually requires policies that curb the influence of powerful corporations in structuring market outcomes.

The example from India that I am about to narrate demonstrates that permeability of the state by private-sector interests may lead to an opposite outcome. In fact, it may facilitate the formulation of progressive policies. In 1987, the state government of Gujarat approved a scheme that made it possible for poor, urban, informal-sector women to have life insurance. This may not seem like a major social policy to an American, but it is, particularly if one takes into account the fact that there are millions of poor, urban, informal-sector women in Gujarat and their life expectancy is barely fifty years!

How did this progressive policy come to be formulated? Interviews with a number of key policy actors revealed the outlines of the following story. In the early 1980s, Gujarat's then labor commissioner, the highest level bureaucrat in the state government's Ministry of Labor, was approached by a grassroots organization, named SEWA (Self-Employed Women's Association), which represented the interests of poor urban informal-sector women. SEWA had approached the commissioner to request that he enforce existing state legislation regarding minimum wages for its members who worked as subcontractors to wholesalers of embroidered clothing. The commissioner became knowledgeable about SEWA members and poor women in other informal-sector trades as a result of prolonged legal battles with the wholesalers. Thanks to the personal intervention of the Minister of Labor, the commissioner was finally successful in enforcing a higher hourly wage for the SEWA members.

Soon after this, the labor commissioner had to leave his job because he had reached the government's mandatory retirement age of fifty-five years.

The commissioner, however, was in good health and needed additional income, beyond what he received as a pension, to marry off his youngest daughter.[10] He decided to become an agent for a major insurance firm. In his new position, he would receive a commission every time he sold an insurance policy. It was at this time that he approached the leader of SEWA and inquired if the SEWA members would be interested in procuring life insurance policies.

The idea of life insurance for the members was very appealing to the leader of SEWA, but she was skeptical that any insurance company would be willing to insure her members, who were very poor and generally suffered from malnutrition and other diseases associated with poor living conditions. The ex-commissioner then suggested to the SEWA leader that she take up this issue with the Ministry of Labor, where he had previously worked. He provided names of people who, he thought, would be sympathetic to such an appeal. In essence, his goal was to make the government put pressure on insurance agencies to create some kind of special group scheme for poor, informal-sector women, which could then be used by SEWA members. Needless to say, the ex-commissioner, now the insurance agent, was ultimately interested in receiving a commission for each member insured under the new scheme.

MEANING, NOT INTERESTS

What lessons can we draw from these three vignettes of progressive planning in India? In answering this question, we need to be cautious about generalizing from the Indian experience because the Indian planners operate within institutional and political contexts that are not typical of all developing countries. For example, the relationship between planners and politicians in India is strongly conditioned by a relatively autonomous bureaucracy that was created during British Colonial rule, long before many of the political parties were formed (Evans 1989). Also, the social composition of the dominant political party in India, namely, the Congress Party of which Rajiv Gandhi was the head at the time of my field work, accounts for the progressive stance of the then Prime Minister vis-à-vis IBAs (Manor 1990). Finally, a factor that influenced the policy outcome in India was the growing organizational strength of NGOs such as SEWA. The NGOs played a key role in drawing the planners' attention to the plight of the poor (Shah 1988).

Having recognized these particular features of the Indian context, we may proceed to draw at least one lesson from the three vignettes. Unlike what public choice theorists or neo-Marxists argue, planners do not necessarily always act to further either their self-interest or the interest of the dominant classes. Nor do they act simply to implement official rules and procedures, as some Weberians suggest. Progressive planners act out of a motivation that is broader in scope and more complex in its purpose than the term "self-interest" conveys. That motivation encompasses the need for personal benefit and the propensity to follow rules, but it is not confined to these two purposes. Several other factors contribute to the structuring of progressive motivations. For example, a concern for public welfare, a sense of social justice, a long-term view of societal trajectory, and more personal factors such as the personal gratification one enjoys in doing well one's share of work toward the collective good—all these factors contribute to the social construction of ethical identities of progressive planners which, in turn, guide their motivation for progressive action. To reduce the multidimensional purposes underlying action to the singular notion of self-interest is, to say the least, rather narrow. It also conveys the incorrect notion that self-interest is self-produced whereas we know that, in reality, how one defines one's self-interest is largely constructed by a host of cultural, political, and social factors (Modell 1992).

Perhaps the main lesson of this study, then, is that we need to go beyond the notion of self-interest and formulate a different concept that better explains the motivations underlying progressive planning. The first step toward that objective is to acknowledge that what guides progressive action is not self-interest but a particular sense of meaning about one's ethical identity and mission in life (Coles 1992). Which particular factors contribute to the social construction of that "meaning," we cannot say for sure as yet, because our understanding of how social and psychological factors influence one another is still quite limited. Nevertheless, my interviews with the progressive planners provide some clues. For example, we know that both social and political acculturation influence the construction of meaning. We also know that major events such as a political assassination, sharp economic downturn, or severe drought also bring to the fore concern for collective interest that is central to progressive thinking. Finally, the relative autonomy of the planner within the bureaucratic structure may strongly influence his or her work capability and the meaning he or she derives from work.

To be sure, cultivation of meaning that draws on a progressive view of social life is not sufficient for progressive planning: Progressive planners must also be strategic in pushing for progressive policies only at certain times and in particular ways (Krumholz and Forester 1990). Having a political boss with a progressive agenda is, of course, helpful in this regard, but that too is not sufficient. As the three vignettes demonstrate, planners must be skillful in creating institutional autonomy for the formulation and implementation of progressive policies.

How does one create institutional autonomy amidst the multiple constraints imposed by a public bureaucracy? These vignettes suggest two lessons. First, as planners we must abandon the notion of the state as a unitary actor with a clearly defined goal and, instead, understand the institutional dynamics within and among the various components of the governing structure in any place. It is this knowledge that led the progressive planner in the second vignette to choose, purposefully, a weak ministry for pushing a progressive policy. It is also this kind of institutional understanding that helps planners anticipate when and how to use their discretionary power to progressive ends.

The second lesson, drawn from the first and third vignettes, is that in creating autonomy for progressive action, planners should not limit their thinking to the domain of state activities. They should look outside their home domain to the market and civil society to take advantage of the interactions and overlaps among the three principal domains of social activities. The strategic use of NGOs to discipline state actors (first vignette) and the use of market actors such as the private insurance agent to influence state policies (third vignette) are examples of how best to utilize for progressive purposes the interactions among the three domains. These examples imply that planners, to be keenly aware of the institutional dynamics of the state, must also understand the institutional dynamics of the market and of civil society. It is my hunch, based on interviews with successful planners, that one of the keys to their success is an astute understanding of the interactions among these domains and how such interactions can be put to good use. This understanding is largely developed through work experience. Planners who best utilize their work experience to reflect and fine-tune their "worldview" never subscribe to the kind of theories of bureaucratic behavior I described at the beginning of this chapter.

Notes

1. I realize that there is a theoretical debate about whether the term "informal" is appropriate for these activities. However, lacking a more precise term, I am using it to refer to small business enterprises that are not officially accounted for and that operate outside the legal and regulatory framework. In developing countries, between 40 and 70 percent of the urban labor force is engaged in these businesses.

2. For a review of this literature, see B. Sanyal, *An Institutional Approach to Urban Informal Sector Policies: Lessons from the Past, Directions for the Future* (United Nations Development Program, 1991).

3. I visited India from January to April 1989 and was based primarily in the state of Gujarat, where a nongovernmental organization, the Self-Employed Women's Association (SEWA), was the focus of my research inquiry. SEWA has played a leading role, since 1972, in influencing government policies toward IBAs. I met with the leaders of SEWA and other top-level bureaucrats and asked them to identify six policy changes in favor of IBAs. For each policy reform, I collected information from both SEWA and the government about why and how such reforms were initiated and, specifically, what role bureaucrats played in the process.

4. For a good review, see B. Jessop, *State Theory: Putting the Capitalist State in its Place* (University Park, PA: Pennsylvania State University Press, 1990).

5. For an elaboration and critique of this approach, see M. Grindle, "The New Political Economy: Positive Economics and Negative Politics," in G. M. Meier, ed., *Politics and Policy Making in Developing Countries* (San Francisco: ICS Press, 1991), pp. 41–68.

6. I spent three months in India gathering detailed information on various pro-IBA policies. I interviewed planners, politicians, business leaders, academics, leaders of grassroots organizations, and international donor agencies that, in one form or another, were involved with the formulation and implementation of these policies. In addition, I studied government reports, office memos, newspaper reports, and published articles related to these policies.

7. Although Gujarat stands out among the Indian states in terms of pro-IBA policies, many other states have also implemented pro-IBA policies. See N. J. Turin, "Anti-poverty Programme—A Reappraisal," unpublished mimeo (New Delhi: Ministry of Rural Development, 1990).

8. The legislation that Rajiv Gandhi had supported and for which he was heavily criticized by Indian feminists allowed Muslim men to practice Islamic marriage laws. According to these laws, Muslim men could marry more than one woman and could opt for a divorce without paying any alimony. The Indian constitution does not permit this. However, Rajiv Gandhi supported the position that social and religious practices of minority groups, such as Muslims in India, should not be dictated by the Hindu majority. Some argue that Rajiv's position was not based on any principle but that he was interested primarily in getting the Muslim votes in the upcoming election.

9. On this issue, see E. A. Nordlinger, "Taking the State Seriously," in M. Weiner and S. P. Huntington, eds., *Understanding Political Development* (Boston: Little, Brown and Company, 1987), pp. 353–90.

10. Although the government of India has formally banned the practice of dowry, it is still prevalent, particularly among middle- and upper-middle-class Indian families.

REFERENCES

Bates, R. 1988. Disaggregating the political. *States and Social Structure Newsletter 6.*

————. 1993. *Essays in the political economy of rural Africa.* Berkeley: University of California Press.

Coles, R. 1992. *The call to service: a witness to idealism.* Boston: Houghton Mifflin.

DeSoto, H. 1989. *The other path: the invisible revolution in the third world.* New York: Harper and Row.

Evans, P. 1989. The state as problem and solution: predation, embedded autonomy and adjustment. Working Paper No. 11, Series on Comparative Development. Providence, RI: Brown University.

Harvey, D. 1978. On planning the ideology of planning. In R. W. Burchell and G. Sternlieb, eds., *Planning theory in the 1980s.* New Brunswick, NJ: Center for Urban Policy Research, 213–34.

Killick, T. 1989. *A reaction too far: economic theory and the role of the state in developing countries.* London: Overseas Development Institute.

Krumholz, N., and J. Forester. 1990. *Making equity planning work: leadership in the public sector.* Philadelphia: Temple University Press, 225–40.

Lipsky, M., and R. Weatherley. 1977. *Street level bureaucrats and institutional innovation: implementing special education reform in Massachusetts.* Cambridge: Harvard University Press.

Manor, J. 1990. How and why liberal and representative politics emerged in India. *Political Studies* 38: 20–38.

Marx, K. 1934. *The eighteenth brumaire of Louis Bonaparte.* Moscow: Progress Publishers.

Modell, A. H. 1992. *The private self.* Cambridge, MA: Harvard University Press.

Portes, A., M. Castells, and L. A. Benton, eds. 1989. *The informal economy: studies in advanced and less developed countries.* Baltimore: Johns Hopkins University Press, 298–311.

Sen, A. K. 1977. Rational fools: critique of the behavioral foundations of economic theory. *Philosophy and Public Affairs* 6: 317–44.

Shah, G. 1988. Grass-roots mobilization in Indian politics. In A. Kohli, ed., *India's democracy: an analysis of changing state–society relations.* Princeton, NJ: Princeton University Press, 262–304.

Stearns, K., and M. Otero, eds. 1990. *The critical connection: governments, private institutions and the informal sector in Latin America.* Monograph Series No. 5. Washington, DC: Accion International.

Tripp, A. 1989. *Defending the right to subsist: the state vs. the urban informal sector in Tanzania.* Helsinki: World Institute for Development Economics Research.

Weber, M. 1958. Bureaucracy. In H. H. Gerth and C. W. Mills, eds., *From Max Weber: essays in sociology.* New York: Oxford University Press.

Andy Thornley

8 Thatcherism and the Swedish "Model": Center/Local Relationships in Urban Planning

INTRODUCTION

Since 1979 Britain has been ruled by governments pursuing a very distinctive ideology based upon the ideas of the New Right. This ideology has come to be termed "Thatcherism."

Of course, there is the question of whether Thatcherism will continue now that Margaret Thatcher herself has left 10 Downing Street. She believes it will: "Thatcherism will live. It will live long after Thatcher has died" (Thatcher 1992, 37). Whatever happens in the future, there is no doubt that over the last decade public policy has been much influenced by the government's ideological position. The field of planning has not escaped this influence and, as a result of constant erosion over the years, the planning system has been significantly reoriented in both its purpose and its procedures (for a full account see Thornley 1993). One aspect of this ideological influence has been a centralization of power. This has led to a reformulation of the role of local government, the arena of most planning activity in the United Kingdom.

The first part of this chapter will describe the effect on local government and the planning system of this centralization. The second part poses the question "How typical is the British experience?" As a partial address

151

to that query, I explore the relationships between ideology, local government, and planning in Sweden. I have chosen Sweden because it has pursued a very different political path although it is at broadly the same level of economic development as Britain. While Britain was experiencing the conflictual market-oriented strategy of Thatcherism, Swedish politics, until 1991, was dominated by the Social Democratic Party with a strong welfare state and consensual ideology. Even the changes in Sweden that now seem to move it closer to the British model are peculiarly revealing of the dynamics of planning in the two societies.

Comparison plays an important role in the formulation of theory and the articulation of practical advice. There is, indeed, a long tradition among both planning scholars and practitioners of comparative inquiry. Working within that tradition, I have chosen to focus on the relationship between political ideology, local government power, and the latitude of planners and planning. Those elements seem to be particularly important in understanding the relationship between economic restructuring and urban development: How far can economic forces be guided by political intervention? Does the global economic drummer leave much space for individual cities to shape their character or choose their niche?

Much of the literature that explores this theme focuses on cities in the United States (Beauregard 1989; Logan and Molotch 1987; Mollenkopf and Castells 1991) and the dynamics of a federal system with strong, though hardly autonomous, local government. In Europe, however, it is hard to make sense of urban development without studying the policies of national (and now transnational) governments. Local finances, participatory modes, and responses to development proposals all are shaped by discrete national mandates and generalized ideologies.

THE BRITISH EXPERIENCE

Thatcherism

It is widely recognized that there are two strands to Thatcherism. The first strand—that of economic liberalism—sanctifies the market as the best decision-making process. In the urban arena, this commitment accedes to the initiatives of developers in shaping the direction and pace of growth. The second strand—authoritarian—praises allegiance to a strong central state.[1] In the urban arena, a strong center implies a lack of concern with local majorities and participatory modes, particularly when local democracy is used to resist the will of national majorities and their agents.

On the face of it, the two strands appear ideologically opposed, being based upon two very different concepts of human nature and the ideal society (Levitas 1986). Economic liberalism rests on individualism and promotes competitive, self-seeking values for which individual freedom from regulation is an important touchstone, and the role of the state is minimized. In contrast, authoritarian writers such as Scruton (1980) see the enemy of conservatism not in socialism but in liberalism "with all its attendant trappings of individual autonomy and the 'natural' rights of man" (Scruton 1980, 16).

These two strands—overtly tugging in different directions—were imaginatively reconciled in the Thatcher governments to form a single ideology. Traditionally, conservatives in Britain have relied on the "One Nation" strategy in which it is the duty of those who rule to sustain the less well-off in order to legitimate the regime. The authoritarian strand in Thatcherism replaced this welfare strategy with a bald appeal to nation, family, and duty to generate legitimacy, deference, and social stability. The strong central state was used to suppress the articulation of welfare demands and to protect the market. Scruton, speaking within this authoritarian strand, refers to democracy as "a menacing disease raging through society" (Scruton 1980, 69).

The resultant "strong state" is not local but national: The center controls the ideological heights (King 1987). Since local government has been the main vehicle for the satisfaction of "social citizen rights," its latitude had to be severely constrained.

The Weakening of Local Government

Over the last decade, a reduction in the power of local authorities has been achieved through financial policies (Duncan and Goodwin 1988). Central government has gained greater and greater ability to control the spending of individual authorities rather than just a reduction in local government spending as a whole. Central government's responses have been pragmatic, complex, and ad hoc within the overall aim of reducing public expenditure, but over the decade a more strategic approach has developed. Some authors have suggested that a more coherent approach can be identified since 1987 (Bulpitt 1989; Stewart and Stoker 1989a). This involves a move away from pure finance to the restructuring of local government itself. The metropolitan authorities and the Greater London Council were removed as a tier of government in 1986 because they were controlled by the Labour Party and were pursuing popular policies that were seen as an ideological threat to Thatcherism (see Allen 1996; Duncan and Goodwin 1988). Currently, further changes to the structure of local government are under consideration but the main impact is occurring through the radical reforms within local government.

This internal restructuring involves the removal of certain services from local government through the separation of the responsibility for provision from the actual act of provision. This shift has been referred to as one of "enabling not providing." A start to this process occurred before 1987 with the "right to buy" policy for council houses, shifting the responsibilities from local authorities to owner occupiers. The Education Acts of the 1980s transferred power from the local authority to parents, head teachers, and governors. However, more recently there has been evidence of a concerted effort to restructure the whole of local government along these lines. This was clearly set out in the pamphlet by Ridley (1988), who was secretary of state at the time. He proposed that local authorities should abandon or reduce many activities that could be better done by the private sector. This would allow government, he argued, to operate on a tighter budget and free resources to concentrate on those activities that only a local authority could undertake successfully: "Inside every fat and bloated local authority there is a slim one struggling to get out" (Ridley 1988, 26). Local authorities, in his scheme, would regulate standards and monitor contractors but would no longer serve as the universal service provider. The right-wing No Turning Back Group (1990) has taken the idea a stage further and suggested that ultimately a local authority would be run like a company, with an annual meeting in which a small number of councillors would meet to decide the allocation of service contracts. The remaining administrative functions would operate under tight financial controls and be run by an elected mayor acting as a manager.

The same strategic commitment is expressed in the Citizen's Charter, proposed by the right-wing pressure group, the Adam Smith Institute, and adopted with great enthusiasm by Prime Minister John Major in 1991. The Charter applied the principle of consumer choice and value for money to the provision of public services. It stressed the publication of performance standards and the monitoring of how well agencies match these standards. A fundamental assumption underlying the approach is that better service would be provided through more competition within the public sector.

The Charter has been applied to a whole range of services including transport, education, and housing. It was implemented through the Local Government Act of 1992 in which the Audit Commission was charged with prescribing a set of indicators for local authority services. Performance would be measured in terms of cost, economy, efficiency, and effectiveness (Audit Commission 1992). The approach is a highly centralized one in which the indicators are decided by the Commission with no regard for local differences. These centrally defined measures of performance prevent local authorities from making their own decisions on how to meet local needs. The disaggregated model of consumer choice that runs through the Charter makes it difficult to assess services that are jointly produced and collectively consumed. The Charter can, and will, measure dog excrement on the pavement but cannot effectively address environmental quality or the alleviation of poverty.

THE IMPACT ON PLANNING

So the "authoritarian decentralism" has led to an increase in the power of central government to relocate formerly public activities into the marketplace. Local government has been deeply implicated in this process, losing many of its powers to the central government and contracting out many of its functions to the private sector. How much has this process affected planning practice?

First, there is a very clear centralization trend running through all the changes to the planning system since 1979. The central government has restricted the scope of planning and the range of criteria used by local authorities. A very direct increase in central control is introduced through regional and strategic guidance memoranda that allow Westminster to set the parameters of all plan making. The Urban Development Corporation initiative is another clear example of the "authoritarian decentralism" principle. Central government has very strong financial controls over planning in affected areas and arbitrates conflict. This authority is then used to ensure that decisions are made according to market priorities. Simplified Planning Zones can be imposed upon local authorities by the secretary of state, and developers can also request such designations. In such zones it is not possible to pursue planning gain, thus one of the remaining mechanisms for local authorities to introduce community-oriented criteria is not available. In 1991, another initiative to deal with the problems of the inner city, City Challenge, was launched. Local authorities were invited to submit bids for money to tackle their problem areas. Again, this program was highly orchestrated by central government, who set out strict guidelines on the kind of proposals it would support: They must be geared to the requirements of private-sector interests, which meant that local authorities had to shift some of their resources away from other community-oriented schemes.

The reduction of opportunities for participation is another thread running through the changes. The attempts to speed up and streamline the planning process have clearly led to a less favorable attitude toward participation and a reduction in opportunities. Many of the new initiatives, such as simplified regimes in Enterprise Zones and Urban Development Corporations, involve reduced participation. The result of the procedures in these areas is a bypassing of local democracy and community involvement and a redefinition of democracy that relies wholly on the general election for legitimacy. Sheltered by the umbrella of electoral legitimacy, decisions are made in the private arenas of the marketplace and within central ministries that are impervious to local opinion.

THE SWEDISH EXPERIENCE

The Consensus Culture

Dahrendorf has suggested that the Swedish "model" exists in the minds of political reformers rather than in the messy reality of life (Dahrendorf 1990, 2–3). The warning is well taken, but it is difficult to deny the distinctive Swedish emphasis on consensus-seeking politics. In the past, this approach as been used to show that there is a middle way between capitalism and communism, for example by Anthony Crosland in his classic statement of socialist reformism (1956), and more recently by the former Soviet Premier Gorbachev. This Swedish approach has been given a variety of labels, including that of "corporate pluralism." The corporative part indicates the structured nature of the consultation process and the pluralist part the opportunities for a wide range of interests to be involved in participation (Heclo and Madsen 1987).

At the national level, Sweden employs a centuries-old system of official investigatory commissions. The deliberations of government are supplemented by these commissions in which specialized groups, professions, experts, and interest groups work out proposals before they are submitted to Parliament. In the process of investigation, ideas are continuously fed back and forth between the commissions, interest groups, and government agencies. It is not surprising that most conflicts are resolved before parliamentary debates begin and that the implementation of policies is very smooth.

A similar approach is adopted at the local level, and in most municipalities there is a great deal of consultation with local groups and organizations of all kinds. In the 1970s local government was consolidated into larger units and, in parallel, the consultation procedures were expanded (Gustafsson 1988).

This system of consultation requires a great deal of organization and incurs high transaction costs. It assumes that social and economic interest groups are organized into national associations with professional staffs that can participate fully in the work of the commissions. Such organizations may exist in other countries, but in Sweden they are more highly institutionalized and given an important status in the consensus-seeking political process.

Until recently, this consensus-oriented political culture seemed to imbue all political parties, although it was closely associated with the long-dominant Social Democrats. Thus, when the alliance of "bourgeois" parties managed to dislodge the Social Democrats from office in 1976, they appeared to be so concerned with demonstrating to the electorate that they would continue to operate within the consensus culture that they were unable to take the strong measures that the declining economic situation required and were subsequently defeated. The picture changed in the 1991 elections when the opposition parties campaigned together, won the election, and formed a government. This time it looks as if they will pursue a more radical ideology and try to break free from the consensus culture of the past.

Decentralizing Government

Compared with Britain, local government in Sweden has a much stronger position in both legal and financial terms. Municipalities can raise and spend their own local taxes. The rates are determined by local councillors, although in recent years central government has prevented any increase.

Whereas Britain has been centralizing government authority, Sweden has been following the more widespread European route of decentralization (Crouch and Marquand 1989). In Sweden, municipalities have been able to set up neighborhood committees since 1979. They have also tried other innovations to increase public participation. An experiment in "free" local authorities was launched in 1985. Several authorities have been allowed to apply for the removal of state controls as a test of local autonomy (Gustafsson 1991; Stewart and Stoker 1989b). Many of these exemptions have been institutionalized in the Planning and Building Act of 1987.

A New Style of Planning

The 1987 act was the product of years of discussion. The act sought to enhance both initiative and the immunity of local authorities, as well as to increase public participation in planning decisions. Except in a few circumstances engaging national security, the act permitted municipalities

to make their own planning decisions without any monitoring or interference by the central government. It also expanded the categories of
persons who had a formal right to appeal the plan.

Both before and after 1987, there has been considerable comment in
Sweden over the way in which planning has changed from a consensus-
seeking, professionalized, and stylistically "rational" activity to one that is
now often described as a politicized "negotiation." This new style has led
to a greater emphasis on politician/developer discussions and, in many
cases, an increase in the importance of the "estate management" departments of local governments. The actors dominating the negotiation approach often have short-term economic objectives that are different from
those of the professional planners. Large, controversial projects in central
city districts are developed in informal discussions between owners and
political leaders. Neither planners nor the public have much influence
when the complex technical, organizational and financial agreements are
finally disclosed (Fog et al. 1990, 9).

The "development agreement"—a bargain between the municipality
and the developer based upon contract law (Mattsson et al. 1989)—is the
vehicle for bypassing the planning system. Although principally geared to
deciding costs and responsibilities for infrastructure and public facilities,
they can be extended to cover a wide range of issues such as design standards, land use, and tenure. The bargains will often be struck prior to the
preparation of a detailed development plan. Reversing the expected order,
the plan will then have to conform to the agreement. Formally, the municipality will not be bound by the agreement until the plan has been adopted.
Something may go awry, but it rarely does. Citizens trying to upset an
agreement are at a serious disadvantage and usually fail. The planning
system seeks to promote a comprehensive, long-term approach enriched
by extensive public participation; the development agreement process creates a second regulatory system without participation or broad interagency
consultation and with much more limited objectives.

SOME CONCLUDING THOUGHTS

On one level, the experience in Britain and Sweden is one of contrast.
Until recently, the political ideology of each country could be said to oc-
cupy opposite ends of the spectrum in Western democracies. Thatcherism—
during and after Margaret Thatcher's tenure—integrated a strong authoritarian strand and a commitment to freeing markets. As a result, power
was centralized and the latitude of local authorities drastically reduced.

In contrast, during the same period, Sweden retained its commitment to a consensus-oriented, participatory political culture incorporating different views and interests. This has involved devolving greater power to both municipal and neighborhood levels. The trend has been to undertake reforms that increase participatory opportunities. The result would seem to be one in which decision making is closer to the community level and is likely to reflect social needs and aspirations.

However, at another level, the developments over the last decade have been very similar. Both countries have experienced economic difficulties leading to fiscal constraints on government. There has been a questioning of the costs of the postwar welfare state in both countries, and the local level of government, being the main provider of these welfare services, has been under particular financial pressure. Greater reliance on efficiency and cost effectiveness in decision making has resulted in market-led solutions. This has been very clear and overt under Thatcherism. There was, however, a similar trend in Sweden with greater reliance on the "negotiation style" of decision making, resulting in the downgrading of social goals.

Elander (1989) has suggested that the decentralization trend in Sweden acts as a cloak for greater central control over finance. The decentralizing process, far from increasing the power of local authority, actually gives the center greater power. His argument is that the center no longer has the ability to control the increasingly complex pressures on government and has utilized the demands for greater local democracy as a means of deflecting the increasing pressures on the national purse. He concludes that what has been happening is a "centralisation of power (and especially of economic power), coupled with a decentralisation of responsibility" (Elander 1989, 46; see also Elander and Montin 1990). Within the municipality itself the decentralization to neighborhoods could be similarly interpreted as giving power to the central coordinating board of the local authority, especially as these neighborhoods have very little decision-making power.

It has also been suggested that the reforms to planning incorporated in the 1987 act are at risk in hard times. As Odmann remarked:

> Vague statements in law, in combination with the complexity of the production process, and economic considerations will allow the building industry—growing and operating within its own logic and dynamics—to find tactics for an implementation of the Planning and Building Act, which fits this industries [*sic*] goals. (Odmann 1987, 264)

Thus, while ideological differences between Britain and Sweden are great, economic imperatives seem to be pushing both countries in the same direction. One perspective that might help to illuminate this disparity is the analysis of post-Fordist society (Harvey 1989; Martin 1988). This perspective maintains that there has been a shift in the organization of advanced economics from one in which economies of scale and mass consumption were paramount to one based on flexibility and segmented markets. Such changes also involve radical restructuring of the organization and management of firms themselves (Peters and Waterman 1982). Some writers are now exploring whether these changes can also be detected in the way governments operate. Thus, Stoker (1989) has suggested that the move by local authorities in Britain to decentralized service delivery and increased responsiveness to customers and clients can be traced to the same post-Fordist trend. The new form of responsive management fits a world that is divided between a strategizing center and a large and often competitive set of firms and agencies that produce the goods and services we associate with government but that have very little influence over public policies.

It could be said that the comparison of Britain and Sweden shows that both countries are responding to the post-Fordist trend. However, the comparison also illustrates that there is scope for variation in the way government might respond to this trend. This is where ideology can have an influence. Sweden, in line with most European countries (Batley and Stoker 1991), has been following the approach of centralizing financial strategy while allowing the periphery considerable scope to make political decisions within these financial limits. In Britain, the center has also been setting fiscal limits but has also been seeking to utilize organizations that are subservient to market pressures as the decentralized unit. These organizations might be private companies, parent associations, or individual home owners, their common characteristic being that they respond to market competition. This has meant removing as much political power as possible from the local government in an effort to achieve this restructuring.

These alternative responses are likely to have different implications for planning. For example, under the first approach there is likely to be a demand for local plans that express the social aspirations and needs of the communities in these decentralized arenas. It would be possible to express these aspirations directly in the political process. Whether they would be successful is another matter. In the second approach, this opportunity is unlikely to arise as social needs are expected to be met as the result of market competition. However, even in this approach it is possible to conceive of some planning role as part of the activity of the "center." Some kind of strategic central guidelines could be envisaged—a strengthening and expanding, maybe, of the British regional guidance approach or the performance targets of the Citizen's Charter.

There may, indeed, be very powerful influences reshaping the relationships between central governments, local politics, and markets across the developed world. The precise patterns of these new relationships are, however, both varied and plastic, subject to design and negotiation. There is nothing inevitable about the worlds we make.

Note

1. Inside Great Britain, the label "authoritarian" is widely used as a description of the Thatcher governments, whereas for many outsiders the term conjures an image of dictatorship. This may say something about the long-standing appeal of strong leadership for the British public.

REFERENCES

Allen, J. 1996. Our town: Foucault and knowledge-based politics in London. In S. J. Mandelbaum, L. Mazza, and R. W. Burchell, *Explorations in planning theory.* New Brunswick, NJ: Center for Urban Policy Research, Rutgers University.

Audit Commission. 1992. *Citizen's charter performance indicators.* London: Audit Commission.

Batley, R., and Stoker, G., eds. 1991. *Local government in Europe.* London: Macmillan.

Beauregard, R., ed. 1989. *Economic restructuring and political response.* Newbury Park, CA: Sage Publications.

Bulpitt, J. 1989. Walking back to happiness? Conservative Party governments and elected local authorities in the 1990s. In C. Crouch and D. Marquand, eds., *The new centralism.* Oxford: Blackwell.

Crosland, A. 1956. *The future of socialism.* London: Cape.

Crouch, C., and D. Marquand, eds. 1989. *The new centralism.* Oxford: Blackwell.

Dahrendorf, R. 1990. *Reflections on the revolution in Europe.* London: Chatto and Windus.

Duncan, S. S., and M. Goodwin. 1988. *The local state and uneven development.* Cambridge: Polity Press.

Elander, I. 1989. Notes on central-local government relations in Sweden. In E. Reade, ed., *Britain and Sweden: current issues in local government.* Gavle: National Swedish Institute for Building Research.

_____, and S. Montin. 1990. Decentralisation and control: central-local government relations in Sweden. *Policy and Politics* 18, 3.

Fog, H., A. Tornqvist, and K. Astrom. 1990. Legitimacy and quality: uses of Swedish planning law. Paper presented at the Planning Theory Conference, Oxford Polytechnic, 2–5 April.

Gustafsson, A. 1988. *Local government in Sweden.* Stockholm: Swedish Institute.

_____. 1991. The changing local government and politics of Sweden. In R. Batley and G. Stoker, eds., *Local government in Europe.* London: Macmillan.

Harvey, D. 1989. *The condition of postmodernity.* Oxford: Blackwell.

Heclo, H., and H. Madsen. 1987. *Policy and politics in Sweden: principled pragmatism.* Philadelphia: Temple University Press.

King, D. S. 1987. *The new right: politics, markets and citizenship.* London: Macmillan.

Levitas, R., ed. 1986. *The ideology of the new right.* Cambridge: Polity Press.

Logan, J., and H. Molotch. 1987. *Urban fortunes.* Berkeley: University of California Press.

Martin, R. 1988. Industrial capitalism in transition: the contemporary reorganisation of the British space-economy. In D. Massey and J. Allen, eds. *Uneven re-development.* London: Hodder and Stoughton.

Mattsson, H., T. Kalbro, and T. Miller. 1989. Development agreements for residential development in Sweden. In D. Porter and L. Marsh, eds. *Development agreements: practice, policy and prospects.* New York: Urban Land Institute.

Mollenkopf, J., and M. Castells, eds. 1991. *Dual city: restructuring New York.* New York: Russell Sage Foundation.

No Turning Back Group. 1990. *Choice and responsibility: the enabling state.* London: Conservative Political Centre.

Odmann, E. 1987. Vague legal norms in a tough reality—some remarks on the new Swedish Planning Act. *Scandinavian Housing and Planning Research* 4.

Peters, T., and R. Waterman. 1982. *In search of excellence.* London: Harper & Row.

Reade, E., ed. 1989. *Britain and Sweden: current issues in local government.* Gavle: National Swedish Institute for Building Research.

Ridley, N. 1988. *The local right.* London: Centre for Policy Studies.

Scruton, R. 1990. *The meaning of conservatism.* Harmondsworth: Penguin.

Stewart, J., and G. Stoker, eds. 1989a. *The future of local government.* London: Macmillan.

_____. 1989b. The "free local government" experiments and the programme of public service reform in Scandinavia. In C. Crouch and D. Marquand, eds., *The new centralism.* Oxford: Blackwell.

Stoker, G. 1989. Creating a local government for a post-Fordist society: the Thatcherite project? In J. Stewart and G. Stoker, eds., *The future of local government.* London: Macmillan.

Thatcher, M. 1992. Don't undo my work. *Newsweek.* 27 April.

Thornley, A. 1993, 2d. ed. *Urban planning under Thatcherism: the challenge of the market.* London: Routledge.

JUDITH ELEANOR INNES

9 Group Processes and the Social Construction of Growth Management: Florida, Vermont, and New Jersey

INTRODUCTION

Consensual group processes are playing a growing role in planning practice in the United States. Nowhere is this trend more evident than in the seven states that since 1985 have instituted statewide growth management programs.[1] These programs entail strategies to coordinate and redirect the actions of the many players whose decisions affect the location, patterns, and types of development, as well as to create patterns of growth that will limit infrastructure costs, provide for economic development and housing, protect natural resources, and improve the quality of community life. In all seven states, governors, state agencies, regional commissions, and legislatures have created group processes to handle many of the key planning tasks. Where no groups were formed to do certain tasks or where groups were poorly designed, implementation of growth management has faltered.

Because growth management is so complex and involves so many actors, actions, and places, no one set of experts can design a successful

Adapted from Judith E. Innes, "Group Processes and the Social Construction of Growth Management: Florida, Vermont, and New Jersey." Reprinted by permission of *Journal of the American Planning Association* 58, 4 (1992).

program nor can any state impose an effective program from the top down. Instead, groups working on the ground and including experts, citizens, and high-level officials must go through a process of mutual learning to create a shared conception of policy intentions and modes of implementation. The groups learn by talking and by doing, articulating, applying and evaluating policy concepts and principles in order to create workable strategies and procedures. In this mutual learning process, problems, policies, and plans are socially constructed.[2]

This chapter—embedded in a long tradition that treats the American states as policy "laboratories"—should be read as a contribution to the comparison of planning modes, complementing Andy Thornley's account of "Thatcherism and the Swedish 'Model'" (chapter 8 in this volume). It may also be read as a study of the design of new forums and arenas as described by John Bryson and Barbara Crosby (chapter 22 of this book) and of the search for ways to unfreeze the constraints on planning that stem from mutual misunderstanding and specious conflicts of interest.

I report on three states—Florida, Vermont, and New Jersey—each of which has passed legislation mandating a distinctive set of institutions for managing growth. I am interested in how and why group processes were invented to implement the legislation, in the tasks the groups undertook, and in the results of their labors. Reviewing the extensive scholarly literature on group processes, I suggest why and when such groups should be expected to be important for growth management. Reflecting on the evidence, I identify the planning tasks for which group processes seem particularly useful. (See Table 9.1 for an outline of the basic growth management program strategies and Table 9.2 for specific group processes and their tasks.)

CONSENSUAL GROUP PROCESS

Difficult conditions must be met for groups to develop workable and widely supported policies and programs.[3] The groups must incorporate the stakeholders who will be affected by a program and can lead it to succeed or fail. Group members must know that their tasks are important and that the agreements they reach will matter. Moreover, deliberations must be conducted in a way that seeks to assure that all members have an equal voice within the group, even if they do not have equal power outside it. Those managing the process must provide all members with access to essential information and prevent a single voice from dominating conversations.

TABLE 9.1

Growth Management Strategies of Three States

Program Feature	Florida	Vermont	New Jersey
OVERALL APPROACH	Top-down bureaucratic	Laissez-faire, quasi-judicial	Collaborative, consensus building
STATE ROLE	State goals and plan. State agency (DCA) writes and enforces implementing rules.	State goals. No implementing agency or commission. Council of Regional Commissions (CORC) reviews plans and has quasi-judicial role.	State Planning Commission (SPC) prepares draft state plan for cross-acceptance.
CONSISTENCY REQUIREMENT	Local and regional plans must be consistent with state goals and plan.	Local planning is voluntary. Consistency of local plans with state goals decided by regional commissions. CORC decides if regional plans are consistent with state goals.	No consistency requirement for local planning. Counties act as mediators between SPC and localities in negotiations over state plan. No regional plans.
COORDINATION OF INFRASTRUCTURE WITH DEVELOPMENT	Adequate infrastructure must be available concurrent with development.	State agency plans must be consistent with state goals and with approved local plans.	State plan to be used as guide to state investment decisions.
SANCTIONS AND INCENTIVES	DCA can withhold local funding from noncompliant localities.	Localities with approved plans can challenge state agency plans.	Participation in cross-acceptance gives localities a voice in the state plan. Local plans in conflict with state plan may not be implementable.
APPEALS PROCEDURES	Administrative Hearing Board decides on challenges to DCA decisions.	CORC hears appeals of regional commission decisions, challenges to state agency plans. Assists in mediation. Supreme Court is final arbiter.	No appeal process above the SPC. Legislature and governor decide whether to implement the state plan.

These are difficult conditions to satisfy, particularly if members are accustomed to playing unequal roles in interactions or have been hostile to one another. Groups typically require training and professional help in facilitating discussion and bridging the gap between technical and everyday knowledge.

Consensual group process involves informal exploratory discussion designed to assure that stakeholders learn about each other's unarticulated interests and perspectives. Participants seek common ground and collaborate on solutions. The process can result in both individual and group learning and can change attitudes and commitments. The groups can be most productive when they challenge accepted views and reformulate problems in ways that allow consensual outcomes or creative new directions for action.[4]

PLANNING AND GROUP PROCESS

The traditional land-use planning process in the United States has sometimes involved consensual groups. John Friedmann (1987) identifies "social learning" as one of the major styles of planning. For example, planning commissions in small communities may include citizens and stakeholders, such as developers and environmentalists, together with planners in informal consensus-seeking discussion. Today, however, legal requirements typically force public bodies into formal, stepwise procedures, with announced meetings, strictly followed agendas and standardized decision criteria (Rudel 1989). Consensus seekers usually cannot march to such a well-ordered drummer. Accordingly, in recent years, only ad hoc task forces and advisory committees that are free of the restraints of highly prescribed procedures are likely to engage in exploratory consensus-building deliberations.

Consensual group process is being discovered in many areas of planning theory and practice. Strategic management and strategic planning in business (Rowe et al. 1989) and in government rely on such groups to envision the future, identify strategic issues and solve problems (Bryson 1988). Ozawa (1990) reports on how consensual groups have helped to integrate science and policy. Others have documented their use in dispute resolution (Amy 1987; Rabinovitz 1989) and community goal setting (Bryson and Einsweiler 1988). The Joint ACSP-AESOP International Conference of U.S. and European planning schools in 1991—the source of many of the chapters in this volume—listed sixteen papers under the category "negotiation, mediation, and group process." No one, however, has yet systematically identified the variety of planning purposes for which group process is particularly well-suited.

TABLE 9.2

Group Processes in Growth Management in Three States

State	Group Process	Tasks
FLORIDA	Negotiation between DCA staff and local officials	Reaching a compliance agreement on a local plan.
	Governor's Task Force on Urban Growth	Defining the problem of sprawl and proposing policies to alleviate it.
	Joint Legislative Committee on Growth Management	Oversight and review of all growth management legislation and its implementation. Proposing revisions.
NEW JERSEY	State Planning Commission (SPC) made up of interests, citizens, and agency heads	Multiple. Policy and plan development, oversight, and review; build and maintain consensus; propose implementation.
	SPC and localities, with counties as mediators	Cross-acceptance of the state plan through negotiation. Development of interim and final plans.
	Advisory committees to SPC, made up of stakeholders, agency staff, and experts	Policy and plan review and development by topic area, such as housing, infrastructure, or agriculture.
VERMONT	Governor's Task Force on Vermont's Future	Identification of a need for growth management.
	Working groups of agency heads and of state agency staff	Creation of principles and practices for the preparation of state agency plans.
	Working groups of stakeholders, potential producers, and users	Design of a statewide geographic information system.
	Legislatively appointed task force of supporters and opponents to review Act 200	Consider need for additional amendments.

THE STATE PROGRAMS

The growth management legislation in all seven states was backed by wide public consensus and by both development and environmental interests. These states typically had experienced rapid growth, visible increases in traffic, problems with air and water quality, and conflict among developers, environmentalists, and local governments. These stakeholders decided that they preferred rules of the game to endless controversy, and they agreed in principle to try to achieve a consensual set of goals.

The legislation in each state established a framework of goals, organizations, and procedures, leaving the development of specific workable policies and implementation procedures to emerge from the next steps. While there are many variations among the state programs, the most common features are:

- broad state goals and a few common state policies and standards;

- requirements for local governments and often state agencies to make plans and demonstrate consistency with state goals and policies;

- review and comment procedures by various players on each other's plans;

- financial assistance and other incentives for local planning;

- provision for conflict resolution; and

- new GIS (geographic information systems) to map land uses and locate environmentally fragile areas (Innes 1992).

These innovative programs are broad and multipurpose rather than focused on one resource, one issue, or a limited set of areas. Moreover, they call for the sharing of power among levels of government, unlike an earlier generation of state land regulations[5] that often preempted local control over land use.[6] The new programs seek to link local governments' land-use planning and regulation with the infrastructure investments and environmental regulations of state agencies.

WHY GROUP PROCESSES ARE IMPORTANT FOR GROWTH MANAGEMENT

Some arguments in the literature anticipate the reliance of growth management programs on group processes. These programs, for one thing, require the most challenging form of coordination. Thompson (1967) contends that in the easiest case, when tasks are repetitive, the technology known and the environment predictable, coordination can be accomplished through the standardization of all parts and inputs. If, however, a task involves sequential interdependence—the output of one part of the system is input to the next—participants can coordinate by making plans that are mutually consistent, as the legislation requires in most growth management programs. If the outputs of one activity are inputs to another and vice versa—for example, highways generate development demand and development generates highway demand—coordination requires mutual adjustment. Face-to-face group discussions are essential to accomplish such adjustment efficiently.[7]

Growth management is also a case of planning under uncertainty, as discussed by Christensen (1985). She argues that when there are multiple goals, as in growth management with its broad purposes and many players, planning requires bargaining or mediation. When the means for accomplishing goals are also uncertain (Landis 1992), then adaptive approaches are needed to facilitate learning by doing. When both goals and means are uncertain, as they are in growth management, charismatic leadership or a social learning strategy is needed. Only when society knows how to do a task and agrees on a single objective is top-down regulation appropriate (de Neufville and Christensen 1980).

The literature on successful innovation also anticipates the importance of group process to growth management. Rogers (1983), in his review of hundreds of innovations in a wide range of organizations, concludes that three of the critical factors in the successful adoption of an innovation are compatibility with values and understandings of the players, observability of the benefits, and comprehensibility. Successful adoption requires adapting the innovation to the context and needs of the users, and it requires creating a shared meaning and purpose for the innovation (Eveland et al. 1977). For such tasks, group process is both an efficient and effective strategy.

Finally, growth management presents a particularly challenging task of linking knowledge and action. It requires many kinds of knowledge: facts and predictions about growth patterns and relationships among activities, estimates of the interests and values of players, and practical understandings of how things work. As knowledge is diffused, the behavior of the players inevitably changes. The first generation of top-down state land-use regulations relied on experts using formal analyses and "objective" research methods to provide information for decision makers.[8] Unfortunately, information generated in that way poorly predicts the effect of a policy in specific contexts and communities. It does not provide the "how to" knowledge of what works in practice, in part at least because it cannot stay abreast of the way the participants change in the process of doing.

Moreover, the issues at stake—property rights, land-use control, quality of life—have symbolic meanings linked to deeply held values, which growth management appears to threaten. Stories told in at least two states suggest the depth of these emotions. A story widely circulated in Vermont that a citizen repeatedly testified at hearings that Act 200 (the growth management law) "scares me to death." Then one day, at the podium, he died. This story might have related only an unfortunate coincidence but the New Jersey plan was also blamed, in a letter to the director of state planning, for the deaths of two of its opponents. When passions are so high, as John Forester's chapters in this volume suggest, it takes more than technical knowledge to overcome shared emotional attachments to existing practices.

Consensual groups and social learning are grounded in a view of knowledge that is different from the positivist underpinning of the standard approach informing policy making. This phenomenological view, implicit in the work of consensual groups, contends that everyday knowledge (including knowledge of stories or myths), rather than expertise, is the appropriate starting point for inquiry. The task of knowing, in this view, is making sense of issues rather than trying to distill principles. Context is important. Learning is inductive rather than deductive, and facts are regarded as socially constructed in a community rather than purely objective.[9] This kind of knowledge has the purposes of understanding and practical action.

RESEARCH APPROACH

The research involved field and telephone interviews, conducted in 1988, 1989, and 1990. In each of the three states, the researchers interviewed in-depth between fifteen and twenty-five people with key roles in the growth management program. The interviews focused on the progress and evolution of the programs and on how and why decisions were made. The purpose was to get an accurate account of events and their logic and to compare and assess the effectiveness of the institutional designs. The inquiry revealed that group processes had an unanticipated importance. Accordingly, the research also noted the membership, focus, and products of the important groups. Informants included state, regional, and local staff, agency heads, citizen commissioners, elected officials, and leaders of environmental and other organized interest groups. The research also reviewed program documents, including guidelines, minutes of meetings, plans and findings of administrative hearings. In New Jersey, the author attended key meetings and observed processes firsthand.

FLORIDA: MODIFYING A TOP-DOWN STRATEGY

The Florida story is one of a state discovering that a top-down strategy backed by ample power was difficult to implement, not only because it did not get the support of local governments but, more importantly, because it lacked the knowledge to create implementable strategies from the top. At various points, group processes helped overcome the difficulties.

Florida's growth management program, passed in 1985, gives authority to the state Department of Community Affairs (DCA) to ensure that local plans conform to state goals. If they do not conform, DCA can withhold significant funding. All local plans go to DCA, along with comments from state and regional agencies. DCA either approves the plans or makes objections in writing. Originally, the locality either had to change its plan to meet DCA requirements or take the issue to the state Administrative Board. The legislation did not set up any group processes, not even a commission to elaborate policy or develop implementation procedures. Instead, DCA prepared detailed rules for assessing local plan compliance and developed a large matrix for staff to use in checking plans.

Negotiating Compliance Agreements

The DCA began by disapproving nearly one-half the local plans, and it seemed likely that many localities would come back a second time with unsatisfactory plans. When it became obvious that the procedure for resolving differences was slow and inflexible, DCA invented "compliance agreements," which involved DCA staff and officials from noncompliant localities in meeting face-to-face to negotiate plan revisions. As of May 1990, this group process had produced agreements in all but three of the more than 100 disputed plans.

Longer-term success and genuine stable agreements, however, are more questionable because the groups negotiating compliance agreements are neither consensual nor stakeholder-based. Local officials are under pressure to settle to avoid losing substantial state funding. They contend bitterly that DCA "gets what it wants." DCA staff agree. They see the negotiations as an efficient procedure for showing the localities that they "mean business," rather than as a way to give localities "voice." Because key stakeholders such as environmentalists, farmers, and developers are not at the table, they later challenge the agreements.

The lack of genuine as opposed to merely formal agreement poses a problem for implementation. DCA can only require plan compliance; it does not control plan implementation or specific development decisions.

Conformance in the implementation phase depends on local watchdogs and on the acquiescence of the localities and the development community.

Oversight and Review

The legislature created the Joint Select Committee on Growth Management in response to the growing legislative responsibility for oversight and revision of the growth management and related laws. The group has become knowledgeable as it monitors experience, discusses issues, hears from lobbyists and experts, and tries to achieve consensus. Staff play a strong role as participants. Committee meetings operate consensually to a considerable degree.

This committee has created partial consensus on various growth management measures, but its effect on legislation has been limited. It is not a true stakeholder group. Instead of participating, some key interests go directly to the legislature, often in direct opposition to the committee. As a legislative body, the committee is not linked into the administrative decision-making structure, but neither does it have the power to report out legislation. The committee's positions sometimes conflict with those of DCA, which is a powerful agency with its own legislative influence. For all these reasons, the committee's recommended reforms are not necessarily adopted.

The Meaning of Sprawl

Strained political relations between DCA and localities were compounded by conceptual difficulties. Though sprawling development and its consequences were among the principal reasons for growth management in Florida, neither the law nor the regulations addressed sprawl directly. Instead, the central regulatory concept is "concurrency": that no plan or development order can be approved unless the locality shows that adequate services and infrastructure will be provided simultaneously with the impacts of development. The legislature intended that this provision would prevent further traffic congestion and degradation of air and water quality, while accommodating growth. When Governor Martinez refused to support new taxes to fund infrastructure, however, the concurrency requirement became a limit on growth. Moreover, it encouraged developers to build sprawling subdivisions at low density in rural areas, where septic systems would be sufficient and unused road capacity existed.[10]

The DCA responded to these perverse incentives by demanding that some localities change their zoning ordinances to permit higher densities.

Other units were told that they must dramatically lower densities. These demands created confusion and engendered intense opposition. One respondent said that anticipating DCA was like "shooting at a moving target." Another said, "Sprawl is like pornography, hard to define."

Defining and stopping sprawl became so central an issue that in 1988 the governor appointed the Task Force on Urban Growth. The members of this group included high-level stakeholders and experts on growth including developers, business representatives, environmental leaders, professors, elected city and state officials, state cabinet secretaries and the head of the American Planning Association state chapter. After thirteen months, the task force released its unanimous report (Florida 1989), which contends that sprawl not only damages the environment, causes traffic congestion, and uses state resources inefficiently but also results in the loss of a sense of community and identity. The report recommends mapping the state into "urban service areas" and "urban expansion areas" and reorganizing state and local agencies to prepare regional transportation strategies that will deal with sprawl.

The group defined a shared and not previously obvious set of meanings for sprawl and its consequences, challenging the assumptions, purposes, and strategies of the growth management legislation in a way that would have been inappropriate for DCA. Key players—local government officials and the heads of major state agencies—were not, however, represented on this task force. Despite the remarkable consensus the group achieved, there was no immediate way to move its strategy forward.

VERMONT: INCENTIVES IN A LAISSEZ-FAIRE MODEL

Vermont's Act 200, passed in 1988, relies on a decentralized approach using quasi-judicial proceedings to determine the consistency of local, regional, and state plans. Liberal rules of standing allow a wide range of interested parties to initiate proceedings challenging plan approvals or disapprovals. The law establishes neither an oversight commission nor a state regulatory bureaucracy. It requires both regional commissions and state agencies with land-use–related responsibility to prepare plans consistent with state goals. Local planning and land regulation are optional. The act originally established thirty-two goals against which the regional planning commissions should evaluate local plans. The legislation permitted plans inconsistent with state goals but allocated new funds and special rights in the state development permitting process (Act 250) to localities with approved plans. Such localities can also challenge state agency plans that do not conform to their own. The one group process set up by the legislation is that of the Council of Regional Commissions (CORC), made up primarily of local and regional representatives and a few other stakeholder representatives. CORC mediates or adjudicates disputes over local plan consistency with Act 200 and disputes between localities and state agencies. It also reviews regional plans and state agency plans and forwards its comments to the legislature.[11]

The Battle over the Meaning of Act 200

Public discussion of growth management in the mid-1980s resulted in the creation of a gubinatorial task force on the state's future. Members included stakeholders from industry, universities, farming, ski operations, the state land trust, the cabinet, the legislature, and the League of Cities. They operated in an exploratory learning mode, meeting for many months and holding twenty-three hearings and focus groups with citizens and interest groups around the state. The task force report was largely a set of stories about the problems Vermonters face from uncontrolled growth. It was a call for action to protect the economy, environment, and quality of life (Vermont 1988). The effort put growth management on the public agenda but did not set a clear policy direction. The legislature put together Act 200 shortly thereafter but without the aid of a special group process.

Within a year the consensus that seemed to be behind the law turned to antagonism and mistrust. The controversy began in the tiny upstate village of Sheffield. Town leaders decided to bring their protest against the act statewide. Calling themselves Citizens for Property Rights, they argued that Act 200 amounted to oppressive state control of local government and protested the regional commissions' right to approve local plans. They feared the act would damage the economy, argued that planning and zoning were confiscation of property, and worried that the process would give environmentalists too much control.

This was a battle over symbols. Far from instituting state control, the act left local planning optional. Towns with approved plans would have access to new resources and new power to challenge state agency plans. Through the earlier Act 250, state-appointed boards already could deny permits to projects of more than ten units or ten acres and to virtually any project in towns without plans when the boards determined that there would be environmental damage. Towns with plans, therefore, had more control over their own development than those without them. Rather than stopping growth, Act 200 gave the state a high rating as an investment risk in the banking community.

Although the founders of the revolt were from a rural, blue-collar, economically depressed community, they found remarkable support in communities under growth pressure and among professionals and environmentalists. Posters went up in Vermont villages saying "Act 200 is a bad law." The broad-based public interest group of business and environmental leaders formed to support the act abruptly fell apart. On town meeting day in 1989, nearly half of the towns voted not to participate in Act 200.

Although most town officials regarded the vote as merely advisory and continued to develop local plans, the state legislature regarded the vote as a sign of discontent. By June, it had reduced the act's goals from thirty-two to twelve. The new goals were more general and less enforceable. The legislature also made the approval of local plans by regional commissions optional for several more years and increased the rights of localities without approved plans.

Why did so many Vermonters oppose a law that corresponded to their values and interests? Why did most community leaders support it while other citizens opposed it? The answer seems to be that the act had no well-understood public meaning. Observers told of leading citizens who opposed the law but could not articulate their reasons and knew little about its provisions. No group—neither commission, legislative committee nor task force—existed during implementation to address questions as they arose.[12]

After amending Act 200 and hoping to forestall further conflict, the legislature established a working committee of representatives of opposing views, including members of Citizens for Property Rights. The legislature assigned the committee the vague task of considering the need for further amendments. The committee, however, brought together emotionally opposed perspectives without group facilitation. One observer said some members appeared uninterested in even discussing the law. The majority concluded that it was too soon to amend the law again, while the minority said that "Act 200 has become a tangible surrogate for the intrusion of state government into our personal life and that of our community" and urged repeal (Vermont Legislature 1990). The differences in views and the fact that the minority continued to adhere to the old symbolism suggest that the group learned little and that the process left deeply held beliefs untouched.

Working Groups

Although group processes have not succeeded in developing shared meaning for Act 200, groups have been more successful in inventing ways to accomplish complex new tasks. The most important example has been in the design of state agency plans. State agencies had not previously prepared plans, much less considered the land-use implications of their actions. They did not know what it would mean to apply the state goals to their own practices nor what form a useful plan would take. In Florida, where the law was similar, many plans developed by the agencies alone had to be returned for revision because they were inadequate.

In Vermont, however, several agency heads guided the process with the assistance of a staff-level working group representing the nineteen agencies. The group defined in operational terms key concepts such as "projects that affect land use," reviewed agency programs influencing land use, clarified the implications of state goals, and worked out ways of dealing with the conflicts between goals. With the inauguration of a new governor, the group abruptly was disbanded but not before completing a full set of agency plans.[13]

Act 200 also set up group processes to design a statewide GIS, which was to use data from many agencies and provide a common database for all players at the state, regional, and local levels. Building a GIS is a complex technical and managerial task (Innes and Simpson 1991) that requires negotiation among participants and agreement on common standards. Working groups in Vermont at state and regional levels have engaged technicians and managers as well as citizens, business people, and planners in this task. Pilot programs allowed users to learn and develop applications and informed state level technicians about practical issues.[14]

NEW JERSEY: CROSS-ACCEPTANCE AND COLLABORATIVE PLANNING

In contrast to Florida and Vermont, New Jersey deliberately developed a program that was fundamentally based on consensual group process. New Jersey's process has identified and resolved many of the issues that remain problematic in other states.[15]

The first significant group was the one that wrote the legislation. The governor had informally agreed that if a consensus bill could be developed for state planning, he would support it. Accordingly, a self-selected and influential group of key stakeholders representing business, environmental concerns, and local government interest groups, after months of discussion, prepared the basic legislation that became law.

The most important group involved in New Jersey's growth management program is the State Planning Commission (SPC). Its members are drawn from the state cabinet, municipal and county governments, and the public, including environmentalists, business interests, Republicans, and Democrats. The Office of State Planning (OSP), in the Department of Treasury, staffs the commission. The SPC's task has been to prepare, adopt, and regularly revise a state plan to carry out such objectives as preventing sprawl, promoting development and redevelopment, and protecting environmental resources. The law requires the SPC to define areas for growth, limited growth, agriculture, and other categories.

New Jersey's most creative contribution to the growth management tool kit is the concept of cross-acceptance. The legislation requires that agreement on the state plan be negotiated with the counties and municipalities.

While this program, like that of Florida and Vermont, aims for consistency among state and local plans, it seeks to achieve this without sanctions or a plan approval process. Participation by localities in cross-acceptance is voluntary. All New Jersey municipalities had master plans and land-use regulations prior to the law, and they are not required to alter these. Cross-acceptance stresses collaboration, bringing localities together at the county level to prepare a report rather than requiring separate local responses. The incentives for local participation and adjustment of plans and zoning are substantial since localities depend heavily on state infrastructure, financing, and environmental regulation. Though local leaders remained skeptical about the ultimate influence of the state plan on state investment decisions, they concluded it was better to be at the negotiating table than not. Moreover, if the state makes a decision to invest in infrastructure in a particular area, it is in the locality's interest to adapt its own plans to reflect that reality. While localities in Vermont also had an interest in preparing consistent plans because they could then challenge state agency plans that did not conform to their own, no process comparable to cross-acceptance informed or convinced community leaders that they might influence the state if they obtained plan approval.[16]

Although the SPC cannot force the governor, the state agencies, or the legislature to implement the plan, its membership includes key cabinet officials who, in assenting to the plan, implicate their agencies. Writers of the legislation believe that if the plan is prepared with "full participation of state, county and local governments as well as other public and private sector interests," it will be carried out. A governor is unlikely to challenge a well-constructed agreement developed among the many constituencies.

State Planning in Practice

The SPC first produced a preliminary plan, a three-volume document of policies, criteria, and standards, that mapped the state into seven land-use categories including "redeveloping cities and suburbs," "suburbanizing areas," "exurban reserves," and "agricultural areas" (New Jersey State Planning Commission 1988). The plan proposed statewide and tier-specific policies on topics such as population densities, housing, and capital facilities.

This plan was controversial. The map relegated some communities to little or no development. Some interest groups and communities challenged the density standards. Other interests contended that the plan would impoverish the state and demanded an economic impact assessment. Business leaders and developers feared having to channel their activities into troubled older cities instead of affluent suburbs. Farming interests said it would unfairly take away their property rights.

The SPC set up a three-phase cross-acceptance process. In phase one, municipalities compared the preliminary plan to their own plans, conditions, and projections. Counties prepared reports incorporating the municipalities' findings and identifying points of agreement and disagreement with the state plan. OSP summarized and organized these into carefully framed issues for discussion. Phase two involved negotiations between a subcommittee of the SPC and representatives of the municipalities in each county. These negotiations transformed the vast majority of differences into agreements through the reframing of issues, clarification, modification of the plan, and even major changes that later became part of the interim plan (New Jersey State Planning Commission 1991). The third phase—issue resolution—addressed the remaining disagreements before the preparation of the final plan.

Another set of group processes also operated throughout cross-acceptance. SPC set up specialized advisory committees, with each one charged to review the plan from a particular perspective such as agriculture, suburban policy, or infrastructure. Members included knowledgeable and interested parties in state and federal agencies, environmental groups, academe, business, and farming. The reports of these committees played an important role in the revision of the plan.

The philosophy of consensual groups permeated the New Jersey planning process. The SPC decided that its seventeen-member commission was unwieldy and divided into smaller working subcommittees to handle policy development. These subcommittees worked through issues, sometimes in day-long retreats. They operated in an open way, usually including members of the public in their discussions. Typically, their recommendations became SPC policy.

The SPC staff gave careful attention to the design and management of groups. The state provided training in mediation and group process to state and county staff and to citizen participants. Staff selected members of certain advisory committees to represent a "microcosm of the larger public debate" in the hope of "building creatively on tensions" among the various interests. In the groups, staff worked to create communication among all parties. They listened, learned, responded to participants, and built trust. They facilitated meetings, provided information, clarified communication, reframed issues, recorded discussions and agreements, and prepared position papers on request. In one meeting, for example, the director frequently articulated and reframed his interpretation of the meaning of group members' statements until all parties were satisfied that they understood one another.

The philosophy of SPC is summed up in a report of one of the advisory committees:

> Wise decision makers know that consensus fares better than edict where there is limited or no authority to enforce. In New Jersey jurisdictional arrangements there is . . . minimal authority for regional growth management. . . . Thus is born the imperative for collaboration. . . . Collaboration involves equality, mutual respect, and full representation to be effective. All levels of government, the private and nonprofit sectors, and citizens and interest groups ought to deal as equal partners. Full representation also includes a wide array of professional assistance, beyond planners, landscape architects, engineers, and lawyers. (New Jersey State Planning Commission 1990, 24)

Content of Group Discussions

Groups across the state raised similar concerns during the cross-acceptance process. Many were the same issues that worried Vermonters and led cities to challenge DCA rulings in Florida. Municipalities and counties were concerned about criteria for land allocation, for example to agriculture or exurban reserves. How would the criteria actually apply in various contexts? Should they depend on the type and viability of the agriculture? What if an island of office development already existed in the center of an agricultural area? Groups discussed standards, both to understand the theory behind such ideas as "carrying capacity" and to explore the implications of applying standards in different contexts. For example, which would be more appropriate in reserve areas: three- to five-acre lots or cluster zoning?

Groups commonly questioned the meaning of concepts and challenged the language in the plan. When is a suburb really "built out"? Were the tiers tantamount to zoning? If so, were they intrusions on home rule? City representatives objected that the "municipal distress index" would harm their image. Many discussions entailed efforts to give meaning to such elusive ideas as "rural character."

Counties and municipalities were concerned that the plan did not spell out implementation procedures and hesitated to agree to the plan without knowing specific costs and effects. They had contradictory fears about both rigidity and ambiguity. The cross-acceptance process allowed them to address these questions by talking them through, developing trust, and compromising.

Simultaneously, the advisory committees were involving players new to planning who were learning about the issues and about each other's concerns and, in the process, developing new ideas. City representatives learned that the state plan was not concerned only with growth at the fringe. The rural policy committee outlined criteria for determining densities in rural areas. The regional design committee proposed making "communities of place," rather than the tiers, focal points for settlement and they outlined a hierarchy of such communities including urban centers, corridor centers, towns, villages, and hamlets, each with its characteristic size, density, jobs, and activities.

In the negotiation phase, SPC staff in consultation with county officials identified not only the issues of disagreement but also the interests of the participants. The focus on interests rather than positions permitted the "getting to yes" model of negotiation (Fisher and Ury 1981). The discussion forced the SPC to clarify its policies and develop more specific implementation strategies. Sometimes talking through the problem revealed that there was less disagreement than participants originally thought and that a minor change would resolve the issue. Sometimes reframing the problem eliminated the conflict.

Evidence of Success

The SPC unanimously adopted the state plan on June 12, 1992. This action was eloquent testimony to the success of their consensual group model of planning. Even the secretary of agriculture supported the plan on behalf of his constituency, which was the last major holdout.[17] All municipalities and counties had participated in cross-acceptance. Supporters of the plan prevented passage of a bill to require legislative approval before the plan could take effect. The executive director of the New Jersey State League of Municipalities testified against the bill, saying the plan was a "remarkable achievement" and, as put together through cross-acceptance, was more representative of the will of the people than it would be if adopted by the legislature.

Cross-acceptance systematically reduced hundreds of disagreements to a small handful. The huge controversy that erupted with the publication of the preliminary plan subsided after a year or two. By June 1992, only some builders and realtors remained as vocal opponents, with virtually all other interests backing the plan.

Results of the Process

Cross-acceptance resulted in significant changes in the state plan. SPC eliminated the term "tiers" and changed the plan to emphasize communities of place as the focus for new development. Group discussions revealed the difficulty of labeling cities as "distressed" and of distinguishing between exurban reserve and agriculture areas. The final plan resolved these ambiguities by outlining a smaller number of planning areas and dropping the distress index. This plan adds statewide policies for agriculture, redevelopment, and overall growth patterns. Standards and guidelines will be in an advisory manual rather than in the plan.

Cross-acceptance engaged at least 50,000 participants in committees, task forces, and public meetings. They were exposed to each other, to the problems of growth, and to the tools of planning. The participants included citizens and professionals in public and private sectors, leaders of the business and environmental communities, and elected officials. These people were directly and intensively engaged at multiple levels of government through their participation during the process in various committees. Public hearings and meetings, however, were attended mainly by professional staff of organizations; average citizens did not extensively participate.

The process has created an alliance of key players and leaders who speak for the plan. Many of these players now have a stake in the plan's implementation because they were part of the negotiations. State agency heads and directors of organizations such as the League of Municipalities can help assure that the plan is backed by action, either because they are influential or because they are decision makers.

If it empowers and engages the participants, group process has its own dynamic. Members come to care about finding a solution that meets each other's concerns. They put creative energy into the invention of new strategies that may run counter to their original assumptions. Group process can be a way of allowing participants to consider the unthinkable and to support dramatic departures from conventional practice.

Len Leiberman, former head of New Jersey's Chamber of Commerce, in his farewell speech on leaving the SPC in May 1990, said:

I think [the plan] will come to be understood as revolutionary in the creative sense. We are moving to a new way of defining the boundary line at the core of representative government, the line between freedom for every individual and the needs of society and between the public and the private interest. . . . I originally came loaded with prejudices. Government was bad and we should beat up on them so they can let brilliant people in the private sector do what they do. For me, learning how good public servants can be was the most transforming experience.

THE ROLES OF GROUP PROCESS IN GROWTH MANAGEMENT

Comparison of growth management programs in the three states suggests that a well-designed group process can be an effective way to accomplish key tasks. By the same token, lack of a group process or a poorly designed one can hinder implementation. For example, while New Jersey was bringing many interests into the plan revision process, Vermont's citizens were in rebellion. Many of the problems DCA had in implementing Florida's anti-sprawl policy were anticipated by New Jersey's cross-acceptance process. While the Florida legislature recognized the need for a group to provide policy oversight, the legislative committee did not include key players who accordingly felt free to challenge its recommendations. And Vermont's committee to review Act 200 produced no useful conclusions, apparently because no one managed the group process to achieve constructive discussion.

The group processes discussed here played a role in the social construction of the growth management program in each state. The processes have been useful in addressing at least six different tasks:

- ☐   framing problems and shaping the public agenda[18]
- ☐   writing legislation that has been widely supported[19]
- ☐   development of implementable policies and strategies
- ☐   oversight and review of the law as it begins to be more precisely formulated and applied
- ☐   negotiation among conflicting groups
- ☐   design of approaches to new tasks

The group processes, however, have been only qualified successes, moving the programs forward somewhat, resolving some disputes, working through some tasks, identifying some new ideas, and achieving some degree of consensus. But the products of the groups often have not been used, and internal agreements have not always been shared with the wider public. In some cases, the groups failed to include key stakeholders, who later sabotaged the effort. In other cases, lack of group facilitation prevented the participants from working constructively on their differences. In some instances, the groups did not operate long enough. In many cases, the groups and their findings were not well linked to the institutionalized procedures and political processes by which decisions are actually made. If group processes are to accomplish the tasks for which they are best suited, the careful design and management of the groups is but one step. The next task for planners will be to design new planning and decision-making institutions in which such groups can play an integral part.

Acknowledgments

The research reported in this paper was partially supported by the Lincoln Institute of Land Policy, where the author was a fellow from 1988 to 1989. John Watts assisted in the literature review and conducted the Florida case study.

Notes

1. These states are Florida, Georgia, Maine, New Jersey, Rhode Island, Vermont, and Washington.

2. The term "social construction" is taken from Berger and Luckmann (1966). They contend that reality is something a society constructs through an interpretive social process that combines both subjective and objective ways of knowing. Reality is what is understood to be real in a community. As the unifying concept of this article, "social construction" provides a way of understanding why the activities of these group processes have become central to the creation of these new strategies for the management of growth.

3. This model of group process draws on literature particularly in the fields of management, psychology, and education. See, for example, Marshall and Peters (1985) for a clearly defined approach. The model also meets the stipulations by Habermas (1981) for communicative action or discussion designed to achieve critical or emancipatory knowledge.

4. Groups typically undergo single-loop learning, in which they develop a new way of solving a problem. In some cases, members may individually and as a group reexamine their assumptions and objectives in a process known as double-loop learning, which can result in both changes in individual commitments and in creative new ways of seeing and doing. This roughly corresponds to the concept of transformation that can occur in communicative action.

5. These include Vermont's Act 250, which requires state permits for developments meeting certain criteria of size and potential environmental impact,

and Florida's Land Management Act, which regulates "developments of regional impact" and "areas of critical concern," as well as a host of other legislation enacted in the early 1970s (Popper 1981; Healy and Rosenberg 1979).

6. Local governments in the United States are creatures of the states and entirely subject to them in theory. In practice, local control of land use is a jealously guarded "right."

7. Mutual adjustment also occurs in well-functioning markets but cases of public goods provision, such as directing growth in the most collectively desirable way, are not adequately handled through markets.

8. This model is outlined in more detail in Innes (1990), which contends that the standard approach to information use is grounded in the positivist/ scientific view of knowledge and is a stepwise procedure in which citizens and policymakers establish goals and frame problems; professionals and experts gather and assess information, searching out facts and principles in a value-neutral way; and policymakers choose on the basis of the information. While this pattern seldom reflects actual practice, it has been the predominant model offered in planning education for linking knowledge and action.

9. Bernstein (1976) provides a good overview comparing these two epistemological perspectives.

10. See Audirac et al. (1990) and Neuman (1991) for a debate that suggests the centrality and ambiguity of the sprawl question.

11. As of June 1992, CORC had reviewed and commented on draft agency plans and several noncontroversial regional plans. CORC had taken only a few minor actions on controversies over local plans. At the time of this writing, it is too soon to evaluate CORC's role in developing shared meaning for Act 200 or in dispute resolution.

12. CORC presumably will play this role but only after localities develop plans and disputes have worked their way up to the commission.

13. In the revisions of these draft plans in 1992, the governor's office sponsored focus groups made up of interest group representatives to give the agencies feedback. Agencies learned and made changes as a result.

14. The state has drastically cut the budget for this program, so its future is somewhat in doubt.

15. See Neuman (1992) for further discussion of the role of groups.

16. As of June 1992, fifty to sixty communities had prepared plans but had not sought approval.

17. After extensive discussions, SPC incorporated a policy to protect landowners' equity as much as possible. This, along with a proposal for equity insurance, satisfied most farming interests.

18. In California, for example, Bayvision 2020 spent a year understanding the issues of regional planning and successfully placed these in the public eye.

19. Georgia used a carefully facilitated yearlong group process to develop its legislation.

REFERENCES

Amy, Douglas. 1987. *The politics of environmental mediation.* New York: Columbia University Press.

Audirac, I., A. H. Shermyen, and M. T. Smith. 1990. Ideal urban form and visions of the good life: Florida's growth management dilemma. *Journal of the American Planning Association* 56, 4: 470–82.

Berger, P., and T. Luckmann. 1966. *The social construction of reality.* Garden City, NY: Doubleday.

Bernstein, R. 1976. *Restructuring of political and social theory.* Philadelphia: University of Pennsylvania Press.

Bryson, J. M. 1988. *Strategic planning for public and nonprofit organizations.* San Francisco: Jossey Bass.

Bryson, J. M., and R. C. Einsweiler. 1988. *Strategic planning: threats and opportunities for planners.* Chicago: Planners Press.

Christensen, K. S. 1985. Coping with uncertainty in planning. *Journal of the American Planning Association* 51, 1: 63–73.

de Neufville, J. I., and K. S. Christensen. 1980. Is optimizing really best? *Policy Studies Journal* 2: 1053–60.

Fisher, R., and W. Ury. 1981. *Getting to yes: negotiating agreement without giving in.* Boston: Houghton Mifflin.

Friedmann, J. 1987. *Planning in the public domain: from knowledge to action.* Princeton, NJ: Princeton University Press.

Habermas, J. 1981. *Reason and the rationalization of society. vol. I. The theory of communicative action.* Translated by Thomas McCarthy. Boston: Beacon Press.

Healy, R. G., and J. S. Rosenberg. 1979. *Land use and the states.* 2d ed. Baltimore: Johns Hopkins University Press.

Innes, J. E. 1990. *Knowledge and public policy: the search for meaningful indicators.* New Brunswick, NJ: Transaction Publisher.

_____. 1992. Implementing state growth management in the U.S.: strategies for coordination. In J. Stein, ed., *Planning for growth management.* Beverly Hills, CA: Sage Publications.

_____, and D. Simpson. 1991. Implementing GIS for growth management: the problem of technological innovation. Paper presented at the Second International Conference on Urban Planning and Urban Management, Oxford, England. July.

Landis, J. 1992. Do growth controls work? A new assessment. *Journal of the American Planning Association* 58, 4: 489–508.

Marshall, J., and M. Peters. 1985. Evaluation and education: the ideal learning community. *Policy Sciences* 18: 263–88.

Neuman, M. 1991. Utopia, dystopia, diaspora. *Journal of the American Planning Association* 57, 3: 344–47.

_____. 1992. A new approach to planning and governing: the Jersey shore experience. Unpublished.

New Jersey State Planning Commission. 1988. *Communities of place: a legacy for the next generation. The Preliminary State Development and Redevelopment Plan for the State of New Jersey.* Trenton, NJ: New Jersey State Planning Commission.

_____. 1990. *Regional design: a report of the Regional Design System State Planning Advisory Committee.* Trenton, NJ: New Jersey State Planning Commission.

_____. 1991. *Communities of place: the Interim State Development and Redevelopment Plan for the State of New Jersey.* Trenton, NJ: New Jersey State Planning Commission.

_____. 1992. *Communities of place: final plan.* Trenton, NJ: New Jersey State Planning Commission.

Ozawa, C. 1991. *Recasting science: consensual procedures in public policymaking.* Boulder, CO: Westview Press.

Popper, F. 1981. *The politics of land-use reform.* Madison, WI: University of Wisconsin Press.

Rabinovitz, F. 1989. The role of negotiation in planning, management, and policy analysis. *Journal of Planning Education and Research* 8: 87–95.

Rogers, E. 1983. *The diffusion of innovation.* 3d ed. New York: Free Press.

Rowe, A. J., R. O. Mason, K. E. Dickel, and N. H. Snyder. 1989. *Strategic management: a methodological approach.* 3rd. ed. Reading, MA: Addison Wesley.

Rudel, T. K. 1989. *Situations and strategies in American land-use planning.* Cambridge, UK: Cambridge University Press.

Thompson, J. D. 1967. *Organizations in action.* New York: McGraw Hill.

Vermont. 1988. *Report of the Governor's Commission on Vermont's Future.*

Vermont Legislature, Act 200 Study Committee. 1990. *Report of the Act 200 study committee.*

Commentary

GLEN MCDOUGALL

The Latitude of Planners

INTRODUCTION

One of the major themes in contemporary planning theory identified by Seymour Mandelbaum in the introduction to this book is the relationship between structure and agency. The chapters in this section focus on different aspects of this relationship. Each, however, is concerned with the degree to which the institutional context of planning is structured by and/or structures the mode of planning and the actions of individual planners.

While most social and planning theorists have maintained that structure and agency are mutually determinant, the weight of explanation between the two has shifted over time. From the early 1970s to the mid 1980s, for example, the planning theory field was dominated by structural explanations of the practice of planning. These frequently neo-Marxist explanations represented planning as providing a supportive role to the processes of capitalist accumulation, urbanization, and control, and the actions of individual planners, regarded essentially as the guard labor of the state, were of little interest. Although some writers persisted throughout this period with more individualistic accounts derived from symbolic interactionism, ethnomethodology or pluralism, they formed a minority tradition. But by the late 1980s, the popularity of one-sided structuralist explanations was waning and more work appeared placing a greater importance on the actions and perceptions of human agents.

This shift in the weight of explanation from structure to agency in planning theory mirrored a wider movement in the social sciences. Such factors as the rise of the New Right and neo-liberalism, the collapse of Eastern European communist states, and the intellectual challenge of post-modernism led to a more general retreat from structuralist explanations and a disillusionment with all "grand narratives." As a consequence, the focus of much writing in the social sciences and planning shifted from society and political economy to culture and individual action, and the search for predictability and regularity in social life was replaced with a sensitivity to difference and the rediscovery of the importance of indi-viduals. The rejection of "grand narrative" also was accompanied by a retreat from the primacy of theory to that of practice and a growth in the appeal of pragmatism and associated philosophical and political positions. Furthermore, the demise of Eastern European communist states led to a more general disgust with all forms of planning that were associated with authoritarian government and centralized control and that seemed to jar with a rekindled desire for democracy, citizenship, and local control and accountability. There was, therefore, a connection between the swing in the explanatory pendulum from structure to agency and the reemergence, at least in popular thought and debate, of the false dichotomies between society/individual, political economy/culture, democracy/planning, and theory/practice.

However, throughout the period a number of social theorists contin-ued to strive to maintain an older tradition that denied these dualisms and particularly that between structure and agency. For example, Giddens's (1984) influential theory of structuration emphasized the Janus nature of social life and the duality—not dualism—of structure and agency. Start-ing from Marx's comment (in *The Eighteenth Brumaire of Louis Bonaparte*) that "Men make history, but not in circumstances of their own choosing," Giddens reformulated an earlier sociological orthodoxy, supported by both Karl Marx and Max Weber, which insisted that structures are both con-straining and enabling and are the conduit and product of human action. Giddens defined *structures* as organized sets of rules and resources that are produced and reproduced through human action. Structural continuity is dependent on the knowledge of human actors who concretize and repro-duce through their thought and action the routinized patterns of social life. This does not mean that single actors can create or control their social sys-tems, for these stretch in both time and space beyond the boundaries of an individual's action space. But through their thought and action, human actors are the agents of structural reproduction and this role, in association with others, gives them the capability for transformation.

Giddens (1984) defines *agency* in terms of the ability of individuals to intervene in social life through their action. This ability rests on the capac-ity to choose to act or not act, or to choose to act differently, and through this actors can, if they wish, exercise control. The capacity to choose does not mean that the intentionality of human action is a prime determinant of the relationship between structure and agency because the unintentional consequences of action can be as important as the intentional for the course of history. But it does imply power, which Giddens sees as lubricating the relationship between structure and agency and which expresses in its two faces (Bachrach and Baratz 1962) this deeper relationship. The study of power and the ability of human agents to act otherwise are, therefore, central to explanation.

The theorizing of actors about their own action, their *knowledgeability*, is also critical to explanation. Again following Marx, Giddens argues that the fact that structures are dependent for their production and reproduction on the knowledgeability of human agents does not mean that these agents appreciate this dependency and their potential power. More frequently, the theories of social life that actors themselves hold and use in their everyday world tend to reify structures and misunderstand the duality of social life. This reification induces a fatalism that prevents actors from realizing their capability to choose otherwise—to make a difference—and results in a self-imposed powerlessness. Therefore, the nature of the knowledge that actors espouse is a key factor in understanding the relations between structure and agency and resultant social action.

This type of conceptualization of the duality of structure provides an important backcloth to the four chapters in this section. Planning by definition involves choices about future action, and the extent to which planners can choose to do otherwise is a central question in planning theory. In this context, the knowledge that planners espouse and their appreciation of power become key issues. My intention in this commentary is to discuss the extent to which the four chapters in this section contribute to our understanding of these issues and by so doing expand the latitude of planning and enable planners to choose to act otherwise.

PLANNING AND KNOWLEDGEABILITY

We have seen already that the knowledgeability of actors is a key variable in understanding the relationship between structure and agency and the amount of power that actors are able to exert in action. This is one of the central themes of the chapter by Michael Brooks. He begins by noting the irrelevance of most contemporary planning theory to planning practice, which he argues is the result of planning theorists overemphasizing the importance of politics and demoting planners "to minor walk-on roles under highly constrained conditions." Brooks sees a clear connection between planning theory and the creative potential of planning practitioners and, therefore, he believes that the main challenge facing theorists and educators is to replace this overdetermined and reified knowledge with a practice-based theory (or strategy) that will enable planners to define a role for themselves in practice that is both efficacious and politically realistic.

The connection that Brooks makes between theory and practice and knowledge and action merits further exploration. He blames the slavish character of much contemporary practice on the disabling power of planning theory and attributes the gap between planning theory and practice to planning theorists and educators. This is somewhat unfair given the rejection of the necessity for theory (in any sense that would be understood by theorists and methodologists) by many practitioners. It has been noted by a number of writers (e.g., Healey et al. 1981) that the shift in planning from a design-based to a social science-based paradigm resulted in many practitioners seeing themselves as technical experts who were interested in "rules of thumb," case notes, and assembling a tool kit, and who were more concerned with "getting things done" and "keeping the show on the road" than grand designs and visions of the future. This pragmatism has similar disabling consequences to one-sided structural explanations: The constraints of structure are overestimated and the freedom of agency underplayed. Connected to this has been the willingness of practitioners to abdicate responsibility for defining goals or ends to politicians or clients. This view of planning as essentially concerned with means, not ends, is endorsed by Brooks's Political Feedback Strategy, for he accepts that goals are supplied by the client although the planning process may facilitate the identification and prioritization of these. This political neutrality (or perhaps "defeatism" may be more appropriate), combined with an anti-theoretical stance, has defined a narrow role for the planner—confined by institutional constraints and the existing political agenda. I would argue that it is this blindness to the power of agency as much as the failures of planning theory that has dulled the creativity and effectiveness of planning and denied planners the choice to act differently.

It is worth noting that this anti-theoretical stance of planning practice reflects a more general devaluation in the last twenty years of the type of knowledge (generated mainly in academia) that involves critical reflection and challenges the taken-for-granted assumptions of everyday social life. This has been pandered to by developments within academia itself, particularly ethnomethodology and, more recently, the relativism and nihilism of postmodernist thought, which have legitimized the view that the ideas that people use in everyday life can be viewed as "theory-in-use," enjoying equal status with other types of theory and knowledge. But the reliability, generalizability, and validity—the knowledge claims—of these ideas are open to extreme doubt. To elevate this type of theory-in-use to a status beyond the limited situations in which it is generated is to misunderstand the status of different types of knowledge and to deny the distinction between ideology and theory, thus giving legitimacy to prejudice and the narrow-minded interest of specific groups. In addition, it fails to take account of the fact (Giddens 1984) that the theories of social life that actors hold and use tend to reify structures, misunderstand the power of agency, and underestimate their room for maneuver.

Brooks also implies that the main source of practitioners' ideas has been the writings of planning theory. This single source of planners' knowledgeability contrasts sharply with the typology of idea sources that Brooks outlines as part of his Political Feedback Strategy, where he identifies four main sources of ideas: one's self, reference groups, influence wielders, and client groups. Although he proceeds to generate an interesting set of questions that can be used to illuminate the significance of various idea sources in particular situations, he does not use these questions to highlight the relationship between planning theory and practitioners' knowledgeability. This is a pity because his questions would have provided a powerful tool for an analysis of contemporary planning theory and practice.

THE RELATIVE AUTONOMY OF PLANNERS

The chapter by Bishwapriya Sanyal addresses another aspect of the relationship between structure and agency, focusing on the relative autonomy of individual planners. His aim is to make planners more aware that although the institutional context of planning is a constraint, it also creates opportunities for choice and change.

From an examination of three dominant models of bureaucratic behavior, Sanyal concludes that each underestimates the power of agency, and consequently they are unable to account for the emergence of what he calls progressive and innovatory planning policies. He maintains that these models are essentially anti-planning for two reasons. Firstly, they deny the possibility that the state, or its functionaries, can act in a wider public interest and, secondly, they view self-interest as the only motivational basis for individual action. Using examples of progressive planning from India, he concludes that planners can formulate progressive and innovative policies in the interest of the poor and excluded if planners reconstruct their ethical identities and create a greater degree of institutional autonomy. It is these strategies for increasing the autonomy and power of planners that are worth examining in further detail because they turn on the tension between structure and agency.

Sanyal's advocacy of the reconstruction of the planner's ethical identity is derived from his observation that "planners do not necessarily always act to further their self-interest or the interests of the dominant classes." The "sense of meaning" of the progressive planner is based on a complex set of motivations including a sense of public interest and altruism, and it is this that enables them to choose to act otherwise and to expand the innovative potential of planning. But Sanyal unfairly presents the models of Marx, Weber, and public choice theory by oversimplifying their views on human intentionality and motivation. He then contrasts them with the complexity of his own model.

The significance of meaning and intentionality in social action has been a major concern of sociology since the nineteenth century. Following Max Weber, a number of writers have made a distinction between subjective and objective meaning. Subjective meaning is that which actors ascribe to their own action, whereas objective meaning is that which can be inferred from behavior by others. In both cases, the search is for motive or intentionality, but whether this is derived observationally or subjectively is important for the outcome. For example, planners may say that they intend to act in the public interest, but observation of their action and its outcomes may lead one to infer that they acted in their own interest. This discrepancy between intention and outcome has been the subject of much planning history, and it might have provided Sanyal with interesting insights into the planning episodes that he discusses.

Another important distinction is the one that Schutz (1974) and others have made between the meaningful grounds for behavior. First, these can be made by reference to future events that an actor may wish to bring about ("I am doing this in order to. . . .") and, second, by reference to past experiences that led to a particular type of behavior ("I am doing it because. . . ."). Sanyal, however, like most planning theorists and practitioners, assumes that behavior is future oriented and therefore confines his analysis to the first type of intentionality. Any review of the history of planning action (e.g., United Kingdom inner-city policy in the postwar period) would clearly demonstrate that a great deal of planning has been aimed at rectifying past mistakes or blunders rather than being directed to future outcomes.

This rectification of past mistakes relates to another important aspect of meaning and intentionality: the question of unintended consequences. Giddens (1982) argues, "According to the theory of structuration, all social action consists of social practices, situated in time-space, and organised in a skilled and knowledgeable way by human agents." But the incompleteness of actors' knowledgeability means that there are unanticipated conditions of action resulting in unintended consequences. Limited knowledgeability is hardly surprising given that structures are embedded in spatio-temporal systems that extend far beyond the horizons of individual actors. As noted in the introduction to this commentary, single actors are unable to exercise control over social structures because structures extend beyond their reach in terms of their action space and knowledgeability. This restriction is the reason why most sociologists, from Marx to Giddens, have emphasized the importance of collective action and understanding for power to be exercised and change implemented in social structures. Agency cannot be equated with individual agents, and for this reason the study of agency in planning requires a wider brief than understanding the meaning and intentionality of individual planners.

Sanyal's discussion of how planners can increase their institutional autonomy offers two related suggestions. First, planners need to develop a more sophisticated concept of the state, based on a better appreciation of its internal institutional dynamics and a greater awareness of the variation that can occur within the state at particular points in time. Second, state autonomy must be considered within the wider context of civil society and the market: The state cannot be separated from wider social processes, for it is embedded within them. Both these suggestions can be seen as an appeal to resist the temptation to reify the state. The state does not exist independently of the actions of human agents: It was initiated, is sustained, and can be changed by their action. This is equally true of civil society and the market: They are social constructions that achieve actuality through the things that people do. The externalization of these social constructions is assisted by a desire on the part of individuals for ontological security and by the routinized and unreflective way in which we carry out our everyday lives. This tendency to reification is at the root of powerlessness, and if human agents are to exercise control in social action, they must first re-imagine institutions, such as the state, as sets of social practices that are dependent on individuals for their realization. If, as we noted earlier, the knowledge that actors espouse is the key to power, lubricating the relationship between structure and agency, then Sanyal is right to emphasize that the autonomy of planners is partly dependent on their conceptual schema.

THE RELATIVE AUTONOMY OF PLANNING

The chapter by Andy Thornley focuses on the relationship between political ideology, local government power, and the mode of planning. By comparing two countries, the United Kingdom and Sweden (which, Thornley claims, have similar levels of economic development), he hopes to highlight the latitude or relative autonomy of planning. According to Thornley, until recently the two countries sat in different ideological camps— New Right conservatism (Thatcherism) and corporate pluralism—but ideological convergence is now occurring. He is interested in understanding why this has happened and its impact on the mode of planning. He concludes that the two countries are responding to similar economic imperatives and that these have overridden many of the differences in ideology and political institutions to produce some similarities in the planning process in terms of a diminution of social goals, an increase in market solutions, and an emphasis on negotiation rather than plan making. Despite this, Thornley insists that there is still some important variation between the two countries that he ascribes to continuing differences in political ideology.

Thornley's position raises a number of interesting questions about ideology and power. First, he assumes that political ideologies tend to be uniformly applied, but this is rarely the case. For example, he presents Thatcherism as imposing a uniform planning style across the United Kingdom planning system, including a retreat from public investment-driven to market-led planning and a reduction in opportunities for public participation in the planning process. This may be true for England but it was not the case for much of the United Kingdom Celtic fringe and particularly Northern Ireland. Throughout the Thatcher years, government intervention and high public spending continued in this United Kingdom province, and public-sector and state-dependent employment grew to embrace the majority of its working population. Within the planning system, a public participation system was established that enabled community groups to receive funding to assist them in preparing and presenting their case at planning inquiries—a demand that consistently has been rejected in England. The priority for Thatcherite governments in Northern Ireland was the containment of violence and the economic, social, and political integration of the greatest number across the sectarian divide. Under these extreme circumstances even they were willing to turn. But they were also willing to trim in less extreme situations. For example, defense contracts were used to assist some local economies, and inducements offered by some local authorities and others to overseas firms to start or continue production in certain peripheral areas were supported. These examples demonstrate that the extent to which political ideologies are operationalized in action is a function of the logic of the situation (which includes the interplay between the various actors) rather than strength of conviction. This dynamic in practice expresses the complex interplay between structure and agency and reveals cracks in apparent ideological monoliths such as Thatcherism. It also opens up the possibility of social and political change.

Secondly, Thornley accepts that Thatcherism rests on a consensus that has been achieved by uniting in action the two main strands of New Right conservatism—economic liberalism and social authoritarianism. This endorses the view that Thatcherism presented of itself: Its strength rested on the ability to achieve unity among the potentially warring elements in the

Conservative Party. This view has enormous political potential in itself, for if it is generally believed that the Right has sunk its internal differences and agreed on a common agenda, then opposition will be perceived as more difficult. Contrast this with the view that Thatcherism presented of other parties and particularly those of the Left. These were seen as at best capable of forming temporary alliances. As their differences were thought to be maintained even when working together, they were projected as prone to schism. If this view is generally accepted, the potential power of these parties is reduced and their opponents are encouraged to believe that their internal differences can be exploited, which further weakens them.

The general point that we can conclude from this is that the external perception of the degree of ideological consensus achieved within a political group can materially affect the amount of power which that group can exercise. The implication is that, in analyzing political ideologies like Thatcherism, we need to deconstruct the consensus that they have constructed for themselves. For example, re-imaging Thatcherism according to its internal differences would have weakened its potential power and would have assisted in the discovery of how and when we might have acted otherwise. In terms of planning, this re-imaging might start by searching for planning practices under Thatcherism that contradicted rather than confirmed (which is Thornley's way) their ideology, and understanding how such practices arose and why they persisted. In addition, this might provide a better appreciation of existing variety within the mode of planning and thus stretch the latitude of planning.

THE PLASTICITY OF PLANNING

The three chapters discussed so far have raised a number of important issues about structure and agency, but it is Judith Innes's work that provides the most evidence of their creative potential. In her chapter, Innes shows a sensitivity to the interaction between institutions/groups and knowledge/action that is unusual in the planning field, and this enables her to observe the fluidity of the structure–agency relationship. By using different empirical examples of growth management programs to compare the effectiveness of various institutional strategies and group processes, she is able to derive a number of useful lessons for planning practice. For example, her New Jersey case confirms that the group processes that produce workable and supported policy possess the following qualities: incorporation of significant stakeholders, knowledge that agreements matter, an equal voice for all, a specific role for experts bridging technical and everyday knowledge. But the main importance of her work is that it moves the theoretical debate forward toward a closer consideration of the plasticity of planning.

The first aspect of this that we can identify in her work is the plasticity of form or structure. The three states that she analyzed created different strategies and institutional designs within a common federal government policy framework and in response to similar economic imperatives. Their overall approaches covered almost the full range of planning styles, from laissez-faire through bureaucratic regulation to collaborative planning. This variety accords with the view of many social scientists (e.g., Unger 1987) that the variability of social forms and social constraint is much greater than previously thought. If we accept Innes's evidence, it means that the structural context of planning provides a far higher degree of latitude than most planning theorists, including those in this section, have suggested.

The second aspect that we can identify is a plasticity of process or agency. Innes outlines the variety of interests and players who were included or excluded in the policy formulation and implementation process in the three states and demonstrates how different group processes produced different policy and institutional outcomes. Innes's evidence demonstrates quite clearly that group processes are open to design and management and that process and agency are fluid under certain conditions. This evidence should discourage any fatalism, or what Unger (1987) calls "false necessity," toward structural constraints that planners may feel and can assist in the discovery of the capability to be creative and perhaps act differently.

The way in which Innes is able to reveal this plasticity or malleability of both structure and agency is partly a product of the subject and methodology of her research. Her subject was an innovative program that stood outside the routinized world of everyday planning practice, and her research method concentrated on the dynamics of group processes and the collective design of new procedures. This emphasis enabled her to expose the choices that had to be made to do this or that, the consequences, intended or otherwise, of decisions taken, and the differential knowledgeability of various groups. In addition, the importance she attached to group processes is in accordance with the sociological orthodoxy that individuals can extend control only over their social worlds and realize their creative potential through collective action. Of course, it could be argued that Innes is analyzing an atypical situation and that her findings, therefore, cannot be generalized to the more normal world of everyday planning practice. But the contrary could also be argued: It is impossible to comprehend the potential plasticity and creative freedom of social life by examining the world of everyday routine where the plastic has set cold and stiff.

The duality of change and order, like that of structure and agency, is a conundrum lying at the heart of the social sciences and individual experience. Reflect on the way in which, when we consider our own biographies, the past and present tend to reveal the ordered hand of necessity while the future offers change and the freedom to choose. Or consider the ability of social scientists to explain and predict past revolutions and upheavals by applying structural models, their skill in revealing the ordered continuity of the present but their failure to capture the discontinuities of the next day. So it may be the case that our capability to make a difference cannot be appreciated by examining the routinized activities of everyday practice and that, in order to transform social structures, we may need to concentrate on understanding structures in transformation. Then we have nothing to lose and all to gain by adopting a methodology that attempts to capture the creative potential of human agency by focusing on the fluidity of innovative situations.

CONCLUSIONS

It can be seen that the four chapters in this section go some way toward articulating the theoretical debate on structure and agency and to expanding the latitude of planning. But in order to extend this understanding of the variability and plasticity of planning, it will be necessary to return to the world of practice and the making of its present history rather than the history of its past-made world.

REFERENCES

Bachrach, P., and M. Baratz. 1962. The two faces of power. *American Political Science Review* 56: 947–52.

Giddens, A. 1984. *The constitution of society: outline of the theory of structuration*. Cambridge: Polity Press.

Healey, P., G. McDougall, and M. Thomas, eds. 1981. *Planning theory: prospects for the 1990s*. Oxford: Pergamon Press.

Schutz, A. 1974. Subjective and objective meaning. In A. Giddens, ed. *Positivism and sociology*. London: Heinemann.

Unger, R. M. 1987. *Politics, a work in constructive social theory*. Cambridge: Cambridge University Press.

PART III

The Planning Encounter and the Plan

Seymour J. Mandelbaum

The Planning Encounter and the Plan

INTRODUCTION

Virtually every chapter in this volume deals in one way or another with two related questions: How should we go about understanding the practices of professional planners? What should we expect of professionals as individuals and from professional planning as an institution?

The five chapters and four authors in this section confront these questions directly and from a broadly shared perspective. Rather than circling around professionals and their work—setting the stage, exploring the context, and defining the constraints—they leap directly into an examination of the day-to-day work of practitioners and the measured language of formal plans. They describe the ways in which planners address even the most abstract cognitive problems within a system of social "inter-actions" (the playful hyphen is John Forester's) and narratives. Every message is an action; every action, a signal.

The four authors are not, however, identical peas in a pod. Charles Hoch and John Forester both rely on the analysis of stories they have collected. At least in these essays, however, they use them quite differently. Hoch is not particularly interested in the story form but in attempting to answer the overtly naive or simple question: "What do planners do?" The stories he has collected—and the two he presents here—create a subtle portrait of that activity. Of course, planners tend to projects and to regulations, to infrastructure and to programs. More pervasively and perhaps

tly, however, Hoch demonstrates how they attend to the
d repair of polities and civil society.

er, in contrast, is engaged by the form of stories themselves.
ode, he argues, is the principal way in which practitioners
their own experiences, speak to one another, and represent
their worlds. The form sustains them in using what he calls "practical judgment." Listening closely to stories in a transcript of a meeting with a developer and in a retrospective account of a hiring decision, he illuminates dimensions of power and passion that shape those judgments and that are
barely touched in the image of planning as a process guided by "rational
choice."

The subtle difference between Forester and Hoch is repeated in the
contrast between Jean Hillier and Patsy Healey. Both tell us that it is worth
reading plans but their interpretive concerns, in these essays at least, are
quite different. Hillier presents eight plans from Western Australia that she
describes as coherent expressions of a sexist society. The rhetoric of a confident "modernist" rationalism is an instrument for rendering women as
an invisible "other" or as adjuncts to men. There is nothing ambiguous,
dilemmatic, or even particularly obscure about these plans or her call for a
transformation of planning in "Western Australia"—wherever it exists.

Healey, in contrast, is interested in the ways in which development
plans are arenas in which a pluralistic society records its multiple conversations and its conflicting preferences. She encourages readers to abandon
the specious assumption that plans speak in a single voice or that they are
uniquely coherent. She encourages writers to explicate that pluralism in a
measured, even "tragic," tone that makes it possible for readers to recognize dilemmas and limits and to communicate across "discourses."

Hillier's account of Western Australia is striking in its stark image of
the intentions and discretion of planners. No "planning in the face of power"
here: just planning with power. In contrast, Hoch, Forester, and Healey
seem optimistic about the domain and possibilities of professional practice. Hoch and Forester seek to demonstrate to novices and jaded "old
hands" alike that ordinary planners, without any pretense of heroism, are
capable of remarkable moral courage and intellectual insight. (They are
also capable of a full litany of sins, but that is not the burden of these three
chapters.) Healey, writing in much the same spirit, imagines that planners,
if they are moved by deep democratic aspirations, are capable of explicating their discursive choices, revealing in their plans both the paths and the
words that have been chosen and those that have been rejected. Her per-
oration is optimistic. The choices of local planners are constrained by the
power of the national government and of the interests of "capital," but the

discipline of those constraints is incomplete. Planners in the United King-dom, she encourages us to believe, enjoy a substantial measure of both latitude and discretion; they are capable of speaking directly and honestly about diverse meanings, alternative strategies, and "tragic" choices. She is heartened by "plans currently in preparation" that respond to the chal-lenge of "interdiscursive" communication, and by an image of a demo-cratic respect for diversity that is both possible and necessary.

It is difficult to know whether Hillier is describing a different place or reads with a different sensibility. In Perth, she reports, a "directive God's-eye view" of professional planning is tightly linked to the discursive forms of "patriarchal power." Adopting new communicative forms and modes of interaction to empower women and "other disadvantaged groups" would require a dramatic transformation of "the whole intellectual and professional tradition" that sustains planning in the region. Planners are afraid of adopting an "untried stance." Even the increasingly "impover-ished" quality of their practice is not likely to open the door to change with-out "the radical restructuring of power relations within the planning pro-cess." She cautions that without restructuring, "a focus on the detail of language and communication" is likely only to obscure the essential sta-bility of exploitative relations.

Hillier's essay is not addressed to professional planners but to their critics—current and potential. The planning processes that are the source of new meanings barely exist and are certainly not institutionalized in the agencies and protocols of urban development in Western Australia. Hoch, Forester, and Healey tell us that studying planners closely should reassure us both that professionals are capable of wisdom and integrity and should be confidently held to a set of democratic ethical standards. That apprecia-tion is too optimistic for Hillier. At present, in her image of Western Aus-tralia, it would force her to treat as friends and allies, planners whom she believes are sexist opponents. In Western Australia, at least, she tells us to expect very little good from professional planners or plans and to redirect our view away from the planners and toward those (largely women) who chip away at the assumption that male meanings constitute the "incontest-able reality" of urban development.

JOHN FORESTER

10 *The Rationality of Listening, Emotional Sensitivity, and Moral Vision*

INTRODUCTION

W e learn from friends as well as from scientists. We learn from historical studies and the experiences of others as well as from philosophical argument and social science. This much is immediately apparent, but it is just as immediately forgotten once we try to understand the rationality of decision making and planning practice more generally.

In planning and policy work, we plainly do learn from astute accounts of particulars, from the dramas of the moral challenges and conflicts of others. Watching and listening closely, we are impressed by some people and dismayed by others, but we often learn from both. Frustrated by some, we nevertheless pick up "tips" from others: We see new ways of going on, ways of handling pressure, ways of presenting information, ways of being careful and persistent. Iris Murdoch (1970) has put this brilliantly: "Where virtue is concerned, we often apprehend more than we clearly understand and we grow by looking."

Paying attention to those around us, we learn about character and our own possibilities at the same time. We may come to see more clearly not so much the brute facts as what seems to matter: what we take to be significant or at stake in the case at hand. To put it simply, we are likely to learn far more in practice from stories than from controlled experiments (Schön 1983).

Listening carefully to practice stories every day, we work to formulate our problems, to empathize with or understand others we hardly know, to deliberate and consider our own responsibilities and interests too (Forester 1989; Hoch 1994; Krieger 1981; Marris 1990). Yet often we reduce "acting rationally" to "choosing well," and so we neglect the challenging practical rationality involved in listening to practice stories astutely and in telling them carefully as well.

The very richness of stories that threatens their "generalizability" may well be what enables them to be so revealing: to show as well as to explain, to connect as well as to predict, to frame in a new light as well as to put an argument in context. Imagine, for example, that we want help before walking into a difficult meeting with a developer's lawyer and architect. Forced to choose, we are more likely to want the particular story of their previous negotiations with our department than we are to want a more general study of architect versus lawyer influence in developer–planner negotiations.[1]

But if stories are so often messy, detailed, particularistic, and unique, how can they help us to learn in practice? They can help precisely when messiness and detail, particulars and uniqueness matter: in an extraordinary number of cases, indeed all cases in which real individuals must be treated not as stereotypes but as the specific people they are. The very messiness of thickly described practice stories has its own lesson to teach: Before problems are solved, they must be constructed. Before we can consider options and choices, we must have a decent sense of what is at stake, who and what are involved, to whom and to what we need to pay attention.[2]

In addition, because practice stories can convey the emotional demands of work in an ambiguous, politicized world, they can enrich our emotional awareness and responsiveness. Articulated in practice stories, emotions may teach us as well as move us. In empathizing with another's fear, for example, our emotional responsiveness may help us to see the world more clearly.[3] We may know abstractly that a developer fears the false assurances of permitting officials, that a neighbor to a site fears the good intentions of City Hall, but we really know quite little here unless we know emotionally what it might be like to feel such fear in the particular circumstances of this developer and this neighbor.

When planners are distrusted and perceived as threatening and aloof, their failure to respond sensitively to those emotions will look not like professionalism but like callous blindness, if not a willful disregard for the well-being of others. More generally, because we suspect those who are emotionally callous to be blind to large parts of what actually matters to those around them, we can recognize emotional sensitivity not only as a source of knowledge and a way of learning, but as a mode of moral vision and recognition too (Coles 1989; Murdoch 1970; Nussbaum 1990).

These claims suggest the agenda of this chapter, which has four main parts. The first part examines a practice story told by a planner, Harry, in a staff meeting of a small city's planning department. Even a quick look at Harry's story reveals it to be far from a simple tale about a multi-use project; it has a good deal to teach us.

The second part sets out the underappreciated aspects of practice stories: the ways they express and render political judgments, the ways their telling and listening require an astute practical rationality and responsiveness to the cases at hand. The next part examines another kind of practice story—a brief reflection by an environmental planner, Wayne, about mistakes he had made as a manager in his planning office. A close look at Wayne's story shows that stories do far more than describe events. To think of telling stories as primarily describing events, we shall see, would be as limited a view as thinking of playing music as primarily making noise. There is more to it!

The fourth example turns in more detail, then, to a brief story taken from a profile of a community development planner, Arthur, who recounts a deceptively simple vignette involving racism, risk taking, and astute political judgment. Arthur's story suggests both the challenges of community development practice and the ways we all may learn from profiles of astute and perceptive planners. The conclusion, finally, summarizes the political, moral, emotional, and deliberative work to be done (well or ineptly) as planners tell and listen to diverse stories every day.

I. THE EXTRAORDINARY RICHNESS OF ORDINARY STORIES IN PLANNING PRACTICE

In a mid-morning staff meeting, called every two weeks to discuss work in progress, the planning director, Tom, says to his half-dozen planners:

> We've got a problem on the Northside. Can someone fill us in, since I have to go at noon?

Harry, his assistant director, responds,

> The problems on the Northside? Let me try. We've got four users here: the Park, the Housing Association, the Nature Center, and the Children's Center. And you've got three different architects working on the project and no overall set of assumptions for what are the constraints for what they're designing. And then you've got Charles [the city attorney] negotiating various land sales, also without regard to any kind of overall design layout (particularly for access and circulation), and that seems to be the crux of the problem right now.

> *There was a very early site plan put together that suggested a portion of Benjamin Street could be used for parking, and that there would also be bus access to the front of the nature center site and the children's center site along Benjamin, and that the bus would probably get there through a new road that would be cut between the park portion and housing portion of the site.*
>
> *In our negotiations with the Housing Association—that is to say, Charles and myself on behalf of the Intergovernmental Relations Committee—we really tried hard to structure a deal that's not going to break their backs. One of the things we said to them is, "Look, your earlier proposal suggested that the city was going to build the street, and that's just not in the cards. The city is not going to build a street; you guys are going to have to build it. And it seems to us that one way to sort of build something that gives you the frontage you need for zoning—because they've got this ridiculous requirement of having to subdivide this site into fourteen individual lots—would be to build a small, private street that would give you frontage and would only be used for the people whose houses front that street."*

Here another planner, Lynn, asks: "What's ridiculous? What's the ridiculous requirement about having to divide this into fourteen lots?", and the staff go on to discuss the project. They ask about the zoning requirements, the actors involved and their commitments, the encompassing political pressures, and so on.

The assistant director here has told a quite ordinary story in an ordinary staff meeting. The staff take his account of what is happening on the Northside as reasonably ordinary too: There are problems, surprises, fights, negotiations, personal frictions, the usual uncertainties. So the planners listen for the relevant details. If they can make no helpful suggestions, at least they can better understand a co-worker's problems—and perhaps his best judgment of what is to be done now.

But this story, like many stories told in practice, is really quite extraordinary. The story not only presents but it also constructs a "problem." It not only identifies "actors" ("four users here") but it also characterizes their collective irrationality: "And you've got three different architects working on the project, and no overall set of assumptions for . . . what they're designing."

There is much more to this story, too: attention to particular actors (Charles, "negotiating various land sales") in the context of more general planning concerns (Charles's negotiating "without regard to any kind of overall design layout"). And more: a mention of relevant institutional and normative history (the "very early site plan") before the account of Harry's own efforts in the recent negotiations: "We really tried hard to structure a deal that's not going to break their backs." The story begins to put the project in its current institutional context, too: "They've got this ridiculous [zoning] requirement of having to subdivide this site into fourteen individual lots," and "The city is not going to build a street; you guys are going to have to build it."

The discussions quoted above, of course, are only one small part of an evolving story of "the problems on the Northside."[4] But the richness of even this segment of the story teaches several lessons.

What appears initially as a report of recent events quickly becomes a complex set of future issues the staff might explore. Harry is not just providing facts; he is presenting the facts that he takes to matter, facts he takes to be significant or even worrisome. What we call ordinarily "setting out the issues" is really quite extraordinary, ethically speaking, for it means making judgments about what is important, what is valuable enough to need further attention and study. This deliberative aspect of storytelling and listening calls for what academics refer to as "deconstruction" and "reconstruction" on the job, practically and ethically. What, for example, is Harry saying about Charles? Is he a "loose cannon," acting willfully "without regard to any kind of overall design layout," or is he being driven by the mayor? What about those "ridiculous" zoning requirements? Just what does Harry mean, and what is really important here (Majone 1989; Manin 1987; Reich 1988; Vickers 1984)?

Such practice stories portray not only issues but a practical world of action and interests, of settings and histories, of strategies and counterstrategies. But notice that Harry cannot define the "context" of the Northside project once and for all because that context is always changing. That context changes as the local economy fluctuates, as the city council becomes more or less attentive, as state legislation evolves, and it changes practically too with every move made in the current negotiations, with every promise or threat.

Harry's account suggests not only several of the actors involved but also the precariousness of their relationships. The architects are working without a shared sense of constraints; the Housing Association had been expecting the city to build a new street but Harry and Charles have told them, on "behalf of the Intergovernmental Relations Committee," "That's just not in the cards." We learn, too, about contingencies: The housing project's success will depend upon a "ridiculous requirement of having to subdivide this site into fourteen individual lots."

So Harry portrays in his story a practical and moral complexity of differing expectations, legal obligations, governmental commitments, historical precedent, and design suggestions as well. Harry's story helps his planning colleagues to understand better not only the Northside but themselves: to appreciate how Harry and, by extension, each of them as the city's planners is morally entangled, morally obliged to listen to the architects, to respect but perhaps attempt to rein in Charles's negotiations, to confront the requirements of the zoning law, to recognize but improve the early site plan, to negotiate successfully with the Housing Association. These entanglements are both moral and practical requirements, each of which can be met well or poorly, each of which may affect the success of the ultimate project. Perhaps most importantly, planners' practice stories can convey the moral complexity of issues and the practical moral entanglements of planners in ways that more abstract accounts of planning cannot.

II. BEYOND DESCRIPTION TO PRACTICAL RATIONALITY: STORIES RENDER JUDGMENTS

We could, of course, still insist on looking at planners' practice stories as descriptive accounts. Seen this way, the stories would be pictures, snapshots, and approximations of events and behaviors. We would often discount these stories a good deal, knowing how much they inevitably leave out.

But we have a better alternative. We can look at these stories no longer primarily as descriptive but as prescriptive: telling us what is important, what matters, to what we should pay attention, what we need to worry about, what is really at stake if we fail to act. When a planner asks a colleague at work, "What happened at the meeting last night?" he or she is far more likely to be asking "What happened last night that I might need to know about?" than "What really happened, step by step?" Seen in this light, these stories set agendas, shape senses of relevance, contribute to priority setting, construct problems, and shape action.

No longer tales told simply to entertain or describe, these stories now appear ethically selective through and through. For if we listen closely not only to the portrayals of fact in planners' stories but rather to their claims of value and significance, we discover an infrastructure of ethics, an ethical substructure of practice, a finely woven tapestry of value being woven sentence by sentence, each sentence not simply adding, description by description, to a picture of the world but adding care by care to a sensitivity to the practical world, to an attentiveness to and a prudent appreciation of that world (Krumholz and Forester 1990, chapter 15; Forester 1992). So we learn from skillful (and perhaps inept) performance as well as from verified (or refuted) propositions. Iris Murdoch (1970, 37) powerfully makes the deeper and more general point:

> [I]f we consider what the work of attention is like, how continuously it goes on, and how imperceptibly it builds up structures of value round about us, we shall not be surprised that at crucial moments of choice most of the business of choosing is already over. This does not imply that we are not free, certainly not. But it implies that the exercise of our freedom is a small piecemeal business which goes on all the time and not a grandiose leaping about unimpeded at important moments. The moral life, on this view, is something that goes on continually, not something that is switched off in between the occurrence of explicit moral choices. What happens in between such choices is indeed what is crucial.

Again: before the rationality of choice comes the prior practical rationality of careful attention, critical listening, setting out issues, and exploring working relationships as pragmatic aspects of problem construction.

Planners build up such structures of value in their stories in institutionally and ideologically staged ways. Certain values seem excluded, to arise only rarely, if at all; others are "impractical" or "not serious" or "out in left field" given the staff's reading of those with whom they work.[5] Planners' stories inevitably express relations of power, reproducing those relations in politically diverse ways (Forester 1993b; Healey 1993a, 1993b; Tett and Wolfe 1991).

We can recognize in planners' practice stories the ongoing rendering of political judgments in institutional settings in which resources can be few and ambiguities many, in which authority can be minimal but vulnerability ample. Planners' practice stories reflect and render political judgments because the planners have not just issues to face but relationships to sustain: with politicians, citizens groups, official boards, legal staff of city and developer alike, architects, adversaries and supporters too. In a conflictual political world, the failure of these relationships can stop the planners' efforts cold. The city council may withdraw support. The head of the housing authority may withdraw cooperation. The supposedly friendly planning board may stall. The citizens group may distrust the staff's promises. And so on.

Sorting through an infinity of fact, facing ambiguous desires, interests and mandates, the planners must search for an account of the issues and actors so they can fashion working agreements with others on this design or that strategy, on that project mix or this schedule. They are neither just describing facts nor simply prescribing values: They are searching for possibilities of agreement and consent, for others' support, for a solution that will make sense to others as well as to themselves (Benhabib 1990).

Tore Sager (1993) quotes Hannah Arendt on this point: "The power of judgment rests on a potential agreement with others, and the thinking process which is active in judging something is not, like the thought process of pure reasoning, a dialogue between me and myself, but finds itself always and primarily, even if I am quite alone in making up my mind, in an anticipated communication with others with whom I know I must finally come to some agreement. From this potential agreement judgment derives its specific validity." Anthony Kronman (1987, 869) puts the other-regarding aspect of political judgment in more pragmatic terms: "(A)nyone wishing to be effective in debate will have an interest in becoming the sort of person whose opinions are respected, . . . a person of good judgment."

But in a staff meeting, how do the planners' stories reflect their "anticipated communication with others with whom [they] know [they] must finally come to agreement?" The planners' time is short; their agendas are full. Politically vulnerable, the planners know that they will have to make a case to citizens, developers, and politicians alike. So thinking through any project's problems, planners are continually under pressure to search not just for what is good in some abstract sense but to find what is good in the political sense of potentially gaining the approval of others.

Harry's story, for example, suggests his search for strategies to move ahead: He recounts his proposal for dealing with the "ridiculous" zoning requirement at the Benjamin Street site. "We tried really hard," Harry says of his and Charles's efforts. Harry does not simply complain about the zoning and portray himself as a victim; he describes the zoning requirement, his effort to respond, and the practical suggestion he has made to move ahead—a suggestion he brings to the staff meeting for discussion and refinement. So, too, the stories planners tell at work can reveal political judgments about opportunities and constraints, about more and less responsible efforts, about more or less supposedly legitimate mandates, about relevant history to be respected and learned, relevant concerns, interests and commitments to be honored.

These processes of judgment are remarkably complex—certainly as complex as the work of description!—and they are as remarkably understudied. We need to learn more about both the kinds of judgments planners must routinely make and the experience, education, and sensitivity planners require to make such practical judgments well (Rorty 1988).

III. AN ENVIRONMENTAL PLANNER'S CONFESSION

The stories that planners tell about their own work suggest the rich variety of judgments they must make in practice. Consider now two excerpts from a series of "profiles of planners" (Forester 1993a; Forester and Kreiswirth 1993a, b, c, d). The first excerpt suggests how much more than description a planner's story can accomplish. The second excerpt suggests ways that planners' practice stories can teach us about the riskiness and opportunities of practice, the moral imagination required, and the kind of practical rationality arguably necessary as well.

To begin, consider a passage from a profile of Wayne, an environmental planner. Let us see if Wayne's story, superficially about management style, is simply a description of facts, or much more.

Speaking of his experience of managing a planning team, Wayne tells us:

> *That stuff I had no clue about. So you'd be real rigid about your management style when it wasn't appropriate, and people resent that. So you learn later to be rigid when you need to be rigid and lax when it's okay. And that way everybody gets a balance. They don't feel so bad about working hard later, because it's been lax other times; and you're getting the most out of it. You're using it when it's appropriate. That's an important lesson."*

Perhaps this little story of learning on the job could be considered a description, but in telling this tale, Wayne does much more than recount facts. We see Wayne self-report, admit, and confess his own ignorance: "That stuff I had no clue about." He identifies his own and, by extension, others' mistakes: "So you'd be real rigid . . . when it wasn't appropriate." He predicts instrumental, psychological, and political costs of a rigid management style: " . . . and people resent that." He also seems to acknowledge a substantive harm of causing staff resentment, independent of its instrumental hindrances.

Yet he recognizes hope and envisions possibility too: "So you learn. . . ." He makes the judgment that contingency counts, and he suggests what can be learned: "to be rigid when you need to be rigid and lax when it's okay." More, too: He empathizes with his staff about their working conditions: "and that way everybody gets a balance." He appreciates staff morale: "They don't feel so bad about working hard later," and he honors a norm he implies his staff shares, a norm of reciprocity and reasonableness, "because it's been lax other times." Nonetheless, he justifies "laxity" strategically: "You're getting the most out of it," and he legitimates his own managerial action: "You're using it when it's appropriate." Then he sums up and evaluates his own short story: "That's an important lesson."

Wayne's story expresses moral imagination as much as empirical description because, as with many planners' stories, it is not just about facts but about facts that matter, facts that are significant to planning practice and citizens' lives. Wayne's work of description is also one of confession, empathy, recognizing possible harm, respecting social norms like reciprocity, and morally imagining possibilities and opportunities.

The point here is not to show how complex an apparently simple paragraph can be but rather to debunk the idea that planners' practice stories are primarily descriptions, pictures of events, mirrors of some unambiguous reality. Telling their stories, planners act in very concrete, very specific ways, making particular practical judgments for which they are often held responsible—recognizing or missing important issues—by those with whom they work.

IV. A Community Development Planner on Racism, Particularity, and Hope

Turn finally to another excerpt from a profile of "Arthur," a planner hired as executive director of a settlement house serving poor white Appalachian and African American communities (Forester and Chu 1990, 20-24). Arthur tells us:

> *The first thing I did was advertise for a home buyer counselor. I remember saying, "If we're going to have an equity program here, we're going to have to buy these houses, rehab them, and sell them." And I needed somebody to advise residents who had never before dealt with banks on how to deal with banks. How to establish credit. That was the first thing I started with.*
>
> *I was also aware of the split between the black community and the Appalachian community. I knew that in order for this arrangement to work, they had to work together and present a unified neighborhood front for the economically poor in that neighborhood. Any differences between groups would be played off by those who didn't want them to succeed in the first place.*

Arthur had moved from a city with a strong history of nonprofit community development work to what seemed to be another world:

> *I found myself in the bastion of the private sector. People [in this city] didn't really respect government, except insofar as it supported the private enterprise movement. The whole rhetoric was different. The city had experience only with a couple of nonprofits that, by and large, had failed. And the only reason they kept pouring money into those institutions was because of straight political deals.*

He continued:

> *The only person I found for this home buyer counseling role was this woman who responded to the ad I put in the paper. She had grown up as a welfare mother herself, broke out of it, and got a home in the private rental market. She was also on the staff of the Housing Authority, counseling public housing tenants on how to get their financial act together when they fell behind in their rent. . . .*

She could understand what I was trying to do to get to the poor Appalachian and black communities, who had no experience in dealing with banks. I was saying, "What we want to do is put together a credit program for the families, give them six months of working with a home buyer counselor before they even set foot in a bank, have the home buyer counselor walk into the bank with the family, with all the documents laid out that the banks are used to, and present a credit-worthy risk so that the banks will finance these individuals." She could understand that. I knew there was a lot of training I had to do, but she could understand the program. She just happened to be black.

The advice I got, though, was: "The Appalachian poor will never work with a black. You're taking a risk with the project."

Well, I didn't have the luxury of asking questions. She was the only person I found who I thought could do the job. The only thing I asked her during the job interview was: Did she mind working in an environment in which a lot of people would be prejudiced against her? I asked her point-blank: How comfortable did she feel in dealing with Appalachian whites? I didn't have to ask that question twice—she knew exactly what I meant. She said she thought she could do it.

I left it up to good faith after that. In any environment, there are prejudices that people face. But when you start to work one-to-one, when you start really to help people who need help and do it in a way that is not heavy-handed and maximizes their options for succeeding, the effort is appreciated. I was banking on the fact that the poor communities would appreciate what we were trying to do, even if they didn't in the beginning. A lot of people in fact wouldn't work with us in the beginning. But ultimately, they did. She was good, sensitive, and not overly aggressive. In fact, she was very quiet. In her own quiet way she plugged along, helped everybody over the two years, and became a very trusted member of the Appalachian community.

How can we learn from these few paragraphs? Certainly we do not learn that the success of the story is generalizable. Neither do we learn that the case is unique. What then?

We learn first, perhaps, about the crucial importance of particular people in particular places and times. Arthur's story leaves us with no doubt that his program might have failed, that his good intentions might have gone disastrously wrong, that another counselor might have done far less well.

We learn, too, about the immediate and pervasive threat of racism to the planning process. Arthur had been told of his chances: "The Appalachian poor will never work with a black." That prediction was no neutral statement of likely fact; it was a direct warning: "You're taking a risk with the project." The pressure—if not the risk—here, and no doubt in other cases, was inescapable, Arthur recounts: "I didn't have the luxury of asking questions," of exploring alternatives, of taking more time.

But Arthur did not take that risk blindly, exposing not only the project but the prospective black counselor to the racism of the poor Appalachian community in which she would have to work. He spoke directly, if not single-mindedly, to the issue to recognize and assess with her the threat of racism from the beginning: "I asked her point-blank: How comfortable did she feel in dealing with Appalachian whites?" This was, he implies, no easy question to ask. We would hardly say ordinarily, for example, "I asked her point-blank if it was raining."

Arthur suggests, too, their developing collaboration: "I didn't have to ask that question twice—she knew exactly what I meant." Here we see less a meeting of minds between a white male planner and a black female home-buying counselor than we see a glimmer of their joint recognition of a common threat.

Arthur thought she could do the job. He acknowledged the threat of racism, asked if she thought she could still work in the face of it, and when she said she thought she could, he tells us, he "left it up to good faith after that." This appeal to "good faith" was pragmatic, not theological: a faith in a sensitive practice and a sensitive, experienced practitioner and not, significantly, a faith in an abstract solution, a way to handle racism in general, a recipe for community development, a "one, two, three" method of community work.

Arthur tells us, instead, of good work in the face of the perversity of racism. He tells us too of the kind of rationality required here: a kind of practical rationality that does not promise grand strategy but responds to particular need, that does not so much fix clearly on an end and choose a means to it as it responds without creating new problems—in a way, Arthur tells us, "that is not heavy handed."

But there is a good deal more going on here. We learn too from the emotional quality of the story. We learn not only about the iffyness of practice, its contingencies and fragility, but also about the planner's and counselor's experience of that iffyness, their experience of real vulnerability. Arthur's efforts to hire a counselor for applicants to the home ownership program brought him an underwhelming pool of one qualified applicant. This might have simplified Arthur's problem of choice but it can hardly have given him any real sense of making a choice at all. Rather than seeing Arthur managing a program, we see him instead being managed by the constraints he faced and feeling vulnerable to the resulting dangers.

But we learn about a kind of emotional particularity here too, for

Arthur's single qualified applicant knew about more than bureaucracy, housing, and banks. Arthur's very first words about her suggest important parts of her story: "She had grown up as a welfare mother herself, broke out of it, and got a home in the private rental market." So she knew personally the poverty of the communities Arthur hoped to serve; she also "broke out of it," an expression suggesting not happenstance but a personal story of struggle. And those personal qualities, we come to learn, were crucial: "sensitivity" to the people she worked with, determination and persistence too ("she plugged along, helped everybody over the two years. . . .").

Particular sensitivities and luck matter as much as technical competence here. Speaking of a different case, Arthur put it succinctly: "You find people all of a sudden. Well—you have to have your eye out. You have to know what you're missing and have an eye out for what you need." So luck matters, but so too does a careful perception, so too does the work of search, knowing what you are missing and having an eye out for what you need. The judgment Arthur had to make here—to hire this applicant or not—involved creating his own program's luck, enabling "the right person to be in the right place at the right time" (Pitkin 1984).

Arthur knew what he needed from his prospective counselor. He saw that she had worked for the housing authority and that she understood his program, but he knew, too, that she and his program both would be vulnerable to racism. So he looked not only for technical qualifications but for what we can call "moral qualifications": the qualities of real responsiveness under pressure that we call good judgment, wisdom, or, more colloquially, "street smarts." Arthur knew to search not for idealistic rule-following, not for a moral saint, but for tested virtues of character: an open-eyed recognition of the threat of racism and a considered response in the face of it. "How comfortable did she feel in dealing with Appalachian whites? I didn't have to ask that question twice. . . . She said she thought she could do it." Arthur tells us a great deal here about himself too. He did not feel the need to ask his question twice. He felt confident that she recognized the problems he was talking about and he accepted her response, her judgment that "she could do it."

Arthur has another lesson to teach us in his emphatic "she knew exactly what I meant." Literally minded theorists might object here: How could Arthur know this? How could he know what she meant, at his distance from her African American, gendered experience? This objection would miss the point besides presuming the kind of full knowledge it seeks to criticize, for Arthur is not making philosophical claims about sameness of meaning or experience. He is making a practical claim about their interaction—and he does it with hindsight, claiming that, given the situation (his words and her response, and their subsequent behavior), she knew exactly what he meant regarding the practical purposes they both recognized.

We learn here about two people's courage and determination, and we know that while one faced the loss of his program's success, the other faced the potential loss of life and limb. We can hardly understand this story, it seems, if we fail to understand the relevant emotions involved here: his directness, her courage, their collaborative "understanding," his confidence in her abilities, her sensitivity, his conviction "that the poor communities would appreciate what we were trying to do," her one-to-one help of people in need, his willingness to move ahead in the face of "a lot of people" who "wouldn't work with us in the beginning."

These emotions are far from irrelevant here and far from irrational. Indeed, only if we recognize these emotions might we even begin to make sense of what has happened, of the actual practice in this case. The risks here were taken, we learn, not blindly or callously but deliberately, if also with "good faith" as well as trepidation on Arthur's part, and no doubt with some combination of hope and fear on the counselor's part as well.

Similarly, we can hardly doubt that the counselor's success grew not just from her competent provision of information about bank practices but also from her particular emotional qualities: her persistence, her sensitivity, and her "not overly" aggressive directness—emotional qualities of attentiveness and responsiveness in practice without which she might well have failed. So Arthur's story suggests the importance of intellect and emotion, technical competence and affective responsiveness, as complementary if not interpenetrating aspects of practice—required of practitioners whatever their class, race, and gender. An important empirical question in any given case is whether, how, and when particular practitioners of varying class, racial, and gender backgrounds might embody differing sensitivities and abilities, given the requirements of working in that case— with immigrant Asian women, with Eastern European gypsies, with African American Baptists, and so on.

These emotional qualities of practice that Arthur sketches for us seem not incidental but crucial. Hardly irrational, these emotional qualities of a black woman's rich responsiveness to poor whites seem to have enabled her to have overcome racist suspicions, to have succeeded programmatically, and to have enabled her, against the apparent odds, to have become "a very trusted member of the Appalachian community."

Arthur's story presents a tale of emotional struggle and judgment interwoven with a program's development. To neglect the emotional character of the story would make it both less subjective, less sensitively nuanced—making us less able to empathize with and understand the characters involved—and less objective too, telling us less of what really mattered in the case at hand, less of the actual qualities that enabled Arthur and the counselor to act effectively.

Arthur's story suggests more, too: that emotional sensitivity and responsiveness work together, along with technical knowledge, as a mode of practical response, and that such sensitivity and responsiveness are not simply incidental accompaniments of cognition, of "thinking." This no more means that any emotion any time will do, any more than it means that any fact is relevant. It means, instead, that in a world of difference, emotional sensitivity can be a form of moral vision, of moral attentiveness to others (Nussbaum 1990; Rorty 1988). It suggests, too, that planners lacking emotional range, emotional maturity, and capacity will likely miss a good deal of what lies before them and are likely to fail as a result.

As Kronman (1987, 858) argues, "To deliberate well—which requires both sympathy and detachment—one must . . . be able not only to think clearly but to feel in certain ways as well. The person who shows good judgment in deliberation will thus be marked as much by his affective dispositions as by his intellectual powers, and *he will know more than others do because he feels what they cannot*" [emphasis added]. So Arthur speaks of the importance, for example, of not being "heavy handed" or "overly aggressive" and of his faith that their efforts would be "appreciated," recognized as valuable and not self-serving, as promising and not as a "con."

Arthur has learned too. He took a substantial risk, and his retrospective story reflects what he has learned—as well as what he can now reconstruct briefly about what really did happen. He has learned, for example, about racism and practical work. He did not seem to take lightly the warning that he was risking the project. Yet he took a risk, and certainly exposed the counselor to greater personal risk, without full information, without a well-developed "means" to his desired "ends." But he was not "flying blind." He tells us what his bets were, what his working theory was: "I was banking on the fact that the poor communities would appreciate what we were trying to do, even if they didn't in the beginning." In hindsight, those bets and that working theory seem to have been vindicated, we learn, as Arthur learned.

We would do well here to explore the kind of judgment, the kind of rationality, that Arthur seems to have brought to bear. He did not simply satisfice, lowering his expectations to find a satisfactory outcome, nor did he act incrementally in the sense of building upon reachable incremental agreements to move ahead. Indeed, he tells us, "A lot of people in fact wouldn't work with us in the beginning." So Arthur did not work by consensus building either; quite the contrary, in hiring a black woman to work in part with a poor white community, he was working directly against the practical advice of others.

So how can we understand Arthur's judgment? Arthur seems to have recognized not just one but several very general but very important facts, encompassing histories, that were operating in the situation he faced: the histories of racism, first, and poverty, second. The poverty of the African American and Appalachian communities had motivated his project in the first place; the racism of the Appalachian community, he tells us, threatened the same project. Yet Arthur was not stuck here. Why not?

In the face of warnings that he was endangering the project, in the face of "a lot of people [who] wouldn't work with" him, what made it possible for Arthur to move forward and not bail out, not wait for another day? His story suggests that he saw not only the facts of poverty and racism but more, too: He recognized the human capacities of others "to appreciate" the effort "to help people who need help" in a way that is "not heavy handed." As Nussbaum (1990) suggests, Arthur's practical judgment reflected a dialogue of antecedent principle and new vision, a recognition of both general normative conditions and the particular possibilities of this case.

Had Arthur initially taken a vote in the affected community, he might have closed up shop. Had he taken a vote later on, he might well have been supported. In the language of rational choice theorists, Arthur bet that the community's initial preferences in this case—refusing to work with a black woman housing counselor—would change, that the general threat of racism could be overcome by "sensitive," "one-to-one" work (March 1988). But this case is what matters if we are to understand the possibilities of case-specific practical judgment, the connections between thinking and acting, learning and doing, perception and action in actual practice.

But did Arthur "bet" that the community's preferences would change? He tells us that after the prospective counselor told him she thought she could work with the white community, he "left it up to good faith after that." With the benefit of hindsight and somewhat glibly now, he tells us that "in any environment, there are prejudices that people face." Had he been that cavalier originally, he never would have asked the counselor "point-blank" how comfortable she felt in dealing with Appalachian whites." If Arthur can now see that these prejudices were not determinant, he hardly knew that with any certainty in the beginning. If Arthur "bet" on the counselor's success, he did so not throwing the project to the winds of chance but as a participant, expecting to do "a lot of training," expecting that the particular person, her particular style, and the particular community's needs could mesh and be helped to fit together successfully. Arthur's story suggests no weighing of commensurable costs and benefits. It suggests instead a careful work of practical rationality, a careful consideration of general facts, including racism and poverty, that would influence the actions of particular people with particular sensitivities and histories and that would, in the specific case, be influenced in turn. This rationality, of Arthur's and the counselor's, is interpretive and practically pitched, responsive to the ambiguity and incommensurability of "real" situations, and it is a rationality powerfully conveyed by practice stories whose messiness and moral entanglements characterize the work that practically rational actors must do all the time.

CONCLUSION

This essay has explored the practical, political, and ethical character of the stories that planners routinely tell—at work and about their work too. The argument in a nutshell has been this: By telling practical stories, for better or worse, planners bring to bear moral imagination and shape the moral imaginations of others.

Telling practice stories, planners render practical and political judgments not "in their minds" but in their deeds, as they come to be responsible for reporting or failing to report events, for recommending or failing to see options, for identifying threats or opportunities or failing to, and so on. In so doing, they search for value, set agendas, characterize others, define constraints and possibilities.

Telling stories at work, planners not only describe events but also explain what has happened, warn of dangers, and identify "benefits." They report relevant details and search for others' meaning ("I think what he meant was. . . ."). They confess mistakes, justify recommendations, prepare others, and do far, far more. Doing moral work, planners' stories characterize others by giving them status or ascribing stigma. Doing political work, planners' stories organize attention, including some concerns and excluding others, invoking or challenging supposedly legitimate norms, pointing to support or opposition, to future problems and possibilities. Doing emotional work, planners' stories allow listeners to empathize at times, to see issues more clearly because they see more sensitively too.

Planners stories do deliberative work as well. Always told in constrained circumstances, these stories reflect their tellers' ongoing search for value, for what matters, for what is relevant here, what is significant. Planners' stories are thus ethical not because they reflect right or wrong decisions but because they reflect appreciation of what matters in the case at hand or blindness to it, because they reflect a responsive awareness (or an insensitivity) to what is at stake, because they reflect a responsible appropriation of norms and precedent or a callous disregard of them.

If we wish to understand the everyday politics, ethics, and rationality of planning, we would do well to listen carefully to the stories planners tell. But if we think of stories simply as descriptive tales, we will miss most of their richness and significance, the challenges and opportunities, the "care-ful" work and the serious blindness, too, of actual planning practice. If we are to interpret the world of planning in order to change it, we should pay attention not just to the partiality of planners' stories but also to the subtle moral and political work those stories do.

Notes

1. This is not to argue that stories are always better than studies: Stories can be more or less relevant, as studies can be, in any given case. Likewise, stories may be better or worse (along many criteria), as studies can be; both may be shown to be riddled with falsehood or not, to attribute causality or responsibility faultily, to be selective in justifiable or unjustifiable ways. To blur boundaries, stories may make reference to studies, and studies may refer to or even share characteristics of stories in their own right. Cf. Gusfield (1981), Van Maanen (1988), Abrams (1991), Hummel (1990, 1991). In addition, stories partially constitute their narrators as well as being told and improvised by them (Forester 1992).

2. So practice stories can teach us about the priority of practical rationality: Before problem solution proceeds, problem construction must be well underway. For the argument applied to medical practice and medical ethics, see Jennings (1990). Cf. George (1994), Forester (1993a) and more generally, Nussbaum (1990, ch. 2). As we shall see below, these practice stories can teach listeners what it may be like to face—in Nussbaum's terms, to "be finely aware and richly responsible to"—the issues they portray (Nussbaum 1990, ch. 5). Such stories provide moral phenomenologies that more abstract philosophical or structuralist accounts do not.

3. Of course, emotions can mislead us, just as some selections of "the facts" can. Nevertheless, failing to respond with emotional sensitivity can lead to as much trouble as failing to provide "the facts." Cf. Nussbaum (1986, 364; 1990, 75-82). So we must try to recognize difference and listen carefully—presuming neither that differences of experience, class, gender, or race, for example, must be unbridgeable and mutually incomprehensible nor that some perfect intersubjectivity will assure equally perfect understanding.

4. Holding aside disputes about true and false stories, any one person might tell an infinite number of different (!) true stories about the same event—

from different angles, with different emphases, with different amounts of detail, for example. We should not confuse the plurality of possible stories with simplistic notions of truth or falsity. We should assess the ways practice stories might be relevant or irrelevant, sensitive or callous, simplistic or nuanced, timely or not, confusing or edifying, and so on. Cf. John Austin's (1961, 131) remark: "(I)f only we could forget for a while about the beautiful and get down instead to the dainty and the dumpy."

5. To say that institutional pressures shape the stories that are told is true, but hardly all determining; it does not yet help us to understand how two planners in the same working environment might tell such different stories, make such differing, even contradictory claims of value, as they work on projects. Nevertheless, the warning of Bruce Jennings (1990, 269) is apt here: "What ethicists do not do is see moral concepts and categories as embedded in ongoing forms of social practice and experience that are structured via particular institutional patterns or the encounter with certain technological constraints. And ethicists do not pay *much attention to the ways in which struggling with a problem or acting within a certain pattern of constraints or power relationships can actually transform the moral perception and understanding of agents*" (emphasis added). Cf. Forester (1989, 1993b). Planners' stories too may be hegemonic or counter-hegemonic, and we need better to assess which they are when.

REFERENCES

Abrams, K. 1991. Hearing the call of stories. *California Law Review* 79, 4 (July): 971–1052.

Austin, J. 1961. A plea for excuses. In *Philosophical papers*. London: Oxford University Press.

Benhabib, S. 1990. In the shadow of Aristotle and Hegel: communicative ethics and current controversies in practical philosophy. In M. Kelly, ed., *Hermeneutics and critical theory in ethics and politics*. Cambridge, MA: MIT Press.

Coles, R. 1989. *The call of stories*. New York: Houghton Mifflin.

Forester, J. 1989. *Planning in the face of power*. Berkeley: University of California.

_____. 1992. On critical ethnography: fieldwork in a Habermasian way. In M. Alvesson and H. Wilmott, eds., *Critical management studies*. Los Angeles: Sage.

_____. 1993a. Learning from practice stories. In F. Fischer and J. Forester, eds., *The argumentative turn in policy analysis and planning*. Durham, NC: Duke University Press.

_____. 1993b. *Critical theory, public policy, and planning practice.* Albany: State University of New York Press.

_____, and L. Chu, eds. 1990. Profiles of planners. Typescript. Profile/Working Papers, 106 W. Sibley Hall, Cornell University, Ithaca, New York 14853. 234 pages.

Forester, J., and B. Kreiswirth, eds. 1993a. Profiles of planners in housing and community development. Typescript. Profile/Working Papers, 106 W. Sibley Hall, Cornell University, Ithaca, New York 14853.

_____. 1993b. Profiles of planners in land use, transportation, and environmental planning. Typescript. Profile/Working Papers, 106 W. Sibley Hall, Cornell University, Ithaca, New York 14853.

_____. 1993c. Profiles of planners in historic preservation planning, typescript, Profile/Working Papers, 106 W. Sibley Hall, Cornell University, Ithaca, New York 14853.

_____. 1993d. Profiles of Women in Planning. Typescript. Profile/Working Papers, 106 W. Sibley Hall, Cornell University, Ithaca, New York 14853.

George, R. V. 1994. Formulating the right planning problem. *Journal of Planning Literature* 8, 3: 240–59.

Gusfield, J. 1981. *The culture of public problems.* Chicago: University of Chicago Press.

Healey, P. 1993a. The communicative work of development plans. *Environment and Planning B: Planning and Design* 20: 83–104.

_____. 1993b. Planning through debate: the communicative turn in planning theory. In F. Fischer and J. Forester, eds., *The argumentative turn in policy analysis and planning.* Durham, NC: Duke University Press, 233–53.

Hoch, C. 1994. *What planners do.* Chicago: APA Planners Press.

Hummel, R. 1990. Uncovering validity criteria for stories managers hear and tell. *American Review of Public Administration* 20, 4: 303–14.

_____. 1991. Stories managers tell: why they are as valid as science. *Public Administration Review* 51, 1: 31–41.

Jennings, B. 1990. Ethics and ethnography in neonatal intensive care. In George Weisz, ed., *Social science perspectives on medical ethics.* London: Kluwer.

Krieger, M. 1981. *Advice and planning.* Philadelphia: Temple University Press.

Kronman, A. 1987. Living in the law. *Chicago Law Review* 54: 835.

Krumholz, N., and J. Forester. 1990. *Making equity planning work.* Philadelphia: Temple University Press.

Majone, G. 1989. *Evidence, argument, and persuasion in the policy process.* New Haven, CT: Yale University Press.

Mandelbaum, S. 1991. Telling stories. *Journal of Planning Education and Research* 10: 209–14.

Manin, B. 1987. On legitimacy and political deliberation. *Political Theory* 15, 3: 338-68.

March, J. 1988. *Organizations and decisions.* New York: Blackwell.

Marris, P. 1990. Witnesses, engineers, or story-tellers? The influence of social research on social policy. In Herbert Gans, ed., *Sociology in America.* Los Angeles: Sage.

Murdoch, I. 1970. *The sovereignty of good.* London: Ark.

Nussbaum, M. 1986. *The fragility of goodness.* Cambridge: Cambridge University Press.

_____. 1990. *Love's knowledge.* New York: Oxford.

Pitkin, H. 1984. *Fortune is a woman.* Berkeley: University of California Press.

Reich, R. 1988. Policy making in a democracy. In R. Reich, ed., *The power of public ideas.* Cambridge: Ballinger.

Rorty, A. 1988. *Mind in action.* Boston: Beacon Press.

Sager, T. 1990. *Communicate or calculate: planning theory and social science concepts in a contingency perspective.* Stockholm: Nordplan.

Schön, D. 1983. *The reflective practitioner.* New York: Basic Books.

Tett, A., and J. M. Wolfe. 1991. Discourse analysis and city plans. *Journal of Planning Education and Research* 10, 3: 195-200.

Van Maanen, J. 1988. *Tales of the field.* Chicago: University of Chicago Press.

Vickers, S. G. 1984. *The art of judgment.* New York: Harper and Row.

CHARLES HOCH

11 *What Do Planners Do In the United States?*

THE PROFESSIONAL PROTOCOL OF EXPERTISE

Planning and policy schools have encouraged beginning professionals to master and apply the methods and techniques of an instrumental rationality grounded in utilitarianism. For the true believers,
everyone applying these methods and techniques properly should arrive
at the identical "rational" choice among policy or project alternatives.

There are, of course, relatively few such true believers these days. But
even those of us who have assimilated the widespread critique of the limits of utilitarianism are likely to think of cost-benefit analysis—both as protocol and symbol—as at the core of our professional expertise. "Rationality" may not be everything but it is peculiarly ours. Students learn to prize
the predictability and precision of their new skills and to embrace the authority conferred upon them by their expertise. The image of the autonomous professional fosters a split in their minds between adversarial democratic politics and technical authority.

Although students tend to modify, abandon, or simply forget specific
techniques when they enter practice—satisficing and muddling through
seem so much more fitting than formal methods of rational analysis—many
of them hold to the aura of professional competence to justify their identity
(Baum 1983; Hoch 1988; Hoch and Cibulskis 1987). They adopt a dualistic
outlook that elevates the apparatus of rationality—even when it is locked

Adapted from Charles Hoch, *What Planners Do* (Chicago: APA Planners Press, 1994). Used
with permission of the American Planning Association.

securely away—over mere political manipulation. Some planners claim to work as pure technicians, others as political advocates, while most try to serve what they perceive as contesting gods.

The frustration and ambivalence practitioners feel are usually not indicators of a lack of individual competence but the product of professional practice that cannot simultaneously meet the expectations of expertise and still serve the public interest in a democratic manner. In a society fragmented by relations of power embedded in large-scale organizations, planners (along with other professionals) practice in institutional settings where the realization of competing instrumental and strategic ends requires adversarial politics. The predominance of instrumentally organized power relations, and the uncertainties these relations pose for practitioners in the organizational world of the bureaucratic system, fragment and displace the social integrity of the kind of democratic community that fosters consensus. The bureaucratic message—the third-person text—ruptures and fragments a democratic communion because the social experience of the message requires that the author and audience separate (as means from ends) or as one individual or group from another, reconnecting only through the abstract medium of hierarchical rules or adversarial political competition.

The organization of such fragmentation centers in relations of power as described by Max Weber and Michel Foucault. Planning practitioners may obtain some organizational security within which they feel free to pursue professional goals, but doing so seems to require that they increase the uncertainty endured by others down the line. Ironically, planning organizations allegedly designed to reduce the collective uncertainties of modern society can end up generating their own set of uncertainties, not only for clients but for employees as well. How do planning professionals pursuing practical plans and democratic consensus cope with the pressures and demands of adversarial settings?

DEMOCRATIC PLANNING IN LIBERAL SOCIETIES

The Powerful Professional: From Self to Others

The rational model justifies the image of the public-serving, independent professional as the proper standard of conduct. This professional protocol adopts conceptions of rationality that overstate the powers of expertise while simultaneously disguising those powers as matters of technique. The presupposition of perfect knowledge in many social science models and even the rational planning model tends either to banish the politics of uncertainty entirely or to translate these political relationships into methodological presuppositions and procedures. Such abstraction has its uses but also imposes a serious impediment. Planners who adopt the model as a practical guide blind themselves to those power relations that shape the identity of their work. This often promotes a naive notion of science that ignores how the social organization and political use of scientific and technical knowledge contribute to new risks and new domains for the exercise of power.

Social and organizational uncertainty in a liberal society is a consequence of the simultaneous pursuit of many individual purposes and developmental journeys. Uncertainty exists as both a prerequisite for, and by-product of, individual freedom and choice. The problem for these analysts is not how we might eliminate such uncertainty—an order and predictability that would threaten the freedoms liberals embrace—but how we might remove forms of uncertainty (i.e., externalities) that no one (or very few) desire and reduce the uneven distribution of uncertainties that favors a few at the expense of the many.

The danger of technocratic rationality comes not from the commitment to reason but from the use of particular technical findings to discredit the legitimate purposes of other individuals as irrelevant, self-interested, or even stupid. Acting as experts, planners can offer advice that is used to dispel or silence the questions and concerns of people worried about the uncertainty they face. The paradox planners face, one they share with other professionals seeking the creation of a public good in organizations, is between the autonomy of expertise and responsibility to others.

THE DEMOCRATIC CONTINUUM

In theory, liberal democracies encourage and protect the purposes of individual citizens. A liberal moral order relies on people self-consciously shaping their own destinies, making informed choices using a reflective moral inquiry that allows them to give "reasons" for their choices: "I voted for her because. . . ." "I moved from one neighborhood to another in order to. . . ." "I decided to get a divorce so that. . . ."

In practice, the liberalism in which we believe and the social world we experience never are fully consonant. Class, race, and gender differences prevent many from obtaining and exercising individual purposes. The idea that we are free to do as we please so long as we do not hurt others misses the dense fabric of our interdependence. Whether with good will or with malevolence, as attentive citizens or as free riders, we inevitably thwart others as we pursue our own interests. Our very diversity frustrates our best efforts to identify shared public problems and purposes.

Democracy Through Adversity

Classical liberal theorists encouraged us to solve these problems through what Jane Mansbridge (1983) describes as "adversarial politics." In the political realm, individuals compete and cooperate as strangers seeking only to maximize their own benefits. They may or may not respect a utilitarian calculation of the welfare of the entire society. The public good is, however, operationally defined by voting within representative institutions and not by cost–benefit analysis. But serious costs accompany the remarkable institutional benefits of adversarial democracy. There are serious costs that accompany the remarkable institutional benefits of adversarial democracy. As Mansbridge argues:

> It replaces common interest with self interest, the dignity of equal status with baser motives of self protection, and the communal moments of face-to-face council with the isolation of a voting machine. (Mansbridge 1983, 18)

If individuals are to plan together effectively they cannot rely only on adversarial forms of representative democracy. And, indeed, they do not! Adversarial democracy has been much oversold in the literature on planning. Meyerson and Banfield (1955) and Altshuler (1966) could so handily dismiss professional planning efforts as ineffective because they based their evaluations on the standards of liberal adversarial politics. Measured against these standards, the actions of city planners pursuing the public interest appeared apolitical, naive, and inept.

The same critique with a different melody ran through the work of the early proponents of advocacy planning. They accurately exposed how many comprehensive plans rationalized the interests of the powerful as if these were the interests of all. They proposed reforms to expand adversarial practices to help remedy the unjust exclusion of the poor, women, and minorities from the planning process (Davidoff 1965). Later critics of the politics of injustice have relied heavily upon adversarial democracy as a description of the institutional context within which the mobilization of disadvantaged groups would redistribute welfare. Rabinowitz (1969), Vasu (1979), and Howe and Kaufman (1979) all tended to equate politics with advocacy. For instance, when Howe and Kaufman described political action, they used measures of adversarial activity as if it were the whole of politics. They classified planners who advocated partisan positions among conflicting parties as "politicians" while labeling those planners seeking a unitary conception of the public good as apolitical "technicians." This dichotomy—deeply embedded in the definition of professional expertise—led Howe and Kaufman to overlook forms of political action that reconcile technical knowledge and political purpose.

RESEARCH ON PLANNING PRACTICE

A number of theoreticians in the 1980s broke the grip of the severe dichotomy of "technical" and "political" planning to adopt what I have called a "pragmatic orientation." Pragmatism allows us to imagine individuals acting in communities (and communities in individuals). It fosters an appreciation of the search for a communal welfare that is not a bargain among strangers but that also cannot be tarred with the brush of a specious utilitarian rationality. Instead of treating professional expertise (the technical) and social values (the political) as exclusive and even antagonistic domains of action, the critical pragmatists recast the two as distinct aspects of practical advice giving. Depending on what is at stake, conflict sometimes emerges that contrasts the technical and the political aspects of a plan. But in other cases, the two work together to inform practical judgments about what actions to take in the face of difficult problems.

Using interviews, case histories, and participant observation methods, these analysts study planners and planning with a critical and interpretive bent. They focus on the relationship between planners and organizations in practical settings, exploring how misleading ideas (Krieger 1981), social and moral dilemmas (Marris 1982, 1987), unconscious psychological fears (Baum 1983, 1987), and rhetorical manipulation (Forester 1989; Throgmorton 1990, 1992) distort efforts to conduct democratic and egalitarian planning. They evaluate how the actions of planners hamper or improve democratic collaboration in planning. They focus especially on the relationship between individual planners and the social institutions they inhabit and serve.

Power and reason are not separate in these analysts but are intimately related. Effective planning in liberal societies—planning that reduces uncertainty for its users and beneficiaries—draws upon power relationships. But this concept of power includes reciprocal as well as unilateral relations, cooperative as well as adversarial relations. The empirical work shifts attention away from images of political effectiveness that emphasize individual success in the democratic competition of adversarial politics. Adversarial relations are not dismissed but are placed within a broader array of democratic political relationships. They emphasize the conventions of unitary democracy to remedy a long-standing imbalance. Their research draws attention to a practical democracy that many planners tacitly use and struggle to cultivate, although it has no name and is rarely acknowledged.

THE RESEARCH

As I began my research on planning practice, I suspected that planners used the rational model as a rhetorical device to justify their work rather than as a guide for practical reasoning, a persona they adopt as professionals working in bureaucracies. I focused on the relationship between the moral quality and practical efficacy of different kinds of actions taken to cope with tension between structural obstacles and individual initiative. As I conducted my interviews and framed my observations, I asked myself how much autonomy planners enjoyed in their efforts to cope with the institutional and moral tensions among power, knowledge, and the public interest. Do individual planners frequently bear greater responsibility than authority? If so, how do they cope? Do their stories reflect ongoing commitments to democratic participation and the public interest, or are these subordinated to the quest for greater organizational autonomy?

As I conducted my research on U.S. planners I expected to find planners identifying with individualistic modes of professional practice in both their accounts and actions, pursuing the public good through the individual act. Did this attachment lead them to overestimate the strength of individual influence in the face of institutional and cultural resistance? Did this attachment lead them to underestimate the value of colleagues and political allies in the conduct of public planning?

In the remainder of this chapter I answer some of these questions drawing on the stories of two planning directors: Jorge Cruz, planning director in an old working-class suburb, and Bill Maloney, working in a prestigious upper-class suburb. The stories were composed from interview notes and are not verbatim transcripts.

THE STORIES

JORGE CRUZ:
> *The incident that precipitated my resignation was a street construction*
> *project using CD funds. We had drawn up the preliminary construction*

plans that go out for bid. But I knew something was wrong when the manager wanted only two and a half weeks allowed for potential bidders to review the plan and prepare their bids. A week before sending the plans out, the manager told me to bring the construction plans to his office. When I got there he asked if I had brought all the documents. I said "Yes." I suspected he was going to give the plans to one of his favorite contractors so they would have an unfair advantage in the bidding process. I went downstairs as if to leave but sort of hung around in the lobby. About a half hour later a contractor friend of the manager arrives. He goes into the manager's office and in no time comes out with the plans I had delivered.

I confronted the manager and told him that I had seen his contractor friend leave with the plans. [This contractor and the manager were longtime associates. The contractor in fact had constructed the City Hall building, which had all sorts of physical problems. He was not all that competent.]

The manager explained to me that this contractor was special. The contractor knew people who could bring the project in under budget. So giving this guy the edge would actually be more efficient for the city than relying on competitive bidding.

I felt frustrated and helpless. I was being used—an accomplice in a sleazy patronage arrangement. I basically told the manager what the rules required. He needed Board authorization to make such exceptions: the illegality of this sort of favoritism, etc.

"I know that, Jorge!" he finally exclaimed. We stared at each other, and I knew that I could not hang around anymore, that I had to leave.

I did not take any direct action against the manager. I was just too new to know what to do. Worse yet, the manager was using the staff to provide all sorts of special services for his trustees—patronage payoffs—to help their re-election campaigns. I felt awful and developed colitis [a stress-related intestinal disorder].

The structure did not allow for much change. The manager held all the strings. The upcoming elections were promising, but I couldn't wait that long. I quit.

I liked planning for older suburbs and learned of a planning job in the nearby municipality of Quincy. At that time (about 1986) the Quincy village board had created a new job of zoning administrator. I did some homework on the place. I asked around about the reputation of the village staff and political leadership. I am Mexican, and I learned that the village had no minority staff. Furthermore, the village had annexed a geographically concentrated Mexican community that was quite poor. I was interested in trying to improve the living conditions of these residents.

I decided to apply for the job. Anticipating discrimination, I wrote my name as George instead of Jorge. When I interviewed I was George Galvan.

The trustees who interviewed me just presumed I was an Italian with the added advantage of being able to speak Spanish. I got the job. After being hired, I appeared before the village board to express my gratitude for being hired and to introduce myself to those I had not met during the interview process. One trustee asked me about my nationality. I told him the truth: I'm Mexican.

I don't think what I did was dishonest. It was a strategy designed to neutralize racism and give me an opportunity to have my selection based on competence and a sensitivity to the kinds of values the citizens and I shared. We really did have the same urban neighborhood social roots.

Unlike my former job, this position does not report to a manager but directly to the mayor. I like the mayor. We have a close relationship. The mayor has enabled me to pursue projects that improve the village. I can identify with the Quincy community because the mayor gives me sufficient discretion to do planning. The mayor and I both benefit.

I have grown closer to the mayor over time because he cares about the entire community. I feel a loyalty to him because we share a concern for the public good. For example, there is one four block subdivision that the city annexed some twenty years ago. It consists of large, low-rent apartment buildings that were poorly built and that lack adequate parking and street improvements. I told him that the village needed to get the mainly Mexican residents involved in efforts to improve their neighborhood.

I wanted to improve the area and knew that long-term success would hinge crucially on developing a group of local activists. Getting these people to act would be greatly assisted by the mayor's presence and support for such a local initiative.

I set up a public meeting in the area that was billed as a community needs meeting—come and tell the mayor what your problems and needs are. This was the first time in over thirty years (since 1957, when the area was annexed) that a mayor had visited the area. At first, when I asked the mayor, he balked. I emphasized that such a meeting was crucial to build community morale and an attachment to the village of Quincy. Other trustees advised the mayor against such a visit. Despite this, he finally decided to go.

I prepared him for the meeting by briefing him about what problems the residents were most likely to mention. I had already met with numerous residents of the area to find out the complaints. I also gave him some concrete proposals to make—things he could do that would address some resident concerns.

The night of the meeting, I arrived early and mingled with people, encouraging them to express their concerns. About fifty people showed up and complained about poor police service and a lack of public improvements—the very issues we had anticipated. This went on for a couple of hours.

The mayor was prepared to offer specific actions that addressed their concerns. So when he told them that he would represent their interest it was believable. The residents left satisfied, and the event launched the formation of a small group of local activists dedicated to seeing that the promises are kept and that residents keep trying to improve their neighborhood.

There has to be a detached approach to my role. I am culturally tied to the Mexicans. The relationship is special, and I feel a kind of kinship. But I also want to remain detached enough to fulfill the needs of others whose cultural values I don't share. I don't want to become the mediator or patron for the neighborhood. That's why I work with them to build their own neighborhood organization. I have been especially active helping get the residents registered as voters. The area is quite dense and could have a significant effect on local elections. I also helped many residents get in touch with amnesty officials to obtain citizenship under the recent changes in the immigration laws. Finally, I worked closely with Census officials to make sure everyone was counted.

I have been here less than five years, but I have managed to create a professional versus patron-based planning department. I hired the first black employee in the village and hired two women staff as well. I encourage quality work, and the competence of the department has given us a good reputation.

Bill Mahoney:

I like it here. The staff is small and the atmosphere friendly and supportive. We definitely share the values of good government. There are a town manager and five department heads: fire, police, public works, finance, and myself—planning. I have no staff and work alone.

I report directly to the manager on most development issues that involve any expenditure of tax funds or involve the extension of public facilities and services to private parcels. The manager is definitely the one who makes the big decisions, although as zoning administrator I have the authority to deny applications I find nonconforming.

This town, like other upper-class suburban towns, has a lot of CEO's who are used to getting their way. These people usually either fire it or buy it. But when it comes to local town affairs they find that these ploys don't work here. Good government means that they must abide by the rules just like anyone else. I believe in open government and due process and this belief is shared by many of the town officials. I care less about having more authority than about ensuring that the local government treats people fairly.

Among town employees, the town attorney is a close confidant and colleague. He sits on the planning commission as an ex officio member and brings a commitment to planning to his job. For instance, when a commission member acts overbearing, stupidly, or in an obviously partisan fashion, I can talk about it with the attorney and develop a strategy about how to anticipate and cope with such outbursts. The attorney has been serving the town for more than twelve years. (I have been here for only a couple of years.) He gets respect in the eyes of the commission while I still have trouble getting their attention. He provides both useful advice and public support.

I share some common values with the attorney. We both come from a working-class background and have struggled hard to achieve professional status. I consider myself more deal- and negotiation- oriented than other planners, and the attorney is that way too. When we encounter a conflict, both of us take this as an opportunity for negotiation. The attorney cares a lot about fairness and equity, just as I do. He puts these values into practice in the way he contributes to planning commission meetings.

Of course, in many public decisions some issues are, regrettably, non-negotiable. For instance, health and safety issues always seem to outweigh development concerns. At one point in my career I was working as an economic development planner in an older industrial city and had put together a proposal for rehabbing a cement plant operation that employed about 300 people. The proposal was in place and awaiting the approval of the fire chief, who refused to grant a permit unless a sprinkler system was installed. The cost of such a system in the existing structure was enormously prohibitive and really unnecessary given the fact that cement manufacture involved little in the way of flammable materials. The fire chief won, and the city lost the plant. I still encounter the same sort of problem here.

The fire chief here comes from a family of firemen. These guys are all crazy. They run into burning buildings. The firemen do enjoy clear choices between life and death. They tend to see the world in terms of worst-case scenarios. The chief adopts a command style of management. He is not very responsive to me. He is local and a long-standing resident. He usually gets his way.

I recently completed a planning review case that involved a scheme to develop a baseball field for a municipal team near the local high school. The project was sponsored by a politically powerful foundation that had hired an architect to design the playing field and facilities. The architect phoned me to get some information, and I informed him of the necessity of getting a permit. He told me that no special commission approval was necessary for the project and complained that the planning commission was ponderous and conservative. The architect and members of the sponsoring foundation called the mayor of the town and requested that the permit review be skipped. I wrote a memo that pointed out how the field was located near a floodplain, could create parking conflicts with the nearby ice arena, and that the lights might create dissatisfaction for residents to the south. I raised enough uncertainty to get the mayor and manager to let the permit hearing take place. Furthermore, this also ensured that the owners within 300 feet would be invited to voice their concerns.

I believe in fairness and felt the architect and foundation should not be given special treatment. The commission and I eventually recommended approval. No residents showed up to protest. We negotiated an arrangement to ensure additional parking and that lights would be turned off at 9:30 P.M.

I am not a firm believer in rules, but everyone should play on even ground. I resented the architect for trying to break the rules. I wanted to make sure he didn't succeed. I wanted to send a message: "Whatever power you enjoy, when it comes to planning for future development, you will not win in this town." Of course this is possible only because there is a public culture of shared values—especially about fairness and good government— that both the mayor and manager live by.

There was some risk involved by my bucking the interests of the architect and foundation members, but I appealed to the values of fair play, the political and practical risks of breaking the rules, and the promise of a negotiated permit agreement. I care about the reasons for the rules. These rules are usually based on real problems. Seeking exceptions from the rules is the worst to me because it is both unfair and is usually done without good reason. My conflicts with the planning commission occur most commonly when they insist on a position without offering any reason, much less a good one.

ANALYSIS

Public Interest and Individual Character

The planners in both cases faced political and institutional barriers to success. Each initiated risky actions using knowledge and information to reframe conventional understanding, favoring their own view of the problem. Neither expected this would matter unless they persuaded others to grasp the moral significance of the problem as they laid it out. Each offered advice about what should be done to serve the public interest, relying on their integrity and craftsmanship as individual professionals.

The planners show a definite moral concern for the use of their official powers. Each cares sincerely about the integrity of his advice. It is less the avoidance of error that they worry about than the avoidance of dishonesty and self-interest. Bill seeks fairness while Jorge abhors political favoritism. Although they pursue different versions of the public good, each perceives individual judgment and reasonable deliberation as their crucial assets. John Forester's comments about listening and design offer an apt account of the careful attention these planners offered to subordinates and superiors alike (Forester 1989, 107–36). But I think Martin Krieger put it best when he summarized what was necessary for advice: "Advice requires that persons be in a relationship with each other, that the advice-giving have a firm basis in how the world works, and that the persons understand each other" (Krieger 1981, 14).

Both directors take great care in cultivating relationships with superiors, colleagues, and even potential adversaries. They establish their character within this network of trust—a network reproduced by listening well, giving reliable information, keeping promises, and otherwise reducing unnecessary sources of social uncertainty (e.g., gossip and lies) that often accompany routine organizational work. They hope to rely on the integrity of their professional reputation, once it is established, as a source of legitimacy for the stories and arguments they offer as advice.

Bill turns to the city manager and especially the city attorney as colleagues who offer not only advice but reassurance and support as well. He considers himself an active member of the local political culture, helping make good government work fairly and efficiently. Jorge explains how he nurtured close ties with the mayor and used the trust he established to persuade the mayor to meet with local Hispanics, despite warnings from the mayor's political advisors. Jorge took actions to build a community of interest and to represent those interests in the form of problems that addressed both the service needs of the people and the political solutions available to the mayor. Even when he cleverly anticipated and avoided discrimination in his own hiring, he did so in a way that built on and appealed to social traditions and experiences that he shared with local citizens and officials.

Both planners offered specific advice in the present, usually proposing selective conditional visions of future consequences. On the one hand, practical, context-specific speculation is crucial for offering useful and meaningful advice. However, much of this planning advice produces invisible effects: congestion avoided, pollution curtailed, or residential quality maintained. On the other hand, the products of practical reasoning, even when successful, will still fall short of accommodating the broad public good in the future. Since people do not know how the future will turn out, they frequently judge the quality of the advice based on the character of the planner who offers it. In effect, the moral integrity of the individual planner provides a foundation for believing the claims about future consequences, both ones that are practically realized (but invisible) and those that remain promises of future public benefit.

Craft and Technique

Both planners used rational arguments to guide their interpretation and application of policies and rules in specific cases. Their reasoning and judgment were not, however, exclusively technical and instrumental. Planning analysts often use the concept of technique to mean improving the fit between an abstract scientific model and its implementation. Jorge and Bill, however, developed their planning knowledge and skills more as craft than technique. They focused less on the fit between means and ends and more on making a familiar, useful, and pleasing object that others could appreciate and use. We certainly expect skilled craftsmen to produce effective objects. There is, however, a quality of their craft that expresses a delight and a pride in the doing that transcends effectiveness, that enhances the experience of everyone who uses the objects or who shares in the performance.

Local officials, superiors, developers, and property owners confront a variety of uncertainties that the planners can render more predictable through the competent and strategic use of their discretion (Marris 1982, 1987). Bill cares deeply about the arts of persuasion and voices frustration that the commission he serves will make decisions without engaging in reasonable deliberations. Jorge, shaped more deeply by the impact of political corruption, engages in a more openly political approach to planning deliberations. He works hard to establish the foundations for "good," i.e., public-serving, government that Bill already enjoys. Both have developed public personas through which the information they collect, the analyses they conduct, the judgments they make, and the advice they offer prove desirable to others.

Power, Character, and Craft

Both stories offer examples, I think, of how planners go beyond a narrow technical instrumentalist as they seek ways to offer critical attention shaping and advice. Both planners admit room for individual improvement since they do enjoy some discretion. Yet, each had a clear sense of his limits, even as each resented how those limits frustrated efforts to plan.

Jorge struggled against forms of political patronage that violated legal boundaries in a perverse and elitist manner. Public resources and planning policies were used to further the purposes of private interests and consolidate the power of a central authority. His individual efforts to resist these illegitimate and unfair practices were not very successful. When deliberations become a charade and bribery and threats mark the relationships between public officials and their employees, then meaningful planning discourse cannot take place.

Jorge was more ambivalent in his present job, moving between a desire to promote the public interest through official planning deliberations and the recognition of organized political power as a crucial prerequisite to obtain fair treatment of a minority neighborhood. In his first job, he adopted the protocols of professional expertise as an awkward and ill-fitting suit of armor, as much a trap as a protection. But now he uses the protocol of the professional civil servant as a moral shield against especially nasty opponents, leaving a hand free to take political initiatives. Bill enjoys greater administrative authority than Jorge but still finds that the planning function is subordinated to the police and fire departments. Regardless of the merits of his argument and the public benefits of planning proposals, he loses when opposed by the police and fire chiefs.

Planning for Bill does not reshape the future but remains faithful to adopted rules and policies. When people try to work around the rules, Bill does not simply enforce the rule; he develops arguments that remind city officials and others of the reasons and purposes that hold them together. Bill's authority and effectiveness flow from the shared values of town officials and staff. Failure to sustain those values would be politically destructive, weakening the foundations of social trust.

The dichotomy between rational action and politics and the association of politics with aggressive advocacy and interests have often blinded us. We fail to see, and we may even disdain, the subtle but pervasive political influence of planners who attend to fairness, the rules of civil society, political legitimacy, and their professional craft. That is, however, what planners do in the United States—not everywhere and not always, but remarkably often.

REFERENCES

Adler, S. 1990. Environmental movement politics, mandates to plan, and professional planners: the dialectics of discretion in planning practice. *Journal of Architectural and Planning Research* 7: 315–29.

Altshuler, A. 1966. *The city planning process: a political analysis.* Ithaca, NY: Cornell University Press.

Baum, H. 1983. *Planners and public expectations.* Cambridge, MA.: Schenkman Publishers.

_____. 1987. *The invisible bureaucracy: the unconscious in organizational problem solving.* New York: Oxford University Press.

Clavell, P. 1986. *The progressive city: planning and participation 1969-1984.* New Brunswick, NJ: Rutgers University Press.

Davidoff, P. 1965. Advocacy and pluralism in planning. *Journal of the American Institute of Planners* 31: 103–14.

Forester, J. 1989. *Planning in the face of power.* Berkeley: University of California Press.

Hoch, C. 1988. Conflict at large: a national survey of planners and political conflict. *Journal of Planning Education and Research* 8: 25–34.

_____, and A. Cibulskis. 1987. Planning threatened: a preliminary report of planners and political conflict. *Journal of Planning Education and Research* 6: 99-107.

Hoffman, L. 1989. *The politics of knowledge: activist movements in planning and medicine.* Albany: State University of New York Press.

Howe, E. 1980. Role choices for planners. *Journal of the American Planning Association* 46, 4: 398–410.

_____, and J. Kaufman. 1979. The ethics of contemporary American planners. *Journal of the American Planning Association* 45, 3: 243–55.

Krieger, M. 1981. *Advice and planning.* Philadelphia: Temple University Press.

Lindblom, C. 1959. The science of muddling through. *Public Administration Review* 19, 79–99.

_____. 1979. Still muddling, not yet through. *Public Administration Review* 39: 517–26.

Mansbridge, J. 1983. *Beyond adversary democracy.* Chicago: University of Chicago Press.

Marris, P. 1982. *Community planning and conceptions of change.* Boston: Routledge and Kegan Paul.

_____. 1987. *Meaning and action.* Boston: Routledge and Kegan Paul.

Meyerson, M., and E. Banfield. 1955. *Politics, planning, and the public interest.* New York: Free Press.

Rabinowitz, F. 1969. *City politics and planning.* New York: Atherton Press.

Throgmorton, J. 1990. Passion, reason, and power: the rhetorics of electric power planning in Chicago. *Journal of Architectural and Planning Research* 7: 330–50.

_____. 1992. Planning as persuasive storytelling about the future: negotiating an electric power rate settlement in Illinois. *Journal of Planning Education and Research* 12: 17–31.

Vasu, M. L. 1979. *Politics and planning: a national study of American planners.* Chapel Hill: University of North Carolina Press.

John Forester

12 *Argument, Power, and Passion in Planning Practice*

INTRODUCTION

This chapter explores the ways planners must negotiate the worlds of analysis, politics, and passion simultaneously.[1] When planners meet with developers or community residents, advisory boards or decision makers, they have to deal with emotion no less than reason, with passion no less than rationality. Addressing options and recommending actions, planners typically try to enlarge other people's visions of what is possible and what is at stake: how a particular project, for example, could be built or redesigned, pushed through or delayed, applauded, modified, or sent back to the drawing boards. By examining a "project review" negotiation between city planners and a developer's team proposing to build a 180-unit apartment complex, we can see how skillful planning requires not only a micro-politics of "what planners say when and how" (Forester 1989), but emotionally perceptive and responsive practical judgment as well (Healey 1992; Hoch 1994; Throgmorton 1992).[2]

This analysis seeks to integrate theory and practice, insight and opportunity. In the applied professions like city planning, theory is what we need when we get stuck, when we need to think differently about what we are doing. But not just any new and different view will do, and we should make several demands of any prospective theoretical picture of planning practice.[3]

Surely, for example, theory that is supposedly relevant to planning analysts should do justice to their everyday experience. Those analysts should be able to read such theory and feel, "Yes, this is what I'm up against. This gives me a better view of problems I face all the time." Such theory should help planning analysts to understand better the messy situations they are getting into: what problems they will be up against, what they might be able to do about them, and what meaning and consequences their strategies might have (Forester 1993a).

In planning and the "policy sciences" more generally, theory should also help planning analysts to understand the relationship between the problems they experience and the larger structural shape of the political economy in which they live. C. Wright Mills called this capacity "the sociological imagination," the ability to understand the connection between personal "troubles" and the social "issues" of the day (Mills 1959).

It follows that such theory should also suggest directions for study and training in planning education. If planners, for example, must regularly be able to negotiate well or fail to have anyone take their ideas seriously, then planning and policy educators should respond accordingly. So planning theory should, at least, insightfully illuminate the political, practical, and ethical challenges of day to day planning.

PLANNING ANALYSIS IN A REAL ESTATE NEGOTIATION: THE BEST PROPERTIES DEVELOPMENT GROUP

Let us now sit in at a metropolitan planning department's conference table and listen as the city planning staff meet with the Best Properties Development Group. We can then explore several questions:

1. What kind of conceptual work do the staff do? Do they perform rational calculations or instead make a series of practical judgments? If the latter, what kinds of judgments must they make?

2. Do the planners apply well-defined means to reach well-defined ends, or do they instead fashion and present practical arguments? If they must create arguments, how do they do that?

3. How does the larger political-economic structure shape planners' actions? Can we see how encompassing social and political-economic institutions influence the very tone of planners' arguments?

4. Finally, what must planners be able to do if they are to make practical arguments? In particular, how does the play of passion enter: as a necessary evil or, quite the contrary, as an essential constituent of their work?

The excerpt of the conversation that follows has roughly three parts. In the introductory section, the Best Properties developer and his architect set out their proposal as it stands. The middle section is devoted to the evaluation of the proposal and options for the site. The final section is devoted to alternative ways that the planners and developer might proceed, given the issues they have raised earlier.

The staff and developer are about to review design issues—without clear guidelines that define staff influence. The staff are advisors to the permit granting board, but they have no formal authority. Nevertheless, they could delay the project substantially. The developer knows that if he has the staff's cooperation, the project can move along more quickly, and time, of course, is expensive. The staff, in turn, understand: 1. that they are unlikely to stop the project; 2. that their agency is under strong pressure from the mayor to get housing units built, including affordable units wherever possible; and 3. that design changes are needed to improve the present project—as long as they do not threaten its very viability.

The developer and his architect have come downtown to the planning department where they are about to meet for a second time with a group of the staff. Their proposal shows a 180-unit apartment building that is set back substantially on a somewhat awkwardly shaped lot that the developer has assembled from several smaller parcels.

The cast of characters includes the developer's team: Don (the developer), Chris (Don's architect), and Don's lawyer; and the planning staff: Jan (the first planner, project coordinator); Barbara (the second planner); Tim (a planner–architect); and Walt (another planner–architect).

The meeting has been scheduled to run from 10:00 A.M. to 11:00 A.M. in the planning department's conference room. The previous meeting in the room has run over a bit and the developer's architect, Chris, has taken time to set up his pictorials and arrange the model that he brought. Walt walks in, and the meeting finally begins, fifteen minutes late.

DON (THE DEVELOPER):
I'd like to start the meeting, as it relates to me personally, to tell you about this building and this site. The site is a combination of six parcels I acquired—two more than the previous developer who'd tried to build here [he describes each quickly]—*and these parcels* [pointing to those adjacent to his] *I can't get. On this one* [pointing], *the owner wants to negotiate a long-term lease with the pharmacy there, and even though I'd love to get that land, I can't, and I don't want to lose the pharmacy. I'm partial to drug stores; they bring in the right kinds of people. . . . So this is the site, and that's what we have to work with. Now, with all due respect—an*

architect doesn't think the way an owner does. [Nodding toward his architect] *Chris wants to put something up here and say, "I built that!"— but here we can't do that—we have to be able to market these units. I want to build something that fits into the East Milton area—and still do it with the pool, the sauna, the underground parking. . . . That's my philosophy. I'm not going to go for luxury units but for a mix, what's economical, what satisfies the bank, what's workable. . . . And that's where we are. Oh yes— since the last meeting we've developed some photo studies too. So please, ask me any questions you have.*

JAN:

Thanks. That's why I've asked Walt and Barbara to join us.

DON:

The reason I wanted to start was to tell you that I'd have loved to get these parcels and I tried, but I can't.

JAN:

Since it seems so late (this morning), let's look at design issues. We can deal with the affordability questions and the financing questions later. I've also looked at the questions of community input; we'll talk later about that. So Chris, go ahead.

CHRIS:

We have three buildings here, at five, eight, and twelve stories, set back [he explains as he points to pictorials and a site plan], *with an oasis here. We've maximized the parking underground; and* {pointing to an adjacent lot] *we'd like to promote development here in the future. These buildings allow entrance from Broad Street and let us put the parking below the buildings; staggered parking around the site didn't make sense. To allow the 180 units, we have the twelve-story tower, which allowed us to maximize the greenery around it. The twelve stories then becomes an issue, so we've done some photo studies.* [He shows a view of the proposed project from the major intersection at one corner of the site.]

TIM:

Is that taken from Broad Street?

JAN:

No, from Commons Avenue.

BARBARA (POINTING):

Is this the Burger King?

CHRIS:

No, here [pointing].

BARBARA:

I see—so the playground is over here [pointing over the plans]?

CHRIS:

Yes [showing the approach to the project on the model]. *We tried to get a picture from here* [pointing] *too.*

[They continue to locate the site and identify surroundings.]

JAN:

Wait. Is that building cantilevered at the fifth floor?

CHRIS:

No. We looked at stepping the building back, but it's much too costly per square foot, so we tried to massage the buildings (into an "L").

TIM:

Can you put the site plan up anywhere off to the side so that we can make references to it?

CHRIS:

Sure.

[They continue to discuss the parking levels and numbers of spaces.]

TIM:

The question I have is why this is so dense and so far back from the street. We think there'd be an opportunity to strengthen the street, to have visual buffers of, say, 20 feet.

DON [INTERRUPTING]:

Conceptually, that's great. But economically, no way. I like the plaza in front; everybody likes that.

TIM:

That's not a plaza, it's a parking lot. And this is not a suburban space; it's an urban space.

DON:

I see where you're coming from, but I can't do that. Those next two lots are in the future. I paid $250,000 for that turnaround; I wanted an elegant turnaround, to give it a hotel-like appearance. [Barbara raises an eyebrow.] If I could have bought those two parcels, it'd have been different, but the owner laughed at me—he laughed at me!—so this is what we feel we can work with.

[They go on to discuss the setback, and continue.]

WALT:

Well, this is complicated. We'd like to see more options; I can see twenty-five footprints that might work here. We want to see some more ideas.

DON'S LAWYER:

You'd like to see the parking in the back?

WALT:

Parking in the front destroys other uses. It's bad for the pedestrian character of the street.

DON:

You'd like to see retail stores there?

WALT:

Not necessarily. We'd like the image of the street to take the pedestrian into account—not to give priority to the car—so we can rebuild the pedestrian fabric of the street.

BARBARA:

Yes, something that addresses pedestrian activities. The square is a high pedestrian-use area—and this discourages those uses. This building doesn't address the uses of the Square, or the Square as built. This is a much more suburban solution than an urban one.

TIM:

I'd like to let your architect come up with a creative solution. There are lots of variables here—cost, the site, and so on. It's still early. We're not interested in hearing that all costs are fixed, that you have to have 12 stories— there are lots of variables. Say you spend more, but you get additional units.

DON (INTERRUPTING, EMPHATICALLY):

I don't mean to be rude, but this is not an early stage. I have a commitment letter—it's a late stage—I have $17 million in this. I have ninety days to do some things, and if I don't get approvals of certain sorts, I can lose that financing. This project let me convince a bank; only when I got the bank behind me could I go to this sort of design. I can't go back to the bank to renegotiate that letter—I'm proud I got that commitment. I can't go back to them—for various architectural reasons—that the units are now going to be $40,000 more, that the whole project is changed. I won't do that.

BARBARA:

We come to this meeting, guarding the community from an urban design viewpoint.

DON (INTERRUPTING AGAIN):

I have limited time; I'll lose the project and you'll lose 180 units!

WALT:

We don't mean to delay you at all. Say you want one parking space per unit and not 1.5 per unit; that's a lot of money to work with. There should be some level of flexibility here.

[They discuss parking, and continue]

BARBARA (RECAPPING):

We've met twice now: once on the pro forma. We really don't want to hold the project back. I think the kind of design changes we're talking about can be done in your time frame.

DON:

When I come back like that, it's emotion. I worry about the budget, the bank, the letter. Chris tells me what we can do. I don't say "No."

Barbara and Chris then arrange a meeting to discuss design issues the following week. Walt and Chris talk briefly about the buildings' shadows, and then as Walt leaves to everyone's "Thanks," the meeting ends. Jan, Don, and Don's lawyer continue for a few moments to talk about community participation later in the planning process, the city's concerns about increasing the numbers of affordable units, and the disposition of a small house standing in the far corner of the developer's property.

THE PLANNERS' EVALUATIONS:
CALCULATION OR ANTICIPATORY JUDGMENT?

We can now ask some simple questions: What sort of practical thinking do we find here? What sort of influential action? What institutional pressures? What sensitivities and skills are required, and what potential failures and opportunities do we see?

The transcript hardly suggests that planners are computing machines, calculating the most efficient means to predetermined ends. This model of rationality is common in our culture, but this view of how planners might or ought to think, before or after acting, is as empirically indefensible as it is analytically weak (Schön 1983). Students of planning have noted for many years that planning problems typically need to be reformulated or selectively defined while they are being addressed, so in many practice settings, the time of rationally calculating the best means to well-defined ends will simply never come (e.g., Churchman 1968; Sager 1994; Seeley 1963; Webber and Rittel 1971).

In the meeting we are considering, for example, what are the planners' ends? They want to expand the city's housing supply. They want to protect the character of the street. They want to maintain a working relationship with the developer. They want to avoid massive apartment towers. They want to avoid scattered parking. They want lots of things, and no calculus exists that will let them mathematically trade off one bit of one end for another bit of another.

Further, the planners are not even clear about the content of the proposal. Much of the developer's opening statement is concerned with two lots that are adjacent to the project site. Should the planners learn more about those lots? Just how much of this proposal is "untouchable"? The developer sounds as if he'd like to build tomorrow, but the planning staff "can see twenty-five footprints" on the site, and they'd like to consider more options. So what is really being evaluated here? This number of units in fact, this layout, this residential–commercial mix, or another configuration altogether?

Not only are the ends not clear and comparable (or commensurate), the means are not clear either. So these planners hardly seem to be performing means–ends calculations as they work. But what sort of estimates, then, are they making?

The planners are constructing practical judgments.[4] They have to work on several fronts at once. In part, they work to construct the relevant context of the project, to ask not only about whatever the developer proposes but about the appropriate setting in which it should be seen (Krieger 1981). How strongly does the mayor want to increase the supply of housing in the city? Are the adjoining two parcels really unobtainable? Is this developer in over his head—without a track record on projects of this scale?

The planners are not simply applying general rules or procedures: Maximize expected return! Expand housing supply! Protect the character of the street! Do these all at once! They are doing much more complicated work than that: They are interpreting the proposal and the context with respect to each other; they are circling back and forth as they see each in light of the other (Dallmayr and McCarthy 1977; Schön 1983). If the project is built as shown, what will that do to the street? If the mayor really wants housing and the staff need to help accomplish that goal, how much design change can really be sought here? The planners interpret the possibilities by fitting part with whole, proposal with context, design with precedent, action with tradition. They assess the rules and particulars too: the size and character of the adjoining lots, the street, the nearby square, and so on (Wiggins 1978). But they do more too.

The planners' practical judgments are particularly challenging and fascinating because they are peculiarly anticipatory in nature. These are not the judgments that a judge must make: "Guilty" or "Not guilty," for example. Judicial judgments, some argue, can be considered backward-looking, even though they create a new narrative about the past (Beiner, 1983). Planners' judgments, in contrast, are more directly forward-looking, anticipatory judgments that must both assess the circumstances at hand and actually propose for others a course of action to address the demands and opportunities of those circumstances.

To make such judgments, the planners must envision the possible configurations of the project (how tall? how dense? what setback? and the like) and its relevant contexts, as we have suggested. But the planners also have to formulate arguments about how the proposal "works" or fails to work, how the proposal fits the real contexts at hand or fails to fit them. Here, for example, one planner argues, "That's not a plaza; it's a parking lot. And this is not a suburban space, it's an urban space." To think this is one thing, but to say it effectively, to make the practical judgment in deed, is another. Whatever they think, planning analysts have to talk or write too—to articulate practical arguments to influence others' actions.[5] This is a basic matter of professional and political literacy (Krumholz and Forester 1990).

The planners also have to negotiate. They must measure their words. However much the space is urban and not suburban, these planners end this particular meeting with encouragement for the project, with reassurances that the developer can meet their objections in the time frame required, and so on. They work not only to criticize and improve the project, they work to keep the developer in the game as well. They protect not only the nearby street and the community, they protect their relationship with the developer too, so they can indeed meet next week and keep working— to get more housing and to improve the design (Susskind and Cruickshank 1987).

ARGUMENTATION IS ACTION

If the planners have to speak articulately in such meetings, their talk is not just "mere talk," but action for which they are responsible—action that can be incompetent or skillful, constructive or wasteful. So when the planning staff asked for more ideas, here the developer heard not only a simple request for information but an official demand—a demand he claimed he could not meet. When the staff said the "plaza" was really a parking lot, they challenged the basic rationale for part of the project's design. When the staff asked to see more options, they asked for time and effort which meant, of course, money. When the staff said that the changes could be made within the time frame the developer claimed was necessary, they may not only have been reassuring the developer, softening their threats of delay with encouragement, but they may have begun caving in to his bluffing as well.

So the staff's words, specific or vague, sensitive or callous, matter here. In a variety of voices, the planners are making practical and political-economic claims upon the scarce attention, the possible investment, of the developer. Shaping attention selectively through their talk, the planners shape the worlds of meaning and political economy as well (Letcher 1994).

That practical talk, furthermore, adds up. In the meeting the staff did not simply ask (Is this Broad Street?), suggest (We think there'd be an opportunity to strengthen the street), challenge (It's a parking lot!), and so on, but their particular claims produced larger units that we can call arguments, for example, about the setback and "pedestrian activities" (Fischer and Forester 1993). The staff wished not to delay the project, they explained, but to improve it while respecting the developer's constraints.

They argued briefly that they sought to "guard the community from an urban design viewpoint," and so on.

But the staff make these arguments as elements of larger strategies to get results. Just as the planners' particular claims—what they choose to say and how, and what not!—can add up into arguments, those arguments can add up into strategies (Bailey 1983; Barber 1984; Forester 1989, 1993a; Bok 1978; Edelman 1977; Kochman 1981; Wardhaugh 1985).

The staff want to consider more design options, but they balance that objective against that of keeping the project on track. They are conciliatory because they know that their arguments calling for design changes can be construed in many ways, and they want not just to point to changes they would like but to keep the developer happy: Their reassurances make clear that they want the project, that they will not push the developer to take substantially more time, to jeopardize his financing, and so on. The planners make design arguments here, but because they also know that those arguments can have a real impact on what the developer does next, they pay attention to political strategy too: Push for the design improvements, but keep the project alive!

POLITICAL STRUCTURE, ACTION, AND EVOLVING CONTRA-DICTIONS

Planners do not work in a political vacuum. Broader social, political, and economic structures influence this planning encounter, but how? Even though the transcript does not directly describe the institutional context at hand, we can learn a good deal (Giddens 1984; Habermas 1984).

How hard the planners push for design change is obviously circumscribed here. They are afraid of losing the project, and the developer has threatened as much: "I have limited time—I'll lose the project and you'll lose 180 units!"

Two major forces operate upon planner and developer alike: 1. the financial requirements faced by the developer (he invokes the bank's requirements, and the planners acquiesce), and 2. the mayor's mandate that the planners help to increase the supply of affordable housing in the city. The mayor, of course, has not told anyone how to trade off housing units for monstrous bulk and oversized projects, but she has made a promise to her constituency and now needs to deliver on it: Her staff is claiming credit for every unit on every project that gets approved.

The planners may be sympathetic both to the developer's desire to satisfy his financiers and make a profit and to the mayor's goals—but that just begins to help them to get the job before them done. For not only do those goals—increase market return and provide affordable housing—

conflict, but the planners must serve other goals and constituencies too. They have strong community associations to satisfy. They have urban design issues to worry about: the setback, the scale, the street, pedestrians, and issues affecting the quality of life of the unorganized, of neighbors, motorists, and passersby.

Seeing the city in part as a system, the planners anticipate and respond to pressures of the market and politics. Seeing the city too as a world of daily life, they try to anticipate the experience of people walking by this site, living around the nearby square, having to pay for housing in the city. Just as the political economy structures contradictions between private gain and public welfare, so do these contradictions show up in practical planning meetings as actual, audible, uttered, and argued contra–dictions (Forester 1993b; Habermas 1984; Mumby 1988). So the developer goes through the roof about going back to the bank for "architectural reasons," and the planners talk about "pedestrian activities." This is no accident, for the planners work on projects whose dramas unfold on institutional stages structured by banks and political bureaucracies, just as the planners must try to understand the everyday, experiential consequences of those projects for the city's residents.

So the contradictions between private accumulation and control of investment on the one hand and broader public welfare on the other get played out in the very speech and diction of planning staff. The planners speak—however weakly here—about "guarding the community," and the developer speaks much more strongly about protecting his financing with the bank. The political-economic contradictions about control of resources and investment show up, though, not just in words but in acts: The planners ask for more investment in public-serving alternatives; the developer threatens the loss of the project. The planners ask questions; the developer interrupts and claims to be tied to the bank; the planners seem to back off, narrowing the scope of their requests to whatever can be done in the developer's "time frame."

Observing how the planners' words build up into arguments which can, in turn, build up into strategies, provides a way to analyze the political and practical richness of planners' ordinary talk. For what is practically uttered or heard at one moment as disagreement or conflict—as quite literally "contrary diction" ("I don't mean to be rude, but. . . . I can't go back to them . . . I won't.")—should be understood as practical moves or actions within conflicting arguments, which work in turn within conflicting political strategies. Political-economic contradictions show up as contra-dictions, conflicting actions within conflicting arguments and strategies.

In this meeting, for example, we saw a planner begin to ask about density and the developer respond, "Conceptually that's great; but economically—no way." The planner began an argument about density, but the developer quickly cut him off by appealing to a presumably more potent argument about economic feasibility.

In a second instance, another planner asked for options, but the developer countered, "I can't go back to the bank to renegotiate." The planners suggested that they could hardly review plans seriously without considering a range of alternatives that explored the shape of the proposed project. The developer countered, then, by arguing not about economic feasibility but about the institutional constraints he faced.

In a third instance, Barbara tried to justify the planners' request to consider further options by invoking the staff's presumed obligations to guard "the community" and to respect the planning tradition of concern with urban design issues. The developer interrupted and argued again that time was limited and that the whole project could be lost, that he could lose the project and the staff would lose their desired housing units.

In each case, the arguments were elements of broader strategies. The planners wanted to consider alternative designs, and they tried at least three strategies to achieve that objective: 1. dealing with the merits (e.g. addressing the density question on its face); 2. dealing with the conventional process (e.g. invoking standard operating procedure and asking for more options); and 3. invoking a moral entity ("the community") and the normative order of a planning tradition ("an urban design viewpoint").

The developer had his own strategies, of course. First, he appealed to a separate normative order, that which respects whatever is economically feasible in the market place and rejects whatever is not. Second, he invoked the (presumed) rigidity of institutional constraints to say that effectively his hands were tied—he was committed, helplessly dependent upon his bank's conditions. Third, he threatened the loss of the project and the planners' own desired ends, the provision of affordable housing.

We will better understand planning practice, then, when we appreciate the intimate relationships between structure and action, strategy and word.

THE RHETORICAL DEMANDS OF PLANNING PRACTICE: PROBLEMS OF SUBSTANCE, POWER, AND PASSION

Because planners always work on problems but in processes, their arguments involve both substantive and procedural matters. For example, the planners here made arguments about plazas and parking lots, about the street and the square, about density and scale—about the site and its potential, evolving project. Uncertainties and ambiguities of substance were central, and without substantive training and knowledge, planners could hardly make serious substantive arguments.

In addition, much of the meeting above was concerned not with the site or the present plans but with the developer himself (his past efforts, his self-esteem, his pride, his feelings about the bank), with time, and with the institutional setting in which both the planners and developer must work. The planners attended not only to the site and the drawings but to the evolving process itself, including, of course, the particular participants themselves.

So, for example, the planners began the meeting by shaping the agenda. Focusing first on design issues, they proposed to discuss questions of affordability and community participation later. To consider design options, they argued, may not really cost the developer time and money but may actually reward him: "Say you spend more, but you get additional units." They also made arguments of reassurance by attending not just to the site, the project, and the bank, but to the developer's feelings, his fear of delay, his anger, and his possible threats. Unlike the substantive questions whose considerations are often technically uncertain, the issues of process are often different, raising ambiguities calling for moral judgments instead (how fast to go? how tough to be?) (Forester 1989).

Clearly, both the substantive project-focused arguments and procedural, process-focused arguments are fully political. Any project description is necessarily selective, calling attention to some aspects and neglecting others. The very language of description is ethically loaded. What seems to be a plaza to one can be a parking lot to another, and the appropriateness of the formulation here is a deeply political and ethical matter (Seeley 1963). Performed under political constraints and guided by political mandates, technical work is virtually always political, but no less vital as a result.

The planners' arguments about the review process itself require political judgment too. Just what constitutes appropriate review is perpetually ambiguous: Who ought to participate, representing whom? How should differences be reconciled—through expert judgment, through community participation, through planner–developer negotiation, through official political decision making, or through a combination of these? Specific regulations and requirements can be quite ambiguous even if they are spelled out on paper: Guidelines and criteria must be interpreted in specific cases. But another more subtle, if equally practical, ambiguity arises: In these arguments about substance and process, who speaks? Whose voices are heard? Whose arguments are pressed, and how (Throgmorton 1992, 1993)?

Every human organization organizes some people in and some people out (Schattschneider 1960; Lukes 1974). Some people can come to meetings and others cannot. Planners may well say that they will talk to anybody—but "anybody" cannot talk to them. Some people are in the business of building buildings and doing the talking that is necessary, often with legal counsel, to build them; but neighbors have other jobs to do. Some people get financing—and control it—and pursue their interests; but other people are too poor, too weak, too powerless to pursue their interests. As a result, planners play roles in a political game in which the deck is stacked. Many affected people cannot play, and some who play have substantially greater power and influence than many others.

So the conversations in which planners must argue are hardly characterized by equality and reciprocity; they do not reflect conditions of equal access, information, expertise, and participation—to say nothing of mutuality, common concern with a public realm or with the obligations of citizenship, membership in a common community or polity. So planners' arguments are inescapably uttered—or suppressed—in institutional contexts structured by voice for some and silence for others, processes responsive to the interests of some and blind to the pain of others. Those with access to capital can come into the planners' offices and do business; they can push their projects forward and threaten planners and public officials with the loss of jobs or housing units as an alternative. But those people most in need, those whom planners often hope to serve, cannot do such business, and for the most part they rarely speak with anything approaching the practical voice—the resources, the level of organization, the information, the political pressure—that project developers or state agencies have. The result: Planners have to learn how to make their arguments under systematically skewed conditions of access, voice, power, and authority. Planners must be able to speak and write astutely even as they know that many comfortable people will not want to listen to accounts of the pressing problems the planners must try to address (Forester 1989; Krumholz and Clavel 1994; Krumholz and Forester 1990).

So in practice, planners often face the perplexing task of being messengers bringing uncomfortable news: This many thousands of housing units are deteriorating; this many fewer units are being added to the housing stock than are being torn down; this many jobs are being lost to capital flight; this many people are standing in lines at soup kitchens; one in four children lives in poverty; and so on. Planners know also that messengers who bring bad news may be ignored, rejected, or dismissed. Just as planners and planning theorists may suppress attention to politics because of the psychological ambivalences it may create, so may attention to issues of real human suffering be suppressed as well: They may be too painful, even for planners whose "professionalism" might not quite shield them from such pain (Baum 1987; Goleman 1985; Krumholz and Forester 1990).

So planners who wish to improve our cities, to alleviate needless suffering, must work against the defenses of many governments and still more established agencies. These planners must manage conflicting senses of their own roles: To get things done, they must in part be bureaucrats, learning the many formal and informal rules of the game and developing the relationships without which seemingly nothing in government would move beyond stalemate. But to call attention to the enormous problems they see around them, they must be not bureaucrats but also educators, or, to overstate the case, uneasy prophets, seeking not to reassure some constituencies but to mobilize them, wishing to promote not complacency but dissatisfaction, hoping to rally support for progressive initiatives rather than to leave everything to the powers that be (Forester 1989).

Planners are not prophets, but they can be more than mere functionaries in the bureaucracy. Because political influence comes in many forms, planners can at times be bureaucratic organizers of information, access, expertise, timing, risk and uncertainty, participation, and pressure in ways that can, to a limited extent, resist the prerogatives of the already powerful and serve the interests of those most in need (Hoch 1994; Krumholz and Clavel 1994; Krumholz and Forester 1990). To understand better the problems and possibilities here, we need to explore further not only how progressive planners argue practically, but how politically astute organizers do so also.[6]

The planners' arguments are not just about projects and processes. Those arguments are articulated, offered, tried, presented, broached, put forth weakly or strongly, or aggressively or reassuringly—to other people with deep interests in the issues at hand. To make those arguments, whether about the site or the bank, the street or the community, planners need to learn about their audience as well as about particular projects and political processes.

The planners need to know not just about project consequences or institutional processes, but also about the people—developers, neighbors, tenant activists, and so on—to whom they must make sense, to whom they as planners must be compelling if they are not to be ineffectual. This simple point has both subtle and directly practical implications. First, it means that if planners are to work effectively with other actors, they will need to learn, and continually to refine their operating theories, about who those others are. They must continually probe what a particular developer will listen to and why; what balance of self and community interest a "neighborhood leader" might have; what emotional makeup a developer or neighbor or politician has; how intemperately, how carefully, or how idly any of them will listen to the planner's arguments and respond.

Second, to work effectively, planners must be able to respond to others' ideas and to their passions: their fears, suspicions, distrust, anger, and so on.[7] But this is emotional work that planners are poorly trained to do. Worse still, planners may even try to ignore just these issues of passion—in the name of remaining "objective," "detached," "neutral," or "professional"—and so ironically guarantee their own planning failure (Krumholz and Forester 1990, ch. 15). One planner put this brilliantly when asked how she worked in the heat of conflicts between project developers and community residents (Forester 1989):

> "In the middle, you get all the flak. You're the release valve. You're seen as having some power, and you do have some. Look, if you have a financial interest in a project, or an emotional one, you want the person in the middle to care about your point of view, and if you don't think they do, you'll be angry!"
>
> "So when planners try to be "professional" by appearing detached, objective, does it get people angry at them?" I asked.
>
> "Sure!" came the answer.

The point here is simple, but fundamental, if too often ignored by students and analysts of planning. People not only have interests; they care about them as well. Merchants and developers wish to protect investments; residents wish to protect their neighborhoods. To work practically in the face of conflict, then, planners will often have to speak sensitively to deeply interested and caring people—people who may be afraid, needy, hurting, greedy, egotistical, civic-minded, ideological, suspicious, defensive, or more. There is just no ignoring this without severely imperiling the possibility that anyone will listen to what the planning staff have to say.

If planners want their words to matter—in meetings such as the one considered above, for example—they will have to pay attention not only to projects, not only to processes, but also to the passions that others bring to the planning process. If developers or residents or politicians do not feel that the planners understand the passions that make the very projects at hand important in the first place, what are they likely to think about the planning staff? How cooperative or even attentive will they then be? How are they likely then to feel and act in the planning process?

The transcript above suggests too that planners inescapably face or ignore questions of passion. Notice how much the developer talked about himself, how he made his character part of the process, part of the project to be negotiated. He began by saying how he tried to obtain the two adjacent lots and could not; how he was partial to drugstores because they brought in the right kinds of people (whoever they are!); he repeated his offended tone as he recounted his experience with the adjacent landowner ("He laughed at me!"); he interrupted with the acknowledgment, "I don't mean to be rude, but . . ."; he said of the bank's letter about financing, "I'm proud I got that commitment"; he interrupted impatiently with, "I have limited time; I'll lose, and you'll lose."

Toward the end of the meeting, the developer made our point about passion in a fascinating way: "When I come back like that [i.e., when I interrupt you, tell you what I will and won't do, what I'm proud of, and then threaten you], it's emotion. I worry about the budget, the bank, the letter. Chris tells me what we can do; I don't say 'No.'"

What are we to make of this? First, the developer pointed to the pressures and emotional stress he faced: He too had feelings, he suggested, and he asked the planning staff to acknowledge them and indeed to forgive him for his outburst. Second, he tried to link his own behavior of interruptions and threats, his strategy in the meeting, to such "emotion"—and he did this quite selectively, of course, not mentioning other strong emotions (pure economic motives, for example) that he also felt. We should not think, then, that emotion and practical strategy have little relationship!

Third, what the developer said next—"Chris tells me what we can do. I don't say 'No'"—is so patently fantastic, so literally incredible, that its very untruthfulness was irrelevant and suggests instead the ceremonial point (Forester 1993a). What he said here, of course, was contradicted by the entire previous discussion: his continued dominance in the meeting, and even his opening—"With all due respect, an architect doesn't think the way an owner does." The developer's claim here was strategically disingenuous: It worked not really to indicate who said "No" to whom, but instead to express ritualistic apology and self-effacement to the planning staff.

Why this denial of his own obvious power? The developer here performed a conventional peacekeeping ritual to restore the cooperation he needed from the staff—to reestablish those same working relations with the planning staff that he himself had just thrown into jeopardy with his threat. He responded to the planners' reassurances by ceremonially reassuring them: in effect, "Yes, now that you've agreed not to slow me down, I'll cooperate" (Bailey 1983). Far from being a necessary evil, then, passion is a central element in the micro-politics of the planning process.

CONCLUSION

This analysis suggests that planners will find themselves facing other parties whose practical arguments are simultaneously quite explicitly emotional, economically strategic, obviously deceptive, and manipulatively ritualistic. This leads to an obvious question: if planning analysts who regularly participate in such meetings will routinely be subject to the full range of others' persuasive argumentative strategies that combine fact and fiction, affect and abstraction, issues of project, process, and passion too, how can these planning analysts be prepared for the onslaught they will face (Forester 1993b)?

Only if practicing analysts and planning and policy educators too will carefully examine the real argumentative work of practice will such preparation be possible. Traditionally taking place in studio and fieldwork courses where the problems of "what to say when" are inescapable, this examination of planning analysts' rhetoric and political literacy needs to be refined still further by integrating field experience with astute theoretical work. As long as we think of planning analysis as the problem of selecting means to ends, we will ignore these problems and pay the price.

Assessing a quite ordinary encounter between planning staff and a developer's team, this chapter has argued that planners have challenging and complex jobs requiring them to speak simultaneously to issues of substance, power, and passion. Plainly, if planners pay attention only to substantive issues and not to process, they are likely to fail (Szanton 1981). But if they attend only to substance and process and ignore the affective and passionate pulse of people's participation, they will be scorned as being insensitive and callous, to say little of being distrusted, if not detested. But planners can meet these challenges: if this analysis of an ordinary meeting can clarify the problems at hand, then the analysis of exemplary practice in turn might suggest the real possibilities of an astute, engaged, progressive planning practice (Krumholz and Clavel 1994; Krumholz and Forester 1990; Thomas and Healey 1992).

Acknowledgments

For comments on an earlier draft, I am grateful to Howell Baum, Kirk Harris, Charles Hoch, Robert Letcher, Sharon Lord, and Thomas Walker.

Notes

1. The research approach taken in this chapter is a form of quasi-ethnographic discourse analysis (see, e.g. Grimshaw 1982, 1987; Gumperz 1982; Labov and Fanshel 1979; Mishler 1985; and cf. Edelman 1977; Goffman 1967; Kochman 1981) supplemented by questions derived from critical social theory (e.g. Habermas 1970, 1975, 1979, 1984). The method might also be called a "structural phenomenology," an analysis seeking to do justice both to practical experience and to structural settings (Forester 1989, 1992, 1993a).

2. The transcript that follows has been excerpted from a longer transcript of a working meeting attended by the author as part of fieldwork research in a large metropolitan planning department. Cf. Robert Coles on his continuing source of inspiration, William Carlos Williams, as a keen observer of the everyday world: "I have put down on paper many times . . . my deep obligation to William Carlos Williams. . . . I simply state it again here, as I conclude twenty-five years of work. 'Catch an eyeful, catch an earful, and don't drop what you've caught,' he'd tell me as he pushed himself from building to building. . . . Those of us who rather obviously lack his talents can at least be glad for his sanction, his encouragement, his example" (Coles 1986, 17; see also Hoch 1994).

3. Here I follow Bernstein (1978) as in Forester (1993a): An adequate planning theory should be empirically applicable, interpretively compelling, and ethically critical. Planning theory cannot offer general answers to be used independent of specific practical settings—but planning theory can be expected to pose significant questions, to point attention selectively and insightfully, so that actors in their own settings can find their own answers. Theory asks, practice answers?

4. This analysis draws on Beiner (1983) who examines Aristotelian and Kantian understandings of judgment. Following Aristotle, Beiner (1983, 95) writes, "[Rhetoric does not merely serve] as means to an independently posited end. The point is not that we use rhetoric to obtain our ends, but that our ends are themselves inextricably situated in a rhetorical medium, and are constitutively shaped by this medium. Our ends are not merely pursued rhetorically, they are themselves constituted rhetorically. This is what it means to say that political ends are subject to deliberation (and not simply manipulation)." Compare also: "One who forms a judgment on any point, but cannot explain himself clearly to the people, might as well have never thought at all on the subject" (not Marx or Lenin, but Thucydides, quoted in Beiner 1983, 83).

5. For views of the place of argument in public policy contexts more broadly, see F. Fischer and J. Forester (1993). Beiner (1983, 85) characterizes the Aristotelian view of the relationship between political judgment and rhetoric when he writes, "The lesson of philosophical hermeneutics is that one does not reach a judgment in abstraction from the opinion of others, but rather in communion with their feelings and desires, and the judgment is communicated with a view to its proper reception. The judgment is never abstracted from the context of the audience for which it is intended. This is the object of philosophical reflection upon rhetoric, and explains why a philosopher writes a Rhetoric."

6. What is critical about a structurally situated argumentative theory of planning practice? Such a theory might help us: 1. to look for the inarticulate member of the community and not presume the voluntariness of silence; 2. to assess the systematic perpetuation of silence and lack of voice; 3. to examine the structural contingencies of patterns of action—neither to reify "the system" nor to "blame the victim"; thus 4. to connect in politically contingent ways speech to argument to strategies to institutional settings to structural dynamics of the encompassing (contingently reproduced) political economy; and 5. thus to anticipate and inform responses to practically unnecessary but

systematic obstacles to ordinary experience, genuine community membership, and political citizenship—with the forms of participation and voice that those imply (Forester 1989).

7. Passion is an almost altogether neglected topic in the planning literature—as if planning practice were unemotional, dull and boring, lacking in any affective depth, free of fear and suspicion, oblivious to conflicts of interests, values, and attachments, so matter-of-fact that no one cared much about anything. All too single-handedly, Howell Baum addresses the psychological dimensions of planners' responses to issues of power, authority, ambiguity, and success (Baum 1983, 1987); with Baum, Peter Marris is virtually alone in exploring the nature of ambiguity and conflict in the context of attachment and loss (Marris 1975). Compare the lucid analysis of Bailey (1983).

REFERENCES

Bailey, F. G. 1983. *The tactical uses of passion.* Ithaca, NY: Cornell University Press.

Barber, B. 1984. *Strong democracy.* Berkeley: University of California Press.

Baum, H. 1983. *Planners and public expectations.* Cambridge, MA: Schenkman.

_____. 1987. *The invisible bureaucracy: the unconscious in organizational problem solving.* New York: Oxford University Press.

_____. 1990. *Organizational membership.* Albany: State University of New York Press.

Beiner, R. 1983. *Political judgment.* Chicago: University of Chicago Press.

Bernstein, R. 1976. *The restructuring of social and political theory.* Philadelphia: University of Pennsylvania Press.

Bok, S. 1978. *Lying.* New York: Pantheon.

Churchman, C.W. 1968. *The systems approach.* New York: Delta.

Coles, R. 1986. *The moral life of children.* New York: Atlantic Monthly Press.

Dallmayr, F., and T. McCarthy. 1977. *Understanding and social inquiry.* Notre Dame, IN: University of Notre Dame Press.

Edelman, M. 1977. *Political language.* New York: Academic Press.

Fischer, F. and J. Forester, eds. 1993. The argumentative turn in policy analysis and planning. Durham, NC: Duke University Press.

Forester, J. 1989. *Planning in the face of power.* Berkeley: University of California Press.

_____. 1992. On critical ethnography: fieldwork in a Habermasian way. In M. Alvesson and H. Willmott, eds., *Critical management studies*. Los Angeles: Sage.

_____. 1993a. *Critical theory, public policy, and planning practice*. Albany: State University of New York Press.

_____. 1993b. Beyond dialogue to transformative learning: how deliberative rituals encourage political judgment in community planning processes. Working Papers in Planning, Technion Faculty of Town Planning, Haifa, Israel, and Cornell University, Ithaca, New York.

Giddens, A. 1984. *The constitution of society*. Berkeley: University of California Press.

Goffman, E. 1967. *Interaction ritual*. Garden City, NY: Anchor Books.

Goleman, E. 1985. *Vital lies, simple truths*. New York: Simon and Schuster.

Grimshaw, A. D. 1982. Comprehensive discourse analysis: an instance of professional peer interaction. *Language in Society* 11: 15–47.

_____. 1987. *Conflict talk*. London: Cambridge University Press.

Gumperz, J. 1982. *Discourse strategies*. Cambridge: Cambridge University Press.

Habermas, J. 1970. *Toward a rational society*. Boston: Beacon Press.

_____. 1975. *Legitimation crisis*. Boston: Beacon Press.

_____. 1979. *Communication and the evolution of society*. Boston: Beacon Press.

_____. 1984. *The theory of communicative action*. Boston: Beacon Press.

Healey, P. 1992. A day's work: knowledge and action in communicative practice. *Journal of the American Planning Association* 58: 9–20.

_____. 1993. The communicative work of development plans. *Environment and Planning B: Planning and Design* 20: 83–104.

Hoch, C. 1994. *What planners do*. Chicago: APA Planners Press.

Kochman, T. 1981. *Black and white styles in conflict*. Chicago: University of Chicago Press.

Krieger, M. 1981. *Advice and planning*. Philadelphia: Temple University Press.

Krumholz, N., and J. Forester. 1990. *Making equity planning work*. Philadelphia: Temple University Press.

_____, and P. Clavel. 1994. *Reinventing cities*. Philadelphia: Temple University Press.

Labov, W., and D. Fanshel. 1979. *Therapeutic discourse*. New York: Academic Press.

Letcher, Robert. 1994. Practical political economy: public planners, practical action, and the construction of political economic institutions. Doctoral dissertation, Cornell University, Department of City and Regional Planning.

Lukes, S. 1974. *Power: a radical view.* New York: Macmillan.

Marris, P. *Loss and change.* 1975. New York: Anchor. (Reprinted RKP, 1986).

Mills, C. W. 1959. *The sociological imagination.* New York: Oxford University Press.

Mishler, E. 1985. *The discourse of medicine: the dialectics of medical interviews.* Norwood, NJ: Ablex.

Mumby, D. K. 1988. *Communication and power in organizations: discourse, ideology, and domination.* Norwood, NJ: Ablex.

Sager, T. 1994. *Communicative planning theory.* Aldershot, UK: Avebury Press.

Schattschneider, E. 1960. *The semi-sovereign people.* New York: Holt, Rinehart, Winston.

Schön, D. 1983. *The reflective practitioner: how professionals think in action.* New York: Basic Books.

Seeley, J. 1963. Social science: some probative problems. In A. Visit and M. Stein, eds., *Sociology on trial.* Englewood Cliffs, NJ: Prentice Hall.

Susskind, L., and J. Cruickshank. 1987. *Breaking the impasse.* New York: Basic Books.

Szanton, P. 1981. *Not well advised.* New York: Russell Sage.

Thomas, H., and P. Healey, eds. 1992. *Dilemmas of planning practice.* London: Pion.

Throgmorton, J. 1992. Planning as persuasive story-telling about the future: the case of electric power rate settlement in Illinois. *Journal of Planning Education and Research* 12, 1: 17–31.

_____. 1993. Survey research as rhetorical trope: electric power planning arguments in Chicago. In F. Fischer and J. Forester, eds., *The argumentative turn in policy analysis and planning.* Durham, NC: Duke University Press.

Wardhaugh, R. 1985. *How conversation works.* New York: Basil Blackwell.

Webber, M., and H. Rittel. 1971. Dilemmas in a general theory of planning. *Policy Sciences* 4: 155–69.

Wiggins, D. 1978. Deliberation and practical reason. In J. Raz, ed., *Practical reasoning.* Oxford: Oxford University Press.

Patsy Healey

13 The Communicative Work of Development Plans

INTRODUCTION

Development plans have a long history as tools of spatial planning. In the United Kingdom (and in many other places) they often represented directives within a model of planning that assumed that public authorities, informed by scientific knowledge and guided by consensual goals, controlled the course of urban growth. That model has been generally rejected in recent years. Planning authorities have had neither the power nor the inclination to ensure that cities develop "according to plan." Both scientific knowledge and a consensual "public interest" are now seen as highly contestable.

The directive model has been replaced—in the minds of theorists if not practitioners—by an interactional, "post-positivist" image of the relations between planning authorities, developers, community groups, and all those concerned with the spatial organization and design of places. In this more pluralist model, plans are seen to perform multiple roles, sending quite different messages to different "audiences." The plan, in turn, may mean different things to different groups.

How, then, are we to "interpret" the development plans we come across? What assumptions do they express; what messages are conveyed? What implications do plans have for the power relations that surround the management of environmental change? How do plans and planning change these relations?

This is a revised version of an original article published in *Environment and Planning B, Planning and Design* 20: 83–104 (London: Pion Ltd., 1993).

THEORETICAL EXCURSION

The "command-and-control" model was sustained by concepts from architecture, engineering, regional science, and scientific rationalism. These directed attention to the internal logic and analytical coherence of a plan's design. As Mazza (1986) has argued, such internal consistency is an unlikely property of plans produced through interaction rather than the intelligence of a single mind. He proposed that plans should be seen as sets of technical and political claims, to be understood in the context of relations external to the text. Specifically, Mazza argues, that we have to attend to the evaluation of political and not merely technical claims. Fischer (1990) argues similarly that policy analysis involves both rational-technical and normative claims: the first may be validated through a "scientific" method, but the second brings us into the domain of moral philosophy.

Evaluation and validation do not, however, exhaust the concerns of theorists with development plans. Who, we should wonder, makes the claims embedded in a plan? To whom are they made? How are they understood, and how should they be interpreted? Critical political economists have traditionally argued that all plans should be understood as political mystifications, protecting property interests in the guise of expressing "the public interest":

> Plans stamp all schemes with a double character: on the one hand, they come to be seen as "reasonable," rational technical solutions to the problems pursued, and, on the other, they appear to bring about a convergence of the various social groups and urban functions. (Castells 1977, 76)

In this conception, the state as the "tool" of capital deliberately obscures its purposes and may seek to persuade "audiences" to accept strategies and projects that are against their own real interests. Jean Hillier's chapter in this volume provides revealing examples of such processes at work.

A more pluralist interpretation sees the text of a plan as an arena of struggle—a game—with different interests competing to determine its content, sentence by sentence, design by design. Within this conception, a range of roles may be defined for plans, varying with the organization of interests. We read the plan to discover who has won and who has lost, issue by issue, page by page.

Mandelbaum (1990) uses a different analogy when he describes how he reads plans. He interprets their texts in three ways: as a set of policy claims, as an account of the creation of the plan, and as a narrative scenario for the future, a drama with many actors:

> The stage is populated by developers and homeless panhandlers, the mayor and city council, the press, the planners. . . . These characters receive the plan that created them and are expected to respond to it and to each other. (Mandelbaum 1990, 355)

This suggests that the focus of analytical attention should be on these "characters" in the plan drama. Throgmorton (1992) has also made use of this dramaturgical analogy in presenting episodes of planning conflict.

Geertz (1983) argues that in order to capture the meaning of games and dramas, we train our attention to the ways in which "the inscription of action is brought about, what its vehicles are and how they work, and on what the fixation of meaning from the flow of events . . . implies for sociological interpretation" (Geertz 1983, 31).

Geertz's image focuses attention on what the text of a plan could mean in the flow of events and relations among the interests who played the game of plan construction and the characters who constituted its drama(s). What forms of language, what imageries and metaphors are used? What meanings do these have in the various "discourses" between writers and readers that permeate plans? What relations of power do these meanings record and promote? Our analytical emphasis thus focuses on the dialogical or communicative work of the plan (see Fischer 1990; Fischer and Forester 1993; Throgmorton 1991).

Such an analysis of meaning can take place only within the context of the social relations and systems of meaning that "make sense" of words and signs. These form discourses, uniting writers and readers in a common system of meaning (Hajer 1993). Potentially, several discourses may coexist within a single plan. The power relations of a plan text may thus find expression in both the exercise of power within a single discourse and in the discordance between discourses in a text. In effect, a plan may contain several parallel conversations. This is one source of the "inconsistencies" in plans that trouble both designers and rational-technical analysts who expect that the parts of a text will fit together coherently and will have one "overall" meaning.

From a critical and normative perspective, we can also use the analysis of textual meanings to "judge" the plan. The game analogy focuses attention only on the identity of winners and losers. A critical analysis leads us to ask about the fairness of the rules and the justice of the patterned outcomes. If we are concerned with the democracy of the planning system, then we ask about the genesis of the task and its style. Does the plan appear to be a product of a broad conversation within the community about possibilities and choices? Does it provide a "position statement" to help a continued process of learning about future options and difficult moral decisions? Does it "speak to" the multiplicity of power games and stories that engage a community? Does it reveal the tensions and ambiguities that any attempt to build agreement out of conflict will face? Does it, rather, seek to impose a single dominant view on a community, manipulating acceptance by "washing out" the richness of social diversity? In this way, we may begin to explain what communicative work plans perform in specific situations. Normatively, such an analysis helps us to advise plan writers and readers how to prepare and use plans skillfully and democratically.

ANALYTICAL EMPHASES

Following this perspective, the analytical task is to identify the system(s) of meaning of a plan—its "discourses"—and the publics who sustain those meanings—its "discourse communities." Systems of meanings are embedded in assumptions, starting points, plots, metaphors, style, format, and "conversational exchanges."

How, then, might these discourses be evaluated? This will depend, of course, on one's analytic concerns and normative commitments. I bring to my reading a long-standing interest in the contribution of plan making to the creation of democratic polities (Healey 1993). My reading has been informed by Forester's (1989) exposition of Habermas's (1984) principles for open public debate. I read a text and ask myself: "Are the conversations centered in the plan comprehensible, sincere, legitimate, and true?" Statements that are comprehensible to participants allow understanding to be shared. Statements that are true help to reveal the intentions of those making them. Statements sincerely made increase the trust listeners have in the speaker.

The issue of legitimacy directs us to the power relations of the plan. A "conversation" in a plan may be accessible and frank but conducted within unequal social relations. The powerful may speak freely only to each other. When the parties are unequal, meanings are shaped by the distribution of power. The principles of open public debate demand that these relations be revealed and that statements are legitimately made in the context of socially accepted rules governing power relations. Legitimate relations may, of course, be contestable. One objective of a plan may be to make certain contestable attitudes legitimate by including them within its framework. This may be done with bold declarations and new visions. In an open conversation, however, legitimation requires a more balanced and subtle advocacy, describing both the new aspirations and the constraints that must be overcome; exposing rather than suppressing conflicts within the goals of the plan's discourse communities.

Explicating political, economic, and moral dilemmas will produce a necessary ambiguity in a plan. The democratic plan should bring this ambiguity to the foreground rather than suppress it in a deceptive presentation of a technically robust consensus. A plan may thus both express established rules and seek to challenge them.

We may locate the systems of meaning of a plan within the relations through which agents acknowledge, reinforce, and challenge established power relations, and we may evaluate the legitimacy of statements in terms of their potential to reinforce or change "structure." Thus, following Giddens (1984), the analyst should not only "read structure" through the statements of a plan, but should explore how the plan may seek to contribute to the constitution of structures.

Three British plans are analyzed here. The Birmingham plan was prepared for discussion with "the public" prior to proceeding through formal procedures to approval. It is for a large metropolitan district capital of the West Midlands conurbation. The Solihull plan is for an adjacent metropolitan district. The Harlow plan is for a small County District in the County of Essex. It has been prepared in the context of the Essex Structure Plan.

Development plans in the United Kingdom typically consist of reports of some 75 to 150 pages. They contain a set of statements describing the purposes, objectives, and strategies of the authors and specific proposals for spatial areas and policy domains. Statements on policies and proposals may include performance criteria for judging land allocations, development proposals, and the management of environmental resources. Policy statements and proposals are usually supported by some kind of explanation and justification.

My review focuses on the general organization of the plan and, specifically, the treatment of economic activity. Each account is preceded by a brief summary of the context of plan preparation and is followed by an analytical commentary on the discourses and discourse communities of the plan, the communicative work undertaken and its accessibility and frankness, and the power relations of the plan. In each case, a reading of the text is supplemented by knowledge acquired through interviews with key actors conducted in connection with other research projects.

THE BIRMINGHAM PLAN

Context

Birmingham is the largest Metropolitan District in England, with a long reputation for pragmatic, proactive municipal government. At the core of

Birmingham and the Nation

Birmingham is the UK's second city—the centre of the largest concentration of people and economic activity outside London. The City Council aims to consolidate the City's status vis-à-vis competing regional centres and to secure for the City a national/international standing equivalent to that of other major European provincial capitals. *(The alternative would be for the City Council to leave the City's status to other agencies and to market forces.)*

Birmingham in Its Region

Birmingham is a strong central place providing higher-level services and specialized functions in the region. The City Council will foster the City's distinctive central roles in relation to spreading regional patterns of economic, physical, and social interaction. *(The alternative would be to accept the general pressures towards dispersal and homogeneity of function.)*

Birmingham's Citizens

Birmingham is home to a million people of diverse cultures, ethnic origins, skills, incomes, and life-styles. The City Council will seek to provide a social and cultural environment to play a satisfying and distinctive part in the City's life. *(The alternative is to accept the pressure towards social and economic polarisation, maintaining distinctiveness, but blighting the life chances of individuals.)*

> *The vision has stability, it has continuity with the past, and it is sufficiently broad-based to command the political and interest group support to survive the inevitable crises and conflicts that will occur over the years ahead. These objectives are intended as a starting point and are not sacrosanct; the vision will be refined and enlarged upon as time progresses, but it will not be either denied or reversed.*

FIGURE 13.1
Birmingham Unitary Development Plan: strategic priorities

Britain's largest conurbation outside London, it is the capital of what was in the postwar period the country's buoyant industrial heartland. Since the 1970s, however, the manufacturing economy has been savagely undermined by international restructuring, exacerbating the problems of a diversity of poorer communities clustered in the inner city and a few peripheral estates. For the past fifteen years, municipal authorities have focused their attention on economic regeneration. Initially, they tried to achieve this by tightening the already restrictive greenbelt around the conurbation, to force development into the inner city. In the early 1980s, they shifted their approach to maximizing the conurbation's regional assets. Urban regeneration of Birmingham meant negotiating a complex balance between promoting the regional economy while limiting peripheral development to protect office and industrial locations within the city itself.

Format

> The City Council's objective in preparing the plan has been to concentrate on the main policy strands and from these to create a framework which will provide clear guidance for decision-making on the myriad detailed land use issues which will come forward over the plan period. (paragraph 1.5, p.3)

The Draft Birmingham Unitary Development Plan (UDP) starts with a "vision" of Birmingham of the future "staked out" in relation to the "key socio-economic forces that have acted upon the city" (paragraph 2.5 p.6). The vision is expressed in relation to the city's role in the region and nation, and to its own citizens. The consequent policies are presented in five topic chapters, followed by summaries of the plan's implications for the twelve political constituencies within the city. It concludes with a very brief statement on "development control policies."

The proposals map contains the main site-specific policy proposals. The text is illustrated with graphs and carefully designed graphics to convey messages about council attitudes and understandings. The cover graphic illustrates Birmingham's thrusting new hotel and convention center, a Victorian civic building, and the map of constituencies: the city as a place of many parts. The graphic at the start of the introduction shows diverse citizens invited to help the planners devise the plan, using desktop publishing technology.

Economy

Reflecting the city's preoccupations, this topic comes first:

> The city's economy will determine the number and type of jobs, the level of population, the amount of wealth created, as well as the extent to which the Council and other agencies are able to tackle wide-ranging inter-dependent urban and social problems. (paragraph 3.1 p.14)

This statement presents the state with the task of working to create the prosperous conditions for capital which, it assumes, will benefit everyone. After a brief review of economic trends, the chapter then outlines general and specific policies within the economic remit. The general policies emphasize that the plan—focused primarily on land use—will seek to "maximise opportunities for economic revitalisation and urban renewal" and ensure that the benefits of this effort will be widely distributed (paragraph 3.13, p.15).

The injunction against doing harm expresses a debate that runs through the text and, indeed, Birmingham's politics. The "disadvantaged" appear in this debate as shadow figures. All the detail—all the thick grain of reality—is attached to capital. The references to the disadvantaged and their needs seem to be "tacked on" to the chapter while the treatment of industrial and office development is integral to the text and highly sophisticated. It is cast in the language of technical analysis, dividing the region into sub-markets, estimating the need for industrial land within each of them, and allocating "premium industrial sites"—some of them in the greenbelt—to accommodate inward investment.

The argument is then presented for allocating greenbelt land for a premium industrial site. Hidden in the text and in a list of sites is the most contentious proposal of this section of the plan, an allocation of up to 50 hectares in the greenbelt somewhere near a proposed relief motorway, adjacent to an affluent and articulate residential neighborhood. The proposal is barely visible on the main proposals map. Even the road largely disappears in the map extract in the "constituency" statement.

Discourses and Discourse Communities

At one level, the Birmingham UDP is a "clear, succinct and understandable" plan.[1] Its style is straightforward and its language relatively simple and largely free of planning jargon. The presentation of technical matters is accessible to lay readers, leaving more complex matters to separate reports. Citizens appear to be the primary audience for the plan. The language, the graphics, and the neighborhood-by-neighborhood presentation all suggest a council that cares about its constituents. There is, however, little indication that the plan is the product of an active debate with citizens. The relations of this discourse community (the city council and its citizens) appear traditionally paternalistic, the council articulating its interests for the people rather than with the people, and explaining in the plan that they have done this.

Two other discourse communities emerge from the plan: business and developers. With its reference to a strategic "vision" and its careful discussion of the economy, the plan seeks to reassure local businesses and the prized "inward investor" that the council understands their needs, can meet its commitments, and is preeminently trustworthy. The development industry, whose contribution is critical in realizing many of the development proposals in the plan, is given less clearly targeted messages. Opportunities for development are indicated broadly in various land allocations, but there is little specificity as to the regulations that will govern them or of the detailed considerations of planning control. (The details will be settled in discussions with planning officers.) In contrast to the confident and assertive tone of the treatment of business, the discourse with developers is muted and muffled.

Despite assertions of independence, the plan is also strongly influenced by the "discourse of procedure" established by central government advice. Central government's power here lies in its capacity to overturn local decisions if these are "appealed against" by property interests. This influence is expressed both in the way central government authority is referred to and in the position the plan takes against central government advice (for example, in the organization of the plan and in the lack of detailed principles for planning control).

Communicative Work

This plan, then, is more a plan of messages than of conversations. In attempting to speak to various audiences, the plan's messages to each appear superficially clear, but on probing, this clarity disappears. Who exactly is the plan for? Who might benefit? What are the real priorities? Will the priority for the disadvantaged really prevail? The plan offers some information and outlines a strategic agenda. But its key communicative effort is essentially about managing ambiguity. This is done in a way that conceals the dilemmas and conflicts the council faces. Much is hidden and inaccessible. The council preserves its own discretion and autonomy to interpret its policies and set its priorities outside the plan framework. But it does not declare this approach or the possible reasons for it. This is not an "open" plan, despite the clarity of the text. Some of its policies "hide" in the text and plan, and it does not declare its discretionary stance.

Power Relations

Birmingham has traditionally been a pro-growth council, managing development in alliance with the business community. Despite the initial statement of concern for its citizens and the disadvantaged, this attitude appears as a superficial gloss on a strategy of growth promotion, supported by assertions of managing the "trickle down" to the disadvantaged. It expresses, despite its clear language and citizen-targeted presentation, an experiment in "caring capitalism." It illustrates Castells's "double-character" plan, combining technical rationality with the presentation of a convergence of interests between capital and community. While using the language of interaction, it remains "technocorporatist" in tone.[2]

Despite this rhetoric, the plan lacks assurance. It acknowledges a shift from the council as a "provider" to an "enabler" but cannot quite identify the difference this will make. It asserts local power to define the plan style, format, and context but does not know its own strength. It is unsure which sections of the business community it can help and is particularly uncertain about its relations with land developers. It refers to "spreading the wealth" generated by economic development but says little about how this can be achieved. Ultimately, the plan's tension lies in the council's pro-capital position in the face of major social problems and, in the affluent suburbs, residents' lobbies opposed to growth.

Birmingham's problems are faced by other big city councils in preparing their development plans. Confronted with growing economic and social problems, and challenges from suburbanization, their ability to control their environment is increasingly limited. Birmingham's plan seems to present the council in its old role of the paternalistic manager of change, while reality has moved elsewhere.

THE SOLIHULL PLAN

Context

Affluent suburban Solihull stretches from Birmingham into the greenbelt toward Coventry. It commands the apex of a triangle whose base stretches from London along the Western Corridor to Bristol. Recent motorway completions have increased the attractiveness of this location for industrial and commercial development while it has long been a sought-after residential location. Birmingham International Airport and the National Exhibition Centre are both in Solihull. The key issue for the Solihull Unitary Development Plan is development versus environment, centering on the release of greenbelt land. Like Birmingham, Solihull has a long history as a pro-growth borough, seeking expansion as a way to sustain its independence from its larger neighbor (Wannop 1985). Having gained this in local government reorganization in 1974, the pro-growth alliance has been repeatedly challenged by anti-growth interests. These won the upper-hand in the late 1970s, but the collapse of the West Midlands' economy in the early 1980s affected Solihull residents' sense of prosperity. Pro-growth strategies reemerged in the mid-1980s, focused primarily on "business" development. Housing, for which there was considerable demand, was viewed with hostility locally, symbolized in large dense high-rise estates for Birmingham incomers.

For the other Metropolitan Districts in the West Midlands in the 1980s, Solihull was a key player in the negotiation of a regional strategy. Within the strategic discourse of positioning with respect to inward investment, Solihull held the most "premium" of the premium sites. If Solihull allocated too much land for development, opportunities in other, poorer boroughs would be undermined; too little, and the regional economy would probably suffer, leading to appeals that would be settled by the central government. Faced with the difficult search for just the right balance, Solihull council and planners felt the need for a plan that would strike a bargain with other districts.[3]

Format

Residents of Solihull saw the council as being in the pockets of developers. Solihull councillors and officers saw themselves as sensitive growth managers, allocating sites as required by regional and local economic demand, but holding a firm line against the pervasive pressures for development. To sustain the growth management strategy against anticipated challenges from developers, the plan preparers sought to follow central government advice in every particular. The resulting plan focuses on land allocations. Every word in the plan is honed to the task of preparing a robust defense against developers' challenges. That the result might not be "easily understood" by other readers of the plan is acknowledged in a short afterthought of a preface:

> Most people might wonder why (the plan) is not in simple, everyday English. They might also wonder why it is not much shorter.

> The answers lie in the principal use to which an approved Plan will be put. It will steer and control the future development of land. This can have significant financial, environmental and social consequences for very many people.

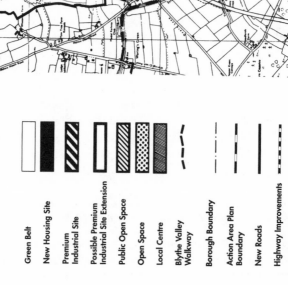

HOCKLEY HEATH PARISH

ACTION AREA PLAN

Green Belt

New Housing Site

Premium Industrial Site

Possible Premium Industrial Site Extension

Public Open Space

Open Space

Local Centre

Blythe Valley Walkway

Borough Boundary

Action Area Plan Boundary

New Roads

Highway Improvements

Highway Improvement Line

Proposal E1/2

Business Site 2 – The Council proposes to designate approximately 100 acres (40 hectares) of land as a Premium Industrial Site in the vicinity of the M42/A34 Junction at Monkspath West.

2.18 The site and the restrictions as to its use are formally identified in the Hockley Heath Parish Action Area Plan.

2.19 The Strategic Guidance also includes the principle that the release of sites should be phased with reference to the level of demand to achieve continuity and choice. It states that a new site should be released when monitoring indicates that the existing site, in this case the Birmingham Business Park, will be over three quarters occupied within three years. The underlying intention is that companies should have the choice of two or three high quality sites in the sub-region at any one time. The Council will therefore give careful consideration to these phasing principles in considering any application for detailed development.

2.20 Further to this, the Council believe that there may be a need to release further high quality business land to meet the needs of the Conurbation in the longer term. On this basis it proposes to include the following proposal.

FIGURE 13.2
Solihull Unitary Development Plan: premium industrial site allocation

As a result, the Plan will be interpreted by lawyers, scrutinised by planners, and picked over by surveyors. For this reason the Plan is lengthy, to explain fully what is intended: the Plan is written in a formal way, for legal clarity; and the Plan contains some planning jargon, because this tends to be the language of the government circulars and guidance to which the Plan relates. (Solihull Metropolitan Borough Council 1990, Preface)

The introduction to the plan is very brief. The statement "Solihull provides a buffer between the cities of Birmingham and Coventry" (paragraph 2, p.1) introduces the borough as an edge, or urban fringe, bordering open countryside. The role of the plan is explained in three paragraphs, followed by a summary of policy agreement with neighboring districts (not our policy but theirs), with respect to housing, the economy (there will be land allocations in the greenbelt), greenbelt (remains a firm element of the plan), and the environment (development will be high quality).

In this way, the plan engages its principal communicative dilemma: how could it justify a land allocation largely shaped by regional requirements and national mandates while purporting to act as the dedicated advocate of its local constituents? The rhetorical approach to this dilemma is to overwhelm the reader with a richness of detail: topic chapters, action area plans, maps, and spending priorities. Underlying all this detail, however, is a relationship between the council and developers viewed from the perspective of the regional and national arenas in which disputes would be engaged and resolved.

Economy

In contrast to Birmingham's plan, this chapter in the Solihull plan is brief. In six pages it focuses on the allocation of "business sites," a term preferred in Solihull to Birmingham's "prime industrial" sites.

The Council believes that . . . the economy of the West Midlands can be guided in such a way as to make a major contribution to the economic regeneration of the conurbation. This will help to maintain the continued wealth and prosperity of Solihull residents . . . . By carefully controlling the quality of all new economic development, there is no reason why the environment of the Borough should be harmed. (paragraph 2.11, p.26)

The concept of a flow of sites underpins these allocations, with one site already in construction (Birmingham Business Park), a second allocated for early development, and a third to be held in reserve. A similar approach is taken to the allocation of smaller sites for local purposes. The chapter concludes with a brief note on hotel developments and the needs of small businesses. (For detailed development guidance, readers are referred to the Action Area maps.) Very little guidance is provided for those interested in expanding existing businesses or taking over premises in existing built-up areas. This section of the plan, as with the housing plan, is primarily targeted at opportunities and debates with large development firms over large sites.

Discourses and Discourse Communities

If the Birmingham plan is speaking, in a rather confused way, to several audiences at once, the Solihull plan makes an implicit choice. It aims to insert itself within the debates between the planning system and developers over which sites to allocate for development. Implicitly also, the conversation is with larger, more sophisticated firms who know the council quite well. The plan sets out the arguments and principles to be used in debates at inquiries and provides a clear indication of the terms on which development will be allowed. Developers will be expected to provide social and physical infrastructure to service development as well as quality layouts and designs. In return, the ground rules are stated clearly. This will help developers in their negotiations over land value with landowners. Although the text is clear and very concise, the issues and context will be readily understood only by the development nexus in Solihull.

Citizens are largely left out. While local people in the greenbelt villages had a role in determining where development should go, they are given little assistance in "reading the plan." Residents' groups within the built-up area are offered no response to their concerns about environmental policy. They have to read each topic of the plan to find out how their interests are affected. It is perhaps small wonder that they have responded with hostility through the ballot box.[4] Councillors and officers argued that consultation with citizens to discover their concerns would only have led to enhanced antagonism to the strategy, the logic of which is regional not local. Instead, Parish councils and Tory politicians were "manipulated" to accept the plan. As a result, the plan has little to say about the needs of existing businesses or even small-scale developers. The dominant discourse is one of strategic economic necessity and practical implementation through effective planner-developer relations, a "technocorporatist" plan par excellence. This crowds out everything else.

Communicative Work

The main communicative work of the plan is to structure the agenda of debate within the ongoing conversation between planners and developers and to impose the strategic agreement on everyone else. It is clear and relatively frank to all those within the conversation (developers and consultants who have worked in the area for some time). Its clarity is such that it even holds out the possibility to developers of reducing the costs of hiring consultants to interpret the plan and lawyers to construct challenges to it. It is largely opaque to everyone else, except to central government officials and inspectors who are accustomed to the debates involved. Citizens and local businesses find little in the plan to advise them on council policy toward small-scale development projects. Nor does the plan help citizens monitor council policy, since once again much is left to the discretion of the local authority.

Power Relations

As far as national government is concerned, the Solihull UDP is an example of "good practice" in plan making. It follows centrally determined rules of procedure. It is clear and succinct and can be understood by civil servants. It holds out the prospect of cutting developers' costs by combining certainty (over strategy) with flexibility (over detail). But it is certainly not a democratic plan. It results from a process that can be described only as strategic political fixing, within which the negotiation of state-market relations between planners and developers can proceed. The plan, in effect, clears a range of development opportunities through the politics of environmental conflict, making them available to developers. Local residents see the situation cynically, as the outcome of a corrupt growth alliance between developers and councillors. Some past episodes appear to give credence to this view. The plan (and Solihull councillors), however, tells a different story, of how a local council can maximize its control over a strategic necessity. Perhaps so. In the end of course, the councillors will not be judged by their strategies but by their tactical success in managing growth. However, the plan says very little about the details of implementation. Indeed, as this is being written, the prospects of the plan seem very uncertain. Designed to preclude developer challenges, it now faces citizen attacks. I wonder whether a broader-based debate would have led to a more politically robust strategy? Are there, perhaps, political and economic advantages in proceeding with a more pluralist form of democracy?

THE HARLOW PLAN

Context

Harlow, formerly one of the London New Towns, is now a district in Essex. The area generally is under heavy development pressure, facilitated

FIGURE 13.3
Harlow Local Plan (front cover)

by infrastructure improvements and the expansion of Stansted Airport. There is, however, very little green field land left to accommodate this pressure.

The plan I reviewed is the bottom layer of a three-tiered hierarchy: the South East Regional Guidance, the Essex Structure Plan, and the District Development Plan. The introduction to the text carefully specifies the relations between the tiers in order to clarify for readers the sources of the plan's policies. Indeed, careful specification is the hallmark of this plan. The authors elaborate the ways in which policy proposals were developed, explaining—sometimes in a painfully pedantic style—the reasons for each choice. The new urban left (Stoker 1988, ch. 9) had strongly influenced the positions of some councillors and of officers in the Planning Section, the economic development department, and the equal opportunities section. The council has also been influenced by the think tank of a grouping of district councils under Labour Party control in the South East (SEEDS) and by the experience of the radical Greater London Council in the early 1980s. Politically, then, the Harlow plan is the product of a new philosophy. The planners faced the task of translating this philosophy into the detail of a formal development plan.

Format

All the plan policies are listed at the start. This is followed by three general sections, nine topic chapters, and two chapters on implementation, resources, and monitoring. The introduction explains the focus of the plan and the consultation that has gone into plan preparation: "The aim of the extensive consultation was to give people a real say in their own environment. Planning 'with the people and not for them,' the consultation aimed to 'inspire the public to air their views.'" (paragraph 1.6, p.9)

The plan first explains its intentions in the formal language of the central government advice and then provides an "ordinary language" translation:

> The local plan is especially useful when applications for planning permission are being dealt with. Harlow Council takes into account whether these follow the plan when making a decision. In this way, the plan helps private developers to see what kinds of changes or new developments are likely to be acceptable to Harlow Council in particular places." (paragraph 1.3, p.8)

This announcement also signals to developers that Harlow is a council seeking to direct development in line with the plan, taking a strong interventionist line in "shaping the future."

The next chapter outlines the policy context of the plan, and the third lists the plan's aims. The seven aims act as reference points throughout the rest of the plan. They center around the need to sustain job opportunities, provide for local housing needs, ensure equal opportunities, and balance development with the maintenance of environmental quality.

These aims are then consolidated into two main elements: a Strategy for Taking Opportunities—for meeting community needs and in particular "enhancing employment prospects"—and a "Strategy for Planning and Equal Opportunities." The latter is articulated as a "fundamental ethos" (paragraph 12) and a practical principle (paragraph 3.24).

This means that policies and decisions will have a differential impact. Unless this is taken into account, "planning practice . . . will perpetuate inequalities and fail to address unequal access to resources." The plan, then, attempts to work this version of a democratic pluralism into each topic of the plan.

Employment

Use of the term "employment" rather than "economy" presents economic activity from the point of view of local people's job needs rather than the concern for wealth creation generally (Newman 1991). The council's existing employment strategy is referred to as aiming to exploit the town's locational and other advantages to promote a "healthy and fair economy," from which local residents will obtain job opportunities at which fair employment practices will be maintained. Developers are to pay attention to the needs of the disabled and women (via child care provision). The plan then turns to calculations of land allocation requirements. The council interprets the structure plan policy as requiring considerable land allocation for industry and offices. Such activity is welcome, so long as firms follow the council's employment strategy principles. These principles include jobs for locals, child care provision and flexible working arrangements, an equal opportunities policy, skill training provisions, and involvement of trade unions. The chapter then continues with policies for small firms, employment practices, existing firms, existing industrial areas, small offices, craft units, training, child care, and environmental aspects. This rather long chapter illustrates the council's attempt to ensure that all the general aims of the plan are followed through, all the interrelations between topics are considered, and that the plan specifies where the policies apply and who will implement them.

Discourses and Discourse Communities

The resultant plan is not easy to read. It interrelates political philosophy, planning theory (the section on monitoring explains why the plan is not a blueprint), legal statutory procedure, and information to developers. Two clear discourse communities coexist within the plan:

1. *The new urban left*, with its concern for a. economic strategies that involve "capital"-making agreements with councils to promote the concerns of "labour" (Cochrane 1988); and b. the promotion of equal opportunities, with a particular emphasis on women's issues—the 1986 Greater London Development Plan has been a significant influence (Wainwright 1985).

2. *The planning administration* as it has been built up in recent years in local planning and development control. The plan contains little innovation here and is not much concerned with the way development works.

Despite the emphasis on plan preparation and public consultation, there is little reference in the plan to the debates that arose in these processes and how these were resolved. So it is not clear whether these discourses connect to either local people or local business, or the development industry in Harlow. Perhaps the most obvious audience for the plan is central government. In seeking to promote equal opportunities policies and good employment practice as well as in other respects (notably the treatment of planning gain), the plan is pushing at the margins of legal and administrative interpretations of the legitimate remit of planning control.

Communicative Work

This plan claims to be derived from the "inspiration" of citizens—to be the product of interaction with local people. In fact, the public consultation process adopted was conventional, with a round of public meetings. There were no specific discussions with groups representing different interests. This plan is possibly no closer interactively to its citizens than Birmingham's plan. A coalition of councillors and officers is trying to push an innovative approach on behalf of citizens and against the nationally dominant administrative plan-making discourse. The primary communicative purpose of the plan may thus be justificatory: to provide the arguments to sustain Harlow's distinctive position in anticipated battles with central government, with developers, and with the courts over the legitimacy of the plan's "directive, promotional" stance. There has to be ambiguity here, as the intention is to attract firms (to create jobs), to persuade developers to contribute to community infrastructure (and planning gain), and to require firms to adopt progressive employment practices.

There is further ambiguity in the style of the plan. It seeks rational consistency, explaining and elaborating its position with laborious care. The resultant style is, however, complex and the language at times a little tortured. It reads in places more like a philosophical treatise than an accessible statement to which various interest groups can refer. The underlying democratic "tone" of the plan is thus compromised by the hermetic style. It remains the style of a closed discourse among committed campaigners and administrators, rather than an open discourse among citizens, the state, and business.

Power Relations

In this plan, self-conscious agents (local politicians and officials) deliberately seek to challenge structures (the central state, the courts, and economic processes). Will the council succeed? If they fail, will it be their fault? (Could their democracy have been more active and their technical competence in translating philosophy into plan more sensitive and sophisticated?)

Or are the cards stacked against them? Central government, the courts, and developers have various means of demolishing their policies as illegitimate interference in private rights. If they continue to negotiate good employment practice and high environmental quality in deals with developers and firms, as they were successful in doing in the late 1980s, will this make any difference to the realization of the council's objectives? Does the council have the power to pursue its ideological commitments? The ambiguity in the plan's assertion of the primacy of its citizens but without a clear strategy for a democratically pluralist debate on plan purpose, strategy, and content also raises questions as to how far the plan is "with" as opposed to "for" the people.

CONCLUSIONS

A development plan is the product of processes of interaction between a range of parties, and in turn becomes an object, a point of reference, for continuing interactions. Within these interactions, one or many discourses may evolve, each with its own "story line." Plan preparation itself may involve a process of "making story lines," although more usually preexisting "stories" and strategies are consolidated in plan making and translated into reference criteria for regulatory decisions and development briefing. The analysis of the communicative work of plans is thus only one part of the more general analysis of the discourses and "discourse making" involved in planning activity.

An analysis of this kind, nevertheless, illustrates what can be revealed by focusing on the discourses and communicative work of a plan, rather than merely on interest competition and the drama among the characters. The planners involved in each case would probably identify the competition and describe the drama but claim that their job was to "balance" competing interests. Their effort is often devoted to producing an agreed-upon "story line." Yet in all these plans, there was more than one possible discourse. Choices were being made not merely between strategies within a common and widely understood framework. They were, implicitly, being made between discourses, understood as systems of meaning.

Several discourses can be identified in these plans. The Birmingham and Solihull plans are dominated by a strategic economic debate over the role of peripheral industrial and commercial sites for urban region economic development and the necessity to release land from the greenbelt. The conception of the local economy was new, but the struggle to capture peripheral land for conurbation needs has a long history in the West Midlands (Healey et al. 1988, ch.2). The debate in this instance had been carefully constructed between councillors and officers, and central government civil servants. Interventionist at the level of strategy with respect to land allocation and infrastructure support, its local benefits were cast within a market liberal form in which the wealth generated by growth was to "trickle down" to local people. The dimensions of the debate were well-known, as were the positions of the developers and consultants with significant property interests in the plan. In effect, there was a discourse consensus among local planners, national government, civil servants, major local politicians, and representatives of the development industry. Well established, the debate could be discussed in clear and precise terms. In the Birmingham plan, this strategic discourse coexists uneasily with a social-needs story line focused on equal opportunities and the disadvantaged. Despite a firm assertion of a social justice principle (no one already disadvantaged should be made more so), there is little indication in the plan that this has been seriously followed through with respect to policy details.

In Harlow, by contrast, a social-needs approach was developed into a version of democratic pluralism. This was made to pervade the plan, driven into its detailed policies and proposals. While Birmingham's social-needs approach seems the product of a slow evolution from a welfarist tradition into a form of multi-culturalism, Harlow's political philosophy is firmly located in the debates of the 1980s "urban left." But this discourse too coexisted uneasily with an administrative discourse, the points of reference of which are the debates surrounding the interpretation of procedures and central government policy (McAuslan 1980). In the Birmingham plan, this discourse is less evident, partly because plan preparers deliberately sought to distance themselves from it. But the plan remains within the strategic "discourse coalition" generated around strategic planning issues in the conurbation.

In Solihull, the strategic debate crowds out everything else. However, in Solihull's case, national government support is so critical for the success of the strategy that the administrative discourse has been merged into it. Local people are offered reasons and promises about environmental quality but are otherwise marginalized by the discourse. Solihull's plan, in effect, is explicitly a plan for property capital.

This tension between discourses within a plan raises questions about how a plan should reflect discourse diversity. The British national government demands that plans be "clear, succinct and easily understood by all those who need to know" (see note 1). But such a comment assumes a common discourse. The tension this generates is clearly evident in the Solihull case. Local residents want specificity, while development interests want what Solihull provides: strategic precision with flexibility over details.

Solihull's plan is judged by developers to be efficient, providing them with reasonable certainty. Its lack of specificity provides accountability only within the terms of the strategic discourse. It may be argued that Solihull is specifically narrow in its discourse, as the most effective way to achieve community purposes. Yet it does not provide a rich account of these purposes as a basis for subsequent discussion or development. The plan thus illustrates how exclusionary central government's apparently democratic intentions really are. "Those who need to know" are implicitly those in the strategic/administrative discourse. National politicians and civil servants tend to come across people ("citizens") who are already skilled in this kind of discourse. This helps to sustain the illusion that, by writing clearly, a local plan dominated by this discourse can be understandable to everyone.

Harlow rejected this approach, operating politically within a different discourse. If Solihull's plan develops a "top-down" argument, Harlow's claims to seek a "bottom-up," people-based approach. It seeks accountability through specificity. It is explicit about its assumptions and dilemmas but lacks the stylistic skill necessary to achieve accessibility. It requires considerable interpretive work to understand it. Further, because it is pushing at the margins of legitimacy in central government's terms, it does not deliver certainty to developers and businesses, as it is unclear whether the policies can survive. The ambiguous tensions of the Birmingham plan achieve neither accountability nor efficiency. Thus, while all the plans are much more explicit about their assumptions and dilemmas than was normal in the early 1980s, and more aware of their audiences, none reflects the diversity of interests and discourses that have a relevant voice in the development and management of an area. In this sense, they do not achieve a democratic form.

What communicative work, then, are these plans performing? All the plans inform readers "who can understand" about land-allocation proposals and performance criteria for development (but with variable degrees of coverage and detail). The plans are also inserted in debates about the goals of development management, offering persuasive rhetorical strategies (Throgmorton 1991). The Solihull plan firmly structures the agenda and imposes its "strategic agreement" on local people. Birmingham's plan seeks to do this in combination with a social-needs approach but is uncertain how this may be achieved. Harlow's plan is strongly influenced by a social-needs approach and seeks to justify this. Thus all the plans present arguments in defense of positions adopted. All the plans perform argumentative work, yet none presents its argument within the context of an open debate among all those "with a right to know."

How far is it possible to produce a plan that reflects richly textured interdiscursive public debate given the power relations within which plan making currently proceeds in Britain? The power of central government to impose its administrative discourse certainly creates difficulties in achieving this ideal. Local authorities also now appreciate that only limited bargains can be made with the interests of "capital." All three plans to an extent aim to facilitate private sector development. With cutbacks in the public sector, there might be no development without this. It may just be impossible to combine the concerns of capital, the community and administrators readily within a single plan. Technocorporate reductionism or uncertainty in style and tone may be the inevitable result.

However, this is not necessarily the conclusion. Some plans currently in preparation are trying hard to make the combination work. But this requires more than a readiness to review a whole package of existing policies (i.e., plan content). It also means developing a communicative strategy for plan making. Public consultation typically exercises focus on "interests in the game," assessing who to consult about what. Some planners now consider carefully how to manage arguments in the formal public "dramas" (inquiries) through which the plan has to pass for approval. This chapter stresses the importance of an awareness of the communicative work a plan is intended to perform and an appreciation of the diverse "communities of discourse" within which the plan may have meaning. Plan makers must choose whether to let their own professional discourse dominate or seek a dominant discourse acceptable to their politicians, key economic interests or their politicians' ideologies, or whether to attempt to prepare a plan through speaking between discourse communities.

What could this mean? One way is to acknowledge the diversity and the dilemmas. This involves, in particular, acknowledging what has been chosen against as well as chosen for; indicating what are still matters of conflict, as well as where there seems substantial agreement. Stylistically, this provides not only a record of a process of collective "learning about choosing," but a record of arguments and conclusions to return to in subsequent debates. Another way is to admit the dilemmas. In this sense, a plan could explicitly reflect on the "tragic" choices with which the community is confronted. A community's development plan thus could become not only a tool in its political game with national government and developers but an expression and record of the strategic choices and moral dilemmas a community has to face. A tragic perspective requires dealing with both the struggles between communities and the struggles within them.

Democracy in the present age has to absorb the diversities and differ-entiations that characterize our contemporary "postmodern" culture. This has to mean recognition of the plurality of discourse communities. With respect to plan making, it means explicitly addressing the challenge of "interdiscursive" communication. This is not to imply that a new discourse is created, since the diversity among us may be too great for each of us to enter into the systems of meaning of the other. We can perhaps only come to understand that we understand things differently and appreciate that we need to give each other space for these different understandings. The task, as Geertz (1983) advises, is to construct conversations within which:

> [P]eople inhabiting different worlds . . . [can] . . . have a genuine, and reciprocal, impact on one another. . . . The first step is usually to accept the depth of the differences; the second to understand what these differences are; and the third to construct some sort of vocabulary in which they can be publicly formulated. (Geertz 1983, 161)

The democratic plan may thus be recognizable not so much through its aims, or its policies, or its "distributive justice." Rather, its identifying character is likely to be its tone, expressing the experience of interdiscursive discussion.

In this chapter, I have attempted to provide some ideas to help identify plans that express a contemporary understanding of democratic plan mak-ing. It is hoped that these ideas may also help the creative efforts of all those currently struggling to realize such an ideal.

Acknowledgments

I am grateful for comments on an earlier version of this chapter to participants at the AESOP/ACSP Congress, Oxford, July 1991, at which this paper was presented, and from Huw Thomas, Roy Darke, Ted Kitchen, Jean Hillier, and Seymour Mandelbaum.

Notes

1. This is a key criterion in advice from central government on the style of plans. "Local plans should be clear, succinct and easily understood by all those who need to know about the planning policies and proposals which apply in the area" (Department of the Environment 1988a, paragraph 9).

2. See Fischer 1990 for the distinction between technocorporate and progressive democratic pluralism in policy analysis.

3. This was negotiated through the medium of a regional strategic framework agreed with central government (Department of the Environment 1988b).

4. In May 1991, just before the Local Public Inquiry was due to start, many Tory councillors were voted out in local elections. The plan was a significant reason for this, and subsequently there was pressure to change some of the policies (Ellerby 1992).

REFERENCES

Castells, M. 1977. Towards a political urban sociology. In M. Harloe, ed., *Captive cities*. London: Wiley.

City of Birmingham. 1990. Draft Birmingham Unitary Development Plan. Birmingham City Council.

Cochrane, A. 1988. In and against the market? The development of Socialist economic strategies in Britain: 1981–1986. *Policy and Politics* 16, 3: 159–68.

Department of the Environment. 1988a. Planning Policy Guidance No. 12. London: HMSO.

_____. 1988b. Planning Policy Guidance No. 10. West Midlands strategic guidance. London: HMSO.

Ellerby, J. 1992. Critical theory and the democratisation of planning practice. BA Town and Country Planning Dissertation, University of Newcastle.

Fischer, F. 1990. *Technocracy and the politics of expertise.* London: Sage.

_____, and J. Forester, eds. 1993. *The argumentative turn in policy analysis and planning.* Durham, NC: Duke University Press.

Forester, J. 1989. *Planning in the face of power.* Berkeley: University of California Press.

Geertz, C. 1983. *Local knowledge: further essays in interpretive anthropology.* New York: Basic Books.

Giddens, A. 1984. *The constitution of society.* London: Polity Press.

Habermas, J. 1984. *The theory of communicative action. Vol. I.* London: Heineman.

Hajer, M. 1993. Discourse coalitions and the institutionalization of practice. In F. Fischer and J. Forester, eds. *The argumentative turn in policy analysis and planning.* Durham, NC: Duke University Press.

Harlow District Council. 1990. Harlow Local Plan: shaping the future. Essex, UK: Harlow District Council.

Healey, P. 1993. Planning through debate. In F. Fischer and J. Forester, eds. *The argumentative turn in policy analysis and planning.* Durham, NC: Duke University Press.

_____, P. F. McNamara, J. J. Elson, and J. Doak. 1988. Land use planning and the mediation of urban change. Cambridge: Cambridge University Press.

McAuslan, P. 1980. *The ideologies of planning law.* Oxford: Pergamon.

Mandelbaum, S. 1990. Reading plans. *Journal of the American Planning Association* 56, 3: 350–56.

Mazza, L. 1986. Guistificazione e automania degli elementi di piano. *Urbanistica* 82: 56–63.

Newman, I. 1991. Surviving in a cold climate: local authority economic strategy today. *Local Economy* 5, 4: 293–304.

Solihull Metropolitan Borough Council. 1990. Solihull Unitary Development Plan. Solihull, West Midlands, United Kingdom.

Stoker, G. 1988. *The politics of land government.* London: Macmillan.

Throgmorton, J. 1991. The rhetorics of policy analysis. *Policy Sciences* 24: 153–79.

_____. 1992. Planning as persuasive storytelling about the future: the case of electric power rate settlement in Illinois. *Journal of Planning Education and Research* 12, 1: 17–31

Wainwright, H. 1985. Sharing power: popular planning and the GLC. *Going Local?* 2 (April): 6–7.

Wannop, U. 1985. The practice of rationality: the case of the Coventry-Solihull-Warwickshire Subregional Planning Study. In M. Breheny and A. Hooper, eds. *Rationality in planning.* London: Pion.

JEAN HILLIER

14 Deconstructing the Discourse of Planning

INTRODUCTION

This chapter provides a reading of eight professional plans produced in Western Australia between 1986 and 1990. I have usually cited them only by number in order to emphasize how similar they are. (See note 1; text citations to numbered plans are set in bold face.)[1] Their specific focus or provenance barely matters. I have read the texts with a sensibility that is both postmodern and feminist. My purpose in reading was to understand the ways in which women are presented in the worlds of these texts.[2] I looked at the substance of the plans, their rhetorical strategies, and the discourse within which they are written.

I discovered quickly that women are virtually invisible in these plans and in the professional discursive forms that characterize them. Insofar as women appear at all—which is not very often—they are represented as a homogenous group defined in relation to men. They are the Other, embedded in a metanarrative that is inattentive to diversity but denies its own biases. Reading the plans makes sense of the built environment of Western Australia. Its forms—its buildings, streets, parks and transit lines —express phallocentric ideologies that support separate and unequal roles for men and women. Consider the following quite typical policy statement:

> In order to preserve amenity and contribute to the quality of life in urban areas, including country towns, the Commission has resolved, as a general policy, to require suitable provision of public open spaces which can be used by people living and/or working in those areas. (**3**, 1.1)

289

In this statement, the depersonalized language names an anonymous body, the "Commission," as responsible for "requiring" (an active verb of direction and compulsion), provision of public open space to contribute to the "quality of life" (planning jargonese with uncertain meaning), for "people" (an assimilative term not recognizing the differing needs of women and other groups in society). Similarly, with regard to local subdivisional issues:

> The first design consideration is to avoid any common boundaries of school sites with residential uses wherever possible. There are a number of activities conducted on school sites which can adversely affect the amenity of residential properties, particularly where they are located very close to a school site. This is a growing problem with the trend towards increased community use of school facilities after hours. It is, therefore, preferable that school sites be surrounded by a combination of roads, public open space and other community recreation facilities. (3, 3.5.1)

The emphasis is on design rather than on those who take children to school—that is, women—and their convenience. Women are subsumed by "design" and "amenity." The unexplained ideology is to be protective of capital as invested in residential properties rather than to facilitate the needs of women. The community, in fact, is viewed as a "problem," using school facilities after hours to make up for the lack of other local facilities in or near the subdivision. The depersonalized "It is, therefore, preferable" avoids responsibility for the lack of provision of local shops, health and dental facilities, and so on that would be convenient for women if located next to a school, thus minimizing journeys. Such facilities represent the Other to the "roads, public open space, and recreation" amenities listed.

Turning to the city center, a consultant's report (6) states that:

> With sustained attention, St. George's Terrace could become a truly great urban street where people could walk in comfort, flanked by exclusive shops. (6, 47)

The depersonalized language, deleting pronouns, begs the question of who will give "sustained attention" to the issue so that the result may be a "truly great" street, but for whom? The answer is for the assimilative "people," walking amongst "exclusive shops." The unquestioned assertion that an undifferentiated mass (people) actually wants or needs "exclusive shops" is made, as it is that such exclusive shops make a street "truly great." Shopping for daily needs is marginalized to the Other, as are women who undertake the bulk of such shopping.

All the documents examined are guilty of not explaining their underlying ideological stance. Consider the following series of statements that illustrate the implicit foundations of planning policy:

> [M]ore efficient planning of open space, rationalising the use of paved footpaths and multiple use of recreational open space for drainage purposes and access (**2**, 114)

is clearly inequitable, as is

> [T]o achieve market viability and economic certainty for each centre (**2**,126)

while

> Real savings can be made in providing new services to the developing suburbs (**1**, 29)

places the emphasis (first position in sentence) on economic savings rather than on the needs of the inhabitants.

The use of depersonalized language and omission of pronouns removes the author from direct responsibility for the statement and the reader from direct association with the intended policy recipient. For example,

> Planning policies are required to . . . (**2**, 114)

and

> Policy DC1.4 establishes a uniform road classification system based on function for use (**3**, 1.3)

combine depersonalization with jargon in a typical modernist policy statement. Other examples follow, such as

> [T]here will be a move towards increasing housing yield in new suburbs (**1**, 6)

and

> [I]ncreasing gross urban densities from the prevailing seven dwellings per hectare to nine dwellings per hectare. This will provide a land-saving in excess of 10,150 hectares. (**1**, 29)

The texts assimilate women into other categories so that gender is hidden. Even the Recreation report with a main term of reference to research the "appropriateness of local government initiatives to satisfy *women's* recreational requirements" (7, 5; my emphasis) presupposes that women's needs are met by community, neighborhood, and Learning Centers, that women all have children, and that children's activities constitute recreation for women. Recreation in Western Australia is regarded primarily as being connected with sport, and if women are considered at all, "the immediate response was to connect firstly women with children and to then connect them to children's play groups, children's libraries" (7, 36).

Transporting Perth into the 21st Century (5) contains photographs of people using bikeways, specialized transport services, public transport facilities and so on, but women, who form the majority of users of such services, are noticeably omitted. The sole photograph of a woman shows her pushing a buggy, accompanied by a toddler, outside a new suburban home. Even though this token photograph may pander to women, women's needs are not addressed anywhere in the document. Statements such as "residents have, of necessity, developed a life-style which is highly dependent upon the private car" (5, 6) do not consider women's general alternative, which is not to go out at all.

Similarly, land use and transport sections refer to transportation to work and to shopping. Women living in outer suburbs with other needs are not considered. Despite their often very difficult situation, they are not treated as "transport disadvantaged" (5, 10), a category reserved for people with physical disabilities. Provision for walking and cycling is covered, but the emphasis is firmly on choice rather than on necessity. In total, the document does not concern itself with the needs of women, the prime users of public transport, who are forced to walk far more than men.

The *Commercial Centres Policy* (4) also reflects a modernist attitude to functional land-use planning rather than people planning. The description of policies for the commercial hierarchy of central area, regional, district, and neighborhood centers makes no mention of shoppers at all, notwithstanding the fact that the majority of shoppers are women. Policies for neighborhood centers do not regard the issues of access and links to schools and other facilities that may minimize women's journeys. Corner stores/delicatessens that provide convenient shopping for women with limited mobility rate no consideration at all.

Central area policies are also notable for their omissions. The *Bunbury Region Plan* (8), for example, contains a regional center policy almost exclusively concerned with traffic. Women (and, indeed, people in general) are entirely absent, even as pedestrians. The *Perth Central Area* report (6) is of similar orientation, concentrating on offices and retailing to the exclusion of residential provisions—the very consideration that might contribute sorely needed life to the city center. "If one has to get into a car to move comfortably from one office to another, a major reason for having a city in the first place disappears" (6, 42). This chicken-and-egg statement of whether offices create cities or cities offices, treats residents, people, and especially women, as the invisible Other.

The highly master-planning–, land-use–oriented policies prevalent in Western Australia refuse to engage with women, to acknowledge women's stories and women's needs. Women thus remain disempowered by the modernist discourse of planning policies that are physically and economically driven. Technical tables of distances to facilities, of setbacks, of space standards, and so on are an easy evasion of the issue. "Function for use" (3, 1.3) is not an adequate policy framework.

WOMEN'S INVISIBILITY AND DOMINATION

So far I have attempted to demonstrate that authoritative views purporting to be neutral actually express the partial and interested perspectives of dominant social groups. The identities and needs the planning discourse and the planning system fashion for their recipients are identities and needs as interpreted by male-oriented planners. Yet, these very needs and identities are not always recognized as being interpretations. "Too often, they simply go without saying and are rendered immune from analysis and critique" (Fraser 1989, 154).

Planning as described generally by Fraser (1989) and as realized in Western Australia links together juridical, administrative, and therapeutic procedures. As a consequence, planners translate contested political interpretations of people's—especially women's—needs into a seemingly neutral legal, administrative, and therapeutic language. This system thus implements political policy in a way that appears to be nonpolitical but is, in fact, subordinating, depoliticizing, and disempowering.

Planning discourse and the resultant policies position its "subjects" as passive clients or recipients rather than as active co-participants involved in shaping their life environments. The state has preempted the power to define and satisfy the public's (as an undifferentiated mass) needs. As Fraser states, "It tends to substitute monological, administrative processes of need definition for dialogical, participatory processes of need interpretation" (Fraser 1989, 156). Plans, as Patsy Healey (chapter 13 in this volume) describes them, are messages *to* their audiences rather than conversations *with* them. Women and women's voices remain the invisible and power-less Other.

Can Planning Be Otherwise?

My deconstructive reading of the eight texts represents women as sys-tematically disempowered, excluded, and marginalized. I recognize, how-ever, that I have adopted a somewhat simplified view of the planned envi-ronment. I have stripped it of the meanings that people—particularly women—attach to it as they go about their daily lives. Fond memories may even be attached by some women to buildings or streets that other women find oppressive.

"Mere recognition of the existence of something," as Massey (1991) notes, "does not empower it." Derridean analysis must not fall into the trap of endorsing a wholesale rejection of modernist planning discourse without a conception of what is to replace it. If women are to be empow-ered or capacitated in the planning process, the content of policies should be reached in discussion with women. Women's knowledge must be shared through communication—"The construction of knowledge involves com-munication, politics, passion" (Sandercock and Forsyth 1990, 73).

Planners in "Western Australia"—or wherever on the globe—should rethink the relations between the state and disempowered groups. They should face the fact that genuine planning means giving up an element of control. They need to challenge the structures of planning practice and to incorporate rather than simply accept difference. Women should challenge the planning experts in order to take control of their lives and institutions (Young 1990).

Planning should be an interpretive and interactive process (see For-ester 1989). Interaction involves different individuals and organizations being engaged with one another in debate and negotiation; each group having its own discourse, knowledge, and meaning systems and telling its own stories. The role of planning should be to engage in "respectful dis-cussion within and between discursive communities, respect implying rec-ognizing, valuing, listening and searching for translative possibilities" (Healey 1992, 154).

Habermas's theory of communicative action offers a way of challenging formal processes of planning, enabling all sides to understand and respect each others' discourses and viewpoints, and to work toward negotiated agreement (Hillier 1993). Such discussions and discourses should be truly open to all Others so that language can function as the "medium of unhindered understanding" (Habermas 1984, 94–5).

Women's voices and language differ from men's and from each others'. All women's voices must be brought out of silence in a reordered planning process that will recognize the commonalities, differences, and conflicts among the diverse stories women tell. The patriarchal, phallocentric order of planning can be defeated.

A recognition of women's specificity requires the cultivation of "other kinds of discourse, different forms of evaluation and new procedures for living in and reflecting on day-to-day life" (Grosz 1989, 126). Femininity cannot simply be added to the existing discursive framework of planning that has been built upon the foundation of patriarchy. Women must be asked for new proposals and reformulations based on their experiences and described in their discursive forms. What gets done in the planning world depends on what gets said, how it is said, and by whom. It is time that women began to have their say.

There should not, in the future, be one meta narrative of planning. Planning discourse as reconstructed should be more than a "metalangue of interference" (Dear 1986, 383) to be comprised of a set of "flexible networks of language games" (Lyotard 1984, 17) that overlap to produce linguistic "knots" (Kristeva 1980, 55–6) binding different groups of women and different sectors of society together. A focus on the detail of language and communication is not, however, an alternative to reordering the structure of the planning process to become capacitating for women. Without such a structural challenge there is a danger that "everything changes but stays the same" (Chapman 1988, 247).

Gender-sensitive planning must recognize that introducing gender as a variable is not what is at stake (Milroy 1991). Rather, we should aim at radical restructuring of power relations within the planning process. Only by according "voice," "ear," and "respect" to all those with an interest in what is at issue can planners arrive at true interactive planning or "planning through debate" in which:

> [I]ts images and metaphors would draw on both the experiential and abstract knowledge and understanding of those involved, recognizing the interweaving of rational-technical, moral and aesthetic life dimensions. It would seek to "reason between" conflicting claims and conflicting ways of validating claims. It would not force one dimension of knowledge to dominate over another. It would be courageous, challenging power relations through deconstructive critique and the presentation of alternative arguments. (Healey 1992, 158–9)

The entire set of planning assumptions in Western Australia should therefore be de-reified in order to create a new framework for planning with which women are engaged and empowered. It will not be an easy task as women have often internalized many of the precepts of the patriarchal reality. In the short term, women must continue to demand that their stories and needs be acknowledged by professional planners. This in itself is a radical change from a situation in which meanings were taken for granted, and where it was assumed that male meanings constituted the incontestable reality.

Policies and plans should represent a collective authorship between people and planners; planning through debate. Women must be fully involved in the dissolution of the universal perspective to bring plurality into being in a way which does not limit that plurality. With apologies to Foucault (1960), planning discourse, planning policies, and above all, the planning system, must be re-created to reflect a situation in which "women's Other must become the same as herself."

Acknowledgments

My grateful thanks to Hubert Law Yone for the courage of my convictions; to Seymour Mandelbaum and Patsy Healey; to Fiona Fisher for braving Word 5.5; and to Leah Marlow for commas and coffee.

Notes

1. The documents analyzed are:

   1 METROPLAN. A PLANNING STRATEGY FOR THE PERTH METROPOLITAN REGION

   1990. Prepared by the Western Australia Department of Planning and Urban Development.

   2 PLANNING FOR THE FUTURE OF THE PERTH METROPOLITAN REGION

   1987. Prepared by the State Planning Commission of Western Australia (now Department of Planning and Urban Development [DPUD]). Superseded by Metroplan.

   3 POLICY MANUAL

   1990. Department of Planning and Urban Development.

   4 PERTH METROPOLITAN REGION COMMERCIAL CENTRES POLICY

   1989. Draft prepared by the State Planning Commission of Western Australia.

   5 TRANSPORTING PERTH INTO THE 21ST CENTURY

   1990. Prepared by the Transport Strategy Committee on Future Perth.

   6 PLANNING PROCEDURES FOR PERTH'S CENTRAL AREA

   1988. Prepared by J. Mant.

7 ARE YOU BEING SERVED? A REPORT ON
LOCAL GOVERNMENT APPROACHES TO RECREATION
1989. Prepared by Learning Centre Link.

8 BUNBURY REGION PLAN
1986. Prepared by the State Planning Commission of Western Australia.

2. "Women" is used in this chapter as an inclusive category, acknowledging that it incorporates a multiplicity of women with varying needs and demands but following Spivak's (1985) argument that in order to advance a feminist program, the category "women" should be treated as an operational essentialism while recognizing it to be a false ontology.

REFERENCES

Chapman, R. 1988. The great pretender: variations on the new man theme. In R. Chapman and J. Rutherford, eds. *Male order.* London: Lawrence and Wishart, 225–48.

Dear, M. 1986. Postmodernism and planning. *Environment and Planning D: Society and Space* 4: 367–84.

Forester, J. 1989. *Planning in the face of power.* Berkeley: University of California Press.

Foucault, M. 1960. *Les mots et les choses.* Paris: Gallimard.

Fraser, N. 1989. *Unruly practices: power, discourse and gender in contemporary social theory.* Cambridge, UK: Polity Press.

Grosz, E. 1989. *Sexual subversions.* Sydney: Allen & Unwin.

Habermas, J. 1984. *The theory of communicative action.* vol. I. *Reason and the rationalization of society.* Boston: Beacon Press.

Healey, P. 1992. Planning through debate. *Town Planning Review* 63, 2: 143–62.

Hillier, J. 1993. To boldly go where no planners have ever. *Environment and Planning D: Society and Space* 11.

Kristeva, J. 1980. *Desire in language.* New York: Columbia University Press.

Lyotard, J-F. 1984. *The post-modern condition.* Manchester, UK: Manchester University Press.

Mant, J. 1988. *Planning procedures for Perth's central area.* A report to the Minister for Planning. Perth, Western Australia: Phillips Fox.

Massey, D. 1991. Flexible sexism. *Environment and Planning D: Society and Space* 9: 31–57.

Milroy, B. M. 1991. Taking stock of planning, space and gender. *Journal of Planning Literature* 6, 3–15.

Sandercock, L., and A. Forsyth. 1990. Gender: a new agenda for planning theory. *Planning Theory Newsletter* (Winter): 61–92.

Spivak, G. 1985. Remarks. Middletown, CT: Wesleyan University, Center for the Humanities.

State Planning Commission of Western Australia. 1986. *Bunbury Region Plan.* Perth, Western Australia: State Planning Commission.

_____. 1989. *Perth Metropolitan Region commercial centres policy.* Perth, Western Australia: State Planning Commission.

State Planning Commission of Western Australia. Review Group. 1987. *Planning for the future of Perth Metropolitan Region.* Perth, Western Australia: State Planning Commission.

Transport Strategy Committee on Future Perth. 1990. *Transporting Perth into the 21st century.* Perth, Western Australia: Transport Strategy Committee on Future Perth.

Western Australia Department of Planning and Urban Development. 1990. *Metroplan: A planning strategy for the Perth Metropolitan Region.* Perth, Western Australia: Department of Planning and Urban Development.

_____. 1990. *Policy manual.* Perth, Western Australia: Department of Planning and Urban Development.

Young, I. M. 1990. *Throwing like a girl.* Bloomington, IN: Indiana University Press.

Commentary

Helen Liggett

Examining the Planning Practice Conscious(ness)

TELL THE TRUTH[1]

The practice movement has made an important contribution to the design disciplines and policy studies by carefully establishing that even when one is so inclined, telling the truth is not such a simple thing. The work of John Forester is exemplary in this respect. It was his initial insight that contemporary language philosophy, represented by theorists such as John Austin, and postwar critical theory, represented by Jürgen Habermas, could be applied to analyzing what "planners really do." Both of his chapters in this section demonstrate this approach in action. At the same time, they incorporate the fruits of Forester's work in moral philosophy. They show the daily discussions in planning agencies as "practical" in the sense that they are not carried on in abstract codes totally detached from or laid over events but rather are constitutive aspects of those events. They also illustrate how policy professionals operate within highly coded discursive practices that have moral components.

Both of Forester's pieces include discussions of planning discourses, inviting readers to participate in reflection. The analysis in "Argument, Power, and Passion in Planning Practice" is a little broader, however, in that more attention is paid to explaining how ongoing discourse operates at several registers and how players do or do not react in kind. Forester uses the notion of "contra-dictions" to describe shifts in kinds of argument. This allows him to broaden the very definition of discussion to bring in what he calls "passion." In other words, people genuinely lose their tempers or feign anger, and this is one mode of establishing the "truth" of a situation. In the illustration he uses, the boundaries for action are established by a series of exchanges involving temper. This addresses the limitations of identifying truth with Rationality and then seeing relations of dominance only in terms of the imposition of instrumental reason. Indeed, all the chapters in this section address multiple rationalities at work rather than a single transcendent Rationality. The case studies by Hoch, Healey, and Hillier illustrate that, in spite of our best efforts, the rationalities "that win" are not necessarily examples of logical discussion in the classic liberal mode.

Once one is keyed to the multilayered aspect of language use and the centrality of various modes of persuasion, it is easier to see the interweaving of practical and moral activities. Hoch provides examples of two planning professionals creating paths for themselves through the moral and practical concerns that constitute commitment to a career path.

Understanding the complexity of the organizational exchange is one achievement of practice research in planning that has a broad reach. It is applicable to policy studies and other disciplines concerned with formulating public issues and their resolution. Although Forester's pedagogical recommendations are aimed principally at training planners, they are relevant to professional training in general. In the context of the findings of his analytic work, Forester's abiding interest in planning education becomes understandably urgent. He puts ethical considerations at the core of professional identity in a way that offers a welcome relief from bounded discussions along the lines of whether professional schools should "also" teach an ethics course.

WHAT COUNTRY SHOULD YOU ADOPT IF YOU HATE POOR PEOPLE?

Recognizing negotiation within the professional practice of planning leads to evaluation by the reader/writer of value on a broader scale. Analysis of the dialogue of planning professionals in action at the scale Hoch and especially Forester present is like a laboratory procedure in its exactness and attention to particular issues. This approach raises further questions about arenas not under the microscope. Healey's careful examination of three British plans widens the circle of inquiry by addressing plans as objects of analysis. She approaches the plan from a theoretical perspective that complements the first chapters in this section. Rather than viewing The Plan as a completed document to be evaluated according to static or formal criteria, she analyzes plans first as enactments of value in concrete spatial/political contexts, and second as the basis for ongoing negotiation. Neither situation is seen as determinate, but both limit and also construct the terms of the debate. They constitute what Dumm (1993, 14) has called "contexts of visibility" for the alteration of spatial arrangements.

Healey avoids the traps of seeing The Plan as the (end) object of planning by using a textual approach to her work. When plans are analyzed textually, arenas that provoke planning dialogue involving practical reasoning, or passion and dilemmas about professional identity, are put in a larger frame that asks directly about how meaning is produced in the text/context interplay. A textual approach highlights the interior and exterior relations in which plans are constructed and implemented. "The Plan" is replaced by "plan formulation," as ongoing practice, and the analysis is concerned about how external forces influence ongoing stages of formulation.

For example, Healey shows how planning discourse justifies preexisting patterns of distribution by analyzing how the language of the planning can promote development in ways that identify successful *economic* development with general well-being. Questions about how increased wealth will be used were not included in the growth-oriented plans she examined. A widely accepted representational sleight of hand allows concern for the future to cover greed and public documents to do the work of private interests.

Like the other authors in this section, Healey is highly self-conscious of her own position as part of the context that shapes her analysis and shoulders the responsibility of making her values explicit. Her particular interest is in a kind of democratic planning that would include affected citizens as participants in plan formulation. When Healey brings this interest in democratic planning to bear on assessing the three plans she studied, she does so by asking about whether the procedures of construction, the amount of play in the language of the plan, and the likely forms of reenacting the plans in space foster or ignore widespread participation. There is variation in how the planning problems are represented for each of the three sites involved, and the position of each plan in the highly structured British planning system is different, but nevertheless she illustrates how each operates more or less independently of citizen participation in the work of planning. Healey separates planning *for* the people from planning *with* the people. This challenges the conventionally simple democratic definition of "the people." Healey shows "the people" to be more complex. Some people (or at least publicly identifiable interests) were included in each plan, usually in the language that presented the goals of the plan and the preferred avenues for reaching those goals. This language did not say "others need not apply"; it just reduced the likelihood of that application.

The bias that follows from Healey's concern with democratic planning is that she sees planning for the good of all as necessary but not sufficient for democratic planning. This bit of intellectual rigor on her part allows her to illuminate some of the restrictions built into the rhetoric of the "New Urban Left" in Britain. The New Left position did dominate one of the plans she analyzed but in a highly paternal way. Healey points to the mechanisms in the plan that systematically disadvantage poorer segments of the population. At the same time, she sees their exclusion as one of the instruments of creating their disadvantage.

WE ARE UNITED IN THE TOLERANCE
OF OUR DIFFERENCES

Hillier uses gender relations to address the relationship between systematic exclusion and systematic disadvantage. The most obvious thing to note about the way she states her position is that she is not shy about it. This can be off-putting until the reader begins to reflect on some of the specific examples she provides. Some biases are easy. How clearly one can see outmoded gender relations embedded in recreational planning that identifies women's leisure needs only in terms of the requirements that their children have access to good sports facilities!

There is more at stake in Hillier's analysis of the spatial routines of women and the spatial routines planners provide for. Her analysis reveals *how* cultural habits enforce identities. Transportation patterns disadvantage women in terms of the kinds of trips they are most likely to make. That is, women are less likely than men to commute to work at 9:00 A.M. and then to return back home at 5:00 P.M. They are more likely to be involved in carpooling (numerous short trips taking children places and shopping) and sandwiching these activities into a work day, if they are also employed outside the home. On one level this is about inconvenience. It also illustrates the intractability of spatial constructions. And it is about what happens when a society admits women to new roles without substantially altering the requirements of their old roles. If viewed from only this perspective, the reforms Hillier's analysis implies could be considerable.

Another one of Hillier's examples seems somewhat bewildering on the surface. She discusses a plan that describes a "good street" as one where pedestrians are drawn. This in not unusual; preference for the walking city has long been a prejudice of urban design. In this case the draw to the street is based on the presence of exclusive shops. We all like upward mobility, and furthering the dynamics of the postmodern city includes festive market places and appropriate shopping experiences. Hillier's choice of this example provokes thinking that connects the ways women are inconvenienced by plans that exclude their routines to the ways in which feminine subjectivity is specified in terms that link gender to presentation rather than participation. Exclusive shopping as successful planning disadvantages women by promoting leisure (tourist) consumption, which is a direct descendent of the industrial city's bourgeois ladies of leisure to the exclusion of the "pick up the milk and dry cleaning on the way home" type of consumption with which most middle-class women are familiar. The latter forms of consumption they do *against* and hence around cultural ideals of what they should *be* (rather than what they should do). This ideal of the feminine subject is costly in both money and in the lost opportunity to construct the kinds of participatory identities Healey identifies with democratic planning and Forester with ideal professional practice.

It is at exactly this point where Hillier's work breaks out of the bounds of her analysis. If we can ask this question about cultural constraints on women, then should we not ask about cultural constraints on the rest of the population? The issue of what mode of planning we want is intimately tied to consideration of the forms of life we wish to create.

IT IS IN YOUR SELF-INTEREST TO FIND A WAY TO BE VERY TENDER

Hillier implicitly raises the question of what kind of subjects the society constructs in a way that shows it to be connected to planning and the larger society in which planning functions. Hoch's discussion of two planners shows them developing the capacity to reflect and act in ways that facilitate their success at making places for themselves in the planning profession. Similarly, Forester addresses broad moral issues within the context of self-conscious participation in constructing selves and worlds that are good and desirable.

All of these pieces ultimately touch on questions concerning the nature of planning and the nature of society. Hillier suggests not just that more women participate in planning or that planning be more "women" oriented. Her critique aims at planning as a form of power. At the core of her critique is the *way* or *mode* or *being* of planning. Thus, gender bias, reflecting and reenacting relations of dominance in the larger culture, is a paradigmatic example of planning itself as it reflects patterns of dominance.

For Hillier the remedy would be at the same level, the mode of being of planning. She virtually leaps to the conclusion that "genuine planning means giving up an element of control."

Genuine planning is a nice notion.

WHAT IF IN YOUR DREAM YOU FOUND A WAY TO SURVIVE AND YOU WERE FULL OF JOY?

The practice movement in planning theory has isolated aspects of planning activity in order to examine planning in play. This has done the great service of moving away from decontextualized discussions of comprehensive planning that combine design principles with the spatial requirements of the larger political economy (Boyer 1983). But to do this necessarily means holding in abeyance issues dealing with the object of the enterprise. "Object of the enterprise" has two meanings here. It refers to the object as the social and physical space of everyday life, and the object as participation in formulating that space.

Concerns about the objects of planning tend to sneak in each chapter. They surface in Forester's concern with planning pedagogy, in Hoch's insistence that readers note the ethical components of professional development and action, in Healey's interrogation of three plans in terms of democratic standards, and in Hillier's call for redress of destructive modes of operation. The call to focus on "what planners really do" may be more compelling in an era of comprehensive planning, but when the plan as an end and singular object of affection dominates, that battle may be won. There is now time/space to develop modes for writing about the relationship between the subjects and objects of planning in a reformulated way. Each of these pieces has began that work.

Spatial theory is a particularly useful tool for continuing this work (LeFebvre 1991). It is firmly based in the sensitivities of theory and postmodern consciousness. From a spatial theory approach, agency and structure are seen as mutually constitutive (one of the strengths of the practice movement). Spatial theory is particularly suited to planning because questions of the play among social and physical domains, which is the realm in which planning operates, are central concerns. Furthermore, it provides a way of bringing together concerns with the fragmentation of urban space and the function of signs in constructing a united cyber-spatial world within which planners must be literate participants. Finally, although spatial theory cannot solve the institutional crisis in the planning profession brought about by the need to keep and find institutional space in a world no longer easily beguiled by the Rational Model, it does contain conceptual tools for recognizing this issue.

From a spatial perspective, planning has been defined as a gerundic activity, what David Perry calls "making space" (Perry 1995). Theoretically, making space can occur at various levels, from "homemaking" to "regional planning." This has the advantage of enlarging the field of planning practice while also recognizing that a realm for planning expertise still exists. One thinks in this context of the African American woman Forester mentions in one of his case studies who successfully educated poor whites out of their prejudices while she was empowering them to manage their finances. The making space model has the advantage of having a built-in grounding in actual practice with the breath of concern that admits questions of external forces or the planning context, including the quality of participation. One thinks here of all the citizens whose "interests" were being represented in the plans Healey analyzed, without they themselves appearing as part of the planning. They were excluded from making space on one level, but the actual social consequences of making space that will proceed from the implementation of the plan will include time, if only in its effects.

Although LeFebvre and some of his followers, such as DeCerteau (1988), are highly critical of planning as a spatial practice imposed on the city, spatial theory is not substantively dictatorial. It merely sets up the analytic framework for asking about the relationships or play among planning, the spatial practices of everyday life, and symbolic meaning. In this regard it can be used to extend the reach of practice research into questions of the relation between planning as a profession and other social formations.

On the surface the question of the relationship between increasingly fragmented urban space and the united cyber-spatial world may not seem a planning practice issue. But if we adopt a position that connects planning practice to "making space," then we have to ask: What kind of space? Françoise Choay (1986) has suggested that one of the characteristics of contemporary urban life is the extent to which signs are organizing components laid over spatial configurations deemed to be outmoded. In a related development, marketing cities has become a major aspect of their economic development (Boyer 1995; Holcomb 1993). The planning profession, then, must develop literacy in the area of the politics of representation, if only to read our own writing.

Stepping off into the area of hyper-reality and cyborgs is not to step away from studying planning as it really works nor is it to move away from developing a self-consciousness about the kinds of planning we wish to promote. Donna Haraway's image of the cyborg is the image of a new hybrid subjectivity in which the distinction between technology and humanity is not easy to make. She counters this with a concrete ideal that only sounds like a contradiction: "The pleasure of being at home in the world" (Penley and Ross 1990, 20). When Hillier finds systematic gender bias in the planning profession in her country embedded in the neutral language of professional practice, she is arguing more than anything for this pleasure: to be at home in the world. When we begin to address the question of the object of planning practice in the sense of what form of life it promotes, what better guideline is there to employ? Planning practice research has helped formulate the question; one can only look forward to further developments.

Acknowledgment

1. The headings for this essay are taken from Jenny Holzer's work, which has appeared in public places in New York and other venues over the last decade.

REFERENCES

Boyer, M. 1983. *Dreaming the rational city.* Cambridge: MIT Press.

_____. 1995. The great frame-up: fantastic appearances in contemporary urban politics. In H. Liggett and D. Perry, eds., *Spatial practices: communities, politics and markets.* Newbury Park, CA: Sage.

Holcomb, B. 1993. Revisioning place: de- and re-constructing the image of the industrial city. In G. Kearns and C. Phils, eds., *Selling place: the city as Cultural capital past and present.* Oxford: Pergamon Press, 133–45.

Choay, F. 1986. Urbanism and semiology. In M. Gottdiener and A. P. Lagopoulos, eds., *The city and the sign.* New York: Columbia University Press, 160–75.

DeCerteau, M. 1988. *The practice of everyday life.* Berkeley: University of California Press.

Dumm, T. 1993. The new enclosures: racism in the normalized community. In R. Williams, ed., *Reading Rodney King, reading urban uprising.* London: Routledge.

LeFebvre, H. 1991. *The production of space.* Oxford: Basil Blackwell.

Penley, C., and A. Ross. 1990. Cyborgs at large: interview with Donna Haraway. *Social Text* 25/26: 8–23.

Perry, D. 1995. Making space: planning as a mode of thought. In H. Liggett and D. Perry, eds., *Spatial practices: communities, politics and markets.* Newbury Park, CA: Sage.

PART IV

The Status and Use of Knowledge

Seymour J. Mandelbaum

The Status and Use
of Knowledge

INTRODUCTION

I n their efforts to express themselves and to persuade or control others,
human beings enjoy a great variety of rhetorical forms. They shout
and they whisper. They wave their arms, draw pictures, write elaborate argumentative texts, speak with a studied detachment or in the caring
tones of intimacy and love. They imperiously defend their personal perceptions or justify their claims as embedded in a shared public logic and
factual order.

The four chapters in this section are all concerned with rhetorical forms
commonly called "rational," "scientific," or "formal." If the authors were
concerned with matters epistemological (as a Gilbert and Sullivan character might describe them), they would be bound to identify precisely the
distinguishing marks of the objects of their attention. In these chapters,
however, the definitional issue is less important. The forms are understood
as social resources and as claims to authority rather than as rules for speech
in an idealized conversation: a finger points to "science," "theory," and
"reason" as loosely defined but critically important tools of social discipline, persuasion, and control.

In the first of these chapters, Giovanni Ferraro quickly concludes that
it is impossible to imagine collective choices that are uniquely rational in
the sense that they follow tightly disciplined formal rules from the
distinctive preferences of individuals. This conclusion—the intractable
necessity of "irrationality"—clears the way for an appreciation of planning
as a process of exploration, reflection, invention, ethical development and,

in the author's summary term, "creative interpretation." It follows that when we act as if the dream of rational collective action were possible, we are likely to impoverish our moral sensibilities and our imaginations.

Judith Allen and James Throgmorton's chapters may be read as bolstering that conclusion although this is neither the explicit subject nor the objective of their work. Both authors describe the two paradoxical faces of the relationship between Knowledge and Power. Allen, writing in the spirit of Michel Foucault, presents the apparatus of social science as part of the armor of bureaucratic states: rewarding "confessions" and then probing, counting, and categorizing so that individuals come to define themselves in terms that allow them to be controlled. The construction of a factual knowledge that often seems natural and beyond dispute sustains the power of the regime.

The discursive commitment to the (linked) forms and the substance of this shared knowledge also, however, renders the state vulnerable. Allen demonstrates that when local political groups master the rhetorical forms, reporting on "facts" and speaking in the appropriate dramaturgical style of British public inquiries, they are able to create their own world and draw attention to it, sometimes mounting successful campaigns against the ordinary "masters of the game."

Throgmorton's account of "impeaching research" in a dispute over the control of the electric power system in Chicago starts out as a study in rhetoric—the craft of persuasive speech—rather than of the deep connections between social inquiry and political power. However, in the end, his story and Allen's converge.

Throgmorton recounts a citizen's attempt to persuade the city of Chicago to buy and operate a portion of Commonwealth Edison's facilities. In the course of the debate, a business group released the results of a survey purporting to demonstrate that the purchase would lead to a massive flight of business firms from the city, entailing a substantial loss of jobs. The proponents of acquisition countered by seeking to impeach the research. Throgmorton leads us through the back-and-forth discussion in which both sides "constituted" themselves and their opponents as they argued over the meaning of terms, the interpretation of data, and the appropriate forms and uses of sample surveys. These disciplines probably helped to temper Commonwealth Edison's dominant political influence. It never, however, completely controlled the discussion, nor did it create a common ground for the rival advocates. Science, concludes the author, is one among many rhetorical modes entering into the craft of planning, whereas social surveys are "like all alleged planning facts, inherently tropal and contestable."

Echoing Ferraro, Throgmorton finds a creative challenge in the surrender of "any further pretense to neutrality, objectivity and universal truth."

Howell Baum, whose chapter closes this section, begins with an intellectual history of the critique of reason in the community of theorists, the emergence of a pervasive interest in communicative action, and the study of practitioners—their self-images, practices, and "theories in use." In a powerful conclusion, however, he turns the current fascination with practitioners in on the theorists: like the practitioners about whom they write, the theorists, he argues, practice denial, protecting themselves against the psychic challenge of action in the world and the confrontation with power. In effect, he challenges the authors represented in this volume to reexamine their own practices: "If we accepted our experiences as valid and as kindred with others, we could better understand what practitioners want from a theory of action." Reexamining the practice of theorizing would, he insists, help theorists protect themselves from projecting their own fantasies upon the planners whom they study and advise.

Although he cannot speak for anyone but himself, Bent Flyvbjerg's critical commentary in this section takes up that challenge.

Giovanni Ferraro

15 *Planning as Creative Interpretation*

INTRODUCTION

P lanners traditionally justify their work by referring to those persons whose "reasons" (usually described as "needs," "wants," "rights," or "values") would be neglected or violated as a consequence of private decisions. Throughout the history of planning, the concerns of neighbors, poor people, or future inhabitants have been evoked to legitimate zoning ordinances, welfare policies, investment programs, and other public acts. In all their activities, planners have claimed that they command a broad and comprehensive "rationality" that counteracts egoistic and myopic private decisions—that they can guide public choices toward a collectively satisfying result.

This is the basic meaning of "rationality" in the talk of planners and the scholarly literature of the field: rationality is a criterion for choosing among courses of action and not merely a technical device for analyzing situations. The criterion is grounded in concern with the welfare of collectivities rather than individuals. Rationality is a special form of decision making: a form that seeks technical tools to improve the efficiency of collective choices within an environment in which many interdependent persons often act independently.

The core of this idea of rationality lies in the possibility of comparing resources, results and ends of an action, according to the basic Weberian definition.[1] Subsequent, more sophisticated, enquiries (Brandt 1983; Elster 1983) have not substantially modified the operational principle that rationality in itself cannot be but consequentialist, though not necessarily utilitarian or self-interested (Sen and Williams 1982). This is especially true for a planning discipline that still legitimizes itself as "essentially an economizing approach to the future, constantly appraising trade-offs among alternative investment strategies in search of the desired welfare return" (Webber 1969, 279). So the first question to be answered is: What are the conditions for rationality in planning as collective decision making?

IMPOSSIBILITIES OF COLLECTIVE DECISION

If I refer to social choice theory as an heuristic frame, I can express the core of the problem in a few short statements. Almost all scholars who have discussed collective choice processes from the point of view of psychology, politics, or economics have come to recognize that every collective action faces paradoxes and difficulties that hinder rational collective decisions on the basis of individual rationalities. I do not mean difficulties stemming from cognitive or resource limitations. I mean the reciprocal inconsistency of individual rationalities, however efficient they may be in themselves. These inconsistencies become more severe as rationality is defined more rigorously. The prisoner's dilemma and the impossibility theorem are the paradigmatical and most famous forms of these difficulties. Both examples show that individual rational courses of action rarely lead unequivocally to a satisfying collective outcome in social life. Collective action itself conflicts with individual intentions and the need for social cooperation.

Since every action produces external effects, it is by nature collective and requires a rational collective evaluation. Unfortunately, there are no constitutions that can guarantee that the collective decision will be stable and will respect individual values (Arrow 1951). Neither are there reliable techniques to evaluate objectively the collective repercussions of individual decisions and to compensate those who have been harmed (Samuelson 1954). If this conclusion applies to the highly simplified world of social choice theory, it holds true even more for the real world crowded with actors who have limited access to information and multiple and unstable preferences.

Nevertheless, we go on in spite of this impossibility. We continue to act in a collective context both as individuals and in groups. Our social actions thus are always to a lesser or greater degree in conflict with the demands of rational justification. We can be sure that even our best-intentioned and best-conceived plans can never be rational. Irrationality is a necessity, not simply a deviation from good intentions.

Here my syllogism produces its paradoxical conclusion: in contrast to the standard individualistic approach, where every action is always—by definition— rational (von Mises 1949), I could say that acting *per se* is irrational, that irrationality is a necessary condition for human (social) action. Here the verse from Goethe's *Faust* suggests the first dictum of my argument: "For man must strive, and striving he must err." At the core of this intractable irrationality lies our inability to obtain "true" information about people's aspirations and to arrange them into consistent collective goals. There is no technological fix for this deep political problem. We have no rational drug for that ailment.

Planners often ignore this paradox. They still refer to collective interest and collective rationality not only as abstract principles but as operational criteria for evaluating and deciding. Planners also define their work as the only or the best way in which a community can express its fullest and amplest rationality.[2] Only a claim to a collective rationality as the technique for making decisions according to the collective interest can give a full social legitimation to their work, as "holding on to the idea of public good" (Friedmann 1973, 7).

I believe that planners should avoid using expressions such as collective rationality or public good. Such expressions are meaningful only if one assumes that collective goals are exogenously given. In every planning situation with which I am familiar, however, this assumption has been shown to be erroneous. Even the simplest decision theory poses many different kinds of impossibilities.

a. Optimal collective outcomes cannot be neutrally derived from individual rational choices. Cooperative solutions in prisoner's dilemmas always involve some degree of perceived redistribution of welfare.

b. Relevant individual values cannot be rationally known. If planning primarily responds to external, unwanted, unpredicted outcomes, information about their effects on individual subjects cannot be transmitted or simulated by any market-like, costless, and truthful channel. Planners must resort to voluntary information, by definition always subject to strategic bias.

c. Individual values cannot be rationally aggregated into a collective value system. As the impossibility theorem demonstrates, constitutions for voting do not always guarantee the respect of individual rationality requirements.

d. However defined, collective values, or individual values relating to collective outcomes, cannot even be supposed to exist before the plan, as operational independent preferences. Consider that a rational decision process will, in time, inevitably require the actor to persist in his/her own ends. But collective subjects are intrinsically ephemeral and unstable. The composition of groups and the kinds of preferences both change over time—often in response to the planning process itself and the options it opens (Veyne 1978). Planners are doomed to fail when they seek to ground their decisions on stable, preexisting preferences.

My central argument is simply that planners cannot presuppose the existence of knowable collective values as independent points of reference for the plan. Values cannot be taken as a starting condition and a source of information for the planning process. To the contrary, values often appear to be a product of the planning process itself and cannot offer any preliminary criteria for drafting guidelines or a rational definition or evaluation of the plan's choices. The term "collective rationality" ultimately proves to be self-contradictory and meaningless.

The argument is not trivial. Rational planning may indeed be interpreted as an effort to place planning practices on the stable ground of some objective and scientific definition of a community's values—as an effort to define a "substantial" rationality that finally proves to be inconsistent (Reade 1985). It could be argued that by doing so, planners are building on sand. Here I suggest an additional reason why planning problems are uninevitably "wicked" (Rittel and Webber 1973). A community's goals do not change merely in response to outside stimuli. Communities also experience internal preference changes since every successive collective decision (e.g., every plan) shapes expectations and values: discovering and adding new possibilities of action, diffusing new routes of access to collective assets, creating new collective actors, adapting preferences *ex post facto* to the perceived results of the action. Adaptiveness and self-deception (Elster 1983) being always possible, planners can never be sure that the cyclical process of planning—from goals to approximated targets, back to goals and so on—has any significant functional or progressive direction. By talking about the public interest as a condition for collective rationality, they cannot avoid errors because there is no knowable object: they are finally constrained to talk "about what one cannot talk" (Wittgenstein 1922, §7).

IRRATIONALITY AS CREATIVITY

Nevertheless, planners act. They act even without the possibility of reaching any truth, without any scientific law, empirical rule, or formal technique to legitimize their action. If not rationality, what then justifies the practices of planners?

As they act, planners implicitly reverse the logical and hierarchical sequence of translating abstract values into goals and operational targets. In that common but unacknowledged order, they create goals through temporary and publicly knowable targets and designs. One might suggest that planning paradoxically is not at all a tool for the improvement of rationality in collective decisions but a procedure for "rushing into the gates of language" (Wittgenstein 1965, 12), for making "irrational" collective decisions, escaping from the dilemmas of egoistic rationality, and relaxing the conditions for rational collective choices.

Here acting "irrationally" does not mean acting incoherently, randomly, or chaotically. It means acting to be free from strict rationality prescriptions, not to be "rational fools" (Sen 1977), that is, slaves of one's own untouchable, unreflected individual preferences. Planning is irrational because it is creative, insofar as it influences people's preferences, shapes their perceived needs and expectations, and finally produces new values. In fact, planning can be said to:

a.   supply technical consistency schemes, through which people can reflect about their own preferences by evaluating the collective effects of pursuing their own individual interests;

b.   suggest ethical agendas of social priorities, where people can compare each other's expected welfare levels;

c.   show alternatives and styles of life that were previously unknown and unthinkable and create new needs and values.

Irrationality as creativity is even more evident if we consider planning action over time. Of course, the authors of every plan hope that it will persist and that it will both serve and survive the preferences and needs of future generations. Even in the absence of rational techniques for *forecasting* future preference systems, planners *act* on them. Not only do planners shape their values *ex post facto*, praising conditions that cannot be altered, each planning alternative will produce a set of future people (Parfit 1984) different from other sets. Planners thus produce not only the actual planning choices but also the future subjects who will evaluate them. Each plan produces its unique evaluators and corresponding rationalities. This is why planners, when discussing choices for the future, necessarily fall into irrational discourses—forced to talk of what they could not talk of, and to do what they could not do.[3]

"Special"—that is to say, intellectually suspect but practically necessary— thinking techniques help in these "irrational" but inescapable tasks. For instance, while designing alternative future scenarios, planners act as if they were inhabitants and evaluators, sharing their relative welfare levels. This is, of course, an impossibility. They cannot be eternal and ubiquitous, living in the skin of every possible person. With similar audacity, planners, who have no way of knowing the needs and preferences of the future inhabitants of their plans, will that these inhabitants have positive rights and desires. By doing this, planners necessarily make impossible interpersonal comparisons of welfare among unborn generations.

Planning is thus much more than a calculation of future benefits. It ultimately is an "irrational" attempt to fulfill, in the course of time, the image of future inhabitants created by the plan itself. It is not only the "art of the possible" (Forester 1989, 16) but the "art of the impossible." Planners persuade people to choose accessible courses of action by suggesting and discussing inaccessible (i.e., rationally irrelevant) alternatives.

Whichever way they turn, planners cannot avoid the traps of irrationality. Their action cannot but be arbitrary and risky. Nevertheless, it can in some way be justified. Here again, Goethe's *Faust* suggests a motto: "For he whose striving never ceases / Is ours for his redeeming." Planners cannot expect redemption to come from some adjectives appended to the word "rationality," for instance "new," "expanded," "existential," "narrative," and the like (Friedmann 1989; Goldberg 1985; Throgmorton 1992; Weaver et al. 1985). Rather, it comes from recognizing arbitrariness as a condition for the creation of new collective values and reasons for action. A century ago, the German philosopher Friedrich Nietzsche suggested that errors are sometimes a condition of life (Nietzsche 1882, §121) and that truth itself is a useful error (Nietzsche 1906, §493) that enables people to talk to each other, to know each other and to act (Nietzsche 1878, II, §107).[4]

In this way, we can escape a cul-de-sac in our search for rationality and address a different question: what does creativity mean in planning? Recall that error in planning fundamentally lies in misunderstanding people's values and aspirations, and that, in the words of the German philosopher Friedrich Schleiermacher, "Where there is misunderstanding, there is hermeneutic" (Ricoeur 1986, 75). This suggests that creativity in planning means the ability to interpret people's values and aspirations. This is what planners actually do. They approach social action, as constituted of discourses, behaviors, objects, as a collective text to be understood. The meaning of the text lies in the intentions of the individual actors producing it.

But social actions face the planner as an object, as a "chose du text" (Ricoeur 1986, 161), separated from their subjective authors.[5] Understanding action also means recognizing individuals' intentions and attributing individuals' responsibilities within a network of intentional and unintentional relations. In this historical science, no predetermined results can be reached through perfect knowledge, independent of the subjectivity of the interpreter (Gadamer 1960).

This conclusion is consistent with collective choice paradoxes that remind us that there are no impersonal ways for filtering and linking the words of individuals in a uniquely coherent discourse. This is why the hermeneutic of planning is explicitly creative, transforming both the text and its interpreter (Eliade 1971). While interpreting people's action, planners engage their own hermeneutic prejudices. Paradoxically, without a biased way of reading, we would be unable to communicate at all. While producing plans, planners shape a community's jumbled and protean values into an orderly hierarchy of collective goals that are conventionally and temporarily accepted. The plan as text is presented to the public to be read and interpreted over and over again in a "conversational process of making sense together" (Forester 1989, 120). The conversation is doomed to remain uncertain and ambiguous. No ultimate truths are revealed: only needs and goals that are continually reinterpreted and reshaped.

Truth is inaccessible—but happily it is unnecessary. In the crowded field of a pluralistic society, we always act under conditions of "radical" uncertainty (Langlois 1986), unable to generate stable and consistent reciprocal expectations. We plan to reduce our uncertainty and to tame the Hobbesian "state of war." Planning creates a sense of security by making sense of collective action, producing a set of consistent beliefs and needs.[6] The players in the planning game are persuaded to move their pieces (and to measure winnings and losses) within new scenarios. Values, after all, are just ways of scoring.

Interpretation as persuasion and reciprocal strategic reassurance is the proper job for planners. Interpretative planning aims at producing certainties for action much more than at revealing truths. This opposition recalls a wide philosophical reflection opposing *veritas* to *certituto*, starting with Plato, through Augustinus and successive scholastic debates, to Vico[7], and to the modern well-known distinction between logic and rhetoric (Perelman and Olbrechts-Tyteca 1958; Barthes 1970). Logic is defined as the science of demonstrating the rationality of propositions by investigating abstract truths or empirical evidences; rhetoric, a technique for producing persuasive local certainties. In the planning domain, "logic" means the capacity to derive consistent targets from a predefined value system; rhetoric is the ability to persuade people to act according to new values suggested by the planner as a public speaker. In a world of radical uncertainty, planners as collective actors do not make exceptions. Since usable information about people's "real" values and welfare is unattainable, planners cannot account for all external collective effects and are constrained to approach present states as if they were Pareto-optimal. Of course, they are not. But they are strategically represented as such by the inhabitants within the bargaining game of the plan (Ferraro 1990). Planners, therefore, can never demonstrate that the states they propose are rationally preferable to the present ones. Rather, they must resort to rhetoric to persuade actors to change their point of view about the game and to allocate their resources in support of some conventional and provisional definition of collective interest. Here rhetoric has a direct influence on the construction of the plan and its choices and is not merely a literary language of presentation.[8] Plans are rhetorical constructions in that their logic proceeds by enthymemes: incomplete approximate syllogisms based on probabilistic commonsense premises that the citizen-readers are invited to complete with their local knowledge (Aristotle, as re-read by Barthes 1970; and Colli 1975). By doing this, planners build not only their professional language of principles and techniques but also a common language to be shared with people. It is only within this language, where projects and designs are reduced to figures of speech, that "rationality" and its inventory of "laws" can finally work as an inexhaustible tank of *topoi*—from which planners can derive arguments to talk to people and to make them believe in arbitrary cooperative scenarios.

Planning rhetoric addresses mainly the future. Producing a plan means presenting a future world as a "common world" (Arendt 1958) populated by future citizens whose preferences, touted as rights, could be shared by contemporaries and could "act back" as meta-preferences (Sen 1977) on their present behaviors. This common world of the future does not provide operational guidance for action, only a scenario within which we may now begin to plan for the future.[9] Here the vicious circle of forecasting techniques becomes justified as an hermeneutic circle—where the arbitrarily chosen rights for future people "act back" on people of today, who can reflect on their own preferences and responsibilities, as in a mirror, and then evaluate and confirm planning choices, and so on, in an endless sequence. Planning tries to translate self-centered, unreflected preferences into negotiable aspirations that allow the game of reciprocal interpretation to continue. Persuasive communication about the future is also the only area where a definition of "collective interest" can be meaningful: as a reminder of moral responsibilities toward people who are underrepresented within the game, and as a conventional and provisional collective target intended to reassure people and to mobilize material and immaterial resources along a time path. But again, since nothing can be said about the direction of this path, this pragmatic belief about collective interest cannot be judged in itself.[10]

ETHICAL REQUIREMENTS AND GOOD MANNERS FOR PLANNERS

A theory of planning based on such premises is possible. Unfortunately, its propositions are mainly negative. It is impossible to derive from it positive and univocal prescriptions. Paradoxically, the thinness of the theory may strengthen the current deep division between theorists and practitioners (Beauregard 1991). Unable to devise a compelling rational method, contemporary theorists largely adopt the styles of micro-ethnographers (Forester 1992), observing planners from the outside, or of literary critics (Mandelbaum 1990) reading plans without explicit prescriptive ambitions.

It may appear that I have left planners to face two dangerous temptations without a compelling alternative to bolster themselves against the Siren's call. Paralyzed by impossibilities, they may renounce choice and pretend that they are neutral advisers interested only in ends, not means. Alternatively, emboldened by creativity, they may attempt to enhance their own images and goals by wrapping themselves in the mantle of a specious, but prestigious, rationality they cannot justify.

There are, I believe, standards planners may adopt to avoid these temptations. It is still possible to define criteria for "better interpretations" as "better conversations" with people. Of course, theory cannot produce technical "instructions" (von Wright 1963) since the relation between text and meaning in interpretation is no more certain than the relation between result and intention in action. There is, however, more to making a plan than the production of optimal solutions within objectively described systems. Plan making basically means speaking with different groups of individuals whose actions can be understood only on the basis of their goals. When they enter the planning arena, planners start their interpretative work with a set of prejudices, embodied in their knowledge of the language. They must submit projects, programs, and policies for discussion, determining focus, shaping perceptions, and deciding among alternatives. The standards that guide professionals in this work of communication are at the core of what I mean by "planning ethics."

Practitioners face moral risks. Risk is an inherent part of planning because of its logical impossibility. Some risks arise from people with whom they work. They can be tempted into convenient deceptions and seduced by power. They can be intimidated and fired. They need not, however, be reduced to silence. Theorists can help practitioners by bolstering their ethical commitments to "good conversations" and to the "manners" that sustain communication. Planners need a philology to inspire their attitude and style as interpreters of the collective text, and a rhetoric that tells the interpreter how to talk with various publics. This is why an appeal to the hermeneutic practical tradition is justified—to help planners become conscious of their prejudices and to manage their responsibilities. Planning hermeneutics *is* rhetoric in that it is an interpretation of future values to be shaped by the interpretation itself. I advance two possible standards:

1. The interpretation must be based on the "text" itself and use all its elements. This kind of "tangram rule" it not trivial; it binds the interpreter to recognize the structure of the situation as a circle of the parts and the whole (Ricoeur 1986) and to refer to the text as a publicly knowable document;

2. The interpretation must produce a revision of the set of prejudices of the interpreters as both a critique of the *auctoritas* the planner refers to as a key for understanding (Gadamer 1960) and a collective reappraisal of past plans as hermeneutic texts exposed in their turn, in time, to the interpretation of people implementing them.

Both examples refer to the basic principle of the hermeneutic circle, as a relation between the parts and the whole of the text and between the interpreter, the text, and the public: an endless relation producing meanings to be subjected to new interpretations. This principle is much more than a simple methodological prescription. It defines the person as a projecting being whose relation with the structure of the world is a "totality of meanings" (Heidegger 1927) to be deciphered by the action. It reminds planners that every new interpretation and every new plan is a test of their intentions, knowledge, and techniques.

In a society of freely intentional individuals, planners will pass that test only if they meet morally acceptable criteria. Again, I give only two examples:

1. *Listening to each other.* The ability to persuade depends upon attention to the aspirations and plans of those with whom we are engaged.

2. *Dialogue as a value in itself.* Good conversations, by definition, do not end with any definitively established result. They are good in that they produce new conversations where an increasing number of interlocutors have the possibility of entering the circle with a chance for winning the day and expressing themselves fully as human beings and as members of a community (Arendt 1969).

In short, persuasive planners do not need rational instructions. They need a "book of good manners" that teaches them how to speak with people, encourage them to enter into a dialogue, and to transform non-cooperative into cooperative games that will allow them to go on talking. "Good manners" may require stability and consistency of language, sharing information about the outer world, and ensuring that the inner workings of the planning process are transparent. Good manners cannot guarantee that the planner's work will be either more rational or more democratic, but they can make choices more comprehensible and help the planner to establish common meanings and reciprocally consistent expectations with the community. Good manners as persuasive philology based on patience (Nietzsche 1888, §52) and on the ability to listen are the only way in which planning conversations that are otherwise threatened by impossibility can proceed. Good manners, finally, meet the basic ethical requirement for hermeneutics as posited by the German thinker Wilhelm Dilthey, which can serve as a basic rule for planning as well: Individuals can understand others only on the basis of some sympathy or recognized similarity as intentionally acting beings (Dilthey 1900).

Here the circle of the argument closes. Sympathy as an irrational, not instrumental, sentiment is also, I believe, the only way by which we can hope to perform our responsibilities toward future people. Plans are endless—risky—interpretations. If planners want to face the challenge of the environmental quality of future life, they cannot derive operational constraints for present actions only from the consideration of objective parameters but rather from the qualitative standards they decide to attribute as rights to future inhabitants and from the range of possible options they decide to keep open to them. Rational investigations of the world cannot suggest unequivocal criteria for action. Since the degree of reversibility of the transformations and the rate of waste of natural resources is not rationally and unambiguously definable, and since there is no possibility of abstractly and uncontroversially deriving rights for future generations, an arbitrary and risky choice regarding our sentiments toward future generations is more and more explicitly required.

Acknowledgments

Originally presented to the Joint ACSP and AESOP International Congress, Oxford, July 1991, under the title "Irrationality in Planning." I am indebted to Pierluigi Crosta, John Forester, Seymour Mandelbaum, Luigi Mazza, and Luciano Vettoretto for many criticisms and suggestions.

Notes

1. "A person acts rationally (when) he rationally assesses means in relations to ends, ends in relation to secondary consequences, and finally the various possible ends in relation to each other" (Weber 1922, I, 1, §2). It is impossible to describe here the evolution of this idea, but it could be shown that it is a generalization of the behavior of the neoclassical *homo oeconomicus*, based on "the measurements of needs and goods" and looking for an "equilibrium between requirements and disposable goods" (Menger 1871, III, §4). Still more deeply, it is rooted in the very foundations of the individualistic approach to the analysis of societies, for instance in Hobbes, where "*ratiocinatio is computatio*" (Hobbes 1655, I, §2).

2. "To serve the public interest" is the "simplistic" (Lucy 1988, 147) first ethical principle of the American Planning Association. A less naive approach, though still optimistic about the possibility of defining public interest as a criterion for action, is in Klosterman (1980). "Public interest" is, of course, susceptible to divergent interpretations. For instance: "The supreme planning agency would act as the guardian of the rationality of the process by which variety is articulated and choices are made" (Faludi 1973, 294); or "Planning is concerned with making decisions and informing actions in ways that are socially rational" (Friedmann 1987, p. 47); or "Planners can indeed work to serve those most in need" (Krumholz and Forester 1990, xv).

3. "We can affect the identities of future people, or *who* the people are who will later live" (Parfit 1984, p. 355).

4. Many authors, from Lösch's (1940) "finiteness" and choosing "with their fingers crossed" to Hirschman's (1967) "hiding hand," have stressed that myopia, errors, and chance are unavoidably connected with behavior in space and, what is more, that they can help actors to make decisions under conditions of uncertainty.

5. "Action is a social phenomenon, not only because it is the product of many actors, so that the role of each cannot be separated from the other's, but also because our actions escape from us and have effects we did not intend" (Ricoeur 1986, 187).

6. Here, again, Nietzsche and William James, not unexpectedly, meet, because if on one side "indeed there are no facts but only interpretations" (Nietzsche 1906, §481), on the other possible alternative worlds can be made true and needs can be fulfilled by trust (James 1897, 59).

7. *"Gli uomini che non sanno il vero delle cose procurano d'attenersi al certo, perché, non potendo soddisfar l'intelletto con la scienze, almeno la volontà riposi sulla coscienza"* (Vico 1744, §137).

8. I use the word "rhetoric" in a slightly different sense than the social sciences have been doing in recent years, for instance in McCloskey (1985). Indeed, I am not interested here in planners' vocabulary within their academic discussion but mainly in planners' language in interacting with people and shaping their values. From my point of view, rhetoric is much more than a literary device intended for *verba colorare* in its medieval definitions (Curtius 1948); it involves the structure of the discourse *(inventio)*, not only its presentation *(elocutio)*. It is closer to the ancient meaning, a way of structuring discourse to produce consent about uncertain matters. Planners discovering that samples are synecdoches and models are metaphors reminds one of M. Jourdain discovering that he is speaking *prose.*

9. Even if a project is not realized, its function is more one of showing in concrete language new possibilities of life and values, and collecting responses to it, rather than one of organizing resources into rationally evaluable paths of action.

10. This means that we cannot ask planners to be "progressive" as Forester (1989) does, since individuals' subjective perception of social equilibria as Pareto-optimal leaves no room for defining unnecessary misinformation and ideal conditions of speech.

REFERENCES

Arendt, H. 1958. *The human condition.* Chicago: University of Chicago Press.

_____. 1969. *Crises of the republic.* New York: Harcourt Brace Jovanovich.

Arrow, K. J. 1951. *Social choices and individual values.* New York: Wiley.

Barthes, R. 1970. L'ancienne rethorique. *Communications* 16.

Beauregard, R. A. 1991. Without a net: modernist planning and the postmodern abyss. *Journal of Planning Education and Research* 10: 189–94.

Brandt, R. B. 1983. The concept of rational action. *Social Theory and Practice* 9: 143-64.

Colli, G. 1975. *La nascita della filosofia.* Milano: Adelphi.

Curtius, E. R. 1948. *Europäische Literatur im lateinischen Mittelalter.* Bern: A. Franke, Ag.

Dilthey, W. 1900. *Die Entstehung der Hermeneutik.*

Eliade, M. 1971. *La nostalgie des origines.* Paris: Gallimard.

Elster, J. 1983. *Sour grapes: studies in the subversion of rationality.* Cambridge: Maison des Sciences de l'Homme and Cambridge University Press.

Faludi, A. 1973. *Planning theory.* Oxford: Pergamon Press.

Ferraro, G. 1990. *La città nell' incertezza e la retorica del piano.* Milano: Franco Angeli.

Forester, J. 1989. *Planning in the face of power.* Berkeley: University of California Press.

_____. 1992. Critical ethnography: on fieldwork the Habermasian way. In M. Alvesson and H. Wilmett, eds. *Critical management studies.* Newbury Park, CA: Sage.

Friedmann, J. 1973. The public interest and community participation: toward a reconstruction of public philosophy. *Journal of the American Planning Association* 39: 2–7.

_____. 1987. *Planning in the public domain: from knowledge to action.* Princeton, NJ: Princeton University Press.

_____. 1989. The dialectic of reason. *International Journal of Urban and Regional Research* 13: 217–36.

Gadamer, H. G. 1960. *Wahrheit und Methode.* Tübingen: J.C.B. Mohr.

Goldberg, M. A. 1985. The "irrationality" of rational planning: exploring broader bases for planning and public decision making. In M. J. Breheny and A. J. Hooper, eds. *Rationality in planning: critical essays on the role of rationality in urban and regional planning.* London: Pion.

Heidegger, M. 1927. *Sein und Zeit.* Halle: Jahrbuch für Philosophie und phänomenologische Forschung.

Hirschman, A. O. 1967. *Development projects observed.* Washington: The Brookings Institution.

Hobbes, T. 1655. *De Corpore.*

James, W. 1887. *The will to believe.* New York: Longman, Green and Co.

Klosterman, R. E. 1980. A public interest criterion. *Journal of the American Planning Association* 46: 323–33.

Krumholz, N., and J. Forester. 1990. *Making equity planning work: leadership in the public sector.* Philadelphia: Temple University Press.

Langlois, R. N. 1986. *Economics as a process.* Cambridge: Cambridge University Press.

Lösch, A. 1940. *Die räumliche Ordnung der Wirtschaft.* Jena: Fischer.

Lucy, W. H. 1988. APA's ethical principles include simplistic planning theories. *Journal of the American Planning Association* 54: 147–49.

Mandelbaum, S. 1980. Reading plans. *Journal of the American Planning Association* 56: 350–56.

McCloskey, D. M. 1985. *The rhetoric of economics*. Madison, WI: University of Wisconsin, Board of Regents.

Menger, C. 1871. *Grundsätze der Volkswirtschaftslehre*.

Mises, L., von. 1949. *Human action: a treatise on economics*. London: Hodge.

Mumford, L. 1961. *The city in history*. New York: Harcourt, Brace & Co.

Nietzsche, F. 1878. *Menschliches, Allzumenschliches*.

_____. 1882. *Die fröhliche Wissenschaft*.

_____. 1888. *Der Antichrist*.

_____. 1906. *Der Wille zur Macht. Versuch einer Umwerthung aller Werthe*. Leipzig: Naumann.

Parfit, D. 1984. *Reasons and persons*. London: Oxford University Press.

Perelman, C., and Olbrechts-Tyteca, L. 1958. *Traité de l'argumentation*. Paris: PUF.

Reade E. 1985. An analysis of the use of the concept of rationality in the literature of planning. In M. J. Breheny and A. J. Hooper, eds. *Rationality in planning: critical essays on the role of rationality in urban and regional planning*. London: Pion.

Ricoeur, P. 1986. *Du texte à l'action. Essais d'herméneutique II*. Paris: Editions du Seuil.

Rittel, H. W., and M. M. Webber. 1973. Dilemmas in a general theory of planning. *Policy Science* 4: 155–69.

Samuelson, P. A. 1954. The pure theory of public expenditure. *The Review of Economics and Statistics* 36: 387–89.

Sen, A. 1977. Rational fools: a critique of the behavioural foundation of economic theory. *Philosophy and Public Affairs* 6: 317–44.

_____, and B. Williams. 1982. *Utilitarianism and beyond*. Paris: Maison des Sciences de l'Homme.

Throgmorton, J. 1992. Planning as persuasive storytelling about the future: the case of electric power rate settlement in Illinois. *Journal of Planning Education and Research* 12: 17–31.

Veyne, P. 1978. *Le pain et le cirque*. Paris: Seuil.

Vico, G. 1744. *La scienza nuova*.

Weaver, C., J. Jessop, and V. Das. 1985. Rationality in the public interest: notes toward a new synthesis. In M. J. Breheny and A. J. Hooper, eds., *Rationality in planning: critical essays on the role of rationality in urban and regional planning*. London: Pion.

Webber, M. M. 1969. Planning in an environment of change: II. Permissive planning. *Town Planning Review* 39: 277–95.

Weber, M. 1922. *Wirtschaft und Gesellschaft*. Tübingen: Mohr.

Wittgenstein, L. 1922. *Tractatus logico-philosophicus*. London: Kegan Paul, Trench, Trubner & Co.

_____. 1965. A lecture on ethics. *The Philosophical Review* 74: 3–12.

Wright, G. H. von. 1963. *Norm and action: a logical enquiry*. London: Routledge & Kegan Paul.

Judith Allen

16 Our Town: Foucault and Knowledge-based Politics in London

INTRODUCTION

E veryday, in myriad ways, the modern European state invites its citizens to subject themselves to its administrative power. There is virtually no activity in daily life that is not touched by the state's constant requests for information. In subjecting themselves to the routines of state administrative power, modern citizens soon grow accustomed to defining themselves within the categories the state uses to regulate them and their relations with each other. Each citizen's sense of her/himself as a unique individual comes, imperceptibly, to be shaped by the methods and techniques the state uses to shape its administration of the social body as a whole and the social bodies within that whole (Foucault 1965, 1973, 1975a, 1975b).

The state's power over its citizens, and its citizens' power over it, come to rest on the knowledge each provides to the other, rather than on superior force or moral hierarchy. Most of the time, in most places, this reciprocal power/knowledge relationship is taken for granted, routinized, accepted without question.

But now and then, here and there, these relationships are questioned. Citizens reserve the right to define themselves as they see themselves, to contest the definitions of themselves inherent in state administration, to challenge the practices and discourses of that administration, and to create new visions of what it means to be a citizen, an individual, an active subject. Sometimes these challenges are small, localized, specialized. Sometimes they mobilize large groups in new and changing perceptions of themselves (Foucault 1982).

If participation is the everyday activity of knowledge exchange between the state and its citizens, organizing and campaigning activities challenge the nature of the discourses and practices that underlie participation. These activities are based on the self-defined identities of its subjects, rather than those arising from subjection to administrative methods of exercising power. Campaigning and organizing seek to alter the relations between state and citizen or to mitigate the effects of existing relations.

These ideas, drawn from Michel Foucault's work, suggest that people act within and challenge state administrative frameworks in planning, housing, education, health services, and the like, not because they are committed to these practices, but because they have quite different objectives related to both their sense of themselves as subjects and to their refusal to allow themselves to be defined as "other" within a power relationship (Foucault 1982, 1988b, 1988c).

I use Foucault's ideas to tell the story of the Paddington Federation of Tenants and Residents Associations, how it came to define itself while campaigning against the administrative power of central and local governments. I will show how a disparate group of people created a set of relations among themselves and how these relations—and the identity they shaped— supported them in contesting subjection to and subjectification by the modern state.

What is remarkable about the story is the failure of the Thatcherite ideological and administrative project to infect the federation's definition of itself, its work, and its members' sense of the necessity of speaking out collectively against oppression. Thus, the federation stands as an example of the strength of people making their own lives together, reflecting the radical root image of democracy wherever it occurs (Fisher 1984; Forester 1989).

MICHEL FOUCAULT: THE MODERN SUBJECT

What does an abstruse, modern French philosopher have to offer in telling the story of the Paddington Federation?

Commenting on the French Revolution, the German philosopher Immanuel Kant remarked that the democratic ideal carried within it a new conceptualization of what it meant to be an "individual." Most subsequent political philosophers have, however, focused on "citizens"—and their relations to the state—rather than "individuals." The concept of the individual and the representation of the ways in which individuals relate to one another has been neglected except, perhaps, as those notions have been necessary to understand the expansion of civil administration in policing social relations (Foucault 1979, 1978b).

Over a lifetime's work, Foucault inverted and subverted this conceptualization of political philosophy, delineating a new concept of the individual focused on a dual concept of "subjectivity," as that which gives each of us a sense of uniqueness as a subject and as that which simultaneously provides the basis of the individual's subjection (Foucault 1978c, Wood 1985).

In order to develop this concept of the individual, Foucault radically reformulated concepts of power. Power, for Foucault, is not something that flows from the "center" to the "peripheries" of society, as in traditional juridical concepts of the nature of the state. Rather, power "circulates" through individuals and links them together in a net or web of relationships (Foucault 1976). To understand power, it is necessary to study the methods and techniques through which individuals seek to control each other. Power is what happens within a relationship in which each party has options, including critically the choice to leave the relationship altogether (Foucault 1982). Relationships between individuals are formed within practices that define, mark, measure, and identify them. These practices are institutionalized in knowledge and discourses the legitimize them (Foucault 1973, 1975a, 1978a).

Tracing out the ways in which knowledge and power are connected through the practices and discourses of specific institutions is crucial to understanding the nature of modern European societies. It is also crucial to understanding how refusing to have one's subjectivity defined by these forms of knowledge creates the space and means for contesting the power of the modern state. Thus, resistance is born in the interplay between subjectivity and subjection. To refuse to be subjected is to insist on one's own subjectivity. To define one's own subjectivity is to refuse subjection (Foucault 1982, Wood 1985, Weeks 1989).

Nevertheless, Foucault rejects any kind of individualistic essentialism as the basis for defining subjectivity. We cannot be ourselves in a free space outside social orders. Rather, he sees complex modern societies as offering a diversity of discourses and practices, organized within broad blocks or disciplines, upon which individuals can draw. We define and know "ourselves" only within these diverse discourses and practices (Foucault 1978a).

To develop the significance of this method of exercising power by defining, measuring, and marking out individuals, Foucault needed a complementary conception of the state and its power. In his view, the modern state is characterized by its concerns with both the whole of the social body and with the bodies of the individuals it governs. It "polices" the social body through administrative means rather than force as in the medieval state, or through the use of "confession" as in Christian ecclesiastical institutions (Foucault 1975b, 1978a, 1988a). The administrative means the modern state uses to govern are based on distinguishing individuals from each other, categorizing them, and intervening in their lives in ways based on these categorizations. In order to do this, the state must acquire detailed knowledge of individuals, which it gathers by encouraging them to report their own characteristics, behaviors, desires, and aspirations. The state has adopted the techniques of "confession" of the Christian church and uses them to constitute its citizens, the individuals it seeks to "govern," whose relationships it seeks to regulate and police (Foucault 1978a, 1988a).

Democracy, within this framework, can best be seen as an incitement to individuals and groups to talk about the ways in which the state's administrative mechanisms, techniques, methods affect them. As the modern state has come to penetrate more and more areas of social and individual life, the tendency within modern democracy is for individuals and groups to define themselves more and more in relation to the state's institutional structures and activities, whether as clients or consumers of particular services, members of pressure groups or political parties, taxpayers, state employees, welfare recipients, and so on (Foucault 1978a, 1982).

This verbal flood has paradoxical consequences. Through verbalization, the individual comes to know her/himself as a unique individual. It is through the processes of self-knowledge—listening to oneself talk—that the individual is able to resist the state's categories. Through the techniques of verbalization, the individual can form her/his own subjectivity in ways that refuse the forms of subjection inherent in the administrative activities of the modern democratic state (Foucault 1988a, 1988b, 1988c).

The assertion of difference is played out on a complex, contested terrain; within a constantly shifting social, economic, and political environment. Within the complex institutional structure of the state, forms of subjection in one arena provide the basis for resistance in others, as when "democratic" practices incite individuals to refuse the methods and techniques of administrative control; when the administrative responsibilities of one part of the state institutional structure conflict with another; when "democratic" practices at different levels point in different directions. Beyond these "internal" complexities, individuals can draw on the subjectivities characterizing other institutional complexes as bases of resistance, such as family, school, religion, occupation, locality. Finally individuals can combine to create new subjectivities, new institutions, new discourses and practices, running with or against preexisting subjectivities, institutions, discourses, and practices (Foucault 1982; Weeks 1989).

There is no center from which power emanates in Foucault's image of social structure, only a complex web or net within which a multiplicity of actors seek to exercise power over each other, interacting, intersecting, altering their purposes, adapting and adopting each other's ideas and practices, and changing themselves and society as a consequence (Foucault 1976; Cousins and Hussain 1984). Nevertheless, this social web is loosely structured into "disciplines" within which power and knowledge are linked through specific practices and discourses, methods and techniques of exercising power. Most crucially for Foucault's epistemologically based concept of social structure, each of these disciplines contains an "ensemble of rules" as to what constitutes "truth." What is considered "true knowledge" within one discipline may well be regarded as irrelevant or false within another discipline (Foucault 1988b, 1988a).

KNOWLEDGE AND CAMPAIGNING: THE PADDINGTON FEDERATION OF TENANTS AND RESIDENTS ASSOCIATIONS

How do Foucault's ideas apply to the experience of a group of tenants associations in Central London between 1974 and 1990? The Paddington Federation was formed in 1974 as an umbrella group for tenants and residents associations throughout the northwest quadrant of the London Borough of the City of Westminster. Its boundaries were those of the Metropolitan Borough of Paddington, one of three metropolitan boroughs that were joined together to become the City of Westminster after local government reorganization in 1964. (The City of Westminster is one of thirty-two London Boroughs that make up the administrative area bounded by the Greater London Council. The Cities of Westminster and London constitute the central core of London.)

Initially, the federation's membership spanned both public and private tenants, as well as owner-occupiers. In 1980, however, local authority tenants formed a separate organization to take advantage of the requirement within the 1980 Housing Act that local authorities must consult their own tenants on a range of policy matters. Thus, the Federation came to represent only private tenants and owner-occupiers. Throughout its life, the Federation sustained a membership of approximately forty groups from the entire area. The Federation sought to represent tenants and residents groups on issues of common concern. These ranged from helping to form tenants associations, supporting individual tenants in negotiations with their landlord, and campaigning around local housing issues to give voice to member associations and to the interests of private tenants more generally.

The individuals associated with the Federation can roughly be divided into four groups: 1. the representatives, "activist" tenants from member associations, largely self-selected with the tacit or explicit endorsement of their associations; 2. tenants from properties where there was no formal tenants association, "individuals" who had been helped by the Federation and who wished to return their appreciation; 3. community workers from other organizations in Paddington, who saw participation in the Federation as part of their job; and 4. the Federation's own workers. Not surprisingly for a socially mixed area, the people involved in the Federation spanned an immense range of class, age, political experience, and affiliation.

The ethos which united these disparate individuals was based on four shared understandings: 1. the power relationship between landlord and tenant is unequal; 2. acting together is more effective than acting individually; 3. all should share a deep concern for the misfortunes any individual might face; and 4. all issues should be discussed together until a common basis for action is found within which each participant can see her/himself (Allen 1986). Most of the discussions that led to this shared understanding took place in the Federation's monthly general meetings, a forum to which everyone who was involved in the Federation could contribute, sharing their experiences, discussing how to proceed together, and supporting each other.

For many, these meetings were as important as a social event as a working meeting. Some members would speak more than others, yet the "listeners" came to have a unique significance for the Federation: as the quiet observers that every political speaker needs at their elbow, as repositories of moral strength, as keen judges of character, and as symbols of those whom the Federation was aiming to help. Their careful listening practices taught the speakers both how to speak and how to listen, thereby contributing to the development of a unique form of discourse within the Federation. Thus, the Federation developed a distinctive set of internal relationships and style of working, which gave it unique stability and cohesion within a highly turbulent, external political environment.

The Federation defined itself in a series of pamphlets and campaigns. It repeatedly sought to present "factual" information in a way that would expose the effects of the state's administrative activities on the lives of tenants and residents in Paddington. My purpose in describing this activity is to explore how "knowledge-based campaigning" works within a modern democracy; how knowledge can be used within different kinds of power relationships to resist subjection to the practices and discourses of the state and landlords; and how knowledge itself is produced by specific practices and discourses. I treat the Federation's publications and public events as "confessions" articulating the Federation's organizational identity and the shared subjectivity of its members. In summary, this chapter is about how the "writing" and "speaking" practices and discourses within the Federation produced the Federation's subjective identity.

This permits me to explore three specific issues Foucault poses about understanding knowledge-based campaigning in a specific context: 1. the extent to which the Federation's self-definition was shaped by the practices and discourses of local government and by the relations among its members—what they knew and how they spoke; 2. the way in which the effects of the Federation's activities were sometimes unpredictable, reflecting the complex webs of relationships that characterize modern democracies; and 3. the ways in which different practices and discourses implicitly define what constitutes "truth" in relationship to knowledge.

SPEAKING OUT: FINDING A VOICE

The Federation engaged in three important identity-defining campaigns: "Home Truths" in 1977, the District Plan Inquiry in 1980, and "Taken for Granted" between 1980 and 1984. All three of these campaigns focused on the City of Westminster. Campaigns with other groups in Paddington and throughout London only built on and extended this identity.

1. Home Truths

In 1974, Paddington was fertile ground for organizing tenants. Its rental housing stock was large, run-down, and overcrowded. The Paddington Federation was created by a group of professional community workers, employed by a number of local organizations, most of which were funded by Westminster City Council as part of its support for community development. The community workers, however, were all strongly inspired by neo-Marxist theory and saw organizing local groups as a form of struggle against the capitalist state (Cockburn 1977).

The Federation's first major campaign publication, "Home Truths: An Investigation into Westminster City Council's Housing Policies," was published in 1977. "Home Truths" established the Federation as a political entity within Westminster City Council housing politics. Nevertheless, the process behind writing the pamphlet and its style did little to challenge the ways in which local government deploys knowledge in support of power.

"Home Truths" was largely written by the group of community workers then supporting the Federation, although it was initiated and supported by an officer at Westminster City Council acting covertly. The liaison with the council officer was kept secret, not only from his employer, but also from the other members of the Federation, reflecting the professional distance between the community workers and the tenants they were organizing, as well as some of the ideological and ethical conflicts of local authority professional officers (Kaufman 1987; Thomas and Healey 1989). The core issue behind the pamphlet was the level of housing capital investment by the City Council. It "played back" to the Council information from its own technical reports, showing how this information could support quite different conclusions. It cited directly the personal experience of tenant members of the Federation but reflected professional stereotypes of that experience. Thus, both the content and the writing process mirrored the professional control over technical information that characterizes political decision-making processes within British local government.

The technical quality of "Home Truths" alone made it difficult for the Council to refute it. However, it was what the Federation did with the report that established its position as a political entity in Westminster. In 1977, the government introduced a national system for controlling public expenditure on housing. Local authorities were asked to submit detailed capital spending plans to the central government, which then allocated national capital spending targets among the authorities (Holmans 1991). In a brilliant tactical move, the Federation submitted an alternative capital spending plan for Westminster based on "Home Truths." This led to a meeting between the Federation (the community workers and two token tenants) and the Labour Housing Minister. As a consequence, the government granted the Conservative City Council permission to spend an extra £1 million on housing. In effect, the conspiratorial aspirations of the community workers were channelled into normal party political networks. The alternative capital spending plan contested neither the right of central government to determine spending limits for local authorities nor the right of local authorities to decide how to spend that money. All it did was argue that more should be spent.

Nevertheless, "Home Truths" did insert the Federation into the housing politics of the City Council at quite a high level of visibility. It built the reputation of the Federation as not just another local pressure group, but as a group with considerable, unusual, and unexpected technical and political skills. Theorists of pluralist politics usually assume that local groups can (or should) only argue about the general objectives municipalities should be pursuing. The monopoly of technical skills and information among their professional workers generally allows councils to play groups off against each other through "technical" considerations (Saunders 1979). "Home Truths" challenged the local authority's monopoly of technical expertise without contesting the general practices and discourses associated with the use of this expertise in local politics. It did nothing to change the relationship between tenant members of the Federation and the power–knowledge processes of local administrators. It simply inserted the community workers as another group of professionals into the existing practices and discourses of local authority administration. It did little to build a subjective identity among tenant members. Instead, and despite tangible results, it simply confirmed their subjection to existing techniques of power by demonstrating their "lack of knowledge."

The District Plan Inquiry

The District Plan Inquiry in 1980 was the key event that shaped the Federation's own identity. Local authority land-use planning documents in Britain are highly formalized. The central government gives clear and strong guidelines about their form and function. Since their main function is to provide a consistent and coherent set of policies to govern applications for new development and/or changing the use of existing properties, plans are structured as a series of separate chapters that lay out the conditions under which development and changes will be permitted.

Plans articulate three different types of power relationships and the planning process contains very clear images of the administrative subjects within it. The heart of any plan is the power relationship between planners granting or refusing planning permission, and developers applying for planning permission. The second power relationship is between the local authority and the population it "governs." In administrative terms, the local authority is responsible for the well-being of all the people who live within its area. However, in a strongly politicized system, this administrative responsibility becomes biased toward those groups that support the ruling party in the local council. There are important contradictions between these two roles, aptly summarized by one Central London activist as "local authorities make policies, local councils make deals." The third power relationship in planning arises from the roles it assigns to individual citizens. They can act only as "objectors" to policies or, if they happen to be adjacent property owners or members of a "recognized" amenity group, to specific planning applications.

The legislation governing planning imposes several participation requirements on local authorities. The last stage of participation is a formal public inquiry, held under the auspices of officials within the central ministry whose function it is to adjudicate conflicts between the local authority and objectors over the content of the plan before it is formally approved by the Secretary of State for the Environment. The problem for the Federation was to break out of these administratively defined roles and to find an idea that would give form and voice to its experiences within a single framework.

When the text of the Draft Plan was circulated for comment, the Federation divided the work of reading it chapter by chapter among its members. However, its organization into separate land use chapters inhibited members from seeing how it related to immediate local housing problems. Then, one member observed that the expansion of hotels in the area seemed to be taking over houses that had previously been let in rooms. This observation allowed the Federation to define the local problem in new terms, that is, to create new planning knowledge based on the idea of "hotelization," defined as the consequence of "creeping conversions," that is, changes in land use without the required planning permission from the local authority. Creeping conversion, in turn, created "quasi-hotels," that is, buildings that were neither fully residential nor fully hotels and so did not fit within the traditional land-use categories. The formal public inquiry process then allowed the Federation to insert this new knowledge into the administrative discourses of planning and to assert the Federation's own subjectivity.

Public inquiries in England are quasi-judicial procedures. To an outsider, they resemble courtroom dramas on television. In preparing for the inquiry, the Federation used this dramatic form to write a play. The script was drafted during a series of meetings in which its members played the roles of "expert witness" and of the examining lawyer. At the first meeting, members described their experiences with hotelization in their own words to the whole group. At the second meeting, other members closely questioned each of the "experts," allowing the group to form a view of how their disparate experiences fitted into the whole. At the final meeting, the "examining lawyer" went through the questions from the previous meeting with the expert witnesses answering, closely observed by all the members to ensure that the answers supported the general line of argument.

The public inquiry went very smoothly, involving well over twenty people in what one of the local authority planners remarked was the "best floor show he had ever seen." In addition to making substantive points about the interaction between housing and tourism, the Federation leaders conveyed three important messages to the local authority as well as to its own members: 1. We seek to make a positive contribution to the governance of Westminster and not simply be carping critics; 2. Each one of us is a person whose life makes sense as a whole and cannot be understood within the administrative categories of planning; 3. We see ourselves as "friends and neighbors who care about each other, no matter how individually disparate you may think we are."

In preparing for the District Plan inquiry, the Federation developed its own discourses and practices, ways of working together, and sets of concepts, which gave it its own identity, formed its own subjectivity. Seeing the inquiry procedures as a part of popular culture subverted the subjectifying experience of participating in the inquiry. By acting on its own terms, the Federation created a new form of knowledge about planning and housing. Finally, the Federation rejected its previous subjectification as a technically sophisticated pressure group within the framework of local authority discourses and practices by presenting tenants as experts within its own practices and discourses. Presenting tenants as experts shaped much of the Federation's later work. The organization's professional members and workers were now cast simply as people skilled in articulating what the experts knew.

The approach to the District Plan inquiry was successful in changing the plan because there was a congruence between the dramatic form used by the Federation and the administrative practices of local authority planning. Without this congruence between subjectification by the local authority and self-defined subjectivity, they could not have influenced one another; without the differences between the two forms, it would not have been possible to change the discussion.

Taken for Granted

After the District Plan inquiry, the Federation turned its attention to how improvement grants to renovate older properties were associated with the harassment of tenants. The 1969 Housing Act had introduced local authority improvement grants. These grants paid a substantial proportion of the costs of improvement and were often concentrated in small action areas. They were intended to make the full renovation of rented property profitable, particularly in areas where rents were insufficient to give an adequate return to landlords. (Grants were also available to owner-occupiers.) The combination of grants and a major house price boom in the early 1970s stimulated gentrification of inner city areas and displacement of poorer populations.

The 1974 Housing Act contained provisions to limit the negative effects of improvement grants. Virtually all private tenants were given security of tenure. In addition, landlords of tenanted properties within the action areas were required to rent the improved property at less than market rents for at least seven years after the works were completed. Local authorities were not obligated to impose these conditions outside the action areas, although in practice virtually all did.

In 1976, Westminster City Council stopped imposing conditions on grants outside the action areas in response to lobbying by the Church Commissioners, who were seeking to gentrify their slum holdings in Paddington. In addition, another type of landlord entered the market in Paddington in the late 1970s. These landlords bought fully tenanted properties and harrassed residents into leaving. Once the buildings were vacant, they were able to apply for grants without being subject to the conditions that would ordinarily apply to occupied buildings.

In 1981, the Federation wrote to senior elected representatives on Westminster City Council, expressing dismay at the scale of harassment in the context of national changes that significantly increased the level and attractiveness of improvement grants. Neither letter was answered. The Federation proceeded to publish one of the letters in the local newspaper. This publicity elicited a response from a senior politician in the newspaper. He stated that conditions on grants were an unnecessary administrative burden on free enterprise and admonished the Federation for seeking "to debate . . . political decisions of the Council" through the local newspaper.

By this time, political control of Westminster's Housing Committee had passed into the hands of the New Urban Right, leading to a new image of the Federation among these councillors. They saw the Federation, somewhat romantically, as an unruly inner city mob and used this image to justify excluding it from local political debate (Young and Kramer 1978). In the early summer of 1981, the Federation met with the chair of the City Council's Private Sector Subcommittee. The Federation's approach to the meeting was simply to affirm an empirical "truth," based on the experience of its members, acting as if the power relationship was simply one between any interest group and an elected councillor with a common interest in good local administration, effectively undermining the Council's attempt to write off the Federation as part of the "loony left."

When the issue came before the Housing Committee, Council officers confirmed that eight of the twenty-two cases of harassment documented by the Federation had been associated with grants and recommended that conditions on grants be reimposed. The Housing Committee made a great show of "compromising" by lowering the amount of money to be paid in grants for landlords who did not wish to accept the conditions. The Federation responded with a pamphlet, "Taken for Granted: Improvement

Grants in Westminster" (1981). It simply recounted the events to date, included the various relevant documents, and asked the next full Council meeting to change the decision of the Housing Committee.

What happened next was totally unexpected. The *Times* published four column inches on its front page, based on the pamphlet, during the Conservative Party conference. The Housing Minister was put under pressure at the conference and, in turn, pressured Conservative councillors in Westminster. The Housing Committee's decision was substantially altered.

In the autumn of 1981, the Federation submitted written evidence to the House of Commons Environment Committee's Inquiry into the Private Rented Housing Sector. The Committee was interested, but its report had very little effect on a Thatcher government committed to freeing private enterprise from the fetters of government regulation (House of Commons, 1982, 1983).

Following the House of Commons inquiry, the Federation tried a different tactic. Each November, local authorities must open their accounts to scrutiny by any elector within their area. From this source, the Federation obtained a list of every improvement grant given in Westminster between 1969 and 1981. Together with the *Sunday Times* Insight Team, the Federation was able to show that in Westminster property renovation was so profitable that there was no need for improvement grants. The Federation then decided to submit a complaint to the district auditor on the legal grounds that the decision to remove conditions on improvement grants was unreasonable; given the knowledge of harassment caused by unconditional improvement grants, no "reasonable" local authority would remove the conditions. The district auditor dismissed the complaint, remarking dryly that "unreasonable" effectively meant "totally loony." Undeterred, the Federation complained again the next year, arguing that the City Council did not monitor whether or not conditions were met. Without monitoring, it could not reclaim grant money when the conditions were broken. Therefore, the City Council was wilfully "losing" money. The complaint was upheld. The subsequent internal audit identified a number of cases of fraud by council officers responsible for administering grants. The Council eventually stopped giving grants altogether outside the small action areas, justifying its decision by referring to central government limits on the level of capital spending against which the grants counted.

Complaining to the district auditor does not provide a basis for asserting a unique subjectivity. Rather, it reinforces the forms of subjection that characterize modern government. Complaints turn on highly technical arguments and occur wholly within the framework of local authority discourses and practices, to which the complainant is subjected. More importantly, the tactic excludes contributions from those who have been directly affected. As a consequence, it could affect the relationships within the Federation in ways that would undermine the subjectivity the Federation had formed for itself, by overvaluing the technical expertise of some of its members and devaluing the significance of the experience of other members. For these reasons, the Federation turned its attention to other equally important local issues after 1984.

After the Greater London Council was abolished in 1986, the Federation received no further funding. Although many groups collapsed at this time (London Voluntary Service Council 1987), the Federation persisted for another four years. It voluntarily dismantled in 1990, because nothing is more painful to activists than enforced passivity. The activists are now all involved in other local organizations. The individual members who sustained the activists are still cared for through the networks of friendship which the Federation established during its life.

Each of the Federation's campaigns had unintended consequences, or rather, consequences that emerged from the social networks of power and knowledge in unexpected ways. The 1988 Housing Act introduced draconian penalties for harassment and illegal eviction, as well as an improved improvement grant system. At the same time, however, it introduced new forms of tenancy that retroactively legalized evasions of the Rent Acts. The concepts of "creeping conversions" and "quasi-hotels" have entered into general planning discourse. In addition, the Federation strongly influenced the planning and housing strategies of the Greater London Council, which still underpin cooperation across the political spectrum of local authorities in London. Beyond this, many of the Federation's ideas have been taken up and used by both campaigning groups and local authorities outside London.

What made all of this work? In the end, it was the relationship between the techniques of debate and the shared subjectivity that grew from those discussions at the Federation meetings. The Federation never defined itself or its members as victims but celebrated the courage and persistence of those who were willing to speak out against state power and the political influence of landlords. This led to discussion and "publication" based on the telling of its members' stories, displaying the Federation's subjective view of itself as "friends and neighbours caring about each other."

CONCLUSIONS

Michel Foucault asked the question, "What does it mean to be an individual?" His answer tells us what it means to be a person located within the social networks of modernity. These networks hold us "in place," subject us to the power of others, and are simultaneously the means through which power flows, articulated by acting as a subject in relationship to others. The social networks of modernity are formed out of relationships that are simultaneously about power and knowledge. They are expressed in the practices and discourses through which individuals seek to exercise power over each other. In this way, Foucault explains how democracy both sustains structures of power and allows for change. The institutional forms of democracy incite confession; they permit individuals to speak to each other, to define themselves as distinctly different from the categories established by administrative power.

Within this framework, specific actors pursue their own programs. However, articulation of social networks throughout society means that what is achieved is most often something different from the initial objectives. Indeterminacy and unforeseen consequences are the result of all action, as ideas circulate through society in unpredictable ways.

Foucault's work, thus, provides a means of analyzing the nature of "knowledge based campaigns." These campaigns use knowledge in two ways: 1. to form relationships within the campaigning group based on distinctive subjectivities; and 2. to subvert the techniques of administrative powers by refusing to act as the kind of subjects they envisage. Such campaigns use the practices and discourses associated with democracy to "speak out," to exploit the divisions within the state's own networks of power, and to alter what happens there by creating new "knowledge" of subjects within the body politic.

Acknowledgments

I would like to thank Pru Posner, Joe Kling, and Bob Fisher for their support and constructive criticism in clarifying the ideas in this chapter.

REFERENCES

Allen, J. 1986. Smoke over the Winter Palace: the politics of resistance and London's community areas. Paper presented at the Conference on Planning Theory in Practice, Politecnico di Torino, Italy.

Allen, J., and L. McDowell. 1989. *Landlords and property: social relations in the private rented sector.* Cambridge: Cambridge University Press.

Cockburn, C. 1977. *The local state.* London: Pluto.

Cousins, M., and A. Hussain. 1984. *Michel Foucault.* Cambridge: Cambridge University Press.

Fisher, R. 1984. *Let the people decide: neighbourhood organizing in America.* Boston: Twayne Publishers.

Forester, J. 1989. *Planning in the face of power.* Berkeley: University of California Press.

Foucault, M. 1965. *Madness and civilization: a history of insanity in the age of reason.* New York: Random House.

_____. 1973. *Birth of the clinic: an archaeology of medical perception.* London: Tavistock.

_____. 1975a. *Discipline and punish: birth of the prison.* London: Allen Lane.

_____. 1975b. Body/power. In C. Gordon, ed., *Michel Foucault: power/knowledge: selected interviews and other writings, 1972–1977.* Hemel Hempstead: Harvester Wheatsheaf.

_____. 1976. Two lectures. In C. Gordon, ed., *Michel Foucault: power/knowledge: selected interviews and other writings, 1972–1977.* Hemel Hempstead: Harvester Wheatsheaf.

_____. 1978a. *The history of sexuality: the will to knowledge.* vol. 1. London: Allen Lane.

_____. 1978b. On power. In L. Kritzman, ed., *Michel Foucault: politics, philosophy and culture: interviews and other writings, 1977–1984.* London: Routledge.

_____. 1978c. The West and the truth of sex. In V. Beechey and J. Donald, eds., *Subjectivity and social relations.* London: Open University Press.

_____. 1979. Politics and reason. In L. Kritzman, ed., *Michel Foucault: politics, philosophy and culture: interviews and other writings, 1977–1984.* London: Routledge.

_____. 1982. The subject and power. *Critical Inquiry* 8: 777–95.

_____. 1988a. Technologies of the self. In L. Martin, ed., *Technologies of the self: a seminar with Michel Foucault.* London: Tavistock.

_____. 1988b. Truth, power, self. In L. Martin, ed., *Technologies of the self: a seminar with Michel Foucault.* London: Tavistock.

_____. 1988c. Political technologies of the self. In L. Martin, ed., *Technologies of the self: a seminar with Michel Foucault.* London: Tavistock.

Holmans, A. 1991. The 1977 national housing policy review in retrospect. *Housing Studies* 6: 206–19.

House of Commons Environment Committee. 1982. *The private rented housing sector.* vol. I: *Report.* vol. II: *Minutes of evidence.* vol. III: *Appendices.* London: Her Majesty's Stationery Office.

_____. 1983. *The private rented housing sector—a report on the memorandum from the Department of the Environment in response to the Committee's first report.* Session 1981-82. London: Her Majesty's Stationery Office.

Kaufman, J. L. 1987. Teaching planning students about strategizing, boundary spanning and ethics: part of the new planning theory. *Journal of Planning Education and Research* 5: 108–15.

London Voluntary Service Council. 1987. After abolition: a report on the impact of abolition of the Metropolitan County Councils and the Greater London Council on the voluntary sector—and the outlook for the future.

Milner Holland. 1965. Report of the Committee on Housing in Greater London, Cmnd. 2605. London: Her Majesty's Stationery Office.

Paddington Federation of Tenants and Residents Associations. 1977. Home truths: an investigation into Westminster City Council's housing policies.

_____. 1981. Taken for granted: improvement grants in Westminster.

Saunders, P. 1979. *Urban politics: a sociological approach.* London: Hutchinson.

Thomas, H., and P. Healey. 1989. Ethics, skills and legitimacy in planning practice in Britain. *Planning Theory Newsletter* 3: 63–5.

Thornley, A. 1991. *Urban planning under Thatcherism: the challenge of the market.* London: Routledge.

Weeks, J. 1989. Uses and abuses of Michel Foucault. In L. Appignanesi, ed., *Ideas from France: the legacy of French theory.* London: Free Association Books.

Wood, N. 1985. Foucault on the history of sexuality: an introduction. In V. Beechey and J. Donald, eds., *Subjectivity and social relations.* London: Open University Press.

Young, K., and J. Kramer. 1978. Local exclusionary policies in Britain: the case of suburban defence in a metropolitan system. In K. Cox, ed., *Urbanisation and conflict in market societies.* London: Methuen.

JAMES A. THROGMORTON

17 "Impeaching" Research: Planning as Persuasive and Constitutive Discourse

INTRODUCTION

Planners, as I have heard them speak, tend to describe rhetoric as "mere words" that simply add gloss to the important stuff, to the objective methods that we use to discover the "facts." On other occasions, they describe rhetoric with suspicion as the use of seductive language to manipulate others into embracing a speaker's preferred values, beliefs, and behaviors. We are not sure, in effect, whether rhetoric is trivial or insidious.

There is a good way to bring together these two definitions. Rather than thinking of rhetoric as gloss or seduction, let us regard it as the study and practice of persuasion, and let us recognize that persuasion is constitutive. Rather than divorcing planning tools from their contexts of application or treating them simply as political ammunition, let us think of surveys, models, and forecasts as rhetorical tropes, as figures of speech and argument that give meaning and power to the larger narratives of which they are a part.

To think of planning in terms of persuasive and constitutive discourse is part of a larger turn toward the importance of language, discourse, and

This chapter is a revised version of my earlier work, "Survey Research as Rhetorical Trope: Electric Power Planning Arguments in Chicago," published in Frank Fischer and John Forester, eds., *The Argumentative Turn in Policy Analysis and Planning* (Durham, NC: Duke University Press, 1993), 117–44; and "Planning as a Rhetorical Activity: Survey Research as a Trope in Arguments About Electric Power Planning in Chicago," *Journal of the American Planning Association* 59 (Summer 1993): 334–46. Permission of the publishers is gratefully acknowledged.

argument in planning thought (e.g., Forester 1989; Goldstein 1987; Healy 1992; Mandelbaum 1990, 1991; Throgmorton 1990). I already presented the details of the rhetorical approach to planning (Throgmorton 1992, 1993) and limit myself here to a brief outline of its major elements.

Drawing on the recent work of Leith and Myerson (1989) and many others, I suggest that an adequately rhetorical approach to planning would emphasize the importance of thinking of surveys and other planning tools as partial efforts to persuade *specific audiences in specific contexts* to accept proposed explanations, embrace inspiring visions, undertake recommended actions, and so on. But it would also acknowledge that such persuasive efforts take place in the context of a flow of utterances, replies, and counter-replies and that each of those utterances and replies is likely to be inter-preted in diverse and often antagonistic ways. Audiences can assign dif-ferent meanings to key terms, fill gaps in the original analysis, and choose to read either with or against the analysis (Fish 1979; Freund 1987; Tompkins 1980).

At the heart of persuasion is the use of *tropes*. These are any literary or rhetorical device—such as metaphor, metonymy, synecdoche, and irony—that involves using words in other than their literal sense (Quinn 1982). As a word, *trope* implies a turn on or toward something, a turn induced by the device itself. When we weave such tropes together into a larger planning narrative, we are engaging in persuasive discourse.

Rhetoric is not, however, simply persuasive. It is also constitutive: to use James Boyd White's (1984, 1985) terms, the ways in which we write and talk shape a planner's character and the community that exists be-tween planners and their audiences. How "we" (as authors) write and talk shapes who "we" (as a community of authors and readers) are and can become. Each time we write or speak, we create "ideal readers or listeners" whom actual readers or listeners—as objects of our planning or even par-ticipants in it—may or may not be, may or may not choose to become. Furthermore, by our choice of how to write and speak, by our choice of tropes, we create images of the kinds of characters we are or want to be-come.

Because rhetoric is constitutive, it connects intimately with narrative. Narratives are crafted stories that establish the context within which tropes are used. Tropes, in turn, lend persuasive power to those larger narratives of which they are a part. Thus, a flow of utterances, replies, and counter-replies can be plotted as a flow of action that can be turned—through the use of particular tropes by particular characters at particular times and places—in a different direction.

To acknowledge that our rhetoric can be both persuasive and con-stitutive should lead us to ask a crucially *ethical* question: what kinds of communities, characters, and cultures do we want to help create? I will argue that we planners should strive, not to speak purely scientifically or purely politically, but to find a persuasive discourse that permits us (and others) to talk coherently about contestable views of what is good, right, and feasible.

With this cursory outline of a rhetorical approach to planning in mind, we can now examine one particular case to see how planning analyses work as rhetorical tropes in planning narratives. The case I have chosen involves the use of survey research in a six-year political conversation about whether the City of Chicago should "take over" part of Commonwealth Edison's (Com Ed's or Edison's) electric power system. Probing deeper into that case, we will observe one survey researcher's effort to persuade a citizens task force that he had produced "accurate" estimates of how Chicago businesses would react to a City "takeover." This lets us turn, in the end, to how a rhetorical approach might improve the theory, pedagogy, and practice of planning.

ELECTRIC POWER PLANNING AND RATEMAKING IN THE CHICAGO AREA, 1985–1991

Com Ed owns and operates the electric power system that serves Chicago and the northern one-third of Illinois. In the early 1970s, the company started the nation's largest nuclear construction program. To the dismay of many, the program proved to be far more expensive and time-consuming than originally planned (Throgmorton 1992).

Edison and its critics explained the delays and overruns in light of two very different stories. Defining themselves as expert managers of an extraordinarily complex enterprise, Edison officials attributed the delays and overruns to inflation and other factors beyond its control, especially excessive government regulation inspired by politically motivated interest groups. Consumer groups told a very different story. In their view, managerial incompetence and profit seeking had caused the delays and overruns. Edison's managers built nuclear power plants that were not needed, made northern Illinois one of the costliest electric power regions in the country, and drove jobs and businesses away.

Mayor Harold Washington of Chicago joined the consumer groups in opposing Edison's rate increases, which he feared would cause jobs and businesses to flee the city. Since the company's franchise was due to expire in 1990, he asked his planning staff to explore the city's energy options.

In November of 1987, a city-sponsored report estimated that Chicago-ans could save $10 billion to $18 billion over a twenty-year period if the city bought and operated a portion of Com Ed's facilities (Beck and Associates 1987). Edison attacked the Beck report vigorously and in diverse ways (Throgmorton and Fisher 1993). Roughly three weeks after release of the Beck report, and shortly before the City Council was to vote on whether to fund additional studies, a business group closely allied with Edison re-leased the results of a survey of Chicago businesses that had been con-ducted by Michael Leard and Associates. According to Sam Mitchell, presi-dent of the Chicago Association of Commerce and Industry (CACI), the survey showed that nearly 30 percent of the 454 firms surveyed would relocate outside of Chicago if the city became the sole provider of electric-ity, thereby costing the city 250,000 jobs. Consumer and community groups condemned the CACI's survey as "sheer propaganda."

In early 1989, Mayor Eugene Sawyer, who had replaced the recently deceased Mayor Washington, appointed an Energy Task Force to help him decide what to do about renewing Edison's franchise. In April 1989 that Task Force listened to a lengthy presentation by Edison officials. There the Task Force heard an Edison vice-president say that the CACI survey showed that the people of Chicago wanted Edison to be their electricity supplier. Three weeks later, consumer groups spoke to that same Task Force. Sam Mitchell of the CACI was the second speaker that day, and he reiterated the results of Leard's 1987 survey of businesses. A community group spokesman immediately criticized the Task Force for allowing Mitchell to speak at that time and urged them to "consider whether or not you don't have a Trojan Horse in your midst" (Energy Task Force 1989).

Consumer groups interpreted the survey as an effort to manipulate public perception, but they were unable to question Leard and his client in public until Sam Mitchell and Michael Leard accepted an invitation to meet with the Task Force and other interested parties on August 16, 1989. Mitchell and Leard would have an opportunity to persuade a key audience that the survey had been conducted in a valid manner, and consumer groups would have a chance to test their challenges to that claim.

THE ENERGY TASK FORCE'S RESPONSE TO A SURVEY OF CHICAGO BUSINESSES

As the meeting began, twenty or so people sat at the outer side of a hexagonal pattern of tables.[1] On the left sat several Task Force members;

on the right, community and consumer group representatives. Another ten to twenty observers were scattered around the perimeter. Robert Wilcox, a conservatively dressed, graying, middle-aged businessman who co-chaired the Mayor's Task Force, called the meeting to order, then asked the consumer representatives to comment on a written question from the Task Force. For the next hour or so, they engaged in a calm and reasoned conversation—one well-suited to the plain, unadorned, modernist room in which the meeting took place.

Wilcox then interrupted the flow of the meeting to give Sam Mitchell of the CACI a chance to speak. Hunched forward, arms crossed, Mitchell read the following statement:

> *Thank you, Mr. Chairman. We appreciate the courtesy. The Task Force in a directed question asked CACI, "Would you provide your survey instrument and the tabulation of results? What sources of information did you use to develop that instrument?" I believe that we have answered that question before both to this body and to others, and that answer is "no." Our rationale is that our research is proprietary and we do not release proprietary information. We release the results of our surveys and the questions concerning those results and the methodology used in conducting that research. . . . While many in this room will not find that answer to their satisfaction, that is the reality of the matter.*
>
> *Another reality is that our research appears to be the only document that has been brought to this body that has been impeached in this manner. To our knowledge no other group's work has been challenged. We believe that in . . . challenging the credibility of this research and the Association's credibility is placed in question. We can only draw the conclusion that some members of this task force did not like the results of our work and seek to discredit it in order to feature their own aims.*
>
> *As I said a moment ago, we have always been willing to answer questions concerning the results of our research and the methodology used in conducting that research. Toward that end we have asked Mr. Michael Leard, of Michael Leard Research, Inc., who conducted this research, to appear here to discuss the methodology and the results. Mr. Leard is well-known and highly regarded in the field of market research and is widely used by business in the region. I feel obliged to point out that Mike came back from vacation on the East Coast to meet with the task force and answer these questions and, if it pleases the Chair, I would like Mike to join us at the table.*

The confrontation, thus, did not begin well. Mitchell indicated that the credibility of his organization (and the research it had sponsored) had been unfairly challenged and that he had no intention of giving the Task Force what it was asking for. But he did give them Michael Leard.

Leard began by indicating that he was unhappy about having to interrupt his vacation in order to speak to the Task Force. Then, interrupting a questioner, he stated:

> Well, basically what the process was, we were requested to do was do a survey of businesses in the Chicago area to see what their feeling was on a study that came out two years ago, the initial one, which called in some cases for I'm not nearly an expert on the stuff which I'm not expected ... I'm expected to test about the public opinions. Basically what we did was, is we had Dunn and Bradstreet generate in three divisions for us random names of companies located in the city of Chicago, based on fifty and under, fifty employees and under, fifty-one to two hundred-fifty employees, and over two hundred-fifty employees. We designed the survey to just basically test their mood on what they felt was the, the results have been released here, on what they felt the prospects of the city running the, having something to do with running, the taking over the electric service, providing electric service and things like that. The research was done under controlled means, statistical probabilities and everything else like that. And, we just ran it. We designed the questionnaire so that we could, so that we got a free flow of information.

At that point Leard shifted topics, angrily portraying himself as an expert whose work had been criticized by politically motivated know-nothings. The issue according to Leard was that he has had success in predicting elections but his critics (his immediate audience) were too ignorant to know it. Furthermore, the quality of his work could be assessed by comparing his pre-election surveys with actual election results.

At that point one of the community representatives—Scott Bernstein, Executive Director of the Center for Neighborhood Technology—asked a question. Bernstein, a thin young man with short, wiry, black hair and beard, wondered whether there might be a significant difference between a survey of business intentions and a survey of voter intentions. "[I]f that's the case," he said, "you were widely quoted in the same newspaper, or your survey was by CACI, as having something to say about the likelihood of businesses' intent to leave should the city act to play some sort of municipal utility role. Would you comment for us on the nature of that question [here Leard tried to interrupt] and what and how, and how you approached it, and whether you feel as strongly about that as you feel about the likelihood of the outcome of the Attorney General's race?"

By this time Leard had become extremely hostile. His anger, coupled with the CACI's refusal to present the actual survey instrument, led to turmoil in the meeting. The confusion concerned the precise wording of the questionnaire and whether that wording had skewed the results in Com Ed's favor. Dodging Bernstein's question about comparability of surveys, Leard focused on whether businesses would be likely to leave the city:

> *Oh, I think there would be significant shifts. I think there were two parts to that question. One ... part of that proposed survey called for fifty percent cogeneration, if you recall²* ... [pointing at Mitchell] *Am I right or wrong?* [Then, after hearing an affirmative answer from Bernstein:] *Fifty percent cogeneration is ... not what ... we threw into the action, but what the report that your study and analysis* [the Beck report] *said was there. Fifty percent cogeneration for the businesses. ... Are you familiar with that? It's in the study. It's in the Beck study* [angrily jabbing his finger toward Bernstein]. *True or false? Are you familiar with that?*

At this point Leard's barrage of hostile comments was interrupted by one of the Task Force members, Michael Bell of Certified Public Accountants for the Public Interest, who sought to bring the conversation back to the initial question. "I haven't made any comments pro or con," Bell said, "but I feel like you're getting in here and boxing with somebody. ... Could we just talk about ... what the issues are here, rather, because it just feels to me ... that this is getting pretty loaded and kind of off the tangent. ... What I am interested [in] right now is in process and in some of the questions the way they were asked. ... We're not getting ... the survey instrument so we're, we want to be able to rely on what you are saying."

After another brief flurry of heated exchanges, during which Leard referred to the Task Force as a "hostile committee," the conversation returned to the 50 percent cogeneration issue. Martin Heckman, an informally dressed older man who represented the Labor Coalition on Public Utilities, asked thrice whether the survey instrument could be made available. Finally, Sam Mitchell of the CACI intervened impatiently: "I'd like to answer that if I may. Mr. Heckman, at the last meeting I saw you in fact carrying a copy of an editorial from *Commerce Magazine* which outlined in totality. ... the results of the survey. You have that material in your possession." Leard then chimed in: "The questions that are on that survey are the questions we asked. Period. There was no other loading, there was no other bias or anything else like that. And so, what you see is what you got. The survey instrument is exactly what's on the poll. Yes, sir" [gesturing to the next questioner].[3]

The Task Force then inquired about the actual phrasing of the questions. David Kraft of Nuclear Energy Information Services, a public interest organization that sought to inform the public about the risks associated with nuclear power, opened the inquiry: "What sort of reliability checks were done on the terms used and the questions, for example, the words *city*, *became*, and *sole provider*, to make sure that that was consistently interpreted from participant to participant in the survey?" Leard had some difficulty answering Kraft's question. After Leard rambled about how the survey had been conducted shortly after Mayor Washington released the Beck report, Kraft responded, "Essentially what you're saying is, the only estimate of reliability was the context of what was going on at the time?" Though calmer now, Leard still did not seem to understand. "All right," said Kraft, "I'll explain more clearly if I can."

> *If that question were given to me now, as opposed to then . . . You see it's a different context first of all. And secondly . . . does the term "city" connote to those participants the aldermen as have been portrayed in the press, did it connote the Department of Planning, did it mean city hall? . . . I mean . . . there are different ways of interpreting it is what I'm . . . driving at. And the same with the word "sole provider," did that mean that they were the ones who are actually going to produce the electrons or did it mean they would be the fiscal backers or the . . . see what I'm driving at, you see what I'm driving at?*

Leard finally seemed to understand:

> *First of all, what I think you have to look at . . . is . . . you're . . . an energy task force that's looking for this, looking for that. What we deal with is public perception. The public has a very limited perception of what's going on. You can talk about energy supplies. Mr. Bernstein talked about, one of his top clients (Sears) moved out of Chicago now, moved to, moved right outside the city where the rates are still the same and everything else like that. . . . When they think of "city," what do they think of? Any kind of municipalization. Now we could have been more negative, we could have said that the Chicago city council is considering taking over the collection company. Right through the roof. My expertise, what I do best (I feel I do it better than anybody else), is we try and make the questions as neutral as possible so what we can get out of it is the people's interpretation of what's going on, not what the clients feel is there or anyone else for that matter.*

Kraft chose not to challenge the validity of Leard's survey results. He did, however, repeat his worries about reliability: "What I'm driving at," he said, "is I needed a better clarification of the reliability of the particular instruments because you said, you say right now, what the name of the game is: it's public perception. . . . Depending on how these words were perceived, people will frame their answers." Undaunted, Leard simply claimed that "they were highly neutral words."

The discussion then turned to another question that was, in the eyes of some participants, "loaded." One of the consumer group representatives asked Leard whether the survey asked a question that indicated the city would *require* businesses to reduce their electricity usage by 50 percent, either through reduction in demand or by replacing utility power with cogenerated power. Leard's answer was difficult to follow:

> *We did the clear first, with "the city of Chicago becomes a sole supplier of your electrical supply, how will this impact your business in your planning?" were the exact terms. OK? After that, we said well, what if they had to come up with cogeneration and things like that and conservation and things? And then the numbers went right off the chart.* [Then, when asked again whether the question indicated that a 50 percent reduction would be required] *What if you relied on 50 percent cogeneration? Yeah . . . that type of thing.*

At last the conversation had turned to something concrete. After scanning through some papers, Scott Bernstein zeroed in on the 50 percent figure that distorted the options and forecasts in the Beck report.

Leard seemed surprised and a bit shaken. "Is there 50 percent?" he asked. "Could that be 50 percent? No? Never could be interpreted so? With the cogeneration it never could be interpreted as 50 percent?" Sam Mitchell stepped in at this point and tried to shift responsibility for the erroneous question to the City. Leard shifted his ground:

> *But this is specious because of the fact that the question before that without even, without the cogeneration still had a ton of people moving out, and what were the numbers on that? It was still there, it was still a negative impact. . . . You can sit and shake your head. . . . If we had asked 20 percent* [gesturing angrily again] *then they'd still have gone. Are you kidding me? You ask any company, do you own businesses around here, any of you own businesses? The city comes up and says, oh, by the way, you might have to do 20 percent cogeneration, what do you think the results are going to be? Do you think the results are going to be any different at 20 percent than 50 percent?* [Jabbing his finger across the table at Bernstein:] *Ask him. You are the one who thought of it? Do you think it's going to be any different at 20 percent than 50 percent?*

Unpersuaded, Bernstein tossed his papers onto the table. Shrugging, he simply said, "I don't think that's the question. You've answered the question that's on the table, how you conducted the study and what your assumptions were. Thanks a lot. It's self-evident."

At that point the meeting appeared to be over. But then, after two or three minutes of side conversation, one other key issue returned: the credibility of the CACI and Leard's research. Sam Mitchell stressed that he had asked Leard to take part in the meeting because the survey research had been "impeached," and that offended Mitchell: "We know of no other document brought before this body that has been impeached. We consider that not only a question of the credibility of the research and the professionals we hire, we consider it a question of credibility of the organization. We . . . "
At this point Michael Bell began objecting while Mitchell was still speaking. "The Beck report was impeached, Mr. Mitchell, too," Bell calmly insisted. "This is an open society. The Beck report was impeached on a number of different points. There is no reason why there should be any higher ground for a survey and the questioning of what the survey is. . . . " "Our point," Mitchell replied, "is there should be no lower ground." Bell found this response deeply irritating and asked Mitchell to drop his adversarial posture.

Mitchell replied by arguing that the Task Force itself was biased and that its reaction to the survey reflected that bias. "I, in my exposure to this body," he said, "have heard this research impeached. I have heard no comments as to the Beck study, in front of this body when I have been here, and I have seen nothing of any importance on the Beck study being impeached by others."

Disturbed by the use of "impeached," Leard made one last comment, addressing Bell: " . . . [I]f the committee is going to operate on fair ground then the members of the committee shouldn't be taking shots in the papers about stuff that you don't even know."

Leard then rose to leave the meeting. But before he left, Martin Heckman of the Labor Coalition made one last comment to co-chair Robert Wilcox. "Bob, I'd like to make one point. The point is the Beck report itself is impeached. The day that the Beck report was released, on that very day within a matter of an hour, Commonwealth Edison threw somebody in to raise the question about the city wants precinct captains to run Commonwealth. So they tried to impeach it within hours."

PLANNING AS PERSUASIVE AND CONSTITUTIVE DISCOURSE

Earlier I claimed that planning is a rhetorical activity and that planners should think of survey research and other tools as rhetorical tropes that reply to prior utterances (and give meaning and power to the larger narratives of which they are a part), seek to persuade specific audiences, create open meanings subject to diverse interpretations, and help to constitute planning characters and communities.

The case just recounted strongly supports such a rhetorical conception of planning. *It shows, first, that the CACI's survey acted as a trope in a larger narrative about the desirability of the city "taking over" Edison's electric power system.* The survey replied to two prior reports prepared for the city, reports that indicated Chicagoans would be better off if the city purchased all or part of the Com Ed system. How Chicago business people felt about (and would react to) such a purchase was unknown. The survey, presented in the scientific terms of "results," supported a claim that the business people would be deeply displeased. But the claim that the survey simply measured attitudes and intentions belied its tropal nature. Given the business person's "limited perception," acknowledged by the survey researcher himself, the survey had to construct their understanding of the situation. Thus, it had to prefigure their sense of how they would respond.

Here is one particularly revealing example. Leard's survey read: "Part of the city's plan for the takeover of the electrical service would require a business to reduce electrical consumption by 50 percent or generate half the electrical power it uses. Under these conditions, what effect would this plan have on your company's future plans?" (*Commerce Magazine* 1988). If we look at the wording carefully, we can see that three particular aspects of this question function as figures of language or argument and prefigured how businesspeople would respond.

First is *the city's plan*. In context, this phrase seems to refer to the Beck report, which was released a few weeks before the survey was conducted. Neither the city nor the Beck report, however, had referred to the report as the city's "plan." The city portrayed the report as a quantitative assessment of the likely economic consequences of alternative courses of action, not as a plan about what to do and how to do it. Indeed, the CACI's release of Leard's survey occurred just a few days before the City Council was to decide whether to fund the additional studies required to help the city decide what to do. Referring to the Beck report as "the city's plan" probably conveyed the misleading impression that the city already knew its intentions.

Second is the claim that the city's plan would *require* businesses to conserve or generate 50 percent of the power they use. As Bernstein's questions tried to demonstrate, nothing in the Beck report or in the city's actions up to December of 1987 indicated that businesses would be "required" to do anything. The city was clearly inclined to encourage electricity conservation and cogeneration, and to do so by offering price and other institutional incentives, much as Edison was then offering numerous incentives for businesses *not* to conserve or cogenerate. But at no point had the city indicated an intention to require businesses to conserve.

Third is the survey's use of the term "takeover." This word implied that the city was on the verge of seizing something that belonged to someone else, that it intended to expropriate property. This trope radically transformed the context and meaning of the city's actions. Though the survey never said so, the city's exploration of options was taking place in the context of an expiring franchise. In 1948 the citizens of Chicago had granted Edison the exclusive right to provide electric power and services to the city in return for payment of an annual franchise fee and other services provided to the city. That franchise agreement was due to expire in December 1990 unless jointly renewed by Com Ed and the city. Thus, the city had every legal and moral right to explore options to remaining on Com Ed's system and continuing the exclusive franchise. Portraying this simply as a takeover twisted the meaning of the city's actions in an objectionable way.

To be sure, the CACI and Mr. Leard might want to defend the accuracy of such terms. But the issue here is more their figurativeness than their accuracy. Planning and its instruments must use these kinds of words. Yet, terms such as "the city's plan," "require," "takeover," "proprietary" can coalesce to make any survey into a powerful trope of argument—not just because such words might mislead readers, but because they shape our understanding of the situations at issue. By using a particular language, the survey made "the city" into a synecdoche, standing for the board of aldermen and the political machine in Chicago. By contrast, community groups used "the city" as a metaphor, meaning "the city is us." We can imagine a case for either construction, so my main point is not that one side is purely right and the other damnably wrong. Instead, the key lesson is that no planning instruments can avoid persuasive, rhetorical construction of characters and communities. Scientistic talk of survey "results" might obscure that crucial feature of planning but cannot eliminate it. The same tropality appears in the survey's division of "the business community" from "the city." Surely this joined with "takeover" and other terms to help survey respondents think in terms of corrupt politicians expropriating private property and forcing private businesses to do what the politicians wanted. Would many businesses leave Chicago under such circumstances? But remember, there can be no neutral words about contested issues. The lesson is not to avoid or debunk surveys but to understand how they must work tropally. Then we can do them well and read them wisely.

The case also shows that the survey researcher and his client had to persuade a specific audience (the Mayor's Task Force) that the survey had been conducted competently and that its "results" were accurate and reliable. When the Mayor's Task Force began meeting in early 1989, it seemed as if that group would play a crucial role in determining what the city would do with regard to its franchise with Com Ed.[4] The economic impact of alternate courses of action was a crucial factor for it to consider. The utility had to persuade this specific audience in this specific context that the economic effects of a city "takeover" would be disastrous for the city. The CACI's survey, and Mitchell's and Leard's subsequent meeting with the Task Force, were efforts to persuade the Task Force about the same things. Whether they succeeded in those efforts, however, depended in large part on the extent to which the survey acknowledged and fairly incorporated opposing views held by (or familiar to) Task Force members.

Therefore, the case also shows the importance of speaking with awareness of differing or opposing views, and how particular audiences can—due to the inherent plasticity of language—read meanings into surveys that differ from the one intended by the survey's client or researchers. The CACI's survey displayed no overt awareness of opposing views, and suppression of that awareness became quite evident during the Task Force's meeting. Intimately familiar with the flow of utterances, replies, and counter-replies of which the survey was a part, consumer groups and several members of the Task Force read the CACI's survey in ways different from the CACI. They challenged the CACI's motivation in producing the survey, and they convinced themselves that the survey was simply an effort to deceive and manipulate the business community. "You've answered the question that's on the table," said Scott Bernstein. "Thanks a lot. It's self-evident." Mr. Leard's inarticulate but indignant response might make us wonder about whether the situation was that simple. And it is interesting that the critics on the Task Force did not challenge the notion that surveys could produce objective results. Their implication was instead that the survey asked the wrong ("loaded") questions. They believed, perhaps with good reason, that other questions—possibly ones based on the views of community groups—would have yielded starkly different, and likely better, responses.

One might think, therefore, that good survey researchers could have obtained a true measure of the business community's response by testing the sensitivity of responses to language. That is the technical fix taught to modern planners, and though not completely incorrect, it typically forgets that any planning survey must figure as a trope of argument. Alternately, we might postulate a survey conducted in the context of a Habermasian "ideal speech community." In that case the CACI and the community groups would gather happily together with a planning researcher to choose questions that would test the sensitivity of business responses to diverse phrasings (Habermas 1987). We can imagine that such a revised survey could have gone a long way toward reducing conflict between Com Ed and consumer groups, and we can hope that creating such a planning forum would have led to a better understanding of what Chicago residents think of a potential takeover. But we must not forget that we have task forces and surveys precisely because they sometimes seem the closest we can get to such undistorted, democratic dialogue. Both the technical and the communitarian utopias are pleasant dreams, but they are dreams and figures nonetheless. Planning is a deeply politicized practice, and no technical fix or ideal speech community is going to overcome that.

Lastly, the case also draws our attention to the ways in which planning rhetoric (in this case Michael Leard's) constitutes character and community. The story reveals important differences between how to *do* survey research (do planning) and how to *be* a survey researcher (be a planner).[5] Most importantly, it encourages us to ask whether the meeting would have gone differently if Leard had adopted a different rhetorical strategy. My sense is that Leard's rhetoric created characters for himself and his audience that were radically inconsistent with the characters embedded in Com Ed's basic story. Furthermore, his rhetoric reaffirmed the expectations of Edison's opponents and thereby reconstituted the community and culture of conflict between them and Com Ed. A planner who understood planning to be persuasive argumentation about the future would have spoken differently.

Recall that Edison's story characterized its officials as expert managers who were being harassed and impeded by politically inspired know-nothings. When coupled with the CACI's description of Leard as a highly regarded market researcher, and Leard's self-portrait as a scientist who uses neutral questions to generate results, this leads us to expect that he would speak as a scientist. As a scientist, however, Leard might have been ethically compelled to reveal much more about his survey.[6] Then his scientific ethos might conflict with the political nature of his commitment to the client, be it the CACI or Com Ed. Leard, like planners in general, would have faced the tragic choice of liberal politics: to be right and do good (in his own view) or to get things done (in his client's view).

So Michael Leard's rhetoric constituted a character for himself that was radically inconsistent with Edison's (and his own) story. He spoke and acted not as a scientist but like a combative Chicago political hack. His dress (unkempt), his gestures (jabbing his finger toward questioners), his vocal intonation (loud, angry), his frequent lapses into grammatical incoherence, all contradicted his claim to scientific character. By acting as a political hack, Leard appeared deceitful and untrustworthy and thereby made the consumer groups' story seem more persuasive: the utility was headed by arrogant incompetents who sought to manipulate the public and its elected representatives.

We can wonder why Leard posed (metaphorically at least) as the "political hack," and why he came into the meeting reeking of such intense hostility. Was this strategy, stress, or something else? Lacking the chance to ask Leard directly, we can only consider some possibilities. Perhaps that is just the way he is, at least under pressure. Most of us have encountered—or have been—such characters at one time or another, so we cannot dismiss that possibility. A second alternative is that Leard truly regarded the Task Force members as technically uninformed and politically motivated meddlers. But if he thought that when he entered the meeting, how did he retain the opinion by the time he left? Bernstein and Kraft asked him too many technically sound questions to be ignorant, and Bell was much too evenhanded to sound politically craven. By acting as a political hack, Leard seemed to expect his audience to respond in a similar way: to be hostile, aggressive, and evasive—and thus to reproduce a (Chicago) culture (of politics) based on deceit and manipulation. Contrary to Leard's invitation, in any event, the Task Force members chose not to "be Leard." Bell, for example, appears three times in the conversation: first, to ask a simple, straightforward question; then, to ask Leard to "stop boxing"; and last, to protest Mitchell's claim that Leard's survey was the only work to be "impeached." He did not allow Leard to go unanswered, but he chose not to respond solely in Leard's terms.

A third, strategic possibility is that Leard and Mitchell jointly agreed that the best defense was a good offense and thus attacked their opponents on grounds of ignorance and politics rather than directly answering questions and objections from the Task Force. My suspicion is that this is a better characterization. Looming behind Leard's research firm, and behind Mitchell's association, was the pervasive shadow of Commonwealth Edison. As a power behind the scenes, it seemed to have nothing to gain and much to lose by revealing the extent to which survey research could shape the attitudes and intentions of Chicago businesses and residents. If Leard had responded openly to Kraft's plea to design a survey that tested the respondents' sensitivity to words like "city" and "sole provider," he might have placed the Edison monopoly at risk. But a final possibility, one that also rings true, is that Mitchell simply threw Leard to the lions. After all, the key question became whether the Task Force would be allowed to see the survey instrument, and Mitchell left Leard in no position to share it.

How, then, might Leard have responded differently to his audience, and what effect might a different rhetoric have had on the meeting, his audience, and the conflict between Edison's and its opponents' stories?

One possibility to consider is that, rather than appearing to be a cartoon of how to fail at persuasion using the mask of science, he might have portrayed himself as a polished deflector of uninformed questions from outside his realms of expertise, as a politically savvy policy analyst perhaps. Presuming rhetoric to be "mere words," he might have spoken in a more polished and dignified way—while remaining just as uncommunicative. My sense is that a more polished researcher could have obscured the central issue—the tropal (and perhaps "loaded") nature of his questions—by saying something like "The majority of our respondents would not fully grasp a technical explanation of the complexity of the Beck report," or "We've learned that trying to fully capture subtle distinctions among options in survey responses diminishes the validity of the response." The polished researcher could then have argued that his survey might have contained some unavoidable, but minor, distortion. By obscuring the central issue, such a polished researcher would have appeared to be less of a "hack" but still would not have persuaded many in his audience. To persuade them, he would have to be willing to discuss details about how the survey questions were selected and how the survey was administered, and he would have to be open to the possibility of modifying his questions to account for his opponents' views. This he was unwilling or unable to do.

A second alternative is one probably unavailable to Leard but one that we planners should strive to make possible: to be planners who seek to promote and facilitate a public, democratic, persuasive discourse about contestable claims on what is good, right, or feasible—in particular contexts. Such planners would "listen" (in advance) to their audience's story, seeking to learn how that audience thinks and feels and what kinds of questions its members are likely to ask. Having discovered the grounds for the audience's claims, such planners would pay closer attention to the alternative meanings that their tropes would have for that audience. They would try to persuade their audience, fully aware that their planning tools configure planning arguments—and such planners would speak in full awareness that their rhetoric has the potential to create new communities and a new culture of interaction between their audiences and themselves. But such planners would not be naive; they would assume that their audience is also speaking persuasively. Thus, such planners would know that political effectiveness often means withholding some information and feigning more legitimacy than they actually have (Kaufman 1990).

Knowing Edison's story and listening to the consumer groups' story, such a planner in Leard's position might have concluded that the consumer groups would continue to obstruct Edison's effort to obtain rate increases and hinder its ability to negotiate a new franchise agreement with the city.

Aware that terms such as "the city's plan," "require," and "takeover" have different meanings for the consumer groups than they do for Edison, and thus configure planning arguments, such a planner might conclude it was in Edison's self-interest to probe the figurativeness of those terms with its opponents. In sum, such a planner would encourage Edison to explore ways to constitute a new community between it and its opponents, and thereby invalidate or change the consumer groups' characterization of the company. Freed by this reorientation, such a planner might provide the Task Force and the consumer groups with the information needed for them to discuss the survey's methodology and the meanings of its "results."

We can imagine such rhetoric and can argue that planners should strive to behave this way, but in the end we find it difficult to believe that a planner in Leard's shoes would be allowed to act this way. Thus, we conclude that Leard's actual rhetorical strategy was vitally important for the people of Chicago because it helped to reconstitute a community and culture of deceit and manipulation and costly conflict. The difficult challenge planners now face, in Chicago and elsewhere, is to find better ways of listening and speaking even when existing structures of power strive to constrain us—and to conceive how we can begin in fact to talk in those ways.

In the end, this story about the uses of survey research in Chicago teaches us that we planners are engaged in a thoroughly rhetorical practice. Accordingly, we should surrender any further pretense to neutrality, objectivity, and universal truth—such as the "true" measure of business response to a city "takeover." Surrendering the pretense to objectivity does not mean, however, that we should flee to the extreme of defining planning as just another form of politics gone amok. We should, instead, embrace persuasive discourse and political conflict—to realize that survey "results" are, like all alleged planning facts, inherently tropal and contestable. They must be scientific *and* rhetorical, professional *and* political, because they—like all other planning "tools"—configure planning arguments.

Acknowledgments

To be fair to participants, I have changed some of the names that appear in this chapter. I wish to acknowledge advice rendered by various people who have read various versions of this paper, including Ernest Alexander, John Friedmann, Helen Liggett, Dowell Myers, Charles Williams, several anonymous reviewers, and numerous participants in the ACSP/AESOP Joint International Planning Congress. I also want to thank Fred Antzack, Ed Arrington, Bob Boynton, Kathleen Farrell, John Nelson, Ira Stauber, and other participants in the University of Iowa's Spring 1991 Scholars Workshop on the Rhetoric of

Political Argumentation, and to acknowledge the support services provided by the University of Iowa Center for Advanced Study. This material is based in part on work supported by the National Science Foundation's Ethics and Values branch under Grant No. DIR-8911870. The government has certain rights in this material.

Notes

1. A reader might wonder about the methods used to select and research this particular case. The first step was to learn about the larger narratives of which the case is a part (see Throgmorton 1992, 1993; Throgmorton and Fisher 1993). The flow of those narratives strongly suggested that the CACI's survey marked a potentially critical turning point in the controversy. Subsequent conversations with CEOC people and Chicago Planning Department staff led me to learn that the department had videotaped the meeting of August 16 and that it had been shown on the Chicago municipal information television channel, WCTV. I obtained a copy of the videotape (Energy Task Force 1989) and watched it four times. I then asked a graduate student, Michelle Javornik, to prepare a verbatim transcript of the meeting, omitting such verbal ticks as "ah" and "uh." I shortened the transcript, adding comments about physical appearances and gestures where appropriate but also trying to remain faithful to the original videotape. To check my own viewing for potential bias, I also showed the tape to four colleagues and to graduate students in one of my courses. Their responses were, in all cases except one, consistent with mine. One major drawback to the tape is that it rarely shows members of the audience reacting to a speaker's comments and gestures.

2. Cogeneration is a technical process that involves the simultaneous generation of electric power and usable heat. A major shift to cogeneration by businesses could have a dramatic effect on Edison's position as the sole provider of electric power in the Chicago area.

3. Mitchell's and Leard's responses seemed to satisfy the Task Force members, for they turned to a new topic. But note that the *Commerce Magazine* editorial (1988) says only that "Selected questions and findings of the CACI survey include the following."

4. In December of 1990, the Task Force recommended that the city terminate its franchise with Edison and state its intention to acquire utility property under the favorable terms specified in the franchise. Leard's and the CACI's failure to persuade the Task Force that the survey truthfully represented business opinion contributed to that recommendation. The city accepted the Task Force's recommendations and terminated the franchise on December 28. In late 1991, after a year of negotiating, Edison and the city adopted a revised franchise agreement (Throgmorton and Fisher 1993).

5. Some readers have argued that the story recounted in the present chapter is not really about planners except in the broadest sense. Michael Leard

surely is not a "planner" in the narrow sense; however, survey research is a vital part of planning and Leard's survey acted as an important trope in the city's effort to explore options. We can learn a great deal by observing practitioners, regardless of whether they are formally trained in planning.

6. Babbie (1973, 362) reflects this ethos when he insists that "each scientist operates under a normative obligation to share his findings with the scientific community, which means sharing them with non-scientists as well." For Babbie that means not just sharing "findings" but providing enough information to enable a reader to replicate the survey.

REFERENCES

Babbie, E. R. 1973. *Survey research methods*. Beaumont, CA: Wadsworth.

Commerce Magazine. 1988. Strong opposition to municipalized electric service. *Commerce Magazine* 84, 12: 15.

Energy Task Force. 1989. Video tape of public meeting held on August 16. Chicago: Department of Planning.

Fish, S. 1979. *Is there a text in this class?* Cambridge, MA: Harvard University Press.

Forester, J. 1989. *Planning in the face of power*. Berkeley, CA: University of California Press.

Freund, E. 1987. *The return of the reader*. New York, NY: Methuen.

Goldstein, H. A. 1984. Planning as argumentation. *Environment and Planning B* 11, 3: 297–312.

Habermas, J. 1987. *The philosophical discourse of modernity* (translation by F. Lawrence). Cambridge, MA: MIT Press.

Healey, P. 1992. A planner's day: knowledge and action in communicative practice. *Journal of the American Planning Association* 58, 1: 9–20.

Hoch, C. 1984. Doing good and being right. *Journal of the American Planning Association* 50, 3: 335–45.

Kaufman, J. 1990. Forester in the face of planners: will they listen to him? *Planning Theory Newsletter* 4 (Winter): 27–33.

Leith, D., and G. Myerson. 1989. *The power of address*. London: Routledge.

Mandelbaum, S. 1990. Reading plans. *Journal of the American Planning Association* 56, 3: 350–56.

_____. 1991. Telling stories. *Journal of Planning Education and Research* 10, 3: 209–14.

Mayor's Task Force on Energy. 1989. Recommendations concerning electric energy policies for Chicago for the 1990s and beyond. Chicago, IL: Mayor's Task Force on Energy.

Quinn, A. 1982. *Figures of speech*. Salt Lake City, UT: Peregrine Smith.

R. W. Beck and Associates. 1987. *Electric supply options study*. Indianapolis, IN: R. W. Beck and Associates.

Rectenwald, W. 1987. Edison buyout could cut jobs, poll says. *Chicago Tribune* (December 14).

Throgmorton, J. A. 1990. Passion, reason, and power: the rhetorics of electric power planning in Chicago. *Journal of Architectural and Planning Research* 7, 4: 330–50.

_____. 1992. Planning as persuasive storytelling about the future: negotiating an electric power rate settlement in Illinois. *Journal of Planning Education and Research* 12, 1: 17–31.

_____. 1993. Planning as a rhetorical activity: survey research as a trope in arguments about electric power planning in Chicago. *Journal of the American Planning Association* 57, 3: 334–46.

_____, and P. S. Fisher. 1993. Institutional change and electric power in the city of Chicago. *Journal of Economic Issues* 27, 1: 117–53.

Tompkins, J. P. 1980. *Reader-response criticism*. Baltimore, MD: The Johns Hopkins University Press.

White, J. B. 1984. *When words lose their meaning*. Chicago: University of Chicago Press.

White, J. B. 1985. *Heracles' bow*. Madison, WI: University of Wisconsin Press.

Ziemba, S. 1986. Edison rates may cut jobs: city study assails proposed increases. *Chicago Tribune* (August 5).

Howell S. Baum

18 *Practicing Planning Theory in a Political World*

I was also aware that my views were the classic ones of every would-be despot who could not have his way and who was "misunderstood." . . . we fought over everything. . . . Certainly my ego was involved. . . . Here was another bureaucrat being gored in the never ending internal political wars. . . . Maybe, indeed, I was somewhat paranoid on the subject. . . . An evening meeting [where] we were being "mau-maued" by neighborhood activists. . . . While I was waiting to answer the first, well-prepared "have you stopped beating your wife" question, I had the strong feeling that at that moment I hated everyone in the room, even those few who "understood." At the same time, I knew that feeling to be unreasonable, that they were doing what they were supposed to do, that they were participating. I had been in situations like that a hundred times before, and though my adrenaline might have been going pretty well, I had not felt anger. Then why did I hate them? . . . Prone to exaggeration, I concluded that maybe I was becoming like a punch-drunk fighter, brain slightly addled, sitting in his corner. The bell had sounded and I came out and did my thing. (Jacobs 1978, 263, 264, 270, 272, 274, 275)

In an interview following his meeting with the planner, the developer revealed that he had decided against going forward with his project because he would have to apply for a single variance. . . . what he thought would be a long, cumbersome process of appeal. He had made this decision during his meeting, but he had chosen not to reveal it. When he learned of the developer's decision, the planner was shocked. He had based his strategy on minimizing variances, but he had assumed that a single, easily obtainable variance on lot size would not stand in the project's way. . . . The planner's and developer's theories of action had combined to produce a behavioral world in which each withheld negative information, tested assumptions privately, and sought to maintain unilateral control over the other. (Schön 1983, 229, 230)

An earlier version of this chapter appeared in *Society* 26, 1 (November/December 1988), Transaction Publishers, New Brunswick, New Jersey.

365

T hese excerpts both describe the politics of planning. Allan Jacobs's colorful rendering of his last years as San Francisco's Planning Director refers to battles with politicians and bureaucrats over who would control development funds and with residents over whether their neighborhood could be given subsidized code enforcement. Donald Schön's analysis of the transcript of a planner-regulator and a developer reveals a negotiation in which the parties employ such obfuscatory strategies that they fail to discover that they agree on building a housing project. The stakes in these cases are money, power, and status.

These vignettes depict planners taking political roles but executing them unsuccessfully. While Jacobs earlier had masterfully drafted and shepherded an urban design plan and height and bulk ordinance, in these later instances he felt so personally involved, attacked, and unappreciated that he could not take the political tacks that had worked for him before. Schön's planner was not so aware of what he was doing. Trying to manage the development process by mediating between the zoning board of appeals and developers, he became more concerned with control than with communicating information that would identify and facilitate good projects, and in this case he defeated a project he favored. Both cases might be considered examples of self-defeating action in political roles.

What do planning theorists have to say about such cases? Do they recognize that they occur? Can they explain them? What advice would they give such planners? In short, what do planning theorists say about and to planners as political actors?

The "rational" planning theorists[1] who dominated the field in the 1950s and 1960s said little about politics and offered little guidance for acting in a political world. In contrast, contemporary theorists write about political economy, the contest of interests, and the course of argumentation in decision making. Yet, while these theorists recognize politics as a context for planning, few have much more than the rationalists to say to planners about their political activity. This chapter explores why planning theorists say so little about or to planners as political actors, and it examines the covert messages of this silence. The key is to understand theorists as practitioners of theorizing.

POLITICS AND PLANNING THEORY: THE RATIONAL VIEW

The theorists of rationality who first articulated and codified "planning theory" did not recognize the politics of planning. They shared planners' distaste for it as a messy, uncontrollable counterforce to efforts to make "rational" decisions. Their strategy for dealing with politics was to ignore it and, instead, to emphasize two "rational" assumptions. Explicitly normative, in the absence of any direct reference to planning practice, these assumptions were implicitly descriptive as well (Altshuler 1965; Banfield 1955; Davidoff and Reiner 1962; Faludi 1973).[2]

One "rational" assumption concerned the nature of planning problems and the environment in which they were addressed. These theorists conceptualized planning issues in terms of their formal characteristics, which were usually quite abstract and which were rarely likely to be the subject of dispute. Their world was a spacescape: a place of infinite information without people except for the expert planner, perhaps a boss or colleague, and, unseen but ready to appreciate rational work, amorphous implementors. In such a place, identifying and solving a problem involved merely collecting and organizing vast amounts of information. By implication or wish, information was power, though referring to "power" would have invoked a more concrete and complex world than the theorists could comfortably accommodate.

The "rational" model for decision making was acontextual. It disregarded the environments in which issues were formulated, contested, and decided. It often favored such "universal" languages as engineering or economics for describing problems. Thus, all land-use issues, for example, could be considered similar merely because they were concerned with land use. Disregarding context meant ignoring political interests. It also helped assure planners that their recommendations were not only scientific but ethical, representing a single "public interest."

Second, traditional theorists emphasized a complementary "rational" conceptualization of planners. Focusing on the formal logical characteristics of issues, rational theorists emphasized the cognitive side of planners, treating them as impersonal calculators of information. In admonishing planners to examine issues without bias, the theorists ignored planners' emotional lives. They assumed planners had no feelings that would affect how they executed a logical model, much less any that would lead them to prefer another approach. By disregarding the feelings of planners, the rational theorists excluded the possibility that planners themselves might have political interests in how issues were addressed.

As part of the emphasis on cognitive reasoning, rational theorists ignored the possibility—denied the existence—of people's subconscious lives. They assumed that planners always knew what they were doing and were never influenced by unconscious or subliminal aims. It is normal for people to devise unconscious plans to avoid situations that make them anxious. People sometimes unconsciously choose magical strategies to solve problems, acting as if their wishes were enough to do the work. The rational theorists assumed that planners were psychologically a different species.

Undistracted calculation seemed possible for these theorists because they imagined planners acting individually. They emphasized individual decision-making models, which excluded not only the complex, often irrational dynamics of groups and organizations but, more broadly, politics and political relationships. They implied that social decision making was only individual decision making writ larger.

Within the rational tradition, critiques commonly cited cognitive and logical limitations to the prototypical formulation of comprehensive rationality (for example, Arrow 1958; Etzioni 1968). However, many in the tradition proceeded simply to elaborate a concept of bounded rationality that retained the two basic assumptions and still tried to exclude politics (for example, Alexander 1984 and 1993; Simon 1976).

As description, the rational theory is unrealistic, though, as we shall see, on an unconscious level it makes for compelling prescription. However, the paradigm could not overtly withstand cumulative evidence of the centrality of politics to planning. Case studies reported the importance of interests and strategy, and they showed that deliberately political planners were often influential (Altshuler 1965; Catanese 1974; Clavel 1986; Fainstein et al. 1983; Hartman 1984; Jacobs 1978; Krumholz and Forester 1990; Meyerson and Banfield 1955; Rabinovitz 1969). Studies of planners found they differ considerably in whether they think or act politically (Baum 1986 and 1988; Forester 1989; Hoch 1988; Howe and Kaufman 1979; Needleman and Needleman 1974; Schön 1983; Vasu 1979). Planning theorists began to write about politics in planning.

POLITICS AND PLANNING THEORY: THE COMMUNICATIVE VIEW

The position of rational theorists on politics is simple: no one is involved in it, and neither are planner. In contrast, contemporary planning theorists recognize that planning is implicated in politics, and they write a great deal about how decisions get made. They also recognize that planners are actors in this world, and they describe planners' interactions. In general, contemporary theory is more empirically grounded than rational theory.

Across a broad range, many contemporary theorists are joined by the recognition that planners' work is communication. Their plans, reports, phone calls, memoranda, and meetings are not "just words" but words that denote or connote specific institutional and political relationships. Forester (1989 and 1993) has most articulately elaborated this Habermasian insight. The label "communicative theorists" will be used here to encompass this admittedly heterogeneous group.

Communicative theorists take plans more seriously than the rationalists: each word matters, implying or creating speakers, audiences, and embracing communities (for example, Mandelbaum 1990). Plans and reports are texts to be analyzed for what they tell about relations of power and strategies for exercising power (for example, Healey 1992a, 1992b; Liggett 1991; Tett and Wolfe 1991; Throgmorton 1990, 1993). The texts can be construed as arguments for concepts of community and relations of power, as well as substantive policies (for example, Goldstein 1984). In general, written documents and oral presentations constitute "stories" about roles, politics, and communities (for example, Healey 1992a, 1992b; Hoch 1994; Mandelbaum 1991; Schön 1983, 1991; Throgmorton 1992).

Communicative theorists manifestly reject the first assumption of the rational theorists. Planning issues are always defined in an environment of competing political interests. Indeed, problems exist only in contexts. Moreover, how decisions are, can be, and should be made depends on the context (see Forester 1989). Communicative theorists believe that planning practice follows a rationality, though not the logic of the "rational" theorists. It is a rationality that reflects the interplay and negotiation of interests, statuses, and meanings.

No simple statement can encompass the range of contemporary theoretical views of planners as political actors. Communicative theorists, by virtue of their interests in relationships, reject the rationalists' assumption that a planner is a lone actor, that social decision making is only an aggregation of similar individual calculations. They emphasize that planners and others find meanings and interests in things—and shape planning processes—as part of inter-subjective understandings among particular persons in particular situations. Their prototypical planner is a "reflective practitioner" (Schön 1983), who is active and who tries to learn from and modify actions in real time. They observe that even mundane conversations can involve negotiations over substance and power, and they urge planners to recognize the stakes and speak more deliberately.

Communication theorists hold widely varying assumptions about how planners should be active—both how activist they should be and how much of themselves they should involve in relations with others. With regard to activism, Forester (1989) argues that planners cannot always succeed with good-faith bargaining and that they should enlarge their role to consider community organization as well. Yet, other theorists limit the planner's role and concerns to verbal activism: speaking with insight and intention but not joining or creating coalitions to exercise power. Still others define planners mainly as astute textual interpreters who understand the linguistic stakes better than traditional rational planners but stay in relatively passive roles.

With regard to how much of themselves planners should involve in interactions, some (for example, Baum 1987, 1990) argue that planners, as others, inevitably act with both conscious and unconscious aims, that the latter may overwhelm the former, and that success at conscious intentions requires watching for the intrusion of unconscious interests. In this view, planners negotiating realistically must also reflect on their own unconscious aims and others' unconscious meanings, make them explicit where helpful, and find resolutions for them as well as for overt conflicts.

In contrast, many other communicative theorists portray planners, if not always others, more simply. If they have unconscious desires, they can control them without thinking about them. Focusing on overt issues, attending to norms of open communication, planners can avoid being distracted by unconscious wishes such as power or control.

Those communicative theorists who endorse mainly reflective roles and who portray planning as easily under conscious control, while recognizing politics, come close to sharing rationalists' assumptions about it. Politics is a matter of interests. Having interests leads to an interest in power, and theorists in both groups distrust power, a number of communicative theorists invoking Foucault in doing so. While, on the one hand, Norman Krumholz (Krumholz and Forester 1990) is a good example of a planner seeking power to serve public interests, Robert Moses (Caro 1975) is a lingering reminder of the dangers. Many communicative theorists, in common with rational theorists, are wary of the emotions that attach individuals to interests and move them to want power. When they characterize planning as "argumentation," they think of planners clearly expounding well-considered positions, not heated speakers talking hurriedly, loudly, or inconsistently.

An indication of this bias is the way some communicative theorists focus on texts without attention to their authors. Authors emerge by inference: if the text can be interpreted to mean something, its author must have meant to say that. Authors are often not interviewed (exceptions include Baum 1990; Forester 1989; Healey 1992a; Hoch 1994; Schön 1983, 1991). Implicitly, "the text speaks for itself."

This tacit world of ideas without people resembles the rationalists' spacescape. One argued position somehow seems to evoke another. Inferred speakers follow reasoned norms, perhaps intending to be duplicitous, but having unambiguous interests, never losing sight of them, and speaking only in their service. They are not overwhelmed by conflicting ideas or emotions, and they do not say things they do not consciously mean. If planners or others slip into mendacity, they can easily retreat. Many communicative theorists assume that people say things that are untrue mainly under the duress of socially constructed (and re-constructable) situations, rather than as a result of deep-seated personality traits or anxieties. They share rational theorists' Enlightenment optimism about planners' nature.

How would these theorists interpret the two texts at the beginning of this chapter: Jacobs's and Schön's planner? They would do so in many ways, but probably few would consider the range of passionate, conflicted, and irrational feelings that accompany Jacobs's ego involvement, paranoia, hatred, and self-acknowledged unreasonable behavior. Nor is it likely that many would inquire what about Schön's planner's personality leads him to construct relationships that inevitably defeat his conscious planning interests. Schön says he has seen variants of this planner's actions everywhere. Healey writes, "Communicative skill is now recognized as an important quality of a trained planner. But we still know little about what it involves. . . ." (1992a, 19).

It is difficult to explain anyone's actions fully; however, theorizing, as teaching and intervention, requires considering a sufficient range of possibilities to make sense of actions. If actions are regrettable, theorists should explain how they might be avoided; if they are effective, how they could be encouraged.

PLANNING THEORY AS PRACTICE

Communicative theorists have done much more than rational theorists to describe planning and planners; yet, many communicative theorists share with their predecessors a rational view of planners (and others) as actors. This assumption limits their ability to interpret actions and to advise planners on how to act. Put simply: the assumption is unrealistic, and yet theorists continue to hold it. How can this be explained?

It is important to interpret these theorists' writings as the texts of authors whose practice requires them to publish theoretical texts. Their books, articles, and chapters are words published in specific contexts for specific purposes. A proper analysis would involve interviewing authors about their lives and work, as well as members of the audience about their understandings of the texts (see Healey 1991). The analysis here is less complete, based on varying degrees of intimacy with authors, relatively little knowledge about their personal lives, and almost no discussion about why they wrote particular pieces, but also years of research with planning practitioners, long familiarity with academic life, publishing, and the invisible college of planning theorists, and reasonable, though imperfect, self-knowledge as a planning theorist. The reader is warned about the limitations of this speculative, but informed, analysis.

The distinction between "espoused theory" and "theory-in-use" helps understand the meanings of theorists' writings as part of their practice (Argyris and Schön 1974, 1978; Argyris 1982). "Espoused theory" refers to public statements about how one should act, how others should act, or how one or others do act. "Theory-in-use," by contrast, comprises principles inherent in action, whether or not the actor is aware of or intends them. People are conscious of their espoused theory but usually not of their theory-in-use. Moreover, the theories typically follow different logics.

Public espousals are actions for an audience. Accordingly, people tend to describe their own actions and to advise others on how to act in ways that imply they know how to act effectively. They are likely to present their actions as reasonable, high-minded, coherent, and successful. In reality, however, people often act inconsistently, selfishly, uncertainly, mistrustfully, and even unsuccessfully. Argyris and Schön believe these incongruities between espoused theories and theories-in-use reflect two intentions: one is to deceive others about one's goodness and efficacy; the other is to deceive oneself.

Most of us are not as competent or effective as we would like to be. We may have unseemly motives, not always be logical, ignore what we recognize to be valid criticism, resist learning from mistakes, and in our endeavors fail. Although we may recognize our shortcomings, we may unsympathetically expect ourselves to do much better, even be perfect. In addition, we often assume others expect the same of us. As a result, many of us are anxious about seeming weak or wrong and being blamed for problems or mistakes. We may then plan our actions to defend ourselves against seeming imperfect or being blamed for failure. The first step is to close off our recognition of our weaknesses, to forget them. Thus we may espouse high-sounding goals to convince ourselves that, not only do we really pursue only these, but we succeed admirably. This self-deception precedes any representation to others.

In these terms, what theorists publish consists of espousals, but their actions in publishing involve theories-in-use. The many ways they act as academics or planners, for instance, involve theory-in-use, which they may or may not recognize, articulate, or espouse. When we ask what planning theory says about the politics of planning practice, we are asking about the relationship of theoretical espousals by one group of practitioners to the theories-in-use of another. Because espousals are usually more rational than theories-in-use, we should expect not only that theorists' published work is a flawed indication of their practice, but also that it poorly addresses the vicissitudes of planners' practice.

Before looking at links between planning theory and planning practice, we will explore what planning theorists' espousals mean as an expression of their practice. One clue comes from the studies of planning practitioners.

STUDIES OF PLANNERS' POLITICS

Research on planners distinguishes four groups in terms of political beliefs and activity (see Baum 1986, 1988). A substantial minority recognize the planning world as political and choose their actions strategically. They are primarily politicians, with relatively few technical skills. A second group, probably also a minority, combine political thinking and action with technical analysis. They may emphasize whichever considerations and skills best fit specific situations. A larger third group consistently act as technicians. They do not recognize politics in planning, they regard issues as technical, and they think of their actions as the appropriate application of technical methods to problems.

Most interestingly, one group of planners is ambivalent about politics. Their conflicts about politics suggest what is difficult about political action for other planners as well. In addition, what they say resembles what many communicative theorists say. They see the planning world as political, involving the allocation of valued goods and services. They understand that interested parties must act strategically to get what they want. They acknowledge that these conditions make it difficult for planners to identify a unitary public interest, be neutral observers, or give disinterested advice, as the traditional rational theorists have proposed. Nevertheless, they draw back from acting politically. They do not want to identify themselves with interests that others might challenge, and they want to be neutral technicians (Vasu 1979).

Although they are cynical about the efficacy of analysis and believe planners should use political tactics, they insist on technical expertise and neutral positions (Howe and Kaufman 1979). Even when they contend they should be protected by licensing and have more power over decisions, they argue against acting politically on their own behalf (Baum 1983). On the one hand, these planners accurately see the planning environment as political but, on the other hand, they want apolitical roles.

When persons make statements that violate conventional logic—for example, both recognizing an inevitably political world and advocating neutrality in it—they mean to say their experience is contradictory. Psychological interpretation helps make sense of the data. It appears that, even though many planners intellectually recognize the political character of planning, emotionally some are afraid of the personal implications. If the world is political, they should act politically. The essence of political action is the exercise of power; yet, here is where these planners seem to stop.

The seemingly paradoxical beliefs about political action may express anxiety about the exercise of power. Attempting to act powerfully against others entails risks of being defeated, losing goods or status, and being humiliated. Moreover, trying to act powerfully with others requires working intimately together, which some people also find uncomfortable. Further, even success is not unambiguous: acting powerfully may mean hurting others and feeling guilty for that, as well as taking responsibility for the outcomes of programs and their effects on others' lives. Planners in this group may believe that these dangers outweigh the potential rewards of power. They may unconsciously rationalize their fears by choosing technician roles so that they do not have to try to exercise power directly against others, or even think about it. By equating a technical role with "professionalism," they give the balance of emotional weight to wishes to deny politics and power.

AN AMBIVALENT PLANNING THEORY

These planners' actions could be articulated into a theory of planning, that might be their theory-in-use. It includes the following rules:

1. Collect information about issues and their environment, including both the substance of issues and political interests.

2. Assess the personal risks in acting in such an environment, with attention to possibilities of conflict with others, especially the powerful.

3. Select a role that avoids risks of conflict, intimacy, defeat, guilt, or responsibility.

4. Take actions consistent with that role, emphasizing technical neutrality and formal rationality as means of avoiding conflict. If necessary, ignore or deny information about political interests that could undermine a technical role.

This theory has two significant characteristics. First, it focuses on the planner's role as actor, rather than the substance or formal aspects of issues. Here, the practitioner's security is the main consideration, with the role to be framed any way that offers it. This choice will affect a planner's language, arguments, and proposals. However, assuming a safe role is more important than finding optimal problem solutions. This norm resembles disjointed incrementalism more than traditional rationality (Lindblom 1959).

The second important characteristic of this theory is that, in concentrating on the planner's relations with interested parties, it is political. It recognizes that powerful actors have interests in the outcomes of issues and recommends strategically choosing a role that offers apparent control without risk from those actors. The model encourages using technical claims for political purposes. However, for this approach to succeed, planners must deny these aims to others as well as to themselves. Without denial, they cannot act. They must push fears about conflict and defeat from their consciousness so that they can think of themselves as acting consistently in rationally choosing a technical role, and they can avoid recognition of the politics that makes them anxious. Thus, there is a hidden fifth step to this theory:

5. Conceal steps 2 and 3 (and this step) from others and oneself.[3]

THE PUZZLE OF PLANNING THEORISTS' ACTIONS

Planners who acknowledge politics but choose apolitical roles resemble those communicative theorists who record the pervasiveness of politics but portray planners as even-minded interpreters free of strong biases or passions—persons who can almost effortlessly measure their political involvement. They describe planners as freer of, or more able to, control emotional attachments than most persons. Even more puzzling, the theorists are political activists themselves yet urge planners to act differently than they do.

Theorists strategize to get manuscripts published, and they strategize to get tenure and promotions, among other things. Editors' claims that they select manuscripts on the basis of their merits and students' complaints that the university is not "the real world" notwithstanding, success in both realms requires political skills. Dispassionate observation does not lead to publication, tenure, and promotion, even if editors, reviewers, and university colleagues share a norm of dispassionate observation. Why do some communicative theorists, following the rationalists, depict planners with little of the feeling and commitment that informs and surrounds their own actions?

One possibility is that the theorists deliberately dissemble, concealing thoughts of activism from anyone who might be offended, such as academic officers who can tolerate faculty members who think deconstruction but not those who act institutional change. Managers generally try to control emotional expression as subversive to organizations (Van Maanen and Kunda 1989). Theorists following a theory-in-use like the one outlined above may find the risks in step 2 sufficient to encourage them to espouse theory that keeps them safe. Dalton (1986) suggests such reasoning helps explain "why the rational paradigm persists" despite its logical and practical shortcomings.

This interpretation treats theorists' actions as rational and perhaps even conscious efforts to deceive potential enemies. Schwartz (1990) suggests that theorists may take step 5 to conceal their thinking also from themselves, deliberately forgetting it. He reports that when he asks students at the beginning of the semester to describe their organizational experiences, they regale him with stories of treachery, confusion, victimization, and anxiety. However, if he tries to look further into this view of organizations ("the snakepit"), students rebel. They insist he teach them the classical rational model of bureaucracy, which in no way resembles the organizations they have discussed. While they describe places out of control, they insist he teach them theories that would fit an organization amenable to rational control.

Schwartz speculates that his students want to maintain the rational ideal because their reality is painful. They feel incompetent in it, and it makes them anxious. Why not, then, espouse a rational idea, as if devotion to it could magically deny everyday reality and substitute something reassuring? His interpretation parallels Argyris and Schön's (1974) and Argyris's (1982) findings among thousands of professionals.

Schwartz's reasoning offers an explanation for the puzzle of many planning theorists: they may choose to espouse rational views of planners that ignore the possibilities of political action because academic, professional, or other politics are too painful to recognize and write about. Theorists may come to these conclusions in steps 2, 3, and 4 unconsciously, or they may choose to forget how they did so in step 5. In either case, espousing a dispassionate, reflective view of planners as actors in a political world is rational, but doing so follows a different logic than most theorists discuss.

PLANNING THEORISTS' RELATIONS WITH PLANNING PRACTITIONERS

Perhaps planning theorists' espousals serve similar functions for planning practitioners. Planners may appreciate the latent functions of abstract rational theories even while criticizing them. Planners often attack these theories as being unrealistic, especially when they are upended by politics at work. Nevertheless, many seem to wish their work were really as the theories had encouraged them to believe (Baum 1983). Thus, despite what some planners say, they may want academics to espouse neat theoretical ideals, because they offer psychic escape from a frustrating world.

In general, emphasis on rationality suggests only planners know what is necessary to oversee public decision making. At the same time, the theories offer a magical escape from troubling work conditions by suggesting that planning "really" is not political. Rational planning theories do this by denying politics altogether. Communicative theories that portray the planner as an unemotional cognitive reasoner imply that planners can get by, even prevail, just by thinking and speaking or writing clearly. Moreover, a planner who is rational, who is innocent of compelling passions, must be judged innocent of all else, such as interest in power, interest in defeating others—in short, anything aggressive that might offend others and provoke retaliation (see Hoch 1988).

Still, the ambiguous juxtaposition of the emphasis on the planner's cognitive activities with the description of a tempestuous world of political power requires resolution. If cognitive reasoning is enough for planners to prevail, then perhaps politicians are not "really" a part of planning and do not have to be taken seriously. Such an unrealistic conclusion may serve a magical purpose. By suggesting there are no powerful politicians in the planning world, theorists take revenge on them, mentally eradicating them and telling planners, as well, to give politicians no mind. Although these theorists do not describe the real world, they respond to its real frustrations, and they know how to satisfy the wishes of planners.

Many planners are ambivalent about rational theory because they need both to believe it and to doubt it. On the one hand, they want it to be true, because it removes them from a troubling world. On the other hand, by criticizing rational theories, they can deny their own unrealistic desires. Paradoxically, this denial may be still one more part of the rational wish. By disowning real fantasies, planners may further subscribe to an ideal world in which anxiety, anger, escape wishes, and other emotions do not exist. They thus deny their troubles and feelings about them.

THEORIZING AND THEORISTS

This analysis suggests that planning theorists who, in presenting rational views of planners, do not seem to acknowledge their own political practice or the politics of planning, tacitly address the feelings aroused in political situations.

A better understanding planning practice requires us to reconceptualize planning theory and practice. First, we must recognize that both theorists and planners are practitioners and that, as such, they confront many similar challenges and respond in similar ways.

Second, we must discard reassuring but simplistic notions of what planners do. The data on ambivalent planners reveal that planners are like other people. They too think and feel about their work. Their activities bring them both pleasure and anxiety. On occasion their logical statements about their work mask "irrational" feelings about it. Sometimes their conscious descriptions of themselves are accurate—for example, that they are analyzing problems to design efficient, equitable interventions. However, at other times, they unconsciously plan to do quite else—for example, avoiding seeing things they think might antagonize politicians. Planners do both, regardless of which is preferable, and if we want to understand planning, we must understand why different planners choose different aims at different times.

Third, we must think more imaginatively about relationships between theorists and planners. Conventionally we argue that theorists should learn about practice from planners and then offer realistic theoretical guidance for them. This statement often rests on simplistic notions of what planners do and what is realistic advice. If planners do both rational and irrational, conscious and unconscious things, theory must explain and offer guidance in relation to the problems of both.

Still, the conventional argument about what theorists should do for planners ignores what theorists may already do for them. If planners have both conscious and unconscious aims, current theorizing that seems irrelevant to the former may persist because it speaks to the latter. If "better" theory will help planners act more effectively in a political world, we must first know more about why many planners now choose to avoid thinking about that world altogether.

Empirical research on how planners think about practice is important. However, we theorists need to understand ourselves better as well, because we can learn about planning from our own practice. We must ask ourselves more seriously why we develop the theories we do. How do our experiences lead us to emphasize specific principles? In particular, how do our thoughts and feelings about acting politically and exercising power affect how we advise others to act? Are our theoretical admonitions consistent with our actions? If not, why?

Planning theorists are people for whom acting is problematic; we do not takes its efficacy for granted. After all, we have chosen to be planning theorists, rather than planners, much less professional politicians. Our doubts about action are not unique to us, nor to planners. What distinguishes us is that we are moved and able to write about some of the problems of action. We should more sympathetically recognize these issues in ourselves and struggle to understand how we experience and respond to them, rather than deny them and write as if action were simply a matter of dispassionate cognition. In particular, we should probe our experiences with the human problems of power.

If we examined the relations between our theorizing and our practice, we could learn immeasurably about the act of theorizing. If we accepted our experiences as valid and as kindred to others', we could better understand what practitioners want from a theory of action. In the end, we could have surer faith that what we advise others represents more than our own fantasies, that, even as idealism, our theories offer realistic direction and hope.

Notes

1. The quotation marks around "rational" indicate that traditional theorists claimed a universal validity for a particular concept of rationality. Quotation marks will be used sparingly in the text, but the reader should keep this point in mind.

2. Some of these writers are describing their own assumptions, some examining those of others. They share a focus on a "rational" model of planning that emphasizes the two assumptions described here.

3. See Baum (1987) for examples and further explanation. Argyris and Schön (1974; Argyris 1982) describe this way of thinking as a "Model I" theory that is common among professionals. Schön's (1983) case example provides a further illustration.

REFERENCES

Alexander, E. R. 1984. After rationality, what? A review of responses to paradigm breakdown. *Journal of the American Planning Association* 50: 62–9.

_____. 1996. After rationality. In S. J. Mandelbaum, L. Mazza, and R. W. Burchell, eds., *Explorations in Planning Theory.* New Brunswick, NJ: Center for Urban Policy Research.

Altshuler, A. A. 1965. *The city planning process.* Ithaca, NY: Cornell University Press.

Argyris, C. 1982. *Reasoning, learning, and action.* San Francisco: Jossey-Bass.

_____, and D. A. Schön. 1974. *Theory in practice: increasing professional effectiveness*. San Francisco: Jossey-Bass.

Arrow, K. 1958. *Social choice and individual values*. New York: Wiley.

Banfield, E. C. 1955. Note on conceptual theme. In M. Meyerson and E. C. Banfield, eds., *Politics, planning, and the public interest*. New York: Free Press, 303–29.

Baum, H. S. 1983. *Planners and public expectations*. Cambridge, MA: Schenkman.

_____. 1986. Politics and ambivalence in planners' practice. In B. Checkoway, ed. *Strategic perspectives on planning practice*. Lexington, MA: D. C. Heath.

_____. 1987. *The invisible bureaucracy: the unconscious in organizational problem solving*. New York: Oxford.

_____. 1988. Problems of governance and the professions of planners. In D. Schaffer, ed., *Principles and policy: urban planning in the United States*. London: Mansell, and Baltimore: Johns Hopkins University Press, 279–302.

_____. 1990. *Organizational membership: personal development in the workplace*. Albany, NY: SUNY Press.

Caro, R. A. 1975. *The power broker*. New York: Vintage.

Catanese, A. J. 1974. *Planners and local politics*. Beverly Hills, CA: Sage.

Clavel, P. 1986. *The progressive city*. New Brunswick, NJ: Rutgers University Press.

Dalton, L. C. 1986. Why the rational paradigm persists—the resistance of professional education and practice to alternative forms of planning. *Journal of Planning Education and Research* 5: 147–53.

Davidoff, P., and T. A. Reiner. 1962. A choice theory of planning. *Journal of the American Institute of Planners* 28: 103–15.

Etzioni, A. 1968. *The active society*. New York: Free Press.

Fainstein, S. S.; N. I. Fainstein; R. C. Hill; D. Judd; and M. P. Smith. 1983. *Restructuring the city*. New York: Longman.

Faludi, A. 1973. *Planning theory*. Oxford: Pergamon.

Forester, J. 1989. *Planning in the face of power*. Berkeley: University of California Press.

_____. 1993. *Critical theory, public policy, and planning practice*. Albany, NY: State University of New York Press.

Goldstein, H. 1984. Planning as argumentation. *Environment and Planning B: Planning and Design* 11: 297–312.

Hartman, C. 1984. *The transformation of San Francisco*. Totowa, NJ: Rowman and Allanheld.

Healey, P. 1991. Researching planning practice. *Town Planning Review* 62: 447–59.

_____. 1992a. A planner's day: knowledge and action in communicative practice. *Journal of the American Planning Association* 58: 9-20.

_____. 1992b. Planning through debate: the communicative turn in planning theory. *Town Planning Review* 63: 143–62.

Hoch, C. 1988. Conflict at large: a national survey of planners and political conflict. *Journal of Planning Education and Research* 8: 25–34.

_____. 1994. *What planners do*. Chicago: Planners Press.

Howe, E., and J. Kaufman. 1979. The ethics of contemporary American planners. *Journal of the American Planning Association* 45: 243–55.

Jacobs, A. B. 1978. *Making city planning work*. Chicago: Planners Press.

Krumholz, N., and J. Forester. 1990. *Making equity planning work*. Philadelphia: Temple University Press.

Liggett, H. 1991. Where they don't have to take you in: the representation of homelessness in public policy. *Journal of Planning Education and Research* 10: 201–8.

Lindblom, C. 1959. The science of muddling through. *Public Administration Review* 19: 78–88.

Mandelbaum, S. 1990. Reading plans. *Journal of the American Planning Association* 56: 350–6.

_____. 1991. Telling stories. *Journal of Planning Education and Research* 10: 209–14.

Meyerson, M., and E. C. Banfield. 1955. *Politics, planning, and the public interest*. New York: Free Press.

Needleman, M. L., and C. E. Needleman. 1974. *Guerrillas in the bureaucracy*. New York: Wiley.

Rabinovitz, F. F. 1969. *City politics and planning*. Chicago: Aldine.

Schön, D. A. 1983. *The reflective practitioner*. New York: Basic Books.

_____, ed. 1991. *The reflective turn*. New York: Teachers College Press.

Schwartz, H. S. 1990. *Narcissistic process and corporate decay*. New York: New York University Press.

Simon, H. A. 1976. *Administrative behavior*. 3d ed. New York: Free Press.

Tett, A., and J. M. Wolfe. 1991. Discourse analysis and city plans. *Journal of Planning Education and Research* 10: 195–200.

Throgmorton, J. A. 1990. Passion, reason, and power: the rhetorics of electric power planning in Chicago. *Journal of Architectural and Planning Research* 7: 330–50.

_____. 1992. Planning as persuasive storytelling about the future: negotiating an electric power rate settlement in Illinois. *Journal of Planning Education and Research* 12: 17–31.

_____. 1993. Planning as a rhetorical activity: survey research as a trope in arguments about electric power planning in Chicago. *Journal of the American Planning Association* 57, 3: 334–46.

Van Maanen, J., and G. Kunda. 1989. "Real feelings": emotional expression and organizational culture. In L. L. Cummings and B. M. Staw, eds. *Research in organizational behavior.* vol. 11. Greenwich, CT: JAI Press.

Vasu, M. 1979. *Politics and planning.* Chapel Hill: University of North Carolina Press.

Commentary

Bent Flyvbjerg

The Dark Side of Planning: Rationality and "Realrationalität"

REAL RATIONALITY

Niccolò Machiavelli, the founder of modern political and administrative thought, made clear that an understanding of politics requires distinguishing between formal politics and what later, with Ludwig von Rochau, would become known as *Realpolitik*. No such distinction has been employed in the study of rationality. Yet I will argue that distinguishing between formal rationality and *"Realrationalität"* is as important for the understanding of rationality and planning as the distinction between formal politics and *Realpolitik* has been for understanding politics.

Having lived most of my life in a part of the world that originated free, universal education, the public library, the public high school, the cooperative movement, the parliamentary ombudsman, and other institutions essential to a well-functioning democracy, I have deep respect for Francis Bacon's dictum that "knowledge is power." Bacon's idea is fundamental to modernity and to that perhaps most modern notion of all, planning.[1] It is basic to the Enlightenment project: "Enlightenment is power." Hence, the more enlightenment—the more rational knowledge—the better. Still there is a problem here, which is also a problem for two of the four articles in this section of the book, just as it is a problem for mainstream planning theory. The problem lies in the naive normativism of many modernists and, indeed, with the modern project itself. Modernity's elevation of rationality as an ideal seems to result in, or at least to coexist with, an ignorance of the real rationalities at work in actual social institutions and in actual planning processes. Many modernists seem unwilling to accept the fact that if we examine how knowledge, rationality, and power work in real life, we may end up standing Bacon on his head.

I am not trying to place myself in any anti-modernist camp here. Rather, I wish to stress that the modern normative attitude—an attitude that has been dominant in planning theory throughout the history of this discipline—does not serve modernity, or planning theory, well. The ideals of modernity, democracy, and planning—ideals that typically are worth fighting for—are better served by understanding *Realrationalität* than normative rationality. Normative rationality may provide an ideal to strive for, but it is a poor guide to the strategies and tactics needed for moving toward the ideal. This, in my analysis, is the quandary of normative idealists, including the majority of planning theorists: they know where they would like to go but not how to get there. The study of *Realrationalität*, on the other hand, provides both. It pursues what Machiavelli called the *verita effettuale* and Nietzsche *wirkliche Historie* of rationality. In doing so, it depicts what the lived, as opposed to the ideal, world of modern democracy and planning looks like and how it operates as a guide to the transformative mechanisms of democracy and planning.

Let us see how each of the four authors under comment deal with the issue of formal rationality versus *Realrationalität*, Enlightenment planning versus real planning.

MANNERS AND PLANNERS

Given my view on modern rationality and *Realrationalität*, I am uncertain about Giovanni Ferraro's statement in "Planning as Creative Interpretation" that the planner's "redemption" cannot be expected from "some additional attribute to the word 'rationality.'" I agree, if by redemption Ferraro means salvation. Salvation is for another world, not inhabited by planners, as far as we know. I disagree, if redemption is taken to mean, more modestly, a change in our understanding of planning for the better. I think that all the additional attributes to rationality that Ferraro mentions— "new," "expanded," "existential," and "narrative"—have improved our understanding of planning. And I think, as said, that this understanding can be further improved by adding the characteristic "real" to "rationality." In fact, some of the authors under review help develop the understanding of rationality in this direction, most notably Howell S. Baum.

Ferraro tends to see rationality and planning as good and power as bad. "Practitioners face moral risks. . . . Some risks arise from people with whom they work," Ferraro writes. "They can be tempted into convenient deceptions and seduced by power. They can be intimidated and fired." All this is true, but it is also a one-sided view that tends to reduce planners to noble victims instead of seeing them as real actors in real political processes. Planners are often much more powerful than Ferraro's characteristic suggests, and the opposite observation to Ferraro's is just as relevant: Those who work with planners—politicians, for instance, and certainly citizens as Allen, Throgmorton, and Baum show in their articles—face risks at the hands of planners.

Given Ferraro's view of power and politics—or lack of view, as Baum would have it—he inevitably ends up in the naive normativism of modernity thinkers. Planners become noble individuals who need "ethical commitments to 'good conversations' and to the 'manners' that sustain communication." Planners must meet "morally acceptable criteria." Yes, but does this hold for planners more than for anybody else? If not, why use it as a characteristic to distinguish planners as a professional group? Planners must "listen" and they must pay "attention." "Dialogue [is] a value in itself" for planners. Planners must promote "[g]ood conversation" to help people "express themselves fully as human beings and as members of a community." Planners need to work with "how to transform non-cooperative into cooperative games," "sharing information" and how to "build a common world of meanings and reciprocally consistent expectations to be shared by the community." In sum, what planners need is a "'book of good manners.'" And the work of planning theorists should be bolstering planners' ethical commitments to the values expressed in this book.

The more I study the real rationalities at work when real planners plan, the less I see such talk as meaningful. Not because I think the ideals depicted are undesirable. I would, in fact, like to see more of Ferraro's noble planners. I would also like to see an end to world hunger, war, and environmental degradation. But such talk is banal without grounding in the *Realrationalität* of planning and politics. It therefore leaves us defenseless against this rationality. It obfuscates our understanding of what planning is and how it works, and developing such an understanding is, in my view, the first task of planning researchers. If you want to change it, get to know it.

Planners and planning theorists have excessively "good manners" in the sense of good intentions. This, too, is the problem with Ferraro's viewpoint. I, quite simply, do not know "the planner" Ferraro and like-minded planning theorists talk about, except from the discourse of planning theorists. As societies go, I think I live in a fairly good society. There is plenty of room for improvement, needless to say; it is not the Good Society of planning theory textbooks. And planners, as any other professional group, are not the good-willed change agents of that society. Instead, they are civil servants or servants to interest organizations and private companies that pay their salaries and expect them to promote their interests. If they do not, there are sanctions. They are the kind of planners Martin Wachs writes about in his impressive body of work on planning ethics and on the *Realrationalität* of forecasting; for instance this one, whom Wachs met when interviewing public officials, consultants and planners who had been involved in transit planning cases:

> [A] planner admitted to me that he had reluctantly but repeatedly adjusted the patronage figures upward, and the cost figures downward to satisfy a local elected official who wanted to compete successfully for a federal grant. Ironically, and to the chagrin of that planner, when the project was later built, and the patronage proved lower and costs higher than the published estimates, the same local politician was asked by the press to explain the outcome. The official's response was to say, "It's not my fault; I had to rely on the forecasts made by our staff, and they seem to have made a big mistake here." (Wachs 1990, 144–5)

It is nice of Wachs to describe the planner as "reluctant" and to give us an example where deception does not seem to pay off for the planner. In this way we can still sympathize with the planner and learn not to do the same. My own research indicates, however, that planners are often not reluctant when deceiving the public and that deception often pays off. Planners participate in deception, weak or strong, so often that they develop their own humor and stories about it.[2] Recently, I carried out a study of the *Realrationalität* of planning and politics in the Danish town of Aalborg. The chief of city planning, a high-ranking civil servant, explained to me in a taped, in-depth interview how he helped manipulate the public debate about alternative locations of a large bus terminal in order to have the terminal built where the mayor wanted it, and the public did not, in the middle of the historical center of town. After telling me this, the chief joyfully related, tape still rolling, the following parable on how rationality was used in this and other decisions in the Aalborg case:

> It's like the story of Little Town, where the bell-ringer calls up the telephone exchange because he has to set the church clock. So he calls the telephone exchange and asks what time it is, and the telephone operator looks out of the window towards the church clock and says, "It's five o'clock." "Good," says the bell ringer, "then my clock is correct." (Flyvbjerg 1991b, 142)[3]

The main difference between Little Town and Aalborg is that where the reasoning regarding time in Little Town was circular by accident, the planners in Aalborg deliberately made their reasoning circular: the bus terminal must be located where passengers transfer, they argued, but they had, at the same time, planned the transportation system so transfers would take place where they and the mayor wanted the terminal. The goal was not to have to "change the time," that is, the location of the terminal. In formal terms, the rationality of this kind of planning process is just as imaginary as the time in Little Town. In real terms, by playing games of power covered up as technical reasoning, the mayor and the planners got what they wanted—a monument to themselves—despite rampant protests from socialists to conservatives, greens to business, the city architect's office to the Danish EPA in Copenhagen. The consequences were also very real in terms of steep increases in traffic accidents and in levels of air and noise pollution and physical blight.

These, then, are the kinds of real and bad-mannered planners that, in my view, we need to study in planning theory if we are to make progress—not Ferraro's noble individuals. As Baum shows us, the first step to being moral is realizing that we are not. This holds true for both planners and planning theorists.

THE LITTLE QUESTION

Judith Allen's chapter, "Our Town: Foucault and Knowledge-based Politics in London," is refreshingly free from wishful thinking about planning and planners. Allen is studying real planning and counter-planning at work in a specific case. In my view, Allen's is the kind of study we need more of in planning research. But I do not think the story Allen wants to tell us, using the ideas she wants to use, can be told within the limited space of a research article. This does not make Allen's choice of subject matter and approach less valuable or less interesting. It just means that she needs a full-scale book in which to unfold her story. This chapter warrants such a book.

Allen says she uses Foucault's ideas "to tell the story" of a group of tenants' associations in central London between 1974 and 1990. Foucault (1982a, 217 [in Dreyfus and Rabinow 1982]) emphasizes the need "to begin the analysis with a 'how.'" For Foucault "the little question, what happens? . . . flat and empirical," is the main question. If the researcher does not address this question, "an extremely complex configuration of realities is allowed to escape." Earlier, Foucault (1971, 76–7 [in Rabinow 1984]) said that his method "requires patience and a knowledge of details," and that it "depends on a vast accumulation of source material" that is interpreted "according to a rigorous method." This explains why Foucault spent a large part of his typical working day in the archive laboring over "entangled and confused parchments, on documents that have been scratched over and recopied many times." It also explains why he chose books and not articles as the main medium to present his research: in each study he needed the space and possibilities of a full-scale monograph to unfold his material.

In my reading, Allen's article is an example of what happens when a Foucauldian approach is not allowed its proper medium of presentation. The author gets in the way of the source material because lack of space necessitates constant summarizing and makes it impossible to employ the perhaps most important expository tactic of Foucauldian methodology: letting the deep metaphorical detail speak directly to the reader without summaries or other pedagogical devises. In short, the problem is that Allen sums up and *tells* us about the Paddington story instead of letting her material *show* us what the story is about.

Consider the following examples. At one point in her story about the Paddington Federation of Tenants and Residents Associations, Allen tells us that "careful listening practices" of the audience at the Federation's monthly general meetings "taught the speakers both how to speak and how to listen, thereby contributing to the development of a unique form of discourse within the Federation." But we, the readers, are not allowed to hear real speakers speak or the "unique form of discourse" to which Allen attaches such importance. At another point, Allen tells us about a major publication from the Federation, *Home Truths*, which "established the Federation as a political entity." But we are not given excerpts to read that would allow us to understand hermeneutically the power of this publication. In yet another part of the case story, Allen explains how "everyone described their experiences with 'hotelization'" in their own words as preparation for a public inquiry. But not one of these experiences is shown to us. We hear of "back-and-forth of question or answer," but we hear no specific questions and answers. And so it goes. Many actors are apparently active in the Paddington case, but Allen does not allow their voices to be heard. The only voice is Allen's own. All this is not only highly un-Foucauldian, it is also, like most didactics, slightly dull. And what is worse, the main purpose of a Foucauldian approach is lost: grasping the complex configuration of realities Foucault talked about, that would allow us to understand the *Realrationalität* and *wirklich* planning of the Paddington case.

However, at the end of the story, there is an important observation for anyone who works within the context of planning and politics to expand the domain of practices of freedom. Allen rightly finds that existing "practices and discourses associated with democracy" and existing "divisions within the state's own networks of power" are where to look if we are searching for effective ways to change politics and planning. This is a far cry from appeals to cognitive or communicative models of rationality, or to planners with good manners. Here, the sobering effect of a Foucauldian approach makes itself felt after all.

INSIGNIFICANT TRUTHS

It is interesting to contrast Allen's chapter with James A. Throgmorton's "'Impeaching' Research: Planning As Persuasive and Constitutive Discourse." Where Allen gets into trouble because of the impossibility of telling a fifteen-year-long story about planning and politics in a Foucauldian manner in a short research article, Throgmorton limits himself to a case a few hours long, with relevant context. Even if Throgmorton is not employing a Nietzschean or Foucauldian approach, his point of departure is, in fact, one of Nietzsche's "discreet and apparently insignificant truths"—a survey of how Chicago business would react to a change from private to public ownership of part of the city's electric power system—that turns out to illuminate what Nietzsche called "cyclopean monuments," in this case the importance of rhetoric to politics and planning and, thus, to planning practice and theory (Foucault 1971, 77 [in Rabinow 1984]).

The result of Throgmorton's approach is that his case comes alive on us, even within the confines of a short chapter. We are there, at the meeting, in the room in Chicago. Furthermore, at the level of detail Throgmorton employs, the dichotomy between the specific and the general tends to dissolve. Phenomena are, at the same time, very specific and very general, as in the best of tales. This, in my view, is no small achievement, and it is something we need more of in planning research.

It is also interesting to compare Throgmorton's article and Baum's "Practicing Planning Theory in a Political World." Baum describes the way some communicative theorists focus on texts without attention to their authors. According to Baum, authors are often—I would say typically—not interviewed about the interpretation of their texts. There is little communication here on the part of communicative theorists. The result is, as Baum rightly points out, a tacit world of ideas without real people, and that world "resembles the rationalists' spacescape." This, too, becomes a problem for Throgmorton. In his case, the "text" is a videotape of a meeting between members of the Chicago Mayor's Energy Task Force, community and consumer group representatives, and the central figure Michael

Leard, a consultant whose company carried out the survey in question. Throgmorton characterizes Leard as "unhappy," "interrupting," "angry," "extremely hostile," "dodging," "rambling," "unkempt," "loud," "incoherent," "deceitful," and "untrustworthy." In short, Throgmorton sees Leard as a "political hack." Indeed, the transcripts of Leard speaking are somewhat rambling and incoherent. But anyone who has transcribed taped conversation and thus has had to transform the spoken to the written word knows that we all sound rambling and incoherent if transcribed verbatim, as Throgmorton says Leard was, only omitting "such verbal ticks as 'ah' and 'uh.'"

By the end of the day we, the readers, may come to agree with Throgmorton's view of Leard. But at present we, and Leard, are entirely at Throgmorton's mercy. This seems neither balanced, fair, nor communicative. It would be interesting to see a dialogue between Throgmorton and Leard about this article, for instance, in a new article about their interaction. As things stand now, Leard does not become a person in Throgmorton's story. He becomes, instead, one of the "ideas without real people" Baum talks about, namely the idea "political hack." In this sense even Throgmorton is not detailed enough, not real enough, too rationalist. And, sure enough, what Throgmorton ends up recommending—despite talk of planners that are not naive—is quite naive and, like Ferraro, dependent on the characteristic modernist leap of faith: " . . . we [sic] planners should strive to make possible: to be planners who seek to promote and facilitate a public, democratic, persuasive discourse"; "[s]uch planners would 'listen'"; and they would seek "to learn how [their] audience thinks and feels." These, again, are noble intentions, and it is the opposite of what I mean by an understanding of planning based on *Realrationalität*. No power base is identified for Throgmorton's "not naive" planners, no strategies and tactics on how to get from today's situation to where he wants them (us) to go. In my analysis, this is opportunity lost for Throgmorton. My hunch is that with the impressive level of detail he works with, the strategies and tactics needed to be non-naive and politically effective are right there at his fingertips, to be found by dialoguing with and digging deeper into his very interesting source material.

DECEIVERS AND LIARS

Howell S. Baum rightly observes that planning theorists say little about planners as political actors and, I would add, therefore say too little of practical relevance to practicing planners. I am in complete agreement with Baum that the way out of this dilemma is to "probe our experiences with the human problems of power." This, in my view, is the single most important piece of advice in the four chapters. Following it is necessary to move planning theory ahead as an academic discipline. When it comes to portraying planners and planning, the quest of planning theorists could be called the escape from power. But if there is one thing we should have learned today from students of power, it is that there is no escape from it. "The problem is not of trying to dissolve [relations of power] in the utopia of a perfectly transparent communication," as Foucault (1982b, 18 [in Bernauer and Rasmussen 1988]) said, but to give "the rules of law, the techniques of management, and also the ethics . . . which would allow these games of power to be played with a minimum of domination," for instance by employing and expanding the strategies and tactics Judith Allen briefly outlines in closing her chapter.

Baum is quite the Nietzschean in pointing out the need for planners and planning theorists to deceive others and themselves. Nietzsche (1967, 451) said that the "world is . . . false, cruel, contradictory, seductive, without meaning." Baum refers to "treachery, confusion, victimization, and anxiety" as basic organizational and, by implication, planning experiences. Nietzsche, who characterized himself as a "psychologist," said "*We have need of lies* in order to conquer this reality, this 'truth,' [that is, the false and cruel world] that is, in order to *live*." Similarly, Baum uses "[p]sychological interpretation" to "make sense of the data" and concludes that the reality of planners and planning theorists may be "too painful to recognize." In Baum's analysis, this may explain both the collective amnesia among planning theorists regarding the real politics of planning and the abundance of normative rational models, be they cognitive or communicative, "as if devotion to [such models] could magically deny everyday reality and substitute something reassuring." These models, then—together with the talk about planners as noble individuals with "good manners," of which Ferraro and Throgmorton have given us examples—are seen as the Nietzschean lies of planning theorists, according to this interpretation.

Baum's incorporation of deception into his "ambivalent planning theory" is most illuminating. In line with my advocacy of a focus on *Realrationalität*, however, I would have liked to see the theory supplemented by rich case stories about real planners and real planning theorists at work, deceiving others and themselves. Again, the space of a book chapter hardly allows for in-depth case studies. This, however, does not alter the fact that we very much need such studies of the phenomena Baum theorizes. I suggest more planning theorists become planning researchers and start working on such studies.

Despite the strengths of Baum's analysis, his emphasis on psychological interpretation results in an idealistic weakness in his theory. According to

Baum's theory, planners and planning theorists deceive because reality is "too painful to recognize." Psychological explanations of deception carry some weight, but they miss out on the political economy of the phenomenon under study. If knowledge is power, then deception influences the distribution of power. It adds to the power of the deceiver, and reduces the power of the deceived. My own research on planning practices confirms Bok's comment (1979, 183, 258) that "most observers would agree that deception is part and parcel of many everyday decisions in government," and, further, that "[t]he social incentives to deceit are at present very powerful; the controls, often weak." Deception, then, is part and parcel of many of the decisions planners are involved in, and the incentives for planners to deceive others are strong. This aspect of planners' activities needs to be included in any descriptive–explanatory–interpretive theory of planning, just as how to curb deception, which in a democratic society will be the purpose of studying deception, should be part of any normative theory; and a general appeal to planners to "speak truthfully" or to have "good manners" will just not do.

The logic of Baum's theory implies that theories and studies of real deception will not see the light of day since the issue is too painful to work with. In my experience this need not be the case. Machiavelli, Nietzsche, and Foucault are examples of outstanding students of deception. Nietzsche (1974) even developed a term for the research needed that says it all: "the gay [fröhliche] science." And, indeed, it can be great fun, if hard work, to track and study real deception at work. Certainly it is interesting, in the way real-lived life is always interesting. Finally, in my view planning theorists are not worth their money—or their words—if they refuse to or are incapable of working with central phenomena like power and politics, lying and deception. Baum will have us believe that this is the case, but his own work excellently disproves him on this point.

TO BE ABSOLUTELY MODERN

To be absolutely modern, Milan Kundera writes in *Immortality*, means never to question the content of modernity. It means to be forever hopeful about the grand ideas of modernity and not to look at modernity as it is lived in actual detail. Planning, and certainly planning theory, seems to me to be absolutely modern in this sense. In *The Prince*, Machiavelli (1984, 91) spells out in no uncertain terms the dangers of the normative attitude when he says "a man who neglects what is actually done for what should be done learns the way to self-destruction." The focus of modernity and of planning theory is on "what should be done." I suggest a reorientation toward the first half of Machiavelli's dictum, "what is actually done," toward *verita effettuale*. In this way, we may gain a better grasp—less idealistic, more grounded—of what planning is and what the strategies and tactics are that may help change it for the better.

Notes

1. By "modernity" I mean the tradition, from the Reformation and the Enlightenment, as it is expressed in attempts to strengthen the domains of cognitive rationality, moral autonomy, and social and political self-determination.

2. Bok (1979, 65), whose view on deception I quote below, also notes the link between deception and humor.

3. The Aalborg study is described in Flyvbjerg (1991a and 1991b); the methodology employed in the study, in Flyvbjerg (1993a). Comments on the methodology can be found in Peattie (1994), Moroni (1993), and Flyvbjerg (1993b).

REFERENCES

Bok, S. 1979. *Lying: moral choice in public and private life*. New York: Vintage Books.

Flyvbjerg, B. 1991a. *Rationalitet og magt* [Rationality and power], vol. I: *Det konkretes videnskab* [The science of the concrete]. Copenhagen: Academic Press.

_____. 1991b. *Rationalitet og magt* [Rationality and power], vol. II: *Et case-baseret studie af planlaegning politik og modernitet* [A case-based study of planning, politics and modernity]. Copenhagen: Academic Press.

_____. 1993a. Aristotle, Foucault and progressive phronesis: outline of an applied ethics for sustainable development. In E. R. Winkler and J. R. Coombs, eds., *Applied ethics: a reader*. Cambridge, MA: Basil Blackwell.

_____. 1993b. *Planning theory, power and progressive phronesis. Reply to Stefano Moroni. Planning Theory 9*.

Foucault, M. 1971. Nietzsche, genealogy, history. In P. Rabinow, ed. [1984], *The Foucault reader*. New York: Pantheon.

_____. 1982a. The subject and power. In H. Dreyfus and P. Rabinow, eds. [1982], *Michel Foucault: beyond structuralism and hermeneutics*. Brighton: Harvester Press.

_____. 1982b. The ethic of care for the self as a practice of freedom. In J. Bernauer and D. Rasmussen, eds. [1988], *The final Foucault.* Cambridge, MA: MIT Press.

Machiavelli, N. 1984. *The prince.* Harmondsworth: Penguin.

Moroni, S. 1993. Planning theory, practical philosophy and phronesis. Comments on Flyvbjerg. *Planning Theory* 9.

Nietzsche, F. 1967. *The will to power.* Translated by W. Kaufmann. New York: Vintage Books.

_____. 1974. *The gay science.* Translated by W. Kaufmann. New York: Vintage Books.

Peattie, L. R. 1994. An approach to urban research in the nineties. In R. Stren, ed., *Urban research in the developing world.* Toronto: Centre for Urban and Community Studies, University of Toronto.

Wachs, M. 1990. Ethics and advocacy in forecasting for public policy. *Business and Professional Ethics Journal* 9, 1 and 2.

PART V

The Status and Use of Ethics

Luigi Mazza

The Status and Use
of Ethics

INTRODUCTION

P lanners' interest in ethics is not recent. It especially developed when the idea of a general theory of planning, capable of ensuring correct choices, began to fade, when the assumption that a good technical choice was necessarily a good choice was called into question, and when the "public interest"—which was, to some extent, a link between technical optimality and ethical good—no longer seemed to provide a compelling normative guide.

The ethical issue of planning—if it is possible to express oneself in these terms—seems to be that of distinguishing between good and bad planning and of replying to the question "How should we play?" In this way, even if planning cannot be identified *tout court* with politics, the issue occurs as the classical problem of the relationship between politics and ethics, of the perpetual tension between an ethics of principles and an ethics of consequences.

I argued in the Introduction to Part I that planning is a blend of two basic types of action to which different forms of rationality and justification correspond. Planning choices are so complex because of the ways in which the ethics of principles and consequences interact with anticipatory and obligatory actions. We must accept the idea that planning decisions may often be made on the basis of a partial rational justification. The differences between these ethical claims can be resolved only by the "complex, inflected, and conflicted" virtue of prudence.

The contributions to this section confront different themes among the boundless field of questions to be explored, but they share the common

397

conviction that only an argumentative approach can solve the ethical knots of planning.

Thomas Harper and Stanley Stein show the theoretical possibility of facing ethical dilemmas through dialogue. The commensurability theme, which is the core of their chapter, is not related to the issue of descriptive homogeneity or the consistent ordering of goods. Rather, it addresses the possibility of communication within and across different moral communities. The authors challenge the premises that communities and culture are incommensurable and that consensus-seeking dialogue is futile, such that power and coercion replace rational persuasion. They think, on the contrary, that a reasonable and meaningful dialogue toward consensus within and between communities is possible when "rationality" and a general agreement on beliefs are in force. Inter-community differences are not different in kind from intra-community differences, and both are commensurable. Non-overlapping instances are extreme cases because most concepts and beliefs are shared between communities.

Harper and Stein regard the incommensurability premise shared by many "post-modernists, communitarians, feminists, and deep ecologists" as essentially incoherent. Even granting that Harper and Stein are right in principle, I do not share their optimism about the promise of "consensus-seeking dialogue." Planning arguments are often grounded in difficult cases in which either moral communities do not overlap or in which they are torn apart by deep conflicts. (It is often difficult in practice to distinguish the two circumstances.)

Sue Hendler's chapter is closer to specific planning themes, concerned with finding a contractual solution to possible conflicts between personal and professional values and circumstances. She offers an outline of ethical decision-making models and focuses in particular on models that seek to integrate the theoretical, ethical, professional, and organizational aspects of ethical decision making.

Hendler's outline serves to introduce three models of planning ethics. The first is a descriptive model of the flows of the decision-making process substantively observed "in terms of its empirical nature, its focus on specific actors, and its emphasis on observed sources of influence on ethical decisions." The second model is a normative one that views the planner as an autonomous actor in a defined context. The third model is a contractual one that seeks a balance between personal values, personal circumstances, professional values, and professional circumstances. This contractual model is intended to integrate the normative and descriptive components of making ethical decisions and "to contribute to the assessment of the 'fit' of the planner" within this context.

The final contribution to this section explores the role of prudence—an old criterion of choice and valuation—in a planning case where strong ethical mandates face the inclination of social groups to use the coercive powers of local governance to shape self-defensive and exclusionary moral orders. Selecting between the ethical and engineering dimensions of the *Mount Laurel* case, the author chooses the ethical dimension and analyzes the court's decision in order to discover the risks of both an expansive application of strong ethical mandates, such as equal protection or general welfare, and a rigid interpretation of the autonomy of local polities in deciding the future of a community. Mandelbaum shows how the interaction between ethical mandates and prudence shapes the necessary web of competition, conflict, and cooperation that develops within jurisdictional levels and how ethical contents are constructed through the engineering of policy. His chapter demonstrates quite clearly what is in practice the interplay between ethics and engineering in planning and how technical decisions— in this case, concerning housing and land-use policies—imply strong ethical choices. Without the assumption of values, technical decisions would be undetermined, but chosen values become visible when they materialize decisions. Interaction between ethics and engineering is continuous and insuppressible.

SUE HENDLER

19 *On the Use of Models in Planning Ethics*

PLANNING ETHICS AS PROFESSIONAL ETHICS [1]

Professional ethics is a recognized part of what is commonly called "applied" or "practical" ethics. In the same way that environmental ethics refers to the application of moral principles and philosophical methods of inquiry to environmental issues, professional ethics pertains to the study of ethical aspects of issues faced by members of professions. While discussions of business, legal, medical, and "bio" ethics dominate the literature, the past decade also has witnessed increasing ethical scrutiny of other fields of endeavour such as education, engineering, and planning.

Several disparate intellectual threads are woven into the fabric of planning ethics. The first of these entails the direct application of formal moral theories to planning practices (Howe 1990). The goal of this work is to test those practices against established ethical principles. If, for example, "justice" is defined in a particular way, are the practices that respond to "preferences" justified as "justice-seeking?"

A second strand integrates planning with philosophy. I have been particularly interested in the ways in which the study of professional ethical codes illuminates both ethics as a field of knowledge and planning as a body of practices (Hendler 1990a, 1990b, 1991a).

Yet another strand is devoted to the empirical investigation of the views on ethics of planners and planning students (Hendler 1991b; Howe and Kaufman 1979, 1981; Kaufman 1985; Lang and Hendler 1990). These studies often contrast what planners believe is morally right or wrong with principles derived from formal ethical theories or those embedded in professional codes.

A fourth strand seeks to clarify choices by subjecting alternatives to an ethical elaboration and analysis. If, for example, you want to manage growth in this fashion, that implies a particular moral order. If that is the moral order you seek, should you then also act in thus-and-so fashion?

A final strand of the fabric is directed to the ethics of planners at work—not their espoused theories but their practices interpreted as ethical principles. These empirical studies—there are several examples in this volume—rely heavily on transcripts of planning encounters, participant observation, and retrospective accounts provided during in-depth interviews with practitioners (Dalton 1989).

This chapter reviews five types of models that attempt to integrate these disparate strands into a coherent body of thought that makes ethical sense of the ways in which planners and other professionals behave. I have labeled them as models of (1) moral development, (2) philosophical substance, (3) professional substance, (4) process, and (5) integration.

Moral Development Models

Models of the first type are variants of Lawrence Kohlberg's familiar work on the stages of moral development. Individuals, Kohlberg argued, develop through a series of moral stages, each with a broader range and a more abstractly principled order than the ones that preceded it. We progress in making moral decisions, he wrote, from simple reactions to pain, pleasure, punishment, and reward to general concepts and principles.

Kohlberg has had an important influence on the study of the moral development of various professional groups (Baxter and Rarick 1989; Pelsma and Borgers 1986). In Kohlberg's spirit, this work typically assumes that the progression from stage to stage is normative, "that the stages of development are more ethically sound or 'higher' as they progress from the stage-one self-centred concerns . . . to the stage-six, universalistic, altruistic considerations" (Williams 1990, 48). As Williams notes, however, such judgments are philosophical, not psychological, and reasoned arguments are needed as to whether one stage is any more or less moral than another (Williams 1990). Those who view Kohlberg's (and related) discussions in a normative fashion and who then seek to derive ways of molding professionals to "create a culture of self-giving love" (Baxter and Rarick 1989, 404) should thus accompany their suggestions for action with appropriate moral arguments. Descriptively ordering an array of ethical practices into a structured set of stages is not sufficient to prescriptively persuade anyone to shift from one practice to another.

Substantive Philosophical Models

I have grouped in this category models that refer explicitly to moral theories and advocate their application to professional ethics. All are normative, most are generic, and few take the form of process-oriented flow charts or lists of questions. Instead, they start with a philosophical position such as John Rawls's theory of justice (Hundert 1987), communitarianism (Forster 1982), or utilitarianism (Kitchener 1984; Zygmond and Boorhem 1989) and apply that position to professional codes and practices.

These philosophically grounded models are normative and, characteristically, formal and abstract. Their formality runs against the common professional sensibility that warns against deriving constrained and contextually rich choices from general theories or from a small set of abstract ethical principles (Bayles 1984).

Substantive Professional Models

From substantive, philosophical models I move to those that are almost entirely profession-specific. In this category are sequences of questions that professionals are to ask when faced with ethical dilemmas. Examples come from gerontology (Hayes et al. 1986), family medicine (Grodin and Burton 1988), psychiatry (Hayes 1986), nursing (Gearhart and Young 1990; Schultz 1987), and child welfare practice (Pine 1987), among others. Typically, the questions are organized into process stages of the sort taught in introductory planning courses. One begins by defining the problems that require solutions, identifying actors and roles, discussing ethical components (including consequences or utilities of actions, rights, duties, and the like), formulating possible options, selecting a preferred alternative, and, finally, implementing, monitoring, and evaluating the outcomes of the decision.

Models in this category contain many or all of these items and may go beyond this skeletal structure. Some are very specific and involve issues or concepts particular to areas such as health care (Hayes 1986). Others include more relational notions of power, needs, and resource availability (Pine 1987). Some contain, or emphasize, questions directly related to moral theories such as Pagano's suggestion that professionals examine their choices as categorical imperatives. Ask yourself, he suggests: "Do I want this to be a universal standard?" (Mathison 1988, 781). Others seek to avoid explicit references to formal ethical theory while they contain them implicitly.

These models identify individuals as professionals in specified roles. This allows the models to include substantive aspects of professional practice and adds depth and texture to philosophy-based representations of practice. The pendulum, however, has swung too far. The implicit theories that characterize these models should be tested explicitly in the light of formal ethics rather than being left to the moral intuitions of users.

Process-driven Models

Another set of models found in the literature is focused on general, non-specific processes related to ethical decision making (Bologna 1987; Cavanagh et al. 1981; Grebe et al. 1989; Kirrane 1990; Tymchuk 1986). Such models are usually presented as flow charts and lists of questions posed to professionals that rarely refer to substantive issues of moral development or ethical theory. Like the philosophic models, these are often counsels of perfection: few professionals are willing to enter into the comprehensive, linear decision making advocated by these models.

Roldan (1988) has presented one of the models in this category that may serve as an illustration of the type. He depicts a linear process (along with mathematical equations) that begins with the identification of whether a proposed action is or is not important and concludes with an assessment of whether this same action is related to "proportionate reasons" (Roldan 1988, 31). If one progresses successfully along this flow of bimodal choices, one achieves the pronouncement that "[he/she] is ethical."

While such models have moved a step beyond the group of moral development models, they are just as prone (if not more so) to turning descriptive information into normative judgments. In his quest for scientific/mathematical legitimacy, he turns questions of ethics into matters of algebra (Walden et al. 1990). Planning theorists will be struck by the leitmotif of a "rational comprehensive planning process" that runs through the models in this category, a melody not likely to charm most of the authors in this volume.

Integrative Models

Models that seek to integrate theoretical, ethical, profession-oriented and relational/organizational aspects of ethical decision making come largely from the business ethics literature. O. C. Ferrell and Shelby Hunt are probably the best-known writers in this area, but they have many colleagues (Cunningham 1991; Dubinsky and Loken 1989; Ferrell and Fraedrich 1989; Ferrell and Gresham 1985; Hunt and Vitell 1986; Mayo and Marks 1990; Randall 1989; Stead et al. 1990; Trevino 1986; Wotruba 1990). Despite the number and diversity of researchers, several themes and components recur in all of these works.

Most of the models refer explicitly to normative and moral beliefs, values, and principles. Some include specific ethical theories while others are more ambiguous. All distinguish between "external" variables that are not subject to the moral will of the professional and "internal" variables that are part of the domain of morally responsible agents. Finally, the components are generally, though not uniformly, linked by way of complex and often conflictual rather than simple linear relationships. The moral density of these models is immediately engaging. They acknowledge the ambiguities, uncertainties, and dilemmas that characterize planning as professionals experience it.

While such models do not contain specific, answerable questions intended to lead to ethical outcomes, their intentions are prosthetic: their authors often want to improve practices rather than merely describe them. Some models in the literature have been empirically tested. The testing has, however, generated a substantial controversy: can prescriptive models be scientifically assessed? Further, have authors confused descriptive and normative objectives in developing integrated models? Despite difficulties, I find models that represent us as complex and often conflicted beings more compelling than those that are simpler and less grounded in experience. I am not surprised that this category of ethical decision-making models is receiving much attention in the literature of professional ethics.

LESSONS LEARNED

What can we learn from this review of ethical decision-making models? Perhaps the clearest way of presenting conclusions is in a list of four criteria for good or at least reasonable models of this sort.

1. Ideas of moral development can be used in a descriptive sense but not with prescriptive intent unless accompanied by a philosophical argument.

2. Models should be clear as to whether they are meant to describe or prescribe ways of making ethical decisions.

3. Models that are intended to be useful to professionals should seek a balance between substance and process. This balance should include notions of ethics as well as particular professional practices so that they are truly *ethical* decision-making models

rather than being about decision making of a more generic nature.

4. While models have the task of representing reality and thus should not attempt to include reference to all of the complexities inherent in their subject, they need to include a sufficient number and breadth of variables to provide an adequate collage of the behavior under scrutiny.

MODELS OF PLANNING ETHICS

The final section of this chapter illustrates how empirical work on planning practices may be reframed as contributions to ethical models.

Planning is characterized by myriad allegiances and responsibilities. When we think of ethical issues planners encounter, we often identify conflicts among competing obligations (e.g., Forester 1992; Lang and Hendler 1990). I have identified at least twelve factors that affect a planner's decision making on normative, ethical issues: the public, the media, administrative staff, politicians, planning director and staff, legislation and established policies, precedents, developers (project proponents), technical information, professional/ethical commitments, personal commitments and, finally, time and resources (Hendler 1990c).[2] Planners I have observed face several questions in making professional decisions.[3] They do not simply ask, "What should I do, given my best judgment based on sound technical and prescriptive information?" Instead, they tend to entertain all or part of a whole spectrum of queries:

- Will the public (and the media) support me if I make this decision in this manner?
- Will I have the time, support staff, and financial resources to carry through my decision?
- Is fighting for what I believe in worth sacrificing my health and/or financial security?
- What did that other municipality do when it was faced with this problem?
- Could I defend my position at a public hearing?
- Will my director and co-workers support my decision?
- What chance do I have to get my decision carried by the planning commission and city council?
- Will my decision contribute to a better or worse relationship with the administration? And so on.[4]

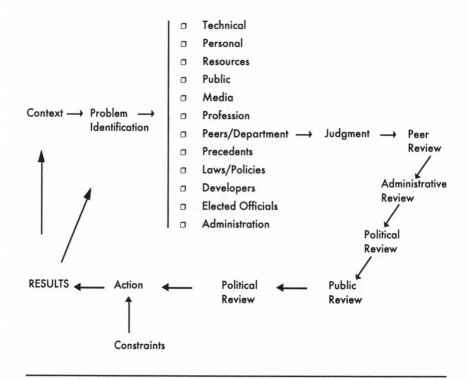

FIGURE 19.1
A descriptive model of planning ethics

A descriptive, substantive professional model of decision making flows directly from this depiction of professional planning life. This model represents the route planning decisions appeared to take during the course of my observations (Figure 19.1). In this model, problems are identified in a complex context of personal, organizational, professional, and moral components that influence the judgments planners make to arrive at solutions. Ethical notions such as rights, duties, and positive or negative consequences may enter into these deliberations but not in any systematic fashion. Individual planning decisions are reviewed by the departmental staff, the city administration, political bodies, and the public. A final decision results in one or more action(s) that are also affected by exogenous variables. "Real" effects of the action follow, and results are fed back into the framework where they are internalized as part of the professional context or lead to identification of the next round of problems requiring attention.

This model (Figure 19.1) conforms to the characteristics of the substantive professional category above in terms of its empirical nature, its focus

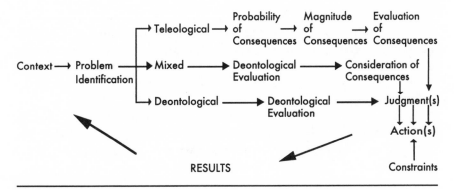

FIGURE 19.2
A normative model of planning ethics

on specific actors, and its emphasis on observed sources of influence on ethical decisions. From a more comprehensive, normative point of view, it lacks a grounding in moral theory and does not indicate preferred directions for the making of such decisions, either in substance or in process. Further, while it delineates the spectrum of individuals and groups involved in planning decisions, it does not indicate relationships among these actors. Thus, while it adequately represents the sorts of processes observed in planning departments, it does not provide much in the way of ethical content.

Is this, then, how these decisions *should* be made? Many of us writing in the area of planning ethics would like to see more emphasis on moral theories and reasoned justifications of ethical activity. A normative model could concentrate on the processes that should be followed by those involved in the decision-making process. Such a model (Figure 19.2) focuses on choices among alternate perspectives of ethics that may, in turn, lead to different processes and perhaps different judgments. This model includes aspects of context in the identification of problems but tends to view the professional as more autonomous than does the descriptive model discussed above. One could, however, apply the normative model to *all* of the actors involved in planning (i.e., administrative officials, politicians, and so on) as opposed to only individual planners. Expanding the use of the model in this way illuminates the difficulties in attaining consensus in an interorganizational field marked by conflicting ethical norms.

This planning model (Figure 19.2) is adapted largely from Hunt and Vitell (1986). It illustrates a process of decision making based in ethical analysis. While grounded in context, it identifies the planner as primarily

an autonomous agent of change. While this model is somewhat more integrative than many of those discussed earlier, it falls mostly within the
bounds of a process-oriented generic or philosophical model. Without more
elaboration of the steps regarding the context, judgment, action, and constraints, the model cannot address the organizational and relational aspects of planning.

Planners recognize that there are discrepancies between what actually
occurs in ethical decision making and that which ought to occur. Those
with whom I have spoken cite several barriers between the descriptive
and normative sequences of events presented here:

    □   perceptions of the role of planning on the part of civil servants,
         politicians, the public and other planners

    □   resources

    □   the political/economic system

    □   education, including planning education

These factors, I believe, can generally be subsumed under the issue of obtaining agreement regarding the role of planners and planning.

The idea of a contract addresses that difficulty. If we accept that different parties involved in planning differ in their views of planning, a way of
reconciling these disagreements becomes crucial, provided we wish to arrive at a coherent position on the role of planning. The notion of a contract—as fact or as metaphor—may help us attain this goal.

Figure 19.3 illustrates how this might work. The relevant variables are:
1. personal values (e.g., ethical positions); 2. personal circumstances (e.g.,
household resource needs); 3. professional values (e.g., professional ethics); and 4. professional circumstances (e.g., departmental resource needs).
These variables are interrelated, and these relationships can be seen, for
lack of better terms, as positive or negative. For example, if a planner's
personal views on ethics do not correspond to those of his/her profession,
ethical dissonance will occur. Alternatively, ethical congruence constitutes
a positive relationship between values.[5]

The model in Figure 19.3 includes four potential "contracts": C1–C4.
C1 is an agreement between a professional and a profession; this may be
seen as a professional code that prescribes the responsibilities of planning
and planners. C2 connects professional values and professional circumstances. It may also be included in a professional code, but I present it here
as a "contract" between planning and political agents who "employ" the
planner. C2 thus determines the role of planning in a local, societal context.
C3 relates personal values and personal circumstances. This may be seen

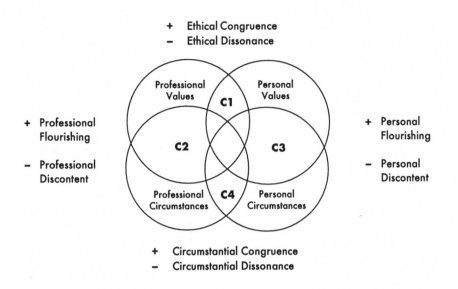

+　Ethical Congruence
−　Ethical Dissonance

+　Professional
　　Flourishing

−　Professional
　　Discontent

+　Personal
　　Flourishing

−　Personal
　　Discontent

+　Circumstantial Congruence
−　Circumstantial Dissonance

FIGURE 19.3
An integrative model of planning ethics

as a personal decision reflecting trade-offs among financial gain, ethical perspectives, familial ties, and so on. Finally, C4 links personal and professional circumstances; a job contract is an illustration of this relationship.

A contractual view of planning (and other professions) helps us to identify and function within these four circles and to strike contractual bargains. The model in Figure 19.3 is intended to integrate the normative and descriptive components of making ethical decisions. Its focus on contract making places primary importance on the relationships in which planners find themselves. This focus also fits well within current emphases in planning theory and research on communication, negotiation, power, and organizational dynamics. Such a model does not attempt to predict decision-making behavior or to prescribe particular decisions; instead, it presents a way of looking at the planner's role within an environment and attempts to contribute to the assessment of the "fit" of the planner within this context.

While this model fulfills some of the expectations of integrative models, I have not provided a compelling account of a better or best way of deriving the needed contracts. I am not alone in this failure (Brody 1988; Brown 1990; Callahan 1988; Hundert 1987; Pelsma and Borgers 1986). I believe, however, that the search for implicit contracts and for new ways of striking bargains promises to create an integrated fabric for planning ethics.

Notes

1. Parts of this chapter are taken or adapted from Hendler (1990c, 1992). An earlier version was presented to the 1991 Joint Congress of the Association of Collegiate Schools of Planning and the Association of European Schools of Planning, in Oxford, England.

2. See Bologna (1987) and Bommer et al. (1987) for analogous lists corresponding to business practices.

3. The observations discussed here are a product of a qualitative research project that focused on how planners make ethical decisions (Hendler 1990c). Participant observation and interviewing techniques were used to gain the information that forms the basis of this section.

4. See also Forester (1992 and other references) for useful analyses of discussions with planners regarding their attempts to deal with ethical issues.

5. See Skinner et al. (1988) for some related ideas from the area of marketing research.

REFERENCES

Baum, H. 1987. *The invisible bureaucracy.* New York: Oxford University Press.

Baxter, G., and C. Rarick. 1989. The manager as Kierkegaard's 'Knight of Faith': Linking ethical thought and action. *Journal of Business Ethics* 8, 5: 399–406.

Bayles, M. 1984. Moral theory and application. *Social Theory and Practice* 10, 1: 97–120.

Bologna, G. 1987. The ethics of managing information. *Journal of Systems Management* 38, 8: 28–30.

Bommer, M., C. Gratto, J. Gravander, and M. Tuttle. 1987. A behavioral model of ethical and unethical decision making. *Journal of Business Ethics* 6, 4: 265–80.

Brody, B. 1988. *Life and death decision making.* New York: Oxford University Press.

Brown, M. 1990. *Working ethics: strategies for decision making and organizational responsibility.* San Francisco: Jossey-Bass.

Callahan, S. 1988. The role of emotion in ethical decision making. *Hastings Center Report* 18: 9–14

Cavanagh, G., D. Moberg, and M. Velasquez. 1981. The ethics of organizational politics. *Academy of Management Review* 6, 3: 363–74.

Cunningham, M. 1991. Walking the thin line: a role stress model of ethical decision-making behaviour by marketing researchers. Doctoral dissertation, Texas A & M University.

Dalton, L. 1989. Emerging knowledge about planning practice. *Journal of Planning Education and Research* 9, 1: 29–44.

Dubinsky, A., and B. Loken. 1989. Analyzing ethical decision making in marketing. *Journal of Business Research* 19, 2: 83–107.

Faludi, A. 1973. *A reader in planning theory.* Oxford: Pergamon.

Ferrell, O., and L. Gresham. 1985. A contingency framework for understanding ethical decision making in marketing. *Journal of Marketing* 49: 87–96.

_____, and J. Fraedrich. 1989. A synthesis of ethical decision models for marketing. *Journal of Macromarketing* 9, 2: 55–64.

Forester, J. 1989. *Planning in the face of power.* Berkeley: University of California Press.

_____. 1992. On the ethics of planning: profiles of planners and what they teach us about practical judgment and moral improvisation. Prepared for the meeting of the American Planning Association, Washington, D.C.

Forster, J. 1982. A communitarian ethical model for public health interventions: an alternative to individual behaviour change strategies. *Journal of Public Health Policy* (June): 150–63.

Gearhart, S., and S. Young. 1990. Intuition, ethical decision making and the nurse manager. *Health Care Supervisor* 8, 3: 45–52.

Grebe, S., K. Irvin, and M. Lang. 1989. A model for ethical decision making in mediation. *Mediation Quarterly* 7, 2: 133–49.

Grodin, M., and C. Burton. 1988. Context and process in medical ethics: the contribution of family-systems theory. *Family Systems Medicine* 6, 4: 421–38.

Harper, T., and S. Stein. 1983. The justification of urban intervention: a moral framework. *Environments* 15, 1: 39–47.

_____. 1989. Normative ethical theory: is it relevant to contemporary planning practice? Presented to the annual meeting of the Association of Collegiate Schools of Planning, Portland, Oregon.

Hayes, J. 1986. Consultation-liaison psychiatry and clinical ethics: a model for consultation and teaching. *General Hospital Psychiatry* 8: 415–18.

Hayes, C., B. Soniat, and H. Burr. 1986. Value conflict and resolution in forcing services on "at risk" community-based older adults. *Clinical Gerontologist* 4, 3: 41–9.

Healey, P. 1990. Planning through debate. Unpublished manuscript.

Hendler, S. 1990a. Professional codes as bridges between planning and ethics: a case study. *Plan Canada* 30, 2: 22–9.

_____. 1990b. Moral theories in professional practice: Do they make a difference? *Environments* 20, 3: 20–30.

_____. 1990c. How planners choose. Paper presented to the annual conference of the Association of Collegiate Schools of Planning, Austin, Texas.

_____. 1991a. Professional codes as bridges between planning and ethics: a conceptual analysis. Unpublished manuscript.

_____. 1991b. Ethics in planning: the views of students and practitioners. *Journal of Planning Education and Research* 10, 2: 99–105.

_____. 1991c. Do professional codes legitimate planners' values? In H. Thomas and P. Healey, eds., *Dilemmas of planning practice*. Aldershot: Avebury Technical.

_____. 1992. Ethical decision making models: a critical, cross-disciplinary review. Unpublished manuscript.

Hendler, S., and J. Kinley. 1990. Ethics and the planning consultant. *Plan Canada* 30, 3: 29–32.

Howe, E. 1990. Normative ethics in planning. *Journal of Planning Literature* 5, 2: 123–50.

_____, and J. Kaufman. 1979. The ethics of contemporary American planners. *Journal of the American Planning Association* 45, 3: 243–55.

_____. 1981. The values of contemporary American planners. *Journal of the American Planning Association* 47, 3: 266–78.

Hundert, E. 1987. A model for ethical problem solving in medicine, with practical applications. *The American Journal of Psychiatry* 144: 839–46.

Hunt, S., and S. Vitell. 1986. A general theory of marketing ethics. *Journal of Macro Marketing* (Spring): 5–16.

Kaufman, J. 1985. American and Israeli planners. A cross-cultural comparison. *Journal of the American Planning Association* 51: 352–64.

Kirrane, D. 1990. Managing values: a systematic approach to business ethics. *Training & Development Journal* 44, 11: 53–60.

Kitchener, K. 1984. Intuition, critical evaluation and ethical principles: the foundation for ethical decisions in counseling psychology. *Counseling Psychology* 12, 3: 43–55.

Lang, R., and S. Hendler. 1990. Ethics and professional planners. In D. Mac-Niven, ed., *Moral expertise: studies in practical professional ethics*. New York: Routledge.

Mathison, D. 1988. Business ethics cases and decision models: a call for relevancy in the classroom. *Journal of Business Ethics* 7, 10: 777–82.

Mayo, M., and L. Marks. 1990. An empirical investigation of a general theory of marketing ethics. *Journal of the Academy of Marketing Science* 18, 2: 163–71.

Pelsma, D., and S. Borgers. 1986. Experience-based ethics: a developmental model of learning ethical reasoning. *Journal of Counseling and Development* 64, 5: 311–14.

Pine, B. 1987. Strategies for more ethical decision making in child welfare practice. *Child Welfare* LXVI, 4: 315–26.

Randall, D. 1989. Taking stock: can the theory of reasoned action explain unethical conduct? *Journal of Business Ethics* 8, 11: 873–82.

Roldan, A. 1988. The ethical manager: analytical tools for ethical problem-solving and decision making. *Organization Development Journal* 6, 4: 25–32.

Schultz, P. 1987. Clarifying the concept of "client" for health care policy formulation: ethical implications. *Family Community Health* 10, 1: 73–82.

Skinner, S., A. Dubinsky, and O. Ferrell. 1988. Organizational dimensions of marketing-research ethics. *Journal of Business Research* 16, 2: 209–23.

Spencer, B., and J. Butler, Jr. 1987. Measuring the relative importance of social responsibility components: a decision modeling approach. *Journal of Business Ethics* 6, 7: 573–77.

Stead, W., D. Worrell, and J. Stead. 1990. An integrative model for understanding and managing ethical behavior in business organizations. *Journal of Business Ethics* 9, 3: 233–42.

Timmerman, P. 1984. *Ethics and waste facility siting.* Toronto: Institute for Environmental Studies, University of Toronto.

Trevino, L. 1986. Ethical decision making in organizations: a person-situation interactionist model. *Academy of Management Review* 11, 3: 601–17.

Tymchuk, A. 1986. Guidelines for ethical decision making. *Canadian Psychology* 27, 1: 36–41.

Walden, T., I. Wolock, and H. Demone, Jr. 1990. Ethical decision making in human services: a comparative study. *Families in Society: The Journal of Contemporary Human Services* 71: 67–75.

Williams, G. 1990. More on ethical reasoning in business. *Training and Development Journal* 44, 1: 47–9.

Wotruba, T. 1990. A comprehensive framework for the analysis of ethical behaviour, with a focus on sales organizations. *Journal of Personal Selling and Sales Management* 10, 2: 29–42.

York, R. 1982. *Human service planning.* Chapel Hill: University of North Carolina Press.

Zygmond, M., and H. Boorhem. 1989. Ethical decision making in family therapy. *Family Process* 28: 269–80.

Thomas L. Harper and Stanley M. Stein

20 *Postmodernist Planning Theory: The Incommensurability Premise*

INTRODUCTION

The influence of postmodernism on planning theory seems to be increasing (Beauregard 1989; Dear 1986; Milroy 1991). Postmodernism is not a well-defined movement or school of thought; it encompasses a variety of views and it shares premises and approach with many communitarians, feminists and deep ecologists. There may well be no such thing as postmodernist planning theory; it is possible that the assumptions of postmodernism[1] preclude the development of any coherent theory.

One reason for the growing influence of the postmodern approach to planning is the demise of the "Rational Comprehensive Planning" model. The foundation of (scientific, instrumental) "rationality" has been undermined but nothing has taken its place. Thus, Beauregard (1989) sees planning theory as suspended between modernism and postmodernism, stuck in the midst of a paradigm shift. With no satisfactory replacement for "rationality," liberal democratic societies are in danger of resorting to power as the means of conflict resolution. We advocate a broader sense of rationality (incorporating communicative and critical rationality) as the replacement for instrumental rationality, with democratic dialogue as the appropriate mechanism for resolving planning issues.

Postmodernists, communitarians, feminists, and deep ecologists have made valuable and valid critiques of planning. They have pointed out that

414

institutional planning processes frequently conceal the disempowerment of certain communities, that not all voices are heard. They have also made credible normative recommendations: planners are urged to empower voiceless communities by ensuring that their voices are heard.

Our concern is that some of the underlying premises of this view have serious implications that could lead to consequences that are just as unfortunate as those that have been criticized. This chapter focuses on one important premise shared by many postmodernists, communitarians, feminists, and deep ecologists. This premise may seem so obviously false that no one would pay attention to it (much less write an entire chapter addressing it). If not dealt with, however, it is likely to infect many future debates arising as we attempt to apply ethics to planning and to unnecessarily muddy the waters of such debates.

THE INCOMMENSURABILITY PREMISE

The premise is that communities are incommensurable. That is, their stories, their discourses, and their language are not understandable to others. The implication of this premise is that "outside" critique is invalid and consensus-seeking dialogue is futile. As we will argue, the grave danger of this view is that power and coercion could come to replace rational persuasion.

For example, Lyotard argues that "the collapse of metaphysics diagnosed by Adorno can be seen as a recognition of 'the multiplicity of worlds of names, the insurmountable diversity of cultures'" (Rorty 1991a, 214). He concludes that because different communities cannot interact through dialogue in a reasonable fashion, the only mode of relation is one of power. There is no longer, he claims, a contrast between force and persuasion. Beauregard emphasizes the "multiplicity of voices and communities which comprise society" and the suppression of those voices by the "planners' totalizing discourse" (1991, 190). Planners are making a "fashionable retreat from grand narrative." "Planning theory is going local and personal," as McDougall says, just when "we are experiencing an intensification of the processes which interlock political, economic, and social structures" (1990, 97).

The issues involved here are at the core of the current fragmentation and relativization of intellectual and practical thought, not only in planning but in society at large. The postmodern rejection of any overarching narrative, of any Archimedean point, of any possibility of universal truth or absolute foundational knowledge, has led many people to believe that dialogue and reasonable agreement between communities are impossible.

The result is power struggles and fragmentation between men and women, black and white, French Canadians and English Canadians, first world and third world.

Thus, the view that cultures (communities) are insurmountably diverse can lead to the dangerous conclusion that it is futile to engage in dialogue and debate because (1) different communities cannot hope to understand each other, and (2) even if they could understand, they could never agree. We want to counter this destructive influence by showing that the postmodern rejection of absolute authority need not lead to fragmentation, that reasonable and meaningful dialogue towards consensus (within and between communities) is still possible. We will argue that coercion need not replace rational persuasion. The method of rational persuasion is not an attempt to establish absolute truth but to use our ordinary shared criteria (arising out of concrete situations) to reach agreement regarding what is true, reasonable, and moral.

In our recent work, we have advocated a "critical liberal" paradigm for planning (Harper and Stein 1992; 1995; 1995). We have based this on three key points:

1. Understanding must arise out of our own community or tradition. (This point is shared by communitarians.)

2. There can be no meta-narrative, Archimedean point, or God's-eye view from which we can independently evaluate a particular community, tradition, or language. (This point is shared by postmodernists.)

3. We all have the resources to critique and to dialogue, both within and between communities,

Those who hold the incommensurability view have argued that if understanding arises out of our own community (#1) and if there is no independent meta-narrative (#2), then objective critique (#3) is impossible. We believe that this is mistaken. Legitimation and reasoned critique do not require appeal to absolute criteria (nor to a meta-narrative or any other form of metaphysical foundation).

Justification must start with the shared beliefs of our community. We must begin from where we are situated—within a tradition, at a particular time, in a particular place. This is exactly what Rawls (1971) does with his process of wide reflective equilibrium (discussed below); he starts with the articulation of deeply embedded intuitions. But this is not where we *end*. While many communitarians believe that "notions of community and shared values mark the *limits* of practical reason" (Kymlicka 1987), we believe they do not. We argue that we do not need a set of absolute criteria or a meta-narrative to go beyond our community and find commensurability with other communities, to be able to critique both our own and other communities. The significant conceptions of different communities are, to a substantial degree, necessarily commensurable (intelligible) to each other. This means that contemporary planning does not need to remain suspended (in Beauregard's terms) between a "foundationalist modernism . . . and a relativist postmodernism" (Forester 1990, 45).

We agree with many contemporary philosophers who reject the traditional philosophical notion (foundationalism) that a judgment must be accompanied by a meta-judgment or meta-narrative that guarantees that it cannot possibly be wrong (Harper and Stein 1992). But it does not follow from this rejection that we cannot have good reasons for believing statements to be true or false (unless there are particular *concrete* reasons for doubting the claim in question). The mere fact that we cannot step "outside" to guarantee the legitimacy of these reasons is not cause to reject good reasons (within a particular context) for a belief.[2]

Rejection of the possibility of a meta-narrative need not imprison each of us within the perspective of our own incommensurable community. It does not mean that transcultural interpretation and translation are impossible. We agree with Richard Rorty that "people can rationally change their beliefs and desires," but they do so "only by holding most of those beliefs and desires constant—even though we can never say in advance just which are to be changed and which retained intact" (1991, 212).

CRITIQUE OF INCOMMENSURABILITY[3]

One way of putting the incommensurability thesis is that "the modern world (conceptually and practically) is highly fragmented and awash in incommensurable private languages" (Dear 1986, 369), with the implication of the "impossibility of connected discourse" (ibid., 370), which has left planning theory an isolated "babel of languages" and planning practice a fantastic "pastiche" of unconnected practices (ibid., 379). We will argue that this view, first, misunderstands the nature of communities alien to our own and, second, functions with a false metaphysical picture (one supposedly rejected by it).

Language and Cross-Cultural Interpretation

Although we reject the notion of incommensurability, we do recognize the intimate connection between community and language. On the whole, language is a reflection of the attributes of a community. Thus, we define community as "a social group whose members share common characteristics of heritage, beliefs, attitudes, hopes, history, and culture, reflected in a common language." Interpretation of what people do (actions) reflects their intentions, beliefs, hopes and even concepts just as much as does interpretation of what they say. Language cannot be separated from meaningful action, from (what Wittgenstein calls) a "form of life."

One way to approach inter-community differences, therefore, is by considering the extreme case of translation into our language from the language of a community with no known affinity to our own.[4] In order to identify beliefs of such a culture, we need to translate their language into our own: "It seems unlikely that we can attribute complex attitudes . . . to a speaker unless we can translate his words into ours" (Davidson 1985, 132). For translation to be possible, several necessary conditions must be met.

1. Rationality. At a minimum, rationality involves (a) assent to statements that are true and dissent from those that are false; (b) a norm of truth telling (necessary for having a language); and (c) concepts of identity and contradiction.

> An anthropologist does not know what he *can* say in a native language unless he also knows what he can *not* say. He . . . must find the word for "no" and to do so must assume that the natives share his concepts of assertion and negation. (Hollis 1970, 231)

In other words, we cannot attribute beliefs and intentions to anyone unless we can distinguish between what a person says and what they do not say:[5] "Yes" must mean yes and "No" must mean no.

2. A bridgehead: general agreement on beliefs. If we are to understand another community's language, we need a bridgehead into that community. Such a bridgehead is created by translating beliefs about ordinary intersubjectively observable material objects and events. These translations form certain patterns. We make errors along the way but in the end, we more or less do get a correct translation. To understand a group's language, we must share a view of the world (i.e., we assume they in general accept the same ontology we do).

> We damage the intelligibility of our readings of the utterances of others when our method of reading puts others into what we take to be broad error. We can make sense of differences alright, but only against a background of shared belief. What is shared does not in general call for comment; it is too dull, trite or familiar to stand notice. But without a vast common ground, there is no place for disputants to have their quarrel.[6] (Davidson 1987, 167)

If the required shared background is absent and there is nothing that we both can identify, then there is nothing to disagree about. To even talk about a community as a community (one with ideas and concepts), there must be an overlap. If a form of expression is truly conceptually different from ours, it is not a form of expression at all. An incommensurable language is not a language; we cannot say anything about it at all. As Wittgenstein says, "Of that which you can not speak, you must remain silent."

So translation requires that most concepts and beliefs that overlap are shared between communities. And translation is, in fact, generally possible between quite alien cultures. Rorty argues that when we come to translate another language, "our form of life and the natives' already overlap to so great an extent that we are already, automatically, for free, participant-observers, not *mere* observers" (Rorty 1991b, 107). The upshot is that inter-community differences are not different in kind from intra-community differences, and both are commensurable. Postmodern writers demonstrate this when they are able to understand, and make intelligible to their readers, not only their own views but also those that they are "interpreting." Weird, non-overlapping cases *between* communities can be treated in the same way as differences *within* a particular community. There may be bizarre, insane, inhuman people (and communities) in the world but they are extreme cases, not the norm.

Mandelbaum believes that the lack of an "Archimedean point outside any constrained social system" creates a contrast:

> Replacing the magical Archimedean Point with an image of a field of communities may lead you quite sensibly to distinguish two quite different critical perspectives. In the first, a community is judged by either members or outsiders against its own standards; in the second, the standards of one community are brought to bear against another. (1992, 17)

These two perspectives (inside and outside) are really the same. There is an ambiguity in Mandelbaum's statement. He may be accepting the notion of incommensurability or he may simply be pointing to the fact that there are sometimes vast differences between communities. Communities may have very different states of knowledge, social customs, social structure, religion, and so on. Although we recognize the existence of such differences, they are usually *not* ones of conceptual incommensurability, nor will they be—as Dear (1986) suggests—the result of the "impossibility of connected discourse."

It is important to note that the foregoing argument for commensurability requires no appeal to any Archimedean point or meta-narrative. So Lyotard (1987) must be mistaken when he claims we need "to come to agreement regarding which rules and meta-prescriptions are universally valid for language games" in order to understand other people's languages.

Different World Views: A False Picture

Underlying the view of incommensurable communities is a deeply held but false metaphysical picture (ironically, one shared with foundationalists/ absolutists) that we believe is incoherent. The idea is that there exists a world (a reality) independent of any conceptualization of it, independent of any language, a reality that different communities and frameworks carve up in different and competing ways. The assumption is that different communities can get different concepts, and different conceptions of "reality," from essentially the same experience. This view is expressed by Benjamin Whorf:

> Language produces an organization of experience . . . we are thus introduced to a new principle of relativity, which holds that all observers are not led by the same physical evidence to the same picture of the universe, unless their linguistic backgrounds are similar. (Whorf 1956, 55)

This is echoed by Dear when he speaks of "incommensurable private languages" (1986, 369), by Milroy talking of "refracting the world through a postmodernist prism" (1991, 183), and by Beauregard claiming "that causal frameworks . . . are incommensurate with and incomprehensible to those whose lives take on meaning in multivalent, multivocal and intentional narratives" (1991, 191).

It is essential to this false picture that reality be neutral between all conceptual frameworks or languages and independent of any conceptual framework. In other words, it must be that reality cannot be incorporated within any conceptual framework. (If it could be incorporated, then it would be part of that framework and not independent of it.) Then this independent reality or experience cannot be the subject of language; if it were, it could be part of a framework. But if it cannot be the subject of language, this independent reality cannot be identified, and the notion is unintelligible and incoherent.

In addition, talk of different conceptual schemes as more true or right presupposes a notion of truth that is extra-linguistic (or extra-community or universal or absolute), such that it is meaningful to attribute truth to a framework completely independent of any conceptual scheme. But this absolute notion of truth is precisely what communitarians and post-modernists reject.

In order to describe or evaluate two (or more) different frameworks A and B, we would need to have a perspective (C) "outside" any framework, that is, a God's-eye view, an Archimedean point, a meta-narrative. Because we lack any such point, the picture evaporates. This picture

> suggests that we can, so to speak, get round behind our descriptions and see how they fit the world, and this makes no sense at all: any conception of the world we can use at all is one that is already expressed in terms that we understand, our terms. The world cannot describe itself for us. (Williams 1991, 12)

To reiterate, there are two paradoxical things wrong with this picture. The first error is to suppose that reality ("the world") is relative to a particular conceptual scheme and that different worlds are represented in different conceptual schemes or linguistic communities. The second error is the claim that when we observe differences, they must always be embedded in intractably different or incommensurable worlds. Once we abandon this false picture, translation and interpretation are seen as possible. The notion that communities must inevitably clash without any hope of resolution can be abandoned. Communities need not be opaque "window-less monads."

The members of communities are usually capable of looking across a communal boundary to understand "strangers" and to be understood by them. Seeking this mutual comprehension, we sensibly assume that human worlds are largely similar and that we can focus our attention on a limited set of differences. Within that frame—limited differences within broad similarities—we are able to speak with one another, debating and learning simultaneously. Since there is commonality, we can map the differences and identify errors in our own and other communities' thinking.

Thus, what seemed to be differences in conceptual frameworks or worldviews can now be seen as a difference in belief or opinion. Inter-cultural differences turn out to be intra-cultural differences (Rorty 1991b, 107). The distinction between "inside" and "outside" is no longer crucial. In an important sense, we can be participant-observers in another community. Dialogue with other communities is similar to dialogue within our own community. In both cases, we debate our differences within a background of shared beliefs regarding the world, human nature, and social relationships. Change takes place within a framework of sameness.

THE ALTERNATIVE: CONSENSUS-SEEKING PROCESSES

Procedural Ethical Theory

Once we acknowledge that translation, communication, and dialogue within and between communities are possible, then different sorts of questions arise. We can conceive of a continuum in the possibility of agreement between people or communities, where one extreme is incommensurability and the other extreme is complete consensus on social, political, and economic institutions, policies, and specific actions. The question, then, is how do we move toward the "consensus" end of the continuum? We have found that procedural ethical theory is helpful and relevant here.

Habermas (1984) believes that, under certain ideal conditions, we could come to a consensus regarding our moral, political, and social disagreements. His "ideal speech situation" has been widely criticized as (1) a naive unrealistic fantasy, and (2) too Kantian and foundationalist. We view it as a heuristic, a regulative ideal toward which we strive without expecting to attain it fully. In particular concrete situations, this means that we should attempt to identify and eliminate communicative and ideological distortions through dialogue and critical reflection.

Our interpretation of Habermas is consistent with the *coherentist* or nonfoundational approach to procedural ethical theory that neither assumes nor seeks to develop abstract or universal moral principles but begins with our own principles, judgments, and intuitions. Using a process often referred to as "Wide Reflective Equilibrium" (WRE) (after Rawls 1971, 48–51; Daniels 1979; and Nielsen 1991), one reflects on one's own ethical principles, judgments, and intuitions and alters them until they are in equilibrium. We believe that WRE is the most practical way to implement Habermas's recommendations, a way that avoids the transcendental, universalistic, foundational aspect of his theory.

Wide Reflective Equilibrium (WRE)[7]

WRE attempts to devise the structure or rules for particular types of situations, independent of one's own interests or position in society. A Wide Reflective Equilibrium has been defined as a coherent set of beliefs that includes the following components:

1. a set of considered moral judgments
2. a set of normative substantive and/or procedural ethical principles

3. a set of background theories that show that the set of normative
    ethical principles is more acceptable than alternative normative
    ethical principles

These background theories may incorporate both (a) very general ethical
notions, such as fairness or a respect for "persons," and (b) empirical theories and observations (Daniels 1979).

The process of seeking a WRE asks the participants in the discussion to
reflect on their own ethical principles, judgments, and intuitions. In the
first phase of the process, the participants try to seek a personal ethical
consistency. They go back and forth, correcting intuitions by reference to
principles and generating principles that are responsive to their moral intuitions. In the second phase, they repeat the process but now they seek
consensual agreements across their differences.

WRE should not be seen as just a method. It is a recognition that intellectual, moral, and social progress occurs, not by reference to absolute foundations but through self-criticism and interactive critique with others. This
recognition, shared by Rawls and Habermas, reflects the thrust of Dewey's
classical pragmatism (Dewey and Tuft 1932). It is closely tied to notions of
participatory democracy.

In advocating consensus seeking, we are not suggesting that it is possible to agree on everything. Rather, we should be seeking a limited consensus on our most basic social, political, and economic institutions, that
is, practical mechanisms for deciding on actions to be taken. (Rawls [1987]
calls this an overlapping consensus.) This is what Rorty (1990) has in mind
with his notion that "Democracy has priority over philosophy." Different
normative ethical theories, political philosophies, or value positions may
still be brought together in a common institutional framework. Within this
basic framework, we can then seek agreement on more specific practical
actions. Note that we are not advocating imposition of any sort of monolithic consensus. Nor should disagreements be glossed over or some voices
muffled to give the illusion of consensus.

Moral Implications

We have already noted that we are not claiming (and we do not believe
it can be shown) that complete consensus is attainable. Moral dilemmas
(e.g., individual freedom versus social benefits) may remain, although it is
desirable to resolve them. Nor are we saying that coercion should never be
used. Sometimes, argument comes to an end and only power can resolve
inter-community differences (or intra-community differences for that

matter). But such situations are not the result of incommensurable communities, nor of disparities between internal versus external critique. People like Heinrich Himmler and Idi Amin should be stopped because their actions are evil: their intentions are all too clear to anyone inside or outside their community.

Nor do we claim that conceptual differences *never* occur. Conceptual differences do show up in isolated cases, for example, our view of (African) Azande magic (Stein 1973). But again, these cases are necessarily the exception, not the rule. In addition, these cases are not differences that we can disagree (or agree) about. Our significant disputes are differences *within* a particular framework. Or to put it more accurately, the contrast between what is within and without a particular framework evaporates, as does the very idea of a conceptual framework. Thus, our significant disputes presuppose shared concepts and beliefs. These differences *can* be resolved through consensus-seeking dialogue.[8]

For example, some feminists claim that women have a different morality based on "responsibility and care linked with an identity formed through relationships" in contrast to a male morality "of rights and abstract justice, more often held by people who saw themselves in terms of autonomy" (Sandercock and Forsyth 1990, 78). They object to Kohlberg's hierarchy that ranks abstract moral principles of justice as the highest level of "moral development"[9] (Gilligan 1977). But these two perspectives are not incompatible. On the one hand, the basic attitude of caring for others is required to motivate individuals to apply moral principles in a particular situation. On the other hand, the historical and contingently rooted web of ongoing relationships must be generalized in order to ensure that those most in need are cared for; this generalization requires an appeal to the principle of universality.

The important question here is not whether a morality of caring is better or more advanced than a morality of abstract justice. The real question is how to bring these two important moral notions together (both recognized by any moral person) in concrete planning situations. We do this by appealing to Rawls's overlapping consensus (1987) and to our shared moral background, attempting to reach a wide reflective equilibrium in particular situations.[10]

Significant Contrast: The Example of Power

We have argued that understanding must arise out of one's own community or tradition and that we all have the resources to critique within and between communities. Thus, Lyotard was wrong to conclude that because different communities cannot interact through dialogue in reasonable fashion, the only mode of relating is one of power, and there is no longer a contrast between force and persuasion. We believe that eliminating this significant contrast is a serious mistake. In a discussion of power, Milroy (1990, 18) suggests that power is what really matters because the powerful make the rules. To this, Forester replies:

> [I]f the powerful make all of the rules, how is it even possible that Milroy recognizes and objects to oppression and hopes to counteract it? Are the rules shaping Milroy's own knowledge so saturated by power that she can neither recognize nor object nor act in any way to counteract the "powerful?" If power is all there is, ... if power is everywhere, then we need to be much more specific about the kinds of power we find oppressive and the kinds we find "empowering." And then we will come back to thinking about the conditions of human interaction that a particular planning practice hopes to foster. (Forester 1990, 55)

Milroy's view here seems identical to Lyotard's: it eliminates the contrast between rational persuasion and coercion. She too has adopted a language of power that abolishes an existing linguistic device for making an important distinction. Forester argues that it is important to express this old distinction, and he is compelled to construct a new device to do the work of the old, that is, different "kinds" of power. We are saying that there is no reason at all to give up—and every reason to maintain—the original distinction between rational persuasion and power.

Democratic Dialogue: Hearing All Voices

The grave danger of the incommensurability thesis is that it can lead to the conclusion that there is nothing left between communities but power. The preservation of democratic dialogue as the means of relating different voices is an alternative that clearly is morally preferable.

A dialogue in which all voices are heard is valuable for three reasons:

1. Intellectual, moral and social progress (both personal and public) requires critique. If all views are represented, the critique will be much richer and the likelihood of approaching "the truth" will be greater.
2. Free and equal persons have an equal right to be heard.
3. Genuine improvements in the "common good" are possible only through active participation (in the communicative process) by all parties.

As Dewey argues

> There is a moral tragedy inherent in efforts to further the common good which prevent the result from being either common or good—not good, because it is at the expense of the active growth of those to be helped, and not common because these have no share in bringing the result about. The social welfare can be advanced only by means which elicit the positive interest and active energy of those to be benefited. . . . It takes time to arouse minds from apathy and lethargy, to get them to thinking for themselves, to share in making plans, to take part in their execution. But without active cooperation both in forming aims and in carrying them out there is no possibility of a common good. (Dewey and Tuft 1932, 385)

Thus, we should encourage all voices to enter the public dialogue of a genuinely democratic planning process with their "competing stories," as Mandelbaum suggests (1991, 211). But these voices should not be received uncritically. We can evaluate, weigh, and judge new voices and thereby enrich our tradition and ensure that our social institutions actually work in a way that is consistent with our liberal democratic ideals. True toleration does not require uncritical acceptance of whatever a community (even a marginalized and oppressed one) says. While the past error was that the wealthy and powerful forced their ideas on other communities, it is equally erroneous to assume that every community is right and should not be challenged or changed.

CONCLUSION

We believe that the postmodern critique of undisputed authority has a great deal of validity. We do lack a meta-narrative and we must start from our own communities. But this does not mean that communities are incommensurable and that all planners can do is empower them by ensuring their voices are heard along with all the other disparate stories. Dialogue and debate are still possible, given our shared view of the world. Good reasons can be given for our beliefs. For example, we believe that good reasons can be advanced for adopting a critical liberal paradigm for planning, a paradigm along the lines of that advocated by Friedmann (1992) or Forester and practiced by Krumholz (Krumholz and Forester 1990).

Notes

1. For a critique of postmodernist assumptions, see Harper and Stein 1992.

2. The fact that a belief is a traditionally received view is not in itself a good reason to reject it.

3. For a more detailed critique of the incommensurability thesis, see Stein (1994).

4. We are assuming that difficulties in interpreting beliefs, attitudes, and meaningful action of a community very different from our own do not involve essentially different principles of interpretation.

5. When a person says "P," it is not the case that they are saying "not P." (This is the law of non-contradiction.)

6. There may be cases where one language lacks words found in another language. For example, some languages (e.g., English) have only one word for "snow," while others have a variety of words for different kinds of snow (Whorf 1956). But this is not evidence for indeterminacy of translation:

> What enables us to make this point in particular is an ontology common to the two languages . . . we can be clear about breakdowns in translation when they are local enough, for a background of generally successful translation provides what is needed to make the failures intelligible. (Davidson 1985, 137)

So this is not an insurmountable problem; we can still generally come up with a description that is an intelligible substitute for the "missing" word. Thus we can learn about different kinds of snow because there is general agreement regarding attributes. We can learn from the other community.

7. For a more complete account of how WRE might be applied to planning, see Harper and Stein (1993).

8. There is no guarantee that all differences will be resolved. We should dialogue in good faith, hoping that we will be able to move toward consensus.

9. This categorization either presupposes a meta-narrative or it begs the question.

10. Of course, this ideal may not always be possible: genuine moral dilemmas may remain.

REFERENCES

Beauregard, R. 1989. Between modernity and postmodernity: the ambiguous position of U.S. planning. *Environment and Planning D: Society and Space* 7: 381–95.

_____. 1991. Without a net: modernist planning and the postmodern abyss. *Journal of Planning Education and Research* 10: 189–94.

Daniels, N. 1979. Two approaches to theory acceptance in ethics. *Journal of Philosophy* 76.

Davidson, D. 1985. On the very idea of a conceptual scheme. In J. Rajchman and C. West, eds., *Post-analytic philosophy*. New York: Columbia University Press, 129–43.

_____. 1987. The method of truth in metaphysics. In K. Baynes, J. Bohman, and T. McCarthy, eds., *After philosophy: end or transformation?* Cambridge: MIT Press, 166–83.

Dear, M. 1986. Postmodernism and planning. *Environment and Planning D: Society and Space* 4: 367–84.

Dewey, J., and , J. Tuft. 1932. *Ethics* (rev. ed.). New York: Henry Holt.

Forester, J. 1990. A reply to my critics. *Planning Theory Newsletter* 4: 43–60.

Friedmann, J. 1992. Educating the next generation of planners. Paper delivered at the annual meeting of the Association of Collegiate Schools of Planning, Columbus, Ohio.

Gilligan, C. 1977. In a different voice: women's conceptions of self and of morality. In M. Pearsall, ed., *Women and values: readings in recent feminist philosophy*. Belmont CA: Wadsworth, 309–39.

Habermas, J. 1984. *The theory of communicative action*. Boston: Beacon Press.

Harper, T. L., and S. M. Stein. 1992. Out of the postmodern abyss: preserving the rationale for liberal planning. Paper delivered at the annual meeting of the Association of Collegiate Schools of Planning, Columbus, Ohio.

_____. 1993. Normative ethical theory: Is it relevant to contemporary planning practice? *Plan Canada* (September): 6–12.

_____. 1994. A neo-pragmatic paradigm: critical liberal planning. Paper delivered at the annual meeting of the Association of Collegiate Schools of Planning, Phoenix, Arizona.

_____. 1995. Contemporary procedural ethical theory and planning theory. In S. Hendler, ed., *Planning ethics: a reader in planning theory, practice and education*. New Brunswick, NJ: Center for Urban Policy Research.

Hollis, M. 1970. Reason and ritual. In B. Wilson, ed., *Rationality*. Oxford: Blackwell.

Krumholz, N., and J. Forester. 1990. *Making equity planning work: leadership in the public sector*. Philadelphia: Temple University Press.

Kymlicka, W. 1987. Liberalism and communitarianism. Paper prepared for the annual meeting of the Canadian Philosophical Association, McMaster University, Hamilton, Ontario.

Lyotard, J.-F. 1987. The postmodern condition. In K. Baynes, J. Bohman, and T. McCarthy, eds., *After philosophy: end or transformation?* Cambridge: MIT Press, 73–94.

Mandelbaum, S. 1991. Telling stories. *Journal of Planning Education and Research* 10: 209–14.

_____. 1992. Deserving communities. CAUS Special Anniversary Celebration Special Lectures: Part I. Blacksburg, VA: Virginia Polytechnic Institute and State University.

McDougall, G. 1990. Planning theory: constructing an agenda for 1992. *Planning Theory Newsletter* 4: 93–100.

Milroy, B. M. 1990. Critical capacity and planning theory. *Planning Theory Newsletter* 4: 12–18.

_____. 1991. Into postmodern weightlessness. *Journal of Planning Education and Research* 10: 181–87.

Nielsen, K. 1991. *After the demise of the tradition: Rorty, critical theory, and the fate of philosophy.* Boulder, CO: Westview Press.

Rawls, J. 1971. *A theory of justice.* Cambridge, MA: Harvard University Press.

_____. 1985. Justice as fairness: political not metaphysical. *Philosophy and Public Affairs* 14, 3: 223–51.

_____. 1987. The idea of an overlapping consensus. *Oxford Journal of Legal Studies* 7, 1: 1–25.

Rorty, R. 1990. The priority of democracy to philosophy. In A. Malachowski, ed., *Reading Rorty.* Oxford: Basil Blackwell, 279–302.

_____. 1991a. Cosmopolitanism without emancipation: a response to John François Lyotard. In R. Rorty, *Objectivity, rationality and truth: philosophy papers.* vol. 1. Cambridge: Cambridge University Press, 211-222.

_____. 1991b. Inquiry as recontextualization: an anti-dualist account of interpretation. In R. Rorty, *Objectivity, rationality and truth: philosophy papers.* vol. 1. Cambridge: Cambridge University Press, 93-110.

Sandercock, L., and A. Forsyth. 1990. Gender: a new agenda for planning theory. *Planning Theory Newsletter* 4: 61-92.

Stein, S. M. 1973. The ontological status of social institutions. Doctoral dissertation, University of Calgary.

_____. 1994. Wittgenstein, Davidson, and the myth of incommensurability. In J. Couture and K. Nielsen, eds., *Reconstruction in philosophy: new essays in metaphilosophy.* Calgary: University of Calgary Press, 181-221.

Whorf, B. 1956. *Language, thought and reality: selected writings of Benjamin Lee Whorf.* J. B. Carroll, ed. Cambridge: MIT Press.

Williams, B. 1991. Terrestrial thoughts, extra-terrestrial science. *London Review of Books* 13, 3 (February 1991): 12–13.

SEYMOUR J. MANDELBAUM

21 *Ethical Mandates and the Virtue of Prudence*

MIND AND MARROW BONE

The Virtue of Prudence occupies a prominent niche in the Temple of Professional Planning. The votaries—among whom I count myself—admonish one another and anyone who will listen that Prudence dictates that we attend to the future, acting now to avoid prospective dangers and to reap the benefits of foresight. We should—prudently—overcome the ubiquitous tendency to calculate our interests so narrowly that we sink our collective ships. Symmetrically, we should regard with prudent skepticism estimates of our intelligence that leave no room for uncertainty or perversity; assessments of our good will that leave no room for egoism and privacy. We should understand that ethical principles are bound to conflict with one another and that it is, therefore, imprudent even to attempt to reconstruct the world or to rewrite our codes as if we could harmonize all interests and all ethical commitments.

As in any religious tradition, the practice of virtue in the Temple of Professional Planning is necessarily more complex and more contested than the simple statement of an ethical principle. Indeed, compared to, say, Justice or Love, Prudence seems all practice and temper with very little in the way of formal text to guide our shared understanding of its ethical or emotional force.[1] Even Machiavelli, as Eugene Garver remarks, "says very little about prudence at all, instead enacting a conception . . . and giving his audience the means of acquiring it" (Garver 1987, 20). In the same way, the concept radiates through professional codes and hortatory literature of planning and public administration, but the word is missing (Wachs 1985).

Even in the absence of canonical texts—or, perhaps, because of their absence—planners (in both Academy and Field) spend a great deal of time cultivating a prudential disposition in new members of the profession, educating them in the theory and training them in the practices of the precious but ambiguous virtue. The recruits must learn when and how it is appropriate to capitalize future goods and bads in the present and when it is not; when it is prudent to avoid risks and when risk aversion is paralyzing; when it is possible to repair the world and when reform is likely to spawn ethical monsters; when formal knowledge enhances intelligence and when it requires that we systematically ignore what we should sensibly regard; when to speak and when to keep silent.

A public order is shaped within organizations and communities, endowing each prudential principle with a local meaning. Only in the simplest groups, however, are these meanings uncontested. The disciplines into which professional planners are socialized characteristically provide ambiguous and conflicting guidelines. We are parties to a grand dilemma that tears us, in the words of the poet William Butler Yeats, between mind and marrow bone, with very little hope of striking other than a temporary balance that is easily disrupted.

> *God guard me from those thoughts men think*
> *In the mind alone.*
> *He that sings a lasting song*
> *Thinks in a marrow bone.*[2]

We believe—in our minds—that it is prudent to articulate and refine our tacit knowledge, to imagine and justify our planning practices ethically, and to construct the world as a series of problems amenable to intelligent solution. But Prudence also dictates—in our marrow bone—that we be cautious; that danger lurks in the detachment of cosmopolitan professions and in the ways they simplify and abstract social worlds and ethical mandates. We sensibly clutch our wallets tightly when—confronting our own language—we are told that a plan is "rational," "comprehensive," "systematic," or "in the public interest."

The dilemma captures us in its toils even when the abstractions are grounded in the experiences of a group and the critics are passionate loyalists rather than outsiders. There are times in the history of every moral community when members insist that prudence requires that an established web of practices and a plurality of moral norms be brought within the discipline of strong ethical mandates. "If the community is to survive," the defenders argue, we must (variously) "renew our ancient faith," "return to first principles," "learn again to speak truthfully with one another," or "pursue justice." Such mandates arouse a prudential counter-response that sometimes appears even in the minds (or the marrow bones) of the proponents of the new discipline. Perhaps, we caution ourselves, we should not be so quick to condemn the petty compromises and the corruption of "everyday" life; perhaps there is a practical wisdom in the ways "ordinary" people balance the virtues so that none completely dominates the others.

The forms of this dilemma are particularly complex and subtle when we represent ourselves as living within a field of open and overlapping communities. In such fields, change in one community does not always require a response from all. Buffers of inattention and tolerance allow us sometimes to move from day to day without reconciling our individual or collective lives to a single coherent moral order.[3]

Some strong ethical mandates, however, spread across a field, threatening the relations between communities and the buffers that divide them. Families, churches, and firms are all challenged when we realign the meaning of privacy in order to reconstruct our conceptions of gender to conform to the demands of Justice (Okin 1989). Similarly, if we all share a common fate as citizens of Planet Earth, how can we, as members of nations, resist the imperatives of a global environmental ethic or the international redistribution of income (Care 1987; Goodin 1985)? If we are all bound to the self-determination of "peoples" as a first political principle, how can multicultural empires survive the ethical challenge unscathed? Strong ethical mandates may be powerfully resisted or they may be embraced, but they cannot be ignored. They change the fields into which they are launched.

Prudence may "demand" the redesign of the communal field we imagine in our minds. Simultaneously, however, the threat of redesign—new boundaries, buffers, and negotiated meanings—appropriately arouses a prudential caution. How will the new field operate? How will it cope with variety, conflict, and change? Might the new ethical imperative be accommodated into the old communal order, or is that order deeply implicated in the immorality we seek to remedy?

Prudent men and women have good reason to be troubled by these questions and to be uncertain in their responses. We enact a concept of Prudence that begins with Aristotle's conception of its compelling role in the array of virtues. Prudence, as he describes it in *The Politics* (1984, 1277b), is the distinguishing mark of public leadership—"the only virtue peculiar to the ruler" in a polity of roughly equal citizens. We temper that grand vision, however, with Prudence as caution and moral skepticism if not outright immorality (Nelson 1991). Indeed, we often have trouble distinguishing the two themes in our own speech, as caution, skepticism, and political capacity are intertwined.

This chapter explores these troubles and these uncertainties as they have been articulated in a series of judicial decisions in the State of New Jersey. The exploration has no conclusion and no simple instrumental message. It is, rather, an appreciation of the Virtue of Prudence and the dilemmas in which it engages us. Caution in the face of an ethical mandate does not necessarily betray moral sloth; nor need hesitation be justified by an equal and countervailing moral imperative. "Simple prudence"—that is to say, "complex, inflected, and conflicted prudence"—shapes our responses to strong ethical mandates: it should lead us to hesitate in the face of "value pluralism" (Mapel 1990) and may (it necessarily follows) sometimes make cowards of us.

The exploration is also an illustration and appreciation of the rhetorical difficulties of arguing within a field of open moral communities. The talk of New Jersey politics and planning in the last two decades has frequently dealt with the challenging image of the state as an association bound by ethical and constitutional imperatives to prevent social groups from using the institutions of local governance to create exclusionary and self-protective moral orders. Within that image, the rights of citizens as members of the New Jersey polity constrain and shape every other communion. Strangely, however, the talk of both the friends and opponents of these imperatives seems stylized and partial as if no one was quite prepared to explicate (in hope or in anger) the dynamics of the imagined field. A major effort to enhance the state as a moral community capable of controlling the pattern of land development was presented under the title *Communities of Place* (New Jersey State Planning Commission 1991). The obscurity in the midst of oceans of words is both protected and protective: we are unable to reshape relations that we do not cogently represent in public.

THE NEW JERSEY PROBLEM[4]

In 1940, roughly 30 percent of the population of New Jersey lived in its six largest cities: Newark, the first of that group, had 430,000 residents. The 1990 Census indicated that the same six cities now contain about 10 percent of the state's population. Newark has shrunk to approximately 70 percent of its 1940 size.

In a spatial form that defies our conventional images of city and suburb, New Jersey is, nevertheless, highly urbanized. A virtually continuous belt of settlement cuts across the state diagonally, from the Philadelphia suburbs in the southwest, into the northeastern region opposite New York City. If Newark—the "metropolis" of the northeast—had annexed its adjacent counties (as Manhattan did at the end of the nineteenth century) it would today be among the nation's largest and richest cities. The belt is, however, politically divided into hundreds of jurisdictions. The edges of these local polities are often virtually invisible, designated only by a street sign in an otherwise seamless landscape, and penetrated by "linear cities"—factories, office buildings, and shopping malls strung along busy highway and rail corridors.

It would be a mistake, however, to imagine that localism is anachronistic or trivial, that it is soon to be overwhelmed by the interdependencies of a dynamic society. Local governments are responsible for choosing, administering, and financing a substantial portion of their own services. That responsibility creates the motive, opportunity, and means for social groups to employ public authority to create and maintain communities: that is, to attract some potential members while effectively excluding others, shaping residents into citizens by framing the conception of rights and obligations. The structure of local government reaches deeply into the design of churches, schools, neighborhood associations, clubs, and Little League teams. The communion may be shaped by what M. P. Baumgartner calls "moral minimalism" but—once threatened—the members rise to its defense (Baumgartner 1988).

The forms of interjurisdictional competition, conflict, and cooperation shape the allocation of initiative and immunity within the political fabric (Clark 1985). The communal winners enjoy considerable discretion in balancing taxes and expenditures. They command resources that allow them to insulate themselves from at least some of the shifting winds of economic fortune. The losers suffer a quite different fate. Former New Jersey Treasurer Clifford Goldman described their situation to an audience at Princeton University in 1987:

> What we have really done is to take a primarily poorer class of people, put them in separate taxing districts, impose on those districts the requirements to support certain services, and essentially in a simplified way, make the poor pay for their own services. We are also taking the property away a little bit each year from property owners in those districts under the burden of 6 to 7 percent tax rates.

"That's not a system," Goldman concluded, "that any moral person would have designed from scratch. It has just evolved over a long period of time" (Council on New Jersey Affairs 1988, 43).

Whatever they would have done "from scratch," men and women who represented themselves as moral have vigorously resisted changes in the system Goldman cryptically sketched. Without the props of an explicit ideology other than "local autonomy," they have sought to create and maintain a social order that legitimates inequality in personal income, affirms the value of winning in life's race by allowing advantages (and, it necessarily follows, disadvantages) to be transmitted across time and generations, and (finally and critically) permits local polities to use their coercive powers to shape and defend local moral orders. The situation of the excluded poor may command sympathy and ethically compel mitigating responses from the state and from the nation. Those responses do not, however, violate the social order in which they are located unless they make it impossible or at least very difficult for local polities to influence the selection of members, to discipline public behavior, and to shape the lives of their children.

Within this order, "urban policy" serves as a reservoir both sustaining and limiting the debate over the mitigating responses. Images of aiding "distressed" cities, working with "urban" schools, and supporting "inner city" neighborhoods shape discussion without allowing it to undermine the principles that legitimate inequality, stratification, and the political construction of communities.

For a time, Newark symbolized urban distress in the United States: New Jersey was a testing ground for the possibilities and the limits of the nationalization of urban governance. In recent years, however, the familiar images of "urban policy" have been overwhelmed; the association of "city" and "social justice" has been attenuated. The attention of political elites in New Jersey has been dominated by a series of overlapping, difficult, and intractably messy questions: How should public services be financed? How should the infrastructure of the politically fragmented urbanized belt be planned? How should endangered ecosystems and natural resources be protected in a political system that multiplies opportunities to externalize the costs of development? How should access to dispersed employment be accommodated in a system that rewards residential exclusion?

Most of the professional planners who have played a central role in these discussions have worn judicial robes and sat on the New Jersey Supreme Court. They have repeatedly focused political attention and forced decisions, bringing to bear the language of social justice upon the design of political institutions and the field in which local moral orders were embedded. For the moment, I am concerned only with the interaction of ethical mandates and prudence in their judicial voice. Planners without robes will, however, recognize their own talk and struggles—that is, will recognize themselves—in the words of the judges.

The robed planners repeatedly represented themselves as reluctant heroes. They entered into this dense tangle of policy issues and persisted only because of a legislative stalemate that compelled them to defend constitutional rights that they could not ignore and to respond to morally compelling social needs.

If the constitutional texts had been explicit—if everyone understood
them in the same way—then lower courts would have suppressed the offending behaviors where and when they appeared. The imperatives, as the
judges read them, were, however, vague and unbounded (though compelling) mandates, simple principles dominating a complex field of subordinate practices. That rhetorical form forced decisions: it also evoked Prudence in response.

Two streams of decisions illustrate this play of strong ethical mandate
and prudential caution. The first challenged the ability of local jurisdictions to use public authority to control their membership. The second challenged their authority and capacity to sustain inequality across generations through the system of financing education. In this chapter, I am concerned only with the first challenge as it appeared in the decisions that
have taken their name from Mt. Laurel, the town in which the legal attack
on established modes of local autonomy was pressed most decisively. Readers who do not follow New Jersey affairs should, however, remember that
my story is very partial. Even within the issues framed by the Mt. Laurel
cases, I have been selective. I am interested in the interplay of ethical mandates and Prudence rather than the substance of housing and land-use
policy; in the minds and marrow bones of the judges rather than the formation or dissolution of political coalitions. Outside the Mt. Laurel frame,
I have not touched the complementary judicial attack on the modes of
school finance nor the vigorous electoral and legislative counterattack on
the idea that New Jersey could—or should—redistribute income and opportunities.

Mt. Laurel[5]

The Mt. Laurel litigation began with a complaint by poor residents of
the town that local zoning and the allocation of public resources effectively
prevented them and their children from replacing their current homes. They
claimed, in effect, that they could not be legitimately exiled from Mt. Laurel by public action setting dues they could not meet. They were joined in
this limited claim by former residents who argued that they had been displaced by those same public decisions. The scope of the case was enlarged
by a complementary assertion that a class of poor residents in adjacent communities also had a right to move to Mt. Laurel although they had never
lived there. Or more carefully: public action could not raise the price of

entry so that no member of the class could hope to bid successfully for shelter in Mt. Laurel.

In 1975, the New Jersey Supreme Court agreed that all of those claims were valid. It insisted that local zoning ordinances are justified only if they do not deny any citizen either "due process" or the "equal protection of the laws" and if they serve the "general welfare." Mt. Laurel, it said, had failed those demanding tests "inherent" in the general wording of Article I, Paragraph 1 of "our Constitution":

> All persons are by nature free and independent, and have certain natural and unalienable rights, among which are those of enjoying and defending life and liberty, of acquiring, possessing, and protecting property, and of pursuing and obtaining safety and happiness.

The judges held that it was constitutionally imperative that each town in which there was a possibility of new development ensure places for a "fair share" of its region's low- and moderate-income residents. Because it was grounded in the state Constitution, that finding could not be overturned by a simple legislative majority.

The Court was unanimous in its findings, but the judges differed among themselves on subtle but important matters. The majority opinion (written by Justice Frederick W. Hall) was complemented by two concurrent statements. The first, a brief note by Justice Worrall F. Mountain, asserted that the result could and should have been grounded in statute rather than constitutional law. The statutory use of the "general welfare" to justify police powers had the same "amplitude" as the constitutional provisions cited by the majority and was sufficient "to justify, if not compel" the decision.

The second concurrent opinion was written by Justice Morris Pashman. He endorsed the principles of the majority but proposed to "go farther and faster" in implementing them. Pashman, however, was not only bolder in his policy recommendations. His description of the enemy embedded in suburban practice was fuller and marked by a broader appreciation of its capabilities and intentions. He was more detailed and more emphatic in his view of a "disaster" imminent in the emergent urban pattern. His rhetoric was hotter, his indictments more severe, and his ethical commandments more pointed.

Nevertheless, I read the Hall and Pashman opinions as tendencies in a single institutional mind: two—or perhaps more—voices in the same body, speaking to the litigants, to larger audiences and (always) to each other. (The New Jersey Supreme Court—in the terms used by John M. Bryson and Barbara C. Crosby in this volume—was simultaneously a *court*, a *forum*, and an *arena*.) Writing for his colleagues, Hall's diction on the bench may have been guarded, but he shared Pashman's moral passions. In a post-retirement speech, he described the exclusion of the poor from suburban jurisdictions and the failure to meet their basic housing "needs" as "social evils that must be corrected if we are to exist as a true democratic society." Having found Mt. Laurel's behavior "immoral," he said, it was not difficult for him to designate it as "unconstitutional" (Rose and Rothman 1977, 3–13).

In both the Hall and Pashman opinions, the Court appears as the reluctant leader of an expedition into morally compelling but practically uncharted territories. The broad direction of that expedition was defined by its origins in a critique of the immorality of established exclusionary practice, its guiding constitutional principles, and its image of a destination in socially diverse communities that would provide (Hall wrote) the "atmosphere" demanded by "a democracy and free institutions." Despite their sense of working against the grain of practice, both Hall and Pashman presented themselves as speaking for a superordinate communal standard. Pashman was particularly insistent on this prophetic role:

> The people of New Jersey should welcome the result reached by the Court in this case, not merely because it is required by our laws but, more fundamentally, because the result is right and true to the highest American ideals.

Perhaps all general principles, even when they meet a congenial and accepting response, are altered in the process of institutionalization. The initial "spirit" is inevitably diminished as it is articulated in bureaucratic rules and detailed legal interpretations. "Fair" distributions lose their glow when they emerge from protracted negotiations rather than leaping from the head of majestic Justice. Our faith in good intentions is eroded by the recognition of the perverse (or at least anomalous) consequences of the ways in which we implement them.[6]

There is, however, something special about the prudential taming of strong ethical mandates that threaten to reorganize a complex field of communities. When the judges in 1975 undertook to discipline their world with the general mandates of Article I, Paragraph 1, they set out a planning task they could not complete without prudently circumscribing their own interpretation of the commanding ethical code. Their circumscription—at the moment the mandate was articulated—illustrates the difficulty of distinguishing between prudential caution and the crafts of practical judgment and leadership that fascinated Aristotle.

The majority opinion framed this planning task clearly but without aggressively specifying its difficulties. Public land-use regulations, Hall simply observed, create amenities and then prevent some citizens from using them. On the face of it, that exclusionary policy offends each individual's right to the "equal protection" of the laws. That denial could never be justified when race was the basis of exclusion.

The majority now insisted that exclusion on the basis of income was also interdicted. Pashman's voice captured the profound implications and the difficulties of that assertion. "Justice," he argued, "must be blind to both race and income." The image of blind justice is, of course, a central icon of the legal system. Pashman was not, however, describing the procedures for the assessment of personal guilt or innocence but a principle guiding not merely land use but the allocation of the benefits of all public action. If Justice were properly blind, the government could not benefit one class without providing an identical or equivalent benefit to every class. Public amenities—including the shared environment of "air and water, flowers and green trees"—could not be arranged or regulated in a way that closed them to anyone simply because they could not afford an illegitimately imposed price of admission.

This expansive view of "equal protection" was complemented by a substantive interpretation of the meaning of "the general welfare." Some human wants, Hall argued, were appropriately understood as politically privileged. The New Jersey constitution implicitly required that public actions be arranged so that these "basic human needs"—including housing—be met. A local polity could not legitimately argue that the basic needs of its members had been satisfied and that its land-use or housing regulations were justified if it had failed to promote the "proper provision for adequate housing of all categories of people." Observing a pattern of exclusionary zoning, the Court held out a Kantian remedy: Every locality must act as if its regulations established a general inclusionary principle. In a field of polities designed to fulfill those principles, each locality would assume its "fair share" of the population of low- and moderate-income residents.

The strong ethical mandates to extend the protection of the law equally to each person and to attend to the general welfare threatened the order of a field of communities in which public and private domains were deeply intertwined. The expansive application of "equal protection" would require either a catastrophic disengagement of government from private realms or an enormous expansion of the capacity of the state to proscribe and, if necessary, redress governmentally supported inequality. The obscure bargain that sustained the image that there was a "private" domain where none existed would be undone.

In a similar way, a patterned, substantive conception of the "general welfare" would require an agency empowered to define politically privileged claims and to oversee and, if necessary, initiate public actions. It would ensure the priority of basic human needs when they could not be satisfied without reducing the political salience of ordinary wants or violating claims based upon rights or deserts. A list of needs that were easily met might be accommodated without difficulty within a pluralistic democratic polity. If, however, the needs challenged deeply embedded practices—if they included, for example, "decent housing," open space, participation in a socially diverse community, equal educational opportunity, and self-respect— then the "general welfare agency" would be a demanding (even a threatening) political master.

Mt. Laurel I, Arnold K. Mytelka (a sympathetic New Jersey lawyer) remarked, "sparkles with kinetic potential, suggesting revolutionary change" without, however, providing fully developed answers to the questions it raises (Rose and Rothman 1977, 150). Hall particularly spoke in the oblique and ambiguous voice of Prudence. Against Pashman's advice, the fair share obligation was confined to "developing" communities, requiring that (in some arena or court) fairness and feasibility would be balanced. Rather than emphasizing its revolutionary possibilities, *Mt. Laurel* was presented as simply a next step in an unfolding series of cases in which the Court had required a "general" rather than "parochial" referent for the "welfare" clause. The constitutional principles the Court evoked were described as limited in their scope: whatever their theoretical reach, as a "matter of policy" they should be applied only to "major questions of fundamental import."

Hall did not, however, simply play Prudence to Pashman. Both judges wrote within a common prudential fabric woven from three distinctive threads. The first thread in the fabric was the concept that the ethical mandate could be satisfied if jurisdictions assumed their "fair shares" within a "region." Hall and Pashman both imagined that each jurisdiction was embedded within a socially diverse territory that was a microcosm of the larger society and a moral object: Mt. Laurel was censured for harming the general welfare of "its" region. If regions were correctly designated and if (as newly enabled polities) they attended to the fair allocations that their own good health required, then a constitutional and moral wall would protect the resulting housing pattern against legal challenge.

In an open social system in which capital, labor, energy, goods, and information all move easily across space, there is, of course, no uniquely compelling—let alone "true"—protocol for the designation of regional boundaries or fair shares. (That, of course, did not prevent the judges from trying to ground regions and shares in the forms and formalities of social science and professional planning.)[7] The meanings we commonly ascribe to such contested and ambiguous notions are necessarily cultivated in complex albeit often tacit negotiations that succeed—as Judith Innes's chapter in this volume illustrates—only as the parties invest themselves in relationships or (as the judges phrased the idea in *Mount Laurel III*), as they try in "good faith" to meet their "obligations." The creation of a "public order" spanning differences in meaning and engendering trust has taken more than fifteen years in New Jersey and is by no means complete. The process has worked through *Mt. Laurel I* and its successors, through legislative debates, the internal dynamics of the Council on Affordable Housing created in 1985, the attempts of the Office of State Planning to create regional polities and to insert them into the process of development planning, and bargaining among jurisdictions and between developers and municipal authorities. Even in *Mt. Laurel I*, however, "region" appears as a process that can contain and limit the destabilizing ethical interpretation of Article I, Paragraph 1: the insistence that there is a substantial, politically privileged, set of basic human needs and that "equal protection" sets an extensive egalitarian standard for public action.

The second thread is nearly transparent. The ethical mandate announced in *Mt. Laurel I* stems from the constitutional obligations of members of the State of New Jersey: the state polity, whatever its conventional practices (or its moral theories-in-practice), was dedicated by its Constitution and its "highest ideals" to the meanings the Court ascribed to Article I, Paragraph 1.

Though cast in this central role, the State of New Jersey is almost wholly invisible in *Mt. Laurel I*. In *Mt. Laurel II*, its salience is reaffirmed in striking sentences that adopt Pashman's earlier characterization of the land as a public resource:

> The basis for the constitutional obligation is simple: the State controls the use of land, all of the land. In exercising that control it cannot favor rich over poor. It cannot legislatively set aside dilapidated housing in urban ghettos for the poor and decent housing elsewhere for everyone else. The government that controls this land represents everyone. While the State may not have the ability to eliminate poverty, it cannot use that condition as the basis for imposing further disadvantages.

The paragraph concludes, however, without specifying either the obligations of the State to meet basic human needs or to redress the inequalities in which it was implicated. The State, the Court announced, had delegated control over land to municipalities. All municipalities that had acted in the exclusionary modes practiced by Mt. Laurel were bound to accept their obligations, remedy their behavior and, in effect, reform their character.

In *Mt. Laurel I,* Hall and Pashman both inveighed against the selfishness and parochialism of exclusionary municipalities. The Court's opinion in *Mt. Laurel II,* written by Chief Justice Robert N. Wilentz, was even more biting:

> Mt. Laurel remains afflicted with a blatantly exclusionary ordinance. Papered over with studies, rationalized by hired experts, the ordinance at its core is true to nothing but Mount Laurel's determination to exclude the poor. . . . We have learned from experience . . . that unless a strong judicial hand is used, *Mount Laurel* will not result in housing, but in paper, process, witnesses, trials and appeals.

The anger directed at "widespread non-compliance" only emphasized, however, how strongly the decisions affirmed the political framework whose failings they sought to rectify rather than shifting to another (statewide) arena. The Court repeatedly announced that it would welcome legislative intervention. In Wilentz's words: "Powerful reasons suggest and we agree, that the matter is best left to the Legislature" in order to "protect" the "interests" created by the Constitution and by "underlying conceptions of fairness in the exercise of governmental power." The Court, however, did not attempt to wrestle with the Legislature so as directly to control its decisions. Instead, it ratified the salience of municipalities, asking them to stretch but not exceed their modest capacity to promote low- and moderate-income housing. The play was scripted so that municipalities—persuaded that the Court was in earnest—would require legislative action in order to create a stable and defensible cartel. The cartel's rules, as realized in the Fair Housing Act of 1985 and accepted by the Court, would require that each jurisdiction permit (though not necessarily create) its fair share of what came to be described as "affordable housing." The rules also ensured that the major community-forming features of localism and its role in a system of stratification would be protected.

The third thread in the prudential fabric was a pervasive confidence in professional planning. Hall and Pashman's initial characterization of the sprawling, low-density urban pattern in New Jersey was written in the terms of the conventional professional critique of ill-planned suburbia. Their remedies were also cast in those professional terms. There is no reason, Hall assured Mt. Laurel and other developing communities, why compliance with the Court's decision would prevent them from becoming and remaining "attractive, viable communities." The fundamental principles of zoning would particularly be undisturbed:

> They can have industrial sections, commercial sections and sections for every kind of housing from low cost and multi-family to lots of more than an acre with very expensive homes. Proper planning and governmental cooperation can prevent over-intensive and too sudden development, insure against future suburban sprawl and slums and assure the preservation of open space and local beauty. We do not intend that developing municipalities shall be overwhelmed by voracious land speculators and developers if they use the powers which they have intelligently and in the broad public interest.

The terms in which the decisions were cast were embedded within a professional discourse that would designate regions, distinguish development opportunities, estimate the impact of regulations on affordability, assess the economic impact of limiting sprawl, and transfer resources rather than people from one jurisdiction to another. The use of "sound planning criteria," Wilentz insisted, would now allow the Court to enrich and vary its conception of fairness:

> There is no reason . . . in our Constitution to make every municipality a microcosm of the entire state in its housing pattern, and there are persuasive reasons based on sound planning not to do so. The Constitution of the State of New Jersey does not require bad planning. It does not require suburban spread. It does not require rural municipalities to encourage large-scale housing developments. It does not require wasteful extension of roads and needless construction of sewer and water facilities for the out-migration of people from the cities and the suburbs. There is nothing in our Constitution that says that we cannot satisfy our constitutional obligation to provide lower income housing and, at the same time, plan the future of the state intelligently.

The commitment to planning, by enriching the conception of fairness, tamed the ethical commitment by grounding it in images of physical design, environmental quality, competitive claims, and budgetary constraints. Planning—as a mode of talking and acting—transformed a fundamental insistence upon blind Justice into a set of goals for "communities of place," "affordable" housing, and the efficient provision of an urban infrastructure. That process began in the decisions of the robed planners and continues in the work of those (less dramatically garbed) engaged in the implementation of the Fair Housing Act and in the preparation and assessment of a new state-wide development plan. Because planners valued ordinary people and the satisfactions of everyday life, policy imperatives have been grounded in banal measures of public preferences and opinions rather than in ethical mandates.

Tutored by Michel Foucault (as described in Judith Allen's chapter in this volume), we often think of the rhetorical forms of professional planning as ways of dominating the citizens of the modern state: as expressions of Mind over Marrow or (what Jürgen Habermas has described as) system over lifeworld.

And so they may be! The talk of planners—the data, the models, the contingent forecasts, the economic calculations, and the policy analyses—are also, however, tributes to the Virtue of Prudence. The constitutional mandates, the moral demands of shared New Jersey citizenship, the radical implications of "equal protection," and even the credibility of regions as anything but an artifice crafted through negotiation, are difficult to discern in the counting and the calculating.

Planning, a moral aristocrat and warrior might observe with disdain, is a *petit bourgeois* craft. In a world in which we value the routines and passions of ordinary people and everyday life, our processes of intelligence and scheming resist the reduction of ethical practices to strong mandates. We deny superordinate or heroic virtues that devalue our (various) "thick" representations of what is good in our lives. Or better, perhaps, we safely elevate ethical mandates so that they can be worshipped without walking among us.

Notes

1. The classic texts are, of course, Aristotle, *The Politics* (1984) and *Nicomachaean Ethics* (1985). My attention recently has been drawn to Prudence by the works of Martha Nussbaum (1990), Edmund L. Pincoffs (1986), and John Dunn (1990). Anthony T. Kronman (1985) reminded me how much my early sense of the concept was shaped by the work of Alexander Bickel.

2. My attention was called to these lines by J. Anthony Lukas (1985, 250-1). Judge Arthur Garrity, a central figure in a difficult school desegregation case in Boston, described how his mentor, Francis Ford, had a "streak of skepticism, even suspicion, lest he embrace a judicial doctrine without an understanding of its practical consequences. In pondering a legal problem he subscribed to the prayer of the poet Yeats."

3. See the treatment of the plurality of "spheres of justice," in Walzer (1983). I read John Rawls's insistence that his theory of justice is "political not metaphysical" (1985) and embraces a rich and varied conception of "goods" (1988)

as an appreciation of Prudence in the face of the superordinate demands of Justice as he first articulated them (1993). For a powerful argument that, even in a liberal regime, the political order that links the field of diverse communities need not—cannot!—be morally neutral, see Galston (1991).

4. For an introduction to New Jersey setting a context for the *Mt. Laurel* decisions, see the relevant chapters in Pomper (1986) and the Council on New Jersey Affairs (1988).

5. The two major decisions I have cited here are *Southern Burlington County NAACP v. Township of Mount Laurel*, 67 N.J. 151, 336 A.2d 713 (1975); and 92 N.J. 158, 456 A.2d 390 (1983)—*Mt. Laurel I* and *Mt. Laurel II*, respectively. In 1986, the Court validated the newly passed Fair Housing Act in *Hills Development Co. v. Township of Bernards*, 103 N.J. 1, 510 A.2d 621—a decision sometimes described as *Mt. Laurel III*. A small cottage industry has grown up around these and related cases. See Rose and Rothman (1977), Burchell et al. (1983), "Symposium" (1984), and Judith Innes's chapter in this volume for signposts along the way.

6. There is a wonderful illustration of this dynamic in the subsequent history of the "Mt. Laurel obligation." The 1985 Fair Housing Act allowed jurisdictions to meet a portion of that obligation by transferring funds to jurisdictions requiring help in housing low- and moderate-income populations. Selig (1988) analyzes the early experience with these Regional Contribution Agreements.

7. There is an account of these toils in Babcock and Siemon (1985) and a vivid illustration of their difficulties in Burchell (1983).

REFERENCES

Aristotle. 1985. *Nicomachean ethics.* Translated by Terence Irwin. Indianapolis: Hackett Publishing Company [Rackham 1984].

_____. 1984. *The politics.* Translation by Carnes Lord. Chicago: University of Chicago Press.

Babcock, R. F., and C. L. Siemon. 1985. *The zoning game revisited.* Boston: Oelgeshlager, Gunn & Hain.

Baumgartner, M. P. 1988. *The moral order of a suburb.* New York: Oxford University Press.

Burchell, R., et al. 1983. *Mount Laurel II: challenge and delivery of low-cost housing.* New Brunswick, NJ: Center for Urban Policy Research.

Care, N. 1987. *On sharing fate.* Philadelphia: Temple University Press.

Clark, G. L. *Judges and the cities.* Chicago: University of Chicago Press.

Council on New Jersey Affairs. 1988. *New Jersey issues: papers from the Council on New Jersey Affairs.* Princeton, NJ: Princeton University.

Dunn, J. 1990. *Interpreting political responsibility: essays, 1981–1989.* Princeton, NJ: Princeton University Press.

Galston, W. A. 1991. *Liberal purposes: goods, virtues, and diversity in the liberal state.* Cambridge: Cambridge University Press.

Garver, E. 1987. *Machiavelli and the history of prudence.* Madison: University of Wisconsin Press.

Goodin, R. E. 1985. *Protecting the vulnerable: a reanalysis of our social responsibilities.* Chicago: University of Chicago Press.

Kronman, A. T. 1985. Alexander Bickel's *Philosophy of prudence. The Yale Law Journal* 94: 1567–1616.

Lukas, J. A. 1985. *Common ground: a turbulent decade in the lives of three American families.* New York: Alfred A. Knopf.

Mapel, D. R. 1990. Prudence and the plurality of value in international ethics. *The Journal of Politics* 52: 433–56.

Nelson, D. M. 1991. *The priority of prudence: virtue and natural law in Thomas Aquinas and the implications for modern ethics.* State College, PA: Pennsylvania State University Press.

New Jersey State Planning Commission. 1991. *Communities of place: the interim state development and redevelopment plan for the State of New Jersey.* Trenton, NJ: Office of State Planning.

Nussbaum, M. 1990. *Love's knowledge.* New York: Oxford University Press.

Okin, S. M. 1989. *Justice, gender, and the family.* New York: Basic Books.

Pincoffs, E. L. 1986. *Quandaries and virtues: against reductivism in ethics.* Lawrence, KS: University of Kansas Press.

Pomper, G., ed. 1986. *The political state of New Jersey.* New Brunswick, NJ: Rutgers University Press.

Rawls, J. 1985. Justice as fairness: political not metaphysical. *Philosophy and Public Affairs* 14: 223–51.

_____. 1988. The priority of right and ideas of the good. *Philosophy and Public Affairs* 17: 251–76.

_____. 1993. *Political liberalism.* New York: Columbia University Press.

Rose, J. G., and R. E. Rothman, eds. 1977. *After Mount Laurel: the new suburban zoning.* New Brunswick, NJ: Center for Urban Policy Research.

Selig, J. M. 1988. Implementing *Mount Laurel*: an assessment of regional contribution agreements. Council on New Jersey Affairs, Working Paper No. 14. Princeton, NJ: Princeton University.

Symposium—*Mount Laurel II* and development in New Jersey. 1984. *Rutgers Law Journal* 15, 3.

Wachs, M. ed. 1985. *Ethics in planning.* New Brunswick, NJ: Center for Urban Policy Research.

Walzer, M. 1983. *Spheres of justice: a defense of pluralism and equality.* New York: Basic Books.

Commentary

Niraj Verma

The Systemic Nature of Professional Ethics

INTRODUCTION

The history of professional education can be seen as the story of successive stages of confidence in, and disavowal of, intellectual knowledge. Influenced by events such as the GI Bill supporting higher education, the mission-oriented science of World War II, and the experience with operations research and management science, professionals in business, law, and planning, as well as the clergy, have sometimes embraced and at other times rejected attempts at intellectualization. That history is too well-known to merit repeating. What is significant, however, is how the intellectualization of the professions has ushered in the professionalization of the academy. Once the bastions of the liberal arts, intellectual fields like epistemology and moral philosophy are reaching out into public policy. Philosophers and social scientists, once shy of less enlightened minds, now increasingly venture into the public domain, and fields like economics and sociology experiment with more professional curricula.

Ethics and moral training are central to this new synthesis. Virtually every professional field has commissioned a committee or group to draw up a code of ethics for the profession, and almost every accreditation process requires evidence of training in ethics. Courses with labels like "business ethics" or "applied ethics" can be found in virtually every professional field, and several professional philosophers are among those who write for journals that cater to these fields. But even as courses proliferate, the debate about the nature and content of professional ethics education is far from over. After all, if unadulterated moral philosophy is unlikely to influence professional practice, neither can we rely on the simple, common-sensical moral maxims that have become the staple of such courses. The question "What should professional ethics comprise?" remains an open one.

The three chapters in this collection offer me an opportunity to develop a response to this question. Together these chapters carve a niche which, to my mind, is neither the traditional intellectualization that accompanies debates within moral philosophy nor is it a vulgar professionalism that disavows serious moral questions in its quest for application. Despite their separate logics and their sometimes differing positions, I see a common thread in their quest for connectivity and in their valuation of the systemic importance of ethical and moral concerns. Ethics, and particularly professional ethics, they seem to suggest, is about systems and system building and not about partitioning or separation. We cannot remove ethics from technical knowledge, nor can we separate it from our obligations as members of communities and as representatives of others. And if these allegiances—to communities or disciplines—are cause for conflict, the primacy of action does not necessitate intellectual disdain or moral disregard. Rather, it requires an extension of our understanding of morality into professional domains.

The modality of this extension varies. Hendler opts for a meta-ethical framework and argues for the necessity of integrating the philosophical with the instrumental. Her framework suggests that differences, however deep, are reconcilable. And she shows her preference for an integrative model of ethics that knits personal with professional, and normative with descriptive. Harper and Stein stress connectivity by denying incommensurability. They argue that our shared language and the basic comprehensibility of others' positions implies commensurability. The metaphysical argument is intricate, but more important are the goals that motivate the analysis. Harper and Stein seek to prevent the nihilism that accompanies a thesis of incommensurability because they fear that such a thesis is an open invitation to the naked exercise of power. Mandelbaum, too, is mindful of the dangers of conflict between rival positions, but he opts for the buffer of prudence, which allows conflicting ethical stances to coexist. Although there are hints of incommensurability here—motivated by the recognition of the undecidability of rival positions that extend beyond the communities that inspire them—the goal is to prevent ethical mandates from becoming so empowering that we demand the annihilation of those mandates with which we disagree. In this sense, prudence performs a systems-building task; it brings sense and order to the seeming disparateness that threatens to make ethical choices arbitrary.

THE CASE FOR A SYSTEMIC ETHICS

The systemic understanding of ethical action is not new to philosophy. Spinoza's *Ethics*, for instance, takes all events to be interrelated because of their underlying moral content. This is not surprising since, for Spinoza, all events are rational inferences emanating from the perfection of God. Aristotle's *Nicomachean Ethics* has systemic links to economics and politics. But if these systemic views of ethics exist—we can also add Kant's categorical imperatives to this list—what is the difference between them and the systemic ethics of professions? The difference, it seems to me, lies in the fragmented nature of contemporary professional knowledge and its intimate connection with technique and technology.

We see this in Mandelbaum's story of the "robed planners" of Mount Laurel, where the ethical commitment was tamed "by grounding it in images of physical design, environmental quality, competitive claims, and budgetary constraints." The fundamental and abstract lessons of moral philosophy have found a vehicle in technology. Hendler's chapter reiterates the point. She reminds us that our model-building expertise has come to dominate our conceptions of good and bad. But although technique, manifest as the "talk of the planners," "ethical models," and the search for "Wide Reflective Equilibrium," may become dominant, it still explains only half the story: the fragmentation of professional knowledge and the intellectual division of labor complete the picture. Specialization, it would seem, demands a price. The synthetic understanding that Renaissance men or women could once boast—"knowledge" as we traditionally knew it—gives way to structural explanations and technical know-how, a situation Edward Wenk has aptly described as "more knowledge but less understanding."

Where does this lead? The gains in our analytic prowess and the delivery of efficiency extract a price that appears variously as the separation of means and ends in planning or as the distancing of facts from values in ethics. Much has been written about these issues, and I have dealt with them elsewhere.[1] For now, I wish to explore whether or not the changes in our craft and in our environment can be "accommodated" within our traditional sense of morality. Or, do we need a revision of some of our most fundamental notions of morality in the form of a new theory of professional ethics?

THREE DEMANDS ON PROFESSIONAL ETHICS

One answer to this question comes from the philosopher Hans Jonas. In *The Imperative of Responsibility* (1984), Jonas argues that the growth of technology has changed the nature of human action and that this demands a change in the focus of ethical theory. These changes are fundamental—so fundamental, claims Jonas, that they shift the focus of professional ethics from an emphasis on moral volition and goodwill to responsibility. That is, the moral demand to be well-intentioned is supplemented by the cognitive demand to know more. The knowledge needed to deal with the uncertainty of the future, the potential for far-reaching effects, and the duty toward future generations calls for, in Jonas's words, "an ethics for an endangered species."

Jonas relies on only one of the two changes we have been investigating: the concern with technology. But equally important for this new ethics, it seems to me, is the fragmentation of our knowledge. If we have become, as Jonas tells us, "captive beneficiaries" of technology, this is as much due to the dominance of a technological force as it is to a nonsystemic growth of our knowledge. If the ethics of responsibility seeks to tame the unchecked march of technology, it must also address the fundamental separation between "thought and wisdom," "knowledge and understanding," and "prudence and calculation." In operational terms, ethics must become instrumental. It must seek not only to admonish against moral indifference or to invoke our cognitive responsibilities, but it must also become the bearer of a synthetic and systemic understanding.

Professional ethics, seen this way, has three simultaneous roles to play: it must be (1) an intention-based volitional ethics, (2) a responsibility-based cognitive ethics, and (3) an instrumentally driven systemic ethics. The first role is the traditional domain of moral philosophy embodied in such theories as the Kantian emphasis on "goodwill" or its modern analog, the Rawlsian invocation of justice. One version of Kant's universal law—considered and then rejected by the planners of Mount Laurel—reads: "The only thing good in itself is goodwill."[2] In an environment where the disengagement of science and technique from morality had not achieved its contemporary proportions, moral philosophy saw no explicit need to step beyond its mandate of moral provisioning to integrate the moral with the technical or scientific. As Kant postulates, "There is no need of science or philosophy for knowing what man has to do in order to be honest and good, and indeed to be wise and virtuous. . . ."[3] Ethics, in this tradition, focuses exclusively on volition and intention, preoccupied largely with questions of freedom of the will. No special knowledge, training, or competence, except purity of the heart, is demanded by it.

BEYOND VOLITION:
COGNITIVELY DEMANDING MORALITY

Volition and goodwill, one suspects, are simply not good enough in a world increasingly fragmented between the various forms of knowledge and dominated by technical knowledge. Indeed, Jonas (1984, 5) tells us that they extract a price in the marginalization of "the cognitive side of moral action." In a technological world, Jonas argues, an imperative of responsibility must supplement the imperative of volition. That is, the cognitive duty of "knowing more" becomes as important a part of morality as the volitional imperative of "intending well." In such a formulation, forecasting, simulating consequences, and similar preparedness become demands of morality and not merely matters of technique and technology.[4]

Such a stance is important for planning. It does not deny the importance of good intention but questions its sufficiency as a criterion for ethical behavior. After all, problems such as pollution, urban sprawl, even poverty and homelessness cannot be explained away by invoking the category of immoral intentions. They are more often than not failures of well-intentioned but poorly designed policies. And since they are as much cognitive flaws as they are intentional moral lapses, the cognitive mandate of designing well becomes part of the moral mandate of doing good.

One example of such cognitive imperatives is found in the chapter by Mandelbaum. "Because planners valued ordinary people and the satisfaction of everyday life," he writes, "policy imperatives have been grounded in banal measures of public preferences and opinions rather than in ethical mandates." These banal measures, as I see them, are not only prudential, they are cognitive as well. In a spirit similar to that of Jon Elster, who suggests that the calculations of reason tell us that "it is rational to be nonrational," Mandelbaum argues that caution in the face of ethical mandate needs no additional ethical justification.[5] Prudence turns out to be a cognitive demand. It is what we turn to when ethical mandates fail us. Prudent disregard of moral imperatives and the decision to move away from "superordinate virtues" or "thick representations," when the situation so demands, put the testing ground of all knowledge not in the hands of a few moral philosophers but in the larger community of everyday practice. Prudence, seen this way, is a democratizing force that rescues us from our dogmatism. It is the final word in critical inquiry, for here the critic is everyone, not only the wearers of academic robes.

If the force of prudence is the cause of Mandelbaum's optimism, Harper and Stein voice similar confidence in their thesis of commensurability. Their metaphysical position on commensurability or incommensurability is less important, I believe, than the motivations behind their claims and the ends that it helps them reach. The Rawlsian Wide Reflective Equilibrium, which they advocate, seeks to bring about an amalgamation of differing positions and a convergence through democratic dialogue. In this respect, curiously, all three authors share a common goal because contracting and bargaining—epitomes of democracy—are also at the center of Hendler's dispensation.

Are these the pathways of a cognitively demanding ethics? In a democratic world, the knowledge of the professional can be tested only at the *agora*. The alternative is what John Stuart Mill called "the peculiar evil of silencing the expression of an opinion." Such concerns are not merely academic nor do they apply only to areas remote from our everyday world. Eisenhower's warnings of the growing power of the military-industrial complex is a poignant reminder. In a communitarian world—and we know no other—cognition must mean the democratization of the generation and development of knowledge.

BEYOND JUSTIFICATION:
THE INSTRUMENTALITY OF A SYSTEMIC ETHICS

The meeting of cognition and volition in professional ethics is justified by the equal roles assigned to responsibility and intention. But while the justification is strong, the implementation is unclear. The operationalization of a cognitively and morally demanding theory of ethics is problematic because professional training distorts our conception of the world. It reconstructs our view of the world in a way that imposes what has been called a "moral blindness."[6] If we agree with Jonas that a cognitively demanding ethics is necessitated by the changing nature of human action, then we must also agree that a systemic ethics is needed due to the changing nature of human cognition.

Seen this way, professional ethics has a synthesizing function. It calls for a renewal of connectivity and broad, more sensitive training. The moral duty here is to oppose the tendency to fragment or to separate. Tunnel vision or the failure to anticipate the consequences of interventions become signs of moral wantonness and not just intellectual incompetence. However, neither the authors of these chapters nor I are alone in contributing toward a systems view of ethics. These concerns have continuously preoccupied systems philosophers, and in planning its best-known exponent is perhaps C. West Churchman.[7] The collective impact of this kind of moral philosophy is to extend professional ethics beyond the bastions of a conventionally defined morality to become an instrument for urging greater responsibility. One measure of responsibility—perhaps its most important measure, I have tried to argue—is in the bringing together of the various elements that comprise professional practice. This is in essence Harper and Stein's call for an integration of a "morality of caring" with a "morality of abstract justice," or Mandelbaum's portrayal of Yeats's song of the relation between mind and marrow bone.

Notes

1. See, for instance, Verma (1994a, 1994b). In a recent essay (Churchman and Verma 1994), I have looked at this in the context of the "theory of the firm" in microeconomics.

2. This is one of three formulations of the Kantian imperative as described in Immanuel Kant's *Groundwork of the Metaphysics of Morals*, translated by H. J. Paton.

3. op. cit., chapter 1.

4. For an early realization of this in planning, see Wachs (1982).

5. I have borrowed this description from Alan Ryan's review of Jon Elster's works in the *New York Review of Books* (October 10, 1991) titled "When It is Rational To Be Non-Rational."

6. This term is from J. Andre (1992).

7. The original sources are Churchman (1979, 1982). For more recent positions and applications, see Churchman and Mitroff (1993) and Werner Ulrich (1994).

REFERENCES

Andre, J. 1992. Learning to see—moral growth during medical training. *Journal of Medical Ethics* 18, 3: 148–52.

Churchman, C. W. 1979. *The systems approach and its enemies.* New York: Basic Books.

_____. 1982. *Thought and wisdom.* Seaside, CA: Intersystems Press.

Churchman, C. W., and I. Mitroff. 1993. *A prospectus for a book: science in the service of humanity.* Berkeley: Center for Research in Management, University of California.

Churchman, C. W., and N. Verma. 1994. Epistemology and the theory of the firm. Working Paper, Lusk Center Research Institute, University of Southern California, Los Angeles, California.

Kant, I. 1786. *Groundwork for the metaphysics of morals.* Translated by H.J.Paton. New York: Harper Torchbooks [1964].

Jonas, H. 1984. *The imperative of responsibility.* Chicago: University of Chicago Press.

Ulrich, W. 1994. Can we secure future-responsive management through systems thinking and design? *Interfaces* 24, 4: 26–37.

Verma, N. 1994a. Organizations and their purposes: a note on Churchman's philosophy of management. *Interfaces* 24, 4: 60–6.

_____. 1994b. A new way of looking at fact and value in planning. Paper presented at the 36th Annual Conference of the Association of Collegiate Schools of Planning, Phoenix, Arizona. November.

Wachs, M. 1982. Ethical dilemmas in forecasting for public policy. *Public Administration Review* 42, 6: 562–67.

PART VI

Designing
Planning Processes

Seymour J. Mandelbaum

Designing
Planning Processes

INTRODUCTION

Virtually all human beings and most social systems are capable of employing a variety of planning modes. Faced with a threat or an opportunity, they choose a mode from their repertoire: here consulting broadly and seeking consensus; there going full speed ahead in pursuit of a grand vision. If one mode fails, they are capable of shifting to another. Indeed, canny adversaries confronting a play in one style recognize that other forms are in reserve. A carrot is offered but a stick lies in reserve; the collapse of comprehensive planning may be followed by aggressive and flexible opportunism. Adversaries sensibly respond both to what they see before them and to tomorrow's possibilities.

For the most part, adults and mature social entities settle into an identity that is defined by a stable planning repertoire. They act "in character." Every once in a while, however, a gap in the repertoire, or an invidious comparison, leads individuals, organizations, polities, and communities of all sorts to attempt to add a new practice to their repertoire, to eliminate a badly flawed one, or to alter the way in which they shift from one planning mode to another.

The enterprise of writing theoretically about planning plays an important role in both the ordinary selection of procedural options within an established array and in the design of procedural innovations. In the simplest case, when things go wrong, theorizing helps us assess whether the fault lies in the capacities of our adversaries, in our substantive decisions, or in the limitations of our planning mode. Theorizing points to alternative

459

modes that we already command. In the more difficult case of innovation, it helps us shape the altered elements within an identity that characteristically remains largely unchanged.

The three chapters in this final section attempt to order our understanding of these occasional—though hardly rare—processes in which we engage to design planning systems rather than simply to act within an established repertoire.

Leaders—the subjects of John Bryson's and Barbara Crosby's chapter—must learn to work within three institutional forms: 1. *forums* in which meanings are shared; 2. *arenas* in which decisions are made; and 3. *courts* in which they are legitimated. The heuristic distinction among forums, arenas, and courts also directs the process of innovation. The three forms are necessarily linked, but Bryson and Crosby alert us to the value of distinguishing among them. A new forum may be destroyed if the search for understanding is curtailed by the demands of a decision-centered arena. Legitimacy may be denied if courts are forced (forum-like) to invent new shared meanings across distinctive discursive frames.

Britton Harris takes a different approach to the design of planning systems. Many of the new practices that promise to enlarge or reform our repertoires appear as bodies of organized knowledge articulated in intellectual techniques and instruments. For most of his professional career, Harris has been particularly interested in the ways in which computerized models and information systems enrich our capacity to represent cities and regions and to explore the implications of our prospective land-use and transportation choices. In effect, these systems—of which the computer itself is only one among many elements—provide us with public access into our own collective mind.

Harris is unique in this volume in reminding us that the theorizing enterprise may play an important role in assessing and shaping technological innovations in planning processes. If technical innovators and planning theoreticians do not talk to one another, then both suffer. Expensive hardware—and lots of trained people and sophisticated software—go unused or are badly distorted. In a cruel version of anti-intellectualism, an anti-technological bias dooms us to rely on old technologies to deal with problems that have already overwhelmed them.

Finally, writing in the shadow of global environmental challenges and the collapse of centralized command planning systems in Central and Eastern Europe, Richard Bolan reflects on the difficulties and methods of designing institutions. A bigger computer or a new organization chart for the central planning agency would not have saved the former Soviet Union in the face of deeply flawed institutional arrangements. There are no simple technological fixes for threatened forests and oceans. Against the weight of a "structuralist" tradition that treats institutions as virtually impervious to design, he offers both more optimistic assumptions and a tentative list of design principles.

The last half of Bolan's chapter articulates "principles of institutional design" that defy ready summary. Each of the individual items points to a complex argument rather than standing unambiguously on a scholarly consensus. His final paragraph captures this quality and may serve as a coda to this volume:

> Planners cannot afford to leave institutional design to a new group of specialists. It is, inevitably, part of the fabric of their daily work lives. Theorists, therefore, must attend to institutionalization. I have laid out a tentative map of a still little-understood intellectual territory. I hope others will join in the exploration. It is a daunting theoretical task but if pursued vigorously, it will profoundly change the nature of planning as practice.

John M. Bryson and Barbara C. Crosby

22 Planning and the Design and Use of Forums, Arenas, and Courts

INTRODUCTION

In today's shared-power, no-one-in-charge, interdependent world, public problems and issues spill over organizational and institutional boundaries. Many people are affected by problems like global warming, AIDS, homelessness, drug abuse, crime, growing poverty among children, and teen pregnancy, but no one person, group, organization, or institution has the power or authority necessary to solve these problems. Instead, organizations and institutions must share objectives, resources, activities, power or some of their authority in order to achieve collective gains or minimize losses (Bryson and Einsweiler 1991). They also must plan but the shared-power context calls for new conceptions of planning.

Historically, the public administration, planning theory, and policy analysis literatures have paid particular attention to procedural, and often rigid, approaches to formulating problems; developing policies, plans or recommendations for addressing those problems; and overseeing implementation of approved solutions. In recent years, attention has focused directly on the various institutional contexts and settings within which procedural aspects of planning occur (Alexander 1992; Brandl 1988; Bryson 1988; Bryson et al. 1990; Eden and Radford 1990; Forester 1989; Friend and Hickling 1987; Healey et al. 1988; Krumholz and Forester 1990; Lynn 1987; Mandelbaum 1985; Weimer and Vining 1989, 1992). Our desire in this chapter is to build on these efforts in order to help planners and policy analysts address important public problems that occur in shared-power contexts more effectively.

We care about planning because we view it as "the organization of hope" (Stephen Blum, quoted in Forester 1989, 20). Planning, in other words, is what makes hope reasonable. However, the planning process in shared-power situations hardly ever follows a rigidly structured sequence from developing problem definitions and solutions to adopting and implementing proposals. Serious difficulties arise when people try to impose rigidly sequential approaches on situations in which no one is in charge. Nonetheless, for hope to be reasonable, it is essential to have an organized approach of some sort. The challenge, therefore, is to instill political, technical, legal, and ethical rationality into these difficult situations; that is, to link knowledge effectively to action (Friedmann 1987). In this chapter we sketch a kind of *procedural* rationality focused on the design and use of shared-power *settings* that can be used to address substantive public problems effectively (Benveniste 1989; Lynn 1987; March and Simon 1958; Stone 1988).

We present a descriptive framework that we think can help planners and policy analysts be more effective in shared-power, no-one-in-charge situations. The chapter is divided into several sections. First, we discuss public action and the three "dimensions" of power. We also identify three basic kinds of public policy-related action:

1.   communication

2.   decision making, particularly as it relates to policy or plan adoption and implementation

3.   adjudication or, more broadly, the management of residual conflicts and the enforcement of the underlying norms in the system.

Second, we show how policy-related action and underlying social structures are intimately linked. Third, combining the dimensions of power with the three basic kinds of public policy-related action, we develop a triply three-dimensional—and holistic—conception of power. This holistic conception of power allows us in the three sections that follow to describe in detail the principal settings and social practices associated with each type of policy-related action—namely, the design and use of forums, arenas, and courts. These settings form the structural basis for public policy-related action, and their design and use provide the principal ways in which planners and policy analysts can affect public policies or plans and their implementation.

In shared-power situations, public leaders, planners and policy analysts rely on forums for discussion, on arenas for policy making and implementation, and on courts to manage residual disputes and enforce the underlying norms in the system. The design and use of these settings have profound effects on how public issues are raised and resolved. They also have profound implications for how planning may most usefully be viewed. Indeed, for purposes of this chapter, *we define planning as the intentional design and use of forums, arenas, and courts to formulate and achieve desired policy outcomes.*

We present several conclusions in the final section. The framework helps make the point that in shared-power, no-one-in-charge settings, planners and policy analysts can have their greatest impact by focusing on the ideas, rules, modes, media, and methods that link action and structure in forums, arenas, and courts. Since the design and use of forums, arenas, and courts can be extremely complex, planners are fortunate to have innumerable opportunities to exert a beneficial influence over both stability and change in social systems.

Due to space limitations, we will offer only brief illustrations. Readers interested in detailed case examples should see Bryson and Crosby (1992, 1993a), which apply the framework to the establishment of the metropolitan government in the Minneapolis–St. Paul region of the United States, and Bryson and Crosby (1993b), which applies the framework to the creation and operation of a public domed sports facility in Minneapolis.

PUBLIC ACTION AND THE DIMENSIONS OF POWER

Based partly on the work of Giddens (1979, 1984), we identify three basic kinds of public policy-related action: 1. communication; 2. decision making, particularly as it relates to policy adoption and implementation; and 3. adjudication or, more broadly, the management of residual conflicts and the enforcement of the underlying norms in the system. Each of these kinds of action is shaped—and biased—by three different dimensions of power (Lukes 1974; cf. Clegg 1989).

The first dimension of power is emphasized by the pluralists (e.g., Dahl 1961). Pluralists argue that the power of public actors in the United States varies with issues, that there are several bases of power (such as wealth, status, knowledge, and skill), and that there is some substitutability among power bases. In other words, winners and losers vary by issue, and society, therefore, is pluralist rather than elitist. The pluralists focus on observable behavior (in our terms, communication, decision making, and adjudication), key issues, and interests, defined as policy preferences revealed by political participation.

In the second dimension, power is exercised more subtly through manipulation of what comes up for decision and action. As Bachrach and Baratz (1962, 949) note: "To the extent that a person or group—consciously or unconsciously—reinforces barriers to the public airing of policy conflicts, that person has power" (see also Bachrach and Baratz 1963, 1970). Various ideas, rules, modes, media, and methods are the principal barriers that bias attention toward some matters and away from others (Forester 1989, 38–89, 150–1; Healey et al. 1988).

The bias of all organizations (Schattschneider 1960, 71) is based on asymmetrically distributed rules and resources (such as control over agendas) that create decision and "non-decision" categories, and define "live" issues versus what must remain, at least for a time, "potential" issues. In other words, the bias has the effect of creating rules (broadly conceived) in power's second dimension that "rule out" certain behaviors—behaviors that, therefore, will not be observed (Bromiley 1981; Bryson and Crosby 1989; Crenson 1971; Gaventa 1980).

The third dimension reveals an even subtler exercise of power, the shaping of felt needs or even consciousness itself (Gaventa 1980). Felt needs are deeply rooted in "bedrock" social, political, and economic structures. These structures provide the "generative" rules, resources, and transformation relations that allow human relations, organizations, and coalitions within and among organizations to exist in the first place (Giddens 1979, 89–91).

The bedrock or "deep" social, political, and economic structures of a society (i.e., the third dimension of power) provide the basis for a potential set of issues, conflicts, policy preferences, and decisions (all rooted in consciously or unconsciously felt needs) that public actors *might* address. In turn, the ideas, rules, modes, media, and methods of the second dimension influence the transformation of that potential set into the actual issues, conflicts, policy preferences, and decisions addressed in the first dimension, and those items that remain in the second dimension as potential issues, covert conflicts, grievances, or nondecisions (Bryson and Crosby 1992).

This three-dimensional view of power reveals how the biases embedded in "layered" structures of rules, resources, and transformation relations (in the second and third dimensions of power) may severely distort communication, policy making, and implementation and adjudication, so that some matters of importance are considered while others are not (Clegg 1981). In particular, action carries with it the conscious and unconscious production and reproduction of these biases.

THE STRUCTURAL BASE FOR PUBLIC ACTION

Within and among organizations, action is linked to rules, resources, and transformation relations—or the dimensions of power—primarily through the design and use of forums, arenas, and courts—the basic social settings humans use in shared-power situations for communication, decision making, and adjudication, respectively. In these settings, human beings interactively draw on social structures or relationships (e.g., organizational and interorganizational rules, resources, and transformation relations) to *produce* tangible effects (such as discussion papers, policy statements, or action plans) at the same time that they *reproduce* organizational and interorganizational social relations and structures. Reproduction in this case implies "ongoing strengthening, altering, or weakening of those social relations without which the production of desired results (e.g., plans, reports, recommendations) would not be possible" (Forester 1989, 71; cf. Giddens 1979, 49–130). In other words, actors draw on rules, resources, and transformation relations, including social relations, to create action, which subsequently recreates the structures (rules, resources, and transformation relations) that permitted the action in the first place. Structures thus are rules, resources, and transformation relations organized as properties of social systems and are characterized by "the absence of the subject" (Giddens 1979, 66, 96–130; 1984, 1–40). Our view of forums, arenas, and courts highlights the central role played by ideas, rules, modes, media, and methods in governing both the continuity and transformation of structures and therefore the production and reproduction—or *structuration*—of social systems (Giddens 1979, 66–73; 1984, 1–40).

An appreciation of structuration implies that planners can have their greatest influence over action and outcomes by focusing on the second dimension of power—that is, by strengthening, weakening, or altering the ideas, rules, modes, media, and methods that divide what is theoretically possible into what is actually possible and what is not. In a shared-power world, planners are rarely able to prescribe actions and dictate terms to other actors. Similarly, planners are unlikely to be able to make significant changes in underlying bedrock social structures. On the other hand, planners may be able to have a significant impact on the ideas, rules, modes, media, and methods used to link action with bedrock social structure, perhaps in part simply because other people may not pay as much attention to these matters. Influence over ideas, rules, modes, media, and methods, in turn, will have a major impact on what is up for discussion, decision, and control and what will remain in a sort of public policy "never-never land."

In other words, in order to raise and resolve public problems constructively, planners must attend to:

1. human interaction that is empowered and influenced by rules, resources, and transformation relations;

2. institutional arrangements of rules, resources, and transformation relations; and

3. how human interaction and social structures are linked through ideas, rules, modes, media, and methods.

A HOLISTIC APPROACH TO POWER

A holistic conception of power requires an understanding of how the three basic types of public policy-related action—communication, decision making and implementation, and adjudication—are connected to the three dimensions of power and how the types interact as part of recurrent social practices. In general, we agree with Giddens's (1979, 1984) view of social practices as the regular dynamics produced by the patterned interaction of human actors empowered and influenced by rules, resources, and transformation relations in specific situations. Social practices may be seen as systems of interaction that have structural properties but are not themselves structures.

All social practices involve communication, decision making, and the sanctioning of conduct, at least to some extent—but that extent depends on the practice (cf. Healey et al. 1988). This leads us in later sections to a more detailed discussion of the design and use of forums, arenas, and courts, practices that differentially emphasize the various kinds of policy-related action.

In order to apply the approach to actual situations, it is necessary to identify and examine those social practices principally associated with each type of policy-related action. We call the social practice that results principally in the creation and communication of meaning *the design and use of forums;* the social practice that results principally in policy or plan adoption and implementation *the design and use of arenas;* and the social practice that results principally in the normative regulation of conduct *the design and use of courts* (Figure 22.1). Traditional procedural approaches to planning are subsumed under these practices, especially the design and use of forums and arenas. In other words, human beings engage in the creation and communication of meaning chiefly through a social practice—the design and use of forums. This process is shaped by what Giddens calls principles

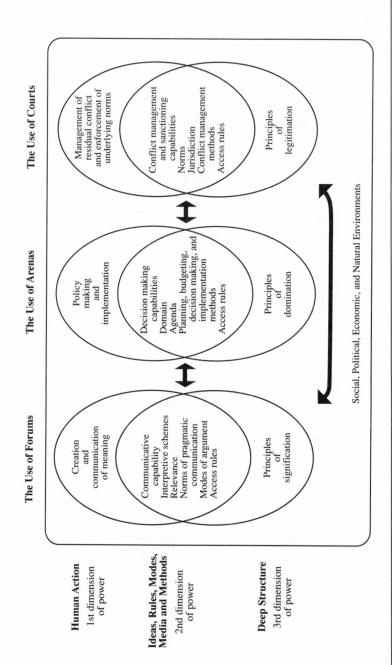

FIGURE 22.1

The triple three-dimensional view of power

of "signification"—that is, bedrock principles of language use and basic ways of looking at the world, or worldviews. Human beings communicate in various settings by using interpretive schemes that draw on these principles.

Decision making for policy or plan adoption and implementation is shaped by aspects and principles of "domination," embodied in or rationalized by unequal distributions of generative rules, resources and transformation relations—for example, social position, skills, intelligence, status, or money. Unequal distributions or rules and resources, in turn, generate individual or group capacities to make and implement policies. Human beings adopt and implement policies through use of particular social practices—the design and use of arenas.

Finally, human beings engage in the normative regulation of conduct through another social practice—the design and use of courts. This process is made possible by the social principles of "legitimation," that is, by bedrock moral or evaluative standards or logics. These standards or logics then generate norms that people use to sanction conduct.

We have chosen the design and use of forums, arenas, and courts as labels for the three major social practices because the common sense generic meanings of forum, arena, and court make them apt descriptors for singling out and understanding these practices in real-world situations. They also draw attention to the settings in which meaning is created and communicated, policies and plans are adopted and implemented, and conduct is sanctioned. By calling these practices the design and use of forums, arenas, and courts, one can more readily identify and analyze them.

Although the design and use of forums, arenas, and courts are analytically separable, in reality these basic practices are in constant interaction. Thus, if one is to understand decision making and implementation, one must also understand the creation and communication of meaning and the normative regulation of conduct. Indeed, it is the interaction of these three basic practices that splits a society's potential decisions, issues, conflicts and policy preferences into two sets—those that will be considered and those that will not. The emphasis on each activity, of course, may vary greatly in different situations—indeed, to the point that it makes sense to use different labels for practices that highlight different kinds of policy-related action (cf. Healey et al. 1988). To arrive at a triply three-dimensional view of power—that is, the capacity to affect and effect change—in real situations where power must be shared, one must locate the pertinent forums, arenas, and courts and understand and explain their operation. The next section describes the design and use of forums, arenas, and courts in more detail.

Forums

Formal and informal forums abound in today's society. Discussion groups and brainstorming sessions; formal debates, public hearings, task forces and conferences; newspapers, television, and radio; plays and other forms of dramatization; and popular and professional journals abound. Forums may be place-bound (e.g., public hearings) or non-place-bound (e.g., newspapers, television, and radio).

Forums link speakers and audiences through discussion, debate, and deliberation in order to create and communicate meaning. They distribute and redistribute access to the creation and communication of meaning and thereby help maintain or change symbolic orders and modes of discourse. How this happens becomes clearer when we apply the three-dimensional view of human action to the use of forums.

In the first dimension (action), people use signs and symbols to discuss, debate, and deliberate various issues. Their ostensible goal (desired outcome) is to advance their views, create shared meaning, or issue framing and, perhaps, shared values in the minds of the relevant publics around a policy issue. In the third dimension are the basic signification principles ("bedrock" signification structures): the requirement of a speaker and an audience (of at least one), plus at least a partly shared set of common linguistic rules and resources, plus one or more basic worldviews.

The second dimension consists of the ideas, rules, modes, media, and methods used to link the other two dimensions. The most important ideas, rules, modes, media, and methods are *communicative capability, interpretive schemes, relevance, norms of pragmatic communication, modes of argument,* and *access rules.*

Communicative capability is simply the capacity to create and communicate meaning. That capability may include, for example, rhetorical skill, the ability to use various print and electronic media, or the potential to pull together a supportive chanting crowd on a moment's notice.

Interpretive schemes (Schutz 1967) are intersubjective organizing frameworks that we humans use to structure cognitions, interpretations, or understandings of events in ways that are meaningful and that allow us to articulate and evaluate elements of those schemes as desired values or interests behind our practical communication (Bolan 1980; Bartunek 1988; Wildavsky 1987). These schemes include beliefs, expectations, and rules through which we interpret our personal experience and the social knowledge we receive. Interpretation is thus based on our own experience and our knowledge of the experiences of others. An individual's set of interpretive schemes is structured by a set of *relevances* determined by his or her concerns (Schutz 1967, 78–86; Bernstein 1976, 146–52). There also is a clearly social aspect to relevance as well, since particular forums are usually not open to the discussion of every topic. Instead, discussion must be germane to the occasion prompting the use of the forum.

Inside forums, competing, conflicting, or contradictory interpretive schemes, or frames, must be at least partially mediated as a necessary condition for the emergence of some sort of concerted action. Norms of relevance and of pragmatic communication, as well as modes of argumentation and access rules, play crucial roles in mediating among incompatible interpretive schemes.

People presume that *norms of pragmatic communication* will be met in communicative interactions (Forester 1989; Habermas 1979). Drawing on the work of Habermas (1979), Forester suggests that these norms lead to four practical criteria for judging speech aimed at influencing subsequent action:

> In every interaction, speakers may be expected to speak more or less (1) comprehensibly, (2) sincerely, (3) appropriately or legitimately in the context at hand, and (4) accurately. In every interaction, too, a listener's subsequent action depends in part on how these same four criteria are satisfied. (Forester 1989, 36)

Social action thus is predicated on communication that is comprehensible, sincere, legitimate, and accurate. When these criteria are violated, listeners feel confusion, distrust, lack of consent, and disbelief (Forester 1989, 147) or, alternatively, "puzzlement, mistrust, anger and disbelief" (Forester 1989, 280).

Argumentation is another important aspect of the mediation of differing interpretive schemes aimed at the creation of at least partially shared meaning and values in forums. Dunn (1981, 40–3), drawing on the work of Toulmin (1958) and Freeley (1976), contends that policy arguments (arguments related to decisions, issues, conflicts, or policy preferences) have several elements. These include the following:

1. policy-relevant information;

2. a policy claim, which is the conclusion of a policy argument;

3. a warrant, which is an assumption permitting the move from information to claim;

4. the backing for a warrant, which consists of additional assumptions or arguments in support of the warrant (often based on scientific laws, the authority of experts, or ethical or moral principles);

5. a rebuttal, or second conclusion, assumption, or argument that indicates the conditions under which the original claim is unacceptable or in need of modification; and
6. a qualifier, which expresses the degree to which the arguer is certain about the policy claim.

The design and use of forums influences what information will be offered, which claims—along with which rebuttals—will be accepted, based on which warrants and backing, and how much weight will be given to the qualifiers (cf. Bozeman 1986; Bozeman and Landsbergen 1989; Landsbergen and Bozeman 1987).

Finally, rules governing *access* to participation in forums strongly influence who speaks what, where, when, why, and how and who listens. In so doing, they strongly influence which decisions, conflicts, issues, and policy preferences get discussed and which do not. For example, having the more senior people in a meeting talk first may inhibit discussion by junior people. Or forcing people to talk about the issue at hand may make it difficult to redefine the issue. But the most powerful rules are those that cause people to be absent from the discussion. For example, holding meetings in places or at times or at a cost that makes attendance by interested parties difficult or impossible can be expected to alter resulting discussions, debates, or deliberation by altering the set of persons among whom communication will develop.

In sum, the design and use of forums in particular circumstances does two things. First, it establishes the structural (collective) basis of a *potential* list of decisions, issues, conflicts, and policy preferences that might be discussed, debated, or deliberated. Second, it mediates the transformation of that list into the *actual* decisions, issues, conflicts, and policy preferences that will be addressed, on the one hand, and into those items that will not be discussed, on the other hand.

Arenas

Formal and informal arenas distribute and redistribute access to participation in policy making and implementation and thereby help maintain or change political and economic relations (cf. Friend et al. 1981; Mintzberg 1985). Examples of arenas are legislatures, city councils, corporate executive committees and boards of directors, the decision-making mechanisms of public bureaucracies, nonprofit organizations and interorganizational networks, and various markets. Arenas may be place-bound (e.g., legislatures) or non-place-bound (e.g., mail-order markets).

Some arenas are primarily political; others are principally economic. The market is the basic form of the economic arena. Deciding what to leave inside and outside of markets is a basic determinant of what happens subsequently in most societies (Giddens 1984; Lindblom 1977; Wildavsky 1979; Williamson 1985).

In the *first dimension* of an arena, actors interact as they use their capabilities to obtain desired outcomes—i.e., preferred policies and their implementation. Policy making in arenas characteristically involves the establishment of rules, laws, norms, principles, policies, standards, or prices that apply generally to a specified population or category of actions. In addition, plans, programs, budgets, or particular recommended actions may be adopted.

The ideas, rules, modes, media, and methods (*second dimension*) used to link action with the basic structure (*third dimension*) include decision-making capabilities; domains; agendas; planning, budgeting, decision making and implementation methods; and rules governing access to participation in the arenas. The basic structure of an arena is a policy maker and at least one other participant. The policy maker must be able to affect a shared resource base that makes policy making necessary and possible.

The *decision-making capabilities* that an actor has available to influence a sequence of policy and plan-related interactions depend on the rules and resources the actor can use and mobilize. These capabilities can range from verbal skill, to the ability to hire and fire, to the capacity to use a computer, to the threat of physical violence. Capability, in other words, refers to an actor's *potential* to affect outcomes through drawing on rules, resources, and transformation relations that offer any kind of advantage. Decision making refers to the *actual* application of some or all of these advantages in interaction. Differential capabilities held by various actors will strongly influence which decisions, issues, conflicts, and policy preferences "count" in particular arenas and which do not.

Domains, agendas, planning, budgeting, decision making and implementation methods help account for how differing, contesting, or conflicting capabilities in arenas are at least partially mediated. Further, rules governing access to participation in arenas strongly influence which persons, groups, organizations, and capabilities are admitted to an arena and thus influence which conflicts, issues, and policy preferences will be considered in the process of policy making and implementation and which will not.

Domain refers to the spatial and substantive extent of an arena's policy making and implementation authority. *Planning, budgeting, decision making, and implementation methods* are the rules used to govern the process of putting together policies and plans, making decisions, and implementing them. The selection of methods will constitute, therefore, some of the most important actions in any arena because different methods will favor different actors' capabilities and purposes (cf. Pfeffer 1992; Friend et al. 1981).

Because time is a limited resource, *agendas* are crucial mediators among competing capabilities. Agendas consist of both general and recurring problems (the systemic or public agenda) as well as those under current serious consideration by authoritative decision makers (the formal agenda) (Cobb and Elder 1972, 82–93). Only capabilities applicable to dealing with agenda items become relevant. Furthermore, the kind of agenda item and its order on the agenda differentially favor the relevant capabilities of competing actors or coalitions (Riker 1986). Agendas are composed of *issues,* which are public problems with at least one attached solution that has pros and cons from the standpoint of various stakeholders (Bryson and Crosby 1992). In other words, they are points of controversy between two or more actors over procedural or substantive matters involving the distribution of resources (Cobb and Elder 1975, 82). The way issues are framed—and here arenas are clearly linked to forums—will dramatically affect coalition formation (Riker 1986).

Rules governing access to participation in arenas strongly influence who decides what, where, when, why, and how. Access may be based on formal rules, position, precedent, reputation, financial resources, rhetorical skill, or some other criterion. But regardless of the particular rules, the mere inclusion of some actors and exclusion of others can be expected to affect what gets on the formal agenda and, subsequently, which decisions get made on which issues, conflicts, and policy preferences. Most societies use rules governing access to establish hierarchies of arenas, reserving more global decision making for those nearer the top. Procedures for appealing decisions to higher-level arenas usually also are established. The rules of access and appeal are basic methods of hierarchical political management, allowing those further up the hierarchy to exercise greater power than those in lower positions.

The design and use of arenas in concrete situations does two things. First, it establishes the structural, or collective, basis for a set of *potential* policies, plans, programs, decisions, budgets, and implementation actions. Second, it transforms that list into the *actual* policies, plans, programs, decisions, budgets, and implementation actions that will be dealt with, and those that will not.

Courts

Courts are used to judge or evaluate decisions or conduct in relation to laws or norms, usually in order to settle disputes. Courts are associated with the organization of laws (or norms, principles, policies, rules, standards, criteria, or decisions) and modes of sanctioning (that is, ways of allowing some conduct and not others). Courts distribute and redistribute access to legitimacy and therefore help maintain or change laws or other modes of sanctioning conduct.

Courts may be formal or informal. Formal courts include the Supreme Court, military tribunals, and local traffic courts. The most important informal court is the "court of public opinion." Courts that fall between the formal courts and the informal court of public opinion include regulatory bodies hearing differing views before issuing or changing regulations, professional licensing bodies involved in disciplinary hearings, deans' offices resolving disputes between college departments or individual professors, binding arbitration, special court-appointed masters dealing with individual cases as part of a class action settlement, and the host of various "alternative dispute resolution" mechanisms that are now receiving serious attention (where these alternatives, such as third-party mediation of differences, are seen as preferable to the use of formal courts). In each instance, the emphasis is on conflict resolution through judging or evaluating decisions or conduct *in relation to laws or norms,* and not on communication or policy making, though each of these is present. The use of courts may or may not be confined to particular places. The "court of public opinion," for example, is not a place-bound construct.

The principal activity (first dimension) in courts is moral evaluation and sanctioning of conduct, especially through conflict management efforts. The disputes that are settled typically are "residual," that is, those that are left over after arenas have established policies and made decisions, or those that cannot be handled for some reason by regular political or economic arenas. The activity of courts either affirms or modifies policies and/or the underlying norms in the system. The basic structure (third dimension) of courts is two disputants plus a third party to help them resolve their dispute, along with at least partially shared norms to govern resolution of the dispute (Shapiro 1975). Action and structure are linked through the mediation of conflict management and sanctioning capabilities, norms, jurisdiction, conflict management methods, and access rules (second dimension).

Conflict resolution and sanctioning capabilities refers to the capacities actors bring to courts to engage in conflict resolution of the sanctioning of conduct. *Norms* in the broadest sense are the standards against which or with which conflicts are resolved. These norms may be formal (e.g., legislative mandates or legal due process rules) or informal (e.g., norms of etiquette or fairness). *Jurisdiction* denotes the spatial and substantive extent of a court's authority to interpret and apply norms to resolve conflicts.

Conflict management methods govern the process of conflict management in specific cases. The methods significantly affect the outcomes of the process, since they sanction some decisions and conduct and rule out others (see, e.g., Filley 1975, 21-34; Fisher and Ury 1981; Susskind and Cruikshank 1987; Fisher and Brown 1988; Gray 1989). Furthermore, since methods of conflict management differ in the manner and extent to which they invoke or refer to specific norms, they differ in their efficacy as methods of social control. The selection of methods, therefore, is one of the more important actions in any court setting, since different methods will favor different actors' objectives. Standard conflict resolution methods include use of a go-between, mediation, arbitration, and the substitution of law and office for consent, which has become the conventional courtroom method in the United States (Shapiro 1981).

Finally, rules governing access to participation in courts strongly influence which residual conflicts will be resolved according to which norms and, therefore, which actions—and especially which decisions and policy preferences—will be allowed and which will not. Access may be based on evidence of rule violation, demonstrated injury, formal rules (including rules of appeal), position, precedent, custom, financial resources, or some other criterion, including appeal procedures that govern access to higher-level courts. But regardless of the particular rules, the mere inclusion of some actors and the exclusion of others will strongly influence which disputes get raised and resolved and who will benefit from the process and who will not (Shapiro 1975, 1981).

In sum, as with forums and arenas, the design and use of courts in particular circumstances does two things. First, it creates a *potential* list of residual conflicts that might be raised and resolved and actions that might be condoned. Secondly, it transforms that list into the *actual* conflicts that are addressed and actions that are morally sanctioned, on the one hand, and those that are not, on the other hand.

CONCLUSIONS

Several conclusions can be drawn from our discussion of power and the design and use of forums, arenas, and courts. The first and, perhaps, distressing conclusion is that social life can be quite complicated. An awful lot is going on, particularly in complex shared-power situations. Furthermore, what one sees on the surface is not the only thing going on and very well may not be the most important thing. Underlying ideas, rules, modes, media, methods, and "bedrock" social structures strongly influence what becomes observable action.

Second, the very complexity of social life—and of forums, arenas, and courts in particular—makes change quite possible. Forums, arenas, and courts are almost always at least partially amenable to design—and the design elements are numerous. Planners, therefore, can and must pay attention to these elements because they are the basic levers of change in situations where no one is fully in charge (Alexander 1982; Bobrow and Dryzek 1987; deLeon 1988-89; Weimer 1993).

In addition to the design of individual forums, arenas, and courts, planners also should pay attention to the separations among, and sequencing of, forums, arenas, and courts. Differing outcomes are likely to emerge from differing separations and sequences. For example, while planners may often bemoan their lack of access to decision-making arenas, they should not underestimate the power that flows from the ability to design and use forums. Indeed, to carry the argument further, planners usually gain leverage through their ability to organize forums in which no one group can dominate. The possibilities are thereby enhanced for the emergence of a collective interest or vision that transcends narrow partisan interests (Stone 1988). Once this collective vision emerges, it can have a profound impact on subsequent decision making in arenas or on conflict management in courts (Bryson and Crosby 1989, 1992).

Third, planners can have their greatest influence over action and outcomes by strengthening, weakening, or altering the ideas, rules, modes, media, and methods that divide what is theoretically possible into what is actually done and what is not. Figuring out what to do in particular circumstances involves attention to both social interaction and institutional arrangements and how they are linked through the design and use of forums, arenas, and courts. Essentially, this means that planning in shared-power situations involves influencing action and outcomes indirectly.

Planning by indirection, however, most certainly does not mean that planning and planners are without influence. For example, the work of Bryson (1988), Bryson and Crosby (1992), Eden and Radford (1990), Friend and Hickling (1987), and Nutt and Backoff (1992) indicates the enormous power to be derived from creative and wise use of planning process methods, a traditional focus of planning theory.

Further, planning by indirection does not mean planning without direction. Indeed, the emergence of a shared-power world, in which what is acceptable to all rather than just the few may prevail, holds considerable promise for the pursuit of values public planners typically hold dear such as efficiency, equity, liberty, and justice. We hope so. We also believe that there are existing or imaginable forums, arenas, and courts that will favor those values, and that planners can help design and use those settings in such a way that virtuous outcomes emerge (Bryson and Ring 1990; Bryson and Crosby 1992; Krumholz and Forester 1989; Stone 1988).

Finally, planners should search for forum, arena, and court designs that result in the continuous production of desirable outcomes, at the same time that the designs are amenable to desirable changes in their constituting elements. This will be no easy task, but the world is crying out for new sets of forums, arenas, and courts that can help us better address the serious public problems that afflict us. The renewed emphasis on institutions in economics (Ostrom 1991; Williamson 1985), political science (Kaufman 1990; Wildavsky 1979, 1987), sociology (Giddens 1984; Sarason 1972), public policy (Brandl 1988; Bryson and Crosby 1992; Bryson and Ring 1990; Lynn 1987), and in planning (Alexander 1992; Bolan 1991; Healey, McNamara, Elson and Doak 1988) offers considerable promise for improving our understanding of how to design better forums, arenas, and courts. We hope the framework offered in this paper is a useful contribution to that effort.

REFERENCES

Alexander, E. 1982. Design in the decision-making process. *Policy Studies* 14: 279–92.

_____. 1992. A transaction cost theory of planning. *Journal of the American Planning Association* 58: 190–200.

Bachrach, P., and M. S. Baratz. 1962. Two faces of power. *American Political Science Review* 56: 947–52.

_____. 1963. Decisions and non-decisions: an analytical framework. *American Political Science Review* 57: 632–42.

_____. 1971. *Power and poverty.* Oxford: Oxford University Press.

Bartunek, J. 1988. The dynamics of personal and organizational reframing. In R. Quinn and K. Cameron, eds. *Paradox and transformation.* Cambridge, MA: Ballinger, 137–62.

Benveniste, G. 1989. *Mastering the politics of planning.* San Francisco: Jossey-Bass.

Bernstein, R. J. 1976. *The restructuring of social and political theory.* Philadelphia: University of Pennsylvania Press.

Bobrow, D. B., and J. S. Dryzek. 1987. *Policy analysis by design.* Pittsburgh: University of Pittsburgh Press.

Bolan, R. 1980. The practitioner as theorist: the phenomenology of the professional episode. *Journal of the American Planning Association* 46: 261–74.

_____. 1991. Planning and institutional design. *Planning Theory* 5/6: 7–34.

Bozeman, B. 1986. The credibility of policy analysis: between method and use. *Policy Studies Journal* 14: 419–39.

Bozeman, B., and D. Landsbergen. 1989. Truth and credibility in sincere policy analysis: alternative approaches for the production of policy-relevant knowledge. *Evaluation Review* 13: 355–79.

Brandl, J. 1988. On politics and policy analysis as the design and assessment of institutions. *Journal of Policy Analysis and Management* 7: 419–24.

Bromiley, P. 1981. Task environments and budgetary decision making. *Academy of Management Review* 6: 277–88.

Bryson, J. 1988. *Strategic planning for public and nonprofit organizations.* San Francisco: Jossey-Bass.

_____, P. Bromiley, and Y. S. Jung. 1990. Influences of context and process on project planning success. *Journal of Planning Education and Research* 9: 183–95.

Bryson, J., and B. Crosby. 1989. The design and use of strategic planning arenas. *Planning Outlook* 32: 5–13.

_____. 1992. *Leadership for the common good: how to tackle public problems in a shared-power world.* San Francisco: Jossey-Bass.

_____. 1993a. Policy planning and the design and use of forums, arenas, and courts. In B. Bozeman, ed., *Public management theory.* San Francisco: Jossey-Bass, 323–44. (*Note:* This version features the establishment of the metropolitan government in the Minneapolis-St. Paul region.)

_____1993b. Policy planning and the design and use of forums, arenas, and courts. *Environment and Planning B: Planning and Design* 20: 175–94. (*Note:* This version features the creation and operation of a public domed sports facility in Minneapolis.)

Bryson, J., and R. Einsweiler. 1991. *Shared power—What is it? How does it work? How can we make it work better?* Lanham, MD: University Press of America.

Bryson, J., and P. Ring. 1990. A transaction-based approach to policy intervention. *Policy Sciences* 23: 205–29.

Clegg, S. 1981. Organization and control. *Administrative Science Quarterly* 26: 545–62.

_____. 1989. *Frameworks of power.* Newbury Park, CA: Sage.

Cobb, R., and C. Elder. 1972. *Participation in American politics: the dynamics of agenda-building.* Boston: Allyn and Bacon.

Crenson, M. 1971. *The unpolitics of air pollution.* Baltimore: The Johns Hopkins University Press.

Dahl, R. 1961. *Who governs?* New Haven: Yale University Press.

de Leon, P. 1988–9. The contextual burdens of policy design. *Policy Studies Journal* 17: 297–309.

Dunn, W. 1981. *Public policy analysis: an introduction.* Englewood Cliffs, NJ: Prentice-Hall.

Eden, C., and J. Radford. 1990. *Tackling strategic problems.* Newbury Park, CA: Sage.

Filley, A. 1975. *Interpersonal conflict resolution.* Glenview, IL: Scott, Foresman.

Fisher, R., and S. Brown. 1988. *Getting together: building a relationship that gets to yes.* Boston: Houghton Mifflin.

_____, and W. Ury. 1981. *Getting to yes: negotiating agreement without giving in.* New York: Penguin.

Forester, J. 1989. *Planning in the face of power.* Berkeley: University of California Press.

Freeley, A. 1976. *Argumentation and debate: rational decision making.* 4th ed. Belmont, CA: Wadsworth.

Friend, J., and A. Hickling. 1987. *Planning under pressure.* Oxford: Pergamon.

_____, M. Laffin, and M. Norris. 1981. Competition in public policy: the structure plan as arena. *Public Administration* 59: 441–63.

Gaventa, J. 1980. *Power and powerlessness: quiescence and rebellion in an Appalachian valley.* Urbana: University of Illinois Press.

Giddens, A. 1979. *A central problem in social theory: action, structure and contradiction in social analysis.* Berkeley: University of California Press.

_____. 1984. *The constitution of society.* Berkeley: University of California Press.

Gray, B. 1989. *Collaborating.* San Francisco: Jossey-Bass.

Habermas, J. 1979. *Communication and the evolution of society.* Boston: Beacon Press.

Healey, P., P. McNamara, M. Elson, and A. Doak. 1988. *Land use planning and the mediation of urban change.* Cambridge: Cambridge University Press.

Kaufman, H. 1990. *Time, chance, and organizations: natural selection in a perilous environment.* 2d ed. Chatham, NJ: Chatham House.

Krumholz, N., and J. Forester. 1990. *Making equity planning work.* Philadelphia: Temple University Press.

Landsbergen, D., and B. Bozeman. 1987. Credibility logic and policy analysis. *Knowledge, Diffusion, Utilization* 8: 625–48.

Lindblom, C. 1977. *Politics and markets.* New York: Free Press.

Lukes, S. 1974. *Power: a radical view.* London: Macmillan.

Lynn, L. 1987. *Managing public policy.* Boston: Little, Brown.

Mandelbaum, S. 1985. The institutional focus of planning theory. *Journal of Planning Education and Research* 5: 3–9.

March, J., and H. Simon. 1958. *Organizations.* New York: Wiley.

Mintzberg, H. 1985. The organization as political arena. *Journal of Management Studies* 22: 133–54.

Nutt, P., and R. Backoff. 1992. *Strategic management of public and third-sector organizations.* San Francisco: Jossey-Bass.

Ostrom, E. 1990. *Governing the commons.* New York: Cambridge University Press.

Pfeffer, J. 1992. *Managing with power.* Cambridge: Harvard Business School.

Riker, W. 1986. *The art of political manipulation.* New Haven: Yale University Press.

Sarason, S. 1972. *The creation of settings and the future societies.* San Francisco: Jossey-Bass.

Schattschneider, E. 1960. *The semi-sovereign people: a realist's view of democracy in America.* New York: Holt, Rinehart, and Winston.

Schutz, A. 1967. *The phenomenology of the social world.* Evanston, IL: Northwestern University Press.

Shapiro, M. 1975. Courts. In F. Greenstein and N. Polsby, eds., *Handbook of political science,* vol. 5: *Governmental institutions and processes.* Reading, MA: Addison-Wesley.

_____. 1981. *Courts: a comparative and political analysis.* Chicago: University of Chicago Press.

Stone, D. 1988. *Policy paradox and political reason.* Glenview, IL: Scott, Foresman.

Susskind, L., and J. Cruikshank. 1987. *Breaking the impasse: consensual approaches to resolving public disputes.* New York: Basic Books.

Toulmin, S. 1958. *The uses of argument.* Cambridge: Cambridge University Press.

Weimer, D. 1993. The current state of design craft: borrowing, tinkering, and problem-solving. *Public Administration Review* 53: 110–20.

_____, and A. Vining. 1989. *Policy analysis: concepts and practice.* Englewood Cliffs, NJ: Prentice-Hall.

Wildavsky, A. 1979. *Speaking truth to power: the art and craft of policy analysis.* Boston: Little, Brown.

_____. 1987. Choosing preferences by constructing institutions: a cultural theory of preference formation. *American Political Science Review* 81: 3–21.

Williamson, O. 1985. *The economic institutions of capitalism.* New York: Free Press.

BRITTON HARRIS

23 *Planning Technologies and Planning Theories*

INTRODUCTION

This chapter attempts to sketch an integrated approach to planning theory, planning practice, and planning technology. In light of the vertiginous expansion of computer technologies and their actual and potential application to planning, I give special attention to the influence of these and other technologies on both theory and practice.

The principal aim is to underscore two major points, both deriving from a concern with making plans which is, in my view, the primary professional goal of planning and the one from which all other planning activities stem. First, I suggest that the nature of planning and the extent of technically accessible rationality reinforces a distinction, already important, between the theory of planning and related theories of morality, politics, and system function. Second, I explore this issue from the viewpoint of making plans. I attempt to show that planning, of necessity, has a basic design component that negates the possibility of any completely scientific form of rationality in planning and, thus, that the supposed distinction between ethically setting goals and technically making plans is not supportable. In considering these themes, I try to sketch some of the implications for planning theory of the interactions between theory and practice mediated by modern computer technology.

THEORIES IN AND OF PLANNING

Planning is the premeditation of action. Because it is oriented to action in a defined area of expertise, city planning is a profession, and any theory

483

that aspires to support it must illuminate the dynamics of social action. There are thus many distinct types of theory involved in planning: moral philosophy or a theory of ethics; political and social theory; a theory of the operation of the system being planned; a theory of the technology used in or available to the profession; a theory of management and decision making; and a theory of planning itself.

I take a simple but not, I hope, simplistic view of theory, practice, and technology. Theory is a coordinated body of knowledge in a defined domain. Theories organize the social understanding of the domain in terms of its most fundamental characteristics and the laws that govern its evolution and the interconnections of its parts. The domain of a body of knowledge is what the knowledge is "of." Practice is the organized application of theory or knowledge, usually from a number of different domains, with the aim of achieving change in conditions to satisfy objectives—such as wellness (medicine), stable flight (aerodynamics) or justice under legal procedures and definitions (the law). Objectives are broadly defined and socially determined. Professional practice is a preeminently social activity. Technology consists of all of the means of devising, studying or undertaking action in a given profession. More narrowly, we might restrict this to means that are external to the individuals and groups engaged in the professions, thus excluding organizations and established professional norms as well as mental and bodily skills.

In this context, it may be apparent that the theory of planning must depend on what planning needs to do and what the technology of planning makes possible. The practice of planning may not define the theory of planning, as it does not necessarily coincide with this need. An understanding of cities does not in itself establish a capacity for city planning. A theory of what is morally right or politically possible is a moral or political theory and not a theory of planning itself.

Most of those who have engaged in or considered the activity of planning know that it is very difficult. This is due in part to the existence of conflicting goals and interests in the body politic, in part to uneven distributions of power, in part to the apparent perversity of complex systems, and in part to uncertainty arising out of many uncontrolled or uncontrollable sources. In the following discussion, these difficulties—however severe—are presented merely as additional complications in an already very complex set of processes. The intrinsic difficulty that concerns me here arises out of the essential characteristics of large complex systems in the current age. The difficulty is pervasive but, unfortunately, it is often neglected by planning theoreticians.

THE CENTRAL DIFFICULTY OF PLANNING

Planning and decision making for complex systems are difficult. Advances in theory and technology for the analysis of large-scale systems arose in the immediate post-World War II period in the fields of operations research and mathematical programming, even before the widespread use of computer methods, and then continued in the field of computer science. Many such complex systems are likely to be in the public sector, for two different reasons. First, their overarching social importance dictates that their planning, management, or control cannot properly be delegated to non-public bodies. Second, there is no automatic or private mechanism that can solve the problems of planning them. So-called market failure is the principal but not the only case in which such private mechanisms fail. Several very important complex systems are outside both the public sector and markets: ecosystems, the human body, and family structure are good examples. Corporations and political structures are intermediate in nature.

Like planning for production and consumption through market mechanisms, planning for accessible complex systems involves coordinating many interacting decisions. But the existence of public goods, indivisibilities, economies of scale, and externalities, together with the public interest in long-term development and non-economic goods, gives this interaction a particular quality that is intractable under analysis and optimization theory. Large bundles of decisions are necessary for the viability of systems such as urban land allotment, health care, education, national defense, energy supply, environmental management, transportation, housing, and science and technology development. For each policy area, and sometimes for many policy areas considered together, these decisions must be taken jointly, and there is typically no automatic mechanism, market or otherwise, which will lead to finding the optimum set. This deficiency arises from the existence of an unmanageable combinatorial explosion.

Problems of this kind have been primarily identified with the design professions—engineering, product, architectural, and urban design, among others. Efforts to establish the scientific bona fides of these activities have been ultimately unsuccessful, so that most professions (including not only these but also others as diverse as medicine and computer programming) are often characterized as both an art and a science. In practice, if not always in the literature, industrial management and public policy making both fall into this category.

The difficulty of finding good approaches to the future development of complex systems is emphasized by the confluence of three major discoveries (or rediscoveries) of the past few decades:

❏   Urban planners have long known that certain types of major
    decisions in complex situations escape automatic and market-
    type choices, just as they can escape incremental and disjointed
    approaches. This conviction has been reinforced by the political
    failures of market planning in the Reagan–Bush years.

❏   An analysis that began in logic (with the "satisfiability prob-
    lem" of propositional calculus) has been widely applied in com-
    puter science. This analysis has shown that there are serious
    limitations (which apply to markets and computational optimi-
    zation alike) to the possibility of automatically finding optimal
    solutions to complex problems.

❏   Economic and social analysis in complexity theory, in this case
    led by the economist Brian Arthur, has shown that major deci-
    sions that escape market guidance and are made with inadequate
    or no planning can lead to the permanent or long-lasting bur-
    den of suboptimal decisions, due to the phenomenon of "lock-
    in" or premature commitment to the wrong solution.

The remarkable convergence of these three relatively independent
views supports the necessity for informed design as a method of planning.
This view is confirmed by practical experience and by the theory of certain
technologies and not, in the first instance, by planning theory and philosophy.

TECHNOLOGY AND THE SCIENCE OF PLANNING

A rational view of planning suggests that every effort must be made to
explore the extent to which planning can be rationalized—that is, made
scientific. Even though planning cannot be fully scientific, there are surely
ways in which science can contribute to good planning. Indeed, the modern technology of information management, analysis, modeling, and presentation adds a great deal to planning and planning theory.

Collecting and Managing Information

Social science information in the form of data provides a major part of
the empirical basis for understanding social systems. Other important bases
are introspection, casual or directed observation, political and legal debates,
journalism, literature, art, and social movements.

Sources of such data in the United States range from the stock markets and financial reports through the decennial census and more frequent governmental statistical series to special studies and their analysis such as, say, the *Kinsey Report*, epidemiological studies of AIDS and cancer, or the Chicago Area Transportation Study. Private statistics such as credit ratings, mailing lists, and utilities billings are also sometimes accessible and some of these data bases are commercialized.

Since about 1960, most of these sources have been computerized and expanded, greatly increasing the volume and accessibility of data. Geographically distributed data is most important for knowledge about the urban and regional systems with which we are concerned, but its availability has been more limited, especially at the disaggregated level of the household and the firm. The emergence of Geographic Information Systems (GIS) has provided frameworks for such spatially distributed data; working as assistants to growth management, permit tracking, and other local functions, these GIS have permitted the regular accumulation of administrative data on a systematic area basis.

From Data to Knowledge

The use of data to support the development of scientific knowledge calls for more than the data themselves. At least a preliminary theory is necessary in each case to organize the data and permit the testing of hypotheses. This necessity extends even to the collection of data—but here the theory must be more tentative and less compelling, or we would be unable to accumulate time series for later use that would enable us to make new comparisons and draw new conclusions over time.

Examples of theories providing a start in understanding data (and vice versa) are abundant in planning. Economic theories underlie many early studies of housing and industrial location. These theories failed to explain transportation demand, however, because behavior appeared more diverse and less uniform than envisioned by economic theory. This contradiction led to the gravity model and ultimately to models of discrete choice, which in turn were applied to the housing market. The presence of urban congestion was widely documented, but its analysis required a theory about trip distributions and the ability to simulate a network by tracing least-cost paths and assigning trips.

Using Knowledge to Test Plans

One ultimate purpose of using scientific methods in planning is to discover the consequences of hypothetical decisions (although this is not the ultimate objective of planning, which is to generate plans). Planning theory should demand that our theories of urban and regional systems support conditional predictions about the probable future outcomes of public and private actions. If we lack the ability to choose among alternative plans by comparing their outcomes, then planning as the premeditation of action has a very weak basis indeed. Planning with disregard for consequences forsakes rationality.

A comparison of outcomes may have to be largely judgmental, relying on a variety of internalized information and theories, calling on experience in other places and times and formulating logical but untested arguments. Indeed, this kind of judgmental choice must be used in testing the design of planning institutions and processes because our knowledge of institutional outcomes is largely limited to that sort of analysis.

In a more prosaic mode of behavioral and locational analysis, we can generate conditional and counterfactual "information about the future" by predicting in a scientific mode the consequences of hypothetical decisions. Equilibrium and, to some extent, dynamic (or non-equilibrium) models of land markets, transportation system use, and locational behavior are available to planning practitioners. These models characteristically are used in simulations that can provide the planner with outcomes flowing from his plans.

The use of these technologies provides interesting challenges to planning theory. The models provide a handle on the extent of interaction in urban and regional systems and highlight the need for a position on the disaggregation of functions and jurisdictions under planning. The interaction between disaggregation and comprehensiveness can be operationally defined, concretely considered, and experimentally manipulated. The theorist will be challenged to provide operational definitions of important values served by planning such as choice, equity, and amenity, since these can now be related to matters of data collection, scientific understanding, and examination under simulated plans. Dynamic models raise problems about the duration of decisions over time and about chaos, instability, and sudden catastrophic changes.

In addition, a class of behavioral problems is now open to a more scientific approach than was the case heretofore. These problems include the role of housing as familial investment, the locational choices of two-worker households, the true choice of routes in transport demand models, the impacted nature of ethnic, racial, and income-segregated neighborhoods, and the effect of lack of empowerment arising from gender, race, disability and discrimination. The unresolved nature of these issues might be taken, from one standpoint, as an indicator of the weakness of system modeling.

I view them instead as matters that have long been on the agenda of ethics in planning theory but have been addressed until now largely in speculative terms on the basis of a priori ethical positions or by pragmatic courses of action roughly informed by these positions. It is now possible to see how the development of planning technology has given practical content to these theoretical topics, challenged their utopian foundations, and brought them closer to realistic study and examination.

Finally, technologically advanced methods for testing intended planning decisions have reopened the prospect for extended sketch planning and have undermined those attitudes of despair that support disjointed incrementalism, market dominance, and the surrender of planning to management. The actual, impending scientific capability for *testing* plans, however, does not necessarily support *making* plans, and this important issue raises a new set of topics in planning theory.

TECHNOLOGY AND THE ART OF PLANNING

The artful side of planning consists of making plans, large or small, that connect many possible actions with many desired outcomes. The underlying reason why this is artful rather than scientific is the explosive combinatorial complexity of multiple decisions. Only by reducing this complexity or restricting search is it possible to arrive at a set of planning alternatives that are feasible, that satisfy public, political, and decision-making goals, and that offer some promise of approaching the best—that is, the most effective and most practically generated—possible solutions.

Planning practitioners, of course, often claim a certain artfulness for their negotiating ability, political astuteness, and understanding of the urban or regional system they are planning. Reflection will show that, in general, these skills embody both personal and social knowledge that has not been reduced to systematic form. Transforming this private knowledge to some public form is a challenge to planning theory. A portion of bargaining and negotiation, however, only begins with the structure of certain types of social interaction and is indeed artful. I would maintain that the limits of this artfulness are established by the larger political and functional system, where the impact of plans is more extensive; hence, I focus on the art of making plans.

The Impossibility of Scientific Design

I already have referred briefly and now return to a major tenet of economics, operations research, and mathematical programming. In various forms, this tenet holds that most decision problems can be solved by optimizing. Despite efforts from many quarters, including mine, this idea has not been widely accepted in planning.

Reasoning on this issue has been confused at best and meretricious at worst. The success of transport planning, for example, is almost never attacked on the basis of its deceptive claim that the plans were generated by scientific and computer-based methods. They are actually produced by hand and by successive approximations. Other shortcomings, such as overemphasis on the private automobile, failure to consider land-use effects, the destruction of inner-city neighborhoods, and the voracious demand by transport planning for information, can be addressed by well-regulated planning approaches using new technology. The difficulty of finding a way to pursue automatic planning cannot be so addressed.

However, many of the analytic models discussed above have optimizing implications that can and should be used in planning. A market-clearing housing model will in general produce a Pareto-optimal distribution of housing types and their occupants, assuming that everything else is taken as fixed. It will not generate a set of laws and subsidies to correct inequities in the distribution, and the optimizing capabilities of the models are weakened if there are externalities within the housing market such as social preferences or discrimination. Similar comments apply to other locational models such as those used for retail trade. Where the use of facilities is controlled and not discretionary, there are numerous optimizing models for establishing their best patterns on various criteria—this applies to schools, fire stations, hospitals, and the like.

Unfortunately, there is one large mathematically defined class of problems that is not amenable to systematic optimization with the use of methods such as linear programming. These include, for example, the problem of optimally assigning triplets of college students to dormitory suites on the basis of compatibility, and the famous traveling salesman problem. These and certain other optimizing problems have a common form that, it is now believed, will always render them computationally intractable even with the most enormous foreseeable increase in computer power and even with constant improvement in algorithms such as branch and bound and dynamic programming. There are ways, however, in which these difficult problems can be forced to yield approximate solutions, and these should play an important role in planning practice.

Two of the most difficult of these problems lie at the base of large-scale planning activities. Network design determines the infrastructure of cities for decades if not centuries in the future, yet it cannot be optimized even for a single point in time. Much more important are the several practices that shape the concentration and internal patterning of populations and activities in urban settlements. A great deal of a typical planner's day is devoted to engaging these practices to improve the "form" of cities, and yet the goal of optimizing form is mathematically intractable.

An important aspect of problems of this type is that they are apt to have many solutions of roughly equal value that cannot be improved by small steps and are therefore stable and locally optimal. At the same time, these solutions may differ widely in their defining characteristics, even though they do not vary in the quality of their outcomes as measured by predefined standards. Thus, plans that seem very different in style may be very similar in effectiveness and offer a wider range of choice. This is evident in the widely varying character of world cities that score equally well on multivariate evaluations despite their differences in structure. These implications from the theory of optimization are part of the technology of computer use and are of major importance for the theory of planning.

The Contingent Nature of Planning Method

Planning is contingent on the resources available for making and executing plans, the goals of the society and polity for which plans are being made, the present state of the systems being planned, and on many other forces and factors. The method used for planning is contingent on these same influences and on the technology in use to support plan making.

The professional planner must be prepared to deal with these contingencies, and in such a way that it is possible to certify that the results are the best achievable under the circumstances. In addition, therefore, to a knowledge of the system being planned, its political environment and the relevant goals and resources, the planner also must understand the implications for the outcome of the work of different planning structures and of all the different methods and their combinations. This last point requires a broad understanding of models, information systems, optimizing algorithms, and approximate methods—together with their costs and effectiveness.

Of course, the planner might choose to forego large classes of methods or may be required to do so by a superior. Rather than certify that these are the "best achievable results," planners might wish to cover their vulnerability with the certification that these methods are "in full conformity with the established standards of professional practice." While this might be a defense against malpractice in medicine, it should not serve as such in planning. The profession of planning has standards governing its ethics but it has not tried to achieve agreement on the specification of method, and certainly not on a contingent basis. In the present state of the art and of the profession, such an attempt could lead to disaster, but the absence of such standards about the technology of practice muddies the waters of professional responsibility.

The contingent nature of planning is perhaps most openly expressed in the idea of "satisficing." In Herbert Simon's original view, this involved settling for solutions that were generally regarded as "good enough" and that were unlikely to be improved significantly by additional effort. The definition of "good enough" was vague, however, and the possibility of having to revise it would open the door to optimization once again. An alternative definition is: to optimize over the resources expended in the planning, and the outcomes of the plans, combined. This amounts to saying that "this is the best plan producible with current resources, and the expenditure of more resources would be unlikely to be justified." It is easy to see that either of these formulations covers a multitude of decisions and judgments in an incompletely defined field, so much so that satisficing is more difficult than optimizing. Yet in some form it seems to be the only method available. A well-conceived planning process that recognizes the contingent nature of choices of method can thus deserve to be called satisficing, but the use of the term does not remove the responsibility for arduous application to the problems it conceals.

POLITICS, ETHICS, AND THE PRACTICE OF PLANNING

The ultimate expression of values and goals in public life is managed through the political process. If the government does not express the goals of the people and provide a method for resolving value conflicts, then alienation results and, in the extreme case, the political process breaks down. In social institutions, less inclusive and less sovereign than national governments, similar observations apply.

Planning thus is subordinated to an institutional structure and most frequently to a governmental structure and a political process. Many of the differences among planning theorists arise over defining the nature and content of these relationships of planning to the larger social milieu. This is not only due to the determining nature of politics for planning but also to the fact that many theorists make a sharp distinction between the activity of determining the goals of planning and making plans per se. It is only fair to add that a mechanistic view of system optimization takes the goals of planning as externally given and thus tends implicitly to endorse this restrictive view.

Substantive versus Technical Rationality

The arbitrary distinction between substantive rationality (having to do with goals) and technical rationality (having to do with methods) works to denature planning. It runs directly counter to the integration of theory and practice that many theorists (and especially Marxist or neo-Marxist theorists) seek to strengthen.

The only way I can see to preserve this vital connection and still separate substantive and technical rationality is to maintain that the practice of planning is essentially non-technical and does not require the mastery of a large-scale and diverse technology. This view, in turn, can be maintained by any of a number of subsidiary arguments. It can be said that every planning decision is political and that technical methods, therefore, are irrelevant. It can be asserted (and supported by observation) that many planning offices are engaged largely in management and thus that the planner's principal role is to validate the activities of a purely technical staff. All of this amounts to a circular argument that says that the important planners do not use technology, while those who do are not planners—or at least not important planners—and thus that the separation is justified by a study of planning itself.

The argument breaks down because, in the face of rising public need and the failure of private markets, planning for a large city can be carried out only with the assistance of up-to-date planning technology. The role of the inspired individualistic planning-designer has been rewritten by the scope of modern operating technology and social organization, the diversity of social groups and individuals, and the emerging need for accountability. At the same time, any neglect of planning technology and its lessons by practitioners and theorists alike would lead to an invasion of the field of planning by computer science and business school technocrats. Practicing planners who are deserted by theorists in their efforts to use technology responsibly can become easy prey for software merchants and irresponsible GIS developers, or they are forced to reinvent theory on their own and ultimately to replace the existing theocracy.

Values in Contingent Planning Decisions

But the matter goes even deeper. The planning professional engaged in the use of technology must be aware from the outset that he or she cannot claim to be engaged in an entirely automatic process. The contingent nature of planning inevitably ensures that one must constantly make decisions about the choice of methods and their application. These choices are permeated by values both in the subjective sense and in the sense that the choices influence the outcomes of the planning process and thus differentially meet the required goals. It is not impossible to imagine the planning practitioner operating like an unimaginative cook using a recipe or an inexperienced machine tool operator looking up each step in a manual. If this were true, modern technology would permit the planner to be replaced by an expert system housed in a computer.

If the values of planning indeed enter intimately in many ways into the procedures of planning, the separation between substantive and technical rationality becomes practically impossible as well as theoretically untenable. But in this case, a grave difficulty arises when the planner's values diverge from those of the employing institution. Such a planner can try to change the values of the institution (possibly by appealing to the public), to cheat or deceive the employer or to suspend disbelief while working to fulfill the "wrong" values. In the last case, planners are often in the long run co-opted by a system that they distrust, while the first two cases perhaps help explain the mobility of professionals in the field. In almost any instance, espousing the meretricious idea that technical rationality is value-free is only a ploy to avoid discussing values.

Planning and the Public

A widely held tenet of planning theory, to which I subscribe, is that planning has a public responsibility and is obligated not only to be accountable to the public but also to invite the public to participate. This view represents a general position about political sovereignty and social justice. Before I make this idea slightly more concrete, two observations are required. First, public participation in planning ought to be distinguished in some way from alternative forms of democratic participation in government. If, as is widely believed, many democratic values are subverted by special interests and failures of the political system, then planning will not cure matters. It may lend itself as a base for political guerrillas but it will not reform the system. The New England (and Swiss) procedures of voting on most local planning decisions bridge this gap but imperfectly.

Second, planning participation as a political good is only vulgarized by repeated reference to consulting all "stakeholders." The most important stakeholders in our society have not yet been born. Therefore, simply canvassing individual interests tends only to undermine and fragment any idea of a public interest and tends to relieve participants of responsibility for the general good and the welfare of unborn generations.

Given these qualifications, public participation in planning should be closely related to the planning process and its technology. Computer technology can make the process of plan evaluation a matter of public record and open the door to counter-planning. Public critics of planning, even friendly ones, can act like second-opinion consultants in medicine or *amici curiae* in court. In any case, they should have access to the original set of facts, rules, and procedures so that they can provide informed views, based on added knowledge (both of facts and their consequences), on an expression of their interests or on a critical reinterpretation of procedures. Public participants can provide planners with wider views of the effects of plans, they can propose new measures or new combinations of measures to be taken in planning, and they can contest the goals served by plans.

Public participation in this mode goes beyond those expressions of interests elicited at the usual public hearing and opens the way to informed discourse rather than subjective opinion on the methods of plan evaluation and the status of alternate plans. Such discourse is difficult without access to a shared technology.

CONCLUSION

The conclusions of this chapter have been developed piecemeal throughout the discussion. From a personal viewpoint, they represent an effort to explain and support my rejection of the sharp division between theory and practice that sometimes arises in the planning community. The texture of these views has a double nature, and each of the extremes is difficult to document within the confines of this format. There is a subtext of extensive, diffuse, and difficult technical discussion that could be summarized only in a long monograph of limited interest to the generalist. The main text sketches a view of planning that touches on many interests but would not be fully endorsed by many of the authors in this volume. To try to satisfy all these interests in detail would require a different kind of prolixity. Each view also presents difficulties in referencing, and I have compromised by listing below a few items on each of several main topics.

REFERENCES

For an exchange of views on types of **rationality**, *see:*

Breheny, M., and A. Hooper, eds. 1989. *Rationality in planning: critical essays on the role of rationality in urban and regional planning.* London: Pion.

Harris, B. 1978a. A note on planning theory. *Environment and Planning A* 10 221–24.

_____. 1978b. *Planning theory: a response to Scott and Roweis. Environment and Planning A* 10: 349–50.

Scott, A. J., and S. T. Roweis. 1977. Urban planning in theory and practice: a reappraisal. *Environment and Planning A* 9: 1097–119.

_____. 1978. A note on planning theory: a response to Britton Harris. *Environment and Planning A* 10: 229–31.

*For material on **urban models**, see:*

Anas, A. 1982. *Residential location markets and urban transportation: economic theory, econometrics, and policy analysis with discrete choice models.* New York: Academic Press.

Batty, M. 1994. A chronicle of scientific planning: the Anglo-American experience. *Journal of the American Planning Association* 59.

Harris, B. 1968. Quantitative models of urban development: their role in metropolitan policy-making. In S. Perloff and L. Wingo, Jr., eds., *Issues in urban economics.* Baltimore: Johns Hopkins University Press.

_____. 1985. Synthetic geography: the nature of our understanding of cities. *Environment and Planning A* 17: 443–64.

_____. 1985. Urban simulation models in regional science. *Journal of Regional Science* 25: 545–67.

Lee, D. Jr. 1973. Requiem for large-scale models. *Journal of the American Institute of Planners* 39, 3: 163–78.

Putman, S. 1983. *Integrated urban models: policy analysis of transportation and land use.* London: Pion.

Wegener, M. 1994. Operational urban models: state of the art. *Journal of the American Planning Association* 60, 1: 17–29.

*For information on **mathematical topics**, see:*

Cook, S. 1971. The complexity of theorem proving procedures. *Proceedings of the third ACM symposium on the theory of computing,* ACM, 151–58.

Waldrop, M. 1992. *Complexity: the emerging science on the edge of order and chaos.* New York: Simon and Schuster.

Wilson, A. 1970. *Entropy in urban and regional models.* London: Pion.

_____. 1981. *Catastrophe theory and bifurcation: applications to urban and regional systems.* London: Croom Helm.

Richard S. Bolan

24 *Planning and Institutional Design*

INTRODUCTION

The desire to anticipate, shape, and control the future is a fundamental condition of human existence for individuals as well as collectivities. At the collective level, planning is embedded in a series of existential dilemmas stemming from our desires for autonomy and community; for spontaneity and predictability; for individual expression and social control. These dilemmas are faced, negotiated, resolved, and renegotiated through historical agreements, norms, customs, rules, laws, rights, and obligations that we represent as "institutions."

Whether our concern is economic, social, or physical planning, the institutional underpinnings of the enterprise are normally taken for granted. There are times, however, when the foundations are exposed to view and are treated as problematic. The collapse of the Soviet bloc command societies, which were so heavily based on central planning, has heightened our sense that difficulties stemming from deeply flawed institutional arrangements cannot be cured by a change in leadership or an improved analytic technology. Other world events also draw our attention to problems that are so deeply grounded in institutional arrangements that it is impossible to "solve" them without redesigning those arrangements. Foremost among these are global environmental problems that spotlight the absence of any institutional regime capable of addressing them. Problems with basic resources such as oil, water, arable land, forests, and fisheries all point to serious deficiencies in existing institutions. Conceiving a more vital collective planning for both public and private enterprises requires an

497

understanding of the institutions in which planning takes place and of the ways of designing institutions—the subject of this chapter.

THE NATURE OF INSTITUTIONS

We know very little about how to design institutions. We continue to be the heirs of an intellectual tradition that pointed to the importance of deeply embedded institutional orders. Within that tradition—structuralism in its various forms—institutions were understood to change over time. The form and pace of change were, however, seen as virtually impervious to strong direction—as if, in a way, institutions were supra-human (Berger and Luckmann 1967). The structuralist sensibility was honed in the study of frustration: even great revolutions promising vast institutional realignments were thwarted at moments of apparent triumph by the power of social patterns they could not control. In a complementary way, overtly rapid changes were presented in the structuralist tradition as only the final visible articulation of glacial shifts.

That tradition does not provide the aspiring institutional designer with many principles although it lays down a trail of appropriately cautious warnings: institutional design is extraordinarily difficult. The search for a fuller body of principles must begin with a simple optimistic assumption: if institutions are socially constructed, then they must be amenable to reconstruction. If institutions are not immutable, then it must be possible to guide them.

The view of institutions as socially constructed derives from pragmatism and phenomenology. In this view, the architectural metaphors of structuralism are replaced with images of "lived events" and the "flux" of experience. Institutions form and re-form in a world that is *becoming* (Sztompka 1991). They change in time through a dialectic process. Opposites coexist, simultaneously opposing and sustaining one another. In a contextual dialectical world, conflict is an endemic characteristic that resolves into synthesis only to encounter new and more complex levels of conflict with new compulsions for synthesis. The resulting world is paradoxical, ambiguous, and uncertain.

This way of framing the institutional problem is essential for there to be any discussion of the design of institutions. In a world that is characterized by accelerating social change, focusing on the enduring (even permanent) qualities of institutional "structures" yields an illusory view that obscures the potential for creating new patterns.

Much of human activity is prone to repetition and habit (Berger and Luckmann 1967). A world of total novelty and unpredictability would be highly unsettling, both psychologically and socially. Two people on a desert island, faced with a world of no rules, would soon forge agreements, divisions of labor, and procedures that would provide the foundation of an informal framework of rules. Actions would be regularized and confirmed in a set of complementary expectations that would make daily life bearable (Luhmann 1987).

Most of us, of course, do not live on desert islands. Our firsthand social worlds are embedded within broader social systems in which we secure employment and income, travel, shop, vote, petition, enter and carry out (or breach) contracts, sue and are sued. This systemic world bestows citizenship, legitimizes marriage (and by that sexual behavior and reproduction), baptizes children, and certifies the beginning and end of life. With all its regularities, this world is also one of flux and constant becoming.

The terms we use to talk about institutions and social systems are often confused. The Firm—as an institution—may shape large parts of our life, but we are paid by a company with a distinctive name. The institution of Higher Education may control the dynamics of certification and learning, but we enroll in a particular college or university. These fine distinctions do not, however, prevent us from speaking of "organizations" as "institutions." ("Remember this glorious institution," the graduation orator pleads, pointing to the statue of Alma Mater.) The confusion of terms is not a simple error that can or should be suppressed. The complex flux we call an "institution" would never be effective in the world of immediate social interaction if it did not appear in well-bounded "organizations" and "communities." The linguistic tangle is accentuated when we realize that many institutions (e.g., the Family, Democracy, Capitalism) are expressed in an interacting set of quite different organizations, that individual organizations are simultaneously elements of many institutions.

When we set out to design, we have to engage this conceptual intertwining of organizations and institutions. Distinctions are important, but it is useful to remember always that neither organizations nor institutions are objectified empirical entities. They both are "lived events" that are simplified, divided, and sorted for particular purposes. They are socially constructed rather than discovered.

Aspects of Institutionalization

The dialectical character of the relations we call "institutions" is rooted in speech and communication (Giddens 1979). Social practices are simultaneously "speech acts" and the outcome of those acts. Humans are both the creators and the products of their social worlds. This dialectic is the foundation of what Giddens has developed as the duality of structure, the foundational mechanism in the shaping of action within a framework of agreements, norms, and rules.

A further tension embedded in the dialectical character of action becomes salient in the institutionalization process. In pursuing our needs, we simultaneously seek controlled, predictable settings in which we can confidently act without fear of being misunderstood or censured, and spaces in which novelty is acceptable and we can sustain the risks inherent in innovative action.

Dynamics of the Institutionalization Process

The interactive behavior of the members of a collective results in two fundamental and dialectically related process vectors: bonding and differentiation. A useful breakdown of the elements involved in the bonding tendency is adapted from Habermas's (1987) work, *The Theory of Communicative Action* (see Figure 24.1). The matrix also portrays the mutations between structure and process aspects of institutionalization. The cells of the matrix with heavy borders situate the primary structural locus of each reproduction process. Socialization focuses primarily on the individual personality, integration on the legitimation of authoritative coordination of interpersonal relations, and cultural reproduction on the constitution of valid knowledge. As suggested by the matrix, the operation of each reproductive process within its primary structural locus has ramifications at all other structural levels.

SOCIALIZATION

Socialization forces arise from the drive for habituation reflecting a push for predictability and control through agreements and rules. For such agreements to be stable, it is necessary to transmit them to newcomers. As Berger and Luckmann point out, a subtle shift takes place from the language of reaching agreement ("let's do it this way") to the language of transmittal to newcomers ("this is the way it is done") (Berger and Luckmann 1967, 59). Moving from a shared understanding toward the sense of an "objective" constraint is a vital step in "incipient" institutionalization. Socialization is completed when the transmitted conduct is internalized by the newcomer, when agreements struck by those in the first generation are projected on to the second. This projection is internalized by the second generation as rules or standards of conduct.

Structural Components / Reproduction Processes	CULTURE	SOCIETY	PERSONALITY
CULTURAL REPRODUCTION	Interpretive Schemes Fit for Consensus ("Valid Knowledge")	Legitimations	Socialization Patterns Educational Goals
SOCIAL INTEGRATION	Obligations	**Legitimately Ordered Interpersonal Relations**	Social Memberships
SOCIALIZATION	Interpretive Accomplishments	Motivations for Actions that Conform to Norms	**Interactive Capabilities** ("Personal Identity")

FIGURE 24.1

Contribution of reproduction processes to maintaining structural components of institutionalized social world

From *The Theory of Communicative Action, Vol. 2*, by Jürgen Habermas. Copyright © 1987 by Beacon Press. Reprinted by permission of Beacon Press.

INTEGRATION

We interpret and cope with new experiences by connecting them to prevailing and accepted social relations. Assimilating new to old is at the core of integration. This is accomplished through the linguistic imposition of logic onto the assimilation process creating an edifice of recursive rationalization and, hence, legitimation. In short, the vehicle of integration is legitimation.

CULTURAL REPRODUCTION

The reproduction of both instrumental knowledge—how to drive a car or open a can of beans—and of shared histories, traditions, myths, and rules brings coherence and continuity to life. Cultural reproduction situates the historical dimension of institutionalization: "It secures for succeeding generations the acquisition of *generalized competencies for action* and sees to it that *individual life histories are in harmony with collective forms of life*" (Habermas 1987, 141).

Differentiation and Segmentation

The dialectically opposite vector entails differentiation and segmentation arising from divisions of labor, specialization of roles, and (by implication) the differentiation of knowledge. The interaction of the two vectors of bonding and differentiation can be seen in the following illustration.

Imagine a continuum. At one pole is a totally institutionalized society and at the opposite pole is a society with minimal or no institutionalization. In Berger and Luckmann's terms, the totally institutionalized society is one with a limited, unified *relevance structure* (Berger and Luckmann 1967; Schutz 1970). All problems and activities are common to all members of the society, and a limited stock of knowledge is uniformly held by everyone. Thus, the institutional framework incorporates and subsumes all behavior. Such an extreme evokes Goffman's (1961) depiction of the "total institution."

At the other end of the continuum are no or only a few shared problems, and thus the least degree of institutionalization. Using the economic sphere as an illustration, the first-described pole of the continuum might be characterized by a central command economy, whereas the opposite pole is a laissez-faire economy conceived with the fewest possible rules.

The processes we associate with economic development usually require a move toward, but never to, the pole of minimal institutionalization. Increasing division of labor, for example, creates subuniverses of meaning that, in turn, push toward the deinstitutionalization of conduct in the general society while pushing for new internal control mechanisms within the specialized groups. These groups become the source of linguistic and skill differentiation whereby knowledge becomes socially fragmented. This fragmentation, in turn, increases the variety of relevance structures around which habituations form (Wittgenstein 1968).

As tasks become more complex or as new ways of carrying out tasks are tried, activities become even further differentiated, creating inducements for further specialization of skills. Each round of change creates more complex demands for organized, authoritative coordination mechanisms and means of exchange. As these processes evolve, there are fewer and fewer society-wide problems held in common. Less and less behavior is communally institutionalized within a single, over-arching frame of reference. Specialists create highly circumscribed institutions that are contextually appropriate to their unique activity. Modernization and technological innovation, in effect, unleash forces that breach the social and psychological bonds of traditional societies.

Figure 24.2 repeats the matrix of Figure 24.1 except that the cells of Figure 24.2 portray the forms of crisis that may appear from the disruptive effects of differentiation and segmentation. Habermas (1987) sees this as the "decoupling" of social systems from the ordinary, immediate social world of individual actors. Thus, we have the paradoxical situation where, on the one hand, social systems have their origins and are anchored in ordinary life experience yet, on the other hand, through specialization and differentiation, the ties of social systems to ordinary life experience become more and more flimsy and remote. Mechanisms of systemic functional integration (such as the organization of economic exchange in a market economy or the power structure of the nation state) are increasingly detached from the forces of social integration in everyday life. Habermas describes this as the "technicizing of the lifeworld" (Habermas 1987, 183).

Giddens, too, elaborates on the separation of systems from ordinary experience. He describes the process as "disembedding"—"the 'lifting out' of social relations from local contexts of interaction and their restructuring across indefinite spans of time-space" (Giddens 1990, 21). For Giddens, this process is a key part of the dynamism of modern institutions. It arises from what he calls "time-space distantiation" which, in turn, emanates from the fact that technology permits not only the objectivation of time but also the separation of "space" from "place."

An additional determinant in the differentiation process is the increased likelihood of distorted communications. While this stems in part from the inherent ambiguity of language, it also arises from the proliferation of highly specialized symbolic language or "language games" (Wittgenstein 1968). With the rising complexity of social systems and the technological complexity of communications media, the chances for distorted communication or miscommunication have become notably enhanced.

We can see, then, the two vectors pushing dialectically in opposite directions on the continuum: bonding pushes toward "total institutionalization," while differentiation (the increasing specialization of labor) and the "decoupling" or "disembedding" of social systems push toward fractured or diffuse institutionalization.

Structural Components / Disturbances in the Domain of	CULTURE	SOCIETY	PERSONALITY
CULTURAL REPRODUCTION	Loss of Meaning	Withdrawal of Legitimation	Crisis in Orientation and Education
SOCIAL INTEGRATION	Unsettling of Collective Identity	**Anomie**	Alienation
SOCIALIZATION	Rupture of Tradition	Withdrawal of Motivation	**Psychopathologies**

FIGURE 24.2

Manifestations of crisis when reproduction processes are disturbed

Adapted from *The Theory of Communicative Action, Vol. 2*, by Jürgen Habermas. Copyright © 1987 by Beacon Press. Reprinted by permission of Beacon Press.

Rules, Resources, and the Duality of Structure

When we speak of a social structure, we refer to the patterning of inter-action plus the continuity of the interaction or, in short, the reproduction of the patterning. In Giddens's work, this patterning is shaped by command over rules and resources. Rules themselves have a dialectical quality: they are simultaneously the medium for the production and reproduction of social practices and the outcome of those practices.

Resources are of two types. Command over allocative resources involves control over material goods and the natural resources that are used in their production. Command over authoritative resources involves control over the activities of human beings themselves. For Giddens, the concentration of social theory on allocative resources has interfered with developing a full understanding of systems of power and domination. He summarizes: "Power may be at its most alarming, and quite often its most horrifying, when applied as a sanction of force. But it is typically at its most intense and durable when running silently through the repetition of institutionalized practices" (Giddens 1985, 9).

Due to the contingent conditions within which human actions take place, the very synthesis of process and product from which social structure emerges contains the seeds for change. Two key elements in this are (1) the unacknowledged conditions of action arising from limits of perception and knowledge; and (2) the unintended consequences of action (Giddens 1979). Institutions shape personality and society simultaneously but never exhaustively. Tension inevitably arises between institutions designed to rationalize system behavior and individual behavior. Focusing on individual rationalization, such as an exchange market, leads to unintended system effects. Alternatively, focusing on system rationalization, such as a hierarchical bureaucracy, leads to unintended effects on individuals.

The Individual and Institutions: Exit, Voice, and Loyalty

The dialect inherent in the evolution of institutions implies an abiding uneasiness between individuals and the institutions of which they are a part. This uneasiness may intensify over time as social practices lose their effectiveness, or "logic," because of changing knowledge, technology, or values. Practices and institutions no longer seem natural. We stumble over them and subject them to critical examination.

Hirschman describes the character of individual responses to this tension in *Exit, Voice, and Loyalty* (1970). Exit is a limited option in most institutional arrangements. The ability to leave or separate oneself from an institution entails migrating from one society to another or from one subgroup to another. Hirschman's prime example of maximal opportunity for exit is a consumer in a competitive marketplace who switches from the product of one producer to that of another. As the breadth and scope of institutionalization widens, however, it is progressively more difficult to exit. One might move from one city to another and even one country to another, but one cannot exit the influence of, say, international money markets.

Voice is a very significant option in the stress between the individual and institutions. Hirschman defines voice as "any attempt at all to change, rather than escape from, an objectionable state of affairs, whether through individual or collective petition" (Hirschman 1970, 30). Historically, this option has been exercised mostly in modern, particularly contemporary, Western democracy.

The loyalty option is subtle and complex. On the surface, every nation–state, every religion, and every economic enterprise seeks a loyal membership. As Hirschman points out, loyalty is interdependent with voice and exit. Attachment to an institution is enhanced when those so attached believe that their voice will help set things straight should the institution move in a wrong direction. In order for loyalty to develop, both exit and voice—particularly voice—must be available and potentially effective.

Deviance

The contingent nature of institutionalization also implies the potential for deviant behavior. As North (1983) has pointed out, this potential obligates the development of mechanisms for measuring or monitoring behavior and for punishing deviance from institutional rules and norms.

At the level of immediate ordinary life experience, there are many informal ways to deal with deviance. In face-to-face interactions, the deviant may suffer social censure, retaliation, or isolation. At the social system level, more formal mechanisms for monitoring, judging, and punishing deviance come into play. These may or may not involve the state (Ostrom 1990).[1] Deviance involving serious crimes falls within the state's role in enforcing the prohibition against violence (Giddens 1985) as well as defining and protecting property rights. Deviance in economic and civil affairs relies on modes of discovery, judgment, and punishment. As North (1983) points out, such mechanisms are part of the transaction costs of maintaining institutional integrity and minimizing free-rider behavior.[2]

PRINCIPLES OF INSTITUTIONAL DESIGN

My purpose in tracking through the terms of Habermas's diagrams (Figures 24.1 and 24.2 in this volume) was not merely to describe how the world *is* but rather to suggest how it *might be changed*. What principles should guide the process of designing and redesigning institutions? I wish I could provide a short and uniquely compelling list grounded in a rich body of experience and consensual scholarly canon. I am afraid, however, that my suggestions are both complex and tentative.

The theoretical literature and historical case studies have led me to think about principles that address four different matters: (1) the primary reasons for creating new or changed institutional arrangements; (2) the design of incentives; (3) ways of minimizing transaction costs; and (4) attitudes toward conflict.

Primary Goals

Institutions are often represented as purposeful entities: they act *as if* they had important goals. They aim, as we construct them in our minds, to bind together the coordinated actions of a collectivity to serve some profound purpose. Markets are concerned with allocation of resources, governments with maintaining social order, marriage and family with ensuring the survival and reproduction of kinship. All of these presumably combine as the vehicles for an enhanced social life. Hurwicz's game-theoretic formulation of the problem facing the institutional designer gives a clue to the complex nature of the design task:

> A possible formulation of the designer's problem might then be the following: given a social choice correspondence expressing the societal goals or desiderata, find game rules (i.e., an outcome function and a specification of permissible moves [behaviors—messages and actions]) implementing (in a non-cooperative game equilibrium sense) that correspondence, subject to the 'validity' of commitments, as well as to restrictions on message space size and on the complexity of computations to be performed by the participants. *It is, of course, quite likely that only an approximate implementation is possible.* (Hurwicz 1987, 401, emphasis added)

In effect, the clarity of societal goals or desiderata and the definition of its boundaries are important first principles in institutional design. Taking the current crisis in environmental protection as an example, can we devise an institution with an appropriate mix of cooperation and competition by which people, immersed in the game and acting in their own interests, behave energetically and creatively in such manner as to protect and enhance environmental resources or minimize damage?

Incentives and Desirable Behavior

Creating new institutional arrangements requires imparting a sense of commitment. Those whose behaviors are expected to be influenced by the new rules and procedures have to be able to perceive the rewards that follow.

There need to be significant incentives for compliance: a strong knowledge of the benefits and costs arising both from compliance and deviation and a strong sense of trust in the behavior of others. An institution needs to engender a sense of loyalty, mutual respect, legitimacy, responsiveness, and competence. Incentives must be arranged to engender spirit, energy, initiative, and creativity. Participants in the institutions need to feel that effort will be rewarded with both material inducements and with the psycho-social benefits of fulfillment, self-actualization, status, power, and security. Like loyalty, spirit and energy cannot be imposed. Coercive institutional authority reaps begrudging conformity at best, at worst commitment to resistance.[3]

A sense of loyalty and obligation characteristically extends not to the institution as a reified object but to the persons who live within and are guided by its framework. Thus, there is an ethical moral dimension that is sensed in its legitimation and realized in communities and organizations, including mutual support in times of adversity. Commitment to the institution is enhanced if this communal and organizational support avoids engendering pathological dependency or resentment (Warren 1963).

Operational Characteristics

The aspiring institutional designer must know a great deal about the operational characteristics of these complex social forms. Ostrom's studies suggest, however, that one normative dictum may simplify the jumble: *minimize transaction costs.* The easier and less expensive the following operational characteristics prove to be in a given institutional context, the better its prospects for survival.

Socialization. An elementary design requirement for any institution is to provide for the learning and internalizing of its rules as well as of proscribed behaviors by the founding members of the institution and any new members subsequently admitted. The ease and rapidity with which this can be done enhances the staying power of the institution.

Legitimation. There needs to be a logic to the framework of interpersonal relations and obligations of integrative character in the design of an institution that is well understood by those who live by its rules and procedures. This requires that congruence between its rules and the material conditions of geography, resources, and other contextual conditions that concretely situate the participants.[4]

Monitoring and Enforcement. A critical feature of successful institutional design is the capacity for monitoring and enforcement that minimizes deviant, opportunistic, or cheating behavior. Capacity may take many forms but it always involves discovery, judgment, and sanction. It oversees both those who are within the domain of the institution and those outsiders who may threaten it.

Means for Conflict Resolution. Due to the intrinsically dialectical character of institutions, conflict is endemic to institutionalized behavior. A new institutional design, therefore, must provide for ways of resolving conflicts that are perceived as fair and legitimate. The imposition of resolutions that are (in the formal language of the law) "arbitrary and capricious" generates resentment. A new institutional design that, in the absence of settled traditions, repeatedly relies on ad hoc modes of conflict resolution tends to amplify rather than moderate the inevitable dialectical flux. In the terms used by John Bryson and Barbara Crosby in chapter 22 of this volume, the designer of arenas must attend to courts.

Qualitative Theoretical Guides

As I argued at the outset of this chapter, the structuralist tradition makes it difficult to design institutions. The alternative tradition, pragmatic and phenomenological, opens opportunities. Embracing that alternative, however, requires an attitude toward conflict that often is jarring to planners, who value neatness and certainty. That attitude is composed of at least four distinctive conceptual elements:

- ❏ Institutional design involves conceiving a process rather than a structure. To do otherwise is to reify institutions and overlook their essence as a web of human relations and legitimated practices. This means keeping in mind the contingent nature of what is being designed.

- ❏ Institutional design requires a method to explore the handling of dialectical, interactive processes as against linear procedures. The design of institutions must acknowledge the alternating play of conflict and synthesis, of differentiation and resolution, of process and product. Design methods must deal with ambiguity and contradiction.

- ❏ Institutional design involves inventing schema of human relations as well as relations to material resources. This means understanding the dialectical, historical processes by which rules come into being, are legitimated, and ultimately are divested of their logic.

☐ Institutional design thus needs to include rules for changing rules. This implies the acknowledgment that, as patterns of human practices, institutions are constantly *becoming*, even if changes at any given moment appear glacial or trivial. Thus, a well-designed institution includes provisions for its own transformation.

IMPLICATIONS FOR PLANNING

Designing institutions calls for a different kind of skill and imagination than planning discrete projects, programs, and policies. On one level, this chapter is a plea for a new sort of specialist practitioner and the cultivation of a new body of theory. I would not be content, however, if readers interpreted it only in that way. The large group of chapters in this volume devoted to the activities of quite ordinary city and regional planners reveals over and over again that practitioners both sustain institutions in their day-to-day practices and war against them. Planners are usually called upon to solve problems that seem to require only a new road, a subsidy package for firms, a housing program, a new way to treat waste, and the like. More and more, however, these conventional products of our craft are useless without new or redesigned institutions. The changing dynamics of human settlements and the growing concern for the physical environment and its sustainable use are but two of the fundamental challenges that should impel us toward a concern for institutional design.

Planners cannot afford to leave institutional design to a new group of specialists. It is inevitable, part of the fabric of our daily work lives. Theorists, therefore, must attend to institutionalization. I have laid out a tentative map of a still little-understood intellectual territory. I hope others will join in the exploration. It is a daunting theoretical task but if pursued vigorously, it will profoundly change the nature of planning as practice.

Notes

1. Many of Ostrom's case studies of institutional creation succeeded more because the state was not involved; participants were able to create their own mechanisms of monitoring and control (Ostrom 1990; see also Wedel 1986).

Business firms or nonprofit enterprises also need to set up internal monitoring and control of deviance. Firing a worker is one extreme measure available, but such organizations also develop a wide array of controls from product quality control procedures to the old-fashioned time clock.

2. There are many variations of deviance; the subject has not been treated well in sociological theory. Deviance has indeed been explored often enough, but the explorations usually focus on serious transgressions from moral codes and law. From the perspective of institutional design, there is deviant behavior that seeks to compensate for weaknesses or failings of primary institutions. Research from the former Soviet Union and Eastern European countries finds various forms of "counter-institutions" that are invented by individuals acting in private capacities (including government and party officials) to fulfill their needs in a framework of official institutions that fail them in important ways (Kaminski 1989; Wedel 1986). There are, in effect, formal, explicitly acknowledged institutions, but there is also a *dual* set of covert, informal, seldom acknowledged institutions. That they existed in communist dictatorships is perhaps not surprising. I would hypothesize that this duality may be found in all societies. The United States long has had an "informal" economy, an economy that often has a primary rule of strictly cash transactions to escape the oversight of taxing authorities. Such economies may indeed embrace organized criminal activity, but some of it includes such middle-class rituals as flea markets and garage sales. Black markets thrive in capitalist and socialist countries, in developed and undeveloped societies alike.

3. See Wedel (1986) for a discussion of private behavior under martial law in Poland in the early 1980s that was intended both to bypass official institutions and to covertly undermine them.

4. Kaminski notes that the political geography of communism is highly significant. Communist institutions gained legitimacy in the former Soviet Union and in China, both of which had been ruled for centuries by traditional aristocratic hierarchies and agrobureaucratic empires. This legitimacy was never earned in Central and Eastern European countries whose histories were linked more closely with Western Europe and the Enlightenment (Kaminski 1989). It should also be noted that Habermas's "uncoupling" and Giddens's "disembedding" processes tend to make the contextual logic more remote.

REFERENCES

Berger, P., and T. Luckmann. 1966. *The social construction of reality*. Garden City, NY: Doubleday [Anchor Books Edition, 1967].

Brandl, J. 1988. On politics and policy analysis as the design and assessment of institutions. *Journal of Policy Analysis and Management* 7, 3: 419–24.

Giddens, A. 1979. *Central problems in social theory*. Berkeley: University of California Press.

_____. 1984. *The constitution of society.* Berkeley: University of California Press.

_____. 1985. *The nation–state and violence.* Berkeley: University of California Press.

_____. 1990. *The consequences of modernity.* Stanford, CA: Stanford University Press.

_____, and J. Turner, eds. 1987. *Social theory today.* Stanford, CA: Stanford University Press.

Goffman, E. 1961. *Asylums: essays on the social situation of mental patients and other inmates.* Garden City, NY: Doubleday Anchor Books.

Habermas, J. 1979. *Communication and the evolution of society.* Boston, MA: Beacon Press.

_____. 1984. *The theory of communicative action: lifeworld and system. Reason and the rationalization of society.* vol. I. Translated by Thomas McCarthy. Boston: Beacon Press.

_____. 1987. *The theory of communicative action: lifeworld and system. A critque of functionalist reason.* vol. II. Translated by Thomas McCarthy. Boston: Beacon Press.

Hirschman, A. 1970. *Exit, voice and loyalty: responses to decline in firms, organizations and states.* Cambridge, MA: Harvard University Press.

Hurwicz, L. 1973. The design of mechanisms for resource allocation. *American Economic Review* 63: 1–30.

_____. 1987. Inventing new institutions: the design perspective. *American Journal of Agricultural Economics* 69, 2: 395–402.

Kaminski, A. 1989. Coercion, corruption and reform: state and society in the soviet-type socialist regime. *Journal of Theoretical Politics* 1, 1: 77–102.

Klosterman, R. 1985. Arguments for and against planning. *Town Planning Review* 56: 5–20.

Luhmann, N. 1987. Modern systems theory and the theory of society. In V. Meja, D. Misgeld, and N. Stehr, eds. *Modern German sociology.* New York: Columbia University Press, 173–186.

March, J., and J. Olsen. 1984. The new institutionalism: organizational factors in political life. *American Political Science Review* 78: 734–49.

North, D. 1983. A theory of institutional change and the economic history of the western world. In M. Hechter, ed. *The microfoundations of macrosociology.* Phildelphia: Temple University Press, 190–215.

Ostrom, E. 1990. *Governing the commons: the evolution of institutions for collective action.* New York: Cambridge University Press.

Ruttan, V., and Y. Hayami. 1984. Toward a theory of induced institutional innovation. *The Journal of Development Studies* 20, 4: 203–23.

Schön, D. 1972. *Beyond the stable state*. New York: Macmillan.

Schutz, A. 1970. *Reflections on the problem of relevance*. New Haven, CT: Yale University Press.

Shepsle, K. 1989. Studying institutions: some lessons from the rational choice approach. *Journal of Theoretical Politics* 1, 1: 131–47.

Sztompka, P. 1991. *Society in action: the theory of social becoming*. Chicago: University of Chicago Press.

Taylor, S. 1989. *Conceptions of institutions and the theory of knowledge*. 2d. ed. New Brunswick, NJ: Transaction Publishers.

Warren, R. 1963. *The community in America*. Chicago: Rand MacNally.

_____. 1977. *Social change and human purpose*. Chicago: Rand MacNally.

Wedel, J. 1986. *The private Poland*. New York: Facts on File.

Weisbrod, B. 1988. *The nonprofit economy*. Cambridge, MA: Harvard University Press.

Wittgenstein, L. 1968. *Philosophical investigations*. 3d ed. Translated by G. E. M. Anscombe. New York: MacMillan.

Wolf, C. 1988. *Markets or governments: choosing between imperfect alternatives*. Cambridge, MA: MIT Press.

Commentary

JOHN FRIEND

Designing Planning Processes

INTRODUCTION

I respond to these three chapters as someone who has always stood outside the academic planning community even though I can claim to have had close associations with that community over the last thirty years. Indeed, I tend to regard myself as belonging to a rare breed of non-academic planning theorist, if that phrase is not to be regarded as a contradiction in terms.

In order to locate myself more clearly within the somewhat amorphous and fluid world of planning theory, I should explain that I was first introduced to the world of urban planning in 1964 when, as an operations research scientist newly recruited to the Tavistock Institute of Human Relations in London, I found myself a member of a mixed OR-social science team working on a four-year research study of urban policymaking, supported by the Nuffield Foundation, in close association with the City Council of Coventry in the English Midlands (Friend and Jessop 1969).

The decision-centered school of planning thought that grew from that and subsequent experiences—many of them concerned with inter-organizational processes (Friend et al. 1974)—has been termed by Faludi (1987) the IOR School. The initials refer to the Institute for Operational Research, which was the group within the Tavistock Institute within which most of the pioneering work was done. The so-called strategic choice approach that emerged from this work (Friend and Hickling 1987) has recently been placed within a broader schema of planning theories by Sager (1993), who sees it as one of the two main influences on British urban and regional planning methodology during the 1960s and as subsequently having had a growing influence on Western European planning.

Faludi has commented that the strategic choice approach appears to have been relatively little influenced by other contemporary work in the field of planning theory. I would not dissent from this view, recognizing that its concepts are grounded more in the direct observation of the behavior of groups engaged in complex planning tasks than in the writings of other theorists, although I would acknowledge the influence during the formative years of such writers as Ashby (1956), Vickers (1965), Gupta and Rosenhead (1968), and Etzioni (1968).

So, if the non-academic planning theorist has any distinctive role to play, it is perhaps to be found in the realm of practice-grounded research. Now, however, I find myself responding to the three chapters as someone who has come to play a somewhat wider range of roles in relation to planning processes, not only as researcher but also as advocate of decision-centered planning methods, consultant to governmental organizations, facilitator of planning groups and—more recently—developer and publisher of software to support planning practice (Cartwright 1992).

THE THREE CHAPTERS: AN INITIAL OVERVIEW

First I should say that, from my non-academic viewpoint, I have found several stimuli to thought in the three chapters that I have been invited to discuss. They all look at the role of urban planners from different but interrelated perspectives: "interface structures" to coin a phrase to embrace Bryson and Crosby's forums, arenas, and courts; technology in the case of Harris; and institutions in the case of Bolan. If I can detect a common thread, it is that of a reinterpretation of the design role of planners. This is a theme to which I should like to return but, first, I should like to offer a few comments on each of the chapters in turn.

Bryson and Crosby: Planning and the Design and Use of Forums, Arenas, and Courts

This chapter is written within an elegant—even a tight—structure. It is built around a 3 x 3 matrix that relates three types of interface structures—termed forums, arenas, and courts—to three dimensions of power. These three dimensions of power are conceptualized as human action; "ideas, rules, modes, media, and methods"; and culturally embedded "deep structure."

Planners are seen as having their greatest potential for influence within the realm of "ideas, rules, modes, media, and methods"—a phrase that recurs frequently and which, I must admit, I found it difficult to keep hold of as an entity. Indeed, I sometimes found myself wondering in what respects it differed from, or overlapped with, Britton Harris's expanded concept of technology or Richard Bolan's expanded concept of institutions.

As the argument of Bryson and Crosby unfolds, there is much discussion of the *design* and *use* of forums, arenas, and courts, and I find myself becoming worried by the lack of any attempt to separate these two terms. For I see opportunities to engage in the *design* of such interface structures as arising much less often than opportunities to engage in their *use*. It is common for many parties to engage deeply with each other in the use of such structures but, in my experience, difficulties arise where many parties also seek to become jointly involved in their design. For then the process of design can start to become an extremely complex process of negotiation, and I begin to wonder at what point "negotiative design" ceases to be a design process in any realistic sense and what kinds of role, if any, planning professionals can then hope to play.

Bryson and Crosby conclude by developing the argument that planners can best hope to exercise influence in such complex, shared-power environments through indirect action, which they call "indirection"—a term with which I am uneasy because I find it hard to shake off an interpretation as lack of direction, which is by no means what is intended. The idea, however, is one that I can readily relate to as a concept that I have often found useful in my work, that of planning as *responsible scheming*.

The implied paradox in this phrase is deliberate. For the activity of scheming is usually thought of as devious, subversive, and underhanded, in contrast with that of planning, which may be variously seen as noble, farsighted, or bureaucratic. Yet, the two nouns *plan* and *scheme* are often treated as synonymous, as reference to any dictionary will confirm.

In my experience, scheming skills are crucial to the effectiveness of practicing planners, whatever difficulties this may raise both for planning education and for public accountability. So I believe that we should debate further what sorts of skills are required on the part of planners if they are to engage responsibly in the design as well as the use of forums, arenas, and courts, in a negotiative—and thus an inherently political—setting. I believe there is no lack of experience on which we can build on either side of the Atlantic, if only we can find the language with which to enable the experience to be more widely shared.

Harris: Planning Technologies and Planning Theories

The chapter by Britton Harris is based on long empirical experience in the art of urban modeling and addresses questions about the technology of planning, defined in a broad sense which I can readily accept. I welcome this emphasis because I have come to the conviction that much contemporary discourse about planning theory, while drawing deeply on other discourses in the worlds of sociology and political science, has little connection with the world of planning practice. There may be practicing planners whose thinking and behavior are influenced by the thought of Habermas, Forester, or Giddens, and perhaps their numbers will gradually increase. But I suspect they are currently few in number, however regrettable we might consider this to be.

While welcoming Harris's concern with technology as offering a potential bridge to the concerns of practicing planners, I found moving from the Bryson and Crosby chapter to the Harris chapter a disconcerting change of style. Rather than being carried along in subtle, sometimes allusive currents of thought, I found myself continually pausing to put to the test a succession of crisp assertions about the nature of planning and the role of technology in planning processes.

I find it hard to disagree with Harris's initial argument that planning is inherently difficult because of the complexity of urban environments. However, I do not so readily accept his description of complexity in terms of complex *systems*, because of what I see as the non-systemic nature of much of the complexity with which planners must grapple in their work.

Indeed, I have begun to see much systems thinking, which has exerted great influence on concepts of corporate planning within the firm, as rooted in a dangerously misleading biological metaphor. Likening a corporate organization—let alone a city—to any kind of biological organism consisting of an assembly of specialized yet genetically identical cells holds many pitfalls, to my mind. I therefore tend to question the role of system-centered modeling technologies in planning. I prefer to search for alternative technological guidelines that are less dependent on information of a systematized, quantitative form and more geared to the perceptions of uncertainty that trouble decision makers and planners as they go about their work.

This leads me to a concern with what might be called the micro-technology as opposed to the macro-technology of planning. Planners in practice must make all kinds of significant day-to-day decisions about where to invest the resources at their disposal in responding to the myriad uncertainties that surround them: whether, for example, to invest their time, energy, and budgetary resources in surveys, either formal and time-consuming or quicker and informal; or in more elaborate forms of predictive modeling; or in political or public consultations; or in negotiations with any of the various contending interest groups with stakes in the issues they must address.

I agree with Harris that the scope for planners to make selective use of what I would describe as data-hungry technologies should not be ignored. However, I would argue that, above all, planners need conceptual tools to help them in evaluating the relative resource-effectiveness of these and other competing—often more political—strategies for responding to the complexities of their wider design role.

Harris concludes with a discussion of the issues of politics and public participation in planning and has some interesting and challenging things to say. I agree wholeheartedly with his view of the need for both theorists and practitioners to address issues of planning technology so that the field is not "invaded by computer science and business school technocrats," for I too see this as an ever-present risk. Those of us who are steeped in public policy have long been engaged with complexities that are only now beginning to come to the attention of business planners. Indeed, if there is to be an invasion of one world by another, I believe that we in the world of public policy and planning are at least as well equipped as those in business schools to mount an offensive that will achieve lasting results.

Bolan: Planning and Institutional Design

Richard Bolan's chapter focuses on the design of institutions rather than on the role of technology or the design of forums, arenas, and courts. However, his definition of the term "institutions" as spanning "historical agreements, norms, customs, rules, laws, rights, and obligations" suggests an equally broad canvas and also suggests a significant overlap with the concept of "ideas, rules, modes, media, and methods" as put forward in the chapter from the Minnesota school.

Bolan draws a careful distinction between institutions and specific organizations, while warning of a tendency toward reification in both cases. This is a warning that I can readily endorse from my own experience both as a researcher and, more recently, in setting up a small corporate organization that is deemed to have its own legal existence, yet which I still find hard to treat, in Bolan's words, as an "objective, empirical entity."

Bolan draws extensively on the work of Habermas in raising general issues about the processes of institutional change. As a non-academic planning theorist, I must admit to not having read any of the work of Habermas firsthand and find some aspects of the analytical framework rather elusive. Yet I am intrigued by the discussion of processes of reproduction in patterns of interaction within societies, and I should like to reflect further on how these ideas might connect with certain aspects of my own thinking about levels of inter-organizational linkage in public policy domains.

In my research on inter-organizational relations, I have tended to separate out three levels of linkage between organizations:

1. interpersonal relationships;

2. locally negotiated links between roles within specific organizations—of a kind that are designed to survive the replacement of one person by another in the same role; and

3. legislated relationships between classes of organization, for example, between the class of all local authorities in an area and a state agency to whose policy guidelines they are expected to conform.

The third category, I suspect, might well be extended and reinterpreted to embrace other types of institutional relations in Bolan's sense.

Perhaps a theory of reproduction—and of impediments to reproduction—in the design of institutions would help me to clarify my thinking about other issues that have long concerned me, such as the paradoxes behind such superficially attractive and widely invoked notions as "partnership" and "trust" in the building of inter-organizational relations. In my experience, one of the most effective ways of building interpersonal trust across corporate boundaries involves a subtle process of "trading in indiscretions." I have observed that one of the most valuable commodities in effective collaboration across boundaries can be sensitive inside information about the internal politics of "life on the other side."

Bolan concludes by arguing prescriptively that planners should become more involved in the little-understood processes of institutional design, and he suggests that this may imply a reappraisal of planning skills. Here, the argument starts to converge with that of Bryson and Crosby, and to some extent with that of Harris, in calling for a fresh interpretation of the planner's traditional design role. We must recognize, with Bryson and Crosby, that planners cannot work alone and must learn to operate by indirect action and, with Harris, that technology cannot guide the design process itself but may nevertheless play a crucial supporting role.

CONCLUDING THOUGHTS

Before we become too ambitious in our speculations, perhaps we should recognize that professional planners are not often very powerful actors in the tangled world of urban politics. Yet, in my experience, the more skilled and experienced planner can still exert significant influence in numerous indirect ways, which can be perceived as benign or malign, depending not only on the ethics of the planner but as well on the political orientation of the observer.

In general, young people who enter the planning profession still have more idealistic motives than those who head for the world of commerce—and I believe that many experienced planners do succeed in finding ways of combining effective scheming skills with an abiding sense of public responsibility. I would draw a distinction here between a personal sense of public responsibility and a visible structure of public accountability, for I believe that the world of public planning is far too complex to enable us to design structures of accountability that will come anywhere near to matching the subtleties of the planner's potentially enhanced design role.

I see planning theory as still relatively unfocused as compared to, for instance, business management theory, and as still lacking in impact on planning practice. I do not believe that we need to feel defensive because of this. After all, public policy processes are much more complex than those of the typical business firm, in which most theories of strategic planning remain rooted in simplifying assumptions relating to the control of corporate operations in what is seen as an inherently competitive environment.

I believe we need all the support we can get from profound thinkers in the social sciences. Yet I also believe that we should strenuously seek to translate whatever wisdom we acquire into language and, indeed, into technological guidance, which practitioners will find directly useful and will be able to relate to their firsthand experiences in their own local environments.

In recent months, I have been rethinking my own stance in relation to the technology of planning. For many years, I have been seen as an advocate of a particular body of methods, with associated ideas on the organization of planning processes, which has come to be known as the "strategic choice" approach. This concept of strategic choice has always been intended to apply to any process of complex choice and not only to processes at a more elevated level within a particular corporate structure. Yet because of the growing cult of strategy and strategic management in business schools, this concept has come to be increasingly misunderstood.

For this reason I am now leaning more toward viewing the work of the IOR School, with which I am associated, as one contribution among others to an emergent field of developmental decision theory. I can see the embryonic field of developmental decision science as drawing to some extent on the micro-level insights of behavior decision theory but also as drawing more widely on all that is understood about the ongoing processes of negotiative, non-recurrent decision making in complex inter-organizational fields, especially in the public policy domain.

Urban and regional planning is by no means the only field of public policy in which important developmental decision processes are found. However, I do believe that the experiences of practicing urban planners and the faltering steps that have been taken so far toward the development of process-oriented planning theory have an important contribution to make to this wider field of scientific endeavor.

I would not be so rash as to try to locate the whole of urban and regional planning theory within this emergent field of developmental decision science. Neither, however, would I seek to belittle the contribution that the experience of urban planning practitioners, if effectively interpreted by ourselves as theorists, can make to the building of understanding within this exciting new domain.

REFERENCES

Ashby, W. R. 1956. *An introduction to cybernetics.* London: Chapman and Hall.

Cartwright, T. J. 1992. STRAD: a new role for computers in planning. *Computers, Environment and Urban Systems* 16: 77–82.

Etzioni, A. 1968. *The active society.* New York: Free Press.

Faludi, A. 1987. *A decision-centered view of environmental planning.* Oxford: Pergamon.

Friend, J. K., and A. Hickling. 1987. *Planning under pressure.* Oxford: Pergamon.

———, and W. N. Jessop. 1969. *Local government and strategic choice.* London: Tavistock. 2d ed. Oxford: Pergamon [1977].

Friend, J. K., J. M. Power, and C. J. L.Yewlett. 1974. *Public planning: the intercorporate dimension.* London: Tavistock.

Gupta, S. K., and J. V. Rosenhead. 1968. Robustness in sequential decisions. *Management Science* 15: 13–18.

Sager, T. 1993. Paradigms for planning: a rationality-based classification. *Planning Theory* 9: 79–118.

Vickers, G. 1965. *The art of judgement.* London: Chapman and Hall.

Contributors

Ernest Alexander is professor of urban planning at the University of Wisconsin—Milwaukee. He is the author of *Approaches to Planning* and *How Organizations Act Together: Interorganizational Coordination in Theory and Practice.*

Judith Allen is principal lecturer in housing in the School of Construction, Housing and Surveying at the University of Westminster in London.

Howell S. Baum is professor of community planning in the Urban Studies and Planning Program at the University of Maryland at College Park.

Robert A. Beauregard is professor in the Milano Graduate School of Management and Urban Policy at The New School for Social Research. His most recent book is *Voices of Decline: The Postwar Fate of U.S. Cities.*

Richard S. Bolan is professor of planning and public affairs at the Hubert H. Humphrey Institute of Public Affairs, University of Minnesota.

Michael P. Brooks is professor of urban planning in the Department of Urban Studies and Planning at Virginia Commonwealth University, Richmond.

John M. Bryson is professor of planning and public affairs in the Hubert H. Humphrey Institute of Public Affairs at the University of Minnesota. He is the author of *Strategic Planning for Public and Nonprofit Organizations* and co-author, with Barbara C. Crosby, of *Leadership for the Common Good.*

Robert W. Burchell, co-editor of *Planning Theory in the 1980s: A Search for Future Directions,* is distinguished professor of urban planning at Rutgers University's Center for Urban Policy Research. A licensed professional planner in the state of New Jersey, Dr. Burchell has authored more than twenty books on fiscal and economic impact analysis as well as housing and public finance issues.

Barbara C. Crosby is a fellow in the Reflective Leadership Center of the Humphrey Institute of Public Affairs, University of Minnesota.

Andreas Faludi is professor of planning at the Institute of Planning and Demography and chairman of the Board of the Amsterdam Study Centre for the Metropolitan Environment, both at the University of Amsterdam.

Giovanni Ferraro is professor of planning theory in the Dipartimento di Pianificazione Urbana e Territoriale, Università di Roma "La Sapienza".

Bent Flyvbjerg, professor of planning in the Department of Development and Planning at Aalborg University, Denmark, is the author of *Rationality and Power*. He visited the United States twice as a Fulbright Scholar.

John Forester is professor in the Department of City and Regional Planning at Cornell University, where he conducts research on the politics and ethics of planning practice and public dispute resolution strategies. He is director of the Program in Urban and Regional Studies at Cornell.

John Friedmann is professor emeritus of urban planning at the University of California, Los Angeles. He currently resides in Melbourne, Australia.

John Friend is honorary professor of Town and Regional Planning at the University of Sheffield. For fifteen years he served as head of the Planning Processes Program in the Tavistock Institute of Human Relations in Britain. He currently directs Stradspan Limited, a consulting and software company.

Thomas L. Harper is associate professor in the Planning Program and Faculty of Environmental Design, University of Calgary, Calgary, Alberta, Canada.

Britton Harris is emeritus professor of planning at the University of Pennsylvania. His special interests are planning theory and modeling for urban planning.

Patsy Healey is professor of town and country planning and director of the Centre for Research in European Urban Environments at the University of Newcastle upon Tyne, United Kingdom.

Sue Hendler is associate professor in the School of Urban and Regional Planning at Queens University, Kingston, Ontario, Canada. Her edited book, *Planning Ethics: A Reader in Planning Theory, Practice, and Education,* was published by CUPR Press in 1995.

Jean Hillier is professor in the Department of Urban and Regional Planning at Curtin University, Perth, Western Australia. Her research interests include public participation in the planning process, communicative planning, planning issues that concern women and youth, and social isolation.

Charles Hoch teaches planning in the College of Urban Planning and Public Affairs at the University of Illinois at Chicago. His recent books include *What Planners Do* and *Under One Roof: Issues and Innovations in Shared Housing* with George Hemmens and Jana Carp, eds.

Judith Eleanor Innes is director of the Institute of Urban and Regional Development and professor of city and regional planning at the University of California, Berkeley. Her current areas of interest include consensus building; land-use planning and growth management; environmental policy; institutional design; information use in planning and policy; planning theory and practice; ethics, values and policy; and community and identity.

Helen Liggett is associate professor of urban studies at Cleveland State University. She writes on the intersections between cultural politics and public policy, with particular emphasis on visual culture and urban design.

Glen McDougall is director of planning studies at the Bartlett School of Planning, University College, London.

Seymour J. Mandelbaum is professor of urban history in the Department of City and Regional Planning at the University of Pennsylvania. He is currently engaged in studies of planning tools and the democratization of access to knowledge.

Luigi Mazza is professor in the Dipartimento di Scienze del Territorio, School of Architecture, at the Politecnico di Milano, Milan, Italy.

Bishwapriya Sanyal is the chair of the Department of Urban Studies and Planning at MIT. He is at work on a new book entitled *Progressive Bureaucrats in Developing Countries*.

Stanley M. Stein is senior instructor in philosophy, Faculty of Environmental Design, University of Calgary, Calgary, Alberta, Canada.

Andy Thornley is director of planning studies at the London School of Economics and Political Science, United Kingdom.

James A. Throgmorton is associate professor of planning in the Graduate Program of Urban and Regional Planning at the University of Iowa in Iowa City, Iowa. He is a former elected member of the Iowa City city council.

Niraj Verma is assistant professor of urban and regional planning at the University of Southern California in Los Angeles. He has a particular interest in applying the ideas of American pragmatism to planning.

Index

A

Aalborg, Denmark, 386, 387, 393n3
abandonment response, 47
Ackoff, Russell, 12, 18
Active Society, The, 15
adjudication, 463, 465, 467
Administrative Behavior, 11, 21, 69
Adorno, Theodor, 415
    Frankfurt School, 40
    influence on planning, 13, 19
advocacy planning, 68–69, 110, 117,
    229, 239
Ahmedabad, India, 140
Albrecht, J., 53
Alexander, Ernest, 57, 59n5, 108
    ethical dimensions
    implementation of plans and
        scientific experiments, 72
    planning doctrine, 4, 75, 76
    rationalist perspective, 106, 107
Alinsky, Saul, 13, 19
Allen, Judith, 310, 385, 387–389, 391, 444
Altshuler, A., 228
American Planning Association,
    174, 225n, 323n2
Amin, Idi, 424
anarchism, 10, 85
    See also social anarchists
anarchist terrorism, 27
Appleby, Paul, 12, 18
Archimedean point, 415, 416, 419, 421

*Are You Being Served: A Report on
    Local Government Approaches to
    Recreation*, 297n1
arenas, 460, 463–464, 466, 467, *468*, 469,
    472–474, 476–478, 515–516
Arendt, Hannah, 210
argument in planning practice, 241–260
*Argumentative Turn in Policy Analysis and
    Planning*, 345n
Argyris, Chris, 372, 376, 379n3
    influence on planning, 12, 14, 18
Aristotle, xiv, 259nn4, 5, 438
    Nicomachean Ethics, 450
    Politics, The, 432, 444n1
Arrow, K., 12, 18
Arthur, Brian, 486
Ashby, W. R., 12, 18
    strategic choice approach, 515
Association of Collegiate Schools
    of Planning (ACSP), ix, xi, 167,
    286, 323, 410n1
Association of European Schools of
    Planning (AESOP), ix, xi, 167,
    286, 323, 410n1
Austin, John, 299
authoritarian, 152, 153, 161nl
    decentralism, 155
autonomy, 36, 37, 271
    "local," 434, 436
    of planning, 194–196
    planners, 135, 136–139, 146, 192–194
    See also institutional autonomy
avoidance response, 47, 48
Ayres, Robert, 12, 18

Note: Italicized page numbers refer to tables and figures. The letter "n" after a page number refers to a note on that page. If several notes appear on a page, the note number is also given (e.g., 134n 12).

- Intro.to Policy
- Land Use
- Planning